The best computer programmers are astonishingly more productive than average. They use good tools, and they use them well.

Clif Flynt's *Tcl/Tk: A Developer's Guide, 2E* helps you improve your effectiveness as a developer in both these ways. Tcl is a software language with a great "return on investment"—it achieves portable, powerful, economical results with great economy. Just a few lines of Tcl are enough to create interesting and useful applications.

Clif draws on his own deep experience as a front-line developer to help you get the most out of Tcl. He writes clearly and has organized his book with instructive examples that teach the essentials of Tcl. He covers the right material too; *Tcl/Tk: A Developer's Guide* packs in not just such long-standing Tcl strengths as its easy networking and graphical user interface but also the latest breakthroughs with internationalization, widget upgrades, and StarPacks. Want to take your programming "to the next level"? Get *Tcl/Tk: A Developer's Guide*.

—Cameron Laird, *Vice President, Phaseit, Inc.*
*and author of "Regular Expressions" column*

Clif Flynt's book *Tcl/Tk: A Developer's Guide, 2E* demonstrates a true mastery of the Tcl programming language, which he ably transmits to the reader in a form that is easy to comprehend and apply immediately to real-world problems. The examples are very clear to read, yet thorough, complete, and relate well to practical situations where the techniques displayed would prove useful. In particular, the sections dealing with data structures, such as lists, arrays, and namespaces, merit special mention for showing the power of Tcl to perform the most complex of tasks. In short, [this is] a great reference that will help readers of all levels understand not just what Tcl does but how to get things done with Tcl.

—David N. Welton, *a Vice President of Apache Tcl with the Apache Software Foundation*

Clif's book is both a pleasure to read and a useful reference.... I'm sure you'll find it a necessary addition to your professional toolkit.

—Marshall T. Rose, *Principal, Dover Beach Consulting, Inc.*

# A Developer's Guide

## Second Edition

## Clif Flynt

MORGAN KAUFMANN PUBLISHERS

AN IMPRINT OF ELSEVIER SCIENCE

AMSTERDAM   BOSTON   LONDON   NEW YORK
OXFORD   PARIS   SAN DIEGO   SAN FRANCISCO
SINGAPORE   SYDNEY   TOKYO

| | |
|---|---|
| *Senior Editor* | Tim Cox |
| *Publishing Services Manager* | Edward Wade |
| *Editorial Coordinators* | Stacie Pierce, Richard Camp |
| *Project Management* | Elisabeth Beller |
| *Cover Design* | Ross Carron |
| *Cover Illustration* | Randy Asplund |
| *Text Design* | Rebecca Evans |
| *Technical Illustration* | Dartmouth Publishing, Inc. |
| *Composition* | CEPHA Imaging |
| *Copyeditor* | Daril Bentley |
| *Proofreader* | Jennifer McClain |
| *Indexer* | Steve Rath |
| *Printer* | The Maple-Vail Book Manufacturing Group |

Designations used by companies to distinguish their products are often claimed as trademarks or registered trademarks. In all instances in which Morgan Kaufmann Publishers is aware of a claim, the product names appear in initial capital or all capital letters. Readers, however, should contact the appropriate companies for more complete information regarding trademarks and registration.

Morgan Kaufmann Publishers
An imprint of Elsevier Science
340 Pine Street, Sixth Floor
San Francisco, CA 94104-3205
*www.mkp.com*

07 06 05 04 03   5 4 3 2 1

**Library of Congress Control Number:** 2003103960
ISBN: 1-55860-802-8

This book is printed on acid-free paper.

# Foreword

## Marshall T. Rose
*Principal, Dover Beach Consulting, Inc.*

It is a pleasure to introduce you to the first revision of Clif's opus on the popular Tool Command Language (Tcl). Tcl has become the Swiss Army knife for the busy programmer—you keep it within easy reach at all times simply because it has lots of uses in many different environments.

Clif's book is both a pleasure to read and a useful reference. Clif is a strong advocate for Tcl, explaining the many different scenarios where Tcl shines and the myriad ways the same facilities can be used over and over again.

In addition to the breadth that Clif brings to the subject, he also knows the details—and, to his credit, he doesn't overwhelm you with them. Instead, each chapter starts with the basics and builds to the fun stuff. There are even self-help questions at the end of each chapter to help you review the lessons Clif has taught.

Whether you're using Clif's book as an introduction to Tcl or as a comprehensive reference, I'm sure you'll find it a necessary addition to your professional toolkit.

# Contents

**CHAPTER 4**

**The File System, Disk I/O, and Sockets**     **87**

**CHAPTER 6**

**CHAPTER 7**

**CHAPTER 8**

# Namespaces and Packages                                                     213

**CHAPTER 11**

### The text Widget and html1ib                                              379

**CHAPTER 12**

## Tk Megawidgets                                                     423

**APPENDIX E**

# Preface

## Tcl/Tk: GUI Programming in a Gooey World

Alan Watts, the Episcopal priest who popularized Buddhist thought in 1960s California, once wrote that philosophical thinkers can be divided into two basic types, which he called "prickly" and "gooey." The prickly people, by his definition, "are tough-minded, rigorous, and precise, and like to stress differences and divisions between things. They prefer particles to waves, and discontinuity to continuity. The gooey people are tender-minded romanticists who love wide generalizations and grand syntheses. . . . Waves suit them much better than particles as the ultimate constituents of matter, and discontinuities jar their teeth like a compressed-air drill."[1]

Watts chose the terms *prickly* and *gooey* carefully, seeking to avoid making one term positive and the other pejorative, and he offered delightful caricatures of the strengths and weaknesses of each type of person. In his view, a constant tension between the two perspectives is healthy in promoting progress toward a more complete understanding of reality.

Western science has long made a similar distinction between two complementary approaches, theoretical and empirical. Prickly theoreticians seek to understand the world through the abstractions of thought, whereas gooey empiricists return ceaselessly to the real world for the ever-more-refined data that methodical experimentation can yield. The complementarity of the two approaches is widely recognized by scientists themselves. Although most scientists would place themselves squarely in either the theoretical or empirical camp, very few would go so far as to argue that the other approach is without merit. A constant dialectic between empiricism and theory is generally seen to promote the integrity and health of scientific inquiry.

More recently, the advent of computer programming has brought with it a new round in the prickly-gooey dialectic. By temperament, there seem to be two types of programmers, who I will call the planners and the doers. Although good programmers will of course plan their software before building it (and will actually build it after planning it), some programmers (the prickly planners) see planning and designing as the primary activity, after which system building is relatively

---

1. Watts, Alan, *The Book: On the Taboo Against Knowing Who You Are*, NY: Vintage Books, 1966, 1989.

automatic. Others (the gooey doers) perceive system design as a necessary and important preparatory stage before the real work of system building.

Both planners and others can be excellent programmers, and the best of them excel at both design and execution. However, they may be categorized as planners or doers by their basic worldview, or primary orientation. They show different patterns of strengths and weaknesses, and they can with skilled management play complementary roles in large project teams. Still, certain tasks cry out for one type of programmer or the other. The design of software systems to control nuclear weapons, for example, is a task that demands exhaustive planning because the risk of unanticipated errors is too high. The design of a throwaway program that needs to be run just once to calculate the answer to a single question, on the other hand, should probably be built by the fastest methodology possible, robustness be damned. Between these extremes, of course, lie nearly all real-world programming projects, which is why both approaches are useful. They are not, however, always equally well appreciated.

The modern managerial mentality thrives on careful organization, planning, and documentation. It should be no surprise that most managers prefer the planners to the doers; if they were programmers, they would probably be planners themselves. Since they are not programmers, they may easily fail to recognize the value of the skills doers bring to the table. Programmers, however, are less likely to make this mistake. In the meager (but growing) literature by and for serious programmers, the role of doers is more generally recognized. Indeed, planning-oriented programmers often still perceive themselves as the underdogs, and programmer humor shows a deeply rooted skepticism regarding overplanned projects.

Historically, the dialectic between planners and doers has been a driving force in the evolution of programming languages. As the planners moved from FORTRAN to Pascal, C, C++, and Java, the doers have moved from COBOL to Lisp, Basic, Perl, and Tcl. Each new generation of language reflected the innovations of both planners and doers in the previous generation, but each made most of its own innovations in a single realm, either planning or doing.

Historically, it has been surprisingly difficult to make money by inventing even the most wildly successful programming languages. Success is typically highly indirect. For example, being the birthplace of C is certainly a claim Bell Labs is proud to make, but it is difficult to argue that the language was spectacularly meaningful for AT&T (or Lucent's) bottom line. ParcPlace has perhaps come the closest to a genuine language-invention success story, but it is clearly no Microsoft. Imagine, then, the dilemma in which Sun Microsystems found itself, circa 1994, when its research labs were polishing up two new languages, one prickly and one gooey, and each a plausible contender for leadership in the next generation of programming languages. Could any corporation really afford two such high-status, low-profit "success" stories?

Sun's decision to promote Java more vigorously than Tcl is difficult to argue with. Because most decision makers are managers, and most managers are planners, Java has always been an easier product to sell. Sun's continued and parallel support for

Tcl was correct, even noble, and probably wiser than one could expect from the average large corporation. Still, in the face of the Java juggernaut, the promotion of Tcl has been left, for the most part, to the gooey doers among us. Pragmatic programmers with dirt on their hands, many of us became Tcl advocates for the most practical of reasons: it helped us get our jobs done, and quickly.

One such gooey doer is the author, a veteran of countless programming languages who has fallen in love with Tcl for all the neat things it lets him do. Java advocates will often praise that language's abstractions, such as its virtual machine model. Tcl advocates such as the author prefer to grab on to the nuts and bolts and show you how quickly you can get real work done. That is what this book is intended to do, walking you all the way from the simplest basics to sophisticated and useful examples. If you are in a "doer" state of mind, you have picked up the right language and the right book. It can help you get a lot of jobs done.

## Acknowledgments

You may like to think of the author sitting alone, creating a book in a few weeks. I'm afraid that this idea has as much to do with reality as the Easter Bunny and Santa Claus. Creating this book took the better part of a year and a lot of help from my friends (some of whom I'd never heard of when I started the project).

The first acknowledgment goes to my wife, Carol. For more than a year she has been putting up with "I can't do any work around the house. I've got to finish this chapter," correcting the grammar on my rough drafts before I sent them out for technical review, editing galleys, making sure I ate occasionally, and keeping life (almost) sane around here. The book would not have happened without her help.

I also want to thank Ken Morton and his editorial assistants Samantha Libby and Jenn Vilaga. If they hadn't been willing to take a chance on an unproven author's ability to finish the first edition of this book, there wouldn't be a second edition.

Tim Cox and Stacie Pierce deserve more thanks than I can give them for dealing with my erratic and unpredictable schedule over the past couple years that it's taken to complete the second edition.

My production editor Elisabeth Beller's tireless devotion to consistency and accuracy is not obvious but improved every section of the book from the front cover to the final index. We both, author and reader, owe her thanks.

Alex Safonov provided the technical review for the first edition. Larry Virden and Leam Hall kept me honest in the second edition. Their comments greatly improved the book and earned more thanks than I can give them.

My heartfelt and sincere thanks to the folks who read and commented on the early drafts. These folks pulled duty way above the call of friendship: reading the truly wretched first drafts. Their comments were all invaluable. My thanks to Margaret Bumby, Clark Wierda, Terry Gliedt, Elizabeth Lehmann, Nick DiMasi,

Hermann Boeken, Greg Martin, John Driestadt, Daniel Glasser, Theresa Arzadon, Lee Cave-Berry, William Roper, Phillip Johnson, Don Libes, Jeffrey Hobbs, John Stump, Laurent Demailly, Mark Diekhans, David Dougherty, Tod More, Hattie Schroeder, Michael Doyle, Sarah Daniels, Ray Johnson, Mellissa Hirschl, Jan Nijtmans, Forest Rouse, Brion Sarachan, Lindsay F. Marshall, Greg Cronau, and Steve Simmons.

And, finally, my thanks to John Ousterhout and his teams at U.C. Berkeley, Sun, Scriptics, and Ajuba, and now to the Tcl Core Team and the host of maintainers. Programming in Tcl has been more productive and given me more pleasure than any tool I've used since I got my first chance to play Lunar Lander on an old IBM 1130.

*Tcl/Tk: A Developer's Guide* could not have existed without a lot of help from my friends, and for the CD-ROM I am even more indebted to a number of folks who contributed their work.

I'm very grateful to the authors of the *Real World* chapters, *;login:* magazine, and *IBM developerWorks* for letting me include these articles with this book.

For allowing me to include tutorials and articles, I am indebted to Will Morse, Robert Hill, Alexandre Ferrieux, Bill Ho, Lakshmi Sastry, Jean-Claude Wippler, Donal K. Fellows, Richard Suchenwirth, Cameron Laird, Mark Roseman, Chris Palmer, Holger Jakobs, Charles Vidal, Ernest Friedman-Hill, Keiichi Takahashi, Chao-Kuei Hung, Thierry Hamon, Steve Landers, Eliseo Vergara, Antonio Bello, César Menéndez, Francisco Ortega, and Satoshi Imai.

For allowing me to include their descriptions on how Tcl can be applied in the real world, I am indebted to David Beazley, Christopher Nelson, De Clarke, Donal K. Fellows, Carsten Zerbst, Doug Hughes, and Andreas Kupries.

For allowing me to include their extensions, packages, code, and extra documentation, I am indebted to Jan Nijtmans, David Beazley, Don Libes, Stephen Uhler, Jon Stump, Raymond Johnson, Ioi Lam, Lindsay Marshall, Dennis Labelle, Jean-Claude Wippler, Steve Landers, Andreas Kupries, Andreas Sievers, Steve Ball, Chang Li, D. J. Hagberg, Artur Trzewik, Scott Beasley, Michael McLennan, Mark Diekhans, Steve Wahle, Tom Poindexter, Cameron Laird, George A. Howlett, Jeffrey Hobbs, John Ousterhout, Paul Raines, Joe Mistachkin, Todd Helfter, Dr. Heiko Itterbeck, Daniel Steffen, and Forest Rouse.

# Introduction

Thanks for purchasing this copy of *Tcl/Tk: A Developer's Guide*. (You did buy this, didn't you?) This book will help you learn Tcl/Tk and show you how to use these tools to increase your programming productivity. By the time you have finished reading this book, you will have a good idea of what the strengths and weaknesses of Tcl/Tk are, how you can use the Tcl/Tk libraries and interpreters, and what constitutes an effective strategy for using Tcl/Tk.

This book is aimed at both computer professionals (from novice to expert level) and students. If you are experienced with computer programming languages, you will be able to skim through the first few chapters, getting a feel for how Tcl/Tk works, and then go on to the chapters on techniques and extensions. If you are less experienced, you should read the first chapters fairly carefully to be sure you understand the Tcl/Tk syntax. Tcl has some features that may not be obvious.

If your primary goal is to learn the Tcl/Tk basics as quickly as possible, examine the tutorials on the companion CD-ROM. There are several text and hypertext tutorials under the *tutorials* directory. The companion CD-ROM also includes TclTutor, a computer-aided instruction package for learning programming languages. It will introduce the Tcl language in 40 short lessons, with interactive examples you can run, modify, and rerun as you learn more about Tcl.

Every language has some simple tricks and techniques specific to that language. Tcl/Tk is no exception. The book discusses how to best accomplish certain tasks with Tcl/Tk: how to use the list and associative array data structures effectively, how to build modular code using Tcl's software engineering features, and what types of programming constructs will help you get your project from prototype to product with the minimal amount of rewriting.

Finally, there are plenty of code snippets, examples, and bits of packages to help you see how Tcl/Tk can be used. These examples are chosen to provide you with some boilerplate procedures you can add to your programs right now, to help you get from scribbles on paper to a working program. The companion CD-ROM includes the following:

- The longer examples
- Extra examples that were too long for the book
- Tutorials on different aspects of Tcl

- A printable reference
- The Tcl style manuals from Scriptics, Sun, and U.C. Berkeley
- Tcl/Tk tools and extensions discussed in Chapters 14 and 15
- The Tcl and Tk source code distributions
- The Tcl and Tk binaries for the Mac, Windows, and Linux platforms
- A collection of articles and an entire bonus book discussing how to use Tcl/Tk in a variety of application domains

This should give you a good idea of what is coming up. Feel free to skip around the book. It is written to be an overview and reference, as well as a tutorial.


## Where to Get More Information

As much as I would like to cover all aspects of Tcl/Tk in this book, it is not possible. Had I but world enough and time, I still would not have enough of either. The Tcl/Tk community and the Tcl/Tk tools are growing too quickly for a book to do more than cover the central core of the language. You can learn more about Tcl/Tk from the following web sources.

*www.tcl.tk/*

The definitive site for Tcl/Tk information.

*http://wiki.tcl.tk/*

The Tcler's Wiki. A collection of brief articles and discussions of Tcl features, tricks, tips, and examples.

*www.noucorp.com*

Noumena Corporation home page. Errata and extensions for this book, and updated Tcl Tutor.

*www.purl.org/NET/Tcl-FAQ/*

Tcl FAQ launch page. URLs for several Tcl/Tk FAQs and `comp.lang.tcl`.

*http://sourceforge.net/projects/tcl/*

Tcl/Tk archives. The official repository for Tcl/Tk distributions.

*www.activestate.html*

ActiveState. Tcl/Tk maintenance, Active Tcl, development tools, and more.

*www.equi4.com/*

Jean-Claude Wippler's corporate site. Information on CriTcl, Starkits, TclKit, and more.

*http://mini.net/cgi-bin/chat.cgi*

The Tcler's chat room. The Tkchat client can be downloaded from *www.sourceforge.net.*

*www.net-quest.com/~ivler/cgibook/refs/index.shtml*

Resources. URLs for mailing lists, newsgroups, and books on Tcl/Tk, Perl, HTML, and more.

*http://cuiwww.unige.ch/eao/www/TclTk.html*

The World Wide Web Virtual Library: Tcl and Tk. URLs for tutorials, FAQs, on-line manual pages, books, extensions, applications, and much more.

*http://bmrc.berkeley.edu/people/chaffee/tcltk.html*

Tcl/Tk for Win32 information. Patches and URLs for OLE and ODBC extensions.

*www.tcl-tk.de/*

Tcl/Tk information in German.

*www.geocities.co.jp/SiliconValley/4137/*

Tcl Scripting Laboratory. Tcl/Tk information in Japanese.

*www.cyut.edu.tw/~ckhung/olbook/*

Chao-Kuei Hung's pages. Tcl/Tk information in Chinese.

# CHAPTER 1

# Tcl/Tk Features

Your first question is likely to be "What features will Tcl/Tk offer me that other languages won't?" This chapter gives you an overview of the Tcl/Tk features. It covers the basics of what Tcl/Tk can offer you and what its strengths are compared to several alternatives.

Tcl is a multi-faceted language. You can use Tcl as a command scripting language, as a powerful multi-platform interpreted language, as a rapid prototyping platform, or as a library of interpreter calls within another project. Tcl's simple syntax makes single-use scripts [to replace repetitive command typing or graphical user interface (GUI) clicking] quick and easy to write. Tcl's modularization and encapsulation features help you develop large projects (100,000 + lines of code). Tcl's extensibility makes it easy to use Tcl as the base language across a broad range of projects, from machine control to database applications to electronic design applications, network test devices, and more.

Dr. John Ousterhout received the 1997 Software System Award from the Association for Computing Machinery (ACM) for inventing Tcl/Tk. This award recognizes the development of a software system that has a lasting influence. The ACM press release says it well:

> The Tcl scripting language and its companion Tk user interface toolkit have proved to be a powerful combination. Tcl is widely used as the glue that allows developers to create complex systems using preexisting systems as their components. As one of the first embeddable scripting languages, Tcl has revolutionized the creation of customizable and extensible applications. Tk provides a much simpler mechanism to construct graphical user interfaces than traditional programming languages. The overall Tcl/Tk system has had substantial impact through its wide use in the developer community and thousands of successful commercial applications.

A researcher at the Software Engineering Institute of Carnegie Mellon University reported in review SEI-2003-TN-001 that Tcl/Tk is practical for developing large systems.

Tcl is both free software and a commercially supported package. The core Tcl language is supported by a worldwide group of volunteers, and support can be purchased from ActiveState, Noumena Corporation, Cygnus, Proc Place, and others.

The current central site for Tcl/Tk information is *www.tcl.tk*. The source code repository and some binary snapshots are maintained at *http://sourceforge.net/projects/tcl/*. Tcl/Tk runtime packages are included with the Linux and FreeBSD packages and with commercial UNIX distributions such as Solaris and HPUX. The current binaries for selected systems (including MS Windows, Linux, and Solaris) are available from ActiveState (*www.activestate.com*).

One of the strengths of Tcl is the number of special-purpose extensions that have been added to the language. The most popular Tcl extension is Tk, which stands for Tool Kit. This extension provides tools for graphics programming, including drawing canvases, buttons, menus, and so on. The Tk extension is considered part of the Tcl core and is included in the source code distributions at SourceForge and most binary distributions.

The next most popular extensions to Tcl are [incr Tcl] (which adds support for object-oriented–style programming to Tcl) and expect, an extension that simplifies controlling other applications and devices and allows many complex tasks to be easily automated.

The proposal to add the [incr Tcl] extension to the standard Tcl distribution was approved in 2001. Adding the [incr Tcl] extension to the standard distribution assures developers that the core interpreter and extension revisions are in sync and work together flawlessly.

The expect, BLT (which includes a very useful graph and bar-chart widget), TclX (which adds new programming tools to the base Tcl language), and many other extensions, packages, and tools are available as source from their primary sites and as binaries on many systems. These packages and others are included on the companion CD-ROM either separately or as part of ActiveState's ActiveTcl release included on the CD-ROM.

## 1.1 Tcl Overview

Tcl (pronounced either as the three letters or as "tickle") stands for Tool Command Language. This name reflects Tcl's strength as a scripting language for gluing other applications together into a new application.

Tcl was developed by Dr. John Ousterhout while he was at the University of California at Berkeley. He and his group developed simulation packages that needed macro languages to control them. After creating a few on-the-fly languages that were tailored to one application and would not work for another, they decided to create an interpreter library they could merge into the other projects. This provided a common parsing package that could be used with each project and a common base language across the applications.

The original design goal for Tcl was to create a language that could be embedded in other programs and easily extended with new functionality. Tcl was also designed to execute other programs in the manner of a shell scripting language. By placing a small wrapper around the Tcl library, Dr. Ousterhout and his group created `tclsh`, a program that could be used as an interactive shell and as a script interpreter.

Dr. Ousterhout expected that this solid base for building specialized languages around a common set of core commands and syntax would be useful for building specialized tools. However, as programmers created Tcl extensions with support for graphics, database interaction, distributed processing, and so on, they also started writing applications in pure Tcl. In fact, the Tcl language turned out to be powerful enough that many programs can be written using `tclsh` as an interpreter with no extensions.

Today, Tcl is widely used for in-house packages, as an embedded scripting language in commercial products, as a rapid prototyping language, as a framework for regression testing, and for 24/7 mission-critical applications. The robustness of the Tcl interpreter is demonstrated by such mission-critical applications as controlling offshore oil platforms, product Q/A and Q/C operations, and running the NBC broadcasting studios. Many companies are open about use of Tcl, and many more consider Tcl their secret competitive edge.

## 1.1.1 The Standard Tcl Distribution

Tcl is usually distributed with two interpreters (`tclsh`, commonly pronounced "ticklish," and `wish`), support libraries, and on-line help. `Tclsh` is a text-based interpreter, and `wish` is the same basic interpreter with Tk graphics commands added.

You can use the Tcl interpreter (`tclsh`) scripts as you would use UNIX shell scripts or MS-DOS batch (*.bat*) scripts to control and link other programs or use `wish` to create GUI interfaces to these scripts. The `tclsh` interpreter provides a more powerful environment than the standard UNIX shell or *.bat* file interpreters.

The ActiveState `ActiveTcl` releases are sometimes called a *Batteries Included* version of Tcl, since the distribution includes the `tclsh` and `wish` interpreters and many more extensions, packages, and tools that have been compiled and tested together. The Tcl on-line help facility integrates into the native look and feel of the platform Tcl is installed on.

On a UNIX/Linux platform, the man pages are installed under *installation Directory/man/mann* and can be accessed using the standard man command.

You may need to add the path to the installed manual pages to your MANPATH environment variable. On Microsoft Windows platforms, you can access the Tcl help from the Start menu, shown in the following illustration.

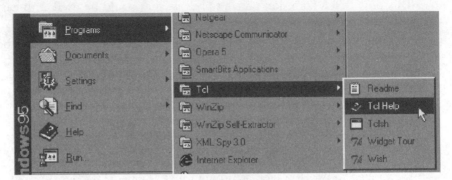

This will open a window for selecting which help you need. The window is shown in the following illustration.

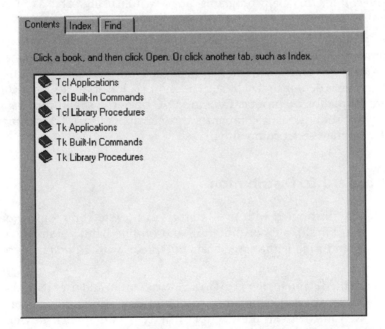

Selecting Tcl Built-In Commands from that menu will open a window like that shown in the following illustration. You can select from this window the page of help you need.

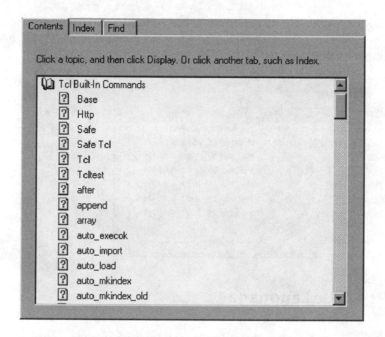

On a Macintosh, the help files are kept in the *Tcl/Tk HTML Manual* folder inside the *Tcl/Tk* folder, as shown in the following illustration.

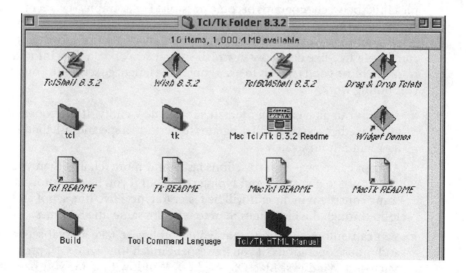

Opening that folder will display a list of the available help files, and selecting one of the help files will open a browser window for displaying the HTML document (see following illustration).

## 1.2 Tcl As a Glue Language

A command glue language is used to merge several programs into a single application. UNIX programmers are familiar with the concept of using the output from one program as the input of another via pipes. With a glue language, more complex links between programs become possible. For example, several programs that report network behavior can be merged with a glue language to create a network activity monitor. Instead of the linear data flow of a set of piped programs, you can have a tree-like data flow in which several sets of data flow into one application. There are good reasons to use simple glue language scripts in your day-to-day computing work:

■ A script can glue existing programs into a new entity. It is frequently faster to glue together several small programs to perform a specific task than it is to write a program from scratch.

■ A script can repeat a set of actions faster and more reliably than you can type. This is not to disparage your typing skills, but if you have to process 50 files in some consistent manner it will be faster to type a five-line script and have that loop through the file names than to type the same line 50 times.

■ You can automate actions that would otherwise take several sets of window and mouse operations. If you have spent much time with GUI programs using Microsoft Windows, Mac OS, or the X Window System, you have probably noticed that there are certain operations you end up doing over and over again, without a hot button you can use to invoke a particular set of button and mouse events. With a scripting language, you can automate a set of actions you perform frequently.

■ The script provides a record of commands and can act as procedure documentation.

For example, I create a new release of the TclTutor package (a copy of which is included on the companion CD-ROM) several times a year. This process involves several steps:

**1.** Copy the correct files to a release directory.

**2.** Create a zip file.

**3.** Convert the zip file to a self-extracting executable.

At each step, there are several mouse selections and button clicks. None of these are particularly difficult or time consuming, but each is a potential error in building the package. I go through this procedure several times while I test that the new distribution works correctly and the new code behaves properly.

I have automated this procedure with a small Tcl script. Since the script will be consistent, I don't have to worry about missing a file because I released a button too early, and the script ensures a consistent release format. The script is better than I am at remembering all the steps in the release process.

If you have written scripts using the Bourne shell under UNIX, or *.bat* files under MS-DOS/MS Windows, you know how painful it can be to make several programs work together. The constructs that make a good interactive user shell don't necessarily make a good scripting language.

Using Tcl, you can invoke other programs, just as you would with shell or *.bat* scripts, and read any output from those programs into the script for further processing. Tcl provides the string processing and math functionality of awk, sed, and expr without needing to execute other programs. It is easier to write Tcl scripts than Bourne shell scripts with awk and sed, since you have to remember only a single language syntax. Tcl scripts also run more efficiently, since the processing is done within a single executable instead of constantly executing new copies of awk, sed, and so on.

Note that you can only use a script to control programs that support a non-GUI interface. Many GUI-based programs have a command line interface suitable for scripting. Others may support script languages of their own or have a dialog-based mode. Under MS Windows, you can also interact applications using Tcl's DDE extension.

You can use a wish script as a wrapper around a set of programs originally designed for a text-based user interaction (query/response, or one-at-a-time menu choices) and convert the programs into a modern GUI-based package. This is a very nice way of adding a midlife kicker to an older package by hiding the old-style interactions from users more accustomed to graphical environments.

For example, we used a text-based problem-tracking system at one company. The user interface was a series of questions, such as "What product is the problem being reported against?" and "What revision is this product?" It took under an hour to write a wish front end that had buttons to select the products, text entry fields for the revisions and problem descriptions, and so on. This GUI invoked the old user interface when the Submit button was pressed and relayed the selected values to that program as the prompts were received.

The GUI interface reduced the time and error count associated with filling out a report by reducing the amount of typing and providing a set of choices for models and revisions. This technique for updating the user interface is faster than rewriting the application and is less prone to introducing new errors, since all original (debugged) code is left untouched.

### 1.2.1 Tcl Scripts Compared to UNIX Shell Scripts

The following are advantages Tcl provides over UNIX shell scripts.

- *Easier handling of program output.* Parsing program output in a shell script is possible but not always easy. With Tcl, it is simple. Instead of saving the original command line variables, changing the field separator, reading a line of output, and using the shell set command to parse the line into new command arguments, or invoking sed or awk to process some text, you can read a line from a program's output just as if it had been entered at a keyboard. Then you can use Tcl's powerful string and list operators to process the input, assign values to variables, perform calculations, and so on.

- *More consistent error handling in Tcl.* It can be difficult to distinguish between an error return and valid output in shell programming. Tcl provides a mechanism that separates the success/failure return of a program from the textual output.

- *Consistent language.* When you write UNIX shell scripts, you end up using copies of awk and sed to perform processing the shell cannot do. You spend part of your time remembering the arcane awk and sed command syntax, as well as the shell syntax. Using Tcl, you can use a single language to perform all of the tasks, such as program invocation, string manipulation, and computations. You can expend your effort solving the original problem instead of solving language issues.

- *Speed.* A single self-contained script running within the Tcl interpreter is faster and uses fewer machine resources than a UNIX shell script that frequently needs to spawn other programs.

  This is not to say that a program written in Tcl is faster than one written in the C language. A string-searching program written in Tcl is probably slower than a string-searching program written in C. But a script that needs to find strings may run faster with a string-searching subroutine in Tcl than one written for the UNIX shell that constantly forks copies of another executable. When it is appropriate to invoke a special-purpose program, it is easily done with the Tcl exec command.

- *GUI support.* You can use Tk to add a graphical interface to your scripts. Under UNIX, wish supports the Motif look and feel. Under Windows and Mac, Tk supports the native Windows or Macintosh look and feel.

According to reports in *comp.lang.tcl*, a GUI written with wish sometimes runs faster than the same GUI written in C with the Motif library. For lightweight GUIs, a Tk GUI is frequently faster than a Java GUI.

### 1.2.2 **Tcl Scripts Compared to MS-DOS** *.bat* **Files**

Tcl has so much more power than *.bat* files that there is actually very little comparison. The power of Tcl/Tk more closely resembles that of Visual Basic. Tcl/Tk is compared to Visual Basic in the next section, in the context of comparison of general-purpose interpreters. The following are advantages a Tcl script provides over an MS-DOS *.bat* file.

- *Access to the output of programs invoked from script.* The *.bat* file interpreter simply allows you to run programs, not to access a program's output. With Tcl you can start a program, read its output into your script, process that data, send data back to that task, or invoke another task with the modified data.

- *Control structures.* Tcl has more control structures than *.bat* files, including while loops, for loops, if/else, and switch.

- *String manipulation.* The *.bat* files do not support any string manipulation commands. Tcl provides a very rich set of string-searching and manipulation commands.

- *Math operations.* Tcl provides a full set of arithmetic functions, including arithmetic, trig, and exponential functions and multiple levels of parentheses.

- *Program control.* An MS-DOS *.bat* file has very limited control of other programs invoked by the *.bat* file. Tcl provides a great deal of control. In particular, when a GUI program is invoked from a *.bat* file under Windows 95 or Windows NT, the control may return to the *.bat* file before the program has ended. This is a problem if you were intending to make use of the results of the first program you invoked in the next program. Tcl can prevent the second program from starting until after the first program has completed its processing, or allow multiple programs to be run simultaneously.

- *GUI support.* You can use Tk to make your scripts into GUIs. Wish supports a look and feel that matches the standard MS Windows look and feel, and thus scripts you write with wish will look just like programs written in Visual C++, Visual Basic, or other Microsoft development environments.

## 1.3 Tcl As a General-Purpose Interpreter

The Tcl/Tk interpreter provides the following advantages over other interpreters.

- *Multi-platform.* The same script can be run under Microsoft Windows 3.1, Microsoft Windows 95/98, Microsoft Windows NT/2000/XP, Apple Mac OS and OS/X, and UNIX or Linux. Tcl has also been ported to Digital Equipment's VMS and real-time kernels, such as Wind River Systems' VxWorks, and even to platforms such as Palm OS and Win CE.

■ *Speed.* Since version 8.0 (released in 1998), the Tcl interpreter performs a run-time compilation of a script into a byte code. Running the compiled code allows a Tcl script to run faster than Visual Basic or Perl.

■ *Power.* Tcl supports most of the modern programming constructs.

  ■ Modularization in the form of subroutines, libraries (including version control), and namespaces.

  ■ Standard program flow constructs: `if`, `while`, `for`, `foreach`, and `switch`.

  ■ Rich set of variable types: integers, floating point, strings, lists, and associative arrays.

  ■ Exception handling. The Tcl `catch` and `error` commands provide an easy method of handling error conditions.

  ■ Support for traditional program flow and event-driven programming.

■ *Rich I/O implementation.* Tcl can perform I/O operations with files, devices, keyboard/screen, other programs, or sockets.

■ *Powerful string manipulation commands.* Tcl includes commands for searching and replacing strings or single characters, extracting and replacing portions of strings, and converting strings into lists, as well as commands that implement regular expressions for searching and replacing text.

■ *Extensibility.* Tcl extensions add a few new commands to the Tcl/Tk language to extend the interpreter into a new application domain. This allows you to build on previous development and greatly reduces startup time when working on a new problem, in that you only need to learn a couple of new commands, instead of an entire new language.

### 1.3.1 Tcl/Tk Compared to Visual Basic

Of the currently available languages, Visual Basic is probably the closest in functionality to Tcl/Tk. The following are reasons Tcl/Tk is a better choice.

■ Tcl/Tk scripts run on multiple platforms. Although the primary market for software may be the MS Windows market, you might also want to have Apple and UNIX markets available to your sales staff.

■ Tcl/Tk scripts have support for Internet-style distributed processing, including a secure, safe interpreter that allows an application to run untrusted applications securely.

■ Tk provides more and finer control of widgets. `Wish` allows you to bind actions to graphics objects as small as a single character in a text window or as large as an application window.

- Tcl has better support for library modules and version levels. A Tcl script can check for a particular version of its support libraries and not run if they are not available.

You might prefer Visual Basic over Tcl if you are writing a package that will only need to interact with the Microsoft applications. Many Microsoft applications use Visual Basic as their scripting language, and there are off-the-shelf components written in Visual Basic you can merge into these applications. Native Tcl supports only the DDE interprocess communication protocol for interacting with other MS Windows applications.

Support for OLE and COM objects can be added to Tcl with the TOCX extension, available at *www.cs.cornell.edu/Info/Projects/zeno/tocx/*, or the TclBridge package from Mistachkin Systems (*www.tclbridge.com/index.html*). A demo version of TclBridge is included on the companion CD-ROM under Tools. Support for SOAP can be added with the Tcl SOAP extension, available at *http://tclsoap.sourceforge.net/*.

### 1.3.2 Tcl/Tk Compared to Perl

Tcl/Tk often competes with Perl as an application scripting language. The following are advantages Tcl/Tk offers over Perl.

- *Simpler syntax.* Tcl code can be more easily maintained than Perl code. The rich set of constructs available to Perl programmers allows some very write-only programming styles. A Perl programmer can write code that strongly resembles UNIX shell language, C code, or awk scripts. Tcl supports fewer syntactic methods of accomplishing the same action, making Tcl code more readable.

- *Speed.* The Tcl 8.0 interpreter byte-compiled code runs as fast or faster than Perl 5 interpreter code.

- *Better GUI support.* Native Perl has no GUI support. A couple of Tk/Perl mergers are available, but Tk is better integrated with Tcl.

- *Internationalization.* Tcl has had fully integrated Unicode support since the 8.1 release (in 1999).

- *Thread safety.* While Tcl does not support multiple threads, the Tcl interpreter is thread safe and can be used with multi-threaded applications.

### 1.3.3 Tcl/Tk Compared to Python

The base Python interpreter is probably the closest to Tcl in functionality and use. Both are interpreted scripting languages designed to either glue other applications into a new super-application or to construct new applications from scratch, and both support easy extension with new C library packages.

The Python and Tcl developers actively adopt each other's ideas, leading to a condition in which the best features of each language are in both languages (and if that is not true at this moment, it will be true again soon). Many programmers know both languages, and the use of one over the other is as much personal preference as anything.

The following are the advantages of Tcl.

- *Simpler syntax.* The Tcl language is a bit simpler and easier to learn than Python.

- *Integrated with Tk.* Both Python and Perl have adopted the Tk graphics library as their graphics package. The integration of Tk with Tcl is cleaner than the integration with either Perl or Python. (After all, Tk was designed to work with Tcl.)

- *Less object oriented.* The base Tcl interpreter supports simple object-oriented programming with the namespace command or a C++/Java style of object-oriented programming with the [incr Tcl] extension, but does not require that you use either.

Python is built around a concept of objects that does not quite match the C++/Java class model, and there is no Python extension to get a complete object-oriented behavior with public, protected, and private data.

### 1.3.4 **Tcl/Tk Compared to Java**

The primary language for multi-platform applications today is Java. Tcl and Java have some similarities but are really designed to solve two different problem sets. Java is a system programming language, similar to C and C++, whereas Tcl is an interpreted scripting language. In fact, you can write Tcl extensions in Java, and Tcl can load and execute Java code. The following are advantages Tcl offers over Java.

- *Better multi-platform support.* Tcl runs on more platforms than Java. Java requires thread support, which is unavailable on many older UNIX platforms. Tcl has also been ported to real-time kernels such as VxWorks and Q-nix.

- *Faster for prototyping.* The strength of an object-oriented language is that it makes you think about the problem up front and to perform a careful design before you code. Unfortunately, for many projects, you do not know the requirements up front and cannot design a class structure until you understand the solutions better. Tcl/Tk is great for whipping out a quick prototype, seeing what truly answers the user's needs and what was not necessary, and then creating a serious design from a solid set of requirements.

- *Better GUI support.* The Tk widgets are easier to work with and provide higher-level support than the Java graphics library.

- *Configurable security levels.* Tcl supports a different security model than the Java Applet model, making Tcl an ideal language for Internet program development. With Tcl, objects with various origins can be given varying levels of access to your system. By default, the Tcl browser plug-in modules come with three security levels: untrusted (no access to file system or sockets), slightly trusted (can read files or sockets, but not both), and fully trusted (can access all I/O types.) With Tcl, you can configure your own security model, allowing access to a subset of the file system or specific devices, for instance.

- *Smaller downloadable objects.* Because the Tcl libraries live on the machine where an application runs, there is less to download with a Tcl/Tk application than a similar set of functionality written in Java.

## 1.4 Tcl As an Extensible Interpreter

Many programming groups these days have a set of legacy code, a set of missions, and a need to perform some sort of rapid development. Tcl can be used to glue these code pieces into new applications. Using Tcl, you can take the existing project libraries and turn them into commands within a Tcl interpreter. Once this is done, you have a language you can use to develop rapid prototypes or even shippable programs.

Merging the existing libraries into the interpreter gives you a chance to hide sets of calling conventions that may have grown over several years (and projects) and thus expose the application developer to a consistent application programmer interface (API). This technique gives you a chance to graft a graphics interface over older, non-GUI–based sets of code.

## 1.5 Tcl As an Embeddable Interpreter

Programs frequently start as a simple proof of concept with hard-coded values. These values quickly evolve into variables that can be set with command line arguments. Shortly after that, the command lines get unwieldy, and someone adds a configuration file and a small interpreter to parse the configuration. The macro language then grows to control program flow as well as variables. Then it starts to get messy.

At the point where you need a configuration file, you can merge in a Tcl interpreter instead of writing new code to parse the configuration file. You can use Tcl calls to interpret the configuration file, and as the requirements expand you will already have a complete interpreter available, instead of hacking in features as people request them.

## 1.6 Tcl As a Rapid Development Tool

Tcl has a simple and consistent syntax at its core, which makes it an easy language to learn. At the edges, Tcl has many powerful extensions that provide less commonly needed functionality. These extensions include the following:

- General-purpose programming extensions such as TclX (new commands to make Tcl more useful for sys-admins) and [incr Tcl] (a full-featured object-oriented extension)

- Application-specific extensions such as OraTcl and SybTcl (for controlling Oracle or Sybase database engines)

- Special-purpose hardware extensions such as the extension for controlling a National Scientific card described in the *Real-World Tcl/Tk* bonus book on the companion CD-ROM

- Special-purpose software libraries such as the TSIPP extension, which lets you generate 3D images using the SIPP library from Tcl

You can think of Tcl as a simple language with a rich set of libraries.

You can learn enough of the core Tcl commands to start writing programs in under an hour and then extend your knowledge as the need arises. When a task requires some new tools (SQL database interface, for instance), you have to learn only those new commands, not an entire new language. This common core with extensions makes your life as a programmer easier. You can take all the knowledge you gained doing one project and apply most of it to your next project.

This simplicity at the core with complexity in the extensions makes Tcl/Tk very suitable for rapid prototype development projects. During the 1995 Tcl/Tk Workshop, Brion Sarachan described the product that General Electric developed for NBC to control television network distribution (the paper describing this work is printed in the Conference Proceedings of the Tcl/Tk Workshop, July 1995).

The first meeting was held before the contract was awarded and included the engineers, management, and sales staff. After discussing the basic requirements, the sales and management groups continued to discuss schedules, pricing, and such, while the engineers went into another room and put together a prototype for what the system might look like. By the time the sales and management staff were done, the engineers had a prototype to show. This turnaround speed had a lot to do with GE being awarded that contract.

The GE group expanded their prototype systems with various levels of functionality for the people at NBC to evaluate. As the project matured, the specifications were changed on the basis of the experience with prototypes. The ease with which Tcl/Tk code can be extended and modified makes it an ideal platform for this type of project.

The ability to extend the interpreter is a feature that separates Tcl from the other multi-platform and rapid development languages. Tcl interpreters can be extended in several ways, ranging from adding more Tcl subroutines (called procs in Tcl) to merging C, Java, or even assembly code into the interpreter.

Studies have found that 80% of a program's runtime is spent in 20% of the code. The extensible nature of Tcl allows you to win at that game by rewriting the compute-intensive portion in a faster language while leaving the bulk of the code in the more easily maintained and modified script language.

This form of extensibility makes Tcl/Tk useful as the basis for a suite of programs. In a rapid prototype phase, a Tcl/Tk project can evolve from a simple set of back-of-the-envelope designs to a quick prototype done entirely in Tcl. As the project matures, the various subroutines can be modified quickly and easily, as they are all written in Tcl. Once the design and the main program flow have stabilized, various Tcl/Tk subroutines can be rewritten in C or Java to obtain the required performance.

Once one project has evolved to this state, you have an interpreter with a set of specialized commands that can be used to develop other projects in this problem domain. This gives you a platform for better rapid prototyping and for code reuse.

## 1.7 GUI-Based Programming

The Tcl distribution includes the Tk graphics extensions of Tcl. The Tk extension package provides an extremely rich set of GUI tools, ranging from primitive widgets (such as buttons, menus, drawing surfaces, text windows, and scrollbars) to complex compound widgets (such as file selectors).

Any visual object can have a script bound to it so that when a given event happens a particular set of commands is executed. For example, you can instruct a graphics object to change color when the cursor passes over it. You can bind actions to objects as trivial as a single punctuation mark in a text document or as large as an entire display.

Chapters 8 through 12 describe using Tk to build simple GUIs, active documents (such as maps and blueprints) that will respond to user actions, and complex, custom graphics objects.

## 1.8 Shipping Products

When it comes time to ship a product, you can either ship the Tcl scripts and Tcl interpreter or merge your Tcl script into an interpreter to create a Tcl-based executable. The advantage of shipping the Tcl scripts is that competent users (or clever programs) can modify and customize the scripts easily. The disadvantages include the need for the user to have the proper revision level of Tcl available for the script to run and the possibility that someone will reverse-engineer your program.

A Tcl script can be wrapped into a copy of the interpreter, to create a binary executable that will run only this script. (See the discussions of starkit, the TclPro wrapper, and Dennis Labelle's Freewrap in Chapter 13.) With this technique, you can develop your program in a rapid development environment and ship a single program that does not require installation of the Tcl interpreter and has no human-readable code.

## 1.9 Bottom Line

Tcl/Tk is

- A shell scripting language
- A multi-platform language
- An extensible interpreter
- An embeddable interpreter
- A graphics programming language

Tcl/Tk is useful for

- Rapid prototyping
- Shippable product
- Use-once-and-dispose scripts
- Mission-critical, 24/7 applications
- GUI-based projects
- Multi-platform products
- Adding GUIs to existing text-oriented programs
- Adding new functionality to old code libraries

## 1.10 Problems

The following numbering convention is used in all Problem sections.

| Number Range | Description of Problems |
| --- | --- |
| 100–199 | These problems review the material covered in this chapter. They can be answered in a few words or a short (1–5-line) script. Each problem should take under a minute to answer. |
| 200–299 | These problems go beyond the details presented in this chapter. They may require some analysis of the material or command details not covered in the chapter. They may require reading a man page or making a web search. They can be answered with a few sentences or a 5–50-line script. Each problem should take under 10 minutes to answer. |
| 300–399 | These problems extend the material presented in this chapter. They may require referencing other sources. They can be answered in a few paragraphs or a few hundred lines of code. Each exercise may take a few hours to complete. |

**100.** Can a Tcl script invoke other programs?

**101.** Can Tcl scripts perform math operations?

**102.** Is Tcl useful for rapid development?

**103.** Who developed the Tcl language? Where? Why?

**104.** Which of these statements is correct? Tcl is

    a. A single language

    b. A language core with many extensions

    c. A graphics language

**105.** How would you deploy a Tcl/Tk program if you could not be certain the client would have the right Tcl/Tk version installed on their system?

**106.** Can a Tcl interpreter be extended with another library?

**107.** Can the Tcl interpreter be embedded into another application?

**200.** Why would you use Tcl instead of C?

**201.** Why would you use C or C++ instead of Tcl?

**202.** Why would you use Tcl instead of a *.bat* file?

**203.** What type of requirement would preclude Tcl as the sole development language?

**300.** Some computer languages were developed to solve problems in a particular domain (SQL for database manipulation, COBOL for business applications, FORTRAN for calculations). Others were developed to support particular programming styles (functional languages such as Scheme and Lisp, object-oriented languages such as C++ and Java). Other groups of languages were created by developers who wanted a new, better tool (C for system development, Perl for systems scripts). Describe the strengths and weaknesses of each of these design philosophies.

**301.** Tcl can be used to glue small applications into a single larger application, to merge the functionality of multiple libraries into a single application, or to write completely self-contained applications. Why would you use one technique over another?

CHAPTER

2

# The Mechanics of Using the Tcl and Tk Interpreters

The first step in learning a new computer language is learning to run the interpreter/compiler and creating simple executable programs. This chapter explores the following:

- The mechanics of starting the interpreters
- Starting `tclsh` and `wish` scripts in interactive mode
- Exiting the interpreter
- Running `tclsh` and `wish` scripts from files

## 2.1 The `tclsh` and `wish` Interpreters

The standard Tcl/Tk binary distribution includes the following two interpreters.

- `tclsh` A text-oriented interpreter that includes the core commands, looping constructs, data types, I/O, procedures, and so on. `Tclsh` is useful for applications that do not require a GUI.
- `wish` A GUI-oriented extension to the `tclsh` interpreter. The `wish` interpreter includes the core Tcl interpreter, with all commands `tclsh` supports plus the Tk graphics extensions.

The simplest way to get started playing with Tcl and Tk is to type your commands directly into the interpreter. If you do not already have Tcl installed on your system, see the instructions in Appendix B for installing Tcl/Tk from the companion CD-ROM.

## 2.1.1 **Starting the** `tclsh` **and** `wish` **Interpreters**

You can invoke the `tclsh` and `wish` interpreters from a command line (with or without additional arguments) or from a menu choice. Invoking the interpreters from a command line without arguments or from a menu choice starts the interpreter in interactive mode: the interpreter evaluates the commands as you type them. Invoking the interpreter with a file name argument will cause the interpreter to evaluate the script in that file instead of starting an interactive session.

The command line to invoke the `tclsh` or `wish` interpreter from a shell prompt under UNIX resembles the following:

```
/usr/local/bin/tclsh ?scriptName? ?options?
```

If you invoke `tclsh` from a *.bat* file, MS-DOS command window, or Run menu under Microsoft Windows, the command would resemble the following:

```
C:\tcl\bin\wish.exe ?scriptName? ?options?
```

The exact path may vary from installation to installation, and the name of the `tclsh` or `wish` interpreter may vary slightly depending on how Tcl was installed. The default installation name for the interpreters includes the revision level (e.g., `wish8.4`), but many sites link the name `wish` to the latest version of the `wish` interpreter. The example paths and interpreter names used throughout this book will reflect some of the variants you can expect.

The command line options can tune the appearance of the `wish` graphics window. You can define the color map, the name of the window, the size of the initial window, and other parameters on the command line. Some of these options are system dependent, so you should check your on-line documentation the options available on your system. See Section 1.1.1 for a discussion on how to access the on-line help on UNIX, Macintosh, and Windows platforms.

If there are flags the Tcl interpreter does not parse, those arguments will be ignored by the `tclsh` or `wish` interpreter and passed directly to the script for evaluation.

A command line such as the following would invoke the `wish` interpreter and cause it to evaluate the code in the file *application.tcl*:

```
wish application.tcl -name "Big application" -config bigconfig.cnf
```

The `wish` interpreter recognizes the -name flag, and thus the arguments -name "Big application" would cause the window to be opened with the string Big application in the window decoration. The interpreter does not support a -config flag, and thus the arguments -config bigconfig.cnf would be passed to the script to evaluate.

### 2.1.2 Starting tclsh or wish Under UNIX

Under UNIX, you start tclsh or wish as you would start any other program: type tclsh at a shell prompt. If the directory containing the interpreter you want to invoke is in your $PATH, you can invoke the interpreter by name, as follows:

```
tclsh ?options? ?scriptName? ?scriptArguments?
```

If your $PATH does not include the directory that contains the tclsh executable, you would use the following:

```
/usr/local/bin/tclsh ?scriptName? ?scriptArguments?
```

When tclsh is run with no command line, it will display a % prompt to let you know the interpreter is ready to accept commands. When wish starts up, it will open a new window for graphics and will prompt the user with a % prompt in the window where you invoked wish. Starting wish and typing a short script at the prompt would resemble the following image.

### *Errors Caused by Improper Installation*

When the tclsh or wish interpreter starts, it loads several Tcl script files to define certain commands. The location for these files is set when the interpreter is installed. If an interpreter is moved without being reinstalled, or the support file directories become unreadable, you may get an error message resembling the following when you try to run tclsh:

```
application-specific initialization failed:
   Can't find a usable init.tcl in the following directories:
   /usr/local/lib/tcl8.4 /usr/local/lib/tcl8.4 /usr/lib/tcl8.4
   /usr/local/library /usr/library /usr/tcl8.4a4/library
   /tcl8.4a4/library /usr/local/lib/tcl8.4

This probably means that Tcl wasn't installed properly.
```

You might obtain the following when you try to run `wish`:

```
Application initialization failed:
  Can't find a usable tk.tcl in the following directories:
  /usr/local/lib/tk8.4 /usr/local/lib/tk8.4 /usr/lib/tk8.4
  /usr/local/library /usr/library /usr/tk8.4a4/library
  /tk8.4a4/library
```

`This probably means that tk wasn't installed properly.`

The `tclsh` and `wish` interpreters try several algorithms to find their configuration files. Sometimes this will result in the same directory being checked several times. This is normal and does not indicate any problem.

If you receive an error message like these, you should reinstall Tcl/Tk or restore the `init.tcl`, `tk.tcl`, and other files to one of the directories listed in the default search paths. Alternatively, you can find the directory that includes the appropriate `init.tcl` and `tk.tcl` and redefine where the interpreters will look for their configuration files by setting the environment variables TCL_LIBRARY and TK_LIBRARY to the new directories.

You can set the environment variable at your command line or in your *.profile*, *.dtprofile*, *.login*, *.cshrc*, or *.bashrc* configuration file. Using Bourne `shell`, Korn `shell`, or bash, this command would resemble

```
TCL_LIBRARY=/usr/local/lib/tcl8.0p1 ; export TCL_LIBRARY
```

Using `csh`, `tcsh`, or `zsh`, the command would resemble

```
setenv TCL_LIBRARY /usr/local/lib/tcl8.0p1
```

### 2.1.3 Starting `tclsh` or `wish` Under Microsoft Windows

When you install Tcl under Microsoft Windows, it will create a Tcl menu entry under the Programs menu, and within that menu entries for `tclsh` and `wish`. When you select the `tclsh` menu item, Tcl will create a window for you with the `tclsh` prompt (%). If you select the `wish` menu item, `wish` will open two windows: one for commands and one to display graphics.

You can also invoke `tclsh` from an MS-DOS prompt by typing the complete path and command name. Note that you may need to use the 8.3 version of a directory name. Windows NT/2000/XP examples follow.

```
C:> \Program Files\tcl\bin\tclsh80.exe
C:> \Program Files\tcl\bin\wish80.exe
```

Windows 95/98/ME examples follow.

```
C:> \Progra~1\tcl\bin\tclsh80.exe
C:> \Progra~1\tcl\bin\wish80.exe
```

Once you see the window with the % prompt (as shown in the following illustration), you can type commands directly to the `wish` shell. The commands you enter will be interpreted immediately. If you start the wish interpreter, and your command creates a graphic widget, it will be displayed in the graphics window. Starting wish from Windows Explorer and typing a short script at the prompt is shown in the following illustration.

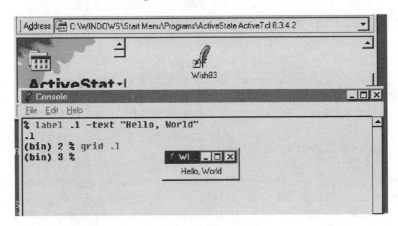

### 2.1.4 **Starting tclsh or wish on the Mac**

When you install Tcl on a Macintosh, it will create an icon that can be double clicked. When you double click the tclsh or wish icon, the tclsh or wish program will be invoked. Invoking tclsh will open up one window for commands. Invoking wish will open two windows: one for commands and one to display graphics. Starting wish from the Wish 8.3.2 icon and typing a short script at the prompt is shown in the following illustration.

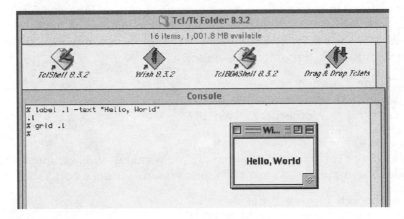

### 2.1.5 **Exiting tclsh or wish**

You can exit a tclsh or wish interactive interpreter session by typing the command exit at the % prompt. Under UNIX, you can also exit a wish program by selecting a Destroy icon from the window manager or selecting Close or Destroy from a pull-down menubutton. Under Microsoft Windows, you can exit a wish task by clicking on the X at the top right-hand corner of the graphics window. To exit tclsh, use the exit command.

## 2.2 Using tclsh/wish Interactively

The default tclsh prompt is a percent sign (%). When you see this prompt either in the window where you started tclsh or in a Tcl command window, you can type commands directly into the interpreter. Invoking tclsh in this mode is useful when you want to check the exact behavior of a command.

### 2.2.1 tclsh As a Command Shell

When tclsh and wish are used interactively, if you type a command that is not part of the Tcl language, such as ls or dir, the interpreter will attempt to invoke that program as a subprocess and will display the child's output on your screen. This feature allows you to use the Tcl interpreter as a command shell, as well as an interpreter.

Under UNIX, the command interpreters also evaluate shell programs. This is the equivalent of having the MS-DOS *.bat* file interpreter and command.com functionality available at the command line. Experienced users use this feature to write small programs from the command line to accomplish simple tasks.

For instance, suppose you give a friend a set of source code, and a few weeks later he returns it with a bunch of tweaks and fixes. You may want to go through all the source code to see what has been changed in each file before you commit the changes to your revision control system. Using a UNIX-style shell, you can compare all files in one directory to files with the same name in another directory and place the results in a file with a DIF suffix. The commands at the Bourne, Korn, or Bash shell prompt are as follows:

```
  $ for i in *.c
do
  diff $i ../otherDir/$i >$i.DIF
done
```

You can use tclsh to gain this power in the Windows and Macintosh worlds. The code to accomplish the same task under Windows using a tclsh shell is

```
% foreach i [glob *.c]{
    fc $i ../otherDir/$i >$i.DIF
}
```

If you install the GNU UNIX tools distribution on your platform, you could use the diff program instead of fc, and have a "compare all files" script that runs on all platforms.

### 2.2.2 **Tk Console (tkcon)— An Alternative Interactive tclsh/wish Shell**

Jeffrey Hobbs wrote a useful console program, tkcon, which provides a nicer interface than the simple % prompt. This program is the default console when you start tclsh or wish under MS Windows or on a Macintosh. Tk Console provides the following:

- A menu-driven history mechanism, to make it easy to find and repeat previous commands
- An Emacs-like editor interface to the command line, to make it easy to fix typos or modify previous commands slightly
- Brace and parenthesis matching, to help you keep your code ordered
- Color-coded text, to differentiate commands, data, comments, and so on
- The ability to save your commands in a file, which lets you experiment with commands and save your work
- A menu entry to load and run Tcl command scripts from files
- Support for opening several new tkcon displays

This program is included on the companion CD-ROM. After you install it, you can invoke it as you would any other script.

Note that although tkcon is easier to work with than the interactive wish interpreter, can be used to invoke wish scripts, and is more powerful than the Windows command interpreter, tkcon does not deal well with programs that use stdin to read user input. It is designed to help develop Tcl scripts and to execute noninteractive or GUI-oriented executables, not as a replacement for the DOS Console or an xterm window.

### 2.2.3 **Evaluating Scripts Interactively**

The tclsh and wish interpreters can be used interactively as Tcl program interpreters. This section will discuss typing a short program at the command prompt. The next section discusses how to run a program saved in a file. The traditional first program, "Hello, world," is trivial in Tcl:

```
% puts "Hello, world"
Hello, world
```

The puts command sends data to an I/O channel. The data may be a printable ASCII string or binary data. The default destination is the standard output device. On Windows and Macintosh systems, the standard output is the tclsh or wish console. On UNIX systems, stdout is the xterm session from which you invoked the interpreter. Windows and Macintosh scripts can display or hide the console with the `console show` and `console hide` commands. The destination for `puts` data can be any Tcl channel, which may be a file, other program, IP socket, or an internal pseudo-device. The Tcl I/O commands are discussed in Chapter 4.

Printing "Hello, world" is a fairly boring little example, so let's make it a bit more exciting by using the Tk extensions to make it into a graphics program. In this case, you need to invoke the `wish` interpreter instead of the `tclsh` interpreter. If you are using the Tk Console program to run this example, you will need to load the Tk package by selecting the Interp menu, then Packages, and then selecting Load Tk from the Packages menu, as shown in the following illustration.

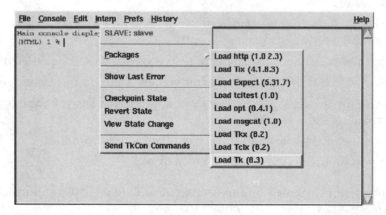

Typing the following code at the % prompt will display "Hello, world" in a small box in the graphics window.

```
label .l -text "Hello, world"
pack .l
```

The `label` command tells the `wish` interpreter to construct a graphics widget named `.l` and place the text "Hello, world" within that widget. The `pack` command causes the label to be displayed. This is covered in Chapter 8. When you run this script you should see a window resembling the following illustration.

## 2.3 Evaluating Tcl Script Files

Typing a short program at the command line is a good start, but it does not create a shippable product. The next step is to evaluate a Tcl script stored in a file on disk.

### 2.3.1 **The Tcl Script File**

A Tcl script file is simply an ASCII text file of Tcl commands. The individual commands may be terminated with a newline marker (carriage return or line feed) or a semicolon. Tcl has no restrictions on line length, but it can be difficult to read (and debug) scripts with commands that do not fit on a single display line. If a command is too long to fit on a single line, making the last character before the newline a backslash will continue the same command line on the next screen line. For example, the following is a simple tclsh script that prints several lines of information.

**Example 2.1**

*Script Code*

```
puts "This is a simple command"
puts "this line has two"; puts "commands on it";
puts "this line is continued \
on the next line, but prints one line"
```

*Script Output*

```
This is a simple command
this line has two
commands on it
this line is continued  on the next line, but prints one line
```

---

Note that there are two spaces between the words continued and on. When the Tcl interpreter evaluates a line with a backslash in it, it replaces the backslash newline combination with a space.

You can write Tcl/Tk programs with any editor that will let you save a flat ASCII file. On the Macintosh, the interactive command window behaves like a standard Macintosh editing window, allowing you to scroll back, copy lines, and save text. Under UNIX and Windows, the interactive command window does not support these options, and you will need to use a separate editor to create and modify your scripts.

In the UNIX world, vi and Emacs are common editors. On the MS Windows platforms, Notepad, Brief, WordPerfect, and MS Word are suitable editors. The Macintosh editors MacWrite and Alpha (and other editors that generate simple ASCII files) are suitable. Note that you must specify an ASCII text file for the output and use hard newlines if you use one of the word processor editors. The Tcl interpreter does not read most native word processor formats.

There are several Tcl integrated development environments (IDEs) available, ranging from commercial packages such as ActiveState's Komodo and Neatware's MyrmocoX, to freeware such as ASED and TclIDE, to tools such as the editor Mike Doyle and Hattie Schroeder developed as an example in their book *Interactive Web Applications with Tcl/Tk* (*www.eolas.com/tcl*). IDEs are discussed in more detail in Chapter 14. Several of these packages are found on the companion CD-ROM.

You can also use the Tk Console to type in Tcl commands and then save them to a file via the File > Save > History menu choice. You will probably need to edit this file after you have saved it, to delete extra lines.

## 2.3.2 Evaluating Tcl Script Files

For the time being, let's assume you have created a file named *foo.tcl* containing the following text:

```
label .l -text "The arguments to this script are: $argv"
pack .l
```

There are several ways to evaluate this wish script file. The following are two that will work on UNIX or Microsoft systems. Other methods tend to be platform specific, and these are covered in the system-specific sections.

You can always evaluate a tclsh or wish script by typing the path to the interpreter, followed by the script, followed by arguments to the script. This works under Windows (from a DOS window or Run menu) or UNIX and would look as follows:

```
C:\tcl8.4\bin\wish84.exe foo.tcl one two three
```

or

```
/usr/local/bin/wish8.4 foo.tcl one two three
```

This will cause a window resembling the following to appear on your display.

You can also cause a script to be evaluated by typing *source foo.tcl* at the % prompt within an interactive wish interpreter session. The source command will read and evaluate a script but does not support setting command line arguments. Using the source command for the previous examples would result in a label that only displayed the text "The arguments to this script are:" with no arguments displayed.

```
$> wish
% source foo.tcl
```

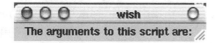

## 2.3.3 Evaluating a Tcl Script File Under UNIX

Under UNIX, you can use the technique of placing the name of the interpreter in the first line of the script file. Unfortunately, the shells will only search your current directory, */bin* and */usr/bin*, for interpreters. If you keep `tclsh` in another directory (for instance, */usr/foo/bin*), you will need to start your script files with the complete path, as follows:

```
#!/usr/foo/bin/tclsh
```

This makes a script less portable, since it will not run on a system that has `tclsh` under */usr/bar/bin*. A clever workaround for this is to start your script file with the following lines:

```
#!/bin/sh
#\
exec wish "$0" "$@"
```

The trick here is that both Tcl and the shell interpreter use the # to start a comment, but the Bourne shell does not treat the \as a line continuation character the way Tcl does.

The first line ( `#!/bin/sh` ) invokes the `sh` shell to execute the script. The shell reads the second line (#\), sees a comment, and does not process the \ as a continuation character, so it evaluates the third line (`exec wish "$0" "$@"`). At this point, the `sh` shell searches the directories in your $PATH to find a `wish` interpreter. When it finds one, the `sh` shell overwrites itself with that `wish` interpreter to execute. Once the `wish` interpreter is running, it evaluates the script again.

When the `wish` interpreter reads the script, it interprets the first line as a comment and ignores it, and treats the second line (#\) as a comment with a continuation to the next line. This causes the Tcl interpreter to ignore `exec wish "$0" "$@"` as part of the comment started on the previous line, and the `wish` interpreter starts to evaluate the script. The last step to making a `tclsh` or `wish` script executable is to `chmod` the file to set the execution bit:

```
chmod +x foo.tcl.
```

## 2.3.4 **Evaluating a Tcl Script File Under Microsoft Windows**

When Tcl is installed under Windows 95/98 or Windows NT/2000/XP, it establishes an association between the `.tcl` suffix and the `wish` interpreter. This allows you to run a `.tcl` script by typing the script name in the Run menu or via mouse clicks using Windows Explorer, the `Find` application, and so on.

If you desire to use other suffixes for your files, you can define `tclsh` or `wish` to process files with a given suffix via the Microsoft Windows configuration menus. The following is an example of adding a file association between the suffix `.tc8` and the `tclsh` interpreter. This association will invoke the `tclsh` interpreter to run scripts that are text driven instead of graphics driven. Select My Computer > View > Options, to get the Options display.

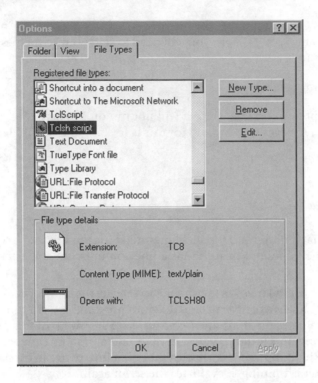

Select the File Types tab from this display and the NewType button from this card.

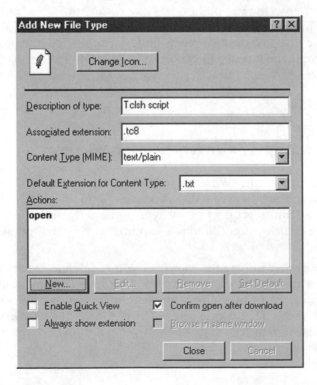

You must provide an open action that points to the interpreter you want to invoke to open files with this suffix. The application to perform the action needs a full path to the interpreter. Clicking the New button opens this window, where you can enter the open action and the application to use to open the file.

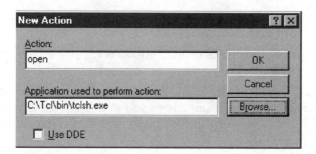

Running scripts via the mouse works well for wish-based programs that do not require any command line arguments. If you need to invoke a script with command line options, you must invoke the script from a DOS command window, the Run selection, or via a shortcut.

You can create a shortcut by right-clicking on an empty space on the Windows screen and selecting the New and Shortcut menu items. In the Shortcut window, enter (or browse to) your Tcl script, followed by whatever options you wish, as shown in the following illustration.

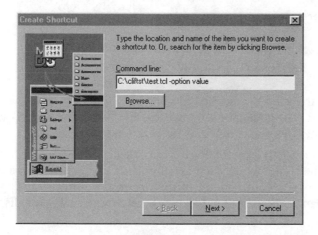

This will create a shortcut on your desktop, and when you click that shortcut Windows will invoke the wish interpreter to evaluate the script with the command line options you entered. Using a shortcut or the Run menu selection, Microsoft Windows will examine the registry to find out how to evaluate your script. If you want to invoke your script from a DOS-style command window, you will need to explicitly tell Windows what interpreter to use for the script. A technique that will always work is typing the complete path to the interpreter and the name of the script, as follows:

```
C:\tcl\bin\wish myscript.tcl
```

If you do not wish to type ungainly long lines whenever you invoke a script, there are several options:

■ You can add the path to the Tcl interpreter to your DOS path:

```
PATH C:\DOS;C:\PROGRA~1\TCL84\BIN;C: \WINDOWS;\
C:\WINDOWS\COMMAND
```

■ You can create a *.bat* file wrapper to invoke tclsh. This is similar to typing out the entire path in some respects, but allows you to put a single small .bat file in *C:\WINDOWS*, while leaving the Tcl interpreter and libraries in separate directories:

```
C:\PROGRA~1\TCL80\BIN\TCLSH  %1 %2 %3 %4 %5 %6 %7 %8 %9
```

■ You can write your Tcl programs as *.bat* files and evaluate them as filename.bat with the following wrapper around the Tcl code:

```
::catch {};#\
@echo off
::catch {};#\
@"C:\tcl\bin\tclsh.exe" %0 %1 %2
::catch {};#\
@goto eof

#your code here

#\

:eof
```

This is similar to the startup described for UNIX Tcl files. The lines with leading double colons are viewed as labels by the *.bat* file interpreter, whereas the Tcl interpreter evaluates them as commands in the global namespace.

These lines end with a comment followed by a backslash. The backslash is ignored by the *.bat* file interpreter, which then executes the next line. The Tcl interpreter treats the next line as a continuation of the previous comment and ignores it. The catch command is discussed in Chapter 6, and namespaces are discussed in Chapter 8.

If you prefer to run your scripts by single word (i.e., filename instead of filename.bat), you can change the line @"C:\tcl\bin\tclsh.exe" %0 %1 %2 to @"C:\tcl\bin\tclsh.exe" %0.bat %1 %2. The problem with the *.bat* file techniques is that *.bat* files support a limited number of command line arguments. On the other hand, if you need more than nine command line arguments, you might consider using a configuration file.

### 2.3.5 **Evaluating a Tcl Script on the Mac**

Mac OS X is built over a UNIX kernel and uses the techniques discussed for UNIX scripts. The concept of the executable script file does not really exist on the traditional Mac OS.

If you wish to evaluate a previously written script on the Mac, you can select the Source entry from the File menu, and then select the file to execute. Alternatively, you can type the command to source the script file at the % prompt. In this case, you must use the complete path, as follows:

```
source :demos:widget
```

The Tcl 8.0 and newer distributions include an application Drag & Drop Tclets that converts Tcl script files into small applications that can be launched normally. The first time you invoke this program, it will launch the standard Macintosh file selection mechanism for you to select the Wish Stub to use in the future and will prompt you for a name and location for the new program. You cannot change the Creator for a script to make the script evaluated by tclsh (or wish) when you double click it.

## 2.4 **Bottom Line**

- Tclsh is an interpreter for text-based applications.
- Wish is the tclsh interpreter with graphics extensions for GUI-based applications.
- These programs may be used as interactive command shells or as script interpreters.
- Either interpreter will accept a script to evaluate as a command line argument. A script is an ASCII file with commands terminated by newlines or semicolons. In a script, commands may be continued across multiple lines by making the final character of a line the backslash character.
- Tclsh scripts may be made executable by wrapping them in .bat files under MS Windows.
- Tclsh scripts may be made executable by setting the execute bit with chmod under UNIX.
- Tclsh scripts may be made executable with the Drag & Drop Tclets application on the Macintosh.
- Wish scripts that need no arguments may be executed from File Explorer under MS Windows.
- Wish scripts that need arguments may be executed from the Run menu under MS Windows.

- Arguments after the script file name that are not evaluated by the interpreter will be made available to the script being evaluated.

- The command to exit the `tclsh` or `wish` interpreters is `exit`.

## 2.5 Problems

The following numbering convention is used in all Problem sections.

**Number Range**  **Description of Problems**

100–199    These problems review the material covered in this chapter. They can be answered in a few words or a short (1–5-line) script. Each problem should take under a minute to answer.

200–299    These problems go beyond the details presented in this chapter. They may require some analysis of the material or command details not covered in the chapter. They may require reading a man page or making a web search. They can be answered with a few sentences or a 5–50-line script. Each problem should take under 10 minutes to answer.

300–399    These problems extend the material presented in this chapter. They may require referencing other sources. They can be answered in a few paragraphs or a few hundred lines of code. Each exercise may take a few hours to complete.

**100.** Can the `wish` shell be used to execute other programs?

**101.** Can the text in the window decoration of a `wish` application be defined from the command line?

**102.** Can a `tclsh` or `wish` script access command line arguments?

**103.** If you have a private copy of `wish` in your personal `bin` account on a UNIX/Linux platform, and have that directory in your search path, can you start scripts with `#!wish` to have them evaluated with this copy of `wish`? Assume the script is located in the `bin` with the `wish` interpreter, and the current working directory is your $HOME?

**104.** If you install Tcl on MS Windows under `D:\Tcl8.4`, will scripts with a file name ending in `.tcl` be evaluated by `wish` when you select them from File Explorer?

**105.** What is the `wish` command to create a window with simple text in it?

**106.** What `wish` command will cause a window to be displayed?

**107.** What `tclsh` command will generate output to a file or device?

**200.** If you type ls during an interactive Tcl session, tclsh will attempt to execute the ls on the underlying operating system. Can you include an ls command in a tclsh script? Why or why not?

**201.** Write a wish script that has a label with your name in it.

**202.** Write a tclsh script that prints out several lines on the standard output.

**203.** What command line would start a wish interpreter with the title "My Wish Application" in the window decoration? (UNIX or MS Windows only.)

**300.** Each window created in wish needs to have a unique name starting with a lower-case letter. Write a wish script that creates labels: one label should contain your name, one your favorite color, and one a numeric value (which might be the air speed of a swallow).

**301.** One of the two standard interpreters (wish and tclsh) was ported to MS-DOS 5.0 (not Windows). Which was ported, and why not the other?

CHAPTER

3

# Introduction to the Tcl Language

The next five chapters constitute a Tcl language tutorial. This chapter provides an overview of the Tcl syntax, data structures, and enough commands to develop applications. Chapter 4 discusses Tcl I/O support for files, pipes, and sockets. Chapters 5 and 6 introduce more commands and techniques and provide examples showing how Tcl data constructs can be used to create complex data constructs such as structures, trees, and classes.

This introduction to the Tcl language gives you an overview of how to use Tcl, rather than a complete listing of all commands and all options. The companion CD-ROM has a Tcl/Tk reference guide that contains brief listings of all commands and all options. The on-line reference pages are the complete reference for the commands. See Chapter 1 for a discussion on how to access the on-line help on UNIX, Macintosh, and Windows platforms.

If you prefer a more extensive tutorial, see the *tutorials* directory on the companion CD-ROM. You will find some HTML-based tutorials and a copy of TclTutor, a computer-assisted instruction program that covers all of the commands in Tcl and most of the command options.

Chapters 9 through 12 constitute the Tk tutorial. If you are performing graphics programming, you may be tempted to skip ahead to those chapters and just read about the GUIs. Don't do it! Tcl is the glue that holds the graphic widgets together. Tk and the other Tcl extensions build on the Tcl foundation. If you glance ahead for the Tk tutorial, plan on coming back to fill in the gaps. This book will print the command syntax using the font conventions used by the Tcl on-line manual and help pages. This convention is as follows.

| | |
|---|---|
| commandname | The command name appears first in this type font. |
| subcommandname | If the command supports subcommands, they will also be in this type font. |

| | |
|---|---|
| *-option* | Options appear in italics. The first character is a dash (-). |
| *argument* | Arguments to a command appear in italics. |
| *?-option?* | Options that are not required are bounded by question marks. |
| *?argument?* | Arguments that are not required are bounded by question marks. |

The following is an example.

**Syntax:** `puts` *?-nonewline? ?channel? outputString*

The command name is `puts`. The `puts` command will accept optional *-nonewline* and *channel* arguments and must include an `outputString` argument.

## 3.1 Overview of the Basics

The Tcl language has a simple and regular syntax. You can best approach Tcl by learning the overall syntax and then learning the individual commands. Because all Tcl extensions use the same base interpreter, they all use the same syntax. This consistency makes it easy to learn new sets of commands when the need arises.

### 3.1.1 Syntax

Tcl is a position-based language, not a keyword-based language. Unlike languages such as C, FORTRAN, and Java, there are no reserved words. The first word of a Tcl command line must always be a Tcl command; either a built-in command, a procedure name, or (when `tclsh` is in interactive mode) an external command.

A complete Tcl command is a list of words. The first word must be a Tcl command name or a subroutine name. The words that follow may be subcommands, options, or arguments to the command. The command is terminated by a newline or a semicolon.

For example, the word `puts` at the beginning of a command is a command name, but `puts` in the second position of a command could be a subcommand or a variable name. The Tcl interpreter keeps separate hash tables for the command names and the variable names, so you can have both a command `puts` and a variable named `puts` in the same procedure. The Tcl syntax rules are as follows.

- The first word of a command line is a command name.
- Each word in a command line is separated from the other words by one or more spaces.
- Words can be grouped with double quotes or curly braces.
- Commands are terminated with a newline or semicolon.

- A word starting with a dollar sign ($) must be a variable name. This string will be replaced by the value of the variable.

- Words enclosed within square brackets must be a legal Tcl command. This string will be replaced by the results of evaluating the command.

The Tcl interpreter treats a few characters as having special meaning. These characters are as follows.

### Substitution Symbols

$   The word following the dollar sign must be a variable name. Tcl will substitute the value assigned to that variable for the `$varName` string.

[]   The words between the square brackets must be a Tcl command string. The Tcl interpreter will evaluate the string as a command. The value returned by the command will replace the brackets and string.

### Grouping Symbols

""   Groups multiple words into a single string. Substitutions will occur within this string.

{}   Groups multiple words into a single string. No special character interpretation will occur within this string. A newline within curly braces does not denote the end of a command, and no variable or command substitutions will occur.

### Other

\   Escapes the single character following the backslash. This character will not be treated as a special character. This can be used to escape a dollar sign to inhibit substitution, or to escape a newline character to continue a command across multiple lines.

;   Marks the end of a command.

`<newline>`   Marks the end of a command.

#   Marks the rest of the line as a comment. Note that the # must be in a position where a Tcl command name could be: either the first character on a line or following a semicolon (;).

## Example 3.1

x=4   Not valid: The string x=4 is interpreted as the first word on a line and will be evaluated as a procedure or command name. This is not an assignment statement.
**Error Message:** `invalid command name "x=4"`

`puts "This command has one argument";`

Valid: This is a complete command.

| | |
|---|---|
| `puts one; puts two;` | Valid: This line has two commands. |
| `puts one puts two` | Not valid: The first puts command is not terminated with a semicolon, so Tcl interprets the line as a `puts` command with three arguments.<br>**Error Message:** `bad argument "two": should be "nonewline"` |

### 3.1.2 Grouping Words

The spaces between words are important. Since Tcl does not use keywords, it scans commands by checking for symbols separated by whitespace. Tcl uses spaces to determine which words are commands, subcommands, options, or data. If a data string has multiple words that must be treated as a single set of data, the string must be grouped with quotes (" ") or curly braces ({}).

**Example** 3.2

| | |
|---|---|
| `if { $x > 2} {`<br>   `set greater true`<br>`}` | Valid: If the value of x is greater than 2, the value of greater is set to "true." |
| `if{ $x > 2} {`<br>   `set greater true`<br>`}` | Not valid: No space between `if` and test left brace.<br>**Error Message:** `invalid command name "if{"` |
| `if {$x > 2}{`<br>   `set greater true`<br>`}` | Not valid: No space between test and body left brace.<br>**Error Message:** `extra characters after close brace` |
| `set x "a b"` | Valid: The variable x is assigned the value a b. |
| `set x {a b}` | Valid: The variable x is assigned the value a b. |
| `set x a b` | Not valid: Too many arguments to set.<br>**Error Message:** `wrong # args: should be "set varName ?newValue?"` |

The Tcl interpreter treats quotes and braces differently. These differences are discussed in Chapter 4.

### 3.1.3 Comments

A comment is denoted by putting a pound sign (#) in the position where a command name could be. The *Tcl Style Guide* recommends that this be the first character on a line, but the pound sign could be the first character after a semicolon.

**Example** 3.3

```
# This is a comment
```
    Valid: This is a valid comment.
```
puts "test" ;# Comment after a command.
```
    Valid: But not recommended style.
```
puts "test" # this is a syntax error.
```
    Not valid: The puts command was not terminated.

---

### 3.1.4 **Data Representation**

Tcl does not require that you declare variables before using them. The first time you assign a value to a variable name, the Tcl interpreter allocates space for the data and adds the variable name to the internal tables.

A variable name is an arbitrarily long sequence of letters, numbers, or punctuation characters. Although any characters (including spaces) can be used in variable names, the convention is to follow naming rules similar to those in C and Pascal; start a variable name with a letter, followed by a sequence of alphanumeric characters.

The *Tcl Style Guide* recommends that you start local variable names with an uppercase letter and global variable names with a lowercase letter. The rationale for this is that items that are intended for internal use should require more keystrokes than items intended for external use. This document is available at the Tcl/Tk resource (*www.tcl.tk/resource/doc/papers/*) and on the companion CD-ROM (*docco/style.ps*).

A variable is referenced by its name. Placing a dollar sign ($) in front of the variable name causes the Tcl interpreter to replace the $*varName* string with the value of that variable. The Tcl interpreter always represents the value of a Tcl variable as a printable string within your script. (Internally, it may be a floating-point value or an integer. Tcl interpreter internals are described in Chapter 13.)

**Example** 3.4

```
set x four
```
    Set the value of a variable named x to four.
```
set pi 3.14
```
    Set the value of a variable named pi to 3.14.
```
puts "pi is $pi"
```
    Display the string: "pi is 3.14."
```
set pi*2 6.28
```
    Set the value of a variable named pi*2 to 6.28.

```
set "bad varname" "Don't Do This"
```
Set the value of a variable named bad varname to Don't Do This.

---

Note that the * symbol in the variable name pi*2 does not mean to multiply. Since the * is embedded in a word, it is simply another character in a variable name. The last example shows how spaces can be embedded in a variable name. This is not recommended style.

### 3.1.5 Command Results

All Tcl commands return either a data value or an empty string. The data can be assigned to a variable, used in a conditional statement such as an if, or passed to another command.

The Tcl interpreter will evaluate a command enclosed within square brackets immediately and replace that string with the value returned when the command is evaluated. This is the same as putting a command inside backquotes in UNIX shell programming.

For example, the set command always returns the current value of the variable being assigned a value. In the example that follows, when x is assigned the value of "apple", the set command returns "apple". When the command set x "pear" is evaluated within the square brackets, it returns "pear", which is then assigned to the variable y.

### Example 3.5

```
# The set x command returns the contents of the variable.
% set x "apple"
apple
% set y [set x "pear"]
pear
% puts $y
pear
```

---

In the previous example, the quotes around the words apple and pear are not required by the Tcl interpreter. However, it is good practice to place strings within quotes.

### 3.1.6 Errors

Like other modern languages, Tcl has separate mechanisms for the status and data returns from commands and functions. If a Tcl command fails to execute for a syntactic reason (incorrect arguments, and so on), the interpreter will generate an error and invoke an error handler. The default error handler will display a message about the cause of the error and stop evaluating the current Tcl script.

A script can disable the default error handling by catching the error with the `catch` command and can generate an error with the `error` command. The `catch` command is discussed in Section 6.3.1.

## 3.2 Command Evaluation and Substitutions

Much of the power of the Tcl language is in the mechanism used to evaluate commands. The evaluation process is straightforward and elegant but, like a game of Go, it can catch you by surprise if you do not understand how it works.

Tcl processes commands in two steps. First, it performs command and variable substitutions, and then it evaluates the resulting string. Note that everything goes through this evaluation procedure. Both internal commands (such as `set`) and subroutines you write are processed by the same evaluation code. A `while` command, for example, is treated just like any other command. It takes two arguments: a test and a body of code to execute if the test is true.

### 3.2.1 Substitution

The first phase in Tcl command processing is substitution. The Tcl interpreter scans commands from left to right. During this scan, it replaces phrases that should be substituted with the appropriate values. Tcl performs two types of substitutions:

- A Tcl command within square brackets (`[...]`) is replaced by the results of that command. This is referred to as command substitution.
- A variable preceded by a dollar sign is replaced by the value of that variable. This is referred to as variable substitution.

After these substitutions are done, the resulting command string is evaluated.

### 3.2.2 Controlling Substitutions with Quotes, Curly Braces, and the Backslash

Most Tcl commands expect a defined number of arguments and will generate an error if the wrong number of arguments is presented to them. When you need to pass an argument that consists of multiple words, you must group the words into a single argument with curly braces or with quotes.

The difference between grouping with quotes and grouping with braces is that substitutions will be performed on strings grouped with quotes but not on strings grouped with braces. Examples 3.6 and 3.7 show the difference between using quotes and curly braces.

The backslash may be used to disable the special meaning of the character that follows the backslash. You can escape characters such as the dollar sign, quote, or brace to disable their special meaning for Tcl. Examples 3.8 and 3.9 show the effects of escaping characters. A Tcl script can generate an error message with embedded quotes with code, as in the following:

```
puts "ERROR: Did not get expected \"+OK\" prompt"
```

The following examples show how quotes, braces, and backslashes affect the substitutions. The first example places the argument to puts within curly braces. No substitutions will occur.

**Example** 3.6

*Script Example*

```
set x 2
set y 3
puts {The sum of $x and $y is returned by [expr $x+$y]}
```

*Script Output*

**The sum of $x and $y is returned by [expr $x+$y]**

In Example 3.7, puts has its argument enclosed in quotes, so everything is substituted.

**Example** 3.7

*Script Example*

```
set x 2
set y 3
puts "The sum of $x and $y is [expr $x+$y]"
```

*Script Output*

**The sum of 2 and 3 is 5**

In Example 3.8, the argument is enclosed in quotes, so substitution occurs, but the square brackets are escaped with backslashes to prevent Tcl from performing a command substitution.

**Example** 3.8

*Script Example*

```
set x 2
set y 3
puts "The sum of $x and $y is returned by \[expr $x+$y\]"
```

*Script Output*

**The sum of 2 and 3 is returned by [expr 2+3]**

Example 3.9 escapes the dollar sign on the variables to prevent them from being substituted and also escapes a set of quotes around the expr string. If not for the backslashes before the quotes, the quoted string would end with the second quote symbol, which would be a syntax error. Sets of square brackets and curly braces nest, but quotes do not.

## Example 3.9

***Script Example***

```
set x 2
set y 3
puts "The sum of \$x + \$y is returned by \"\[expr \$x+\$y\]\""
```

***Script Output***

```
The sum of $x + $y is returned by "[expr $x+$y]"
```

### 3.2.3 Steps in Command Evaluation

When a Tcl interpreter evaluates a command, it makes only one pass over that command to perform substitutions. It does not loop until a variable is fully resolved. However, if a command includes another Tcl command within brackets, the command processor will be called recursively until there are no further bracketed commands. When there are no more phrases to be substituted, the command is evaluated, and the result is passed to the previous level of recursion to substitute for the bracketed string.

The next example shows how the interpreter evaluates a command. The indentation depth represents the recursion level. Let's examine the following command:

```
set x [expr [set a 3] + 4 + $a]
```

- The expr command performs a math operation on the supplied arguments and returns the results. For example, expr 2+2 would return the value 4.

  The interpreter scans the command from left to right, looking for a phrase to evaluate and substitute. The scanner encounters the left square bracket, and the command evaluator is reentered with that subset of the command.

  ```
  expr [set a 3] + 4 + $a
  ```

  - The interpreter scans the new command, and again there is a bracket, so the command evaluator is called again with the following subset:

    ```
    set a 3
    ```

    - There are no more levels of brackets and no substitutions to perform, so this command is evaluated, the variable a is set to the value 3, and 3 is returned. The recursive call returned 3, so the value 3 replaces the bracketed command, and the command now resembles the following:

```
expr 3 + 4 + $a
```

- The variables are now substituted, and $a is replaced by 3, making the following new command:

```
expr 3 + 4 + 3
```

- The interpreter evaluates this string, and the result (10) is returned. The substitution is performed, and the command is now as follows:

```
set x 10
```

The interpreter evaluates this string, the variable x is set to 10, and tclsh returns 10. In particular, note that the variable a was not defined when this command started but was defined within the first bracketed portion of the command. If this command had been written in another order, as in the following,

```
set x [expr $a + [set a 3] + 4 ]
```

the Tcl interpreter would attempt to substitute the value of the variable a before assigning the value 3 to a.

- If a had not been previously defined, it would generate an error.
- If a had been previously defined, the command would return an unexpected result depending on the value. For instance, if a contained an alphabetic string, expr would be unable to perform the arithmetic operation and would generate an error.

A Tcl variable can contain a string that is a Tcl command string. Dealing with these commands is discussed in Section 7.4.2.

## 3.3 Data Types

The primitive data type in Tcl is the string, and the composite data types are the list and the associative array. The Tcl interpreter manipulates some complex entities such as graphic objects, I/O channels, and sockets via handles. Handles are introduced briefly here, with more discussion in the following chapters.

Unlike C, C++, or Java, Tcl is a typeless language. However, certain commands can define what sort of string data they will accept. Thus, the expr command, which performs math operations, will generate an error if you try to add 5 to the string "You can't do that."

### 3.3.1 Assigning Values to Variables

The command to define the value of a variable is set. It allocates space for a variable and data and assigns the data to that variable.

*Syntax:* set *varName ?value?*

> Define the value of a variable.
>
> *varName*  The name of the variable to define.
>
> *value*  The data (value) to assign to the variable.

set always returns the value of the variable being referenced. When set is invoked with two arguments, the first argument is the variable name and the second is a value to assign to that variable. When set is invoked with a single argument, the argument is a variable name and the value of that variable is returned.

## Example 3.10

```
% set x 1
1
% set x
1
% set z [set x 2]
2
% set z
2
% set y
can't read "y": no such variable
```

*Syntax:* append *varName ?value1? ?value2?*

> Append one or more new values to a variable.
>
> *varName*  The name of the variable to which to append the data.
>
> *value*  The data to append to the variable content.
>
> Note that append appends only the data you request. It does not add any separators between data values.

## Example 3.11

```
% set x 1
1
% append x 2
12
% append x
12
% append x 3 4
1234
% append y newvalue
newvalue
```

### 3.3.2 **Strings**

The Tcl interpreter represents all data as a string within a script. (Within the interpreter, the data may be represented in the computer's native format.) A Tcl string can contain alphanumeric, pure numeric, Boolean, or even binary data.

Alphanumeric data can include any letter, number, or punctuation. Tcl uses 16-bit Unicode to represent strings, which allows non-Latin characters (including Japanese, Chinese, and Korean) to be used in strings. A Tcl script can represent numeric data as integers, floating-point values (with a decimal point), hexadecimal or octal values, or scientific notation.

You can represent a Boolean value as a 1 (for true) and 0 (for false), or as the string "true" or "yes" and "false" or "no". Any capitalization is allowed in the Boolean string: "TrUe" is recognized as a Boolean value. The command that receives a string will interpret the data as a numeric or alphabetic value, depending on the command's data requirements.

**Example** 3.12

> *Legitimate Strings*
>
> *set alpha "abcdefg"*
>
> > Assign the string "abcdefg" to the variable alpha.
>
> *set validString "this is a valid string"*
>
> > Assign the string "this is a valid string" to the variable validString.
>
> *set number 1.234*
>
> > Assign the number 1.234 to the variable number.
>
> *set octalVal 0755*
>
> > Assign the octal value 755 to the variable octalVal. Commands that interpret values numerically will convert this value to 493 (base 10).
>
> *set hexVal 0x1ed*
>
> > Assign the hex value 1ED to the variable hexVal. Commands that interpret values numerically will convert this value to 493 (base 10).
>
> *set scientificNotation 2e2*
>
> > Assign the string 2e2 to the variable scientificNotation. Commands that interpret values numerically will convert this value to 200.
>
> *set msg {Bad input: "Bogus". Try again.}*
>
> > Assign the string Bad input: "Bogus". Try again. to the variable msg. Note the internal quotes. Quotes within a braced string are treated as ordinary characters.

*set msg "Bad input: \"Bogus\". Try again."*

> Assign the string Bad input: "Bogus". Try again. to the variable msg . Note that the internal quotes are escaped.

### Bad Strings

*set msg "Bad input: "Bogus". Try again."*

> The quotes around Bogus are not escaped and are treated as quotes. The quote before Bogus closes the string, and the rest of the line causes a syntax error.
>
> **Error Message:** extra characters after close-quote

*set badstring "abcdefg*

> Has only one quote. The error message for this will vary, depending on how the missing quote is finally resolved.

*set mismatch {this is not a valid string"*

> Quote and brace mismatch. The error message for this will vary, depending on how the missing quote is finally resolved.

*set noquote this is not valid string*

> This set of words must be grouped to be assigned to a variable.
>
> **Error Message:** wrong # args: should be "set varName ?newValue?"

## 3.3.3 String Processing Commands

The string, format, and scan commands provide most of the tools a script writer needs for manipulating strings. The regular expression commands are discussed in Section 5.6. The string subcommands include commands for searching for substrings, identifying string matches, trimming unwanted characters, and converting case. The format command generates formatted output from a format descriptor and a set of data (like the C library sprintf function). The scan command will extract data from a string and assign values to variables (like the C library scanf function).

All Tcl variables are represented as strings. You can use the string manipulation commands with integers and floating-point numbers as easily as with alphabetic strings. When a command refers to a position in a string, the character positions are numbered from 0, and the last position can be referred to as end.

There is more detail on all of the string subcommands in the Tcl reference and the companion CD-ROM tutorials. The following subcommands are used in the examples in the next chapters. The string match command searches a target string for a match to a pattern. The pattern is matched using the glob match rules.

The rules for glob matching are as follows:

| | |
|---|---|
| * | Matches 0 or more characters |
| ? | Matches a single character |
| [] | Matches a character in the set defined within the brackets |
| [abc] | Defines abc as the set |
| [m-y] | Defines all characters alphabetically between m and y (inclusive) as the set |
| \? | Matches the single character ? |

Note that the glob rules use [ ] in a different manner than the Tcl evaluation code. You must protect the brackets from tclsh evaluation, or tclsh will try to evaluate the phrase within the brackets as a command and will probably fail. Enclosing a glob expression in curly braces will accomplish this.

> **Syntax:** string match *pattern* *string*
>
> Returns 1 if *pattern* matches *string*, else returns 0.
>
> *pattern* The pattern to compare to *string*.
>
> *string* The string to match against the *pattern*.

## Example 3.13

```
% set str "This is a test, it is only a test"
This is a test, it is only a test
% string match "*test*" $str
1
% string match {not present} $str
0
```

The string tolower command converts a string to lowercase letters. Note that this is not done in place. A new string of lowercase letters is returned. The string toupper command converts strings to uppercase using the same syntax.

> **Syntax:** string tolower *string*
>
> **Syntax:** string toupper *string*
>
> *string* The string to convert.

## Example 3.14

```
% set upper [string toupper $str]
THIS IS A TEST, IT IS ONLY A TEST
% set lower [string tolower $upper]
this is a test, it is only a test
```

The string length command returns the number of characters in a string. With Tcl 8.0 and newer, strings are represented internally as 2-byte Unicode characters. The value returned by string length is the number of characters, not bytes.

> **Syntax:** string length *string*
>
> Return the number of characters in *string*.
>
> *string*   The string.

## Example 3.15

```
% set len [string length $str]
33
```

---

The string first command returns the location of the first instance of a substring in a test string or −1 if the pattern does not exist in the test string. The string last returns the character location of the last instance of the substring in the test string.

> **Syntax:** string first *substr string*

> **Syntax:** string last *substr string*
>
> Return the location of the first (or last) occurrence of *substr* in *string*.
>
> *substr*   The substring to search for.
>
> *string*   The string to search in.

## Example 3.16

```
% set st_first [string first st $str]
12
% set st_last [string last st $str]
31
```

---

The string range command returns the characters between two points in the string.

> **Syntax:** string range *string first last*
>
> Returns the characters in *string* between *first* and *last*.
>
> *string*   The string.
>
> *first*   The position of the first character to return.
>
> *last*   The position of the last character to return.

**Example** 3.17

```
% set subset [string range $str $st_first $st_last]
st, it is only a tes
```

---

The format command generates formatted strings and can perform some data conversions. It is equivalent to the C language sprintf command.

**Syntax:** format *formatString ?data1? ?data2?* ...

Return a new formatted string.

*formatString*    A string that defines the format of the string being returned.

*data#*    Data to substitute into the formatted string.

The first argument must be a format description. The format description can contain text strings and % fields. The text string will be returned exactly as it appears in the format description, whereas the % fields will be substituted with formatted strings derived from the data that follows the format descriptor. A literal percent symbol can be generated with a %% field.

The format for the % fields is the same as that used in the C library. The field definition is a string consisting of a leading percent sign, two optional fields, and a formatDefinition, as follows:

*% ?justification? ?field width? formatDefinition*

- The first character in a % field is the % symbol.
- The *field justification* may be a plus or minus sign. A minus sign causes the content of the % field to be left justified. A plus sign causes the content to be right justified. By default the data is right justified.
- The *field width* is a numeric field. If it is a single integer, it defines the width of the field in characters. If this value is two integers separated by a decimal point, the first integer represents the total width of the field in characters, and the second represents the number of digits to the right of the decimal point to display for floating-point formats.
- The formatDefinition is the last character. It must be one of the following.

s    The argument should be a string.

     Replace the field with the argument.

```
% format %s Oxf
```

**Oxf**

c    The argument should be a decimal integer.

     Replace the field with the ASCII character value of this integer.

```
% format %c 65
```
**A**

d or i      The argument should be a decimal integer.

Replace the field with the decimal representation of this integer.

```
% format %d 0xff
```
**255**

u      The argument should be an integer.

Replace the field with the decimal representation of this integer treated as an unsigned value.

```
% format %u -1
```
**4294967295**

o      The argument should be a decimal integer value.

Replace the field with the octal representation of the argument.

```
% format %o 0xf
```
**17**

X or x      The argument should be a decimal integer.

Replace the field with the hexadecimal representation of this integer.

```
% format %x -1
```
**ffffffff**

f      The argument should be a numeric value.

Replace the field with the decimal fraction representation.

```
% format %3.2f 1.234
```
**1.23**

E or e      The argument should be a numeric value.

Replace the field with the scientific notation representation of this integer.

```
% format %e 0xff
```
**2.550000e+02**

G or g      The argument should be a numeric value.

Replace the field with the scientific notation or floating-point representation.

```
% format %g 1.234e2
```
**123.4**

**Example** 3.18

```
% format {%5.3f} [expr 2.0/3]
0.667
% format {%c%c%c%c%c} 65 83 67 73 73
ASCII
```

The scan command is the flip side to format. Instead of formatting output, the scan command will parse a string according to a format specifier. The scan command emulates the behavior of the C sscanf function. The first argument must be a string to scan. The next argument is a format description, and the following arguments are a set of variables to receive the data values.

**Syntax:** scan *textString formatString ?varName1? ?varName2? ...*

Parse a text string into one or more variables.

| | |
|---|---|
| *textString* | The text data to scan for values. |
| *formatString* | Describes the expected format for the data. The format descriptors are the same as for the format command. |
| *varName\** | The names of variables to receive the data. |

The scan command returns the number of percent fields that were matched. If this is not the number of percent fields in the formatString, it indicates that the scan command failed to parse the data. The format string of the scan command uses the same % descriptors as the format command and adds a few more.

[...]    The value between the open and close square brackets will be a list of characters that can be accepted as matches.

Characters can be listed as a range of characters ([a-z]). A leading or trailing dash is considered a character, not a range marker.

All characters that match these values will be accepted until a nonmatching character is encountered.

```
% scan "a scan test" {%[a-z]} firstword
1
% set firstword
a
```

[^...]    The characters after the caret (^) will be characters that cannot be accepted as matches. All characters that do not match these values will be accepted until a matching character is encountered.

```
% scan "a scan test" {%[^t-z]} val
1
```

```
% set val
```
**a scan**

In the following example, the format string {%s %s %s %s} will match four sets of non-whitespace characters (words) separated by whitespace.

## Example 3.19

```
% set string {Speak Friend and Enter}
```
**Speak Friend and Enter**
```
% scan $string {%s %s %s %s} a b c d
```
**4**
```
% puts "The Password is: $b"
```
**The Password is: Friend**

---

A format string can also include literal characters that will be included in a format return or must be matched by the scan command. For instance, the scan command in the previous example could also be written as follows:

```
% scan $string {Speak %s} password
```

This would extract the password from Speak Friend and Enter, but would not extract any words from "The password is sesame", since the format string requires the word *Speak* to be the first word in the string.

### *String and Format Command Examples*

This example shows how you might use some string, scan, and format commands to extract the size, from, and timestamp data from an e-mail log file entry and generate a formatted report line.

## Example 3.20

### *Script Example*

```
# Define the string to parse.
set logEntry {Mar 25 14:52:50 clif sendmail[23755]:
g2PJqoG23755: from=<tcl-core-admin@lists.sourceforge.net>,
size=35362, class=-60, nrcpts=1,
msgid=<E16paVh-0003Px-00@usw-sf-list1.sourceforge.net>,
bodytype=8BITMIME, proto=ESMTP, daemon=MTA,
relay=IDENT:root@bastion.noucorp.com [192.168.9.4]}

# Extract "From" using string first and string range
set openAnglePos [string first "<" $logEntry]
```

```
set closeAnglePos [string first ">" $logEntry]
set fromField [string range $logEntry $openAnglePos $closeAnglePos]

# Extract the date using scan
scan $logEntry {%s %d %d:%d} mon day hour minute

# Extract the size using scan and string cmds.
set sizeStart [string first "size=" $logEntry]
set substring [string range $logEntry $sizeStart end]

# The formatString looks for a word composed of the
# letters 'eisz' (size will match) followed by an
# equals sign, followed by an integer. The word
# 'size' gets placed in the variable discard,
# and the numeric value is placed in the variable
# sizeField.

scan $substring {%[eisz]=%d} discard sizeField

puts ""
puts [format {%-12s %-40s %-s} "Timestamp" "From" "Size"]
puts [format {%s %d %d:%d %-40s %d} \
    $mon $day $hour $minute $fromField $sizeField]
```

***Script Output***

```
Timestamp       From                                      Size
Mar 25 14:52    <tcl-core-admin@lists.sourceforge.net>    35362
```

---

### 3.3.4 Lists

A Tcl list can be represented as a string that follows some syntactic conventions. (Internally, a string is represented as a list of pointers to Tcl objects, which are discussed later.)

- A list can be represented as a set of list elements enclosed within curly braces.
- Each word is a list element.
- A set of words may be grouped with curly braces.
- A set of words grouped with curly braces is a list element within the larger list and also a list in its own right.
- A list element can be empty (it will be displayed as {}).

For example, the string {apple pear banana} can be treated as a list. The first element of this list is apple, the second element is pear, and so on. The order of the elements can be changed with Tcl commands for inserting and deleting list elements, but the Tcl interpreter will not modify the order of list elements as a side effect of another operation.

A list may be arbitrarily long, and list elements may be arbitrarily long. Any string that adheres to these conventions can be treated as a list, but it is not guaranteed that any arbitrary string is a valid list. For example, "this is invalid because of an unmatched brace {" is not a valid list.

With Tcl 8.0, lists and strings are treated differently within the interpreter. If you are dealing with data as a list, it is more efficient to use the list commands. If you are dealing with data as a string, it is better to use the string commands.

The following are valid lists:

```
{This is a six element list}
{This list has {a sublist} in it}
{Lists may {be nested {arbitrarily deep}}}
"A string like this may be treated as a list"
```

The following are invalid lists:

```
{This list has mismatched braces
{This list {also has mismatched braces
```

### 3.3.5 List Processing Commands

A list can be created in the following ways:

- By using the set command to assign a list to a variable
- By grouping several arguments into a single list element with the list command
- By appending data to an unused variable with the lappend command
- By splitting a single argument into list elements with the split command

The list command takes several units of data and combines them into a single list. It adds whatever braces may be necessary to keep the list members separate.

**Syntax:** list *element1 ?element2? ... ?elementN?*

Creates a list in which each argument is a list element.

*element\** A unit of data to become part of the list.

**Example** 3.21

```
%set mylist [list first second [list three element sublist] fourth]
first second {three element sublist} fourth
```

The lappend command appends new data to a list, creating and returning a new, longer list. Note that this command will modify the existing list, unlike the string commands, which return new data without changing the original.

> **Syntax:**  lappend *listName ?element1? ... ?elementN?*
>
> Appends the arguments onto a list
>
> listName    The name of the list to append data to.
>
> *element*\*    A unit of data to add to the list.

## Example 3.22

```
% lappend mylist fifth
first second {three element sublist} fourth fifth
```

The split command returns the input string as a list. It splits the string wherever certain characters appear. By default, the split location is a whitespace character: a space, tab, or newline.

> **Syntax:**  split *data ?splitChar?*
>
> Split data into a list.
>
> *data*            The string data to split into a list.
>
> *?splitChar?*    An optional character (or list of characters) at which to split the data.

## Example 3.23

```
% set commaString "1,2.2,test"
1,2.2,test
% # Split on commas
% set lst2 [split $commaString ,]
1 2.2 test
% # Split on comma or period
% set lst2 [split $commaString {,.}]
1 2 2 test
% # Split on empty space between letters
% # (each character becomes a list element)
% set lst2 [split $commaString {}]
1 , 2 . 2 , t e s t
```

Tcl also includes several commands for manipulating lists. These include commands to convert a list into a string, return the number of elements in a list, search a list for elements that match a pattern, retrieve particular elements from a list, and insert and replace elements in a list.

**Syntax:** join *list ?separator?*

Joins the elements of a list into a string.

*list* The list to convert to a string.

*separator* An optional string that will be used to separate the list elements. By default, this is a space.

The join command can be used to convert a Tcl list into a comma-delimited list for import into a spreadsheet.

## Example 3.24

```
% set numbers [list 1 2 3 4]
1 2 3 4
% join $numbers :
1:2:3:4
% join $numbers ", "
1, 2, 3, 4
```

**Syntax:** llength *list*

Returns the length of a list.

*list* The list.

The llength command returns the number of list elements in a list. Note that this is not the number of characters in a list but the number of list elements. List elements may be lists themselves. These lists within a list are each counted as a single list element.

## Example 3.25

```
% set mylist [list first second [list three element sublist] fourth]
first second {three element sublist} fourth
% llength $mylist
4
```

**Syntax:** lsearch *?mode? list pattern*

Returns the index of the first list element that matches *pattern* or -1 if no element matches the pattern. The first element of a list has an index of 0.

*?mode?* The type of match to use in this search. *?mode?* may be one of

|         |                                                                                   |
|---------|-----------------------------------------------------------------------------------|
| -exact  | List element must exactly match the pattern.                                      |
| -glob   | List element must match pattern using the glob rules. This is the default matching algorithm. |
| -regexp | List element must match pattern using the regular expression rules.               |
| *list*    | The list to search.                                                             |
| *pattern* | The pattern to search for.                                                      |

The lsearch command uses the glob-matching rules by default. These are described with the previous string match discussion. The regular expression rules are discussed in Chapter 5.

**Example** 3.26

```
%set mylist [list first second [list three element sublist] fourth]
first second {three element sublist} fourth
% lsearch $mylist second
1
% # three is not a list element - it's a part of a list element
% lsearch $mylist three
-1
% lsearch $mylist "three*"
2
% lsearch $mylist "*ou*"
3
```

---

**Syntax:** lindex *list index*

Returns a list entry. The first element is element 0. If the requested element is larger than the list length, an empty string is returned.

*list*   The list.

*index*   The position of a list entry to return.

**Example** 3.27

```
%set mylist [list first second [list three element sublist] fourth]
first second {three element sublist} fourth
% lindex $mylist 0
first
% lindex $mylist 2
three element sublist
% lindex $mylist [lsearch $mylist *ou*]
fourth
```

---

*Syntax:* `linsert` *list position element1 ... ?elementN?*

Inserts an element into a list at a given position.

*list* The list to receive new elements.

*position* The position in the list at which to insert the new list elements. If this value is end or greater than the number of elements in the list, the new values are added at the end of the list.

*element\** One or more elements to be inserted into the list.

The `linsert` command returns a new list with the new elements inserted. It does not modify the existing list.

## Example 3.28

```
% set mylist [list first second [list three element sublist] fourth]
first second {three element sublist} fourth
% set longerlist [linsert $mylist 0 zero]
zero first second {three element sublist} fourth
% puts $mylist
first second {three element sublist} fourth
```

*Syntax:* `lreplace` *list first last element1 ... ?elementN?*

Replaces one or more list elements with new elements.

*list* The list to have data replaced.

*first* The first position in the list at which to replace elements. If this value is end, the last element will be replaced. If the value is greater than the number of elements in the list, an error is generated.

*last* The last element to be replaced.

*element\** Zero or more elements to replace the elements between the *first* and *last* elements.

Like `linsert`, the `lreplace` command returns a new list, but does not modify the existing list. The difference between the *first* and *last* elements need not match the number of elements to be inserted. This allows the `lreplace` command to be used to increase or decrease the length of a list.

## Example 3.29

```
% set mylist [list first second [list three element sublist] fourth]
first second {three element sublist} fourth
% set newlist [lreplace $mylist 0 0 one]
one second {three element sublist} fourth
```

```
% set shortlist [lreplace $mylist 0 1]
{three element sublist} fourth
```

The next example demonstrates using the list commands to split a set of colon-
and newline-delimited data (an export format of a common spreadsheet program)
into a Tcl list and then reformat the data for display.

**Example** 3.30

*List Commands Example*

```
# Define the raw data
set rawData {Package:Major:Minor:Patch
Tcl:8:3:4
}

# Split the raw data into a list using the newlines
#   as list element separators.
# This creates a list in which each line becomes a
#   list element
set dataList [split $rawData "\n"]

# Create a list of the column names.
set columnNames [split [lindex $dataList 0] ":"]

# Convert the first line of data into a list
set rowValues [split [lindex $dataList 1] ":"]

# Create a new list from $rowValues that includes
# all the elements after the first (package name).

set revList [lreplace $rowValues 0 0]
set revision [join $revList "."]

# Display a reformatted version of the data line
puts [format "%s: %s Revision: %s" [lindex $columnNames 0] \
[lindex $rowValues 0] $revision]
```

*Script Output*

**Package: Tcl Revision: 8.3.4**

### 3.3.6 Associative Arrays

The associative array is an array that uses a string to index the array elements,
instead of a numeric index the way C, FORTRAN, and Basic implement arrays.

A variable is denoted as an associative array by placing an index within parentheses after the variable name.

For example, `price(apple)` and `price(pear)` would be associative array variables that could contain the price of an apple or pear. The associative array is a powerful construct in its own right and can be used to implement composite data types resembling the C struct or even a C++ class object. Using associative arrays is further explored in Chapter 6.

**Example** 3.31

| | |
|---|---|
| `set price(apple) .10` | `price` is an associative array. The element referenced by the index `apple` is set to .10. |
| `set price(pear) .15` | `price` is an associative array. The element referenced by the index `pear` is set to .15. |
| `set quantity(apple) 20` | `quantity` is an associative array. The element referenced by the index `apple` is set to 20. |
| `set discount(12) 0.95` | `discount` is an associative array. The element referenced by the index 12 is set to 0.95. |

### 3.3.7 Associative Array Commands

An array element can be treated as a simple Tcl variable. It can contain a number, string, list, or even the name of another array element. As with lists, there is a set of commands for manipulating associative arrays. You can get a list of the array indices, get a list of array indices and values, or assign many array indices and values in a single command. Like the `string` commands, the `array` commands are arranged as a set of subcommands of the `array` command.

> **Syntax:** `array names` *arrayName* `?pattern?`
>
> Returns a list of the indices used in this array.
>
> *arrayName*  The name of the array.
>
> *pattern*  If this option is present, `array names` will return only indices that match the pattern. Otherwise, `array names` returns all the array indices.

The list of indices returned by the `array names` command can be used to iterate through the content of an array.

**Example** 3.32

```
set fruit(apples) 10
set fruit(pears) 5
```

```
foreach item [array names fruit *] {
    puts "There are $fruit($item) $item."
}
```

**There are 5 pears.**
**There are 10 apples.**

---

*Syntax:* `array get` *arrayName*

Returns a list of the indices and values used in this associative array.

*arrayName*    The name of the array.

The `array get` command returns the array indices and associated values as a list. The list is a set of pairs in which the first item is an array index and the second is the associated value. The third list element will be another array index (first item in the next pair), the fourth will be the value associated with this index, and so on.

## Example 3.33

```
% array get fruit
pears 5 apples 10
```

---

*Syntax:* `array set` *arrayName* {*index1 value1 ... indexN valueN*}

Assigns each value to the appropriate array index.

*arrayName*    The name of the array.

*index\**       An index in the array to assign a value to.

*value\**       The value to assign to an array index.

The `array set` command accepts a list of values in the format that `array get` generates. The `array get` and `array set` pair of commands can be used to copy one array to another, save and restore arrays from files, and so on.

## Example 3.34

```
% array set fruit [list bananas 20 peaches 40]
% array get fruit
bananas 20 pears 5 peaches 40 apples 10
```

---

The next example shows some simple uses of an array. Note that while the Tcl array does not explicitly support multiple dimensions, the index is a string and you can define multidimensional arrays by using a naming convention such as separating fields with a comma, period, dash, and so on that does not otherwise appear in the index values.

**Example** 3.35

*Array Example*

```
# Initialize some values with set
set fruit(apple.cost) .10
set fruit(apple.count) 5

# Initialize some more with array set
array set fruit {pear.cost .15 pear.count 3}

# At this point the array contains
# Index       Value
# apple.cost  .10
# pear.cost   .15
# apple.count 5
# pear.count  3
# Count the number of different types of fruit in the
# array by getting a list of unique indices, and then
# using the llength command to count the number of
# elements in the list.
set typeCount [llength [array names fruit *cost]]
puts "There are $typeCount types of fruit in the fruit array"

# You can use another variable to hold all or a part of an
# array index.

set type apple
puts "There are $fruit($type.count) apples"

set type pear
puts "There are $fruit($type.count) pears"

# Clone the array fruit into the array newFruit
array set newFruit [array get fruit]

set type pear
puts "There are $newFruit($type.count) pears in the new array"
```

*Script Output*

**There are 2 types of fruit in the fruit array**
**There are 5 apples**
**There are 3 pears**
**There are 3 pears in the new array**

### 3.3.8 **Binary Data**

Versions of Tcl prior to 8.0 (pre-1998) used NULL-terminated ASCII strings for the internal data representation. This made it impossible to use Tcl with binary data that might have NULLs embedded in the data stream.

With version 8.0, Tcl moved to a new internal data representation that uses a native-mode data representation. An integer value is saved as a long integer, a real value is saved as an IEEE floating-point value, and so on. The new method of data representation supports binary data, and a command was added to convert binary data to integers, floats, or strings. Tcl is still oriented around printable ASCII strings, but the binary command makes it possible to handle binary data easily.

The binary command supports two subcommands to convert data to and from a binary representation. The format subcommand will transform an ASCII string to a binary value, and the scan subcommand will convert a string of binary data to one or more printable Tcl variables. These subcommands require a descriptor to define the format of the binary data. Examples of these descriptors follow the command syntax.

**Syntax:** binary format *formatString arg1 ?arg2? ... ?argN?*

Returns a binary string created by converting one or more printable ASCII strings to binary format.

*formatString*    A string that describes the format of the ASCII data.

*arg**    The printable ASCII to convert.

**Syntax:** binary scan *binaryData format arg1 ?varName1? ... ?varNameN?*

Converts a string of binary data to one or more printable ASCII strings.

*binaryData*    The binary data.

*formatData*    A string that describes the format of the ASCII data.

*varName**    Names of variables to accept the printable representation of the binary data.

The components of *formatString* are similar to the format strings used by scan and format in that they consist of a descriptor (a letter) and an optional count. If the count is defined, it describes the number of items of the previous type to convert. The count defaults to 1. Common descriptors include the following.

h    Converts between binary and hexadecimal digits in little endian order.

binary format h2 34 - returns "C" (0x43).

binary scan "4" h2 x - stores 43(0x43) in the variable x

H   Converts between binary and hexadecimal digits in big endian order.

binary format H2 34 - returns "4" (0x34).

binary scan "4" H2 x - stores 34(0x34) in the variable x

c   Converts an 8-bit value to/from ASCII.

binary format c 0x34 - returns "4" (0x34).

binary scan "4" c x - stores 52(0x34) in the variable x

s   Converts a 16-bit value to/from ASCII in little endian order.

binary format s 0x3435 - returns "54" (0x35 0x34).

binary scan "45" s x - stores 13620 (0x3534) in the variable x

S   Converts a 16-bit value to/from ASCII in big endian order.

binary format S 0x3435 - returns "45" (0x34 0x35).

binary scan "45" S x - stores 13365 (0x3435) in the variable x

i   Converts a 32-bit value to/from ASCII in little endian order.

binary format i 0x34353637 - returns "7654" (0x37 0x36 0x35 0x34).

binary scan "7654" i x - stores 875902519 (0x34353637) in the variable x

I   Converts a 32-bit value to/from ASCII in big endian order.

binary format I 0x34353637 - returns "4567" (0x34 0x35 0x36 0x37).

binary scan "7654" I x - stores 926299444 (0x37363534) in the variable x

f   Converts 32-bit floating-point values to/from ASCII.

binary format f 1.0 - returns the binary string "0x00803f."

binary scan "0x00803f" f x - stores 1.0 in the variable x

## Example 3.36

*Script Example*

```
binary scan "Tk" H4 x
puts "X: $x"
# Assign three integer values to variables
set a 1415801888
set b 1769152615
set c 1919246708

# Convert the integers to ASCII equivalent
puts [binary format {I I2} $a [list $b $c]]
```

*Script Output*

```
X: 546b
Tcl is great
```

The string used to define the format of the binary data is very powerful and allows a script to extract fields from complex C structures.

## Example 3.37

*Script Examples*

*C Code to Generate a Structure*

```c
#include <stdio.h>
#include <fcntl.h>

main () {
  FILE *of;
  // Define the structure

  struct a {
    int i;
    float f[2];
    char s[20];
    } aa;


  // Assign values to structure
  // elements

  aa.i = 100;
  aa.f[0] = 2.5;
  aa.f[1] = 3.8;
  strcpy(aa.s, "This is a test");

  // Open file and save data
  of = fopen("tstStruct", "w");
  fwrite(&aa, sizeof(aa), 1, of);
  fclose(of);
}
```

*Tcl Code to Read the Structure*

```tcl
# Open the input file, and read data
set if [open tstStruct r]
set d [read $if]
close $if



# scan the binary data into variables.

binary scan $d "i f2 a*" i f s

# The string data may include
# binary garbage after the NULL
# byte. Trim off the extra data.

set zero [binary format c 0x00]
set zeroPos [string first $zero $s]
incr zeroPos -1
set s [string range $s 0 $zeroPos]

# Display the results
foreach var {i f s} {
  puts "$var: [set $var]"
}
```

*Script Output*

```
i: 100
f: 2.5 3.79999995232
s: This is a test
```

### 3.3.9 **Handles**

Tcl uses handles to refer to certain special-purpose objects. These handles are returned by the Tcl command that creates the object and can be used to access and manipulate the object. When you open a file, a handle is returned for accessing that file. The graphic objects created by a `wish` script are also accessed via handles, which will be discussed in the `wish` tutorial. The following are types of handles.

channel
: A handle that references an I/O device such as a file, serial port, or TCP socket. A `channel` is returned by an `open` or `socket` call and can be an argument to a `puts`, `read`, `close`, `flush`, or `gets` call.

graphic
: A handle that refers to a graphic object created by a `wish` command. This handle is used to modify or query an object.

http
: A handle that references data returned by an `http::geturl` operation. An `http` handle can be used to access the data that was returned from the `http::geturl` command or otherwise manipulate the data.

There will be detailed discussion of the commands to manipulate handles in sections that discuss that type of handle.

## 3.4 **Arithmetic and Boolean Operations**

The commands discussed so far directly manipulate particular types of data. Tcl also has a rich set of commands for performing arithmetic and Boolean operations and for using the results of those operations to control program flow.

### 3.4.1 **Math Operations**

Math operations are performed using the `expr` and `incr` commands. The `expr` command provides an interface to a general-purpose calculation engine, and the `incr` command provides a fast method of changing the value of an integer.

The `expr` command will perform arbitrarily complex math operations. Unlike most Tcl commands, `expr` does not expect a fixed number of arguments. It can be invoked with the arguments grouped as a string or as individual values and operators. Arguments to `expr` may be grouped with parentheses to control the order of math operations. The `expr` command can also evaluate Boolean expressions and is used to test conditions by the Tcl branching and looping commands.

> **Syntax:** `expr` *mathExpression*

Tcl supports the following math operations (grouped in decreasing order of precedence).

$- + \sim !$     Unary minus, unary plus, bitwise NOT, logical NOT.

|  |  |
|---|---|
| * / % | Multiply, divide, modulo (return the remainder). |
| + − | Add, subtract. |
| ≪ ≫ | Left shift, right shift. |
| < > <= >= | Less than, greater than, less than or equal, greater than or equal. |
| == != | Equality, inequality. |
| & | Bitwise AND. |
| ^ | Bitwise exclusive OR. |
| \| | Bitwise OR. |
| && | Logical AND. Produces a 1 result if both operands are nonzero; 0 otherwise. |
| \|\| | Logical OR. Produces a 0 result if both operands are zero; 1 otherwise. |
| x?y:z | If-then-else, as in C. If $x$ evaluates to nonzero, the result is the value of $y$. Otherwise, the result is the value of $z$. The $x$ operand must have a numeric value. The $y$ and $z$ operands may be variables or Tcl commands. |

Note that the bitwise operations are valid only if the arguments are integers (not floating-point or scientific notation). The expr command also supports the following math functions and conversions.

### *Trigonometric Functions*

| | |
|---|---|
| sin | sin (*radians*)<br>set sin [expr sin($degrees/57.32)] |
| cosine | cos (*radians*)<br>set cosine [expr cos(3.14/2)] |
| tangent | tan (*radians*)<br>set tan [expr tan($degrees/57.32)] |
| arcsin | asin (*float*)<br>set angle [expr asin(.7071)] |
| arccosine | acos (*float*)<br>set angle [expr acos(.7071)] |
| arctangent | atan (*float*)<br>set angle [expr atan(.7071)] |
| hyperbolic sin | sinh (*radians*)<br>set hyp_sin [expr sinh(3.14/2)] |
| hyperbolic cosine | cosh (*radians*)<br>set hyp_cos [expr cosh(3.14/2)] |
| hyperbolic tangent | tanh (*radians*)<br>set hyp_tan [expr tanh(3.14/2)] |
| hypotenuse | hypot (*float, float*)<br>set len [expr hypot($side1, $side2)] |

arctangent of ratio    atan2 (*float, float*)
```
set radians [expr atan2($numerator, $denom)]
```

### Exponential Functions

natural log    log (*float*)
```
set two [expr log(7.389)]
```

log base 10    log10 (*float*)
```
set two [expr log10(100)]
```

square root    sqrt (*float*)
```
set two [expr sqrt(4)]
```

exponential    exp (*float*)
```
set seven [expr exp(1.946)]
```

power    pow (*float, float*)
```
set eight [expr pow(2, 3)]
```

### Conversion Functions

Return closest int    round (*float*)
```
set duration [expr round($distance, $speed)]
```

Largest integer less    floor (*float*)
than a float
```
set overpay [expr ceil($cost/$count)]
```

Smallest integer    ceil (*float*)
greater than a float
```
set each [expr ceil($cost/$count)]
```

Floating-point    fmod (*float, float*)
remainder
```
set missing [expr fmod($cost, $each)]
```

Convert int to float    double (*int*)
```
set average [expr $total / double($count)]
```

Convert float to int    int (*float*),
```
set leastTen [expr (int($total) / 10) * 10]
```

Absolute value    abs (*num*)
```
set xDistance [expr abs($x1 - $x2)]
```

### Random Numbers

Seed random number    srand (*int*)
```
expr srand([clock seconds])
```

Generate random number    rand()
```
set randomFloat [expr rand() ]
```

**Example** 3.38

```
% set card [expr rand()]
0.557692307692
% set cardNum [expr int($card * 52)]
29
```

```
% set cardSuit [expr int($cardNum / 13)]
2
% set cardValue [expr int($cardNum % 13)]
3
% expr floor(sin(3.14/2) * 10)
9.0
% set x [expr int(rand() * 10)]
4
% expr atan(((3 + $x) * $x)/100.)
0.273008703087
```

The incr command provides a shortcut to modify the content of a variable that contains an integer value. The incr command adds a value to the current content of a given variable. The value may be positive or negative, thus allowing the incr command to perform a decrement operation. The incr command is used primarily to adjust loop variables.

**Syntax:**   incr *varName* *?incrValue?*

| | |
|---|---|
| incr | Add a value (default 1) to a variable. |
| *varName* | The name of the variable to increment. |
| | Note: This is a variable name, not a value. Do not start the name with a $. This variable must contain an integer value, not a floating-point value. |
| *?incrValue?* | The value to increment the variable by. May be a positive or negative number. The value must be an integer between −65,536 and 65,535, not a floating-point value. The default value is 1. |

**Example** 3.39

```
% set x 4
4
% incr x
5
% incr x -3
2
% set y [incr x]
3
% puts "x: $x y: $y"
x: 3 y: 3
```

## 3.4.2 Conditionals

Tcl supports both a single-choice conditional (if) and a multiple-choice conditional (switch).

### The *if* Command

The if command tests a condition, and if that condition is true, the script associated with this test is evaluated. If the condition is not true, an alternate choice is considered, or alternate script is evaluated.

*Syntax:* if {*testExpression1*} {

    *body1*

    } ?elseif {*testExpression2*} {

    *body2*

    }? ?else {

    *bodyN*

    }?

| | |
|---|---|
| if | Determine whether a code body should be evaluated based on the results of a test. If the test returns true, the first body is evaluated. If the test is false and a body of code exists after the else, that code will be evaluated. |
| *testExpression1* | If this expression evaluates to true, the first body of code is evaluated. The expression must be in a form acceptable to the expr command. These forms include the following. |
| | An arithmetic comparison {$a < 2}. |
| | A string comparison { $string != "OK"}. |
| | The results of a command { [eof $inputFile]}. |
| | A variable with a numeric {$AnalysisResult} value. Zero (0) is considered false, and nonzero values are true. |
| *body1* | The body of code to evaluate if the first test evaluates as true. |
| elseif | If *testExpression1* is false, evaluate *testExpression2*. |
| *testExpression2* | A second test to evaluate if the first test evaluates to false. |
| *body2* | The body of code to evaluate if the second test evaluates as true. |
| ?else *bodyN?* | If all tests evaluate false, this body of code will be evaluated. |

In the following example, note the placement of the curly braces ({}). The *Tcl Style Guide* describes the preferred format for if, for, proc, and while commands. It recommends that you place the left curly brace of the body of these commands on the line with the command and place the body on the next lines, indented four spaces. The final, right curly brace should go on a line by itself, indented even with the opening command. This makes the code less dense (and more easily read).

Putting the test and action on a single line is syntactically correct Tcl code but can cause maintenance problems later. You will need to make some multi-line choice statements, and mixing multi-line and single-line commands can make the action statements difficult to find. Also, what looks simple when you start writing some code may need to be expanded as you discover more about the problem you are solving. It is recommended practice to lay out your code to support adding new lines of code.

A Tcl command is normally terminated by a newline character. Thus, a left curly brace must be at the end of a line of code, not on a line by itself. Alternatively, you can write code with the newline escaped, and the opening curly brace on a newline, but this style makes code difficult to maintain.

### Example 3.40

**A Simple Test**

```
set x 2
set y 3
if {$x < $y} {
    puts "x is less than y"
}
```

**Script Output**

```
x is less than y
```

---

### The switch Command

The switch command allows a Tcl script to choose one of several patterns. The switch command is given a variable to test and several patterns. The first pattern that matches the test phrase will be evaluated, and all other sets of code will not be evaluated.

**Syntax:**    switch *?opt? str pat1 bod1 ?pat2 bod2 ...? ?default defltBody?*

Evaluate 1 of N possible code bodies, depending on the value of a string.

*?opt?*        One of the following possible options:

-exact    Match a pattern string exactly to the test string, including a possible "-" character.

-glob     Match a pattern string to the test string using the glob string match rules. These are the default matching rules.

-regexp Match a pattern string to the test string using the regular expression string match rules.

-- Absolutely the last option. The next string will be the string argument. This allows strings that start with a dash (-) to be used as arguments without being interpreted as options.

*str* The string to match against patterns.

*pat\** A pattern to compare with the string.

*bod\** A code body to evaluate if patN matches string.

default A pattern that will match if no other patterns have matched.

*defltBody* The script to evaluate if no other patterns were matched.

The options -exact, -glob, and -regexp control how the string and pattern will be compared. By default, the switch command matches the patterns using the glob rules described previously with string match. You can use regular expression match rules by including the -regexp flag.

The regular expression rules are similar in that they allow you to define a pattern of characters in a string but are more complex and more powerful. The regexp command, which is used to evaluate regular expressions, is discussed in the next chapter. The switch command can also be written with curly braces around the patterns and body.

***Syntax:*** switch *?option? string* {
    *pattern1 body1*
    *?pattern2 body2?*

    ?default *defaultBody?*
}

When the switch command is used without braces (as shown in the first switch statement that follows), the pattern strings may be variables, allowing a script to modify the behavior of a switch command at runtime. When the braces are used (the second example following), the pattern strings must be hard-coded patterns.

### • Example 3.41

***Script Example***

```
set x 7
set y 7
```

```
# Using no braces substitution occurs before the switch
# command looks for matches.
# Thus a variable can be used as a match pattern:

switch $x \
    $y {puts "X=Y"} \
    {[0-9]} {puts "< 10"} \
    default {puts "> 10"}

# With braces, the $y is not substituted to 7, and switch looks
# for a match to the literal string "$y"

switch -glob $x {
    "1" {puts "one"}
    "2" {puts "two"}
    "3" {puts "three"}
    "$y" {puts "X=Y"}
    {[4-9]} {puts "greater than 3"}
    default {puts "Not a value between 1 and 9"}
}
```

***Script Output***

**X=Y**
**greater than 3**

---

If you wish to evaluate the same script when more than one pattern is matched, you can use a dash (-) in place of the body to cause the switch command to evaluate the next body, instead of the body associated with the current pattern. Part of a folk music quiz might resemble the following.

## Example 3.42

***Script Example***

```
puts "Who recorded 'Mr Tambourine Man' "
gets stdin artist   ;# User types Bob Dylan
switch $artist {
    {Bob Dylan} -
    {Judy Collins} -
    {Glen Campbell} -
    {William Shatner} -
    {The Chipmunks} -
    {The Byrds} {
        puts "$artist recorded 'Mr Tambourine Man' "
    }
    default {
```

```
        puts "$artist probably recorded 'Mr Tambourine Man' "
    }
}
```

***Script Output***

**Who recorded 'Mr Tambourine Man'**
Bob Dylan
**Bob Dylan recorded 'Mr Tambourine Man'**

---

## 3.4.3 Looping

Tcl provides commands that allow a script to loop on a counter, loop on a condition, or loop through the items in a list. These three commands are as follows:

for       A numeric loop command

while     A conditional loop command

foreach   A list-oriented loop command

### The for Command

The for command is the numeric loop command.

***Syntax:*** for *start test modify body*

Set initial conditions and loop until the *test* fails.

*start*   Tcl statements that define the start conditions for the loop.

*test*    A statement that tests an end condition. This statement must be in a format acceptable to expr.

*modify*  A Tcl statement that will be evaluated after each pass through the loop. Normally this increments a counter.

*body*    The body of code to evaluate on each pass through the loop.

The for command is similar to the looping for in C, FORTRAN, Basic, and so on. The for command requires four arguments; the first ( *start* ) sets the initial conditions, the next ( *test* ) tests the condition, and the third ( *modify* ) changes the state of the test. The last argument ( *body* ) is the body of code to evaluate while the *test* returns true.

## Example 3.43

***Script Example***

```
for {set i 0} {$i < 2} {incr i} {
  puts "I is: $i"
}
```

*Script Output*

```
I is: 0
I is: 1
```

## The while Command

The while command is used to loop until a test condition becomes false.

**Syntax:** while *test body*

Loop until a condition becomes false.

*test* A statement that tests an end condition. This statement must be in a format acceptable to expr.

*body* The body of code to evaluate on each pass through the loop.

**Example** 3.44

*While Loop Example*

```
set x 0;
while {$x < 5} {
  set x [expr $x+$x+1]
  puts "X: $x"
}
```

*Script Output*

```
X: 1
X: 3
X: 7
```

## The foreach Command

The foreach command is used to iterate through a list of items.

**Syntax:** foreach *listVar list body*

Evaluate *body* for each of the items in *list*.

*listVar* This variable will be assigned the value of the list element currently being processed.

*list* A list of data to step through.

*body* The body of code to evaluate on each pass through the loop.

**Example** 3.45

*Script Example*

```
set total 0
```

```
foreach num {1 2 3 4 5} {
  set total [expr $total + $num]
}
puts "The total is: $total"
```

***Script Output***

**The total is: 15**

---

With Tcl release 7.5 (1996) and later, the foreach command was extended to handle multiple sets of list variables and list data.

> ***Syntax:*** foreach *valueList1 dataList1 ?valueList2 dataList2?...* {
> > *body*
> > }

If the *valueList* contains more than one variable name, the Tcl interpreter will take enough values from the *dataList* to assign a value to each variable on each pass. If the *dataList* does not contain an even multiple of the number of *valueList* elements, the variables will be assigned an empty string.

## Example 3.46

***Script Example***

```
foreach {pres date} { {George Washington} {1789–1797}
                      {John Adams}        {1797–1801}
                      {Thomas Jefferson}  {1801–1809}
                      {James Madison}     {1809–1817}
                      {James Monroe}      {1817–1825}
              } state  {  Virginia
                          Massachusetts
                          Virginia
                          Virginia
                          Virginia} {
     puts "$pres was from $state and served from $date"
}
```

***Script Output***

**George Washington was from Virginia and served from 1789–1797**
**John Adams was from Massachusetts and served from 1797–1801**
**Thomas Jefferson was from Virginia and served from 1801–1809**
**James Madison was from Virginia and served from 1809–1817**
**James Monroe was from Virginia and served from 1817–1825**

## 3.5 Modularization

Tcl has support for all modern software modularization techniques:

- Subroutines (with the proc command)
- Multiple source files (with the source command)
- Libraries (with the package command)

The source and package commands are discussed in detail in Chapters 6 and 8, respectively.

### 3.5.1 Procedures

The procedure is the most common technique for code modularization. Tcl procedures

- Can be invoked recursively.
- Can be defined to accept specific arguments.
- Can be defined to accept arguments that have default values.
- Can be defined to accept a variable number of arguments.

The proc command defines a Tcl procedure.

> **Syntax:** proc *procName argList body*
>
> Defines a new procedure.
>
> *procName*   The name of the procedure to define.
>
> *argList*   The list of arguments for this procedure.
>
> *body*   The body to evaluate when this procedure is invoked.

Note how the argument list and body are enclosed in curly braces in the following example. This is the normal way for defining a procedure, since you normally do not want any substitutions performed until the procedure body is evaluated. Procedures are discussed in depth in Chapter 7.

**Example** 3.47

> ### Proc Example
>
> ```
> # Define the classic recursive procedure to find the
> # n'th position in a Fibonacci series.
> proc fib {num} {
>   if {$num <= 2} {return 1}
>   return [expr [fib [expr $num -1]] + [fib [expr $num -2]] ]
> }
> ```

```
for {set i 1} {$i < 6} {incr i} {
  puts "Fibonacci series element $i is: [fib $i]"
}
```

*Script Output*

```
fibonacci series element 1 is: 1
fibonacci series element 2 is: 1
fibonacci series element 3 is: 2
fibonacci series element 4 is: 3
fibonacci series element 5 is: 5
```

## 3.6 Bottom Line

This covers the basics of the Tcl language. The next chapter introduces the Tcl I/O calls, techniques for using these commands, and a few more commands.

- Tcl is a position-based language rather than a keyword-based language.
- A Tcl command consists of
  - A command name
  - Optional subcommand, flags, or arguments
  - A command terminator [either a newline or semicolon (;)]
- Words and symbols must be separated by at least one *whitespace* (space, tab, or escaped newline) character.
- Multiple words or variables can be grouped into a single argument with braces ({}) or quotes ("").
- Substitution will be performed on strings grouped with quotes.
- Substitutions will not be performed on strings grouped with curly braces ({}).
- A Tcl command is evaluated in a single pass.
- The Tcl evaluation routine is called recursively to evaluate commands enclosed within square brackets.
- Some Tcl commands can accept flags to modify their behavior. A flag will always start with a hyphen. It may proceed or follow the arguments (depending on the command) and may require an argument itself.
- Values are assigned to a variable with the set command.
  *Syntax:* set *varName value*
- Math operations are performed with the expr and incr commands.
  *Syntax:* expr *mathExpression*
  *Syntax:* incr *varName ?incrValue?*

- The branch commands are if and switch.

  *Syntax:* if {*test*} {*bodyTrue*} ?elseif {*test2*} {*body2*}? ?else {*bodyFalse*}?

  *Syntax:* switch *?option? string pattern1 body1\ ?pattern2 body2? ?default defaultBody?*

- The looping commands are for, while, and foreach.

  *Syntax:* for *start test next body*

  *Syntax:* while *test body*

  *Syntax:* foreach *listVar1 list1 ?listVar2 list2...? body*

- The list operations include list, split, llength, lindex, and lappend.

  *Syntax:* list *element1 ?element2? ... ?elementN?*

  *Syntax:* linsert *list position element1 ... ?elementN?*

  *Syntax:* lappend *listName ?element1? ... ?elementN?*

  *Syntax:* split *data ?splitChar?*

  *Syntax:* join *list ?joinString?*

  *Syntax:* llength *list*

  *Syntax:* lindex *list index*

  *Syntax:* lsearch *list pattern*

  *Syntax:* lreplace *list position1 position2 element1 ?... elementN?*

- The string processing subcommands include first, last, length, match, toupper, tolower, and range.

  *Syntax:* string first *substr string*

  *Syntax:* string last *substr string*

  *Syntax:* string length *string*

  *Syntax:* string match *pattern string*

  *Syntax:* string toupper *string*

  *Syntax:* string tolower *string*

  *Syntax:* string range *string first last*

- Formatted strings can be generated with the format command.

  *Syntax:* format *formatString ?data? ?data2? ...*

- The scan command will perform simple string parsing.

  *Syntax:* scan *textstring formatString ?varName1? ?varName2? ...*

- The array processing subcommands include array names, array set, and array get.

  *Syntax:* array names *arrayName ?pattern?*

  *Syntax:* array set *arrayName {index1 value1 ...}*

  *Syntax:* array get *arrayName*

- Values can be converted between various ASCII and binary representations with `binary scan` and `binary format`.

## 3.7 Problems

The following numbering convention is used in all Problem sections.

| Number Range | Description of Problems |
|---|---|
| 100–199 | These problems review the material covered in this chapter. They can be answered in a few words or a short (1–5-line) script. Each problem should take under a minute to answer. |
| 200–299 | These problems go beyond the details presented in this chapter. They may require some analysis of the material or command details not covered in the chapter. They may require reading a man page or making a web search. They can be answered with a few sentences or a 5–50-line script. Each problem should take under 10 minutes to answer. |
| 300–399 | These problems extend the material presented in this chapter. They may require referencing other sources. They can be answered in a few paragraphs or a few hundred lines of code. Each exercise may take a few hours to complete. |

**100.** What will the following code fragments display?

a. 
```
set a 1
puts "$a"
```

b. 
```
set a 1
puts {$a}
```

c. 
```
set a 1
puts [expr $a + 1]
```

d. 
```
set a b
set $a 2
puts "$b"
```

e. 
```
set a 1
puts "\$$a"
```

**101.** What are the Tcl's three looping commands?

**102.** What conditional commands does Tcl support?

**103.** What command will define a Tcl procedure?

**104.** Can a Tcl procedure be invoked recursively?

**105.** What is the first word in a Tcl command line?

**106.** How are Tcl commands terminated?

**107.** Can you use binary data in Tcl?

**108.** How does a Tcl procedure return a failure status?

**109.** What commands can modify the content of a variable?

**110.** How could you change an integer to a floating-point value with the append command?

**111.** Write a pattern for `string match` to match

    a. Strings starting with the letter A.

    b. Strings starting with the letter A followed by a number.

    c. Strings starting with a lowercase letter followed by a number.

    d. Strings in which the second character is a number.

    e. Three character strings of uppercase letters.

    f. A question.

**112.** What characters are returned by

    a. `string range "testing" 0 0`

    b. `string range "testing" 0 1`

    c. `string range "testing" 0 99`

    d. `string range "testing" 0 end`

    e. `string range "testing" 99 end`

    f. `string range "testing" end end`

**113.** Write a format definition that will

    a. Use 20 spaces to display a string, and left-justify the string.

    b. Use 20 spaces to display a string, and right-justify the string.

    c. Display a floating-point number less than 100 with two digits to the right of the decimal point.

    d. Display a floating-point number in scientific notation.

    e. Convert an integer to an ASCII character (i.e., convert 48 to "0", 49 to "1", and so on).

**114.** What is the second list element in the following lists?

    a. {one two three four}

    b. {one {two three} four}

    c. { {} one two three}

    d. { {one two} {three four} }

**115.** Which array command will return a list of the indices in an associative array?

**116.** Which Tcl command could be used to assign a value to a single element in an associative array?

**117.** Which Tcl command could be used to assign values to multiple elements in an associative array?

**118.** What `binary scan` format definition would read data that was written as this C structure?: struct { int i[4]; char c[25]; float f; }

**119.** If x and y are two Tcl variables containing the length of the opposite and adjacent sides of a triangle, write the expr command that would calculate the hypotenuse of this angle.

**200.** The classic recursive function is a fibonacci series, in which each element is the sum of the two preceding elements, as in the following:

```
1 1 2 3 5 8 13 21 ..
```

Write a Tcl proc that will accept a single integer and will generate that many elements of a fibonacci series.

**201.** Write a procedure that will accept a string of text and will generate a histogram of how many times each unique word is used in that text.

**202.** Write a procedure that will accept a set of comma-delimited lines and will generate a formatted table from that data.

**203.** Write a procedure that will check to see whether a string is a palindrome (if it reads the same backward and forward). Examples of palindromes include the words *noon* and *radar*, and the classic sentence *Able was I ere I saw Elba*.

**300.** The bubble sort works by stepping through a list and comparing two adjacent members and swapping them if they are not in ascending order. The list is scanned repeatedly until there are no more elements in the wrong position.

    a.  Write a recursive procedure to perform a bubble sort on a list of data.

    b.  Write a loop-based procedure to perform a bubble sort on a list of data.

**301.** Tcl has an `lsort` command that will sort a list. Use the `lsort` command to check the results of the bubble sort routines constructed in the previous exercise.

**302.** A trivial encryption technique is to group characters in sets of four, convert that to an integer, and print out the integers. Write a pair of Tcl procedures that will use the `binary` command to convert a plaintext message to a list of integers, and convert a list of integers into a readable string.

# CHAPTER 4

# The File System, Disk I/O, and Sockets

This chapter describes the Tcl tools for

- Navigating a file system
- Finding files and their attributes
- Reading and writing data to files or other applications
- Using client- and server-side sockets

## 4.1 Navigating the File System

Most modern operating systems represent file systems as some form of tree-structured system, with a single root node, and drives and directories descending from that single node. They represent the trees as a string of words defining the drives and subdirectories separated by some character. Most operating systems provide a library of system calls to interact with the file system. Unfortunately, most modern operating systems use something different for the directory separator, have different conventions for naming drives and subdirectories, and may provide different library calls for interacting with the file system.

The Tcl solution to multiple platforms is to provide a set of Tcl commands to generalize the interface between Tcl scripts and the underlying libraries. Interactions with the file system are handled by the cd, pwd, glob, and file commands. Your script can determine or change its current working directory with the pwd (Print Working Directory) and cd (Change Directory) commands.

*Syntax:* pwd

Returns the current working directory.

*Syntax:*  cd *newDirectory*

Changes the default working directory.

newDirectory   A directory to make the current default directory for open, glob, and so on.

## Example 4.1

*Script Example*

```
puts "Working Directory: [pwd]"
cd /tmp
puts "Working Directory: [pwd]"
```

*Script Output*

```
Working Directory: /home/clif
Working Directory: /tmp
```

---

The Tcl glob command allows a script to search a path for items with names or types that match a pattern. You can use glob to write scripts that will perform some action on each file in one or more directories without knowing in advance what files will be present. The glob command matches file names using the glob-style patterns described with the string match command in Section 3.3.3.

*Syntax:*  glob ?-nocomplain? ?-types *typeList*? ?--? *pattern*

-nocomplain        Do not throw an error if no files match the pattern.

-types *typeList*   Return only the items that match the *typeList*. The *typeList* is a string of letters that describes the types of file system entities available. If the *typeList* includes these elements, they are combined with a logical OR operation.

b    A block-mode device

c    A character device

d    A directory

f    A normal file

l    A symbolic link

p    A named pipe

s    A socket

If the *typeList* includes these elements, they are combined with a logical AND operation.

r    A file with read access.

w    A file with write access.

| | |
|---|---|
| ???? | On Mac only: A four-letter type is the type or creator of the file. For instance, TEXT for a TEXT-type file, or APPL for an Application-type file. |
| - - | Identifies the end of options. All following arguments are patterns even if they start with a dash. |
| pattern | A glob-style pattern to match. |

## Example 4.2

***Script Example***

```
foreach fileName [glob *.c *.h] {
  puts "C Source: $fileName"
}
```

***Script Output***

```
...
C Source tclUtil.c
C Source tclVar.c
C Source: regcustom.h
C Source: regerrs.h
...
```

The -types option can be used to select only those types of file system entities you want to deal with.

## Example 4.3

***Script Example***

```
puts "The subdirectories under /usr are: [glob -types d /usr/*]"
```

***Script Output***

```
The subdirectories under /usr are: /usr/bin /usr/lib /usr/libexec
/usr/sbin /usr/share /usr/X11R6 /usr/dict /usr/etc /usr/games
/usr/include /usr/local /usr/src /usr/kerberos /usr/i386-glibc21-linux
/usr/man
```

The pwd, cd, and glob commands provide an interface to services that all operating systems support. The file commands provide an interface to services that may be platform specific. Like the string commands, the file commands are implemented as subcommands from the main file command.

The file command includes many subcommands. The two primary subcommands for navigating a file system are file split *path*

Returns the path as a list, split on the OS-specific directory markers.

file join *list*

Merges the members of a list into an OS-specific file path, with each list member separated by the OS-specific directory markers.

These commands will split a file path into its components and reassemble them for the current platform. A script that uses these commands to build file paths will run without modification on all platforms.

On Windows and Linux systems, you can build file paths with the string commands by using forward slashes to separate directories. Do not use the Windows-style backward slash. In Tcl, the backward slash escapes the character following it, and you will end up confusing yourself with multiple layers of backward slashes escaping more backward slashes. For example, open "C:/data/datafile r" will work, but open "C:\data\datafile" will return an error that C:datadatafile cannot be opened.

File paths built with slash separators instead of file join will run under Windows or Linux/UNIX, but may not run on a Macintosh or other platforms. Use the file join and file split commands to create paths.

The file command includes several subcommands to simplify manipulating file paths. You can also manipulate a file path by converting a path to a list with file split and using the list and string commands to manipulate the parts. Using the file commands will probably be simpler.

file dirname *path*

Returns the portion of path before the last directory separator.

file tail *path*

Returns the portion of path after the last directory separator.

file rootname *path*

Returns the portion of path before the last extension marker.

## Example 4.4

### *Script Example*

```
set path [file join "PB 1400" "program files" Tcl bin wish.exe]"
puts "join: $path"
puts "dirname: [file dirname $path]"
puts "root: [file rootname $path]"
puts "tail: [file tail $path]"
```

### *Script Output*

```
# On Windows:
join: PB 1400/program files/Tcl/bin/wish.exe
```

```
dirname: PB 1400/program files/Tcl/bin
root: PB 1400/program files/Tcl/bin/wish
tail: wish.exe

# On Unix/Linux:
join: PB 1400/program files/Tcl/bin/wish.exe
dirname: PB 1400/program files/Tcl/bin
root: PB 1400/program files/Tcl/bin/wish
tail: wish.exe

# On a Macintosh:
join: PB 1400:program files:Tcl:bin:wish.exe
dirname: PB 1400:program files:Tcl:bin
root: PB 1400:program files:Tcl:bin:wish
tail: wish.exe
```

Note that the MS Windows and UNIX output is the same. Because Tcl uses the backslash (\) to escape characters, it can use the forward slash for file paths on both systems. Tcl automatically maps the forward slash in file paths to a backward slash under MS Windows.

## 4.2 Properties of File System Items

Before a script attempts to open a file, it may need to know information about the file: its size, creation date, permissions, whether it has been backed up, and so on. The system library calls that report this data differ from platform to platform. The information can be accessed within a Tcl script using some of the file subcommands.

>    *Syntax:* file *subcommand arguments*

The file command supports the following subcommands that return information about files.

### Reporting a File's Existence
file exist *path*

>    Returns true if a file exists and false if it does not exist.

### Reporting a File's Type
file type *path*

>    Returns the type of file referenced by path.

>    The return value will be one of the following.

>> file          $*path* is the name of a normal file.

directory         *$path* is the name of a directory.

characterSpecial  *$path* is the name of a UNIX character I/O device (such as a tty).

blockSpecial     *$path* is the name of a UNIX block I/O device (such as a disk).

fifo            *$path* is the name of a UNIX fifo file.

link            *$path* is the name of a hard link.

socket         *$path* is the name of a named socket.

For common tests, the file command includes the following subcommands.

file isdirectory *path*

Returns 1 if *path* is a directory; 0 if not.

file isfile *path*

Returns 1 if *path* is a regular file; 0 if not.

### *Reporting Statistics About a File*

file stat *path varName*

Treats varName as an associative array and creates an index in that array for each value returned by the stat library call. If the underlying OS does not support a status field, the value will be −1. The new indices (and values) will be

| | |
|---|---|
| atime | Time of last access |
| ctime | Time of last change to directory information |
| mtime | Time of last modification of file content |
| dev | Device type |
| gid | Group ID of owner |
| ino | Inode number for file |
| mode | Protection mode bits |
| nlink | Number of hard links |
| size | Size in bytes |
| type | Type of file |
| uid | User ID number of owner |

file attributes *path*

Returns a list of platform-specific attributes of the item referenced by *path*. These values are returned as a name value list. The values returned on a UNIX system are group, owner, and permissions. The values returned on a Windows system are archive, hidden, longname, readonly, shortname, and system. The values returned on a Mac system are creator, readonly, hidden, and type.

file attributes *path attributeName*

Returns the value of a named platform-specific attribute of the item referenced by *path*.

file attributes *path attributeName newValue*

Sets the value of the named attribute to newValue.

file nativename *path*

Returns pathName in the proper format for the current platform.

## Example 4.5

*Script Example*

```
proc reportDirectory {dirName} {

# file join merges the existing directory path with
#   the * symbol to match all items in that directory.

foreach item [glob -nocomplain [file join $dirName *]] {
  if { [string match [file type $item] "directory"]} {
      reportDirectory $item
  } else {

      puts "$item is a [file type $item]"
      puts "Attributes are: [file attributes $item]"
      file stat $item tmpArray
      set name [file tail $item]
      puts "$name is: $tmpArray(size) bytes\n"
    }
  }
}


# Start reporting from the current directory
reportDirectory {}
```

*Script Output*

```
# Unix output resembles:

html/index.html is a file
Attributes are: -group root -owner root -permissions 00644
index.html is: 1945 bytes

html/poweredby.png is a file
Attributes are: -group root -owner root -permissions 00644
poweredby.png is: 1154 bytes

# Windows output resembles:

C:/WINDOWS/Favorites/Personal Files.LNK is a file
```

```
Attributes are: -archive 1 -hidden 0
  -longname {C:/WINDOWS/Favorites/Personal Files.LNK}
  -readonly 0 -shortname C:/WINDOWS/FAVORI~1/PERSON~1.LNK
  -system 0
Personal Files.LNK is: 247 bytes

C:/WINDOWS/Favorites/Graphics.LNK is a file
Attributes are: -archive 1 -hidden 0
  -longname C:/WINDOWS/Favorites/Graphics.LNK
  -readonly 0 -shortname C:/WINDOWS/FAVORI~1/GRAPHICS.LNK
  -system 0
Graphics.LNK is: 379 bytes

# Mac output resembles:

:Build:Drag Drop Tclets is a file
Attributes are: -creator WIsH -hidden 0 -readonly 0 -type APPL
Drag Drop Tclets is: 257683 bytes

:Build:Tclapplescript.shlb is a file
Attributes are: -creator TclL -hidden 0 -readonly 0 -type shlb
Tclapplescript.shlb is: 21056 bytes
```

Note that names of the attributes in the `file attributes` command include the dash (-) character and are returned as key/value pairs. Many Tcl extensions use this format to return collections of data. Data returned as key/value pairs can be easily assigned to an array using the `eval` and `array set` commands:

```
array set dataArray [file attributes $filePath]
```

## 4.3 Removing Files

The last thing a program needs to do with a file is remove it. The `file` command also provides access to the operating system function that will remove a file.

*file delete pathName*

> Deletes the file referenced by *pathName*.

## 4.4 Input/Output in Tcl

It is difficult to perform any serious computer programming without accepting data and delivering results. Tcl generalizes the input and output commands into two input commands and one output command. Using these three commands, you can read or write to any file, pipe, device, or socket supported by `tclsh` or `wish`. A GUI-based `wish` script can perform user I/O through various graphics widgets but will use these three commands to access files, pipes to other programs, or sockets.

All I/O in Tcl is done through channels. A channel is an I/O device abstraction similar to an I/O stream in C. The Tcl channel device abstraction is extended beyond the stream abstraction to include sockets and pipes. The Tcl channel provides a uniform abstract model of the UNIX, Mac OS, and MS Windows socket calls, so they can be treated as streams.

The Tcl commands that open a channel return a handle that can be used to identify that channel. A channel handle can be passed to an I/O command to specify which channel should accept or provide data. Three channels are predefined in Tcl, as follows.

| | |
|---|---|
| `stdin` | Standard input: keyboard or a redirected file. |
| `stdout` | Standard output: usually the screen or console. |
| `stderr` | Error output: usually the screen. Note that Mac OS and MS Windows do not distinguish between `stdout` and `stderr`. |

### 4.4.1 Output

The `puts` command sends output to a channel. It requires a string to output as an argument. By default, this command will append a newline character to the string.

*Syntax:* `puts ?-nonewline? ?channel? outputString`

Send a string to a channel.

| | |
|---|---|
| *?-nonewline?* | Do not append a newline character to the output. |
| *?channel?* | Send output to this channel. If this argument is not used, send to standard output. |
| *outputString* | The data to send. |

**Example** 4.6

```
% puts "Hello, "; puts "World "
Hello,
World
  % puts -nonewline "Hello, "; puts "World"
Hello, World
```

---

### 4.4.2 Input

The Tcl commands that input data are the `gets` and `read` commands. The `gets` command will read a single line of input from a channel and strip off any newline character. The gets command may return the data that was read or the number of characters that were read. The read command will read a requested number of characters, or until the end of data. The read command always returns the data that was read.

The gets command is best for interactive I/O, since it will read a single line of data from a user. The read command is best used when there is a large body of text to read with a single read command, such as a file or socket, or when there is a need for single-character I/O.

*Syntax:*  gets *channelID ?varName?*

Read a line of data from a channel up to the first newline character. The newline character is discarded.

*channelID*  Read from this channel.

*?varName?*  If this variable name is present, gets will store the data in this variable and will return the number of characters read. If this argument is not present, gets will return the line of data.

## Example 4.7

```
% gets stdin       # A user types "Hello, World" at keyboard.
Hello, World
% gets stdin inputString # A user types "Hello, World" at keyboard.
12
% puts $inputString
Hello, World
```

A Tcl script can invoke the read command to read a specified number of characters or to read data until an End-Of-File is encountered. If a script invokes the read command to read a specified number of characters and read encounters an End-Of-File before reading the requested number of characters, the read command will return the available characters and not generate an error. The read command returns the characters read. The read command may strip off the final newline character but by default leaves newlines intact.

*Syntax:*  read *channelID numBytes*

Read a specified number of characters from a channel.

*channelID*  The channel from which to read data.

*numBytes*  The number of bytes to read.

*Syntax:*  read *?-newline? channelID*

Read data from a channel until an End-Of-File (EOF) condition.

*?-newline?*  Discard the last character if it is a newline.

*channelID*  The channel from which to read data.

**Example** 4.8

```
# Read from stdin until an End-Of-File is encountered
#
% read stdin    # A user types Hello, World EOF
Hello, World
# Read 5 characters from stdin
% read stdin 5 # A user types Hello, World
Hello
```

When the output channel is the standard output device, Tcl buffers text until it has a complete line (until a newline character appears). To print a prompt and allow a user to enter text on the same line, you must either reset the buffering with fconfigure or use the flush command (see Section 4.5.2) to force Tcl to generate output.

**Example** 4.9

*Script Example*

```
puts -nonewline "What is your name? "
flush stdout
gets stdin name ;# User types name
puts "Hello, $name. Would you like to play a game?"
```

*Script Output*

```
What is your name? Dr. Falken
Hello, Dr. Falken. Would you like to play a game?
```

### 4.4.3 Creating a Channel

A Tcl script can create a channel with either the open or socket command. The open command can be used to open a channel to a file, a device, or a pipe to another program. The socket command can be used to open a client socket to a server or to open a server socket that will listen for clients. The open command is used to create a channel to a file, device, or another program.

*Syntax:* open *fileName* *?access?* *?permissions?*

Open a file, device, or pipe as a channel and return a handle to be used to access this channel.

*fileName*    The name of the file or device to open.

If the first character of the name is a pipe (|), this argument is a request to open a pipe connection to a command. The first word in the file name will be the command name, and subsequent words will be arguments to the command.

*?access?*  How this file will be accessed by the channel. The *access* option may be one of

r  Open file for read-only access.

r+  Open file for read and write access. File must already exist.

w  Open file for write-only access. Truncate file if it exists.

w+  Open file for read and write access. Truncate the file if it exists, or create it if it does not exist.

a  Open file for write-only access. New data will be appended to the file. For versions of Tcl before 8.3, the file must already exist. With Tcl8.3, the behavior was changed to create a new file if it does not already exist.

a+  Open file for read and write access. Create the file if it does not exist. Append data to an existing file.

*?permissions?*  If a new file is created, this parameter will be used to set the file permissions. The *permissions* argument will be an integer, with the same bit definitions as the argument to the creat system call on the operating system being used.

## Example 4.10

*Script Example*

```
# Open a file for writing - Note square brackets cause the Tcl command
#  to be evaluated, and the channel handle returned by open
#  is assigned to the variable outputFile.
set outputFile [open "testfile" "w"]

# send 3 lines to the output file.
puts $outputFile "This is line 1"
puts $outputFile "This is line 2"
puts $outputFile "This is line 3"

# Close the file.
close $outputFile

# Reopen the file for reading
set inputFile [open "testfile" "r"]
```

```
# Read a line of text
set numBytes [gets $inputFile string]
# Display the line read
puts "Gets returned $numBytes characters in the string: $string"

# Read the rest of the file
set string2 [read $inputFile]
puts "Read: $string2"

# Announce intent
puts "\nOpening a Pipe\n"

# and open a pipe to the ls command
set pipe [open "|ls /" "r"]

# Equivalent command under MS-Windows is:
# set pipe [open "|command.com /c dir" "r"]

# read the output of the ls command:
while {![eof $pipe]} {
    set length [gets $pipe lsLine]
    puts "$lsLine is $length characters long"
}
```

***Script Output***

**Gets returned 14 characters in the string: This is line 1**
**Read: This is line 2**
**This is line 3**
**Opening a Pipe**
**bin is 3 characters long**
**boot is 4 characters long**
**bsd is 3 characters long**
**dev is 3 characters long**
**...**

### 4.4.4 Closing Channels

The Tcl interpreter supports having multiple channels open simultaneously. The exact number is defined at compile time and by the underlying operating system. In order to process many files, your script will need to close channels after it has completed processing them.

**Syntax:** close *channel*

Close a channel.

channel    The handle for the channel to be closed.

When a file that was opened for write access is closed, any data in the output buffer is written to the channel before it is closed.

## 4.5 Sockets

Most client/server applications such as Telnet, ftp, e-mail, web browsers, large database systems, chat programs, and so on use TCP/IP sockets to transfer data. The Tcl socket command creates a channel connected to a TCP/IP socket. The socket command returns a channel handle that can be used with gets, read, and puts just as a file channel is used. Unlike connections to files or pipes, there are two types of sockets:

- Client socket (very much like a connection to a file or pipe)
- Server socket (waits for a client to connect to it)

Using the socket command to establish a client socket is as straightforward as opening a file.

*Syntax:*   socket *?options? host port*

Open a socket connection.

*?options?*     Options to specify the behavior of the socket.

| | | |
|---|---|---|
| | *-myaddr addr* | Defines the address (as a name or number) of the client side of the socket. This is not necessary if the client machine has only one network interface. |
| | *-myport port* | Defines the port number for the server side to open. If this is not supplied, the operating system will assign a port from the pool of available ports. |
| | *-async* | Causes the socket command to return immediately, whether the connection has been completed or not. |
| *host* | The host to open a connection to. May be a name or a numeric IP address. | |
| *port* | The name or number of the port to open a connection to on the host machine. | |

### 4.5.1 Using a Client Socket

The skeleton for a Tcl TCP/IP client is as follows:

```
set server SERVERADDRESS
set port PORTNUMBER
```

```
set connection [socket $server $port]

puts $connection "COMMAND"
flush $connection
gets $connection result

analysisProcedure $result
```

The next example demonstrates how to open a socket to a remote Post Office Protocol (POP) server to check for mail and shows how Tcl I/O and string commands can be used to develop an Internet client. The POP 3 message protocol is an ASCII conversation between the POP 3 client (your machine) and the POP 3 server (the remote machine). If you used POP from a Telnet client to learn if you have mail waiting, the conversation would resemble the following:

```
$>  telnet pop.example.com pop3
Trying 123.456.789.012
Connected to 123.456.789.012
Escape character is '^]'.
+OK POP3 pop.cflynt.com v2000.70rh server ready
user ImaPopper
+OK Password required for ImaPopper.
pass myPassword
+OK ImaPopper has 1 message (1668 octets).
```

The following example will contact a remote machine and report if any mail is waiting. The machine name, user name, and password are all hard-coded in this example. The test for +OK is done differently in each test to demonstrate some different methods of checking for one string in another.

## Example 4.11

### *Script Example*

```
# Open a socket to a POP server. Report if mail is available

# Assign a host, login and password for this session

set popHost example.com

set popLoginID myID
set popPasswd SecretPassword

# Open the socket to port 110 (POP3 server)

set popClient [socket $popHost 110]

# Get the first line:
#   +OK QPOP (version ..) at example.com starting...
```

```tcl
set line [gets $popClient]

# We can check for the 'OK' reply by confirming that 'OK'
# is the first item in the string
if {[string first "+OK" $line] != 0} {
   puts "ERROR: Did not get expected '+OK' prompt"
   puts "Received: $line"
   exit;
}

# send the user name
# Note that the socket can be used for both input and output

puts $popClient "user $popLoginID"

# The socket is buffered by default. Thus we need to
#   either fconfigure the socket to be non-buffered, or
#   force the buffer to be sent with a flush command.

flush $popClient

# Receive the password prompt:
#    +OK Password required for myID.

set response [gets $popClient]
# We can also check for the 'OK' using string match
if {[string match "+OK*" $response] == 0} {
   puts "ERROR: Did not get expected '+OK' prompt"
   puts "Received: $response"
   exit;
}

# Send Password

puts $popClient "pass $popPasswd"
flush $popClient

# Receive the message count:
#    +OK myID has 0 messages (0 octets).

set message [gets $popClient]

if {![string match "+OK*" $message]} {
  puts "ERROR: Did not get expected '+OK' prompt"
  puts "Received: $message"
  exit;
}

puts [string range $message 3 end]
```

*Script Output*

```
myID has 2 messages (2069 octets).
```

You can put together a client/server application with just a few lines of Tcl. Note that the error messages use an apostrophe to quote the +0K string. In Tcl, unlike C or shell scripts, the apostrophe has no special meaning.

## 4.5.2 **Controlling Data Flow**

When a script tries to read past the end of a file, Tcl will return −1 for the number of characters read. A script can test for an End-Of-File condition with the eof command:

eof *channelID*

Returns true if the channel has encountered an End-Of-File condition.

By default, Tcl I/O is buffered, like the stream-based I/O in the C standard library calls. This is usually the desired behavior. If this is not what your project needs, you can modify the behavior of the channel or flush the buffer on demand.

The fconfigure command lets you define the behavior of a channel. You can modify several options, including whether to buffer data for this channel and the size of the buffer to use. The fconfigure command allows you to configure more options than are discussed in this book. Read the on-line documentation for more details.

*Syntax:* fconfigure *channelID ?name? ?value?*

Configure the behavior of a channel.

*channelID*  The channel to modify.

*name*   The name of a configuration field, which includes the following:

-blocking *boolean*

If set true (the default mode), a Tcl program will block on a gets or read until data is available.

If set false, gets, read, puts, flush, and close commands will not block.

-buffering *newValue*

If *newValue* is set to full, the channel will use buffered I/O.

If set to line, the buffer will be flushed whenever a full line is received.

If set to none, the channel will flush whenever characters are received.

By default, files and sockets are opened with full buffering, whereas stdin and stdout are opened with line buffering.

The fconfigure command was added to Tcl in version 7.5. If you are writing code for an earlier revision of Tcl, or if you want to control when the buffers are flushed, you can use the flush command. The flush command writes the buffered data immediately.

**Syntax:** flush *channelID*

Flush the output buffer of a buffered channel.

*channelID*    The channel to flush.

The previous POP client example could be written without the flush $popClient commands if the following lines had been added after the socket command:

```
# Turn off buffering
fconfigure $popClient -buffering none
```

You can write simple applications using the traditional top-to-bottom flow of initiating a read and blocking until the data is available. If necessary, you could implement a round-robin loop by using the fconfigure command to set a channel to be non-blocking. More complex applications (perhaps with multiple open channels) require some sort of event-driven programming style. The Tcl fileevent command allows you to implement event-driven I/O in a script. The fileevent command registers a script to be evaluated when a channel either has data to read or is ready to accept data in its write buffer. Registering a callback script is a common paradigm for event-driven programming in Tcl.

**Syntax:** fileevent *channel direction script*

channel    The channel to watch for file events on.

direction    The direction of data flow to watch. May be readable or writable.

script    A script to invoke when the condition becomes true. (A channel has data or can be written to.)

We can write a simple syslog daemon, as shown in the next example. Pay attention to the use of quotes and backslashes in the fileevent script. The quotes are used because the $logFile and $socket substitution must be done before the script is registered. The square brackets are escaped because that substitution must be done when the script is evaluated. The script that is registered with the fileevent will look something like the following:

```
puts file2 [gets sock123].
```

If the script were enclosed in curly braces, instead of quotes, no substitution would occur, and the script to be evaluated would be "puts $logFile \[gets $socket\]". When data becomes available on the channel, this script would be evaluated and would throw an error, since the logFile variable is a local variable that was destroyed when the createLogger procedure stopped being active.

**Example** 4.12

```
proc createLogger {socket} {
  # Open a file for data to be logged to
  set logFile [open C:\event.log w]

  # When the socket is written to, read the data
  # and write it to the log file.
  fileevent $socket readable "puts $logFile \[gets $socket\]"
}
```

### 4.5.3 **Server Sockets**

Creating a TCP/IP server is a little different from a client-side socket. Instead of requesting a connection, and waiting for it to be established, the server-side socket command registers a script to be evaluated when a client socket requests a connection to the server.

    *Syntax:* socket -server *script port*

        *script*    A script to evaluate when a connection is established.

                This script will have three arguments appended to the script before it is evaluated:

                *channel*    The I/O channel that is assigned to this session.

                *IP Address*    The address of the client requesting a connection. (You can use this for simple Access List security tests.)

                *port*    The port being used by the client-side socket.

        *port*    The port to accept connections on.

The outline for a Tcl TCP/IP server follows. Note the test for the End-Of-File in the readLine procedure and the vwait command at the end of the script. When the other end of a socket is closed, it can generate spurious readable events that must be caught in the file event-handling code. If not, the server will receive continuous readable events, the gets command will return an empty string (and -1 characters), and the system will be very busy doing nothing. This test (or something

similar) will catch that condition and close the channel, which will unregister the
fileevent.

The normal tclsh script is read and evaluated from top to bottom, and then the
program exits. This behavior is fine for a filter-type program, but not good for
a server. A server program must sit in an event loop and wait for connections,
process data, and so on. The vwait command causes the interpreter to wait until
a variable is assigned a new value. While it is waiting, it processes events.

>*Syntax:* vwait *varName*
>
>>*varName*   The variable name to watch. The script following the
>>vwait command will be evaluated after the variable's
>>value is modified.

The skeleton for a Tcl TCP/IP client is as follows:

```
proc serverOpen {channel addr port} {

    # Set up fileevent to be called when input is available

    fileevent $channel readable "readLine $channel"
}

proc readLine {channel} {

    set len [gets $channel line]

    # if we read 0 chars, check for EOF. Close the
    #    channel and delete that client entry if we've
    #    hit the end of the road.

      if {($len <= 0) && [eof $channel]} {
          close $channel
          } else {
          # Process Line of Data
      }
}

set serverPort PORTNUMBER
set server [socket -server serverOpen $serverPort]

# Initialize a variable and wait for it to change
# to keep tclsh from exiting.
set running 1
vwait running
```

The next example shows a simple server that will watch a file and send a notice
whenever the file is changed. This type of script might be used on a firewall to
report if the registry, or files in /bin or C:/winnt, are modified. In this case, the
script is watching the UNIX password file. If this file changes size, it means a new
user has been added to the system.

The after command will register a script to be evaluated after a time interval. This is discussed in more detail in Chapter 9. There are more discussions of client/server and other socket applications in the *Tclsh Spot* articles on the companion CD-ROM.

**Example** 4.13

```
proc serverOpen {channel addr port} {
  # Collect the initial statistics
  initializeData /etc/passwd

  # After 2 seconds, check /etc/passwd
  after 2000 "examineFiles $channel /etc/passwd"
}

proc initializeData {filename} {
  global fileData

  # Read statistics
  file stat $filename fileData
}

proc examineFiles {channel filename} {
  global fileData

  # Read current statistics
  file stat $filename newData

  # Compare new data with original data
  # Report if not a match
  foreach index [array names newData] {
    if {$newData($index) != $fileData($index)} {
        puts $channel "$filename: $index has changed"
        puts $channel "   old: $fileData($index)"
        puts $channel "   now: $newData($index)"
        flush $channel
    }
  }

  # Reset the old statistics to avoid continuous
  # notices after a change.

  file stat $filename fileData

  # In 2 seconds, check again.
  after 2000 "examineFiles $channel $filename"
}
```

```
# Assign a port to listen on
set serverPort 12345
# Initialize the server socket
set server [socket -server serverOpen $serverPort]

# Wait forever
set done 0
vwait done
```

To test this program, you might telnet to the server in one window and modify the test file in another to see if you get a report. The IP address 127.0.0.1 is always your current host computer. This is called the loopback address. This example watches the /etc/passwd file and will report whenever the file is modified. When someone attempts to log into the system, or a program checks that a user name is valid, the access time (-atime) attribute will change.

```
C:> telnet 127.0.0.1 12345
Trying 127.0.0.1...
Connected to localhost (127.0.0.1).
Escape character is ']'.
/etc/passwd: atime has changed
 old: 1023112769
 now: 1023112872
/etc/passwd: atime has changed
 old: 1023112872
 now: 1023112888
```

## 4.6 Bottom Line

- The pwd command will return the current working directory.
- The cd newDir command will change the current working directory.
- The glob command will return file system items that match a pattern or type.
- Multi-platform file system interactions are supported with the following file commands.

file exist *path*

Returns true if a file exists and false if it does not exist.

file type *path*

Returns the type of file referenced by path. The return value will be file, directory, characterSpecial, blockSpecial, fifo, link, or socket.

file attributes *path*

Returns a list of platform-specific attributes of the item referenced by path.

file stat *path varName*

Treats varName as an associative array and creates an index in that array for each value returned by the stat library call.

file split *path*

Returns the path as a list, split on the OS-specific directory markers.

file join *list*

Merges the members of a list into an OS-specific file path, with each list member separated by the OS-specific directory markers.

file dirname *path*

Returns the portion of path before the last directory separator.

file tail *path*

Returns the portion of path after the last directory separator.

file rootname *path*

Returns the portion of path before the last extension marker.

file attributes *path attributeName*

Returns the value of a named platform-specific attribute of the item referenced by *path*.

file attributes *path attributeName newValue*

Sets the value of the named attribute to *newValue.*

- The open command will open a channel to a file or pipe.
- The socket command will open a client- or server-side socket.
- The puts command will send a string of data to a channel.
- The gets command will input a line of data from a channel.
- The read command will input one or more bytes of data from a channel.
- The fconfigure command will modify the behavior of a channel.
- The fileevent command will register a script to be evaluated when a channel has data to read or can be written to.
- The eof command returns true if the End-Of-File has been reached or a socket has been closed.
- The close command will close a channel.

## 4.7 Problems

The following numbering convention is used in all Problem sections.

| Number Range | Description of Problems |
|---|---|
| 100–199 | These problems review the material covered in this chapter. They can be answered in a few words or a short (1–5-line) script. Each problem should take under a minute to answer. |
| 200–299 | These problems go beyond the details presented in this chapter. They may require some analysis of the material or command details not covered in the chapter. They may require reading a man page or making a web search. They can be answered with a few sentences or a 5–50-line script. Each problem should take under 10 minutes to answer. |
| 300–399 | These problems extend the material presented in this chapter. They may require referencing other sources. They can be answered in a few paragraphs or a few hundred lines of code. Each exercise may take a few hours to complete. |

**100.** Can a Tcl script change the current working directory?

**101.** Can a Tcl open command be given a relative path to the file to open, or must it be an absolute path?

**102.** What Tcl command will return a list of all the files in a directory?

**103.** What features of a file are reported by the file attributes command?

**104.** Why should you use file join instead of assembling a file path using the string commands?

**105.** Can Tcl be used for event-driven programming?

**106.** Can a TCP/IP server written in Tcl have more than one client connected at a time?

**107.** What Tcl command or commands would convert /usr/src/tcl8.4.1/generic/tcl.h to the following:
   a. tcl.h
   b. /usr/src/tcl8.4.1/generic/tcl
   c. tcl
   d. /usr/src/tcl8.4.1/generic
   e. generic

**108.** Can a single Tcl puts command send data to more than one channel?

**109.** What Tcl command can be used to input a single byte of data from a channel?

**110.** Given an executable named `reverse` that will read a line of input from `stdin` and output that line of text with the letters reversed, what commands would be used to open a pipe to the `reverse` executable, send a line of text to the `reverse` process, and read back the reply?

**111.** Which two commands will cause an output buffer to be flushed?

**112.** If you want your application to flush the output buffer whenever a newline is received, what Tcl command would you include in the script?

**200.** Example 4.13 watches a single file. Modify this example so that the `initializeData` and `examineFiles` procedures can accept a list of files to watch.

**201.** Write a Tcl script that will read lines of text from a file and report the number of words in the file.

**202.** Write a script that will examine a given directory and list the object files that are older than their source file.

**203.** Write a script that will list files in a directory in size order.

**204.** Write a script that will report the oldest file in a set of directories by recursively searching subdirectories under a parent directory.

**205.** Write a script that will recursively search directories for files that contain a particular pattern.

**206.** Write a TCP/IP server that will accept a line of text and will return that line with the words in reverse order.

**300.** Write a TCP/IP client that will

   a. Prompt a user for a port

   b. Open a client socket to IP Address 127.0.0.1 and the port provided by the user

   c. In a loop:
      i.   Prompt the user for input
      ii.  Send the text to a server
      iii. Accept a line of data from the server
      iv.  Display the response to the user

   Do not forget to append a newline character to the user input and `flush` the output socket.

**301.** Write a TCP/IP server that will send three questions (one at a time) to a client, accept the input, and finally generate a summary report. The conversation might resemble the following.

```
Server: What is your name?
Client: Lancelot
Server: What is your quest?
Client: To find the holy grail
Server: What is your favorite color?
Client: Blue
Server: Your name is Lancelot.
        You like Blue clothes.
        You wish To find the holy grail.
```

Test this server by connecting to it with a Telnet client or using the test client described in the previous example.

**302.** Write a TCP/IP server that will accept a line of numbers and will return the sum of these values. Write a client that will exercise and test this server. The conversation might resemble the following.

```
Client: 1 2 3 9 8 7
Server: 30
```

**303.** Modify the previous server so that it will return the wrong answer if the correct sum is 30. Confirm that your client will catch this error.

CHAPTER

5

# Using Strings and Lists

This chapter describes how to use Tcl strings and lists for common data-searching applications. A common programming task is extracting one piece of information from a large mass of data. This section discusses several methods for doing that and introduces a few more Tcl concepts and commands along the way.

For the application, we will find the Noumena Corporation home page in a list of uniform resource locators (URLs) for some Tcl information and archive sites. The following is the starting data, extracted and modified from a browser's bookmark file.

```
% set urls {
mini.net/tcl/ "Tcler's Wiki"
members1.chello.nl/~j.nijtmans/ "Jan Nijtmans' Home page"
sourceforge.net/projects/freewrap/ "Freewrap at Sourceforge"
sourceforge.net/projects/tcl/ "Tcl/Tk at Sourceforge"
www.noucorp.com "Noumena Corporation"
www.activestate.com "ActiveState"
www.tcl.tk/ "Tcl Developer's Exchange"
www.sco.com/Technology/tcl/Tcl.html "SCO Tcl/Tk info"
expect.nist.gov/ "Expect Home Page"
zazu.maxwell.syr.edu/nt-tcl/ "NT Extensions for TCL"
}
```

## 5.1 Converting a String into a List

Since the data has multiple lines, one solution is to convert the lines into a list and then iterate through the list to check each line.

**Example** 5.1

*Splitting Data into a List*

```
# Split data into a list at the newline markers
set urlList [split $urls "\n"]
# display the list
puts $urlList
```

*Script Output*

```
{} {mini.net/tcl/ "Tcler's Wiki" }
{members1.chello.nl/~j.nijtmans/ "Jan Nijtmans' Home page" }
{sourceforge.net/projects/freewrap/ "Freewrap at Sourceforge" }
{sourceforge.net/projects/tcl/ "Tcl/Tk at Sourceforge" }
{www.noucorp.com "Noumena Corporation" }
{www.activestate.com "ActiveState" }
{www.tcl.tk/ "Tcl Developer's Exchange" }
{www.sco.com/Technology/tcl/Tcl.html "SCO Tcl/Tk info" }
{expect.nist.gov/ "Expect Home Page" }
{zazu.maxwell.syr.edu/nt-tcl/ "NT Extensions for TCL" }
{}
```

Note that the empty lines after the left bracket and before the right bracket were converted to empty list entries. This is an artifact of the way the starting data was defined. If it had been defined as

```
% set urls {mini.net/tcl/ "Tcler's Wiki"
members1.chello.nl/~j.nijtmans/ "Jan Nijtmans' Home page"
sourceforge.net/projects/freewrap/ "Freewrap at Sourceforge"
sourceforge.net/projects/tcl/ "Tcl/Tk at Sourceforge"
www.noucorp.com "Noumena Corporation"
www.activestate.com "ActiveState"
www.tcl.tk/ "Tcl Developer's Exchange"
www.sco.com/Technology/tcl/Tcl.html "SCO Tcl/Tk info"
expect.nist.gov/ "Expect Home Page"
zazu.maxwell.syr.edu/nt-tcl/ "NT Extensions for TCL"}
```

the empty list elements would not be created, but the example would be a bit less readable. This example code will not be bothered by the empty lists, but you may need to check for that condition in other code you write.

## 5.2 Examining the List with a for Loop

Now that the data is a list, we can iterate through it using the numeric for loop introduced in Chapter 3.

*Syntax:* for *start test next body*

## Example 5.2

### Search Using a for Loop

```
for {set pos 0} {$pos < [llength $urlList]} {incr pos} {
    if {[string first "Noumena" [lindex $urlList $pos]] >= 0} {
      puts "NOUMENA PAGE:\n [lindex $urlList $pos]"
    }
}
```

### Script Output

```
NOUMENA PAGE:

www.noucorp.com "Noumena Corporation"
```

The next section explains in detail what happens when this script is evaluated, followed by more techniques for searching strings.

```
for {set pos 0} {$pos < [llength $urlList]} {incr pos} {
```

This line calls the for command. The for command takes four arguments: start, test, next, and a body to evaluate. You will note that this line shows only three arguments (start, test, and next) but no body. There is only a left curly brace for the body of this command.

The curly braces cause all characters between the braces to be treated as normal text with no special processing by the Tcl interpreter. Variable names preceded by dollar signs are not replaced with their value, the code within square brackets will not get evaluated, and the newline character is not interpreted as the end of a command. So placing the curly braces at the end of the for line tells the Tcl interpreter to continue reading until it reaches the matching close bracket and to treat that entire mass of code as the body for this for command. The following code would generate an error:

```
% for {set i 1} {$i < 10} {incr i}
  {
  set x [expr $x + $i]
  }
```

A Tcl interpreter reading the line for {set i 1} {$i < 10} {incr i} would find a for command (and start, test, and next arguments) and would then see the End-Of-Line and nothing to tell the interpreter that the next line might be part of this command. The interpreter would return the following error to inform the programmer that the command could not be parsed correctly:

```
% wrong # args: should be "for start test next command"
```

The *Tcl Style Guide* developed by the Tcl development group at Sun Microsystems recommends that you place the body of an if, for, proc, or while command on a separate line from the rest of the command, with just the left bracket on the line with the command to inform the compiler that the body of the command is continued on the following lines. The following code is correct:

```
for {set i 0} {$i < 100} {incr i} {
    puts "I will write my code to conform to the standard"
}
```

Note that the arguments to the for command in both sets of example code are grouped with curly braces, not quotes. If the arguments were grouped with quotes, a substitution pass would be performed on the arguments before passing them to the for command. The variable pos has not been defined, so attempting a substitution would result in an error. If pos had already been defined as 10 (perhaps in a previous for loop), variable substitutions would be performed and the first line would be passed to the for command, as in the following:

```
for {set pos 0} "10 < 10" {incr pos} {
```

With the variables in the test already substituted, the test will always either fail or succeed (depending on the value of the variable), and the loop will not do what you expect. For the same reason, the body of a for command should be grouped with braces instead of quotes. You do not want any variables to be substituted until the loop body is evaluated. Given that no substitution happens to the variables enclosed in curly braces, you may be wondering how the code in one scope (within the for command) can access the variables in another scope (the code that invoked the for command).

The Tcl interpreter allows commands to declare which scope they should be evaluated in. This means that commands such as for, if, and while can be implemented as procedures and the body of the command can be evaluated in the scope of the code that called the procedure. This gives these commands access to the variables that were enclosed in curly braces and allows the substitution to be done as the command is being evaluated, instead of before the evaluation.

For internal commands such as for, if, and while, the change of scope is done within the Tcl interpreter. Tcl script procedures can also use this facility with the uplevel and upvar commands, which are described in Chapter 7. There are examples using the uplevel and upvar commands in Chapters 7–10, 12, 14, and 16.

The start and next arguments to the for command are also evaluated in the scope of the calling command. Thus, pos will have the last value that was assigned by the next phrase when the for loop is complete and the line of code after the body is evaluated.

```
if {[string first "Noumena" [lindex $urlList $pos]] >= 0} {
```

Like the for command, the if command accepts an expression and a body of code. If the expression is true, the body of code will be evaluated. As with the for command, the test expression goes on the same line as the if command, but only the left brace of the body is placed on that line. The test for the if is grouped with brackets, just as is done for the for command.

Within the test expression, there are two nested Tcl commands. These will be evaluated, innermost command first, before the expression is evaluated. The command [lindex $urlList $pos] will be replaced by the item at position $pos in the list. Then the command [string first "Noumena" *listItem* ] will be replaced by either the position of the string Noumena in the target string or −1 if Noumena is not in the *listItem* being examined.

```
puts "NOUMENA PAGE:\n [lindex $urlList $pos]"
```

If the test evaluates to true, the puts command will be evaluated; otherwise, the loop will continue until $pos is no longer less than the number of entries in the list. The argument to puts is in quotes rather than curly braces to allow Tcl to perform substitutions on the string. This allows Tcl to replace the \n with a newline, and [lindex urlList $pos] with the list element at $pos.

## 5.3 Using the foreach Command

Using a for command to iterate through a list is familiar to people who have coded in C or FORTRAN, which are number-oriented languages. Tcl is a string- and list-oriented language, and there are better ways to iterate through a list. For instance, we could use the foreach command instead of the for command to loop through the list.

> **Syntax:** foreach *varname list body*

**Example** 5.3

> ### Search Using a foreach Loop
> ```
> foreach item $urlList {
>   if {[string first "Noumena" $item] >= 0} {
>     puts "NOUMENA PAGE:\n  $item"
>   }
> }
> ```
>
> ### Script Output
> ```
> NOUMENA PAGE:
>   www.noucorp.com "Noumena Corporation"
> ```

Using the foreach command the code is somewhat simpler, because the foreach command returns each list element instead of requiring the lindex commands to extract the list elements.

## 5.4 Using string match Instead of string first

There are other options that can be used for the test in the if statement.

**Example** 5.4

*Search Using a string match Test*

```
% foreach item $urlList {
       if {[string match {*[Nn]oumena*} $item]} {
           puts "NOUMENA PAGE:\n  $item"
    }
}
```

*Script Output*

```
NOUMENA PAGE:
   www.noucorp.com "Noumena Corporation"
```

Note that the pattern argument to the string match command is enclosed in braces to prevent Tcl from performing command substitutions on it. The pattern includes the asterisks because string match will try to match a complete string, not a substring. The asterisk will match to any set of characters. The pattern {*[Nn]oumena*} causes string match to accept as a match a string that has the string noumena or Noumena with any sets of characters before or after.

## 5.5 Using lsearch

We could also extract the Noumena site from the list of URLs using the lsearch command. The lsearch command will search a list for an element that matches a pattern.

**Syntax:**  lsearch *?mode? list pattern*

Return the index of the first list element that matches pattern or −1 if no element matches the pattern.

?mode?    The type of match to use in this search.

?mode? may be one of

-exact      The list element must exactly match the pattern.

-glob      The list element must match pattern using the glob rules.

-regexp      The list element must match pattern using the regular expression rules.

list      The list to search.

pattern      The pattern to search for.

## Example 5.5

*Search Using an lsearch*

```
set index [lsearch -glob $urlList "*Noumena*"]
if {$index >= 0} {
    puts "NOUMENA PAGE:\n  [lindex $urlList $index]"
}
```

*Script Output*

```
NOUMENA PAGE:
  www.noucorp.com "Noumena Corporation"
```

Note that this solution will only find the first element that matches *Noumena*. If there are multiple matches, you will need a loop as follows.

## Example 5.6

*Script Example*

```
set l {phaser tricorder {photon torpedo} \
  transporter communicator}

# Report all list elements with an 'a' in them.

while {[set p [lsearch $l "*a*"]] >= 0} {
  puts "There's an 'a' in: [lindex $l $p]"
  incr p
  set l [lrange $l $p end]
}
```

*Script Output*

```
There's an 'a' in: phaser
There's an 'a' in: transporter
There's an 'a' in: communicator
```

## 5.6 The regexp Command

The regular expression commands in Tcl provide finer control of string matching than the glob method, more options, and much more power.

### 5.6.1 Regular Expression Matching Rules

A regular expression is a collection of short rules that can be used to describe a string. Each short rule is called a *piece* and consists of an element that can match a single character (called an *atom*) and an optional count modifier that defines how many times this atom may match a given character. The count modifier might tell the regular expression engine to match an atom one or more times in the target string. If there is no count modifier, the atom will match exactly one atom (which may be multiple characters) in the target string.

### *Basic Regular Expression Rules*

An atom may be as outlined in the following table.

| Definition | Example | Description |
| --- | --- | --- |
| A single character | x | will match the character x. |
| A range of characters enclosed in brackets | [a-q] | will match any lowercase letter between a and q (inclusive). |
| A period | . | will match any character. |
| A caret | ^ | matches the beginning of a string. |
| A dollar sign | $ | matches the end of a string. |
| A backslash sequence | \^ | inhibits treating *, , $, +, ^, and so on as special characters and matches the exact character. |
| A regular expression enclosed in parentheses | ([Tt]cl) | will match that regular expression. |

A regular expression could be as simple as a string. For example, this is a regular expression is a regular expression consisting of 28 atoms, with no count modifiers. It will match a string that is exactly the same as itself. The range atom ([a-z]) needs a little more explanation, since there are actually several rules to define a range of characters. A *range* consists of square brackets enclosing the following.

| Definition | Example | Description |
| --- | --- | --- |
| A set of characters | [tcl] | Any of the letters within the brackets may match the target. |

| Two characters separated by a dash | [a-z] | The letters define a range of characters that may match the target. |
| A character preceded by a caret, if the caret is the first letter in the range | [^,] | Any character *except* the character after the caret may match the target. |
| Two characters separated by a dash and preceded by a caret, if the caret is the first letter in the range | [^a-z] | Any character *except* characters between the two characters after the caret may match the target. |

The regular expression [Tt][Cc][Ll] would match a string consisting of the letters T, C, and L, in that order, with any capitalization. The regular expression [TtCcLl]* would match one of the characters t, c, l, T, C, or L.

A count modifier may follow an atom. If a count modifier is present, it defines how many times the preceeding atom can occur in the regular expression. The count modifier may be the following.

| *Definition* | *Example* | *Description* |
| --- | --- | --- |
| An asterisk | a* | Match 0 or more occurrences of the preceding atom (a). |
| A plus | a+ | Match 1 or more occurrences of the preceding atom. |
| A question mark | [a-z]? | Match 0 or 1 occurrence of the preceding atom. |
| A *bound* | {3} | An integer that defines exactly the number of matches to accept. |
| | {3,} | The comma signifies to match at least three occurrences of the previous atom and perhaps more. |
| | {3,5} | A pair of numbers representing a minimum and maximum number of matches to accept. |

Note that support for bounds was added in Tcl 8.1. Versions of Tcl earlier than that support only the asterisk, plus, and question mark count modifiers. The regular expression A* would match a string of a single letter A, a string of several letter As, or a string with no A at all.

The regular expression [A-Z]+[0-9A-Z]* is more useful. This regular expression describes a string that has at least one alphabetic character, followed by 0 or more alphanumeric characters. This regular expression describes a legal variable name in many programming languages.

Regular expression pieces can be placed one after the other (as previously) to define a set of items that must be present, or they can be separated by a vertical bar to indicate that one piece or the other must be present. Pieces can be grouped with parentheses into a larger atom. To match a literal parentheses, you must escape the character with a backslash.

The regular expression (Tcl)|(Tk) will match either the string Tcl or the string Tk. The same strings would be matched by the regular expression T((cl)|k). The regular expression ((Tcl)|(Tk)|/)+ will match a set of Tcl, Tk, or slash. It would match the string Tcl, Tk, Tcl/Tk, Tk/Tcl, TclTk/, and so on, but not Tlc-kT or other variants without a Tcl, Tk, or slash.

The regular expression \([^ \)]*\) would match a parenthetical comment (like this). The backslashed left parenthesis means to match a literal left parenthesis, then 0 or more characters that are not right parentheses, and finally a literal right parenthesis.

## 5.6.2 Advanced and Extended Regular Expression Rules

This defines most of the basic regular expression rules. These features (with the exception of the *bounds* count modifier) are supported by all versions of Tcl. The 8.1 release of Tcl included a large number of modifications to the string handling. The largest change was to change the way strings were stored and manipulated. Prior to 8.1, Tcl used 8-bit ASCII for strings. With version 8.1, Tcl uses 16-bit Unicode characters, giving Tcl support for international alphabets. Part of revamping how strings are handled required reworking the regular expression parser to handle the new-style character strings. Henry Spencer, who wrote the original regular expression library for Tcl, also did the rewrite, and while he was adding support for 16-bit Unicode, he also added support for the advanced and extended regular expression rules.

The rest of this discussion concerns the rules added in Tcl version 8.1. This is an overview. More discussion and examples can be found in the *Tclsh Spot* articles on the companion CD-ROM.

### Minimum and Maximum Match

When the regular expression parser is looking for matches to rules, it may find multiple sets of characters that will match a rule. The decision for which set of characters to apply to the rule is

**1.** The set of characters that starts furthest to the left is chosen

**2.** The longest set of characters that match from that position is chosen

This behavior is sometimes referred to as *greedy* behavior. You can change this behavior to match the minimum number of characters by placing a question mark after the count modifier. For example, the following regular expression

```
<.*>
```

would match an HTML tag. It would work correctly with a string such as <IMG SRC="comic.gif">, but would match too many characters (the entire string) when compared to a string such as `<IMG SRC="comic.gif"><P>`. Adding the question mark after the star will cause the minimal matching algorithm to be used, and the expression will match to a single HTML tag, as follows:

```
<.*?>
```

### Internationalization

Prior to version 8.1, all Tcl strings were pure ASCII strings, and the content of a regular expression would also be ASCII characters. Several new features were added to support the possible new characters. Unicode support is discussed in more detail in Chapter 10.

### Non-ASCII Values

You can search for a character by its hexadecimal value by preceding the hex value with \x. For example, the æcharacter is encoded as 0xe6 in hexadecimal and could be matched using a script such as the following:

```
% set s [format "The word salvi%c is Latin" 0xe6]
% regexp {([^ ]*\xe6[^ ]*)} $s a b
1
% puts $a
salviæ
```

### Character Classes, Collating Elements, and Equivalence Classes

Another part of reworking the regular expression engine was to add support for named character classes, collating elements, and equivalence classes. These features make it possible to write a single regular expression that will work with multiple alphabets.

A named character class defines a set of characters by using a name, instead of a range. For example, the range [A-Za-z] is equivalent to the named character class [[:alpha:]]. A named character class is defined by putting a square bracket and colon pair around the name of the character class.

The advantage of named character classes is that they automatically include any non-ASCII characters that exist in the local language. Using a range such as [A-Za-z] might not include characters with an umlaut or accent. The named character classes supported by Tcl include those outlined in the following table.

| | |
|---|---|
| alpha | The alphabetic characters |
| lower | Lowercase letters |
| upper | Uppercase letters |
| alnum | Alphabetic and numeric characters |
| digit | Decimal digits |
| xdigit | Hexadecimal digits |

graph    All printable characters except blank

cntrl    Control characters (ASCII values < 32)

space    Any whitespace character

<       The beginning of a word

>       The end of a word

A word is a set of alphanumeric characters or underscores preceded and followed by a non-alphanumeric or underscore character (such as a whitespace). A collating element is a multi-character entity that is matched to a single character. This is a way to describe two-letter characters such as æ. A collating element is defined with a set of double square brackets and periods: [[. .]]. Thus, the Latin word *salviæ* would be matched with the regular expression salvi[[.ae.]].

An equivalence class is a way to define all variants of a letter that may occur in a language. It is denoted with a square bracket and equal sign. For example, [[=u]] would match to the character u, û ,or ü. Note that the internationalization features are only enabled if the underlying operating system supports the language that includes the compound letter. If your system does not support a collating element or equivalence class, Tcl will generate the following error:

**couldn't compile regular expression pattern: invalid collating element**

### Tcl Commands Implementing Regular Expressions

Regular expression rules can be used for pattern matching with the switch and lsearch commands. Tcl also provides two commands for parsing and manipulating strings with regular expressions.

regexp    Parses a string using a regular expression, may optionally extract portions of the string to other variables.

regsub    Substitutes sections of a string that match a regular expression.

*Syntax:*    regexp *?opt? expr string ?fullmatch? ?submatch?*

Returns 1 if expr has a match in string . If matchVar or subMatchVar arguments are present, they will be assigned the matched substrings.

opt      Options to fine-tune the behavior of regexp. Options include

-nocase    Ignores the case of letters when searching for a match.

-indices    Stores the location of a match, instead of the matched characters, in the submatch variable.

| | | |
|---|---|---|
| | -line | Performs the match on a single line of input data. This is roughly equivalent to putting a newline atom at the beginning and end of the pattern. This option was added with Tcl release 8.1. |
| | -- | Marks the end of options. Arguments that follow this will be treated as a regular expression even if they start with a dash. |
| expr | | The regular expression to match with string. |
| string | | The string to search for the regular expression. |
| ?fullmatch? | | If there is a match, and this variable is supplied to regexp, the entire match will be placed in this variable. |
| ?submatch? | | If there is a match, and this variable is supplied to regexp, the Nth parenthesized regular expression match will be placed in this variable. The parenthesized regular expressions are counted from left to right and outer to inner. |

## Example 5.7

### *Example Script*

```
# Match a string of uppercase letters,
# followed by a string of lowercase letters
# followed by a string of uppercase letters
regexp {([A-Z]*)(([a-z]*)[A-Z]*)} "ABCdefgHIJ" a b c d e
puts "The full match is: $a"
puts "The first parenthesized expression matches: $b"
puts "The second parenthesized expression matches: $c"
puts "The third parenthesized expression matches: $d"
puts "There is no fourth parenthesized expression: $e"
```

### *Script Output*

```
The full match is: ABCdefgHIJ
The first parenthesized expression matches: ABC
The second parenthesized expression matches: defgHIJ
The third parenthesized expression matches: defg
There is no fourth parenthesized expression:
```

---

*Syntax:* regsub *?options? expression string subSpec varName*

Copies string to the variable varName. If expression matches a portion of string, that portion is replaced by subSpec.

| | |
|---|---|
| options | Options to fine-tune the behavior of regsub. May be one of: |

-all    Replaces all occurrences of the regular expression with the replacement string. By default, only the first occurrence is replaced.

-nocase    Ignores the case of letters when searching for match.

--    Marks the end of options. Arguments that follow this will be treated as regular expressions, even if they start with a dash.

| | |
|---|---|
| expression | A regular expression that will be compared with the target string. |
| string | A target string with which the regular expression will be compared. |
| subSpec | A string that will replace the regular expression in the target string. |
| varName | A variable in which the modified target string will be placed. |

## Example 5.8

***regsub Example***

```
set bad "This word is spelled wrung"
regsub "wrung" $bad "correctly" good
puts $good
```

***Script Output***

**This word is spelled correctly**

---

The portions of a string that match parenthesized atoms of a regular expression can also be captured and substituted with the regsub command. The substrings are named with a backslash and a single digit to mark the position of the parenthesized atom. As with the regexp parenthesized expressions, they are numbered from left to right and outside to inside. The subexpressions are numbered starting with \1, with \0 being the entire matching string.

## Example 5.9

***regsub Example***

```
set wrong {Don't put the horse before the cart}
```

```
regsub {(D[^r]*)(h[^ ]*)( +[^c]*)(c.*)} $wrong {\1\4\3\2} right
puts $right
```

*Script Output*

**Don't put the cart before the horse**

---

The regular expression (D[^r]*)(h[^ ]*)( +[^c]*)(c.*)} breaks down to the following.

| Piece | Description | Matches |
|---|---|---|
| (D[^r]*) | A set of characters starting with D and including any character that is not an r | Don't put the |
| (h[^ ]*) | A set of characters starting with h and including any character that is not a space | horse |
| ( +[^c]*) | One or more spaces, followed by a set of characters that are not c | before the |
| (c.*) | A set of characters starting with c, followed by one or more of any character until the end of the string | cart |

The substitution phrase {\1\4\3\2} reorders the piece such that the first piece is followed by the fourth (cart) and the second piece (horse) becomes the last.

### 5.6.3 Back to the Searching URLs

We could use the regexp command in place of the string command to search for Noumena. This code would resemble the following.

**Example** 5.10

*Search Using a regexp Test*

```
foreach item $urlList {
  if {[regexp {[Nn]oumena} $item]} {
    puts "NOUMENA PAGE:\n  $item"
  }
}
```

*Script Output*

**NOUMENA PAGE:**
  **www.noucorp.com "Noumena Corporation"**

---

Alternatively, we could just use the regexp command to search the original text for a match rather than the text converted to a list. This saves us a processing step.

**Example** 5.11

> *Search All Data Using regexp*
>
> ```
> set found [regexp "(\[^\n]*\[Nn\]oumena\[^\n]*)" $urls\
>   fullmatch submatch]
> if {$found} {
>   puts "NOUMENA PAGE:\n  $submatch"
> }
> ```
>
> *Script Output*
>
> ```
> NOUMENA PAGE:
>   www.noucorp.com "Noumena Corporation"
> ```

Let's take a careful look at the regular expression in Example 5.11.

First, the expression is grouped with quotes instead of braces. This is done so that the Tcl interpreter can substitute the \n with a newline character. If the expression were grouped with braces, the characters\n would be passed to the regular expression code, which would interpret the backslash as a regexp escape character and would look for an ASCII n instead of the newline character.

However, since we have enclosed the regular expression in quotes, we need to escape the braces from the Tcl interpreter with backslashes. Otherwise, the Tcl interpreter would try to evaluate [^\n] as a Tcl command in the substitution phase.

Breaking the regular expression into pieces, we have

| | |
|---|---|
| [^\n]* | Match zero or more characters that are not newline characters |
| [Nn]oumena | Followed by the word Noumena or noumena |
| [^\n]* | Followed by zero or more characters that are not newline characters |

This will match a string that includes the word Noumena and is bounded by either newline characters or the start or end of the string. If regexp succeeds in finding a match, it will place the entire matching string in the fullmatch variable. The portion of the string that matches the portion of the expression between the parentheses is placed in submatch. If the regular expression has multiple sets of expressions within parentheses, these portions of the match will be placed in submatch variables in the order in which they appear.

The -line option will limit matches to a single line. Using this option, we do not need the \n to mark the start and end of the line, so we can simplify the regular expression by using curly braces instead of quotes and simple atoms instead of ranges for the character matches, as follows:

```
set found [regexp -line {(.*[Nn]oumena.*)} $urls fullmatch submatch ]
```

Adding the -nocase option will further simplify the regular expression, as follows:

```
set found [regexp -line -nocase {(.*noumena.*)} \
    $urls fullmatch submatch ]
```

Alternatively, we could use the submatching support in regexp to separate the URL from the description, as follows.

**Example** 5.12

*Script Example*

```
set found [regexp -line -nocase {(.*) +(.*noumena.*)} \
    $urls full url desc]
if {$found} {
    puts "full: $full"
    puts "url: $url"
    puts "desc: $desc"
}
```

*Script Output*

```
full: www.noucorp.com "Noumena Corporation"
url: www.noucorp.com
desc: "Noumena Corporation"
```

## 5.7 Creating a Procedure

Identifying one datum in a set of data is an operation that should be generalized and placed in a procedure. This procedure is a good place to reduce the line of data to the information we actually want.

### 5.7.1 The proc Command

A Tcl subroutine is called a proc, because it is defined with the proc command. Note that proc is a Tcl command, not a declaration.

The proc command takes three arguments that define a procedure: the procedure name, the argument list, and the body of code to evaluate when the procedure is invoked. When the proc command is evaluated, it adds the procedure name, arguments, and body to the list of known procedures. The command looks very much like declaring a subroutine in C or FORTRAN, but you should remember that proc is a command, not a declaration.

The proc command is introduced in a simple form here. It is discussed in much more detail in Chapter 7.

*Syntax:* proc *name args body*

## Example 5.13

*Script Example*

```
# Define a proc

proc demoProc {arg1 arg2} {
    puts "demoProc called with $arg1 and $arg2"
}

# Now, call the proc
demoProc 1 2
demoProc alpha beta
```

*Script Output*

```
demoProc called with 1 and 2
demoProc called with alpha and beta
```

### 5.7.2 A findUrl Procedure

This proc will find a line that has a given substring, extract the URL from that string, and return just the URL. It can accept a single line of data or multiple lines separated by newline characters.

## Example 5.14

*Script Example*

```
# findUrl -
#       Finds a particular line of data in a set of lines
# Arguments:
#   match    A string to match in the data.
#   text     Textual data to search for the pattern.
#            Multiple lines separated by newline
#            characters.
# Results:
#   Returns the line which matched the target string
#

proc findUrl {match text} {
    set url " "
    set found [regexp -line -nocase "(.*) +(.*$match.*)" \
        $text full url desc]
    return $url
}

# Invoke the procedure to
# search for a couple of well known sites
#
```

```
puts "NOUMENA SITE: [findUrl Noumena $urls]"
puts "SCO SITE: [findUrl sco $urls]"
if {[string match [findUrl noSuchSite $urls] " "]} {
   puts "noSuchSite not found"
}
```

*Script Output*

```
NOUMENA SITE: www.noucorp.com
SCO SITE: www.sco.com/Technology/tcl/Tcl.html
noSuchSite not found
```

### 5.7.3 Variable Scope

Most computer languages support the concept that variables can be accessed only within certain scopes. For instance, in C, a subroutine can access only variables that are either declared in that function (local scope) or have been declared outside all functions (the extern, or global, scope).

Tcl supports the concept of local and global scopes. A variable declared and used within a proc can be accessed only within that proc, unless it is made global with the global command. The Tcl scoping rules are covered in detail in Chapters 7 and 8.

Tcl also supports namespaces, similar in some ways to the FORTRAN named common (a set of variables that are grouped) or a C++ static class member. The namespace command is discussed in Chapter 8.

Global variables must be declared in each procedure that accesses a global variable. This is the opposite of the C convention in which a variable is declared static and all functions get default access to that variable. The global command will cause Tcl to map a variable name to a global variable, instead of a local variable.

> *Syntax:* global *varName1 varName2...*
>
> Map a variable name to a global variable.
>
> varName*    The name of the variable to map.

## Example 5.15

*Script Example*

```
set a 1
set b 2
proc tst {} {
  global a
  set a "A"
  set b "B"
  puts "$a $b"
}
```

*Script Output*

```
% tst
A B
% puts "$a $b"
A 2
```

Within the proc tst the variable a is mapped to the a in the global scope, whereas the variable b is local. The set commands change the global copy of a and a local copy of b. When the procedure is complete, the local variable b is reclaimed, whereas the variable a still exists. The global variable b was never accessed by the procedure tst.

### 5.7.4 Global Information Variables

Tcl has several global variables that describe the version of the interpreter, the current state of the interpreter, the environment in which the interpreter is running, and so on. These variables include the following.

| | |
|---|---|
| argv | A list of command line arguments. |
| argc | The number of list elements in argv. |
| env | An associative array of environment variables. |
| tcl_version | The version number of a Tcl interpreter. |
| tk_version | The version number of the Tk extension. |
| tcl_pkgPath | A list of directories to search for packages to load. |
| errorInfo | After an error occurs, this variable contains information about where the error occurred within the script being evaluated. |
| errorCode | After an error occurs, this variable contains the error code of the error. |
| tcl_platform | An associative array describing the hardware and operating system the script is running under. The tcl_platform associative array has several indices that describe the environment the script is running on. These indices include |

| | | |
|---|---|---|
| | byteOrder | The order of bytes on this hardware. Will be LittleEndian or BigEndian. |
| | osVersion | The version of the OS on this system. |
| | machine | The CPU architecture (i386, sparc, and so on). |
| | platform | The type of operating system. Will be macintosh, unix, or windows. |
| | os | The name of the operating system. On a UNIX system this will be the value returned by uname -s. For MS Windows systems it will be |

Win32s (DOS/Windows 3.1 with 32-bit DLL), Windows NT, or Windows 95. Microsoft Windows platforms are identified as the base version of the OS. Windows 2000 is identified as Windows NT, and Windows 98 and ME are identified as Windows 95.

## 5.8 Making a Script

As a final step in this set of examples, we will create a script that can read the bookmark file of a well-known browser, extract a URL that matches a command line argument string, and report that URL. This script will need to read the bookmark file, process the input, find the appropriate entry or entries, and report the result. Because the bookmark files are stored differently under UNIX, Mac OS, and MS Windows, the script will have to figure out where to look for the file.

We will use the tcl_platform global variable to determine the system on which the script is running. Once we know the system on which the script is running, we can set the default name for the bookmark file, open the file, and read the content.

### 5.8.1 The Executable Script

Aside from those additions, this script uses the code we have already developed.

**Example** 5.16

```
#!/bin/sh
#\
exec tclsh "$0" "$@"
################################################################
# geturl.tcl
# Clif Flynt -- clif@cflynt.com
#
# Extracts a URL from a netscape bookmark file
#
################################################################
# findUrl --
#
#     Finds a line in the text string that matches the
#     pattern string. Extracts the URL from that line.
#
# Arguments:
#     match    The pattern to try and match.
#     text     The string to search for a match in.
#
```

```
# Results:
#       Returns the matched URL, or " "
proc findUrl {match text} {
    set url " "
    set expression \
        [format {"http://(.*?%s.*?)"} $match]
    regexp -line -nocase $expression $text full url
    return $url
}

######################################################################
#
# Check for a command line argument
#
if {$argc != 1} {
    puts "geturl.tcl string"
    exit -1;
}

#
# Set the bookmark file name depending on the current system.
#
switch $tcl_platform(platform) {
    unix        {
      set bookmarkName [file join $env(HOME) .netscape bookmarks.html]
     }
     windows        {
       set path [file join C: / "program files" netscape Users *]
       set path [glob [file join $path bookmark.htm]]

       # If there are multiple personalities, return the first file
       set bookmarkName [lindex [glob $path] 0]
}
mac          -
macintosh  {
        # Find the exact path, with possible unprintable
        # characters.
        set path [file join $env(PREF_FOLDER) Netsc* * Bookmarks.html]

        # If there are multiple personalities, return the first file
        set path [lindex [glob $path] 0]

        # Strip the { and } from the name returned by glob.
        set bookmarkName [string trim $path "{}"]
}
```

```
default     {
    puts "I don't recognize the platform:\
         $tcl_platform(platform)"
    exit -1;
  }
}

#
# Open the bookmark file, and read in the data
#

set bookmarkFile [open "$bookmarkName" "r"]

set bookmarks [read $bookmarkFile]
close $bookmarkFile

#
# print out the result.
#

puts "[findUrl $argv $bookmarks]"
```

## 5.9 Speed

One question that always arises is "How fast does it run?" This is usually followed by "Can you make it run faster?" The time command times the speed of other commands.

**Syntax:** time *cmd ?iterations?*

Returns the number of microseconds per iteration of the command.

cmd                The command to be timed. Put within curly braces if you do not want substitutions performed twice.

?iterations?    The number of times to evaluate the command. When this argument is defined, the time command returns the average time for these iterations of the command.

The time command evaluates a Tcl command passed as the first argument. The cmd argument will go through the normal substitutions when time evaluates it, so you probably want to put the cmd variable within curly braces. We have tried several methods of extracting a single datum from a mass of data. Now, let's look at the relative speeds, as depicted in the following illustration.

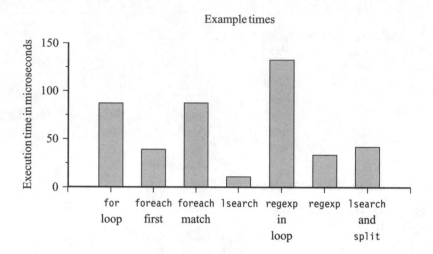

### 5.9.1 Comparison of Execution Speeds (Tcl 8.3.2, Linux, PIII at 1GHz)

The last column in this graph is the combined time it takes to perform the split and lsearch. Given a set of data that must be split into a list before it can be searched with the lsearch command, an accurate comparison between searching with a regular expression and searching with lsearch should include the time for converting the data to a list. Note that the simple comparison used by string first is considerably faster than the glob rules used by string match, which is faster than a regular expression.

Regular expressions are very powerful, but slow. Most of the time consumed in a regular expression search is used by the regular expression compilation (the setup time). However, when you can perform a single search over an entire string, regular expressions can be faster than iterating through a list or converting a string to a list and using lsearch.

The graph was created with the BLT extension. BLT is discussed in Chapter 14. Using procedures will also improve the speed of a Tcl script. Tcl compiles code that appears in a procedure, but not code outside procedures, since that code will only be evaluated once.

## 5.10 Bottom Line

There are some tricks in Tcl that may not be apparent until you understand how Tcl commands are evaluated.

- Tcl variables exist in either a local or global scope or can be placed in private namespaces.
- A Tcl procedure may execute in its default scope or in the scope of a procedure in its call tree.

- Searching a list with `lsearch` is faster than iterating through a list, checking each item.
- The `time` command can be used to tune your code.

  ***Syntax:*** `time cmd ?iterations?`
- Regular expression string searches are performed with the `regexp` command.

  ***Syntax:*** `regexp ?opt? expr str ?fullmatch? ?submatch?`
- Regular expression string substitutions are performed with the `regsub` command.

  ***Syntax:*** `regsub? opt? expr str subSpec varName`
- You can search a set of data for items matching a pattern with

  ***Syntax:*** `string match pattern string`

  ***Syntax:*** `string first pattern string`

  ***Syntax:*** `string last pattern string`

  ***Syntax:*** `lsearch list pattern`

  ***Syntax:*** `regexp ?opt? expr str ?fullmatch? ?submatch?`

## 5.11 Problems

The following numbering convention is used in all Problem sections.

| *Number Range* | *Description of Problems* |
|---|---|
| 100–199 | These problems review the material covered in this chapter. They can be answered in a few words or a short (1–5-line) script. Each problem should take under a minute to answer. |
| 200–299 | These problems go beyond the details presented in this chapter. They may require some analysis of the material or command details not covered in the chapter. They may require reading a man page or making a web search. They can be answered with a few sentences or a 5–50-line script. Each problem should take under 10 minutes to answer. |
| 300–399 | These problems extend the material presented in this chapter. They may require referencing other sources. They can be answered in a few paragraphs or a few hundred lines of code. Each exercise may take a few hours to complete. |

**100.** Some operations are well suited to a `for` loop, whereas others are better suited to a `foreach` or `while` loop. Which loop construct is best suited to each of the following operations?

   a. Calculating the Y coordinate for a set of experimentally derived X values

   b. Calculating the Y coordinate for X values between 1 and 100

    c. Examining all files in a directory

    d. Scanning a specific port on a subnetwork to find systems running software with security holes

    e. Waiting for a condition to change

    f. Inverting a numerically indexed array

    g. Iterating through a tree

    h. Reversing the order of letters in a string

**101.** Can you use a single lsearch command to find two adjacent elements in a list?

**102.** Can you use an lsearch command to find the third occurrence of a pattern in a list?

**103.** What regular expression atom will match the following?

    a. One occurrence of any character

    b. One occurrence of any character between A and L

    c. One occurrence of any character except Q

    d. The word *Tcl*

    e. A single digit

**104.** Given the following Tcl command

`regexp $exp $s full first`

with the variable s assigned the string "An image is worth $5 \times 10^3$ pixels," what string would be assigned to the variable first for the following values of exp?

    a. `{(({0-9]+)}`

    b. `{(({0-9]{2})}`

    c. `{A[^ ]* +(i[^ ]*)}`

    d. `{(w.*?[[:>:]])}`

**105.** What global variable contains a list of command line arguments?

**106.** What global variable can be used within a script to discover if the script is being evaluated on a Windows or UNIX platform?

**200.** The lsearch command will return the index of the first match to a pattern. Write a one-line command (using square brackets) to return the first list element that matches a pattern, instead of the index.

**201.** Write an lsearch command that would find the element that

    a. Starts with the letter A and has other characters

    b. Starts with the letter A followed by 0 or one integer

    c. Starts with the letter A followed by one or more integers

    d. Starts with the letter A followed by one or more integers, with the final integer either 0 or 5

    e. Is a number between 0 and 199

    f. Is a string with five characters

    g. Is a string with less than three characters

**202.** Write a `regexp` command that will extract the following substrings from the string "`Regular expressions are useful and powerful`". Note that these substrings can be matched by a regular expression that is not a set of atoms identical to the substring.

    a. Regular expressions are us

    b. expressions

    c. pow

    d. useful and powerful

**203.** Write a `regexp` command that will extract

    a. The first word from a string

    b. The second word from a string

    c. A word with the letters `ss` in it

    d. A word of two to four letters long

**300.** Write a Tcl procedure that will split a set of data into a list on multi-character markers, instead of the single-character marker used by `lsearch`. For example, this procedure should split `aaaSPLITbbbSPLITcccSPLITddd` into the list `{aaa bbb ccc ddd}`.

**301.** Write a procedure that will accept a list and return the longest element in that list.

**302.** The `lsearch` command will return the index of the first match to a pattern. Write a procedure that will return the index of the Nth match. The procedure should accept a list, pattern, and integer to define which match to return.

**303.** Modify the procedure from the previous exercise to return the Nth list element that matches a pattern, instead of the Nth index.

**304.** Write a procedure that will accept a list and two patterns and return a list of the indices for the element that matches the first pattern followed by the element that matches the second pattern.

**305.** Modify the procedure from the previous exercise to return the indices of the elements that match the two patterns when the elements are adjacent. This may not be the first occurrence of either element.

# CHAPTER

# 6

# Building Complex Data Structures with Lists and Arrays

This chapter demonstrates how lists and arrays can be used to group data into constructs similar to structures, linked lists, and trees. The first examples show how lists can be used to group data in ordered and unordered formats. The next section explores using associative arrays instead of structures. The final set of examples shows how associative arrays and naming conventions can be used to create a tree-structured container object.

Tcl has been accused of being unsuited for serious programming tasks because of the simplicity of its data types. Whereas C++ has integers, floats, pointers, structs, and classes, Tcl has just strings, lists, and associative arrays. These simple constructs are usually sufficient. This chapter will show some techniques for using Tcl data constructs in place of the more traditional structs, linked lists, and so on.

For some applications, such as dealing with an interface to a relational database management system (RDBMS), the Tcl data constructs are more suited to the interface than a C structure. Tcl handles an empty return from a database query more intuitively than some other languages.

If you are familiar with compiled languages such as C or Pascal, you may want to consider why you use particular constructs in your programs instead of others. Sometimes, you may do so because of the machine and language architecture, rather than because the problem and the data structure match. In many cases the Tcl data types solve the problem better than the more familiar constructs.

When programming in compiled languages such as C or Pascal, there are several reasons for using linked lists:

- Linked lists provide an open-ended data structure; you do not need to declare the number of entries at compile time.
- Data can be added to or deleted from linked lists quickly.

- Entries in a linked list can be easily rearranged.
- Linked lists can be used as container classes for other data.

The Tcl list supports all of these features. In fact, the internal implementation of the Tcl list allows data items to be swapped with fewer pointer changes than exchanging entries in a linked list. This allows commands such as lsort to run very efficiently.

The important reason for using linked lists is that you can represent the data as a list of items. The Tcl list is ideal for this purpose, allowing you to spend your time developing the algorithm for processing your data, instead of developing a linked list subroutine library.

A binary tree is frequently used in C or Pascal to search for data efficiently. The Tcl interpreter stores the indices of an associative array in a very efficient hash table. Rather than implementing a binary tree for data access purposes, you can use an associative array and get the speed of a good hash algorithm for free. As a tree grows deeper, the hash search becomes faster than a binary search, without the overhead of balancing the tree.

Most applications that use Tcl are not speed critical, and the speed of the list or array is generally adequate. If your application grows and becomes speed bound by Tcl data constructs, you can extend the interpreter with other faster data representations. Extending the interpreter is covered in Chapter 13.

## 6.1 Using the Tcl List

A Tcl list can be used whenever the data can be conceptualized as a sequence of data items. These items could be numeric (such as a set of graph coordinates) or textual, such as a list of fields from a database or even another list.

### 6.1.1 Manipulating Ordered Data with Lists

Lists can be used to manipulate data in an ordered format. Spreadsheet and database programs often export data as strings of fields delimited by a field separator. The Tcl list is an excellent construct for organizing such data. You can treat a list as an ordered set of data and use the lindex command to retrieve data from fixed locations within a list.

Code maintenance becomes simpler if you use a set of variables to define the locations of the fields in a list, rather than hard-coding the positions in the lindex commands. The mnemonic content of the variable names makes the code more readable. This technique also allows you to add new fields without having to go through all your code to change hard-coded index numbers.

Chapters 3 and 5 showed how a comma-delimited line could be split into a Tcl list, with each field becoming a separate list element. The next example manipulates three records with fields separated by colons, similar to data exported by a spreadsheet or saved in a system configuration file (such as /etc/passwd).

In this example, each record has four fields in a fixed order: unique key, last name, first name, and e-mail address. The example converts the records to lists with the split command and then merges the lists into a single list with the lappend command. After the data has been converted to a list, the lsearch command is used to find individual records in this list, the lreplace command is used to modify a record, and then the list is converted back to the original format. The join command is the flip side of the split command. It will join the elements of a list into a single string.

**Syntax:** join *list ?joinString?*

Join the elements of a list into a single string.

| | |
|---|---|
| list | The list to join into a string. |
| ?joinString? | Use this string to separate list elements. Defaults to a space. |

The lreplace command will replace one or more list elements with new elements or can be used to delete list elements.

**Syntax:** lreplace *list first last ?element1 element2 ...?*

Return a new list, with one or more elements replaced by zero or more new elements.

| | |
|---|---|
| *list* | The original list. |
| *first* | The position of the first element in the list to be replaced. |
| *last* | The position of the last element in the list to be replaced. |
| *element\** | A list of elements to replace the original elements. If this list is shorter than the number of fields defined by first and last, elements will be deleted from the original list. |

## Example 6.1

### *Position-Oriented Data Example*

```
# Set up a list
lappend data [split "KEY1:Flynt:Clif:clif@cflynt.com" : ];
lappend data [split "KEY2:Doe:John:jxd@example.com" : ];
lappend data [split "KEY3:Doe:Jane:janed@example.com" : ];

# data is a list of lists.
```

```
# { {KEY1 Flynt Clif clif@cflynt.com}
#   {KEY2 Doe John jxd@example.com} ...}

# Find the record with KEY2

set position [lsearch $data "KEY2 *"]

# Extract a copy of that record

set record [lindex $data $position]

# Assign the record positions to mnemonically named variables

set keyIndex 0;
set lastNameIndex 1;
set firstNameIndex 2;
set eMailIndex 3;

# Display fields from that record

puts "The Email address for Record [lindex $record $keyIndex] \
  ([lindex $record $firstNameIndex]) was \
    [lindex $record $eMailIndex]"

# Modify the eMail Address

set newRecord [lreplace $record $eMailIndex $eMailIndex \
  "joed@example.com"]

# Confirm change
puts "The Email address for Record [lindex $newRecord $keyIndex] \
  ([lindex $newRecord $firstNameIndex]) is \
    [lindex $newRecord $eMailIndex]"

# Update the main list

set data [lreplace $data $position $position $newRecord]

# Convert the list to colon-delimited form, and display it.
foreach record $data {
  puts "[join $record :]"
}
```

### Script Output

```
The Email address for Record KEY2 (John) was jxd@example.com
The Email address for Record KEY2 (John) is joed@example.com

KEY1:Flynt:Clif:clif@cflynt.com
KEY2:Doe:John:joed@example.com
KEY3:Doe:Jane:janed@example.com
```

### 6.1.2 **Manipulating Data with Keyed Lists**

In some applications information may become available in an indeterminate order, some fields may have multiple sets of data, and some fields may be missing. It may not be feasible to build a fixed-position list for data such as this. For example, the e-mail standard does not define the order in which data fields may occur, some fields (such as Subject) need not be present, and there may be multiple Received fields.

One solution to representing data such as this is to use a string to identify each piece of data and create pairs of identifiers and data. As the data becomes available, the identifier/data pair is appended to the list.

Since a Tcl list can contain sublists, you can use the list to implement a collection of key/value pairs. The records in the next example consist of two-element lists. The first element is a field identifier, and the second element is the field value. The order of these key/value pairs within a record is irrelevant. There is no position-related information, because each field contains an identifier as well as data.

The following example shows a set of procedures to store and retrieve data in a keyed list. The sample script places information from an e-mail header into a keyed list and then retrieves portions of the data.

**Example** 6.2

*Keyed Pair List Example*

```
########################################################
# proc keyedListAppend {list key value}
#    Return a list with a new key/value element at the end
# Arguments
#    list: Original list
#    key: Key for new element
#    value: Value for new element

proc keyedListAppend {list key value} {
  lappend list [list $key $value]
  return $list
}

########################################################
# proc keyedListSearch {list keyName}
#    Retrieve the first element that matches $keyName
# Arguments
#    list:    The keyed list
#    keyName: The name of a key

proc keyedListSearch {list keyName} {
  set pos [lsearch $list "$keyName*"]
```

```tcl
        return [lindex [lindex $list $pos] 1]
}

######################################################
# proc keyedListRetrieve {list keyName}
#   Retrieve all elements that match a key
# Arguments
#   list:    The keyed list
#   keyName: The name of key to retrieve
#

proc keyedListRetrieve {list keyName} {
  set start 0
  set pos [lsearch [lrange $list $start end] "${keyName}*"]
  while {$pos >= 0} {
    lappend locations [expr $pos + $start]
    set start [expr $pos + $start + 1]
    set pos [lsearch [lrange $list $start end] "${keyName}*"]
  }
  foreach l $locations {
    lappend rtn [lindex [lindex $list $l] 1]
  }
  return $rtn
}

# Define a simple e-mail header

set header {
Return-Path: <root@bastion.prplastics.com>
Received: from firewall.example.com
Received: from mailserver.example.com
Received: from workstation.noucorp.com
Date: Tue, 6 Aug 2002 04:13:38 -0400
Message-Id: <200208060813.g768DcP30231>
From: root@firewall.example.com (Cron Daemon)
To: root@firewall.workstation.com
Subject: Daily Report
}

# Initialize a keyed list

set keyedList ""

# Parse the e-mail header into the keyed list.
#   The first ":" marks the key and value for each line.
#
# Note that [split $line :] won't work because of lines
#   with timestamps.
```

```
foreach line [split $header \n] {
  set p [string first : $line]
  if {$p < 0} {continue}
  set key [string range $line 0 [expr {$p - 1}]]
  set value [string range $line [expr {$p + 2}] end]
  set keyedList [keyedListAppend $keyedList $key $value]
}

# Extract some data from the keyed list

puts "Mail is from: [keyedListSearch $keyedList From]"
puts "Mail passed through these systems in this order:"
foreach r [keyedListRetrieve $keyedList Received] {
  puts " [lindex $r 1]"
}
```

*Script Output*

```
Mail is from: root@firewall.example.com (Cron Daemon)
Mail passed through these systems in this order:
  firewall.example.com
  mailserver.example.com
  workstation.noucorp.com
```

For most lists, this technique works well. However, the time for the lsearch command to find an entry increases linearly with the position of the item in the list. Lists longer than 5,000 entries become noticeably sluggish. The pairing of data to a key value can also be done with associative arrays. The arrays use hash tables instead of a linear search to find a key, so the speed does not degrade as more records are added.

## 6.2 Using the Associative Array

The Tcl associative array can be used just like a C or FORTRAN array by setting the indices to numeric values. If you are familiar with FORTRAN or Basic programming, you might be familiar with coding constructs such as the following.

| *C Arrays* | *Tcl Array* |
|---|---|
| `int values[5];` | `set values(0) 1;` |
| `char desc[5][80];` | `set desc(0) "First"` |
| `values[0] = 1;` | |
| `strcpy(desc[0], "First");` | |

When programming in Tcl, you can link the value and description together more efficiently by using a nonnumeric index in the associative array.

```
set value("First") 1;
```

Data that consists of multiple items that need to be grouped together is frequently collected in composite data constructs such as a C struct or a Pascal record. These constructs allow the programmer-to-group–related data elements into a single-data entity, instead of several entities. The data elements within a struct or record can be manipulated individually.

Grouping information in a struct or record is conceptually a naming convention the compiler enforces for you. When you define the structure, you name the members and define what amount of storage space they will require. Once this is done, the algorithm developer generally does not need to worry about the internal memory arrangements. The data could be stored anywhere in memory, as long as a program can reference it by name. You can group data in an associative array variable by using different indices to indicate the different items being stored in that associative array, which is conceptually the same as a structure.

| *C Structure* | *Tcl Array* |
|---|---|
| `struct {` | `set var(value) 1` |
| `  int value;` | `set var(desc) "First"` |
| `  char desc[80];` | |
| `} var;` | |
| `var.value = 1;` | |
| `strcpy(var.desc,"First");` | |

It may not be immediately obvious, but the Tcl variable var groups the description and value together just as a struct would do. The var.value and var(value) are just different semantics for the same high-level data grouping.

Another common C data construct is the array of structs. Again, so far as your algorithm is concerned, this is primarily a naming convention. By treating the associative array index as a list of fields, separated by some obvious character (in the following example, a period is used), this functionality is available in Tcl.

| *Array of C Structures* | *Tcl Array* |
|---|---|
| ```struct {``` | ```set var(0.value) 1``` |
| ```  int value;``` | ```set var(0.desc) "First"``` |
| ```  char desc[80];``` | ```set var(1.value) 2``` |
| ```} var[5];``` | ```set var(1.desc) "Second"``` |
| ```var[0].value = 1;``` | |
| ```strcpy(var[0].desc, "First");``` | |
| ```var[1].value = 2;``` | |
| ```strcpy(var[1].desc, "Second");``` | |

You can create naming conventions to group data in Tcl. The Tcl interpreter does not require that you adhere to any naming convention. You can enforce a convention by writing procedures that will hide the conventions from people using a package. The following sections describe a more complex set of naming conventions that are hidden from the application programmer behind a set of procedures.

## 6.3 Exception Handling and Introspection

Before we get into the next set of examples, there are some new commands to discuss. The next examples use the Tcl exception-handling calls catch and error, the introspection command info, and the file load command source.

### 6.3.1 Exception Handling in Tcl

The default action for a Tcl interpreter when it hits an exception condition is to halt the execution of the script and display the data in the errorInfo global variable. The information in errorInfo will describe the command that failed and will include a stack dump for all the procedures that were in process when this failure occurred. The simplest method of modifying this behavior is to use the catch command to intercept the exception condition before the default error handler is invoked.

> **Syntax:** catch *script ?varName?*
>
> Catch an error condition and return the results rather than aborting the script.
>
> *script*    The Tcl script to evaluate.
>
> *varName*   Variable to receive the results of the script.

The catch command catches an error in a script and returns a success or failure code rather than aborting the program and displaying the error conditions. If the script runs without errors, catch returns 0. If there is an error, catch returns 1, and the errorCode and errorInfo variables are set to describe the error.

Sometimes a program should generate an exception. For instance, while checking the validity of user-provided data, you may want to abort processing if the data is obviously invalid. The Tcl command for generating an exception is error.

**Syntax:** error *informationalString* *?Info?* *?Code?*

| | |
|---|---|
| *error* | Generate an error condition. If not caught, display the *informationalString* and stack trace and abort the script evaluation. |
| *informationalString* | Information about the error condition. |
| *Info* | A string to initialize the errorInfo string. Note that the Tcl interpreter may append more information about the error to this string. |
| *Code* | A machine-readable description of the error that occurred. This will be saved in the global errorCode variable. |

The next example shows some ways of using the catch and error commands.

## Example 6.3

*Script Example*
```
proc errorProc {first second} {
  global errorInfo

  # $fail will be non-zero if $first is non-numeric.
  set fail [catch {expr 5 * $first} result]

  # if $fail is set, generate an error

  if {$fail} {
    error "Bad first argument"
  }

  # This will fail if $second is non-numeric or 0

  set fail [catch {expr $first/$second} dummy]

  if {$fail} {
    error "Bad second argument" \
    "second argument fails math test\n$errorInfo"
  }

  error "errorProc always fails" "evaluating error" \
    [list USER {123} {Non-Standard User-Defined Error}]
}

# Example Script

puts "call errorProc with a bad first argument"
set fail [catch {errorProc X 0} returnString]
```

```
if {$fail} {
  puts "Failed in errorProc"
  puts "Return string: $returnString"
  puts "Error Info: $errorInfo\n"
}

puts "call errorProc with a 0 second argument"
if {[catch {errorProc 1 0} returnString]} {
  puts "Failed in errorProc"
  puts "Return string: $returnString"
  puts "Error Info: $errorInfo\n"
}

puts "call errorProc with valid arguments"

set fail [catch {errorProc 1 1} returnString]

if {$fail} {
  if {[string first USER $errorCode] == 0} {
    puts "errorProc failed as expected"
    puts "returnString is: $returnString"
    puts "errorInfo: $errorInfo"
  } else {
    puts "errorProc failed for an unknown reason"

  }
}
```

*Script Output*

**call errorProc with a bad first argument**
**Failed in errorProc**
**Return string: Bad first argument**
**Error Info: Bad first argument**
  **while executing**
**"error "Bad first argument""**
  **(procedure "errorProc" line 10)**
  **invoked from within**
**"errorProc X 0"**

**call errorProc with a 0 second argument**
**Failed in errorProc**
**Return string: Bad second argument**
**Error Info: second argument fails math test**
**divide by zero**
  **while executing**
**"expr $first/$second"**
  **(procedure "errorProc" line 15)**

```
      invoked from within
"errorProc 1 0"

call errorProc with valid arguments
errorProc failed as expected
returnString is: errorProc always fails
errorInfo: evaluating error
   (procedure "errorProc" line 1)
   invoked from within
"errorProc 1 1"
```

Note the differences in the stack trace returned in `errorInfo` in the error returns. The first, generated with error *message*, includes the error command in the trace, whereas the second, generated with error *messageInfo*, does not.

If there is an *Info* argument to the `error` command, this string is used to initialize the `errorInfo` variable. If this variable is not present, Tcl uses the default initialization, which is a description of the command that generated the exception. In this case, that is the `error` command. If your application needs to include information that is already in the `errorInfo` variable, you can append that information by including $errorInfo in your message, as done with the second test.

The `errorInfo` variable contains what should be human-readable text to help a developer debug a program. The `errorCode` variable contains a machine-readable description to enable a script to handle exceptions intelligently. The `errorCode` data is a list in which the first field identifies the class of error (ARITH, CHILD-KILLED, POSIX, and so on), and the other fields contain data related to this error. The gory details are in the on-line manual/help pages under `tclvars`.

If you are used to Java, you are already familiar with the concept of separating data returns from status returns. If your background is C/FORTRAN/Basic programming, you are probably more familiar with the C/FORTRAN paradigm of returning status as a function return or using special values to distinguish valid data from error returns. For example, the C library routines return a valid pointer when successful and a NULL pointer for failure.

If you want to use function return values to return status in Tcl, you can. Using the `error` command (particularly in library procedures that application programs will invoke) provides a better mechanism. The following are reasons for using `error` instead of status returns.

■ An application programmer must check a procedure status return. It is easy to forget to check a status return and miss an exception. It takes extra code (the `catch` command) to ignore bad status generated by `error`.

   This makes the fast and dirty techniques for writing code (not checking for status or not catching errors) the more robust technique.

■ If a low-level procedure has a failure, the intermediate code must propagate the failure to the top level. Doing this with status returns requires special code to propagate the error, which means all functions must adhere to the error-handling policy.

The `error` command automatically propagates the error. Procedures that use a function that may fail need not include exception propagation code. This moves the policy decisions for how to handle an exception to the application level, where it is more appropriate.

## 6.3.2 Examining the State of the Tcl Interpreter

Any Tcl script can query the Tcl interpreter about its current state. The interpreter can report whether a procedure or variable is defined, what a procedure body or argument list is, the current level in the procedure stack, and so on. The next examples will use only a few of the `info` subcommands. See the on-line documentation for details of the other subcommands.

**Syntax:** info *subCommand arguments*

Provide information about the interpreter state.

*subCommand*    Defines the interaction. Interactions include

| | |
|---|---|
| `exists` *varName* | Returns True if a variable has been defined. |
| `proc` *globPattern* | Returns a list of procedure names that match the `glob` pattern. |
| `body` *procName* | Returns the body of a procedure. |
| `args` *procName* | Returns the names of the arguments for a procedure. |
| `nameofexecutable` | Returns the full path name of the binary file from which the application was invoked. |

The `info exists` command, for example, can be used to query whether a variable has been initialized. This will be used in the next examples to confirm that variables have been properly initialized.

## 6.3.3 Loading Code from a Script File

The `source` command loads a file into an existing Tcl script. It is similar to the `#include` in C, the `source` in C-shell programming, and the `require` in Perl. This command lets you build source code modules you can load into your scripts when you need particular functionality. This allows you to modularize your programs. This is the simplest of the Tcl commands that implement libraries and modularization. The `package` command is discussed in Chapter 8.

> ***Syntax:*** `source` *fileName*
>
> Load a file into the current Tcl application and evaluate it.
>
> *fileName*   The file to load.

Macintosh users have two options to the `source` command that are not available on other platforms:

> ***Syntax:*** `source -rsrc` *resourceName* *?fileName?*

> ***Syntax:*** `source -rsrcid` *resourceId* *?fileName?*

These options allow one script to source another script from a TEXT resource. The resource may be specified by `resourceName` or `resourceID`.

## 6.4 Trees in Tcl

You do not need to use a binary tree in Tcl for data access speed. The associative array provides fast access to data. However, sometimes the underlying data is best represented as a tree. A tree is the best way to represent a set of data that subdivides into smaller and smaller subsets. For example, a file system is a single large disk divided into directories, which are further divided into subdirectories and files. A tree can represent a set of data that has inherent order (with possible branches), such as the steps in an algorithm.

Tcl does not provide a tree construct as a built-in data type. However, it is not difficult to create one using the associative array and a naming convention. This section will build a library of subroutines and data to construct and manipulate trees. Using this library would be difficult if a programmer were required to learn the naming convention and write code that conforms to this convention. Therefore, the procedures in this library use a naming convention internally and return a handle the programmer uses to access the trees and nodes.

### 6.4.1 Tree Library Description

This section describes how to use and implement a tree data object in Tcl. A few procedures will be shown and discussed in this chapter to demonstrate how the procedures work. The complete code for the tree library is found on the companion CD-ROM under *examples/Tree*.

If you were constructing a tree in C, you might use a structure such as the following, with pointers to parent and child nodes:

```
struct node {
    struct node *parent;
    struct node *left;
    struct node *right;
    char *data;
};
```

You might use #define macros to access the elements, as follows:

```
#define treeParent(x) x->parent
#define treeLeft(x) x->left
#define treeRight(x) x->right
#define makeNode() (struct node *) malloc(sizeof (struct node))
#define setLeft(x, l) x->left = l
#define setRight(x, r) x->right = r
```

Tcl does not support the concept of reference by address (a pointer), but it does support reference by name, which is the equivalent in a string-oriented language. We can use an associative array and a naming convention to get the same behavior as this C code and get some added versatility in the bargain.

The naming convention used in this example lets us create multiple trees, each of which has parent and child references. A parent node can reference multiple child nodes (making it easy to create a B tree, quad tree, and so on). A child node references a single parent. Nodes can have multiple sets of data associated with them, or data values can be associated with an entire tree. Trees can be as deep as the data requires.

When the library creates a new node, it returns a handle. The application code passes this handle to the procedures that manipulate the tree. The programmer never needs to see the naming conventions.

## 6.4.2 **Tree Library Naming Conventions**

Since this library is built around a naming convention, we will examine that first. The naming convention is to divide an index into multiple fields using a dot. The first two fields identify the tree and node identifiers, and subsequent fields identify the type of data stored in this array element. The handle returned by various commands (and used to reference a node) is the first two fields: $tree.$node.

For example, tree1.node4.parent would be the index that contains the parent handle for the node with the handle tree1.node4. The value will be a tree handle resembling tree1.node2. The indices used in this array are as follows.

| Index | Description |
| --- | --- |
| *treeID.nodeID*.parent | The handle for the parent of this node |
| *treeID.nodeID*.children | A list of handles of child nodes of this node |

| | |
|---|---|
| `treeID.nodeID.node.key` | Data associated with this node, indexed by *key* |
| `treeID.tree.key` | Data associated with the entire tree, indexed by *key* |

In fact, the only requirement to make a tree is that the nodes be uniquely identified. There is no need to use a tree identifier if each node name is unique. Having both tree and node identifiers makes it easy to confirm that nodes are being added to the proper tree.

This library defines a single associative array to hold the trees and their nodes. This array is a global variable (which makes the data persistent and allows all procedures to access it) named `Tree_Array`. The library consists of several `procs` that can be accessed from a user script and a few internal `procs` that are used only by other tree `procs`, not by an application programmer.

The *Tcl Style Guide* developed by the Sun Microsystems Tcl group recommends that you start procedure names intended for use within a package with an uppercase letter and use lowercase letters to start the procedures intended for external use. It also recommends that all entry points in a package start with a recognizable string, to avoid name conflict when someone needs to load several packages.

The `procs` that provide the program interface to this library all start with `tree`. The internal variables and procedures start with the word `Tree`. The commands this library implements are as follows.

| | |
|---|---|
| `treeCreate` | Create a new, empty tree and return a handle for the root node. |
| `treeCreateChild` *parent* | Create a new node attached to this parent. Add the new node to the parent's list of children, and set the new node's parent address to point to this parent. Return the handle for the new node. |
| `treeGetChildList` *parent* | Return a list of all children attached to a parent node or an empty list if the parent has no children. |
| `treeGetParent` *node* | Return the parent of a node if the node has a parent. |
| `treeSetNodeValue` *node key value* | Set a key and `value` pair in a node. |
| `treeGetNodeValue` *node key* | Returns the value associated with a key in this node. |
| `treeSetTreeValue` *anyNode key value* | Set a key and `value` pair for an entire tree. |
| `treeGetTreeValue` *anyNode key* | Returns the value associated with a key in this tree. |

A script for using these commands would resemble the following.

**Example** 6.4

*Script Example*

```
# Load the script file that defines the procedures and
# Tree_Array
source tree.tcl

# Create a Tree. The root node is returned.
set root [treeCreate]

# attach some data to the key "displayText" of the root node

treeSetNodeValue $root displayText "We can see"

# Create a child attached to the root
# and attach some data to the "displayText" key in the child

set child1 [treeCreateChild $root]
treeSetNodeValue $child1 displayText "the forest for"

# Create another child attached to the root
# and attach some data to "displayText" key in the new child

set child2 [treeCreateChild $root]
treeSetNodeValue $child2 displayText "the trees."

puts "[treeGetNodeValue $root displayText]"

foreach child [treeGetChildList $root] {
    puts "[treeGetNodeValue $child displayText]"
}
```

*Script Output*

```
We can see
the forest for
the trees.
```

The previous script produces a tree that resembles that shown in the following illustration.

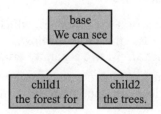

## 6.5 Tree Library Implementation

Now that we have introduced a simple application of the tree library, let's look at the implementation.

### 6.5.1 Getting the Parts of a Name

Most of the procedures in this library will need to separate a node handle into parts. Since this operation is so pervasive and generic, it should be placed in a proc. This proc is named TreeGetNameParts. It will split a node name at the periods and return the *treeID* and the *nodeID*.

Since every other procedure will end up evaluating TreeGetNameParts, this is a good place to perform a validity check on the name. Since the validity check is not the primary purpose of this procedure, the check should be optional.

#### *Procedures with Optional Arguments*

The common way to handle an optional section of code is to pass a flag to the procedure and then branch to evaluate the optional code based on the setting of the flag. We could do this with a proc invocation such as the following:

```
proc TreeGetNameParts {name treeVarName nodeVarName doCheck}
```

This would require that each invocation of TreeGetNameParts include the flag for whether or not to perform the check.

The Tcl proc command also allows you to define a procedure with arguments that can have default values. If a value is provided, the procedure gets that value; but if no value is provided, the default value is used. This is done by defining the variable with a list of the variable name and default value, as in the following:

```
proc TreeGetNameParts {name treeVarName nodeVarName {doCheck 1}}
```

In this case, the default value for the doCheck variable will be 1. If TreeGet-NameParts is invoked with four arguments, the fourth value will be assigned to doCheck.

#### *Procedures Using Call-by-Name Arguments*

Usually, a Tcl proc will return a single value, or a list of values, which the calling script will parse appropriately. In this case, the program flow is simpler if TreeGetNameParts returns the *treeID* and *nodeID* in two separate variables.

To do this, we will use the Tcl upvar command. The upvar command allows a Tcl procedure to link a variable in a higher level of scope than the current scope.

This is conceptually the same as passing a variable by reference in C and C++. The upvar command is discussed in more detail in Chapter 7.

**Syntax:** upvar *?level? varName1 localName1 ?varName2? ?localName2?*

Links a variable from a higher variable scope into the current variable scope.

*?level?*    An optional level to describe the level from which the variable should be linked. This value may be a number or the # symbol followed by a number.

If this is a number, it represents the number of levels higher in the procedure stack to link this variable from. If 1, the variable will be linked from the scope of the calling process; if 2, it will be linked from the scope of the process above that.

If the number is preceded by a # sign, it represents the procedure call level down from the global scope (#0). In this form, #0 is the global scope, #1 is a proc called from the global scope, #2 is a proc called from that proc, and so on.

The level defaults to 1, the level of the script that invoked the current proc.

*varName\**    The name of a variable in the higher scope to link to a local variable.

*localName\**    The name of a variable in the local scope. This variable can be used in this script as a local variable. Setting a new value to this variable will change the value of the variable in the other scope.

## Example 6.5

*Script Example*

```
set variable "A simple variable"
set array(index1) "An array with index1"
set array(index2) "An array with index2"

proc callByName {varName arrayName} {
    upvar $varName localVar
    upvar $arrayName localArray

    puts "VARIABLE: $localVar"
    puts "ARRAY: [array get localArray]"
}
callByName variable array
```

*Script Output*

```
VARIABLE: A simple variable
ARRAY: index1 {An array with index1} index2 {An array with index2}
```

Note that an individual array index may be passed by value to a procedure, but Tcl does not pass entire arrays by value. Whenever you need to pass an entire array to a procedure, you must pass the array by name, either using the upvar command to link to the array in the calling script's scope or the global command (if the array exists in the global scope).

## Example 6.6

*Script Example*

```
#######################################################
# proc TreeGetNameParts \
#    {name treeVarName nodeVarName {doCheck 1}} --
#  Internal proc for splitting a name into parts
# Arguments:
# name:         Node handle to split
# treeVarName:  Name of the variable to receive the tree name
# nodeVarName:  Name of the variable to receive the node name
# doCheck:      If set, will confirm that the handle is valid.
#
# No valid Return, sets two variables in the calling proc.

proc TreeGetNameParts \
  {name treeVarName nodeVarName {doCheck 1}} {
  global Tree_Array

  upvar $treeVarName tree
  upvar $nodeVarName node

  set namelst [split $name "."]
  set tree [lindex $namelst 0]
  set node [lindex $namelst 1]

  if {$doCheck} {
    if {![info exists Tree_Array($tree.$node.parent)]} {
      error \
        "$tree.$node does not exist - did you treeCreate it?" \
        "$tree.$node does not exist - did you treeCreate it?"
    }
  }
}
```

```
# Script usage Example

TreeGetNameParts tree1.node2 treeName nodeID 0
puts "Tree Name is: $treeName. Node ID is: $nodeID"
```

***Script Output***

**Tree Name is: tree1. Node ID is: node2**

---

## 6.5.2 **Creating a New Tree**

The command for creating a new tree in this library is treeCreate. It generates a unique name for the tree and creates a new node to be the base node for this tree. The handle for the new node is returned. The unique procedure is discussed later. This procedure returns a unique value for generating unique names.

**Example** 6.7

***Script Example***

```
#########################################################
# proc treeCreate {} --
#    Create a root node for a tree
# Arguments:
#
# Results:
#    Creates a new root node in Tree_Array
#    Initializes a unique counter for this tree.
#    Returns the name of the root node for use as a handle
#
proc treeCreate {} {
  global Tree_Array

  # Create the unique name for this tree.

  set treeName "tree[unique]"

  # Can't have two trees with the same name.
  # This should never happen, but just in case...

  if {[array name Tree_Array $treeName.*] != ""} {
      error "$treeName already exists"
  }

  # Looks good, return a new base node for this tree.

  return [TreeCreateNode $treeName]
}
```

```
# Example

set tree [treeCreate ]
puts "The root node for this tree is: $tree"
```

***Script Output***

**The root node for this tree is: tree0.node1**

---

### 6.5.3 **Creating a New Child Node**

The treeCreate invokes the TreeCreateNode procedure to create a new node. This creates a new node and initializes the parent and children indices to empty strings.

Application code will create new nodes using the treeCreateChild procedure. This procedure creates a node, adds its handle to the parent node's list of children, and puts the parent's handle in the parent index of the new node. The treeCreateChild procedure calls two internal procedures:

TreeCreateNode     Create an empty node.

TreeAddChild       Link the node to the parent.

***Syntax:*** TreeCreateNode *nodeName*

Create a new node and initialize the parent and children indices to empty strings.

*nodeName*     The name of the tree.

***Syntax:*** TreeAddChild *parent child*

Confirms that parent and child are valid handles. Adds the child's handle to the parent's list of children and sets the child's parent index to the handle for the parent node.

*parent*     The parent to receive this child node.

*child*     The new child node to be added to the parent.

The following example shows the three procedures used to create a new child: the public entry point and the two internal procedures, and how to create a new tree and add two child nodes to the parent node. An application programmer will never need to know what array indices are used to create nodes. However, to make it more obvious what's going on under the hood, the following example displays them.

**Example** 6.8

*Script Example*

```
######################################################
# proc treeCreateChild {parent} --
#   Creates a child of a given parent
#
# Arguments:
#     parent: The parent node to contain this new node
# Results:
#     Creates a new node.
#     Adds the child to the parent node.
#     Sets parent index in new child.
#     Returns the handle for the new node.
#
proc treeCreateChild {parent} {
  global Tree_Array

  TreeGetNameParts $parent tree node

  set child [TreeCreateNode $tree]

  TreeAddChild $parent $child
  return $child
}

######################################################
# proc TreeCreateNode {nodeName} --
# Create a new node (unattached) in this tree
# Arguments:
#     nodeName: The name of a node in the tree
#
# Results:
#     Creates a new node.
#     Returns a handle to use to identify this node.
#
proc TreeCreateNode {nodeName} {
  global Tree_Array

  # The existence of the tree is checked in TreeGetNameParts

  TreeGetNameParts $nodeName tree node 0

  set childname "$tree.node[unique]"
  array set Tree_Array [list \
      $childname.parent "" $childname.children "" ]

  return $childname
}
```

```
#########################################################
# proc TreeAddChild {parent child} --
#    Adds a node to the child list of the parent node, and
#    sets child's parent pointer to reflect the parent node.
#
# Arguments:
#     parent: The parent node
#     child:  New child node being added to the parent.
#
# Results:
#     Adds the child and updates parent pointer
#     No valid return.
#
proc TreeAddChild {parent child} {
    global Tree_Array

    TreeGetNameParts $parent parentTree parentNode

    TreeGetNameParts $child childTree childNode

    if {![string match $parentTree $childTree]} {
      error "Can't add nodes from different trees! \n \
        $parentTree != $childTree"
    }

    if {![string match \
      $Tree_Array($childTree.$childNode.parent) ""]} {
        error "$child already has parent: \
          $Tree_Array($childTree.$childNode.parent)"
    }

    lappend Tree_Array($parentTree.$parentNode.children) \
      $childTree.$childNode

    set Tree_Array($childTree.$childNode.parent) \
      $parentTree.$parentNode
}

# Example Script
#
# Create a tree
#
set root [treeCreate]

# Create 2 child nodes attached to the root
set child1 [treeCreateChild $root]
set child2 [treeCreateChild $root]
```

```
puts "Tree_Array has these indices:"

foreach index [lsort [array names Tree_Array]] {
  puts "INDEX: $index -- VALUE: $Tree_Array($index)"
}
```

***Script Output***

```
Tree_Array has these indices:
INDEX: tree1.node2.children -- VALUE: tree1.node3 tree1.node4
INDEX: tree1.node2.parent -- VALUE:
INDEX: tree1.node3.children -- VALUE:
INDEX: tree1.node3.parent -- VALUE: tree1.node2
INDEX: tree1.node4.children -- VALUE:
INDEX: tree1.node4.parent -- VALUE: tree1.node2
```

The Tcl tree example demonstrates what can be done with naming conventions. Because the naming convention is so important to this library, we will examine it in detail. The base node has the handle tree1.node2, and handles for the two children: tree1.node3 and tree1.node4.

The first word in each index is tree1, the name of the tree. If we created a second tree, it would have a new name, such as tree2. The second word is a unique name for each node; in this case, these are node2, node3, and node4. These two fields are combined to form a handle that is a unique identifier for each node.

The final field is the identifier for the data in this variable. If this value is children, the values are a list of the handles for children of this node. If the final field is parent, it contains the handle of the parent of this node.

The base node, tree1.node2, has two children: tree1.node3 and tree1.node4. These handles are contained in tree1.node2.children. Since this node is the top of the tree, it has no parent, so the tree1.node2.parent index contains an empty string. The child nodes have the parent handle, tree1.node2, in their tree1.*nodeID*.parent index and empty strings in their list of children.

## 6.5.4 Tree Library As a Container Class

The tree library also allows the programmer to attach data to a node and access it via a key. This lets you use the tree data structure as you would use a container class in C++ or Java.

The procedures that implement this are treeSetNodeValue and treeGetNodeValue, which set and retrieve values attached to a node using a key as an index. Similar code implements the procedures treeSetTreeValue and treeGetTreeValue, which set and retrieve values that are attached to the entire tree and are available to all nodes.

*Syntax:* `treeSetNodeValue` *name key value*

Assign a value to a key attached to this node.

*name*  The handle for the node to attach a value to.

*key*  The key to use to access this value.

*value*  A value to assign to the node.

*Syntax:* `treeGetNodeValue` *name key*

Retrieve a data value from this node.

*name*  The handle for this node.

*key*  The key for the data to be returned.

## Example 6.9

*Script Example*

```
#########################################################
# proc treeSetNodeValue {name key value} --
#      Sets the value of a key/value pair in a node.
#
# Arguments:
#      name:  The node to set the key/value pair in
#      key:   An identifier to reference this value
#      value: The value for this identifier
#
# Results:
#      Sets a key/value pair in this node.
#      Returns the value.
#
proc treeSetNodeValue {name key value} {
    global Tree_Array

    TreeGetNameParts $name tree node

    set Tree_Array($tree.$node.node.$key) $value

    return $value
}

#########################################################
# proc treeGetNodeValue {name key} --
#      Returns a value from a key/value pair
#      if it has previously been set.
#
# Arguments:
#      name: The node to get the key/value pair from
#      key:  The identifier to get a value for
```

```
#
# Results:
#      Returns the value from a previously set key/value pair

proc treeGetNodeValue {name key} {
    global Tree_Array

    TreeGetNameParts $name tree node

    if {![info exists Tree_Array($tree.$node.node.$key)]} {
        error "treeGetNodeValue: Key $key does not exist"
    }

    return $Tree_Array($tree.$node.node.$key)
}

# Example Script

# Create a tree

set tree [treeCreate]

# Create two nodes attached to the root node

set node1 [treeCreateChild $tree]
set node2 [treeCreateChild $tree]

# Set values in node1 and node2

treeSetNodeValue $node1 keyA "Value for node1:KeyA"
treeSetNodeValue $node2 keyA "Value for node2:KeyA"

treeSetNodeValue $node1 keyB "Value for node1:KeyB"
treeSetNodeValue $node2 keyB "Value for node2:KeyB"

# Retrieve the values

puts "node1 has values:"
puts " keyA: [treeGetNodeValue $node1 keyA]"
puts " keyB: [treeGetNodeValue $node1 keyB]"

puts "\nnode2 has values:"
puts " keyA: [treeGetNodeValue $node2 keyA]"
puts " keyB: [treeGetNodeValue $node2 keyB]"

# Set a value for the entire tree, via node 1

treeSetTreeValue $node1 TreeKeyA "Value A for tree"

# Retrieve it via node 2

puts "\nTreeKeyA: [treeGetTreeValue $node2 TreeKeyA]"
```

*Script Output*

```
node1 has values:
keyA: Value for node1:KeyA
keyB: Value for node1:KeyB

node2 has values:
keyA: Value for node2:KeyA
keyB: Value for node2:KeyB

TreeKeyA: Value A for tree
```

## 6.5.5 Generating Unique Names

A program can generate a unique string in many ways. One of the simplest is to use a numeric value that is incremented each time it is accessed. The unique procedure used in the tree library could be written as follows.

```
proc unique {} {
    global Tree_Array
    if {![info exists Tree_Array(base)]} {
        set Tree_Array(base) 0
    }
    return [incr Tree_Array(base)]
}
```

Using this technique requires a global variable, which may not be a suitable solution for all situations. One of the interesting features of the Tcl language is that it allows you to redefine a procedure within a running program. Each time an existing procedure is redefined, the old body and argument list is replaced with the new body and arguments.

The info body command (the info commands are also discussed in Chapter 7) will return the body of a procedure. For example, after defining the unique procedure, shown previously, the info body unique command would return

```
% puts [info body unique]
{
    global Tree_Array
    if {![info exists Tree_Array(base)]} {
        set Tree_Array(base) 0
    }
    return [incr Tree_Array(base)]
}
```

Using these two features, we can write a unique procedure that uses no external data, as shown in the next example.

```
proc unique {{val 0}} {
    incr val
    proc unique "{val $val}" [info body unique]
    return $val
}
```

Each time this unique procedure is invoked, it redefines the unique procedure with the same body as before but a new default value for the variable val.

**Example** 6.10

*Script Example*

```
puts "first: [unique] next: [unique] next [unique]"
```

*Script Output*

```
first: 1 next: 2 next 3
```

## 6.6 Using the Tree Library

Now that we have gone over the internals of the tree library, let's see a simple example of how it can be used. This example builds a tree structure from the first two levels of a file directory and then prints out that directory tree.

The tree library is contained in a file named tree.tcl. The source tree.tcl command loads tree.tcl into the script and makes the treeCreate, treeSet-NodeValue, and other procedures available for use. In this example, we use the catch command to examine directories without aborting the program if the directory is empty or our script does not have read permission.

**Example** 6.11

*Script Example*

```
#!/bin/sh
#\
exec tclsh "$0" "$@"

# dirtree.tcl
#     demonstrate using a tree

source tree.tcl

#####################################################
# proc addDirToTree
#     Add a directory to a node.
```

```
#      Create children for each directory entry, and set
#         the name and type of each child.
#
# Arguments:
#     parent       The parent node for this directory.
#     directory    The directory to add to the tree.
#
# Results:
#     The tree is made longer by the number of entries
#     in this directory.

proc addDirToTree {parent directory} {

    # If this isn't a directory, it has no subordinates.

    if {[file type $directory] != "directory"} {
      error "$directory is not a directory"
    }

    # If the parent directory hasn't been updated with name
    #  and type, do so now.

    if {[catch {treeGetNodeValue $parent name}]} {
      treeSetNodeValue $parent name $directory
      treeSetNodeValue $parent type directory
    }

    # An empty or unreadable directory will return a fail
    #  for the glob command
    # If the directory can be read, the list of names
    #  will be in fileList.

    set fail [catch {glob $directory/*} fileList]

    if {$fail} {
       return;
    }

    # Loop through the names in fileList

    foreach name $fileList {
       set node [treeCreateChild $parent]
       treeSetNodeValue $node name $name
       treeSetNodeValue $node type [file type $name]
    }
}
```

```
# Create a tree

set base [treeCreate ]

# Add the initial directory and its directory entries
#  to the tree

addDirToTree $base [file nativename /]

# If any children are directories, add their entries to the
#  tree under as subchildren.

foreach entry [treeGetChildList $base] {
  if {[treeGetNodeValue $entry type] == "directory"} {
    addDirToTree $entry [treeGetNodeValue $entry name]
  }
}

#
# Print out the tree in the form:
# Dir1
#    Dir1/Entry1
#    Dir1/Entry2
# Dir2
#    Dir2/Entry3
#    Dir2/Entry4
#

foreach entry [treeGetChildList $base] {
   puts "[treeGetNodeValue $entry name]"
   if {[treeGetNodeValue $entry type] == "directory"} {
       foreach sub [treeGetChildList $entry] {
           puts "   [treeGetNodeValue $sub name]"
       }
   }
}
```

***Script Output***

```
...
/usr
    /usr/bin
    /usr/lib
    /usr/libexec
    /usr/sbin
/home
    /home/clif
    /home/visitor
/var
    /var/lib
```

```
/var/log
...
```

## 6.7 Speed Considerations

So, how do lists and associative arrays compare when it comes to accessing a particular piece of data? The following example shows the results of plotting the list and array access times using Tcl 8.3.

The time to access the last element in a list increases linearly with the length of the list. In Tcl 8.3, the list-handling code was rewritten to improve the performance, but even with that performance improvement the access speed for array elements is much faster and does not degrade as the number of elements increases.

Note that the performance between lsearch and an array access is not significantly different with Tcl 8.3 until you exceed 500 elements in the list. If your lists are shorter than 500 elements, you can use whichever data construct fits your data best.

This timing test was done on a 1-GHz PIII platform running Linux. The graph was generated using the BLT extension discussed in Chapter 14.

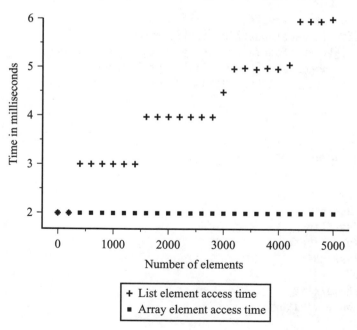

Comparison of list and array element access time

**Example** 6.12

> *List Element Access Time*
> ```
> for {set i 0} {$i < 5100} {incr i 200} {
>   set x "abcd.$i.efg"
>   lappend lst $x
>   puts "$i [lindex [time {lsearch $lst $x} 50] 0]"
> }
> ```
>
> *Array Element Access Time*
> ```
> for {set i 0} {$i < 5100} {incr i 200} {
>   set x "abcd.$i.efg"
>   set arr($i) $x
>   puts "$i [lindex [time {set y $arr($i)} 50] 0]"
> }
> ```

Note that although accessing a known index in an associative array is very fast, using the array names command builds a list of array indices and extracts the list of names that match a pattern. This operation becomes slower as the number of indices increases. If you need to deal with applications that have thousands of nodes, it may be better to use multiple arrays rather than indices with multiple fields.

# 6.8 Bottom Line

This chapter has demonstrated several ways to use Tcl lists and associative arrays.

- Lists can be used to organize information as position-oriented data or as key/value pairs.
- Naming conventions can be used with associative array indices to provide the same functionality as structures, arrays of structures, and container classes.
- A variable can contain the name of another variable, providing the functionality of a pointer.
- The catch command is used to catch an error condition without causing a script to abort processing.

  *Syntax:* catch *script ?varName?*
- The file command provides access to the file system.

> *Syntax:* `file type` *pathName*

> *Syntax:* `file nativename` *pathName*

> *Syntax:* `file delete` *pathName*

> *Syntax:* `file exists` *pathName*

> *Syntax:* `file isdirectory` *pathName*

> *Syntax:* `file isfile` *pathName*

- The `glob` command returns directory entries that match a particular pattern.

  *Syntax:* `glob` *?-nocomplain? ?--? pattern ?pattern?*

- The `source` command loads and evaluates a script.

  *Syntax:* `source` *fileName*

- The `upvar` command causes a variable name in a higher-level scope to be linked to a variable in the local scope.

  *Syntax:* `upvar` *?level? varName1 localVar1 ?varName2? ?localVar2?*

- The `error` command generates an error condition.

  *Syntax:* `error` *infoString ?newErrInfo? ?newErrCode?*

- The `lreplace` command replaces one or more list elements with 0 or more new elements.

  *Syntax:* `lreplace` *list first last ?element element ...?*

- The `info` command returns information about the current state of the interpreter.

  *Syntax:* `info proc`

  *Syntax:* `info args`

  *Syntax:* `info body`

  *Syntax:* `info exists`

  *Syntax:* `info nameofexecutable`

- The `join` command will convert a list into a string, using an optional character as the element separator.

  *Syntax:* `join` *?joinString?*

- Accessing an array element is frequently faster than using `lsearch` to find a list element.

## 6.9 Problems

The following numbering convention is used in all Problem sections.

| Number Range | Description of Problems |
| --- | --- |
| 100–199 | These problems review the material covered in this chapter. They can be answered in a few words or a short (1–5-line) script. Each problem should take under a minute to answer. |
| 200–299 | These problems go beyond the details presented in this chapter. They may require some analysis of the material or command details not covered in the chapter. They may require reading a man page or making a web search. They can be answered with a few sentences or a 5–50-line script. Each problem should take under 10 minutes to answer. |
| 300–299 | These problems extend the material presented in this chapter. They may require referencing other sources. They can be answered in a few paragraphs or a few hundred lines of code. Each exercise may take a few hours to complete. |

**100.** Given a large amount of data, which is likely to be faster: using `lsearch` to search a list or indexing the data in an associative array?

**101.** What Tcl command would convert a Tcl list into a string with commas between the list elements?

**102.** What associative array indices would provide a data relationship similar to the following?

```
struct {
    char *title;
    char *author;
    float price;
} books[3];
```

**103.** What will be the first Tcl command in the error stack generated by the Tcl command `error "Illegal value"`?

**104.** The code fragment `set result [expr $numerator/$divisor]` will fail if the numerator or divisor is an illegal value. Write a code fragment to divide one value by another without generating an error. If the numerator or divisor is an illegal value, set `result` to the phrase `Not-A-Number`.

**105.** What Tcl command will report the type of file (a normal file or directory, for example) given a file name?

**106.** A tree can be used to organize sorted data. In a balanced binary tree, the root node is in the center of the sorted data, and all nodes containing data less than the root are on the left, while nodes containing data greater than the root are on the right. The tree shown below contains data pairs sorted alphabetically by the first element of each pair.

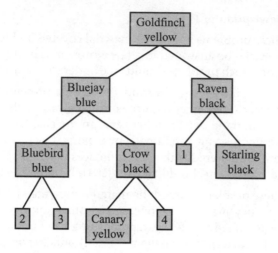

What position would be correct for the following data pairs?

a. Partridge brown

b. Owl brown

c. Auk brown

d. Rooster red

e. Falcon gray

f. Dodo gray

g. Seagull gray

h. Turkey brown

i. Parrot green

j. Junco gray

k. Eagle white

**107.** What Tcl command will return a list of procedure names that match a pattern?

**108.** If the procedure `treeCreate` is defined in a file named `tree.tcl`, what Tcl command should you place in a script before invoking the `tree.tcl` code procedure?

**200.** Given a set of data in which each line follows the form `Name:UserName:Password`, write a `foreach` command that will split a line into the variables `name`, `user`, and `passwd`.

**201.** Given the following list:

```
{
{ {Name {John Doe}} {UserName johnd} {Password JohnPwd} }
{ {UserName jdoe}   {Name {Jane Doe}} {Password JanePwd} }
{ {Name {John Smith}} {Password JohnPwd} {UserName johns} }
{ {UserName jonnjonzz} {Password manhunter} {Name {John Jones}} }
}
```

a. What combination of lsearch and lindex commands would find the password for John Jones?

b. Write a short script that will list users with identical passwords.

c. Will you get the record with John Doe's password using an lsearch pattern of John*?

d. Write a short script that would change John Smith's user name to jsmith.

**300.** The kitchen in an automated restaurant might receive orders as patrons select items from a menu via a format such as the following:

```
{{Table 2} {burger} {ketchup mustard}}
   {{Table 3} {drink} {medium}}
   {{Table 2} {fries} {large}}
   {{Table 1} {BLT}   {no mayo}}
   {{Table 3} {Complete} {} }
   {{Table 1} {drink} {small}}
   {{Table 1} {Complete} {} }
```

Write a script that will accept data in a format such as this, collecting the items ordered at a table and reporting a table's order when the Complete message is received. After reporting an order, it should be ready to start assembling a new order for that table.

**301.** Write a script that will accept multiple lines in the form "author, title, and so on."

```
Clif Flynt, Tcl/Tk: A Developer's Guide
Richard Stevens, TCP/IP Illustrated
Donald Knuth, The Art of Computer Programming: Vol 1
Donald Knuth, The Art of Computer Programming: Vol 2
Donald Knuth, The Art of Computer Programming: Vol 3
John Ousterhout, Tcl and the Tk Toolkit
Richard Stevens, Unix Network Programming
```

Place this data in an associative array that would allow you to get lists of books by an author.

**302.** A tree data structure can be implemented as nested lists. Implement the tree procedures described in this chapter using lists instead of associative arrays.

**303.** Write a "Safe Math" procedure that will accept a mathematical expression, evaluate it, and return the result without generating an error. If any of the values in the math expression are illegal, return the phrase "Illegal Expression" instead of a numeric answer.

**304.** Using the tree commands described in Section 6.4.2 (implemented in the file `examples/Tree/tree.tcl` on the companion CD-ROM), write a Tcl script that would create the tree shown in Problem 106.

**305.** Using the naming convention described in this chapter, write a procedure that will move a child node from one parent to another.

*Syntax:* `treeMoveNode child originalParent newParent`

**306.** Using the tree API described in this chapter, write the insert and delete procedures that would maintain a balanced binary tree in which nodes are inserted into the tree alphabetically based on a data value. The new procedures should resemble the following.

*Syntax:* `treeInsert treeid key value`

*Syntax:* `treeDelete handle`

**307.** Modify the `addDirToTree` procedure from Example 6.12 to support a third argument `recursive` with a default value of 0. If this value is non-zero, the `addDirToTree` should run recursively, adding all subdirectories to the tree.

# CHAPTER 7

# Procedure Techniques

One key to writing modular code is dividing large programs into smaller sub-routines. Tcl supports the common programming concept of subroutines — procedures that accept a given number of arguments and return one or more values. Tcl also supports procedures with variable numbers of arguments and procedures with arguments that have default values.

The Tcl interpreter allows scripts to rename procedures and create new procedures while the script is running. When a new procedure is created by another procedure, the new procedure is defined in the global scope and is not deleted when the procedure that created it returns.

Previous chapters introduced some of these capabilities. This chapter expands on that discussion with more details and examples, including the following:

- Defining the arguments to procedures
- Renaming and deleting procedures
- Examining a procedure's body and arguments
- Performing Tcl variable and command substitutions on a string
- Constructing and evaluating command lines within a script
- Turning a set of procedures and data into an object

The last example in this chapter shows how to extend the tree example from Chapter 6 into a tree object.

## 7.1 Arguments to Procedures

When the proc command is invoked to create a new procedure, the new procedure is defined with a name, a list of arguments, and a body to evaluate when the procedure is invoked. When a procedure is called, the Tcl interpreter counts the arguments to confirm that there are as many arguments in the procedure call as there were in the procedure definition. If a procedure is called with too few arguments, the Tcl interpreter generates an error message resembling this:

```
no value given for parameter "arg1" to "myProcedure"
```

If a procedure is called with too many arguments, the Tcl interpreter generates an error message resembling this:

```
called "myProc" with too many arguments
```

This runtime checking helps you avoid the silent errors that occur when you modify a procedure to take a new argument and miss changing one of the procedure calls.

However, there are times when you do not know the number of arguments (as with the expr command) or want an argument to be optional, with a default value when the argument is not present (as 1 is the default increment value for the incr command). You can easily define a procedure to handle a variable number of arguments or define a default value for an argument in Tcl.

### 7.1.1 **Variable Number of Arguments to a Procedure**

You can define a procedure that takes a variable number of arguments by making the final argument in the argument list the word args. When this procedure is called with more arguments than expected, the Tcl interpreter will concatenate the arguments that were not assigned to declared variables into a list and assign that list to the variable args, instead of generating a too many arguments error.

Note that args must be the last argument in the argument list to get the excess arguments assigned to it. If there are other arguments after the args argument, args is treated as a normal argument. In the following example, the procedure showArgs requires at least one argument. If there are more arguments, they will be placed in the variable args.

**Example** 7.1

*Script Example*
```
# A proc that accepts a variable number of args

proc showArgs {first args} {
    puts "first: $first"
    puts "args: $args"
}

# Example Script

puts "Called showArgs with one arg"
showArgs oneArgument
```

```
puts "\nCalled showArgs with two args"
showArgs oneArgument twoArgument

puts "\nCalled showArgs with three args"
showArgs oneArgument twoArgument threeArgument
```

***Script Output***

```
Called showArgs with one arg
first: oneArgument
args:

Called showArgs with two args
first: oneArgument
args: twoArgument

Called showArgs with three args
first: oneArgument
args: twoArgument threeArgument
```

## 7.1.2 Default Values for Procedure Arguments

The technique for setting a default value for an argument is to define the argument as a list; the first element is the argument name, and the second is the default value. When the arguments are defined as a list and a procedure is called with too few arguments, the Tcl interpreter will substitute the default value for the missing arguments, instead of generating a no value given for parameter error.

**Example** 7.2

***Script Example***

```
# A proc that expects at least one arg, and has defaults for 2

proc showDefaults {arg1 {numberArg 0} {stringArg {default string}}} {
  puts "arg1: $arg1"
  puts "numberArg: $numberArg"
  puts "stringArg: $stringArg"
}

# Example Script
puts "\nCalled showDefaults with one argument"
showDefaults firstArgument
puts "\nCalled showDefaults with two arguments"
showDefaults firstArgument 3
puts "\nCalled showDefaults with three arguments"
showDefaults firstArgument 3 "testing"
```

*Script Output*

```
Called showDefaults with one argument
arg1: firstArgument
numberArg: 0
stringArg: default string

Called showDefaults with two arguments
arg1: firstArgument
numberArg: 3
stringArg: default string

Called showDefaults with three arguments
arg1: firstArgument
numberArg: 3
stringArg: testing
```

The procedure showDefaults must be called with at least one argument. If only one argument is supplied, numberArg will be defined as 0, and stringArg will be defined as default string.

Note that the order of the arguments when a procedure is invoked must be the same as the order when the procedure was defined. The Tcl interpreter will assign the values in the order in which the variable names appear in the procedure definition. For example, you cannot call procedure showDefaults with arguments for arg1 and stringArg, but must use the default for numberArg. The second value in the procedure call is assigned to the second variable in the procedure definition.

You cannot create a procedure that has an argument with a default before an argument without a default. If you created a procedure such as the following,

```
proc badProc {{argWithDefault dflt} argWithOutDefault} {...}
```

and called it with a single argument, it would be impossible for the Tcl interpreter to guess for which variable that argument was intended. Tcl would assign the value to the first variable in the argument list, and the error return would resemble the following:

```
% badProc aa
no value given for parameter "argWithOutDefault" to "badProc"
```

## 7.2 Renaming or Deleting Commands

The proc command will create a new procedure. Sometimes you may also need to rename or delete a procedure. For example, if you need to use two sets of

Tcl code that both have a processData procedure, you can load one package, rename the processData procedure to package1processData, and then load the second package. (A better solution is to use a namespace, as described in Chapter 8.)

If you have had to deal with name collisions in libraries and DLLs before, you will appreciate this ability. When you use the technique shown later in this chapter to extend a data item into an object, you will want to delete the object method procedure when the data object is destroyed.

The rename command lets you change the name of a command or procedure. You can delete a procedure by renaming it to an empty string.

**Syntax:**   rename *oldName ?newName?*

Rename a procedure.

*oldName*   The current name of the procedure.

*?newName?*   The new name for the procedure. If this is an empty string, the procedure is deleted.

The following example shows the procedure alpha renamed to beta and then deleted.

## Example 7.3

### Script Example

```
proc alpha {} {
  return "This is the alpha proc"
}

# Example Script

puts "Invocation of procedure alpha: [alpha]"
rename alpha beta
catch alpha rtn
puts "Invocation of alpha after rename: $rtn"
puts "Invocation of procedure beta: [beta]"
rename beta ""
beta
```

### Script Output

```
Invocation of procedure alpha: This is the alpha proc
Invocation of alpha after rename: invalid command name "alpha"
Invocation of procedure beta: This is the alpha proc
invalid command name "beta"
```

## 7.3 Getting Information About Procedures

The Tcl interpreter is a very introspective interpreter. A script can get information about most aspects of the interpreter while the script is running. The `info` command that was introduced in Chapter 6 provides information about the interpreter. These four `info` subcommands will return the names of all commands known to the Tcl interpreter, and can return more information about procedures that have been defined by Tcl scripts using the `proc` command.

info commands *pattern*
> Returns a list of commands with names that match a pattern. This includes both Tcl procedures and commands defined by compiled C code.

info procs *pattern*
> Returns a list of procedures with names that match a pattern. This will return only the names of procedures defined with a `proc` command, not those defined with compiled C code.

info body *procName*
> Returns the body of a procedure. This is valid only for Tcl commands defined as a `proc`.

info args *procName*
> Returns the arguments of a procedure. This is valid only for Tcl commands defined as a `proc`.

The `commands` subcommand will list the available commands that match a `glob` pattern. This can be used to confirm that an expected set of code has been loaded.

**Syntax:** info commands *pattern*

**Syntax:** info procs *pattern*

> Returns a list of command or procedure names that match the pattern. If no command names match the pattern, an empty string is returned.
>
> *pattern* A `glob` pattern to attempt to match.

**Example** 7.4

```
# Check to see if md5 command is defined. If not, load a
#   Tcl version
if {[string match [info commands md5] ""]} {
    source "md5.tcl"
}
```

The `info body` command will return the body of a procedure. This can be used to generate and modify procedures at runtime or for distributed applications to exchange procedures.

*Syntax:* `info body pattern`

Returns the body of a procedure.

`procName` The procedure from which the body will be returned.

## Example 7.5

*Script Example*

```
proc example {one two} {
    puts "This is example"
}
# Display the body of the proc:
puts "The example procedure body is: \n[info body example]"
```

*Script Output*

```
The example procedure body is:

    puts "This is example"
```

---

The `info args` command returns the argument list of a procedure. This is useful when debugging code that has generated its own procedures.

*Syntax:* `info args procName`

Returns a procedure's argument list.

*procName* The procedure from which the arguments will be returned.

## Example 7.6

*Script Example*

```
puts "The example proc has [llength [info args example]] arguments"
```

*Script Output*

```
The example proc has 2 arguments
```

---

The next example shows how you can check that a procedure exists and create a slightly different procedure from it.

## Example 7.7

*Script Example*

```
# Define a simple procedure.

proc alpha {args} {
  puts "proc alpha is called with these arguments: $args"
}
```

```
# Confirm that the procedure exists

if {[info commands alpha] != ""} {
  puts "There is a procedure named alpha"
}

# Get the argument list and body from the alpha procedure

set alphaArgs [info args alpha]
set alphaBody [info body alpha]

# Change the word "alpha" in the procedure body to "beta"

regsub "alpha" $alphaBody "beta" betaBody

# Create a new procedure "beta" that will display its arguments.

proc beta $alphaArgs $betaBody

# Run the two procedures to show their behavior

alpha How 'bout
beta them Cubs.
```

***Script Output***

**There is a procedure named alpha**
**proc alpha is called with these arguments: How 'bout**
**proc beta is called with these arguments: them Cubs.**

---

# 7.4 Substitution and Evaluation of Strings

Section 3.2 discussed how the Tcl interpreter evaluates a script: the interpreter examines a line, performs a pass of command and variable substitutions, and then evaluates the resulting line. A Tcl script can access these interpreter functions to perform substitutions on a string or even evaluate a string as a command. This is one of the unusual strengths in Tcl programming. Most interpreters do not provide access to their parsing and evaluation sections to the program being interpreted. The two commands that provide access to the interpreter are subst and eval.

## 7.4.1 Performing Variable Substitution on a String

The set command returns the current value of a variable as well as assigning a value. A common use for this is to assign and test a variable in one pass, as shown in the following:

```
while {[set len [string length $password]] < 8} {
  puts "$len is not long enough. Use 8 letters"
  set password [gets stdin]
}
```

This capability is also useful when you have a variable that contains the name of another variable and you need the value from the second variable, as shown in the following:

```
% set a 1
% set b a
% puts "The value of $b is [set $b]"
The value of a is 1
```

If you need to perform more complex substitutions, you can use the subst command. The subst command performs a single pass of variable and command substitutions on a string and returns the modified string. This is the first phase of a command being evaluated, but the actual evaluation of the command does not happen. If the string includes a square-bracketed command, the command within the brackets will be evaluated as part of this substitution.

> **Syntax:** subst *string*
>
> Perform a substitution pass upon a string. Do not evaluate the results.
>
> string   The string upon which to perform substitutions.

The subst command can be used when you need to replace a variable with its content but do not want to evaluate it as a command. The previous example could be written as follows, using subst:

```
% set a 1
% set b a
% puts [subst "The value of $b is $$b"]
The value of a is 1
```

In this example, the $$b is replaced by $a in the usual round of substitutions, and then $a is replaced by 1 by the subst command. In this case, you can obtain the same result with either set or subst. As the string becomes more complex, the subst command becomes a better option, particularly when combined with the eval command, as discussed in the following section.

## 7.4.2 Evaluating a String as a Tcl Command

The eval command concatenates its arguments into a string and then evaluates that string as if it were text in a script file. The eval command allows a script to create its own command lines and evaluate them.

You can use eval to write data-driven programs that effectively write themselves based on the available data. You can also use the eval command to write agent-style programs, where a task on one machine sends a program to a task on another machine to execute. These techniques (and the security considerations) are described in later chapters.

**Syntax:** eval *arg ?args?*

Evaluate the arguments as a Tcl script.

*arg ?args?*   These arguments will be concatenated into a command line and evaluated.

## Example 7.8

*Script Example*

```
set cmd(0) {set a 1}
set cmd(1) {puts "start value of A is: $a"}
set cmd(2) {incr a 3}
set cmd(3) {puts "end value of A is: $a"}

for {set i 0} {$i < 4} {incr i} {
  eval $cmd($i)
}
```

*Script Output*

```
start value of A is: 1
end value of A is: 4
```

Because the arguments to eval are concatenated, the command that is evaluated will lose one level of grouping. Discarding a level of grouping is a common use of the eval command. For example, in the next example, the regexpArgs variable has three options for the regexp command. If this command is invoked as regexp $regexpArgs, the three options are presented to the regexp command as a single argument, and the regexp command generates an error, since it does not support a "-line -nocase --" option.

The eval command can be used to separate the list of options into three separate options, as the regexp command requires. However, we do not want to separate the string the regular expression is being compared to into separate words. When using eval to split one set of arguments, you must also add a layer of grouping to elements you do not want to split.

■ The following generates a runtime error:

```
set regexp Args {-line -nocase --}
regexp $regexpArgs $exp $string m1
```

```
# After Substitution
# regexp {-line -nocase --} {is.*} {This is a test} m1
```

- The following is legal, but the string is also split into separate arguments:

```
eval regexp $regexpArgs $exp $string m1
# After Substitution:
# regexp -line -nocase -- is.* This is a test m1
```

- The following is legal code, which works as expected:

```
eval regexp $regexpArgs $exp {$string} m1
# After Substitution:
# regexp -line -nocase -- is.* {This is a test} m1
```

- The following is legal code, which works as expected and is preferred style:

```
eval regexp $regexpArgs $exp [list $string] m1
# After Substitution:
# regexp -line -nocase -- is.* {This is a test} m1
```

## Example 7.9

### *Script Example*

```
set regexpArgs {-line -nocase --}
set str "This is a test"
set exp {is.*}
set m1 ""
set fail [catch {regexp $regexpArgs $exp $str m1} message]
if {$fail} {
    puts "regexp failed: $message"
}
set rtn [eval regexp $regexpArgs $exp [list $str] m1]
puts "Second regexp returns: $rtn"
puts "Matched: $m1"
```

### *Script Output*

```
regexp failed: bad switch "-line -nocase --": must be -all,
    -about, -indices, -inline, -expanded, -line, -linestop,
    -lineanchor, -nocase, -start, or --
Second regexp returns: 1
Matched: is is a test
```

# 7.5 Working with Global and Local Scopes

The Tcl variable scope rules provide a single global scope and private local scopes for each procedure being evaluated. This facility makes it easy to write robust, modular programs. However, some applications require scripts being evaluated in one local scope to have access to another scope. The upvar and uplevel commands allow procedures to interact with higher-level scopes.

This section discusses scopes and the upvar and uplevel commands in more detail than previously, and shows how to use the uplevel and upvar commands. This discussion is expanded upon in Chapter 8, which discusses the namespace command. For now, a namespace is a technique for encapsulating procedures and variables in a named, private scope.

### 7.5.1 Global and Local Scope

The global scope is the primary scope in a Tcl script. All Tcl commands and procedures that are not defined within a namespace are maintained in this scope. All namespaces and procedures can access commands and variables maintained in the global scope.

When a procedure is evaluated, it creates a local scope. Variables are created in this scope as necessary and are destroyed when the procedure returns. The variables used within a procedure are visible to other procedures called from that procedure, but not to procedures outside the current call stack.

Any variable defined outside of the procedures or identified with the global command is maintained in the global scope. Variables maintained in the global scope persist until either the script exits or they are explicitly destroyed with the unset command.

These variables can be accessed from any other scope by declaring the variable to exist in the global scope with the global command. Note that the global command must be evaluated before that variable name is used in the local scope. The Tcl interpreter will generate an error if you try to declare a variable to be global after using it in a local scope.

```
set globalVar "I'm global"
proc goodProc {} {
  global globalVar
  # The next line prints out
  # "The globalVar contains: I'm global"
  puts "The globalVar contains: $globalVar"
}

proc badProc {} {
  set globalVar "This defines 'globalVar' in the local scope"
  # The next line causes an error
  global globalVar
}
```

Each time a procedure invokes another procedure, another local scope is created. These nested procedure calls can be viewed as a stack, with the global scope at the top and each successive procedure call stacked below the previous ones.

A procedure can access variables within the global scope or within the scope of the procedures that invoked it via the upvar and uplevel commands. The upvar command will link a local variable to one in a previous (higher) stack scope.

*Syntax:* upvar *?level? varName1 localName1 ?Name2? ?localName2?*

## Example 7.10

### Script Example

```
proc top {topArg} {
  set localArg [expr $topArg+1]
  puts "Before calling bottom localArg is: $localArg"
  bottom localArg
  puts "After calling bottom, localArg is: $localArg"
}

proc bottom {bottomArg} {
  upvar $bottomArg arg
  puts "bottom is passed $bottomArg with a value of $arg"
  incr arg
}
top 2
```

### Script Output

```
Before calling bottom localArg is: 3
bottom is passed localArg with a value of 3
After calling bottom, localArg is: 4
```

---

The uplevel command will concatenate its arguments and evaluate the resulting command line in a previous scope. The uplevel is like eval, except that it evaluates the command in a different scope instead of the current scope.

The following example shows a set of procedures (stack1, stack2, and stack3) that call each other and then access and modify variables in the scope of the procedures that called them. All of these stack procedures have a local variable named x. Each is a separate variable. Note that procedure stack1 cannot access the variables in the scope of procedure stack2, although stack2 can access variables in the scope of stack1.

## Example 7.11

### Script Example

```
# Create procedure stack1 with a local variable x.
# display the value of x, call stack2, and redisplay the
```

```
# value of x
proc stack1 {} {
  set x 1;
  puts "X in stack1 starts as $x"
  stack2
  puts "X in stack1 ends as $x"
  puts ""
}

# Create procedure stack2 with a local variable x.
# display the value of x, call stack3, and redisplay the
# value of x

proc stack2 {} {
  set x 2;
  puts "X in stack2 starts as $x"
  stack3
  puts "X in stack2 ends as $x"
}

# Create procedure stack3 with a local variable x.
# display the value of x,
# display the value of x in the scope of procedures that
# invoked stack3 using relative call stack level.
# Add 10 to the value of x in the proc that called stack3
#    (stack2)
# Add 100 to the value of x in the proc that called stack2
#    (stack1)
# Add 200 to the value of x in the global scope.
# display the value of x using absolute call stack level.

proc stack3 {} {
  set x 3;
  puts "X in stack3 starts as $x"
  puts ""
  # display the value of x at stack levels relative to the
  # current level.
  for {set i 1} {$i <= 3} {incr i} {
    upvar $i x localX
    puts "X at upvar $i is $localX"
  }
  puts "\nx is being modified from procedure stack3\n"
  # Evaluate a command in the scope of procedures above the
  # current call level.
  uplevel 1 {incr x 10}
  uplevel 2 {incr x 100}
```

```
    uplevel #0 {incr x 200}
    puts ""

    # display the value of x at absolute stack levels
    for {set i 0} {$i < 3} {incr i} {
      upvar #$i x localX
      puts "X at upvar #$i is $localX"
    }
    puts ""
}

# Example Script

set x 0;
puts "X in global scope is $x"
stack1
puts "X in global scope ends as $x"
```

***Script Output***

**X in global scope is 0**
**X in stack1 starts as 1**
**X in stack2 starts as 2**
**X in stack3 starts as 3**

**X at upvar 1 is 2**
**X at upvar 2 is 1**
**X at upvar 3 is 0**

**x is being modified from procedure stack3**
**X at upvar #0 is 200**
**X at upvar #1 is 101**
**X at upvar #2 is 12**

**X in stack2 ends as 12**
**X in stack1 ends as 101**

**X in global scope ends as 200**

---

The scopes in the preceding example resemble the diagram that follows, in which the procedure stack3 is being evaluated. Each local procedure scope is nested within the scope of the procedures that called it.

When the uplevel 1 {incr x 10} command is evaluated, it causes the string incr x 10 to be evaluated one scope higher than the current stack3 scope, which is the stack2 scope. The uplevel #0 {incr x 200} command is evaluated at absolute scope level 0, or the global scope. The evaluation level for a command uplevel #1 would be the first level down the call stack, stack1 in this example. This example is not a recommended technique for using the command. It is intended only to demonstrate how uplevel works.

Global Scope

All procedure and command names are visible
All global variables are visible

Procedure stack1 { }

Local procedure scope for stack1

upvar #0 maps variables in the global scope to the local scope

upvar 1 maps variables in the global scope to the local scope

stack1 variables are local
global variables are visible using global command

Procedure stack2 { }

Local procedure scope for stack2

upvar #0 maps variables in the global scope to the local scope
upvar #1 maps variables in the stack1 scope to the local scope

upvar 1 maps variables in the stack1 scope to the local scope
upvar 2 maps variables in the global scope to the local scope

stack2 variables are local
stack1 variables are visible using upvar or uplevel
global variables are visible using global command

Procedure stack3 { }

Local procedure scope for stack3

upvar #0 maps variables in the global scope to the local scope
upvar #1 maps variables in the stack1 scope to the local scope
upvar #2 maps variables in the stack2 scope to the local scope

upvar 1 maps variables in the stack2 scope to the local scope
upvar 2 maps variables in the stack1 scope to the local scope
upvar 3 maps variables in the global scope to the local scope

stack3 variables are local
stack1 and stack2 variables are visible using upvar or uplevel
global variables are visible using global command

The main use for the uplevel command is to implement program flow control
structures such as for, while, and if. Using the uplevel command as a macro
facility to change variables in a calling scope (as done here) is a bad idea that leads
to hard-coded variable names and code that is difficult to maintain. If you need

to modify a variable in the current scope, you should use upvar in your procedure rather than uplevel.

The preceding example demonstrates how procedures can access all levels above them in the call stack but not levels below. The global command works well if you have a single global variable that a procedure will manipulate. If your application requires several variables to describe the system's state, the best technique is to use a single associative array and multiple indices to hold the different values.

If your application has multiple entities that each have their own state, you may use a different associative array to describe each entity's state and use the upvar command to map the appropriate array into a procedure.

The next example shows a simple two-person game with the players' positions kept in separate global variables. The move procedure may be invoked with the name of either variable, which it maps to a local variable called player and makes a move for that player.

## Example 7.12

*Script Example*

```
set player1(position) 0
set player2(position) 0

proc move {playerName} {
    upvar #0 $playerName player

    # Move the piece a random number of spaces
    #   between 0 and 9.
    set move [expr int(rand() * 10)]
    incr player(position) $move
}

while {($player1(position) < 20) &    ($player2(position) < 20)} {
        move player1
        move player2
        puts "\nCurrent Positions:"
        puts " 1: $player1(position)"
        puts " 2: $player2(position)"
}

if {$player1(position) > $player2(position)} {
    puts "Player 1 wins!"
} else {
    puts "Player 2 wins!"
}
```

*Script Output*

```
Current Positions:
  1: 2
  2: 6

Current Positions:
  1: 8
  2: 14

Current Positions:
  1: 9
  2: 15

Current Positions:
  1: 13
  2: 15

Current Positions:
  1: 16
  2: 21
Player 2 wins!
```

## 7.6 Making a Tcl Object

This section describes how you can perform simple object-style programming in pure Tcl. This discussion, and the discussion of namespaces in the next chapter, deals with a subset of a complete object programming environment. The [incr Tcl] extension supports full object-oriented programming.

Chapter 3 mentioned that Tcl keeps separate hash tables for commands, associative array indices, and variables, and that the first word in a Tcl command string must be a command name. These features mean that any name can be defined as both a variable name and a procedure name. The interpreter will know which is meant by the position of the name in the command line.

This section discusses techniques for using the same label as a variable name or array index and a procedure name. In this example, the newTreeObject procedure will define an array index and create a procedure with the same name. It will return the name of the procedure.

This lets us implement the object-oriented programming concept of having methods attached to a data object. The implementation of a Tcl object is different from the implementation of a C++ or Java object, but the programming semantics are very similar.

```
C++                           Tcl
object = new Object(arg);      set myTree [newTreeObject]
object->method(arg1, arg2);    $myTree method arg1 arg2
```

### 7.6.1 An Object Example

For a simple example, the following code creates variables with the name of a common fruit and then creates a procedure with the same name that tests whether or not its argument is a valid color for this fruit.

**Example** 7.13

*Script Example*

```
# Define a set of fruit names and colors

set fruitList [list {apples {red yellow green}} \
                    {bananas yellow} \
                    {grapes {green purple}}]

foreach fruitDefinition $fruitList {

  # 1) Extract the name and possible colors from the
  #     fruit definition.

  foreach {fruitName fruitColors} $fruitDefinition {break;}

  # 2) Create a global variable named for the fruit, with
  #     the fruit colors as a value

  set $fruitName $fruitColors

  # 3) Define a procedure with the name of the fruit
  #     being checked. The default value for "name" is
  #     also the name of the fruit, which is also the name
  #     of the global variable with the list of fruit colors.

  proc $fruitName [list color [list name $fruitName]] {
    upvar #0 $name fruit
    if {[lsearch $fruit $color] >= 0} {
        return "Correct, $name can be $color"
    } else {
        return "No, $name are $fruit"
    }
  }
}

# 4) Loop through the fruits, and ask the user for a color.
#     Read the input from the keyboard.
```

```
#    Evaluate the appropriate function to check for correctness.

foreach fruit [list apples bananas grapes ] {
  puts "What color are $fruit?"
  gets stdin answer
  puts [$fruit $answer]
}
```

*Script Output*

```
What color are apples?    # User types red
Correct, apples can be red
What color are bananas?    # User types red
No, bananas are yellow
What color are grapes?    # User types red
No, grapes are green purple
```

In section 3 of the preceding example, procedures are generated with the same name as the various fruits. The argument list for these procedures is constructed using the list command rather than the more common technique of putting the arguments within curly braces. This allows $fruitName to be substituted into the list of arguments, making the name of the fruit (and the global variable containing the fruit's colors) the default value for the argument name.

The first procedure defined resembles the following:

```
proc apple {color {name apple}} {
  upvar #0 $name fruit
  if {[lsearch $fruit $color] >= 0} {
    return "Correct, $name can be $color"
  } else {
    return "No, $name are $fruit"
  }
}
```

When this procedure is invoked as apple red, the default value of apple is assigned to the variable name and the upvar #0 $name fruit maps the global variable apple to the local variable fruit.

## 7.6.2 **Creating a Tree Object**

The tree subroutines discussed in Chapter 6 returned an index into the global associative array Tree_Array. This index is used as a handle to identify the node being referenced.

This handle name can also be used as the name of a newly defined procedure, just as the variable names were used in the previous example. Rather than adding code to convert the handle into a procedure each time we create a new tree or add a node, we can write a new procedure (newTreeObject) that will

**1.** Call the treeCreate procedure to create a new tree.

**2.** Define a procedure with the same name as the handle treeCreate returned.

**3.** Return that name for the program to use as a procedure for manipulating the tree.

In the previous example, we created a procedure that had a single purpose. We can also make a procedure that will perform any of several actions based on a subcommand name. In the next examples, that procedure will be named TreeObjProc, which will be discussed after describing the newTreeObject procedure. The following code shows the newTreeObject procedure.

**Example** 7.14

```
source tree.tcl

#######################################################
# proc newTreeObject {} --
#  Creates a new tree object, and returns an object for
#    accessing the base node.
# Arguments:
#   NONE

proc newTreeObject {} {
    set treeId [treeCreate]
    proc $treeId {args} " \
        return \[TreeObjProc $treeId \$args]\
    "

    return $treeId
}
```

The first line in this procedure is a call to the treeCreate proc that we created in Chapter 6, which returns a handle for the base node of this tree. The second and third lines are a proc command that defines the new procedure to evaluate for this node. This command adds a new procedure to the interpreter with the same name as the handle. The new procedure

**1.** Takes at least one argument (treeId) and may have an undefined number of other arguments (args).

**2.** Returns the results of evaluating the procedure TreeObjProc, with the new handle passed to TreeObjProc as the first argument.

This example uses the backslash to inhibit substitutions from occurring on certain strings. Note what is escaped in the body of the new procedure.

The entire body is enclosed with quotes, not braces. This allows substitutions to occur within the body before the proc command is evaluated. The variable substitution on the variable $treeId places the handle for this node in the body of the procedure.

Because the body is enclosed in quotes, not braces, the opening square bracket before TreeObjProc must be escaped to prevent TreeObjProc from being evaluated during the substitution phase of evaluating the proc command. The backslash will leave the square brackets as part of the procedure body, causing TreeObjProc to be evaluated when the new procedure is evaluated.

The same is true of the dollar sign preceding the args argument to TreeObjProc. If not for the backslash, the interpreter would try to replace $args with the content of that variable while evaluating the proc command. This would generate an error, because args will be defined when the new procedure is evaluated, but is not defined while newTreeObject is being evaluated. After the substitutions, the body passed to the proc command resembles the following:

```
{return [TreeObjProc tree1.node2 $args]}
```

### 7.6.3 Defining the Object's Method

The TreeObjProc is the largest part of the tree object module. This procedure takes two arguments: the name of the node to manipulate (which is set when the node's procedure is defined) and a list of arguments. The first entry in the list will be a subcommand that defines which tree.tcl procedure to evaluate, and the rest of the list will be arguments that will be passed to that procedure. All of the procedures that were defined in the tree example in Chapter 6 are supported in TreeObjProc.

**Example** 7.15

```
##########################################################
# proc TreeObjProc {node methodArgs} --
#     Primary method for tree objects.
#     Parses the subcommand and calls the appropriate tree.tcl
#       procedure.
#
# Arguments:
#     node:        The internal name for this node.
#     methodArgs:  A list, the first member is the subcommand
#                  name, and subsequent (optional) members are
#                  arguments to be passed to the tree.tcl
#                  command.
#
# Results:
#     Calls other procedures that may produce output,
```

```
#       create new objects, delete objects, etc.

proc TreeObjProc {node methodArgs} {

    set subCommand [lindex $methodArgs 0]
    set cmdArgs [lrange $methodArgs 1 end]

    switch $subCommand {
    {set} {
        # Set the key/value pair associated with this node.
        # could be set -node key value
        #           set -tree key value
        #           set key value  -- Default to node.
        if {[llength $cmdArgs] == 3} {
            set option [lindex $cmdArgs 0]
            set key [lindex $cmdArgs 1]
            set val [lindex $cmdArgs 2]
        } elseif {[llength $cmdArgs] == 2} {
            set option "-node"
            set key [lindex $cmdArgs 0]
            set val [lindex $cmdArgs 1]
        } else {
          error "$node set ?-node? ?-tree? key value"
        }
        switch -- $option {
          -node {
            return [treeSetNodeValue $node $key $val]
            }
          -tree {
            return [treeSetTreeValue $node $key $val]
            }
          default {
            error "$node set ?-node? ?-tree? key value"
          }
        }
      }

    {get} {
        # return the value associated with this node/key.
        # May be:
        # get -node key -- return node value
        # get -tree key -- return tree value
        # get -best key -- return node value as first
        #                   choice.
        #                   Return tree value if no node
        #                   value is defined.
```

```
                        # get key        -- treat as best.

                    if {[llength $cmdArgs] == 2} {
                       set option [lindex $cmdArgs 0]
                       set key [lindex $cmdArgs 1]
                    } elseif {[llength $cmdArgs] == 1} {
                       set option "-best"
                       set key [lindex $cmdArgs 0]
                    } else {
                        error "$node get ?-node? ?-tree? key value"
                    }
                    switch -exact -- $option {
                      -node {
                        return [treeGetNodeValue $node $key]
                       }
                      -tree {
                        return [treeGetTreeValue $node $key]
                       }
                      -best {
                        set fail [catch \
                             {treeGetNodeValue $node $key} returnVal]
                        if {!$fail} {
                            return $returnVal
                        }
                        return [treeGetTreeValue $node $key]
                       }
                    default {
                        error "$node get ?-node? ?-tree? key value"
                       }
                    }
                }

        {add} {
             # Add a child node to this node.
             set newNode [treeCreateChild $node]
             proc $newNode {args} "
                  return \[TreeObjProc $newNode \$args]
                "
             return $newNode
          }

        {delete} {
             # remove this node
             # and remove the proc from the proc hash table
             # If cmdArgs == "-r", delete recursively.
             if {[string match $cmdArgs "-r"]} {
```

```
            foreach child [$node childList] {
               $child delete -r
               catch {rename $child ""}
            }
        }

        # delete this node.
        treeDeleteNode $node
        rename $node ""
    }

{destroyTree} {
        # destroy this tree completely
        # Find the base of the tree, and delete all
        # nodes and their associated procs

        set base [$node base]
        $base delete -r

        treeDestroyTree $base
    }

{childList} {
        # return a list of children
        return [treeGetChildList $node]
    }

{parent} {
        # returns the parent of a node
        return [treeGetParent $node]
    }

{dump} {
        # dump the contents of this node
        return [treeDump $node $cmdArgs]
    }

default {
        # Should not be here, this is an error
        set methods {set, get, add, delete, destroyTree, \
             childList, parent, dump}

        error "Bad method: $subCommand\n use $methods"
    }
  }
    return ""
}
```

There are a few points to note about this code. The TreeObjProc procedure uses rename to delete the procedure associated with a node when the node is deleted. Once a node is deleted, there is no longer a procedure call with that name.

The subcommand strings are shorter and simpler than the procedures defined in tree.tcl. The tree.tcl procedures need to use long names, starting with a unique string to avoid conflicts with other procedures that may be loaded. (Imagine how many packages might have a procedure named "processData".) Within the TreeObjProc, however, there are no conflicts with other Tcl commands or procedures, so simple subcommand names can be used.

The set and get commands use an option (-tree or -node ) to declare whether the key being set should be attached to a single node or to the complete tree. In the tree.tcl script, setting a value in the tree and setting one in a node are two separate procedures. By default, the set and get commands set the key/value pair for a node. The following example uses the default action for these commands. It is the example from Chapter 6 rewritten to use the treeObj class instead of the tree functions.

This version of the example has also been tweaked slightly to run on Macintosh, MS Windows, and UNIX/Linux. The previous version, in Chapter 6, would run correctly on MS Windows or UNIX/Linux, but had problems with some files on a Macintosh.

To maintain backward consistency, Tcl treats things that look like a UNIX path as a file path. The particular problem on the Macintosh is file names with a forward slash in them (for instance, the Tcl/Tk directory).

The convention to distinguish between a path and a file name on the Macintosh is that if the name starts with a colon it is a file name, regardless of any internal slashes. This version of the addDirToTree procedure checks the tcl_platform global variable to see if the script is being run on a Macintosh, and if so, sets the following two variables.

*nm*  If the platform is Macintosh, this variable will contain a colon; otherwise, it will contain an empty string.

*pre*  A precursor for the directory name. If the platform is not a Macintosh, or the value of the *directory* variable starts with a colon, this will be an empty string. If the platform is Macintosh, and the directory name does not start with a colon, this variable will contain a colon.

These variables contain a string that is prepended to the directory and file names to mark them properly for the Macintosh.

## Example 7.16

### *Script Example*

```
#!/bin/sh
#\
```

```
exec tclsh "$0" "$@"

# dirtreeObj.tcl
#       demonstrate using a tree Object

source treeObj.tcl

##########################################################
# proc addDirToTree
#       Add a directory to a node.
#       Create children for each directory entry, and set
#          the name and type of each child.
#
# Arguments:
#       parent          The parent node for this directory.
#       directory       The directory to add to the tree.
#
# Results:
#       The tree is made longer by the number of entries
#       in this directory.

proc addDirToTree {parent directory} {
    global tcl_platform

    if {[string match $tcl_platform(platform) macintosh]} {
     set nm ":"
     if {[string first : $directory] == 0} {
        set pre ""
     } else {
        set pre ":"
     }
    } else {
        set nm ""
        set pre ""
    }

    # If this isn't a directory, it has no subordinates.

    if {[file type $pre$directory] != "directory"} {
        error "$directory is not a directory"
    }

    # If the parent directory hasn't been updated with name
    #  and type, do so now.

    if {[catch {$parent get name}]} {
        $parent set name $directory
```

```
            $parent set type directory
            }

    # An empty or unreadable directory will return a fail
    #  for the glob command
    # If the directory can be read, the list of names
    #  will be in fileList.

    set fail [catch {glob [file join $pre$directory *]} \
                fileList]
    if {$fail} {
        return;
    }

    # Loop through the names in fileList

    foreach name $fileList {
      set node [$parent add]
      $node set name $name
      set type [file type [file join $pre$directory $nm$name]]
      $node set type $type
    }
}

# Create a tree

catch {$base destroyTree}
set base [newTreeObject]
# Add the initial directory and its directory entries
#  to the tree

if {[string match $tcl_platform(platform) macintosh]} {
    set root ":"
} else {
    set root "/"
}

addDirToTree $base [file nativename $root]

# If any children are directories, add their entries to the
#  tree as subchildren.

foreach entry [treeGetChildList $base] {
  if {[$entry get type] == "directory"} {
      addDirToTree $entry [$entry get name]
  }
}
```

```
# Print out the tree in the form:
# Dir1
#    Dir1/Entry1
#    Dir1/Entry2
# Dir2
#    Dir2/Entry3
#    Dir2/Entry4

foreach entry [$base childList] {
    puts "[$entry get name]"
    if {[$entry get type] == "directory"} {
        foreach sub [$entry childList] {
            puts " [$sub get name]"
        }
    }
}
```

***Script Output (Macintosh)***

```
Browse the Internet
CommuniCard
    :CommuniCard:CommuniCard Installer 2.3
    :CommuniCard:Dayna Diagnostics
    :CommuniCard:ReadMe 2.3
    :CommuniCard:SimpleText
Fetch 3.0.3
Mail
QuickTime Player
Register with Apple
Sherlock 2
Tcl/Tk Folder 8.3.2
    :Tcl/Tk Folder 8.3.2:Build
    :Tcl/Tk Folder 8.3.2:Drag Drop Tclets
    :Tcl/Tk Folder 8.3.2:Mac Tcl/Tk 8.3.2 Readme
    :Tcl/Tk Folder 8.3.2:MacTcl README
    :Tcl/Tk Folder 8.3.2:MacTk README
    :Tcl/Tk Folder 8.3.2:tcl
    :Tcl/Tk Folder 8.3.2:Tcl README
    :Tcl/Tk Folder 8.3.2:Tcl/Tk HTML Manual
    :Tcl/Tk Folder 8.3.2:TclBOAShell 8.3.2
    :Tcl/Tk Folder 8.3.2:TclShell 8.3.2
    :Tcl/Tk Folder 8.3.2:TclTk Installer Log File
    :Tcl/Tk Folder 8.3.2:test
    :Tcl/Tk Folder 8.3.2:tk
    :Tcl/Tk Folder 8.3.2:Tk README
    :Tcl/Tk Folder 8.3.2:Tool Command Language
    :Tcl/Tk Folder 8.3.2:Widget Demos
```

```
        :Tcl/Tk Folder 8.3.2:Wish 8.3.2
dirTreeObject.tcl
tree.tcl
treeObj.tcl
```

The preceding example is very similar to the example in Chapter 6, since most of the code deals with the file system, not with the tree. However, it is a bit easier to follow with the shorter subcommand names used instead of the long tree procedures. There are two problems with this tree object:

■ The associative array Tree_Array sits at the global scope, where any code can access it easily.

■ The script that wishes to use the treeObject needs to know the directory where treeObj.tcl is stored, and treeObj.tcl needs to be able to find tree.tcl.

Chapter 8 will discuss the namespace and package commands. The examples will show how to use the namespace command to hide the Tree_Array in a private namespace and how to use the package command to create a package that can be used without the script needing to know the location of the files it loads.

## 7.7 Bottom Line

■ A procedure can be defined as taking an undefined number of arguments by placing the args argument last in the argument list.

■ A procedure argument with a default value is defined by declaring the argument as a list. The second list element is the default value.

■ When a Tcl procedure is evaluated, it creates a local scope for variables. This local scope stacks below the scope of the code that invoked the procedure.

■ A Tcl procedure can access all of the scopes above it in the procedure call stack.

■ Tcl procedures can be constructed and evaluated in a running program.

■ Data items can be treated as objects by creating a procedure with the same name as the data item and using that procedure to manipulate the data item.

■ The rename command renames or removes a command or procedure.

   ***Syntax:*** rename *oldName ?newName?*

■ The subst command performs a pass of command and variable substitutions upon a string.

   ***Syntax:*** subst *string*

- The eval command will evaluate a set of arguments as a Tcl command.

  *Syntax:* eval *arg ?args?*

- The info subcommands that report information about procedures include the following.

  *Syntax:* info procs pattern

  > Return a list of procedures that are visible in the current scope and match a pattern.

  *Syntax:* info commands pattern

  > Return a list of commands that are visible in the current scope and match a pattern.

  *Syntax:* info args procName

  > Return the arguments of a procedure.

  *Syntax:* info body procName

  > Return the body of a procedure.

- The global command declares that a variable exists in the global scope.

  *Syntax:* global *varName1 ?varName2...varNameN?*

- Simple objects can be created by using the same word for both a variable name (or associative array index) and the procedure that will manipulate that data.

- Macintosh users may need to prepend file names with a colon to allow Tcl to recognize file names with embedded forward slashes.

## 7.8 Problems

The following numbering convention is used in all Problem sections.

| Number Range | Description of Problems |
|---|---|
| 100–199 | These problems review the material covered in this chapter. They can be answered in a few words or a short (1–5-line) script. Each problem should take under a minute to answer. |
| 200–299 | These problems go beyond the details presented in this chapter. They may require some analysis of the material or command details not covered in the chapter. They may require reading a man page or making a web search. They can be answered with a few sentences or a 5–50-line script. Each problem should take under 10 minutes to answer. |

300–399         These problems extend the material presented in this chapter. They may require referencing other sources. They can be answered in a few paragraphs or a few hundred lines of code. Each exercise may take a few hours to complete.

**100.** What would be the arguments portion of a proc command that duplicated the behavior of the Tcl format command?

**101.** What would be the arguments portion of a proc command that duplicated the behavior of the Tcl incr command?

**102.** After a procedure has returned, can you access any of the local variables that were used in that procedure?

**103.** If procA invokes procB, can procB local variables be accessed from procA?

**104.** If procA invokes procB, can procA local variables be accessed from procB?

**105.** Can you use the rename command to rename Tcl commands, such as while or for?

**106.** Under what circumstances would the subst command be preferable to using the set command?

**107.** What Tcl command will return the argument list for a procedure?

**108.** What Tcl command will define a procedure named foo

     a. with a single required argument?

     b. with a single optional argument with a default value of 2?

     c. that accepts zero or more arguments?

     d. that accepts two or more arguments?

     e. that has one required argument, one optional argument with a default value of 2, and may accept more arguments?

**109.** What Tcl command could be used to determine if a procedure has been defined?

**200.** Write a procedure that will accept one or more numeric arguments and return their sum.

**201.** Write a procedure that will accept zero or more numeric arguments and return the sum if there are multiple arguments or a 0 if there were no arguments.

**202.** Write a procedure that will duplicate the functionality of the incr command using the upvar command.

**203.** Write a procedure that will duplicate the functionality of the incr command using the uplevel command.

**300.** Write a procedure that will rename the following Tcl commands to new commands. Write a short script to test the new commands.

```
if -> if,like
for -> so
expr -> fuzzyNumbers
```

**301.** Write a script that will display all permutations of the values of a list of variable names, as suggested by the following:

```
set a 1
set b 2

set list {a b}

showPermutations $list

...
```

Output would be

```
1 1
1 2
2 1
2 2
```

**302.** Given a procedure report {data} {...} that uses puts to print a report to the screen, write a short script to create a new procedure reportFile {data outputChannel} that will send an identical report to an open Tcl channel.

**303.** Write a short script that will compare the bodies of all visible procedures and generate a list of procedures with identical bodies.

**304.** Write a procedure for the tree.tcl module described in Chapter 6 that will return a list of node siblings (the other child nodes to this node parent). Add a new method to the treeObjectProc described in this chapter to evaluate the treeGetSibling procedure.

**305.** Write a procedure that will create simple objects. The procedure should accept a variable name, value, and body to evaluate when the variable's procedure is invoked.

**306.** Write two procedures, as follows.

> ***Syntax:*** class *className body*

> Adds a new class name to a a collection of known classes and associates the *body* with that class.

> ***Syntax:*** new *className value*

> Creates a variable with a unique name in the global scope, and assigns *value* to it. Creates a new procedure with the same name and single argument args, and uses the *body* that was defined with the class command as the body for the procedure.

When complete, code such as follows should function:

```
class test {return "args are: $args"}
set x [new test 22]

puts "Value of test: [set $x]"
puts "Results of test: [$x a b c]"
```

The script output would look as follows:

```
Value of test: 22
Results of test: args are: a b c
```

# CHAPTER
# 8

# Namespaces and Packages

The namespace and package commands implement two different concepts that work together to make it easier to write reusable, modular, easily maintained code. The namespace command provides encapsulation support for developing modular code. The package command provides tools for organizing code modules into libraries.

The namespace command collects persistent data and procedure names in a private scope where they will not interact with other data or procedure names. This lets you load new procedures without cluttering the global space (avoiding name collisions) and protects private data from unintentional corruption.

The package command groups a set of procedures that may be in separate files into a single logical entity. Other scripts can then declare which packages they will need and what versions of those packages are acceptable. The Tcl interpreter will find the directories where the packages are located, determine what other packages are required, and load them when they are needed. The package command can load both Tcl script files and binary shared libraries or DLLs. This chapter discusses the following:

- The namespace scope
- Encapsulating Tcl procedures and data in namespaces
- Nesting one namespace within another
- Modularizing Tcl scripts into packages
- Assembling a namespaced library within a package
- Some guidelines for writing modules with relative namespace paths

The final example will extend the tree script to a package using nested namespaces for the data and procedures.

## 8.1 Namespaces and Scoping Rules

Chapter 7 discussed the Tcl global and procedure variable scopes. This section expands on that discussion and introduces the namespace and variable commands. These commands allow the Tcl programmer to create private areas within the program in which procedure and variables names will not conflict with other names.

### 8.1.1 Namespace Scope

Namespaces provide encapsulation similar to that provided by C++ and other object-oriented languages. Namespace scopes have some of the characteristics of the global scope and some characteristics of a procedure local scope. A namespace can be viewed as a global scope within a scope. Namespaces are similar to the global scope in that

- Procedures created at any procedure scope within a namespace are visible at the top level of the namespace.
- Variables created in a namespace scope (outside a local procedure scope) are persistent and will be retained between executions of code within the namespace.
- Variables created in a namespace scope (outside a local procedure scope) can be accessed by any procedure being evaluated within that namespace.
- While a procedure defined within a namespace is being evaluated, it creates a local scope within that namespace, not within the global namespace.

Namespaces are similar to local procedure scopes in that

- Code being evaluated within a namespace can access variables and procedures defined in the global space.
- All namespaces are contained within the global scope.
- Namespaces can nest within each other.

Namespaces also have the following unique features.

- A namespace can declare procedure names to be exportable. A script can import these procedure names into both the global and other namespace scopes.

- A nested namespace can keep procedures and variables hidden from higher-level namespaces.

The following diagram shows the scopes in a script that contains two namespaces (`example` and `demo`), each of which contains procedures named `proc1` and `proc2`. Because the procedures are in separate namespaces, they are different procedures. If a script tried to define two `proc1` procedures at the global level, the second definition would overwrite the first.

In this example, `::example::proc1` and `::example::proc2` are procedures that are both called independently, whereas `::demo::proc2` is called from `::demo::proc1`. The `::demo::proc2` is displayed within `::demo::proc1` to show that the procedure local scopes nest within a namespace just as they nested within the `stack` example (Example 7.11).

Global Scope

All command names are visible in this scope
All global variables are maintained in this scope
Imported namespace procedures and variables are visible in this scope

namespace ::example

defines the namespace scope ::example

::example variables are maintained here
::example::proc1 is defined at this scope
::example::proc2 is defined at this scope
can access global scope

Can export variables and procedure names

proc ::example::proc1

local ::example::proc1 scope

can access local (proc1) scope
can access ::example namespace variables
can access ::example procedures
can access global scope

proc ::example::proc2

local ::example::proc2 scope

can access local (proc2) scope
can access ::example namespace variables
can access ::example procedures
can access global scope

namespace ::demo

defines the namespace scope ::demo

::demo variables are maintained here
::demo::proc1 is defined at this scope
::demo::proc2 is defined at this scope
can access global scope

Can export variables and procedure names

proc ::demo::proc1

local ::demo::proc1 scope

can access local (proc1) scope
can access ::demo namespace variables
can access ::demo procedures
can access global scope

proc ::demo::proc2

local ::demo::proc2 scope

can access local (proc2) scope
can access ::demo::proc1 local variables
can access ::demo namespace variables
can access ::demo procedures
can access global scope

**Example** 8.1

```
# Define namespace example with two independent procedures.

namespace eval example {
  proc proc1 {} {puts "proc1"}
  proc proc2 {} {puts "proc2"}
}

# Define namespace demo with a procedure that invokes
#  another procedure within the namespace.

namespace eval demo {
  proc proc1 {} {proc2}
  proc proc2 {} {puts "proc2"}
}
```

## 8.1.2 Namespace Naming Rules

A namespace can contain other namespaces, creating a tree structure similar to a file system. The namespace convention is similar to the file system naming convention.

- Instead of separating entities with slashes (/ or \), namespace entities are separated with double colons (::).

- The global scope is the equivalent of a file system "/" directory. It is identified as "::".

- Namespace identifiers that start with a double colon (::) are absolute identifiers and are resolved from the global namespace.

  An entity identified as ::foo::bar::baz represents an entity named baz, in the bar namespace, which was created within the foo namespace, which was created in the global scope.

- Namespace identifiers that do not start with a double colon are relative and are resolved from the current namespace.

  An entity identified as bar::baz represents an entity named baz that is a member of the namespace bar, which was created in the current namespace. The current namespace may be the global namespace (::) or another namespace.

## 8.1.3 Accessing Namespace Entities

In C++, Java, or other strongly object-oriented languages, private data is completely private and other objects cannot access it. In Tcl, the namespace encapsulation is advisory. An entity (procedure or data) in a namespace can always be accessed if your script knows the full path to that entity.

A script can publish the procedures within a namespace it considers public with the `namespace export` command. Other scripts can import procedure names from the namespace into their local scope with the `namespace import` command. These commands are discussed later in this section. Your scripts should access namespace procedures by their full identifier, instead of importing the procedures into the global scope.

- Using the namespace identifier for an entity makes it easier to figure out what package a procedure or data originated from.
- Using the namespace identifier removes the possibility of name collisions when you load a new package with the same procedure and data names.

### 8.1.4 **Why Use Namespaces?**

If you always access namespace members by their full path, and namespaces do not provide truly private data, why should you use a namespace instead of having your own naming convention?

- The namespace naming conventions are enforced by the interpreter. This provides a consistent naming convention across packages, making it easier to merge multiple packages to get the functionality you need.
- Namespaces nest. Scripts being evaluated in one namespace can create a nested namespace within that namespace and access the new namespace by a relative name.
- Namespaces conceal their internal structure from accidental collisions with other scripts and packages. Data and procedures named with a naming convention exist in the global scope.
- A set of code within a namespace can be loaded multiple times in different namespaces without interfering with other instantiations of the namespace.

### 8.1.5 **The `namespace` and `variable` Commands**

The `namespace` command has many subcommands, but most Tcl applications will only use the `eval`, export, and `import` commands. The `children` command is discussed in this chapter, and although not required for using namespaces, it provides some information that is useful in determining what namespaces exist within which scopes. The `namespace scope` and `namespace current` commands are useful when namespace procedures may be invoked by an event handler. These subcommands are discussed in Chapters 10 and 12.

The `namespace eval` command evaluates a script within a namespace. The namespace is created, if it does not already exist. The script evaluated by the `namespace eval` command can define procedures and variables within the namespace.

*Syntax:* `namespace eval namespaceID arg1 ?argN...?`

Create a namespace, and evaluate the script arg in that scope. If more than one `arg` is present, the arguments are concatenated into a single script to be evaluated.

*namespaceID*    The identifying name for this namespace.

*arg\**    The script or scripts to evaluate within namespace *namespaceID.*

## Example 8.2

```
# Create a namespace named 'demo'
namespace eval demo {
  proc PrivateProc {} {
    # Do stuff
    ...
  }
  proc publicProc {} {
    # Do other stuff
    ...
  }
}
```

Once a namespace has been created, new procedures can be added to the namespace by either defining them within another `namespace eval` command or naming them for the namespace they occur in, as follows:

```
namespace eval demo {}

proc demo::newProc {} {
  # Do stuff
  ...
}
```

Note that `namespace eval` must be evaluated before defining a procedure within the namespace. Namespaces are created only by the `namespace eval` command.

It is often necessary to permit certain procedures in one namespace to be imported into other scopes. You will probably want to allow the procedures that provide the application programmer interface (API) to your package to be imported into other namespaces but not allow the importation of internal procedures.

The `namespace export` command defines the procedures within one namespace that can be imported to other scopes. By convention, procedures that will be exported are given names starting with a lowercase letter, whereas procedures for internal use have names starting with capital letters.

**Syntax:** `namespace export pattern1 ?patternN...?`

Export members of the current namespace that match the patterns. Exported procedure names can be imported into other scopes. The patterns follow `glob` rules.

*pattern\**    Patterns that represent procedure names and data names to be exported.

## Example 8.3

```
# Create a namespace named 'demo'
namespace eval demo {
  namespace export publicProc publicAPI
  proc PrivateProc {} {
    # Do stuff
    ...
  }
  proc publicProc {} {
    # Do other stuff
    ...
  }
}

proc demo::publicAPI {} {...}
```

The `namespace import` command imports a procedure from one namespace into the current namespace. When a procedure that was defined within a namespace is imported into the global namespace, it becomes visible to all scopes and namespaces.

**Syntax:** `namespace import ?-force? ?pattern1 patternN...?`

Imports variable and procedure names that match a `pattern`.

*-force*    If this option is set, an import command will overwrite existing commands with new ones from the `pattern` namespace. Otherwise, `namespace import` will return an error if a new command has the same name as an existing command.

*pattern\**    The patterns to import. The pattern must include the `namespaceID` of the namespace from which items are being imported. There will be more details on naming rules in the next section.

**Example** 8.4

```
# Create a namespace named 'demo'
namespace eval demo {
  namespace export publicProc publicAPI
  proc PrivateProc {} {
    # Do stuff
    ...
  }
  proc publicProc {} {
    # Do other stuff
    ...
  }
}

proc demo::publicAPI {} {...}
# import all public procedures.
namespace import demo::pub*
```

---

When naming procedures that may be imported into other namespaces, it is a good rule to avoid names that may have collisions. In particular, avoid names that already exist as core Tcl commands. For example, a script that imports a modified version of set will develop some difficult-to-debug problems.

Importing procedures using a glob pattern can be fragile. If a namespace imports from multiple namespaces, you can get unexpected collisions. It is usually better to explicitly name the procedures you need to import.

For example, if namespace A imports all exported procedures from namespaces B and C, and B and C both import procedures from namespace D, there will be an import collision with the B::D:: procedures and C::D:: procedure names.

The Tcl interpreter generates an error when a script attempts to import a procedure that is already defined in the current namespace. If the script should redefine the procedures, you can use the -force flag with import to force the interpreter to import over existing procedures.

The namespace children command returns a list of the namespaces that are visible from a scope.

*Syntax:* namespace children *?namespaceID? ?pattern?*

Returns a list of the namespaces that exist within namespaceID. (If namespaceID is not defined, the current namespace is used.)

*?namespaceID?*  The namespace scope from which the list of namespaces will be returned. If this argument is not present, the list of namespaces visible from the current namespace will be returned.

| *?pattern?* | Return only namespaces that match a `glob` pattern. If this argument is not present, all namespaces are returned. |

## Example 8.5

```
if {[lsearch ::demo:: [namespace children]] == -1} {
    # The demo namespace was not found
    # Create a namespace named 'demo'
    namespace eval demo {
        ...
    }
}
```

The `variable` command declares that a variable exists and will be retained within a namespace. A variable defined with the `variable` command is equivalent to a variable defined in the `global` scope, except that the variable name is visible only within the scope of the namespace. The variables declared with the `variable` command will not be destroyed when the namespace scope is exited. This allows you to define persistent data within a namespace. These variables are easily accessed by the procedures in the namespace, but are not visible from the global namespace.

Note that the syntax for the `variable` command is different from the `global` command. The `variable` command supports setting an initial value for a variable, whereas the `global` command does not.

*Syntax:* `variable` *varName ?value? ?varNameN? ?valueN?*

Declare a variable to exist within the current namespace. The arguments are pairs of name and value combinations.

*varName* The name of a variable.

*?value?* An optional value for the variable.

## Example 8.6

```
# Create a namespace named 'demo'
namespace eval demo {
    # name1 has no initial value
    variable name1

    # name2 and name3 are initialized
    variable name2 initial2 name3 initial3
}
```

## 8.1.6 **Creating and Populating a Namespace**

The namespace eval command creates a new namespace. Because all arguments with a namespace eval command are evaluated as a Tcl script, any valid command can be used in the argument list. This includes procedure definitions, setting variables, creating graphics widgets, and so on.

A namespace can be populated with procedures and data either in a single namespace eval command or in multiple invocations of the namespace eval command. The following example shows a namespace procedure that provides a unique number by incrementing a counter. The uniqueNumber namespace contains the counter variable, staticVar. The getUnique procedure, which is also defined within the uniqueNumber namespace, can access this variable easily, but code outside the uniqueNumber namespace cannot.

**Example** 8.7

*Script Example*

```
# Create a namespace.

namespace eval uniqueNumber {

    # staticVar is a variable that will be retained between
    # evaluations. This declaration defines the variable
    # and its initial value.

    variable staticVar 0;
    # allow getUnique to be imported into other scopes

    namespace export getUnique

    # return a unique number by incrementing staticVar

    proc getUnique {} {
      # This declaration of staticVar is the equivalent of a
      #  global - if it were not here, then a staticVar
      #  in the local procedure scope would be created.
      variable staticVar;

      return [incr staticVar];
    }
}

# Example Script

# Display the currently visible namespaces:

puts "Visible namespaces from the global scope are:"
puts " [namespace children]\n"
```

```
# Display "get*" commands that are visible in the global
#   scope before import

puts "Before import, global scope has these \"get*\" commands:"
puts "   [info commands get*]\n"

# Import all exported members of the namespace uniqueNumber

namespace import ::uniqueNumber::*

# Display "get*" commands that are visible in the global
#   scope after importing

puts "After import, global scope has these \"get*\" commands:"
puts "   [info commands get*] \n"

# Run getUnique a couple times to prove it works

puts "first Unique val: [getUnique]"
puts "second Unique val: [getUnique]"

# Display the current value of the staticVar variable

puts "staticVar: [namespace eval uniqueNumber {set staticVar}]"
puts "staticVar: $uniqueNumber::staticVar"

# The next line generates an error condition because
#   staticVar does not exist in the global scope.

puts "staticVar is: $staticVar"
```

*Script Output*

```
Visible namespaces from the global scope are:
  ::uniqueNumber ::tcl

Before import, global scope has these "get*" commands:
  gets
After import, global scope has these "get*" commands:
  gets getUnique

first Unique val: 1
second Unique val: 2
staticVar: 2
staticVar: 2

  can't read "staticVar": no such variable
```

There are a few points to note in this example:

- The procedure getUnique can be declared as an exported name before the procedure is defined.

- After the uniqueNumber namespace is defined, there are two namespaces visible from the global scope: the ::uniqueNumber namespace and the ::tcl namespace. The ::tcl namespace is always present when the Tcl interpreter is running.

- The namespace import ::uniqueNumber::* command imports all exported entities from ::uniqueNumber into the global scope.

- The value of the staticVar variable can be accessed via the namespace eval. It can also be accessed as ::uniqueNumber::staticVar.

- The staticVar variable is initialized by the line

  ```
  variable staticVar 0
  ```

  when the namespace is created. This code is roughly equivalent to placing

  ```
  set staticVar 0
  ```

  within the arguments to namespace eval, which would cause the variable to be defined at the top scope of the uniqueNumber namespace.

- Using the variable varName initValue construct is safer than initializing variables with the set command. When the Tcl interpreter searches for a variable to assign the value to, it looks first in the local namespace, then in the global namespace. If the variable exists in the current namespace, the value is assigned to the variable in the current namespace. If the variable does not exist in the current namespace, but does exist in the global namespace, the global variable will be assigned the value. If the variable exists in neither namespace, it is created in the current namespace. The variable varName initValue will always initialize a variable within the namespace.

## 8.1.7 Namespace Nesting

Tcl namespaces can be nested within one another. This provides lightweight equivalents of the object-oriented concepts of inheritance (the is-a relationship) and aggregation (the has-a relationship). Note that even using namespaces, pure Tcl is not quite a *real* object-oriented language. The [incr Tcl] and Object-Tcl extensions use namespaces to support the complete set of object-oriented functionality, and smaller packages such as stooop and snit provide frameworks for lighter-weight (and fewer-featured) object-style programming. The [incr Tcl] extension is discussed in Chapter 14.

A namespace can be used to create an object. It can inherit functionality and data from other namespaces by nesting those namespaces and importing procedures into itself. Procedures can be imported from any namespace, regardless of where the namespace is located in the hierarchy. If the namespace being imported from includes only procedures, your script can create a single copy of that namespace in the global scope and import from there to as many objects as it creates.

However, if the namespace being imported from also includes variables, you need a copy of the namespace to hold a separate copy of the variables for each object your script creates. In this case, it is simplest to nest the namespaces, rather than keep multiple copies at the global scope.

Note that using namespaces to implement inheritance is accomplished in the opposite way as C++ or Java-style inheritance. In C++ and Java, a child class inherits functionality down from a parent, whereas in Tcl a primary namespace can inherit functionality up from a nested namespace.

If two or more namespaces need functionality that exists in a third namespace, there are a couple of options. They can create a shared copy of the third namespace in the scope of the first two namespaces, or each can create a copy of the third namespace nested within its own namespace.

One advantage of nesting the third namespace is that it creates a unique copy of the persistent data defined within the third namespace. If a namespace is shared, that data is also shared.

Note that whereas procedures can be imported from any namespace, regardless of parent/child relationship, variables cannot be imported. If your design requires separate copies of data, you must have separate copies of the namespace. The namespace copies can be placed at any position in the namespace hierarchy, but it is simplest to inherit the functionality from child namespaces.

The next example shows the uniqueNumber namespace being nested within two separate namespaces (Package1 and Package2). This allows each procedure in Package1 and Package2 to get unique numbers with no gaps between numbers. If the uniqueNumber namespace were created at the global level and shared by Package1 and Package2, whenever either package called getUnique the unique number would be incremented.

## Example 8.8

### Script Example

```
# This procedure creates a uniqueNumber namespace in the scope of
# the script that invokes it.
proc createUnique {} {
  uplevel 1 {
    namespace eval counter {
      variable staticVal 0
      namespace export getNext;
      proc getNext {} {
        variable staticVal
        return [incr staticVal]
      }
    }
  namespace import counter::*
  }
}
```

```
# Create the unique1 namespace,
# Create a counter namespace within the unique1 namespace
# The Package1 namespace includes a procedure to return unique
# numbers

namespace eval unique1 {
  createUnique
  proc example {} {
    return "unique1::example: [getNext]"
  }
}

# Create the unique2 namespace,
# Create a counter namespace within the unique2 namespace
# The unique2 namespace includes a procedure to report unique
# numbers

namespace eval unique2 {
  createUnique
  proc example {} {
    return "unique2::example: [getNext]"
  }
}

# Example Script
puts "unique1 example returns: [::unique1::example]"
puts "invoking unique1::getNext directly returns:\
  [unique1::getNext]"
puts "unique1 example returns: [::unique1::example]"
puts ""
puts "unique2 example returns: [::unique2::example]"
puts "unique2 example returns: [::unique2::example]"
puts "unique2 example returns: [::unique2::example]"
```

**Script Output**

```
unique1 example returns: unique1::example:  1
invoking unique1::getNext directly returns:  2
unique1 example returns: unique1::example:  3

unique2 example returns: unique2::example:  1
unique2 example returns: unique2::example:  2
unique2 example returns: unique2::example:  3
```

Note that the createUnique process uses the uplevel to force the namespace eval to happen at the same scope as the code that invoked createUnique. By default, a procedure will be evaluated in the scope in which it was defined. Since the `createUnique` procedure is created in the global scope, it will default to creating the `getNext` namespace as a child namespace of the global space. By using the `uplevel` command, we force the evaluation to take place in the scope of the calling script: within the package namespace. The following illustration shows what the namespaces look like after evaluating the previous example.

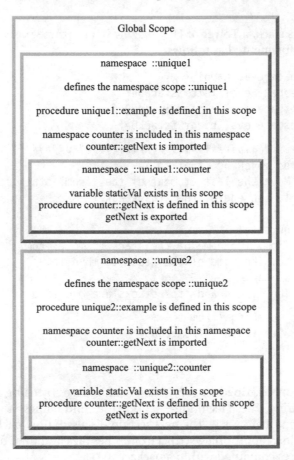

Namespaces can be used to implement aggregation by including multiple copies of another namespace (complete with data) in child namespaces. For example, a simple stack can be implemented as follows.

```
set stackDef {
  variable stack

  proc push {value} {
    variable stack
    lappend stack $value
  }

  proc pop {} {
```

```
        variable stack
        set rtn [lindex $stack end]
        set stack [lrange $stack 0 end-1]
        return $rtn
    }
}
```

Using this stack, a Tower of Hanoi game board (three posts with stacks of disks) can be implemented as follows.

```
namespace eval Hanoi {
  namespace eval left $stackDef
  namespace eval center $stackDef
  namespace eval right $stackDef

  ###############################################
  # proc moveRing {from to}--
  #   Move the last element of the "from" stack
  #   to the end of the "to" stack.
  #
  # Arguments
  #   from: The name of the stack to move from.
  #   to: The name of the stack to move to.
  # Results
  #   The "from" and "to" stacks are modified.

  proc moveRing {from to} {
      $to::push [$from::pop]
  }
}
```

This section described creating nested namespaces by using a procedure or using a script string. These techniques require the child namespace code to be resident in the script that uses it. The next section discusses how packages can be used to find and load appropriate scripts from other files and then describes how to nest namespaces contained within a package.

# 8.2 Packages

The namespace command allows you to assemble related information and procedures within a private area. The package commands allow you to group a set of procedures that may be in multiple files and identify them with a single name. The namespace command provides encapsulation functionality, whereas the package command provides library functionality. This section describes how to turn a set of procedures into a package other scripts can load easily.

People frequently refer to any collection of procedures and variables that work together to perform related functions as a package. A *real* Tcl package is a collection of procedures that can be indexed and loaded easily.

The package provide command changes a simple set of procedures to a Tcl package. This command defines a set of procedures as part of a package identified by the package name and a revision number. These procedures can be indexed and can be loaded automatically when they are needed by another script. The Tcl package command provides a framework for the following:

- Finding and loading the code modules a script requires
- Tracking the version numbers of packages and loading the proper version
- Defining whether the file to be loaded is a script file (discussed here) or shared library/DLL (discussed in Chapter 13)

### 8.2.1 How Packages Work

A Tcl package includes an index file that lists the procedures and commands defined in the package. The Tcl interpreter resolves unknown procedures by searching the index files in the directories listed in the global variable auto_path for required packages. The auto_path variable is defined in the init.tcl script, which is loaded when a Tcl or Tk interpreter is started.

This section describes creating the index files and adding your package directories to the list of places the interpreter will search. Note that when you create an index for a package that has procedures defined within a namespace, only the procedure names listed in a namespace export command will be indexed.

### 8.2.2 Internal Details: Files and Variables Used with Packages

The following files and global variables are used to find and load a package.

pkgIndex.tcl     file

This file contains a list of procedures defined by the packages in the directory with it. The pkgIndex.tcl file is created with the pkg_mkIndex command.

auto_path        global variable

The auto_path variable contains a list of the directories that should be searched for package index files.

The auto_path variable is defined in the init.tcl script, which is loaded when a tclsh interpreter is started.

On UNIX systems, init.tcl will probably be found in /usr/local/lib /tcl8.4, or some variant, depending on your installation and the revision number of your tclsh.

On Windows systems, `init.tcl` is stored in `\Program Files\Tcl\lib\tcl8.4`, or some variant, depending again on your version of Tcl and the base directory in which you installed the Tcl interpreter.

On the Macintosh, `init.tcl` may be stored in `Tcl/Tk Folder 8.4:Tcl:library`, again depending on installation options.

When the Tcl interpreter is trying to find a package to fulfill a `package require` command, it will search all of the directories listed in the `auto_path` variable, and all of the children in those directories, but not second-level sub-directories of the directories listed. This makes it possible to place a single directory in the `auto_path` list and use separate directories under that for each supported package.

## 8.2.3 Package Commands

The `package` functionality is implemented with several commands. These commands convert a simple script into a package. The `pkg_mkIndex` command creates a package index file. It is evaluated when a package is created rather than when a script is being evaluated.

The `pkg_mkIndex` command scans the files identified by the `patterns` for `package provide` commands. It creates a file (`pkgIndex.tcl`) in the current directory. The `pkgIndex.tcl` file describes the commands defined in the package and how to load the package when a script requires one of these commands.

***Syntax:*** `pkg_mkIndex ?-option? dir pattern ?pattern?`

Creates an index of available packages. This index is searched by `package require` when it is determining where to find the packages.

*?-option?* An option to fine-tune the behavior of the command. The option set has been evolving, and you should check the documentation on your system for details.

*dir* The directory in which the packages being indexed reside.

*pattern\** Glob-style patterns that define the files that will be indexed.

When the `pkg_mkIndex` command has finished evaluating the files that match the `pattern` arguments, it creates a file named `pkgIndex.tcl` in the `dir` directory. The `pkgIndex.tcl` file contains the following:

- The names of the packages defined in the files that matched the patterns
- The version level of these packages
- The name of the command to use to load the package
- Optionally, the names of the procedures defined in those packages

The `pkg_mkIndex` will overwrite an existing `pkgIndex.tcl` file. If you are developing multiple packages in a directory, you will need to enter the name of each file every time you update the index. In this case, it may become simpler to create a two-line script that lists all files, as follows:

```
#!/usr/local/bin/tclsh
pkg_mkIndex [pwd] file1.tcl file2.tcl file3.tcl
```

The package provide command defines the name and version of the package that includes these procedures. This command makes the procedures defined within the file available to other scripts.

**Syntax:** package provide *packageName ?version?*

Declares that procedures in this script module are part of the package packageName. Optionally declares which version of packageName this file represents.

*packageName*     The name of the package that will be defined in this script.

*?version?*     The version number of this package.

The pkg_mkIndex command looks for a package provide command in a file. It uses the package name and version information to generate an entry in the pkgIndex.tcl file with the name and version of the package and a list of procedures defined in this file.

The package provide command tells the Tcl interpreter that all of the procedures in the file are members of a package. You can use multiple files to construct your package, provided there is a package provide command in each file. Note that if you have multiple package provide commands with different *packageName* or *version* arguments in a source file, the pkg_mkIndex will not be able to generate an index file and may generate an error.

```
# Declare this file part of myPackage
package provide myPackage 1.0
```

The package require command declares that this script may use procedures defined in a particular package. Scripts that require procedures defined in other files will use this command.

**Syntax:** package require *?-exact? packageName ?versionNum?*

Informs the Tcl interpreter that this package may be needed during the execution of this script. The Tcl interpreter will attempt to find the package and be prepared to load it when required.

*-exact*     If this flag is present, versionNum must also be present. The Tcl interpreter will load only that version of the package.

*packageName*     The name of the package to load.

*?versionNum?*  The version number to load. If this parameter is provided, but -exact is not present, the interpreter will allow newer versions of the package to be loaded, provided they have the same major version number (see Section 8.2.4 for details of version numbering). If this parameter is not present, any version of packageName may be loaded.

**Example** 8.9

```
# This program needs to load myPackage
package require myPackage 1.0
```

The package require command checks the pkgIndex.tcl files in the search path (defined in auto_path) and selects the best match to the version number requested. If the -exact flag is used, it will select an exact match to that version number. If versionNum is defined and the -exact is not set, the largest minor revision number greater than versionNum will be selected. If versionNum is not defined, the highest available version will be selected. If an acceptable revision cannot be found, package require will generate an error.

If the Tcl interpreter can locate an appropriate package, it will load the required files as necessary to resolve the procedures defined in the package. Older Tcl versions (prior to 8.2) deferred loading packages until the procedures were needed. Since 8.2 the default behavior is to load packages immediately. The older, Just-In-Time style of loading can still be used by including the -lazy option to the pkg_mkIndex command when you create the pkgIndex.tcl file.

The packages loaded by package require are loaded into the global namespace. If you wish to load a package into a namespace other than the global namespace, you can use the module command, described later in the chapter.

## 8.2.4 Version Numbers

The package command has some notions about how version numbers are defined. The rules for version numbers are as follows.

- Version numbers are one or two positive integers separated by periods (e.g., 1.2 or 75.19).
- The first integer in the string is the major revision number. As a general rule, this is changed only when the package undergoes a major modification. Within a major revision, the API should be constant and application code should behave the same with later minor revision numbers. Between major revisions, there may be changes such that code that worked with one major revision will not work with another.
- The second integer is the minor revision number. This corresponds to an intermediate release. You can expect that bugs will be fixed, performance enhanced,

and new features added, but code that worked with a previous minor revision should work with later minor revisions.

- The Tcl interpreter compares revision numbers integer by integer. Revision 2.0 is more recent than revision 1.99.

### 8.2.5 **Package Cookbook**

This section describes how to create and use a Tcl package. The next section will show a more detailed example.

#### *Creating a Package*

**1.** Create the Tcl source file or files. You can split your package procedures across several files if you wish.

**2.** Add the command

```
package provide packageName versionNumber
```

to the beginning of these Tcl source files.

**3.** Invoke tclsh. If you have several revisions of Tcl installed on your system, be certain to invoke the correct tclsh. The package command was introduced with revision 7.5 and has been modified slightly in successive versions of Tcl.

**4.** At the % prompt, type

```
pkg_mkIndex directory fileNamePattern ?Pattern2...?
```

You may include multiple file names in this command. The pkg_mkIndex command will create a new file named pkgIndex.tcl, with information about the files that were listed in the pkg_mkIndex command.

In Tcl version 8.2 and more recent, the default option is to create a pkgIndex.tcl file that loads packages immediately. Older versions of Tcl created pkgIndex.tcl files that would defer loading until a procedure was needed. This behavior can be duplicated in newer interpreters with the -lazy option to pkg_mkIndex.

#### *Using a Tcl Package*

**1.** If the package is not located in one of the Tcl search directories listed by default in the auto_path variable, you must add the directory that contains the package's pkgIndex.tcl file to your search list. This can be done with one of the following techniques.

- Add a line resembling
  ```
  lappend auto_path /usr/project/packageDir
  ```
  to the beginning of your Tcl script.

- Set the environment variable TCLLIBPATH to include your package directory. The environment variable need not include the path to the default Tcl library. Note that TCLLIBPATH is a Tcl-style whitespace-delimited list, rather than the shell-style colon-delimited list.

- Add your package directory to the auto_path definition in the init.tcl file. This file is located in the Tcl library directory. The location of that directory is an installation option.

   Modifying the init.tcl script will require continuing the nonstandard modification every time the Tcl interpreters are updated. This can make a system fragile.

**2.** Add the line

```
package require packageName ?versionNumber?
```

to load the package into the global namespace. Alternatively, if you wish the package to load in the current namespace, your script can use the module command described later in this chapter (and included on the companion CD-ROM).

## 8.3 A Tree Object Package with Namespaces

This section describes how to turn the tree.tcl and treeObject.tcl scripts we have developed into a pair of scripts that implement a tree object package with most of the commands protected within namespaces.

### 8.3.1 Adding Namespace and Package to tree.tcl

The first step in this process is to make the procedures defined within the tree.tcl file into a package with the procedures and variables enclosed within a namespace. The beginning code for tree.tcl (which had been a set of Tcl procedure definitions) now looks as shown in the following example.

**Example** 8.10

```
package provide tree 2.5

namespace eval tree {

  # Export the public entry points

  namespace export treeCreate treeCreateChild treeDestroyTree
  namespace export treeDeleteNode treeGetChildList treeGetParent
  namespace export treeSetNodeValuetreeGetNodeValue
  namespace export treeSetTreeValue treeGetTreeValue
```

```tcl
    variable Tree_Array

    ############################################################
    # proc treeCreate {} --
    #     Create a root node for a tree
    # Arguments:
    #
    # Results:
    #     Creates a new root node in Tree_Array
    #     Initializes a unique counter for this tree
    #     Returns the name of the root node for use as a handle
    #
    proc treeCreate {} {
      variable Tree_Array

      # Create the unique name for this tree.

      set treeName "tree[unique]"

      # Can't have two trees with the same name.
      # This should never happen, but just in case...

      if {[array name Tree_Array $treeName.*] != ""} {
          error "$treeName already exists"
      }
      #
      # Looks good, return a new base node for this tree.
      #
      return [TreeCreateNode $treeName]
    }

    # The rest of the procedures...

}
```

The package provide tree 2.5 line informs Tcl that this file defines the tree package, revision level 2.5. The namespace eval tree evaluates all following code within the tree namespace. This creates all of the tree* procedures within the namespace and places the Tree_Array variable (that was maintained in the global namespace) in the tree namespace.

It is a common convention in Tcl programming to use the same name for a package and the namespace that holds the code and data to implement the package's functionality. The namespace export commands allow the entry points to be accessed (and namespace imported) by other programs.

Note that the pkg_mkIndex command will put only exported names into the pkgIndex.tcl file. All procedures that can be called from code outside the package should be listed here. The internal tree procedure TreeGetNameParts is not exported. This procedure should not be used by application code and should not be indexed by pkg_mkIndex.

The Tree_Array is declared to be a namespace variable with the variable Tree_Array command. This line is not required. Simply defining a value for Tree_Array would be sufficient. Explicit declarations of variables makes a package easier to understand, and avoids the possible failure mode of having a variable named Tree_Array in the global scope overwritten by mistake. (See the discussion of mapping names in the example discussion in Section 8.1.6.)

The procedure definition for treeCreate is identical to the original, except that the line global Tree_Array has been changed to variable Tree_Array. The other procedure definitions follow this pattern: the only change between the original procedure and the procedure within a namespace is that the word global is changed to variable.

If the Tree_Array definition were left global, instead of being changed to variable, the variable Tree_Array would be created in the global scope instead of the namespace scope. The code would still work correctly, but we would not gain the encapsulation the namespace command provides.

### 8.3.2 The Tree Object in a Namespace

It is a bit trickier to put a namespace around the tree object described in Section 7.6. The tree namespace is nested within the treeObject namespace, rather than placing both namespaces at the global level. One entry point, (newTreeObject), is in the global scope where all scripts can access it. The other procedure (TreeObjProc) is inside the treeObject namespace, where it is hidden from most scripts.

By nesting the tree namespace within the treeObject namespace, the treeObject acquires a private copy of the tree data and functions. This insulates the treeObject from possible collisions with other packages that might also be using the tree package. The set of namespaces will resemble the following illustration after the treeObject package is loaded.

```
┌─────────────────────────────────────────────────────────┐
│                      Global Scope                        │
│                                                          │
│        newTreeObject is defined in this scope            │
│            Node commands are defined here                │
│   ┌──────────────────────────────────────────────────┐  │
│   │                 treeObject Scope                  │  │
│   │                                                   │  │
│   │        TreeObjProc is defined in this scope       │  │
│   │                                                   │  │
│   │    tree* procedures are imported from tree scope  │  │
│   │         (treeCreate, treeSetNode, etc.)           │  │
│   │  ┌─────────────────────────────────────────────┐  │  │
│   │  │                 tree Scope                   │  │  │
│   │  │                                              │  │  │
│   │  │       tree* procedures are defined here      │  │  │
│   │  │        tree* procedures are exported         │  │  │
│   │  │        (treeCreate, treeSetNode, etc.)       │  │  │
│   │  │                                              │  │  │
│   │  │     Tree* procedures defined in this scope   │  │  │
│   │  │  Procedures for internal use only are not    │  │  │
│   │  │                  exported                    │  │  │
│   │  │ (TreeCreateNode, TreeAddChild,               │  │  │
│   │  │              TreeGetNameParts)               │  │  │
│   │  └─────────────────────────────────────────────┘  │  │
│   └──────────────────────────────────────────────────┘  │
└─────────────────────────────────────────────────────────┘
```

## Nesting Packages

Namespaces that contain data that should not be shared with other code modules are good candidates to be nested. However, not all sets of code that exist in a namespace are capable of being nested within another namespace, and not all scripts should be designed to be nested within other namespaces.

A Tcl script that is designed to be nested within another namespace will be referred to as a module. A module is a package that conforms to the following rules.

- Modules are pure Tcl scripts, not object code.
- Modules are written to be namespace independent.
- Modules use package provide to identify themselves as packages.

The tree package in the previous section is an example of a module. The end of this chapter provides guidelines for writing modules. A script can use the source command to load a script that defines one namespace into another namespace. For example, the following would work to nest the tree namespace described previously into a treeObject namespace.

```
namespace eval treeObject {
    source treeName.tcl
```

```
        # Rest of code defining treeObject
        ...
    }
```

The disadvantage is that your script will need to know the complete path to `treeName.tcl`, which may not be the current directory. The `package` command allows your scripts to load new modules without knowing the exact path. One technique for nesting a package within an arbitrary namespace is to use the `module load` command to load the package. The `module` package provides a facility for loading modules within other namespaces independently of the Tcl release. The `module` package is included on the companion CD-ROM.

The `module load` command provides hooks to load a package into the current namespace, global scope, immediately, or deferred (as with pre-8.1 Tcl). It also provides a hook for finding the package on a local or remote system, or providing your own search-and-load procedure. This discussion will focus on loading modules from the local file system into the current namespace.

> **Syntax:** `module load` *?-policy policyList? packageName packageRevision*
>
> Load a Tcl package as a relocatable module.
>
> `-policy policyList`
> A list of policy arguments to define how this module should be loaded. Options include
>
> > `CURRENT | GLOBAL`
> > Load into the current or global namespace scope.
> >
> > `IMMEDIATE | DEFERRED`
> > Load immediately, or configure the interpreter for deferred loading.
> >
> > `LOCAL | REMOTE | customProc`
> > Load the module from a locally mounted file system (listed in the `auto_path` global variable) or remote site (with optional address), or search and load the module using a custom procedure defined within your script.
>
> *packageName*
> The name of the module, as declared with the `package provide` command.
>
> *packageRevision*
> The revision number of the module, as declared with the `package provide` command.

## Loading the *tree* Module into the *treeObject*

Using the `module load` command is the easiest way to merge the `tree` namespace into the new `treeObject` package and namespace.

**Example** 8.11

```
package require module

package provide treeObject 2.5
########################################################
# proc newTreeObject {} --
# Creates a new Tree object, and returns an object for
#    accessing the base node.
# Arguments:
#    NONE

proc newTreeObject {} {
    set treeId [treeObject::tree::treeCreate]

    proc $treeId {args} "
        return \[treeObject::TreeObjProc $treeId \$args]
    "

    return $treeId

}

########################################################
namespace eval treeObject {

    module load -policy {CURRENT IMMEDIATE LOCAL} tree 2.5
    namespace import tree::*

########################################################
# proc TreeObjProc {node methodArgs} --
#    Primary method for tree objects.
#    Parses the subcommand and calls the appropriate
#    tree.tcl proc.
#
# Arguments:
#    node:        The internal name for this node.
#    methodArgs:  A list, the first member is the subcommand
#                 name, subsequent (optional) members are
#                 arguments to be passed to the tree.tcl
#                 command.
# Results:
#    Calls other procedures that may produce output,
#        create new objects, delete objects, etc.

proc TreeObjProc {node methodArgs} {
    set subCommand [lindex $methodArgs 0]
    set cmdArgs [lrange $methodArgs 1 end]
```

```
switch $subCommand {
...
```

Again, the package provide command defines this package as being the treeObject package. The newTreeObject procedure has been changed from the original version to reflect the fact that this procedure is defined in a different namespace from the other procedures in the treeObject package, and the procedures in the tree package are defined in a namespace nested within the treeObject namespace.

The treeCreate procedure is invoked by its relative namespace path. The relative path from the current scope is used here because the current scope could be the global scope, or the treeObject namespace could be nested within another namespace. For the same reason, the procedure definition for the new tree node that is defined within newTreeObject invokes treeObject::TreeObjProc by a relative path.

The next line, namespace eval treeObject {..., starts the definition of the treeObject namespace. The next line nests the tree namespace into the treeObject namespace. The module load command will load the tree package (and the tree namespace) into the treeObject namespaces.

After loading the new namespace, the script imports procedures from the tree namespace into the treeObject namespace. This is done with the command namespace import tree::*, which will import all entities exported from tree. Note that these procedure names are being imported into the treeObject namespace, not into the global namespace. Importing into this space simplifies writing the treeObject code without polluting the global space.

### 8.3.3 Procedures and Namespace Scopes

What happens if you evaluate a command in a namespace in which that command is not defined? When Tcl evaluates a command, it tries first to evaluate the command in the requested namespace. If that fails, it attempts to evaluate the command in the global namespace. Tcl does not promote a command through a series of nested namespaces.

The following example creates a tree object, adds a child, and then displays what tree procedures are available at which scopes. The procedures created for the new tree nodes, tree0.1 and tree0.2, are available at the global scope, along with the procedure for creating new trees, newTreeObject. All other procedures in this package are hidden in the namespaces. Notice that TreeAddChild and TreeCreateNode are not exported from the tree namespace. They are visible within the tree namespace but not the treeObject namespace.

Note that when info commands is evaluated in the ::treeObject::tree namespace, the output includes the tree commands in the ::treeObject::tree and global scopes, but not in the ::treeObject scope. The info commands command reports only the procedures visible in the scope where the command is evaluated. Tcl will not search the parent namespace to find a procedure. Thus, commands in the parent namespace are not visible from a child namespace.

**Example** 8.12

*Script Example*

```
# Include the Tree directory in the auto search path
lappend auto_path "../Tree"
package require treeObject 2

# Create a new tree and a child node - two nodes total.

set base [newTreeObject]
set child1 [$base add]

# Display the commands defined in the global scope

puts "\nTree Commands defined in global scope:\n\
   [lsort [info commands *ree*]]"

# Display the commands defined in the
#   treeObject namespace scope

set treeObjCmds [lsort [info commands ::treeObject::* ]]

# The regsub command replaces the string "::treeObject::"
# with "" in each of the commands listed in treeObjCmds
# to make the names more readable.

regsub -all {::treeObject::} $treeObjCmds "" treeObjCmds
puts "\nTree Commands defined in treeObject scope:\n \
   $treeObjCmds"

# Display the commands defined in the
#   treeObject::tree namespace scope
set treeCmds [lsort [info commands ::treeObject::tree::*]]

regsub -all {::treeObject::tree::} $treeCmds "" treeCmds

puts "\nTree Commands defined in treeObject::tree scope:\n\
   $treeCmds"

set treeCmds [lsort [namespace eval ::treeObject::tree \
   {info commands *ree*}]]

puts "\nTree Commands visible from treeObject::tree scope:\n\
   $treeCmds"

puts "\ntree1.node2 body: [info body tree1.node2]"
```

*Script Output*

```
Tree Commands defined in global scope:
 newTreeObject tree1.node2 tree1.node3

Tree Commands defined in treeObject scope:
 TreeObjProc treeCreate treeCreateChild treeDeleteNode treeDestroyTree
 treeDump treeGetAllNodes treeGetChildList treeGetNodeKeyList
 treeGetNodeValue treeGetNodeValueList treeGetParent treeGetRoot
 treeGetSiblingList treeGetTreeKeyList treeGetTreeValue
 treeGetTreeValueList treeMoveNode treeSearchKey treeSetNodeValue
 treeSetTreeValue treeUnsetNodeValue treeUnsetTreeValue

Tree Commands defined in treeObject::tree scope:
 TreeAddChild TreeCreateNode TreeGetNameParts treeCreate
 treeCreateChild treeDeleteNode treeDestroyTree treeDump
 treeGetAllNodes treeGetChildList treeGetNodeKeyList
 treeGetNodeValue treeGetNodeValueList treeGetParent
 treeGetRoot treeGetSiblingList treeGetTreeKeyList
 treeGetTreeValue treeGetTreeValueList treeMoveNode
 treeSearchKey treeSetNodeValue treeSetTreeValue treeUnsetNodeValue
 treeUnsetTreeValue unique

Tree Commands visible from treeObject::tree scope:
 TreeAddChild TreeCreateNode TreeGetNameParts newTreeObject
 tree1.node2 tree1.node3 treeCreate treeCreateChild treeDeleteNode
 treeDestroyTree treeDump treeGetAllNodes treeGetChildList
 treeGetNodeKeyList treeGetNodeValue treeGetNodeValueList
 treeGetParent treeGetRoot treeGetSiblingList treeGetTreeKeyList
 treeGetTreeValue treeGetTreeValueList treeMoveNode treeSearchKey
 treeSetNodeValue treeSetTreeValue treeUnsetNodeValue treeUnsetTreeValue

tree1.node2 body:
        return [treeObject::TreeObjProc tree1.node2 $args]
```

---

## 8.4 Namespaces and Packages

Namespaces and packages provide different features to the Tcl developer, with namespaces providing encapsulation support and packages providing modularization/library support. A package can be written with or without using a namespace. (In fact, packages were added to Tcl a couple years before namespace support was added.) The three namespace options when developing a package are

- *Use no namespaces.* The package can be loaded into the global scope or merged into a script-defined namespace. This option is suitable for small special-purpose packages that will not conflict with other packages, or are intended to always be merged into another namespace. This is not a recommended technique, but may be appropriate under some circumstances.

- *Require that the package be created in a given namespace.* The package uses an absolute name for the namespace in the namespace eval command and uses absolute names to define procedures used within the namespace. This is appropriate for packages that add new language features (for example, communications protocols, database connections, and http support) that do not include data structures that are specific to a given instantiation.

- *Allow the package to be created in an arbitrary namespace.* The package uses a relative name for the namespace in the namespace eval command and uses relative names to define procedures used within the namespace. This is appropriate for code modules that contain state information that is specific to a given instantiation of the namespace. Complex data structures (such as trees and stacks or GUI objects that maintain state information) are examples of this type of design.

Note that nesting namespaces requires that code be duplicated as well as data. If you have an application that creates many objects, you may run into memory constraints. In that case, you may need to separate procedures and variables into separate namespaces in order to have nested copies of the namespaces with data, and import procedures from a single copy of the code namespace. There are a few techniques that can be used to ensure a script will be namespace neutral:

- *Use only relative namespace identifiers.* Namespace names that start with a double colon (::) are absolute and are rendered from the global scope. Namespaces that start with a letter are relative names and are resolved from the current namespace.

- *Define procedures within the namespace eval or with relative namespace names.*

```
namespace eval bad {
  variable badVar
}
proc ::bad::badProc {} {
  variable badVar
  set badVar "Don't Do This"
}

namespace eval good {
  variable goodVar
  proc goodProc1 {} {
    variable goodVar
    set goodVar "OK"
  }
}
proc good::goodProc2 {} {
  variable goodVar
  set goodVar "Also OK"
}
```

- *Use namespace* current *or a relative name to identify the current namespace. The* namespace current command *is discussed in Chapters 10 and 12.*

- *Use the* variable *command to map namespace variables into procedures within the namespace rather than using namespace path names for variables.*

```
namespace eval bad {
    variable badVar
    proc badProc {} {
        set ::bad::badVar "Don't Do This"
    }
}

namespace eval good {
    variable goodVar
    proc goodProc {
        variable goodVar
        set goodVar OK
    }
}
```

## 8.5 Bottom Line

- Tcl namespaces can be used to hide procedures and data from the global scope.

- One namespace can be nested within another.

- The namespace commands manipulate the namespaces.

- The namespace eval command evaluates its arguments within a particular namespace.

  ***Syntax:*** namespace eval *namespaceID arg ?args?*

- The namespace export command makes its arguments visible outside the current scope.

  ***Syntax:*** namespace export *pattern ?patterns?*

- The namespace import will make the entities within a namespace local to the current scope.

  ***Syntax:*** namespace import *?-force? ?pattern?*

- The namespace children command will list the children of a given namespace.

  ***Syntax:*** namespace children *?scope? ?pattern?*

- The variable command declares a variable to be static within a namespace. The variable is not destroyed when procedures in the namespace scope complete processing.

  ***Syntax:*** variable *varName ?value? ... ?varNameN? ?valueN?*

- Tcl libraries (packages) can be built from one or more files of Tcl scripts.
- The package commands provide support for declaring what revision level of a package is provided and what revision level is required.
- The package commands provide methods for manipulating packages.
- The package provide command declares the name of a package being defined in a source file.

    **Syntax:** package provide *packageName ?version?*

- The pkg_mkIndex command creates the pkgIndex.tcl file that lists the procedures defined in appropriate files.

    **Syntax:** pkg_mkIndex *dir pattern ?pattern?*

- The package requires command declares what packages a script may require.

    **Syntax:** package require *?-exact? packageName ?versionNum?*

## 8.6 Problems

The following numbering convention is used in all Problem sections.

| Number Range | Description of Problems |
|---|---|
| 100–199 | These problems review the material covered in this chapter. They can be answered in a few words or a short (1–5-line) script. Each problem should take under a minute to answer. |
| 200–299 | These problems go beyond the details presented in this chapter. They may require some analysis of the material or command details not covered in the chapter. They may require reading a man page or making a web search. They can be answered with a few sentences or a 5–50-line script. Each problem should take under 10 minutes to answer. |
| 300–399 | These problems extend the material presented in this chapter. They may require referencing other sources. They can be answered in a few paragraphs or a few hundred lines of code. Each exercise may take a few hours to complete. |

**100.** What Tcl commands provide encapsulation functionality?

**101.** What Tcl commands can be used to build an index of available procedures?

**102.** What Tcl commands support building modular programs?

**103.** Can a Tcl namespace be used in a package?

**104.** Can a Tcl namespace be nested within another namespace?

**105.** What Tcl command is used to create a new namespace?

**106.** Can more than one file be included in a package?

**107.** What Tcl command will build a package index file?

**108.** Can procedure names be imported from one namespace to another?

**109.** Can a directory contain files that define multiple packages?

**110.** Can a directory contain files that comprise multiple versions of a package?

**200.** A LIFO stack can be implemented with a Tcl list. Create a stack namespace in which the Tcl list is a namespace variable. Implement push, pop, peek, and size procedures within the namespace.

**201.** Make a stack package from the script developed in Problem 200.

**202.** Given this code fragment

```
namespace eval pizza {
    variable toppingList
    variable size medium
    variable style deep-dish
}
```

add procedures to

a. Add toppings to a pizza.

b. Set a pizza size.

c. Set a pizza style.

d. Report the size, style, and toppings on a pizza.

e. Report the price of a pizza. (Define a base price and a price per topping. Ignore style and size.)

**203.** Convert the pizza namespace developed in the previous problem to a pizza object, similar to the treeObject described in this chapter. Implement a newPizza procedure to create a new pizza object in the global namespace. All procedures defined in the previous exercise should be available as object subcommands. When complete, the following code should work:

```
set pizza [newPizza]
$pizza addTopping sausage
$pizza addTopping mushrooms
$pizza setSize medium
$pizza setStyle thick-crust
puts "The pizza is: [$pizza describePizza]"
puts "This pizza costs: [$pizza returnCost]"
```

**204.** Write a script that will query a user for size, style, and toppings and generate a pizza using the pizza object from the previous exercise. When a user's order is complete, display all of the pizza objects defined. A dialog might resemble the following.

```
Would you like to order a Pizza (Y/N)? Y
What toppings would you like? sausage mushrooms
What size pizza (S/M/L)? M
What style pizza (deep-dish, thick, crispy)? crispy
Would you like to order a Pizza (Y/N)? N
Your order is:
   pizza 1: crispy medium with sausage and mushrooms
```

**300.** Use the `treeObject.tcl` script described in this chapter to construct a script that will print out the names of the files in two layers of subdirectories under a given directory.

**301.** Add a new procedure to the tree namespace that will return the topmost node, given any node name. Recursively find the parent node until there is no parent.

**302.** Merge the procedure developed in Problem 301 into the `treeObject` namespace.

**303.** Write a script using the `treeObject` namespace that will generate a tree with the names of the namespaces in a running script attached as the data for each node. The child/parent relationships of nodes in the tree should match the child/parent relationships of the namespaces.

**304.** Add an output procedure to the script developed in Problem 303 to display the content of the `treeObject`. The program output should resemble the following.

```
::
::tcl
::treeObject
  ::tree
```

**305.** Place the procedures developed in Problems 303 and 304 into a new namespace called `namespaceTree`. Add a procedure to the namespace to fill the tree. Allow the display procedure to be imported into another namespace.

**306.** Using the Tower of Hanoi name described in Section 8.1.7, write a script that will solve the puzzle. Information about the Tower of Hanoi puzzle is available at *www.dcs.napier.ac.uk/a.cumming/hanoi/* and *www.cut-the-knot.com/recurrence/hanoi.shtml.*

# CHAPTER 9

# Introduction to Tk Graphics

Everyone knows the fun part about computer programming is the graphics. The Tk graphics package lets a Tcl programmer enjoy this fun too. Tk is a package of graphics widgets that provides the tools to build complete graphics applications. Tk supports the usual GUI widgets (such as buttons and menus), complex widgets (such as color and file selectors), and data display widgets (such as an editable text window and an interactive drawing canvas).

The user interaction widgets include buttons, menus, scrollbars, sliders, pop-up messages, and text entry widgets. A script can display either text or graphics with the text and canvas widgets. Tk provides three algorithms, for controlling the layout of a display, and a widget for grouping widgets.

Finally, if none of the standard widgets do what you want, the Tk package supports low-level tools at both the script and C API levels to build your own graphical widgets. You can create either simple stand-alone widgets (similar to those provided by Tcl), or you can combine the simple widgets into complex widgets, sometimes called *compound widgets*, or *megawidgets*.

The Tk widgets are very configurable, with good default values for most settings. For many widgets, you can set your own background colors, foreground colors, and border widths. Some classes of widgets have special-purpose options such as font, line color, and behavior when selected. This chapter discusses some of the more frequently used options. Consult the on-line manual pages with your installation for a complete list of options supported with your version of Tcl/Tk.

Like most GUI packages, the Tk package is geared toward event-driven programming. If you are already familiar with event-driven programming, skip to Section 9.1. If not, the following paragraphs will give you a quick overview of event-driven programming.

Using traditional programming, your program watches for something to happen and then reacts to it. For instance, user interface code resembles the following:

```
while {![eof stdin]} {
  gets command
  switch command {
    "cmd1" {doCmd1}
    "cmd2" {doCmd2}
    default {unrecognized command}
  }
```

The user interface code will wait until a user types in a command and will then evaluate that command. Between commands, the program does nothing. While a command is being evaluated, the user interface is inactive.

With event-driven programming there is an event loop that watches for events, and when an event occurs it invokes the procedure that was defined to handle that event. This event may be a button press, a clock event, or data becoming available on a channel. Whenever the program is not processing a user request, it is watching for events. In this case, the user interface pseudocode resembles the following:

```
REGISTER exit TO BE INVOKED UPON exitCondition
REGISTER parseUserInput TO BE INVOKED UPON CarriageReturn
REGISTER processButton TO BE INVOKED UPON ButtonPress
```

With Tk, the details of registering procedures for events and running an event loop are handled largely behind the scenes. At the time you create a widget, you can register a procedure to be evaluated whenever the widget is selected, and the event loop simply runs whenever there is no other processing going on.

## 9.1 Creating a Widget

The standard form for the command to create a Tk widget is as follows.

*Syntax:* `WidgetClass` *widgetName* `requiredArguments ?options?`

| | |
|---|---|
| `WidgetClass` | A widget type, such as `button`, `label`, `scrollbar`, or `tk_chooseColor`. |
| *widgetName* | The name for this widget. Must conform to the naming Tk conventions described in the next section. |
| *requiredArguments* | Some Tk widgets have required arguments. |
| *?options?* | Tk widgets support a large number of options that define the fonts, colors, and actions to be taken when the widget is selected, and so on. As with the other command options, these are defined as `-keyword value` pairs. |

For example, this line,

```
label .hello -text "Hello, World."
```

will create a label widget named *.hello*, with the text Hello, World.

As part of creating a widget, Tcl creates a command with the same name as the widget. After the widget is created, your script can interact with the widget via this command. This is similar to the way the tree object was created and manipulated in Chapter 7. Tk widgets support commands for setting and retrieving configuration options, querying the widget for its current state, and other widget-specific commands such as scrolling the view, selecting items, and reporting selections.

The label in the preceding example will appear in the default window. When the wish interpreter starts, it creates a default window for graphics named ".".

## 9.2 Conventions

There are a few conventions for widgets supported by Tk. These conventions include naming conventions for widgets and colors and the conventions for describing screen locations, sizes, and distances.

### 9.2.1 Widget Naming Conventions

The Tk graphics widgets are named in a tree fashion, similar to a file system or the naming convention for namespaces. Instead of the slash used to separate file names, widget and window names are separated by periods. Thus, the root window is named ".", and a widget created in the root window could be named .widget1.

A widget or window name must start with a period and must be followed by a label. The label may start with a lowercase letter, digit, or punctuation mark (except a period). After the first character, other characters may be uppercase or lowercase letters, numbers, or punctuation marks (except periods). It is recommended that you use a lowercase letter to start the label.

Some widgets can contain other widgets. In that case, the widget is identified by the complete name from the top dot to the referenced widget. Tk widgets must be named by absolute window path, not relative. Thus, if widget one contains widget two, which contains widget three, you would access the last widget as .one.two.three.

A widget path name must be unique. You can have multiple widgets named .widget1 if they are contained in different widgets (e.g., .main.widget1 and .subwin.widget1 are two different widgets).

### 9.2.2 **Color Naming Conventions**

Colors may be declared by name (red, green, lavender, and so on) or with a hexadecimal representation of the red/green/blue intensities. The hexadecimal representation starts with the # character, followed by 3, 6, 9, or 12 hexadecimal digits. The number of digits used to define a color must be a multiple of 3. The number will be split into three hexadecimal values, with an equal number of digits in each value, and assigned to the red, green, and blue color intensities in that order. The intensities range from 0 (black) to 0xF, 0xFF, 0xFFF, or 0xFFFF (full brightness), depending on the number of digits used to define the colors. Thus, #f00 (bright red, no green, no blue) creates deep red, #aa02dd (medium red, dim green, medium blue) creates purple, and #ffffeeee0000 (bright red, bright green, no blue) creates a golden yellow.

### 9.2.3 **Dimension Conventions**

The size or location of a Tk object is given as a number followed by an optional unit identifier. The numeric value is maintained as a floating-point value. Even pixels can be described as fractions. If there is no unit identifier, the numeric value defaults to pixels. You can describe a size or location in inches, millimeters, centimeters, or points (1/72 of an inch) by using the unit identifiers shown in the following examples.

| *Unit Identifier* | *Meaning* |
| --- | --- |
| 15.3 | 15.3 pixels |
| 1.5i | 1-1/2 inches |
| 10m | 10 millimeters (1 cm) |
| 1.3c | 1.3 centimeters (13 mm) |
| 90p | 90 points (1-1/4 inches) |

## 9.3 **Common Options**

The Tk widgets support many display and action options. Fortunately, these options have reasonable default values associated with them. Thus, you do not need to define every option for every widget you use.

The following are some common options supported by many Tk widgets. They are described here, rather than with each widget that supports these options. Widget-specific options are defined under individual widget discussions. The complete list of options and descriptions is found in the Tcl/Tk on-line documentation under *options*.

| | |
|---|---|
| -background *color* | The background color for a widget. |
| -borderwidth *width* | The width of the border to be drawn around widgets with 3D effects. |
| -font *fontDescriptor* | The font to use for widgets that display text. Fonts are further discussed in Chapter 10, in regard to the canvas widget. |
| -foreground *color* | The foreground color for a widget. This is the color in which text will be drawn in a text widget or on a label. It accepts the same color names and descriptions as -background. |
| -height *number* | The requested height of the widget in pixels. |
| -highlightbackground *color* | The color rectangle to draw around a widget when the widget does not have input focus. |
| -highlightcolor *color* | The color rectangle to draw around a widget when the widget has input focus. |
| -padx *number*<br>-pady *number* | The -padx and -pady options request extra space (in pixels) to be placed around the widgets when they are arranged in another widget or in the main window. |
| -relief *condition* | The 3D relief for this widget: condition may be raised, sunken, flat, ridge, solid, or groove. |
| -text *text* | The text to display in this widget. |
| -textvariable *varName* | The name of a variable to associate with this widget. The content of the variable will reflect the content of the widget. For example, the textvariable associated with an entry widget will contain the characters typed into the entry widget. |
| -width *number* | The requested width of the widget in pixels. |

## 9.4 Determining and Setting Options

The value of an option can be set when a widget is created, or it can be queried and modified after the widget is created (using the cget and configure commands). The cget subcommand will return the current value of a widget option.

**Syntax:**  *widgetName* cget *option*

Return the value of a widget option.

| | |
|---|---|
| *widgetName* | The name of this widget. |
| cget | Return the value of a single configuration option. |
| *option* | The name of the option to return the value of. |

## Example 9.1

### *Script Example*

```
button .exit_button -text "QUIT" -command exit
puts "The exit button text is: [.exit_button cget -text]"
puts "The exit button color is: [.exit_button cget -background]"
```

### *Script Output*

```
The exit button text is: QUIT
The exit button color is: #d9d9d9
```

---

The configure subcommand will return the value of a single configuration option, return all configuration options available for a widget, or allow you to set one or more configuration options.

**Syntax:** *widgetName* configure *?opt1? ?val1? ... ?optN? ?valN?*

| | |
|---|---|
| *widgetName* | The widget being set/queried. |
| configure | Return or set configuration values. |
| *opt\** | The first option to set/query. |
| *?val\*?* | An optional value to assign to this option. |

If configure is evaluated with a single option, it returns a list consisting of the option name, the name and class that can be used to define this option in the windowing system resource file, the default value for the option, and the current value for the option.

## Example 9.2

### *Script Example*

```
button .exit_button -text "QUIT" -command exit
puts "The exit button text is:"
puts "  [.exit_button configure -text]"
puts "The exit button color is:"
puts "  [.exit_button configure -foreground]"
```

### *Script Output*

```
The exit button text is:
  - text text Text {} QUIT
The exit button color is:
  - foreground foreground Foreground Black Black
```

---

If configure is evaluated with no options, a list of lists of available option names and values is returned.

## Example 9.3

*Script Example*

```
puts [join [.exit_button configure] "\n"]
```

*Script Output*

```
-activebackground activeBackground Foreground #ececec #ececec
-activeforeground activeForeground Background Black Black
-anchor anchor Anchor center center
-background background Background #d9d9d9 #d9d9d9
-bd -borderwidth
-bg -background
-bitmap bitmap Bitmap {} {}
-borderwidth borderWidth BorderWidth 2 2
-command command Command {} exit
-compound compound Compound none none
-cursor cursor Cursor {} {}
-default default Default disabled disabled
-disabledforeground disabledForeground DisabledForeground #a3a3a3 #a3a3a3
-fg -foreground
-font font Font {Helvetica -12 bold} {Helvetica -12 bold}
-foreground foreground Foreground Black Black
-height height Height 0 0
-highlightbackground highlightBackground HighlightBackground #d9d9d9 #d9d9d9
-highlightcolor highlightColor HighlightColor Black Black
-highlightthickness highlightThickness HighlightThickness 1 1
-image image Image {} {}
-justify justify Justify center center
-overrelief overRelief OverRelief {} {}
-padx padX Pad 3m 3m
-pady padY Pad 1m 1m
-relief relief Relief raised raised
-repeatdelay repeatDelay RepeatDelay 0 0
-repeatinterval repeatInterval RepeatInterval 0 0
-state state State normal normal
-takefocus takeFocus TakeFocus {} {}
-text text Text {} QUIT
-textvariable textVariable Variable {} {}
-underline underline Underline -1 -1
-width width Width 0 0
-wraplength wrapLength WrapLength 0 0
```

If configure is evaluated with option value pairs, it will set the options to the defined values. The following example creates a button that uses the configure command to change its label when it is clicked. The -command option and pack command are discussed later in this chapter.

**Example** 9.4

*Script Example*

```
set clickButton [button .b1 -text "Please Click Me" \
  -command {.b1 configure -text "I've been Clicked!"}]
pack .b1
```

*Script Output*

Before click         After click

Please Click Me      I've been Clicked!

## 9.5 The Basic Widgets

These basic widgets, as follows, are supported in the Tk 8.0 (and later) distributions.

button
: A clickable button that may evaluate a command when it is selected.

radiobutton
: A set of on/off buttons and labels, one of which may be selected.

checkbutton
: A set of on/off buttons and labels, many of which may be selected.

menubutton
: A button that displays a scrolldown menu when clicked.

menu
: A holder for menu items. This is attached to a menubutton.

listbox
: Creates a widget that displays a list of strings, one or more of which may be selected. The listbox may be scrolled.

entry
: A widget that can be used to accept a single line of textual input.

label
: A widget with a single line of text in it.

message
: A widget that may contain multiple lines of text.

text
>A widget for displaying and optionally editing large bodies of text.

canvas
>A drawing widget for displaying graphics and images.

scale
>A slider widget that can call a procedure when the selected value changes.

scrollbar
>Attaches a scrollbar to widgets that support a scrollbar. Will call a procedure when the scrollbar is modified.

frame
>A container widget to hold other widgets.

toplevel
>A window with all borders and decorations supplied by the Window manager.

## 9.6 Introducing Widgets: `label`, `button`, and `entry`

The `label`, `button`, and `entry` widgets are the easiest widgets to use. The `label` widget simply displays a line of text, the `button` widget evaluates a Tcl script when it is selected, and the `entry` widget accepts user input. All Tcl widget creation commands return the name of the widget they create. A good coding technique is to save that name in a variable and access the widget through that variable rather than hard-coding the widget names in your code.

**Syntax:** `label` *labelName ?option1? ?option2?* ...

Create a `label` widget.

*labelName*  The name for this widget.

*option*  Valid options for `label` include

-font *fontDescriptor*

>Defines the font to use for this display. Font descriptors are discussed in Section 10.4.5.

-textvariable *varName*

>The name of a variable that contains the display text.

-text *displayText*

>Text to display. If -textvariable is also used, the variable will be set to this value when the widget is created.

Note that the options can be defined in any order in the following example.

**Example** 9.5

*Script Example*

```
set txt [label .la -relief raised -text \
  "Labels can be configured with text"]
pack $txt
set var [label .lb -textvariable label2Var -relief sunken]
pack $var
set label2Var "Or by using a variable"
```

*Script Output*

Labels can be configured with text
Or by using a variable

---

The button widget will evaluate a script when a user clicks it with the mouse. The script may be any set of Tcl commands, including procedure calls. By default, a script attached to a widget will be evaluated in the global scope. The scope in which a widget's -command script will be evaluated can be modified with the namespace current command, discussed in Section 12.6.

**Syntax:** button *buttonName* ?option1? ?option2? ...

Create a button widget.

*buttonName*    The name to be assigned to the widget.

*?options?*    Valid options for button include

-font *fontDescriptor*
   Defines the font to use for this button. Font descriptors are discussed in Section 10.4.5.

-command *script*
   A script to evaluate when the button is clicked.

-text *displayText*
   The text that will appear in this button. A newline character (\n) can be embedded in this text to create multi-line buttons.

**Example** 9.6

*Script Example*

```
set theLabel [label .la -text "This is the beginning text"]

set myButton [button .b1 -text "click to modify label"\
  -command "$theLabel configure -text \
```

```
                 {The Button was Clicked}"]
pack $theLabel
pack $myButton
```

**Script Output**

Before click

After click

| This is the beginning text | The Button was Clicked |
|:---:|:---:|
| **click to modify label** | **click to modify label** |

The `entry` widget allows a user to enter a string of data. This data can be longer than will fit in the widget's displayed area. The widget will automatically scroll to display the last character typed and can be scrolled back and forth with the arrow keys or by attaching the widget to a scrollbar (scrollbars are discussed later in this chapter). The `entry` widget can be configured to reflect its content in a variable, or your script can query the widget for its content.

**Syntax:** entry *entryName* *?options?*

Create an `entry` widget.

*entryName*    The name for this widget.

*?options?*    Valid options for `label` include

-font *fontDescriptor*
Defines the font to use for this display. Font descriptors are discussed in Section 10.4.5.

-textvariable *VarName*
The variable named here will be set to the value in the entry widget.

-justify *side*
Justify the input data to the left margin of the widget (for entering textual data) or the right margin (for entering numeric data). Values for this option are `right` and `left`.

## Example 9.7

**Script Example**

```
set input [entry .e1 -textvariable inputval]
set action [button .b1 -text "Convert to UPPERCASE" \
  -command {set inputval [string toupper $inputval]} ]
pack $input
pack $action
```

*Script Output*

Before click

| new and improved |
| --- |
| **Convert to UPPERCASE** |

After click

| NEW AND IMPROVED |
| --- |
| **Convert to UPPERCASE** |

---

Note that the button command in Example 9.6 was enclosed within quotes, whereas the command in Example 9.7 was enclosed within curly braces. In Example 9.6 we want the variable theLabel to be replaced by the actual name of the widget when the button creation command is being evaluated. The command being bound to the button is

```
.la configure -text {The Button was Clicked}
```

If our script changes the content of the variable theLabel after creating the button, the command will still configure the original widget it was linked to (.la), not the window now associated with $thelabel. In Example 9.7, we do not want the substitution to occur when the button is created; we want the substitution to occur when the button is clicked. When the command is placed within brackets, the command bound to the button is

```
set inputval [string toupper $inputval]
```

The variable $inputval will be replaced by the content of the inputval variable when the button is selected. If the command for Example 9.7 were enclosed in quotes, the command bound to the button would have been been evaluated, $inputval would be replaced by the current value (an empty string), and the string [string toupper ""] would be evaluated and replaced by an empty string. The command bound to the button would be

```
set inputval ""
```

In this case, clicking the button would cause the entry field to be cleared.

The script associated with a button can be arbitrarily long and complex. As a rule of thumb, if there are more than three or four commands in the script, or if you are mixing variables that need to be substituted at widget creation time and evaluation time, it is best to create a procedure for the script and invoke that procedure with the button -command option.

For example, you can make an application support multiple languages by using an associative array for a translation table.

## Example 9.8

*Script Example*

```
array set english {Nom Name Rue Street}
array set french {Name Nom Street Rue}
```

```
grid [label .name -text Name]
grid [label .street -text Street]

button .translate -text "En Francais" -command {
  foreach w {.name .street} {
    $w configure -text $french([$w cget -text])
  }
}
```

```
grid .translate
```

You can also make the button change text and command when it is clicked, to translate back to English, but the command starts to get unwieldy.

```
array set english {Nom Name Rue Street "In English" "En Francais"}
array set french {Name Nom Street Rue "En Francais" "In English"}
```

```
grid [label .name -text Name]
grid [label .street -text Street]

button .translate -text "En Francais" -command {
  if {[string match [.translate cget -text] "En Francais"]} {
    foreach w {.name .street .translate} {
      $w configure -text $french([$w cget -text])
    }
  } else {
    foreach w {.name .street .translate} {
      $w configure -text $english([$w cget -text])
    }
  }
}
```

```
grid .translate
```

***Script Output***

In English          En Français

| Name | Nom |
|------|-----|
| Street | Rue |
| En Francais | In English |

Using a procedure instead of coding the translation in-line simplifies the code and makes the application more maintainable.

**Example** 9.9

```
proc translate {widgetList request} {
  if {[string match "En Francais" $request]} {
      upvar #0 french table
  } else {
      upvar #0 english table
  }
  foreach w $widgetList {
    $w configure -text $table([$w cget -text])
  }
}

array set english {Nom Name Rue Street}
array set french {Name Nom Street Rue}

grid [label .name -text Name]
grid [label .street -text Street]

button .convert -text "En Francais" -command {
    translate {.convert .name .street } [.convert cget -text]
}

grid .convert
```

## 9.7 Widget Layout: frame, place, pack, and grid

Stacking one widget atop another is useful for extremely simple examples, but real-world applications need a bit more structure. Tk includes a widget (frame) to group other widgets and three layout managers (place, pack, and grid) to give you total control over your application interface. The frame widget is useful for collecting a set of related widgets into a single unit. This makes complex layouts easier to create or modify.

The layout managers allow you to describe how the widgets in your application should be arranged. The layout managers use different algorithms for describing how a set of widgets should be arranged. Thus, the options supported by the managers have little overlap.

All of the window managers support the -in option, which defines the window in which a widget should be displayed. By default, a widget will be displayed in its immediate parent widget. For example, a button named .mainButton would be packed in the root (.) window, whereas a button named .buttonFrame.controls.offButton would default to being displayed in the .controls widget, which is displayed in the .buttonFrame widget.

Using the tree-style naming conventions and default display parent for widgets makes code easier to read. This technique documents the widget hierarchy in the widget name. However, the default display parent can be overridden with the -in option if your program requires this control.

### 9.7.1 The frame Widget

You frequently need to group a set of widgets when you are designing a display. For instance, you will probably want all buttons placed near each other and all results displayed as a group. The Tk widget for grouping other widgets is frame. The frame widget is a rectangular container widget that groups other widgets. You can define the height and width of a frame or let it automatically size itself to fit the content.

**Syntax:**  frame *frameName* *?options?*

Create a frame widget.

*frameName*   The name for the frame being created.

*?options?*   The options for a frame include

| | |
|---|---|
| -height *numPixels* | Height (using units, as described in Section 9.2.3). |
| -width *numPixels* | Width (using units, as described in Section 9.2.3). |
| -background *color* | The color of the background (see Section 9.2.2). |
| -relief *value* | Defines how to draw the widget edges. Can make the frame look raised, sunken, outlined, or flat. The *value* may be one of sunken, raised, ridge, or flat. The default is flat, to display no borders. |
| -borderwidth *width* | Sets the width of the decorative borders. The width value may be any valid size value (as described in Section 9.2.3). |

A display can be divided into frames by functionality. For example, an application that interfaces with a database would have an area for the user to enter query fields, an area with the database displays, an area of buttons to generate searches, and so on. This could be broken down into three primary frames: .entryFrame, .displayFrame, and .buttonFrame. Within each of these frames would be the other widgets, with names such as .entryFrame.userName, .displayFrame.securityRating, and .buttonFrame.search.

## 9.7.2 **The place Layout Manager**

The place command lets you declare precisely where a widget should appear in the display window. This location can be declared as an absolute location or a relative location based on the size of the window. Applications that use few widgets or need precise control are easily programmed with the place layout manager. For most applications, however, the place layout manager has too much programmer overhead.

*Syntax:* place *widgetName option ?options?*

Declare the location of a widget in the display.

*widgetName*   The name of the widget being placed.

*option*   The place command requires at least one X/Y pair of these placement options:

-x *xLocation*
-y *yLocation*   An absolute location in pixels.

-relx *xFraction*
-rely *yFraction*   A relative location given as a fraction of the distance across the window.

-in *windowName*   A window to hold this widget. The window *windowName* must be either the immediate parent or lower in the window hierarchy than the window being placed. That is, for example, Window .frame1.frame2.label can be placed -in .frame1.frame2 or frame1.frame2.frame3.frame4, but not .frame1.

The following example uses the place command to build a simple application that calculates a 15% sales tax on purchases. As you can see, there is a lot of overhead in placing the widgets. You need a good idea of how large widgets will be, how large your window is, and so on in order to make a pretty screen.

## Example 9.10

*Script Example*

```
# Create the "quit" and "calculate" buttons
set quitbutton [button .quitbutton -text "Quit" -command "exit"]
set gobutton [button .gobutton -text "Calculate Sales Tax" \
  -command {set salesTax [expr $userInput * 0.15]}]

# Create the label prompt and entry widgets
set input [entry .input -textvariable userInput]
set prompt [label .prompt -text "Base Price:"]
```

```
# Create the label and result widgets
set tax [label .tax -text "Tax :"]
set result [label .result -textvariable salesTax -relief raised]

# Set the size of the main window
. configure -width 250 -height 100

# Place the buttons near the bottom
place $quitbutton -relx .75 -rely .7
place $gobutton -relx .01 -rely .7

# Place the input widget near the top.
place $prompt -x 0 -y 0
place $input -x 75 -y 0

# Place the results widgets in the middle
place $tax -x 0 -y 30
place $result -x 40 -y 30
```

**Script Output**

---

### 9.7.3 **The pack Layout Manager**

The pack command is quite a bit easier to use than place. With the pack command, you declare the positions of widgets relative to each other and let the pack command worry about the details.

**Syntax:** pack *widgetName ?options?*

Place and display the widget in the display window.

*widgetName*    The widget to be displayed.

*?options?*    The pack command has many options. The following options are the most used:

-side *side*    Declares that this widget should be packed closest to a given side of the parent window. The side argument may be one of top, bottom, left, or right. The default is top.

| | |
|---|---|
| -anchor *edge* | If the space assigned to this widget is larger than the widget, the widget will be anchored to this edge of the space. The *edge* parameter may be one of n, s, e, or w. |
| -expand *boolean* | If set to 1 or yes, the widget will be expanded to fill available space in the parent window. The default is 0 (do not expand to fill the space). The boolean argument may be one of 1, yes, 0, or no. |
| -fill *direction* | Defines whether a widget may expand to fill extra space in its parcel. The default is none (do not fill extra space). The direction argument may be |

| | |
|---|---|
| none | Do not fill |
| x | Fill horizontally |
| y | Fill vertically |
| both | Fill both horizontally and vertically |

| | |
|---|---|
| -padx *number* | Declares how many pixels to leave as a gap between widgets. |
| -pady *number* | Declares how many pixels to leave as a gap between widgets. |
| -after*widgetName* | Pack this widget after (on top of) *widgetName*. |

The packer can be conceptualized as starting with a large open square. As it receives windows to pack, it places them on the requested edge of the remaining open space. For example, if the first window is a label with the -side left option set, pack would place the left edge of the label against the left side of the empty frame. The left edge of the empty space is now the right edge of the label, even though there may be empty space above and below this widget.

If the next item is to be packed -side top, it will be placed above and to the right of the first widget. The following code shows how these two widgets would appear. Note that even though the anchor on the top label is set to west, it only goes as far to the west as the east-most edge of the first widget packed.

### Example 9.11

#### *Script Example*

```
label .la -background gray80 -text LEFT
label .lb -background gray80 -text TOP
```

```
pack .la -side left
pack .lb -side top -anchor w
. configure -background white -relief ridge -borderwidth 3
# wm interacts with the window manager - discussed later
wm geometry . 80x50
```

**Script Output**

---

The pack algorithm works by allocating a rectangular parcel of display space and filling it in a given direction. If a widget does not require all available space in a given dimension, the parent widget will "show through" unless the -expand or -fill option is used.

The following example shows how a label widget will be packed with a frame with various combinations of the -fill and -expand options being used. The images show the steps as new frames are added to the display.

## Example 9.12

*Script Example*

```
# Create a root frame with a black background, and pack it.

frame .root -background black
pack .root

# Create a frame with two labels to allocate 2 labels worth of
# vertical space.
# Note that the twoLabels frame shows through where the top
# label doesn't fill.

frame .root.twoLabels -background gray50
label .root.twoLabels.upperLabel -text "twoLabels no fill top"
label .root.twoLabels.lowerLabel -text "twoLabels no fill lower"

pack .root.twoLabels -side left
pack .root.twoLabels.upperLabel -side top
pack .root.twoLabels.lowerLabel -side bottom
```

```
 twoLabels no fill top 
twoLabels no fill lower
```

```
# Create a frame and label with no fill or expand options used.
# Note that the .nofill frame is completely covered by the
```

```
# label, and the root frame shows at the top and bottom

frame .root.nofill -background gray50
label .root.nofill.label -text "nofill, noexpand"
pack .root.nofill -side left
pack .root.nofill.label
```

```
# Create a frame and label pair with the -fill option used when
# the frame is packed.
# In this case, the frame fills in the Y dimension to use all
# available space, and the label is packed at the top of
# the frame. The .fill frame shows through below the label.

frame .root.fill_frame -background gray50
label .root.fill_frame.label -text "fill frame"

pack .root.fill_frame -side left -fill y
pack .root.fill_frame.label
```

```
# Create a label that can fill, while the frame holding it will not.
# In this case, the frame is set to the size required to hold
# the widget, and the widget uses all that space.

frame .root.fill_label -background gray50
label .root.fill_label.label -text "fill label"

pack .root.fill_label -side left
pack .root.fill_label.label -fill y
```

```
# Allow both the frame and widget to fill.
# The frame will fill the available space,
# but the label will not expand to fill the frame.

frame .root.fillBoth -background gray50
label .root.fillBoth.label -text "fill label and frame"

pack .root.fillBoth -side left -fill y
pack .root.fillBoth.label -fill y
```

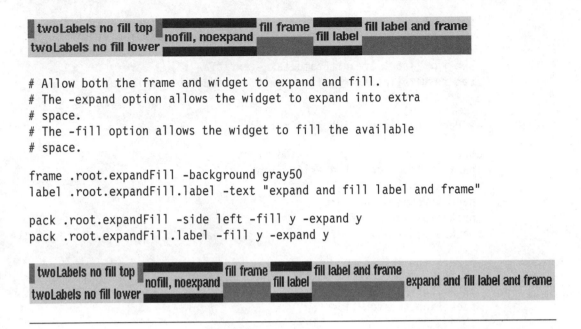

```
# Allow both the frame and widget to expand and fill.
# The -expand option allows the widget to expand into extra
# space.
# The -fill option allows the widget to fill the available
# space.

frame .root.expandFill -background gray50
label .root.expandFill.label -text "expand and fill label and frame"

pack .root.expandFill -side left -fill y -expand y
pack .root.expandFill.label -fill y -expand y
```

The pack command is good at arranging widgets that will go in a line or need to fill a space efficiently. It is somewhat less intuitive when you are trying to create a complex display. The solution to this problem is to construct your display out of frames and use the pack command to arrange widgets within the frame, and again to arrange the frames within your display. For many applications, grouping widgets within a frame and then using the pack command is the easiest way to create the application. The following example shows a fairly common technique of making a frame to hold a label prompt and an entry widget.

### Example 9.13

***Script Example***

```
# Create the frames for the widgets

set buttonFrame [frame .buttons]
set inputFrame [frame .input]
set resultFrame [frame .results]

# Create the widgets

set quitbutton [button .buttons.quitbutton -text "Quit" \
  -command "exit"]

set gobutton [button .buttons.gobutton -text \
  "Calculate Sales Tax" \
  -command {set salesTax [expr $userInput * 0.15]}]
```

```
set input [entry $inputFrame.input -textvariable userInput]
set prompt [label $inputFrame.prompt -text "Base Price:"]

set tax [label $resultFrame.tax -text "Tax :"]
set result [label .results.result -textvariable salesTax \
  -relief raised]

# Pack the widgets into their frames.

pack .buttons.quitbutton -side right
pack .buttons.gobutton -side right
pack $input -side right
pack $prompt -side left
pack $tax -side left
pack $result -side left

# Pack the frames into the display window.

pack .buttons -side bottom
pack $inputFrame -side top

# The left example image is created by setting
#   withFill to 0 outside this code snippet.
# The right example image is created by setting
#   withFill to 1 outside this code snippet.

if {$withFill} {
pack $resultFrame -after $inputFrame -fill x
} else {
pack $resultFrame -after $inputFrame
}
```

### Script Output

With -fill

| Base Price: 12.00 |
|---|
| Tax : 1.8 |
| Calculate Sales Tax | Quit |

Without -fill

| Base Price: 12.00 |
|---|
| Tax : 1.8 |
| Calculate Sales Tax | Quit |

Note the way the -side option is used in the previous example. The buttons are packed with -side set to right. The pack command will place the first widget with a -side option set against the requested edge of the parent frame. Subsequent widgets will be placed as close to the requested side as possible without displacing a widget that previously requested that side of the frame.

The -fill x option to the pack $resultFrame allows the frame that holds the $tax and $result widgets to expand to the entire width of the window, as shown in the With -fill result. By default, a frame is only as big as it needs to be to contain its child widgets. Without the -fill option, the resultFrame would be the narrowest of the frames and would be packed in the center of the middle row, as shown in the Without -fill result. With the -fill option set to fill in the X dimension, the frame can expand to be as wide as the window that contains it, and the widgets packed on the left side of the frame will line up with the left edge of the window instead of lining up on the left edge of a small frame. If you want a set of widgets .a, .b, and .c to be lined up from left to right, you can pack them as follows:

```
pack .a -side left
pack .b -side left
pack .c -side left
```

### 9.7.4 The grid Layout Manager

Many graphic layouts are conceptually grids. The grid layout manager is ideal for these types of applications, since it lets you declare that a widget should appear in a cell at a particular column and row. The grid manager then determines how large columns and rows need to be to fit the various components.

*Syntax:* grid *widgetName ?widgetNames? option*

Place and display the widget in the display window.

*widgetName* The name of the widget to be displayed.

*?options?* The grid command supports many options. The following is a minimal set.

-column *number* The column position for this widget.

-row *number* The row for this widget.

-columnspan *number* How many columns to use for this widget. Defaults to 1.

-rowspan *number* How many rows to use for this widget. Defaults to 1.

-sticky *side* Which edge of the cell this widget should "stick" to. Values may be n, s, e, w, or a combination of these letters (to stick to multiple sides).

The -sticky option lets your script declare that a widget should "stick" to the north (top), south (bottom), east (right), or west (left) edge of the grid in which it is placed. By default, a widget is centered within its cell. Any of the options for the grid command can be reset after a widget is packed with the `grid configure` command.

> **Syntax:** `grid configure` *widgetName* `-option` *optionValue*
>
> Change one or more of the configuration options for a widget previously positioned with the `grid` command.
>
> *widgetName* The name of the widget to have a configuration option changed.
>
> *-option ?value?* The option and value to modify (or set).

### Example 9.14

#### Script Example

```
set quitbutton [button .quitbutton -text "Quit" -command "exit"]
set gobutton [button .gobutton -text "Calculate Sales Tax" \
    -command {set salesTax [expr $userInput * 0.15]}]
set input [entry .input -textvariable userInput]
set prompt [label .prompt -text "Base Price:"]
set tax [label .tax -text "Tax :"]
set result [label .result -textvariable salesTax -relief raised]

grid $quitbutton $gobutton -row 3
grid $prompt $input -row 1
grid $tax $result -row 2 -sticky w
```

#### Script Output

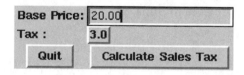

## 9.7.5 Working Together

The different layout managers can be used together to get the screen layout you desire. In the rules defined in the following, `.f1` and `.f2` are frames that contain other widgets.

- Within a single frame, any single layout manager can be used. The following is valid:

```
pack .f1.b1 -side left
grid .f2.b1 -column 1 -row 3
```

- Within a single frame, the grid and pack cannot be mixed. The following is not valid:

```
pack .f1.b1 -side left
grid .f1.b2 -column 1 -row 3
```

- The place can be used with either the grid or pack command. The following is valid:

```
pack .f1.b1 -side left
place .f1.label -x 25 -y 10
grid .f2.b1 -column 1 -row 3
place .f2.label -xrel .1 -yrel .5
```

- Frames can be arranged with either grid or pack, regardless of which layout manager is used within the frame. The following is valid:

```
pack .f1.b1 -side left
grid .f2.b1 -column 1 -row 3
grid .f1 -column 0 -row 0
grid .f2 -column 1 -row 0
```

## 9.8 Selection Widgets: radiobutton, checkbutton, menu, and listbox

Allowing the user to select one (or more) items from a list is a common program requirement. The Tk graphics extension provides the selection widgets radiobutton, checkbutton, menu, and listbox.

### 9.8.1 radiobutton and checkbutton

The radiobutton and checkbutton widgets are very similar. The primary difference is that radiobutton will allow the user to select only one of the entries, whereas checkbutton will allow the user to select multiple items from the entries.

#### radiobutton

The radiobutton widget displays a label with a diamond-shaped status indicator next to it. When a radiobutton is selected, the indicator changes color to show which item has been selected, and any previously selected radiobutton is deselected.

*Syntax:* radiobutton *radioName* *?options?*

Create a radiobutton widget.

*radioName*    The name for this radiobutton widget.

| | |
|---|---|
| *?options?* | Options for the radiobutton include |

-command *script*      A script to evaluate when this button is clicked.

-variable *varName*      The variable defined here will contain the value of this button when the button is selected. If this option is used, the -value must also be used.

-value *value*      The value to assign to the variable.

The -variable and -value options allow the radiobutton widget to be attached to a variable that will be set to a particular value when the button is selected. By using the -command option, you can assign a script that will be evaluated when the button is selected. If the -variable and -value options are also used, the script will be evaluated after the new value has been assigned to the widget variable.

The following example shows how the magic shop in a computerized Fantasy Role Playing game can be modernized. Note the foreach {item cost} $itemList command. This style of the foreach command (using a list of variables instead of a single variable) was introduced in Tcl version 7.4. It is useful when stepping through a list that consists of repeating fields, such as the *name price name price* data in itemList.

## Example 9.15

### Script Example

```
# Update the displayed text in a label

proc updateLabel {myLabel item} {
  global price;
  $myLabel configure -text \
  "The cost for a potion of $item is $price gold pieces"
}

# Create and display a label

set l [label .l -text "Select a Potion"]
grid $l -column 0 -row 0 -columnspan 3

# A list of potions and prices

set itemList [list "Cure Light Wounds" 16 "Boldness" 20 \
  "See Invisible" 60]
set position 0

foreach {item cost} $itemList {
```

```
      radiobutton .b_$position -text $item -variable price \
         -value $cost -command [list updateLabel $1 $item]
      grid .b_$position -column $position -row 1
      incr position
}
```

***Script Output***

Before selecting

| Select a Potion | | |
|---|---|---|
| ◇ Cure Light Wounds | ◇ Boldness | ◇ See Invisible |

After selecting

| The cost for a potion of Boldness is 20 gold pieces | | |
|---|---|---|
| ◇ Cure Light Wounds | ◆ Boldness | ◇ See Invisible |

All of the radiobutton widgets in this example share the global variable price. The variable assigned to the -variable option is used to group radiobutton widgets. For example, if you had two sets of radiobuttons, one for magic potions and one for magic scrolls, you would need to use two different variable names, such as potionPrice and scrollPrice.

If you assign each radiobutton a different variable, the radiobuttons will be considered as separate groups. In this case, all buttons can be selected at once and cannot be deselected, since there would be no other button in their group to select. Note that the variable price is declared as a global in the procedure updateLabel. The variables attached to Tk widgets default to being in the global scope.

The updateLabel procedure is called with an item name and uses the variable price to get the price. The $price value could be passed to the procedure by defining the -command argument as

```
      -command [list updateLabel $1 $item $cost]
```

This example used the variable for demonstration purposes. Either technique for getting the data to the procedure can be used.

### *checkbutton*

The checkbutton widget allows multiple items to be selected. The checkbutton widget displays a label with a square status indicator next to it. When a checkbutton is selected, the indicator changes color to show which item has been selected. Any other check buttons are not affected.

The checkbutton widget supports a -variable option, but unlike the case of radiobutton you must use a separate variable for each widget, instead of sharing a single variable among the widgets. Using a single variable will cause all buttons to select or deselect at once, instead of allowing you to select one or more buttons.

*Syntax:* checkbutton *checkName* *?options?*

Create a checkbutton widget.

*checkName*  The name for this checkbutton widget.

*?options?*  Valid options for the checkbutton widget include

-variable *varName*          The variable defined here will contain the value of this button when the button is selected.

-onvalue *selectValue*       The value to assign to the variable when this button is selected. Defaults to 1.

-offvalue *unselectValue*    The value to assign to the variable when this button is not selected. Defaults to 0.

## Example 9.16

*Script Example*

```
# Update the displayed text in a label

proc updateLabel {myLabel item} {
  global price;
  set total 0
  foreach potion [array names price] {
    incr total $price($potion)
  }
  $myLabel configure -text "Total cost is $total Gold Pieces"
}

# Create and display a label
set l [label .l -text "Select a Potion"]
grid $l -column 0 -row 0 -columnspan 3

# A list of potions and prices

set itemList [list "Cure Light Wounds" 16 "Boldness" 20 \
 "See Invisible" 60 "Love Potion Number 9" 45]

set position 1
foreach {item cost} $itemList {
  checkbutton .b_$position -text $item \
    -variable price($item) -onvalue $cost -offvalue 0 \
    -command "[list updateLabel $l $item]"
```

```
    grid .b_$position -row $position -column 0 -sticky w
    incr position
}
```

*Script Output*

Before selecting          After selecting

| Select a Potion | Total cost is 76 Gold Pieces |
| --- | --- |
| ☐ Cure Light Wounds | ■ Cure Light Wounds |
| ☐ Boldness | ☐ Boldness |
| ☐ See Invisible | ■ See Invisible |
| ☐ Love Potion Number 9 | ☐ Love Potion Number 9 |

## 9.8.2 **Pull-Down Menus: menu, menubutton, and menubars**

The Tk menu command creates the ubiquitous pull-down menu that we have all become so fond of. A Tk menu is an invisible holder widget that can be attached to a menubutton widget or used as a window's menubar. The menubutton is similar to the button widget, described in Section 9.6. The differences include the following:

- The default relief for a menubutton is flat, whereas a button is raised.
- A menubutton can be attached to a menu instead of a script.

Most of the examples that follow will use the -relief raised option to make the menubutton obvious.

*Syntax:* menubutton *buttonName* *?options?*

Create a menubutton widget.

*buttonName*    The name for this menubutton.

*?options?*    The menubutton supports many options. Some of the more useful are

-text *displayText*    The text to display on this button.

-textvariable *varName*    The variable that contains the text to be displayed.

-underline *charPosition*    Selects a position for a hot key.

-menu *menuName*    The name of the menu widget associated with this menubutton.

The -text and -textvariable options can be used to control the text displayed on a button. If a -textvariable option is declared, the button will display the content of that variable. If both a -text and -textvariable are defined, the -textvariable variable will be initialized to the argument of the -text option.

The -underline option lets you define a hot key to select a menu item. The argument to the -underline option is the position of a character in the displayed text. The character at that position will be underlined. If that character and the Alt key are pressed simultaneously, the menubutton will be selected. A menu widget is an invisible container widget that holds the menu entries to be displayed.

**Syntax:** menu *menuName* *?options?*

Create a menu widget.

*menuName*    The name for this menu widget. Note that this name must be a child name to the parent menubutton. For example, if the menubutton is .foo.bar, the menu name must resemble .foo.bar.baz.

*?options?*    The menu widget supports several options. A couple that are unique to this widget are

| | |
|---|---|
| -postcommand *script* | A script to evaluate just before a menu is posted. |
| -tearoff *boolean* | Allows (or disallows) a menu to be removed from the menubutton and displayed in a permanent window. This is enabled by default. |

Once a menu widget has been created, it can be manipulated via several widget subcommands. Those that will be used in these examples are as follows.

**Syntax:** *menuName* add *type* *?options?*

Add a new menu entry to a menu.

*type*    The type for this entry. May be one of

| | |
|---|---|
| separator | A line that separates one set of menu entries from another. |
| cascade | Defines this entry as one that has another menu associated with it, to provide cascading menus. |
| checkbutton | Same as the stand-alone checkbutton widget. |
| radiobutton | Same as the stand-alone radiobutton widget. |
| command | Same as the stand-alone button widget. |

*?options?*   A few of the options that will be used in the examples are

-command *script*
> A script to evaluate when this entry is selected.

-accelerator *string*
> Displays the string to the right of the menu entry as an accelerator. This action must be bound to an event. Binding is covered in Chapter 10.

-label *string*
> The text to display in this menu entry.

-menu *menuName*
> The menu associated with a cascade-type menu element. Valid only for cascading menus.

-variable *varName*
> A variable to be set when this entry is selected.

-value *string*
> The value to set in the associated variable.

-underline *position*
> The position of the character in the text for this menu item to underline and bind for action with this menu entry. This is equivalent to the -underline option the menubutton supports.

## Example 9.17

***Script Example***

```
# Create a "Settings" menubutton
menubutton .mb -menu .mb.mnu -text "Settings" \
  -relief raised -background gray70
menu .mb.mnu

# Add font selectors
.mb.mnu add radiobutton -label "Large Font" \
    -variable font -value {Times 18 bold}

.mb.mnu add radiobutton -label "Small Font" \
    -variable font -value {Times 8 normal}

pack .mb
```

***Script Output***

Alternatively, the command *menuName* insert can be used to insert items into a menu. This command supports the same options as the add command. The insert command allows your script to define the position to insert this entry before. The insert and delete commands require an *index* option. An index may be specified in one of the following forms.

| | |
|---|---|
| *number* | The position of the item in the menu. Zero is the topmost entry in the menu. |
| end or last | The bottom entry in the menu. If the menu has no entry, this is the same as none. |
| active | The entry currently active (selected). If no entry is selected, this is the same as none. |
| @number | The entry that contains (or is closest to) the Y coordinate defined by number. |
| *pattern* | The first entry with a label that matches the glob-style pattern. |

**Syntax:** *menuName* insert *index* *type* *?options?*

Insert a new entry before position *index*.

| | |
|---|---|
| *index* | The position to insert this entry before. |
| *type* | Type of menu item to insert. As described for add. |
| *?options?* | Options for this menu item. As described for add. |

In the following example, the Open selection will always be the first menu entry, and Exit will always be last.

## Example 9.18

### Script Example

```
# Create a "Files" menu
menubutton .mb -menu .mb.mnu -text "Files" \
  -relief raised -background gray70
menu .mb.mnu

# Insert open and exit as first and last
# selections

.mb.mnu insert 0 command -label "Open" \
  -command openFile
#... Other menu entries...

.mb.mnu insert end command -label "Exit" \
  -command quitTask

pack .mb
```

*Script Output*

---

*Syntax:* *menuName* delete *index1 index2*

Delete menu entries.

    *index1 index2*   Delete the entries between the numeric indices index1 and index2, inclusive.

## Example 9.19

*Script Example*

```
menubutton .mb -menu .mb.mnu -text "Files" \
    -relief raised -background gray70

menu .mb.mnu

.mb.mnu insert 0 command -label "Open" \
    -command openFile

.mb.mnu add separator

.mb.mnu add command -label "Save" \
    -command saveData
.mb.mnu add command -label "SaveAs" \
    -command saveDataAs

pack .mb
# ... In file open code.

# Check write permission on file. If not
# writable, set 'permission' to 0, else 1.
# ...

# Remove save option if no write permission
if {!$permission} {
    .mb.mnu delete Save
}
```

### Script Output

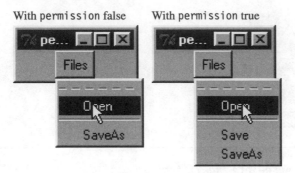

With permission false    With permission true

Tcl also provides support for retrieving the index of a menu entry based on an index pattern.

---

**Syntax:** *menuName* index *pattern*

> Return the numeric index of the menu entry with the label *string*.
>
> *pattern*   An index pattern, as described previously.

## Example 9.20

### Script Example

```
menubutton .mb -menu .mb.mnu -text "Files" \
    -relief raised
menu .mb.mnu

.mb.mnu add command -label Open
.mb.mnu add separator
foreach {label cmd} {Save saveCmd AutoSave autoSaveCmd \
    SaveAs saveAsCmd} {
.mb.mnu add command -label $label -command $cmd
}
.mb.mnu add separator
.mb.mnu add command -label Exit

# ... much code.

# If running in demo mode, remove "Save" menu items

if {$demo} {
  set first [.mb.mnu index Save]
  # Delete the first separator as well
  incr first -1
```

```
    set last [.mb.mnu index SaveAs]
    .mb.mnu delete $first $last
}

pack .mb
```

### Script Output

With demo true          With demo false

The following example shows how the various menus are created and how they look. In actual fact, you cannot pull down all menus at once. You can, however, use the tear-off strip (select the dotted line at the top of the menus) to create a new window and have multiple windows displayed.

## Example 9.21

### Script Example

```
# -------------------------------------------------------------
# Create a checkbutton menu - Place it on the left

set checkButtonMenu [menubutton .mcheck \
  -text "checkbuttons" -menu .mcheck.mnu]
set checkMenu [menu $checkButtonMenu.mnu]
grid $checkButtonMenu -row 0 -column 0
$checkMenu add checkbutton -label "check 1" \
  -variable checkButton(1) -onvalue 1
$checkMenu add checkbutton -label "check 2" \
  -variable checkButton(2) -onvalue 2

# -------------------------------------------------------------
# Create a radiobutton menu - Place it in the middle
set radioButtonMenu [menubutton .mradio \
  -text "radiobuttons" -menu .mradio.mnu]
set radioMenu [menu $radioButtonMenu.mnu]
grid $radioButtonMenu -row 0 -column 1
```

```
$radioMenu add radiobutton -label "radio 1" \
  -variable radioButton -value 1
$radioMenu add radiobutton -label "radio 2" \
  -variable radioButton -value 2

# ------------------------------------------------------------
# Create a menu of mixed check, radio, command, cascading, and
# menu separators

set mixButtonMenu [menubutton .mmix -text "mixedbuttons" \
  -menu .mmix.mnu]
set mixMenu [menu $mixButtonMenu.mnu]
grid $mixButtonMenu -row 0 -column 2

#------------------------------------
# Two command menu entries

$mixMenu add command -label "command 1" -command "doStuff 1"
$mixMenu add command -label "command 2" -command "doStuff 2"

#------------------------------------
# A separator and two radiobutton menu entries

$mixMenu add separator
$mixMenu add radiobutton -label "radio 3" \
  -variable radioButton -value 3
$mixMenu add radiobutton -label "radio 4" \
  -variable radioButton -value 4

#------------------------------------
# A separator and two checkbutton menu entries

$mixMenu add separator
$mixMenu add checkbutton -label "check 3" \
  -variable checkButton(3) -onvalue 3
$mixMenu add checkbutton -label "check 4" \
  -variable checkButton(4) -onvalue 4

#------------------------------------
# A separator, a cascading menu, and two submenus
# within the cascading menu

$mixMenu add separator
$mixMenu add cascade -label "cascader" \
  -menu $mixMenu.cascade
menu $mixMenu.cascade
$mixMenu.cascade add command -label "Cascaded 1"\
  -command "doStuff 3"
```

```
$mixMenu.cascade add command -label "Cascaded 2"\
  -command "doStuff 3"

# Define a dummy proc for the command buttons to invoke.

proc doStuff {args} {
  puts "doStuff called with: $args"
}
```

### Script Output

Select checkbuttons

Select radiobuttons

Select mixedbuttons

Note that the radio buttons in Example 9.21 all share the variable radioButton, even though they are in separate menus. Selecting a radio item from the mixedbuttons window deselects an item selected in the radiobuttons menu.

### Menubars

A menu widget can be attached to a menubutton (as shown previously), designated as the menubar in a top-level window (such as the main window), or designated as a window created with the toplevel command (discussed in Section 9.11). The -menu option will designate a menu as a window's menubar.

A menubar will be displayed and implemented in a platform-specific manner. For example, when the script is evaluated on a Macintosh, the menubar of the window with focus will be displayed as the main screen menu. On an MS Windows or X Window platform, the menubar will be displayed at the top of the window that owns the menubar.

### Example 9.22

```
# Add a menubar to the main window
. configure -menu .menubar
# Create a new top-level window with a menubar
toplevel .top -menu .top.mnu
```

Once a menubar has been created, new menu items can be added as with normal menus.

### Example 9.23

#### Script Example

```
. configure -menu .mbar

# Create the new menu
menu .mbar

.mbar add cascade -label Files -menu .mbar.files
menu .mbar.files
.mbar.files add command -label Open -command "openFile"

.mbar add cascade -label Help -menu .mbar.help
menu .mbar.help
.mbar.help add command -label About -command "displayAbout"

.mbar add cascade -label Settings -menu .mbar.set
menu .mbar.set
.mbar.set add command -label Fonts -command "setFont"

.mbar add cascade -label System -menu .mbar.system
menu .mbar.system
.mbar.system add command -label "Windows System"
```

```
.mbar add cascade -label Apple -menu .mbar.apple
menu .mbar.apple
.mbar.apple add command -label "Apple Menu"

.mbar add command -label Run -command "go"
```

**Script Output**

| Files | Settings | System | Apple | Run | | Help |

Note that the Help menu is on the far right, even though it was the second menu added. Tcl supports some special naming conventions to access platform-specific conventions. The previous example was run on a Linux platform, so the .bar.help menu follows the X Window convention of placing Help on the far right.

| Name | Platform | Description |
|---|---|---|
| .menubar.system | MS Windows | Adds items to the System menu. |
| .menubar.help | X Window | Will make a right-justified Help menu. |
| .menubar.help | Macintosh | Will add entries to the Apple Help menu. |
| .menubar.apple | Macintosh | Items added to this menu will be the first items on the Apple menu. |

When the previous example is run on an MS Windows or Macintosh system, the special menus will be displayed, as shown in the following illustration. Note the (Tear-off) items in these menus. On X Window–based systems, a menu can be turned into a top-level window by clicking the top (dotted) line. This line is referred to as the "tear-off" line. You can inhibit creating this menu entry by creating the menu with the -tearoff 0 option.

Macintosh; Apple Menu added to top of special menu

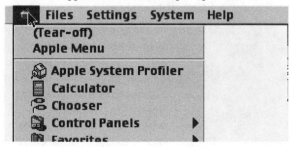

MS Windows; Microsoft System added to bottom of special menu

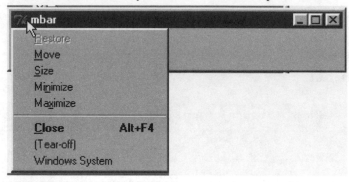

### 9.8.3 **Selection widgets: listbox**

The listbox widget allows the user to select items from a list of items. The listbox widget can be configured to select one entry (similar to a radiobutton) or multiple entries, similar to a check button.

The listbox can be queried to return the positions of the selected items. This can be used to index into a list or array of information, or the listbox can be queried about the text displayed at that position.

| | |
|---|---|
| ***Syntax:*** | listbox *listboxName ?options?* |
| | Create a listbox widget. |
| *listboxName* | The name for this listbox. |
| *?options?* | The listbox widget supports several options. Three useful options are |

-selectmode *style*

Sets the selection style for this listbox. The default mode is browse. This option may be set to one of

single     Allows only a single entry to be selected. Whenever an entry is clicked, it is selected, and other selected entries are deselected.

browse     Allows only a single entry to be selected. Whenever an entry is clicked, it is selected, and other selected entries are deselected. When the cursor is dragged across entries with the left mouse button depressed, each entry will be selected when the cursor crosses onto it and deselected when the cursor passes off.

multiple Allows multiple entries to be selected. An entry is selected by clicking it (if not already selected). A selected entry can be deselected by clicking it.

extended Allows a single entry to be selected, or multiple contiguous entries to be selected by dragging the cursor over the entries.

-exportselection *bool*

If this is set true, the content of the listbox will be exported for other X11 tasks, and only a single listbox selection may be made. If you wish to use multiple list-box widgets with different selections, set this option to FALSE. This defaults to TRUE.

-height *numLines*

The height of this listbox in lines.

When a listbox widget is created, it is empty. The listbox widget supports several commands for manipulating listbox content. The following are used in the chapters that follow.

**Syntax:** *listboxName* insert *index element ?elements?*

Inserts a new element into a listbox.

*index* The position to insert this entry before. The word end causes this entry to be added after the last entry in the list.

*element* A text string to be displayed in that position. This must be a single line. Embedded newline characters are printed as backslash-N, instead of generating a new line.

## Example 9.24

### Script Example

```
# Create and display an empty listbox
listbox .l
pack .l

# Add 3 elements to the listbox
# Note - insert at position 0 makes the display order the
#   opposite of the insertion order.

.l insert 0 first
.l insert 0 second
.l insert 0 third
```

*Script Output*

---

**Syntax:** `listboxName` delete `first ?last?`

Delete entries from a `listbox`.

`first`   The first entry to delete. If there is no `last` entry, only this entry will be deleted.

`last`   The last entry to delete. Ranges are deleted inclusively.

## Example 9.25

*Script Example*

```
# Create and display an empty listbox
listbox .l
pack .l

# Add 3 elements to the listbox
# Note - insert at end position - order is as expected

.l insert end first
.l insert end second
.l insert end third

# Delete the second listbox entry (count from 0)

.l delete 1
```

*Script Output*

---

**Syntax:** `listboxName` curselection

Returns a list of the indices of the currently selected items in the `listbox`.

## Example 9.26

*Script Example*

```
# Create and display an empty listbox
listbox .l
pack .l

# Add 3 elements to the listbox
# Note - insert at end position - order is as expected

.l insert end first
.l insert end second
.l insert end third

### User selects second item
puts "Selected: [.l curselection]"
```

*Script Output*

**Selected: 1**

---

*Syntax:* *listboxName* get *first ?last?*

Returns a list of the text displayed in the range of entries identified by the indices.

*first*　The first entry to return.

*last*　The last entry to return. If this is not included, only the first entry is returned. The range returned is inclusive.

## Example 9.27

*Script Example*

```
# Create and display an empty listbox
listbox .l
pack .l

# Add 3 elements to the listbox
# Note - insert at end position - order is as expected

.l insert end first
.l insert end second
.l insert end third
```

```
### User selects second item
puts "Selected Text: [.l get [.l curselection]]"
```

*Script Output*

**Selected Text: second**

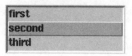

In the next example, some selections were made before the graphic and report were created.

## Example 9.28

*Script Example*

```
# Create the left listbox, defined to allow only a single
# selection

listbox .lSingle -selectmode single -exportselection no

grid .lSingle -row 1 -column 0
.lSingle insert end "top" "middle" "bottom"
# Create the right listbox, defined to allow multiple items
# to be selected.

listbox .lMulti -selectmode multiple -exportselection no

grid .lMulti -row 1 -column 1
.lMulti insert end "MultiTop" "MultiMiddle" "MultiEnd"

# Create a button to report what's been selected

button .report -text "Report" -command "report"
grid .report -row 0 -column 0 -columnspan 2

# And a procedure to loop through the listboxes,
#    and display the selected values.

proc report {} {
  foreach widget [list .lSingle .lMulti] {
    set selected [$widget curselection]
    foreach index $selected {
      set str [$widget get $index]
```

```
            puts "$widget has index $index selected - $str"
        }
    }
}
```

*Script Output*

```
.1Single has index 1 selected - middle
.1Multi has index 0 selected - MultiTop
.1Multi has index 2 selected - MultiEnd
```

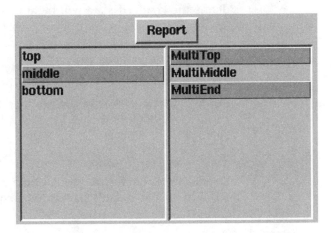

## 9.9 Scrollbar

Since the listbox does not allow variables or commands to be associated with its selections, it seems less useful than the button or menu widgets. The listbox becomes important when you need to display a large number of selection values and you connect the listbox with a scrollbar widget.

### 9.9.1 The Basic scrollbar

The scrollbar widget allows you to show a portion of a widget's information by using a bar with arrows at each end and a slider in the middle. To change the information displayed, a user clicks the arrows or bar or drags the slider. At this point, the scrollbar informs the associated widget of the change. The associated widget is responsible for displaying the appropriate portion of its data to reflect that change.

*Syntax:* `scrollbar` *scrollbarName ?options?*

Create a `scrollbar` widget.

*scrollbarName*The name for this `scrollbar`.

*options*  This widget supports several options.

-*command "cmdName ?args?"*

This defines the command to invoke when the state of the `scrollbar` changes. Arguments that define the changed state will be appended to the arguments defined in this option. Most commonly, the *cmdName* argument is the name of the widget this `scrollbar` will interact with.

-*orient direction*

Defines the orientation for the scrollbar. The *direction* may be `horizontal` or `vertical`. Defaults to `vertical`.

*troughcolor color*

Defines the color for the trough below the slider. Defaults to the default background color of the frames.

A `scrollbar` interacts with another widget by invoking the defined command whenever the state of the `scrollbar` changes. The widgets that support scrolling (`listbox`, `text`, and `canvas`) have subcommands defined to allow them to be scrolled. The commands that control the behavior of the scrollable widget and the scrollbar are discussed in more detail later in this chapter.

The options that must be used to make a widget scrollable are -`xscrollcommand` and/or -`yscrollcommand`. These are the equivalent of the scrollbar's -`command` option.

*Syntax:* *widgetName* -`xscrollcommand` *script*

*Syntax:* *widgetName* -`yscrollcommand` *script*

Defines the script to be evaluated when the widget view shifts, so that the scrollbar may reflect the state of the scrollable widget. Information about the change will be appended to this script.

In the next example, the command to create the scrollbar includes the following option:

`-command {.box yview}.`

This registers the script {.box yview} with the scrollbar. When the scrollbar changes state (someone moves the slider, clicks the bar, and so on), the scrollbar will append information about the change to that script and evaluate it. The listbox, canvas, and text widgets each support a yview subcommand that understands the arguments the scrollbar will append.

The command to create the listbox includes the following option:

```
-yscrollcommand ".scroll set".
```

This registers the script .scroll set with the listbox. When the listbox changes state (for example, when lines are added or deleted), this information will be appended to that script, and the script will then be evaluated. The scrollbar supports a set subcommand to be invoked by this script.

Note the -fill y option to the pack command. This informs the pack layout manager that this widget should expand to fill the available space and that it should expand in the Y direction. Without this option, the scrollbar would consist of two arrows with a 1-pixel-tall bar, to use the minimal space.

The equivalent grid option is -sticky ns, to tell the grid layout manager that the ends of the widget should stick to top and bottom of the frame. The following example shows a scrollbar connected with a listbox.

## Example 9.29

### *Script Example*
```
# Create the scrollbar and listbox.

scrollbar .scroll -command ".box yview"
listbox .box -height 4 -yscrollcommand ".scroll set"
# Pack them onto the screen - note expand and fill options

pack .box -side left
pack .scroll -side right -fill y
# Fill the listbox.

.box insert end 0 1 2 3 4 5 6 7 8 9 10
```

### *Script Output*

## 9.9.2 `scrollbar` Details

In normal use, the programmer can just set the `-command` option in the scrollbar and the `-yscrollcommand` or `-xscrollcommand` in the widget the scrollbar is controlling, and everything will work as expected. For some applications, though, you need to understand the details of how the scrollbar works. The following is the sequence of events that occurs when a scrollbar is clicked.

1. The user clicks an arrow or bar or drags a slider.
2. The scrollbar concatenates the registered script (`.box yview`) and information about the change (`moveto .2`) to create a new script to evaluate (`.box yview moveto .2`).
3. The scrollbar evaluates the new script.
4. The widget changes its displayed area to reflect the change.
5. The widget concatenates its registered script and information that describes how it changed to create a new script (`.scroll set .2 .5`).
6. The widget evaluates that script to reconfigure the scrollbar to match the widget.

The information the scrollbar appends to the script will be in one of the formats outlined in the following table.

| Command Subset | Description | Action |
|---|---|---|
| `scroll ?-?1 unit` | Scroll the displayed widget by one of the smallest units (a line for a listbox or text widget, or a single pixel for a canvas). | Click an arrow. |
| `scroll ?-?1 page` | Scroll the displayed widget by the displayed area. For example, if four lines of a listbox are displayed, the listbox would scroll by four lines. | Click the bar. |
| `moveto` *fraction* | Set the top of the displayed area to start at the requested percentage. For example, in a 100-line listbox, `.box yview moveto .2` would start the display with line 20. | Drag the slider. |

In the preceding example, when the scrollbar is manipulated, a command of the form

```
.box yview scroll 1 unit
```

or

```
.box yview moveto .25
```

would be created by the `scrollbar` widget and then evaluated. The scrollbar's `set` command will modify the size and location of the scrollbar's slider.

*Syntax:* *scrollbarName* set *first last*

Sets the size and location of the slider.

*first*    A fraction representing the beginning of the displayed data in the associated widget (e.g., 0.25) informs the scrollbar that the associated widget starts displaying data at that point (e.g., the 25% point). The scrollbar will place the starting edge of the slider one-fourth of the way down the bar.

*end*    A fraction representing the end of the displayed data in the associated widget (e.g., 0.75) informs the scrollbar that the associated widget stops displaying data at that point (e.g., the 75% point). The scrollbar will place the ending edge of the slider three-fourths of the way down the bar.

## Example 9.30

### Script Example

```
# Create and grid a scrollbar with no -command option

scrollbar .sb
grid .sb -row 0 -column 0 -sticky ns

# Create and grid a listbox (to fill space and expand the
#       scrollbar)

listbox .lb
grid .lb -row 0 -column 1

# The scrollbar slider will start at the 1/3 position,
#  and stop at the 9/10 position.

.sb set .3 .9
```

### Script Output

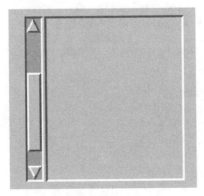

A script can also query a scrollbar to learn the positions of the slider with the get subcommand.

**Syntax:** *scrollbarName* get

Returns the current state of the widget. This will be the result of the most recent set command.

## Example 9.31

*Script Example*

```
scrollbar .sb
.sb set .3 .8
puts "Start and end fractions are: [.sb get]"
```

*Script Output*

```
Start and end fractions are: 0.3 0.8
```

---

## 9.9.3 Intercepting scrollbar Commands

The next example shows how you can use this knowledge about how the scrollbar works to use a single scrollbar to control two listbox widgets. This example uses a previously unmentioned subcommand of the listbox widget.

**Syntax:** *listboxName* size

Returns the number of entries in a listbox.

## Example 9.32

*Script Example*

```
# Create two listboxes

listbox .leftbox -height 5 -exportselection 0
listbox .rightbox -height 5 -exportselection 0

# And fill them. The right box has twice as many entries as
# the left.

for {set i 0} {$i < 10} {incr i} {
  .leftbox insert end "Left Line $i"
  .rightbox insert end "Right Line $i"
  .rightbox insert end "Next Right $i"
}

# Display the listboxes.

grid .leftbox -column 0 -row 0
grid .rightbox -column 2 -row 0
```

```
# Create the scrollbar, set the initial slider size, and
# display

scrollbar .scroll -command \
  "moveLists .scroll .leftbox .rightbox"

# The right listbox is displaying 5 of 20 lines
.scroll set 0 [expr 5.0 / 20.0]

grid .scroll -column 1 -row 0 -sticky ns

##########################################################
# proc moveLists {scrollbar listbox1 listbox2 args}--
#  Controls two listboxes from a single scrollbar
#  Shifts the top displayed entry and slider such that both
#  listboxes start and end together. The list with the most
#  entries will scroll faster.
#
# Arguments
# scrollbar The name of the scrollbar
# listbox1 The name of one listbox
# listbox2 The name of the other listbox
# args The arguments appended by the scrollbar widget
#
# Results
#  No valid return.
#  Resets displayed positions of listboxes.
#  Resets size and location of scrollbar slider.

proc moveLists {scrollbar listbox1 listbox2 args} {

   # Get the height for the listboxes - assume both are the same.

   set height [$listbox2 cget -height]

   # Get the count of entries in each box.

   set size1 [$listbox1 size]
   set size2 [$listbox2 size]

   if {$size1 > $size2} {
      set size ${size1}.0
   } else {
      set size ${size2}.0
   }

   # Get the current scrollbar location

   set scrollPosition [$scrollbar get]
   set startFract [lindex $scrollPosition 0]
```

```
# Calculate the top displayed entry for each listbox

set top1 [expr int($size1 * $startFract)]
set top2 [expr int($size2 * $startFract)]

# Parse the arguments added by the scrollbar widget

set cmdlst [split $args]

switch [lindex $cmdlst 0] {

"scroll" {

  # Parse count and unit from cmdlst
  foreach {sc count unit} $cmdlst {}

  # Determine whether the arrow or the bar was
  # clicked (is the command "scroll 1 unit"
  # or "scroll 1 page")

  if {[string first units $unit] >= 0} {
  # set increment [expr 1 * $count];
  } else {
    set increment [expr $height * $count];
  }

  # Set the new fraction for the top of the list

  set topFract1 [expr ($top1 + $increment)/$size]
  set topFract2 [expr ($top2 + $increment)/$size]
  if {$topFract1 < 0} {set topFract1 0}
  if {$topFract2 < 0} {set topFract2 0}

}

"moveto" {
  # Get the fraction of the list to display as top

  set topFract [lindex $cmdlst 1]
  if {$topFract < 0} {set topFract 0}

  # Scale the display to the number of entries in
  #  the listbox

  set topFract1 [expr $topFract * ($size1/$size)]
  set topFract2 [expr $topFract * ($size2/$size)]
  }
}

# Move the listboxes to their new location

$listbox1 yview moveto $topFract1
$listbox2 yview moveto $topFract2
```

```
    # Reposition the scrollbar slider

    set topFract [expr ($topFract1 > $topFract2) ? \
      $topFract1 : $topFract2 ]

    if {$topFract > (1.0 - ($height-1)/$size)} {
      set topFract [expr (1.0 - ($height-1)/$size)]
    }
    set bottomFract [expr $topFract + (($height-1)/$size)]

    $scrollbar set $topFract $bottomFract
}
```

***Script Output***

```
Left Line 2      △   Right Line 4
Left Line 3          Next Right 4
Left Line 4      □   Right Line 5
Left Line 5          Next Right 5
Left Line 6      ▽   Right Line 6
```

Note the calls to yview in the previous example. The yview and xview subcommands set the start location for the data in a listbox. The first argument ( scroll or moveto ) is used to determine how to interpret the other arguments.

When a scrollbar and a listbox are connected in the usual manner, with a line resembling

```
scrollbar .scroll -command ".box yview"
```

the scrollbar widget will append arguments describing how to modify the data to the arguments supplied in the -command argument, and the new string will be evaluated. The arguments appended will start with either the word scroll or the word moveto. For example, if an arrow were clicked in scrollbar .scroll, the command evaluated would be

```
.box yview scroll 1 unit
```

The .box procedure would parse the first argument ( yview) and evaluate the yview procedure. The yview code would parse the argument scroll 1 unit to determine how the listbox should be modified to reflect scrolling one unit down.

In the previous example, the slider does not behave exactly as described for the default scrollbar procedures. Because we are scrolling lists of two different sizes, the slider size is set to reflect the fraction of data displayed from the larger listbox. The position of the slider reflects the center of the displayed data, rather than the start point. By changing the parameters to $scrollbar set, you can modify that behavior. For instance, you could position the slider to reflect the condition of one `listbox` and treat the other listbox as a slave.

## 9.10 The `scale` Widget

The `scale` widget allows a user to select a numeric value from within a given range. It creates a bar with a slider, similar to the `scrollbar` widget, but without arrows at the ends. When the user moves the slider, the `scale` widget can either evaluate a procedure with the new slider location as an argument or set a defined variable to the new value, or perform both actions.

*Syntax:*  scale *scaleName* *?options?*

Create a `scale` widget.

*scaleName*  The name for this `scale` widget.

*?options?*  There are many options for this widget. The minimal set is

-orient *orientation*  Whether the scale should be drawn horizontally or vertically. *orientation* may be horizontal or vertical. The default orientation is vertical.

-length *numPixels*  The size of this scale. The height for vertical widgets and the width for horizontal widgets. The *height* may be in any valid distance value (as described in Section 9.2.3).

-from *number*  One end of the range to display. This value will be displayed on the left side (for horizontal `scale` widgets) or top (for vertical `scale` widgets).

-to *number*  The other end for the range.

-label *text*  The label to display with this `scale`.

-command *script*  The command to evaluate when the state changes. The new value of the slider will be appended to this string, and the resulting string will be evaluated.

-variable *varName*  A variable that will contain the current value of the slider.

-resolution *number*  The resolution to use for the scale and slider. Defaults to 1.

-tickinterval *number*  The resolution to use for the scale. This does not affect the values returned when the slider is moved.

The next example shows two scale widgets being used to display temperatures in Celsius and Fahrenheit scales. You can move either slider and the other slider will change to display the equivalent temperature in the other scale.

**Example** 9.33

*Script Example*

```
# Convert the Celsius temperature to Fahrenheit

proc celsiusTofahren {ctemp} {
  global fahrenheit
  set fahrenheit [expr ($ctemp*1.8) + 32]
}

# Convert the Fahrenheit temperature to Celsius

proc fahrenToCelsius {ftemp} {
  global celsius
  set celsius [expr ($ftemp-32)/1.8]
}

# Create a scale for fahrenheit temperatures

set fahrenscale [scale .fht -orient horizontal \
  -from 0 -to 100 -length 250 \
  -resolution .1 -tickinterval 20 -label "Fahrenheit" \
  -variable fahrenheit -command fahrenToCelsius]

# Create a scale for celsius temperatures

set celscale [scale .cel -orient horizontal \
  -from -20 -to 40 -length 250 \
  -resolution .1 -tickinterval 20 -label "Celsius" \
  -variable celsius -command celsiusTofahren]

# Pack the widgets
pack $fahrenscale -side top
pack $celscale -side top
```

*Script Output*

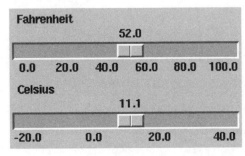

## 9.11 New Windows

When the wish interpreter is initialized, it creates a top-level graphics window. This window will be drawn with whatever decorations your display system provides and will expand to fit whatever other widgets are placed within it. If you find you need another, separate window, one can be created with the toplevel command.

*Syntax:* toplevel *windowName ?options?*

Creates a new top-level window.

| | |
|---|---|
| *windowName* | The name for the window to create. The name must start with a period and conform to the widget naming conventions described in Section 9.2.1. |
| *?options?* | Valid options for the toplevel widget include |

| | |
|---|---|
| -relief *value* | Sets the relief for this window. The value may be raised, sunken, ridge, or flat. The default is flat. |
| -borderwidth *size* | Sets a border to be size wide if the -relief option is not flat. The size parameter can be any dimensional value, as described in Section 9.2.3. |
| -background *color* | The base color for this widget. The color may be any color value, as described in Section 9.2.2. |
| -height | The requested height of this window, in units as described in Section 9.2.3. |
| -width | The requested width of this window, in units as described in Section 9.2.3. |

**Example** 9.34

*Script Example*

```
# Create a label in the original window

label .l -text "I'm in the original window"

# Create a new window, and a label for it

toplevel .otherTopLevel
label .otherTopLevel.l -text "I'm in the other window"
```

```
# Display the labels.

pack .l
pack .otherTopLevel.l
```

***Script Output***

Original window                        New top-level window

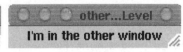

By default, the window name is shown in the top window decoration. This can be modified with the wm title command. For example, wm title."My Application" will change the name in a main application window. The wm command gives the Tk programmer access to the services provided by the window manager. These services vary slightly between window managers and operating systems. You should read the on-line documentation for the subcommands supported by the wm command.

## 9.12 Interacting with the Event Loop

The Tk event loop is processed whenever the interpreter is not evaluating a command or procedure. It is best to write your code to spend as little time as possible within procedures. However, some tasks just plain take a while, and you may need to schedule passes through the event loop while your procedure is running.

A classic error in event-driven GUI programming is to place a command that modifies the display inside a loop but not to force the display to update. (For example, a loop that performs some lengthy calculation might update a completion bar.) If the event loop is not entered, only the final graphic command will be evaluated. The loop will run to completion without modifying the display, and then, suddenly, the display will show the completed image. You can force the Tcl interpreter to evaluate the event loop with the update command.

***Syntax:*** update *?idletasks?*

Process the event loop until all pending events have been processed.

*idletasks*    Do not process user events or errors. Process only pending internal requests, such as updating the display.

The next example shows a simple loop to put characters into a label. Without the update in the loop, the task would pause for several seconds and then display the complete string. The update command causes the characters to be displayed one at a time.

**Example** 9.35

*Script Example*

```
# Create the label.

label .l -text "" -width 25
pack .l

# Assign some text.

set str "Tcl makes programming Fun"

# And add new text to the label one character at a time.

for {set i 1} {$i < [string length $str]} {incr i} {
  .l configure -text [string range $str 0 $i]
  update

  # Mark time for a second or so.
  #  (Better delay technique described in the next section)

  for {set j 0} {$j < 1000} {incr j} {
     set x [expr $j.0*2]
  }
}
```

*Script Output*

Starting                    Middle                          End

| Tcl mak | Tcl makes programming | Tcl makes programming Fun |

---

# 9.13 Scheduling the Future: after

The previous example uses a busy loop to cause the script to pause between inserting characters into the label. This is a pretty silly waste of CPU time, and Tcl provides a better way to handle this. The after command will perform one of three tasks:

- If invoked with a single numeric argument, it will pause for that many milliseconds.

- If invoked with a numeric argument and a script, it will schedule that script to be run the requested number of milliseconds in the future and continue processing the current script.

- If invoked with a subcommand, it provides facilities to examine and cancel items from the list of scheduled tasks.

***Syntax:*** after *milliseconds* *?script?*

***Syntax:*** after *subcommand option*

Pause processing of the current script, schedule a script to be processed in the future, or manipulate the scheduled queue.

*milliseconds*    The number of milliseconds to pause the current processing, or the number of seconds in the future to evaluate another script.

*script*    If this argument is defined, this script will be evaluated after *milliseconds* time has elapsed. The after command will return a unique key to identify this event.

*subcommand*    If the second argument is a subcommand name, that subcommand is evaluated. Some of these are discussed in the next section.

The next example shows the after command being used instead of the busy loop. Then it shows events being scheduled in the future to remove the characters from the label.

## Example 9.36

***Script Example***

```
# Create the label.

label .l -text "" -width 40
pack .l

# Assign some text.

set str "Tcl makes programming Fun"

# And add new text to the label one character at a time.

for {set i 1} {$i < [string length $str]} {incr i} {
  .l configure -text [string range $str 0 $i]
  update
  after 1000
}

###########################################################

# proc shortenText {widget}--
#    Remove the first character from the displayed string of a
#    widget
# Arguments
#    widget The name of a widget with a -text option
```

```
#
# Results
# Removes the first character from the text string of the
# provided widget if one exists.
#
# Schedules itself to run again if the -text string wasn't
# empty.

proc shortenText {widget} {
  # Get the current text string from the widget

  set txt [$widget cget -text]

  # If it's empty, we're done.

  if {$txt == ""} {
    return;
  }

  # shorten the string

  set txt [string range $txt 1 end]

  # Update the widget

  $widget configure -text $txt
  # And schedule this procedure to be run again in 1 second.

  after 1000 shortenText $widget
}

shortenText .l
```

### Script Output

Starting fill

| Tcl makes |
|---|

Middle fill

| Tcl makes programmi |
|---|

Starting empty

| kes programming Fun |
|---|

Middle empty

| ing Fun |
|---|

---

The first loop (filling the widget) is the type of process that occurs immediately to programmers who are used to working in nonevent-driven paradigms. The style of programming demonstrated by the shortenText procedure's use of the after command is less intuitive but more versatile.

In the first style, the event loop is checked only once per second. If there were an ABORT button, there would be a noticeable lag between a button click and the task being aborted. Using the second style, the GUI will respond immediately.

## 9.13.1 **Canceling the Future**

Sometimes, after you have carefully scheduled things, plans change and schedules need to change. When the `after` command is evaluated, it returns a handle for the event that was scheduled. This handle can be used to access this item in the list of scripts scheduled for future evaluation.

*Syntax:* `after cancel` *handle*

Cancel a script that was scheduled to be evaluated.

*handle* The handle for this event that was returned by a previous `after` *milliseconds script* command.

We will use the `after cancel` command in the next chapter.

**Example** 9.37

```
# Schedule the task to exit in 10 seconds
set exitEvent [after 10000 exit]
button .b -text "Click me to cancel exit!" \
  -command "after cancel $exitEvent"
pack .b
```

If your script needs information about events in the `after` queue, you can query the queue with the `after info` command.

*Syntax:* `after info` *?handle?*

Returns information about items in the `after` queue.

*?handle?* If `after info` is invoked with no *handle*, it will return a list of all the handles in the queue. If invoked with a *handle* argument, `after info` will return a list consisting of

1. The script associated with this item.

2. The word `idle` or `timer`. The word `idle` indicates that this script will be evaluated when the idle loop is next run (no other script requires processing), whereas `timer` indicates that the event is waiting for the timer event when the requested number of milliseconds has elapsed.

**Example** 9.38

```
# ... many events added to timer queue

# Delete the exit event from the queue
```

```
foreach id [after info] {
  if {[string first exit [after info $id]] >= 0} {
    after cancel $id
  }
}
}
```

## 9.14 Bottom Line

This chapter has introduced most of the Tk simple widgets. The text widget, canvas widget, and megawidgets (file boxes, color selectors, and so on) are covered in the next three chapters.

- The Tk primitive widgets provide the tools necessary to write GUI-oriented programs with support for buttons, entry widgets, graphics display widgets, scrolling listboxes, menus, and numeric input.

- Widget names must start with a period followed by a lowercase letter. (See Section 9.2.1.)

- Colors can be declared by name, or red/green/blue intensity values. (See Section 9.2.2.)

- Dimensions and sizes can be declared as pixels, inches, millimeters, or points. (See Section 9.2.3.)

- The default widget configuration options are adequate for most uses. Options can be set when the widget is created with -option value pairs, or modified after a widget is created with the *widgetName* configure command.

  ***Syntax:*** *widgetName* configure *?opt1? ?val1?... ?optN? ?valN?*

- The value of a widget's option is returned by the *widgetName* cget command.

  ***Syntax:*** *widgetName* cget *option*

- A label will display a single line of text.

  ***Syntax:*** label *labelName ?option1? ?option2?...*

- A button widget will evaluate a script when it is clicked.

  ***Syntax:*** button *buttonName ?option1? ?option2?...*

- The entry widget will allow the user to enter text.

  ***Syntax:*** entry *entryName ?options?*

- A frame widget can be used to hold other widgets. This makes it easier to design and maintain a GUI.

  ***Syntax:*** frame *frameName ?options?*

- Radio and check buttons let a user select from several options.

  ***Syntax:*** `radiobutton` *radioName* *?options?*

  ***Syntax:*** `checkbutton` *checkName* *?options?*

- A menu contains elements that can be activated or selected. The elements can be commands, radio buttons, check buttons, separators, or cascading menus.

  ***Syntax:*** `menu` *menuName* *?options?*

- A menu can be attached to a `menubutton` or to a window's `menubar`.

  ***Syntax:*** `menubutton` *buttonName* *?options?*

  *$windowname* `configure` `-menu` *$menuName*

- A listbox displays multiple text elements and allows a user to select one or more of these elements.

  ***Syntax:*** `listbox` *listboxName* *?options?*

- A scrollbar can be connected to a `listbox`, `text`, or `canvas` widget.

  ***Syntax:*** `scrollbar` *scrollbarName* *?options?*

- The `scale` widget lets a user select a numeric value from a range of values.

  ***Syntax:*** `scale` *scaleName* *?options?*

- Tk widgets can be arranged on the display using the `place`, `grid`, or `pack` layout manager.

- New independent windows are created with the `toplevel` command.

  ***Syntax:*** `toplevel` *windowName* *?options?*

- The `update` command can be used to force a pass through the event loop during long computations.

- The `after` command can be used to pause an application or to schedule a script for evaluation in the future.

- The `after cancel` command can be used to cancel a script that was scheduled to be evaluated in the future.

## 9.15 Problems

The following numbering convention is used in all Problem sections.

| *Number Range* | *Description of Problems* |
|---|---|
| 100–199 | These problems review the material covered in this chapter. They can be answered in a few words or a short (1–5-line) script. Each problem should take under a minute to answer. |

| *Number Range* | *Description of Problems* |
|---|---|
| 200–299 | These problems go beyond the details presented in this chapter. They may require some analysis of the material or command details not covered in the chapter. They may require reading a man page or making a web search. They can be answered with a few sentences or a 5–50-line script. Each problem should take under 10 minutes to answer. |
| 300–399 | These problems extend the material presented in this chapter. They may require referencing other sources. They can be answered in a few paragraphs or a few hundred lines of code. Each exercise may take a few hours to complete. |

**100.** Which of the following are valid window names? What is the error in the invalid names?

   a. .b

   b. .Button

   c. .button

   d. .b2

   e. .2b

   f. .buttonFrame.b1

   g. .top.buttons.b1-quit

   h. ..button

   i. .b.1-quit

**101.** What conventions does Tcl use to define colors?

**102.** What conventions does Tcl use to define screen distances?

**103.** What option will set the color of the text in a button?

**104.** What is the difference between the return value of

```
$widget cget -foreground
```

and

```
$widget configure -foreground
```

**105.** How many lines of text can be displayed in a `label` widget?

**106.** Can a button's `-command` option contain more than one Tcl command?

**107.** Can you use `place` to display a widget in a frame in which you are also using the `pack` command?

**108.** How many items in a set of `radiobuttons` can be selected simultaneously?

**109.** What types of items can be added to a menu?

**110.** What widgets include scrollbar support by default?

**111.** What is the time unit for the `after` command?

**112.** What command will check for pending events?

**200.** Write a GUI widget with an entry widget, label, and button. When the button is clicked, convert the text in the `entry` widget to pig Latin and display it in the label. The pig Latin rules are as follows:

- Remove the first letter.

- If the first letter is a vowel, append *t* to the end of the word.

- Append the first letter to the end of the word.

- Append the letters *ay* to the end of the word.

**201.** Create a button and command pair in which each time the button is clicked it will change its background color. The text will inform the user of what the next color will be. The color change can be done with a list of colors or by using an associative array as a lookup table.

**202.** Write a data entry GUI that will use separate entry widgets to read First Name, Last Name, and Login ID. When the user clicks the Accept button, the data will be merged into proper location in a listbox. Insert new entries alphabetically by last name. Attach a scrollbar to the listbox.

**203.** Add a Save button to the previous exercise. The command associated with this button will open a file and use Tcl commands to insert data into the listbox. Add a Restore button with a command to clear the listbox and load the data using the `source` command. Information in the Save file will resemble the following:

```
.listbox insert end "Doe, John: john.doe"
.listbox insert end "Flynt, Clif: clif"
```

**204.** Write a busy-bar application that will use a label to add characters to the text in a `label` widget to indicate a procedure's progress.

**205.** Turn Example 6.11 into a GUI application. Add an entry widget to set the starting directory, a button to start searching the directories, a label to show the directory currently being examined, and a scrolling listbox to display the results. The text in the listbox should have leading spaces to denote which files are within previous directories. You may need to create the listbox with `-font {courier}` to display the leading spaces.

**206.** Write a GUI with two sliders and a label. The label will display the result of dividing the value in the first slider by the value in the second slider.

**207.** Write a procedure that will create a pop-up window with an information label, and an OK button that will destroy the pop-up when clicked.

**208.** A top-level window can appear anywhere on the screen. Write a procedure named `frame-toplevel` that will accept as a single argument the name of a frame to create. The procedure should create the frame, place it in the center of the parent window, and return the name of the new frame. Change the `toplevel` command in the previous exercise to `frame-toplevel`. What is different between the two implementations?

**209.** Modify the `frame-toplevel` procedure from the previous exercise to accept an undefined number of arguments (for example, `-background yellow -relief raised -borderwidth 3`) and use those arguments to configure the new frame widget.

**210.** A Pizza object was created in Problem 203, Chapter 8. Make a GUI front end that will allow a user to select a single size or style, and multiple toppings with a Done button to create a new Pizza object.

**211.** Add a button to the result of the previous exercise that will generate a description of all Pizza objects in a scrolled listbox within a new top-level window.

CHAPTER

10

# Using the canvas Widget

Chapter 9 described many of the Tk widgets that support GUI programming. This chapter discusses the canvas widget, Tcl events, interaction with the window manager, and use of the Tcl image object. You will learn how events can be connected to a widget or an item drawn on a canvas and how to use a canvas to build your own GUI widgets.

The canvas is the Tk widget drawing surface. You can draw lines, arrows, rectangles, ovals, text, or random polygons in various colors with various fill styles. You can also insert other Tk windows, or images in X-Bitmap, PPM (Portable Pixmap), PGM (Portable GrayMap), or GIF (Graphical Interface Format) (other formats are supported in various Tk extensions, discussed in Chapter 14). If that is not enough, you can write C code to add new drawing types to the canvas command.

As mentioned in Chapter 9, Tk is event oriented. Whenever a cursor moves or a key is pressed, an event is generated by the windowing system. If the focus for your window manager is on a Tk window, that event is passed to the Tk interpreter, which can then trigger actions connected with graphic items in that window.

The bind command links scripts to the events that occur on graphic items such as widgets or displayed items in a canvas or text widget. Events include mouse motion, button clicks, key presses, and window manager events such as refresh, iconify, and resize. After an examination of the canvas and bind command, you will see how to use them to create a specialized button widget, similar to those in Netscape, IE, and other packages.

## 10.1 Overview of the canvas Widget

Your application may create one or more canvas widgets and map them to the display with any of the layout managers pack, grid, or place. The canvas owns all items drawn on it. These items are maintained in a display list, and their position in that list determines which items will be drawn on top of others. The order in which items are displayed can be modified.

### 10.1.1 Identifiers and Tags

When an item is created on a canvas, a unique numeric identifier is returned for that item. The item can always be identified and manipulated by referencing that unique number. You can also attach a `tag` to an item. A tag is an alphanumeric string that can be used to group canvas items. A single tag can be attached to multiple items, and multiple tags can be attached to a single item.

A set of items that share a tag can be identified as a group by that tag. For example, if you composed a blueprint of a house, you could tag all of the plumbing with `plumbing` and then tag the hot water pipes with `hot`, the cold water pipes with `cold`, and the drains with `drain`. You could highlight all of the plumbing with a command such as the following:

```
$blueprint configure plumbing -outline green
```

You could highlight just the hot water lines with a command such as the following:

```
$blueprint configure hot -outline red
```

The following two tags are defined by default in a canvas widget.

`all`         Identifies all of the drawable items in a canvas

`current`   Identifies the topmost item selected by the cursor

### 10.1.2 Coordinates

The canvas coordinate origin is the upper left-hand corner. Larger Y coordinates move down the screen, and larger X coordinates move to the right. The coordinates can be declared in pixels, inches, millimeters, centimeters, or points (1/72 of an inch), as described for dimensions in Section 9.2.3.

The coordinates are stored internally using floating-point format, which allows a great deal of flexibility for scaling and positioning items. Note that even pixel locations can be fractional.

### 10.1.3 Binding

You can cause a particular script to be evaluated when an event associated with a displayed item occurs. For instance, when the cursor passes over a button, an `<Enter>` event is generated by the window manager. The default action for the enter event is to change the button color to denote the button as active. Some widgets, such as the `button` widget, allow you to set the action for a button click event during widget creation with the -command option. All widgets can have actions linked to events with the bind command, discussed in detail later in the chapter.

The canvas widget takes the concept of binding further and allows you to bind an action to events that occur on each drawable item within the canvas display list. For instance, you can make lines change color when the cursor passes over them, or bind a procedure to a button click on an item.

You can bind actions to displayed items either by tag (to cause an action to occur whenever an item tagged as plumbing is clicked, for instance) or by ID (to cause an action when a particular graphic item is accessed). For instance, you could bind a double mouse click event to bringing up a message box that would describe an item. A plumber could then double click on a joint and see a description of the style of fitting to use, where to purchase it, and an expected cost.

## 1O.2 Creating a canvas Widget

Creating a canvas is just as easy as creating other Tk widgets. You simply invoke the canvas command to create a canvas and then tell one of the layout managers where to display it. As with the other Tk commands, a command will be created with the same name as the canvas widget. You will use this command to interact with the canvas, creating items, modifying the configuration, and so on.

*Syntax:* canvas *canvasName ?options?*

Create a canvas widget.

*canvasName*  The name for this canvas.

*?options?*  Some of the options supported by the canvas widget are

-background color
> The color to use for the background of this image. The default color is light gray.

-closeenough distance
> Defines how close a mouse cursor must be to a displayable item to be considered on that item. The default is 1.0 pixel. This value may be a fraction and must be positive.

-scrollregion boundingBox
> Defines the size of a canvas widget. The bounding box is a list, left top right bottom, which defines the total area of this canvas, which may be larger than the displayed area. These coordinates define the area of a canvas widget that can be scrolled into view when the canvas is attached to a scrollbar widget. This defaults to 0 0 width height, the size of the displayed canvas widget.

-height size
> The height of the displayed portion of the canvas. If
> -scrollregion is declared larger than this and scrollbars are
> attached to this canvas, this defines the height of the win-
> dow into a larger canvas. The size parameter may be in pixels,
> inches, millimeters, and so on.

-width size
> The width of this canvas widget. Again, this may define the size
> of a window into a larger canvas.

-xscrollincrement size
> The amount to scroll when scrolling is requested. This can be
> used when the image you are displaying has a grid nature, and
> you always want to display an integral number of grid sections
> and not display half-grid sections. By default, this is a single
> pixel.

-yscrollincrement size
> The amount to scroll when scrolling is requested. This can be
> used when the image you are displaying has a grid nature, and
> you always want to display an integral number of grid sections
> and not display half-grid sections. By default, this is a single
> pixel.

## 10.3 Creating Displayable Canvas Items

As with other Tk widgets, when you create a canvas widget you also create a
procedure with the same name as the widget. Your script can use this procedure
to interact with the canvas to perform actions such as drawing objects, moving
objects, reconfiguring height and width, and so on.

The subcommand for drawing objects on a canvas is the create subcommand. This
subcommand creates a graphic item in a described location. Various options allow
you to specify the color, tags, and so on for this item. The create subcommand
returns the unique number that can be used to identify this drawable item.

The create subcommand includes a number of options that are specific to the
class of item. Most drawable items support the following options, except when
the option is not applicable to that class of drawable. For instance, line width is
not applicable to a text item.

| | |
|---|---|
| -width width | The width of line to use to draw the outline of this item. |
| -outline color | The color to draw the outline of this item. If this is an empty string, the outline will not be drawn. The default color is black. |

| | |
|---|---|
| `-fill color` | The color with which to fill the item if the item encloses an area. If this is an empty string (the default), the item will not be filled. |
| `-stipple bitmap` | The stipple pattern to use if the `-fill` option is being used. |
| `-tag tagList` | A list of tags to associate with this item. |

The items that can be created with the `create` subcommand are examined in the sections that follow.

## 10.3.1 **The Line Item**

**Syntax:** `canvasName create line x1 y1 x2 y2 ?xn yn? ?options?`

Create a polyline item. The x and y parameters define the ends of the line segments. Options for the `line` item include the following.

| | |
|---|---|
| `-arrow end` | Specifies which end of a line should have an arrow drawn on it. The end argument may be one of |

| | |
|---|---|
| `first` | The first line coordinate. |
| `last` | The end coordinate. |
| `both` | Both ends. |
| `none` | No arrow (default). |

| | |
|---|---|
| `-fill color` | The color to draw this line. |
| `-smooth boolean` | If set to `true`, this will cause the described line segments to be rendered with a set of Bezier splines. |
| `-splinesteps number` | The number of line segments to use for the Bezier splines if `-smooth` is defined `true`. |

## 10.3.2 **The Arc Item**

**Syntax:** `canvasName create arc x1 y1 x2 y2 ?options?`

Create an arc. The parameters `x1 y1 x2 y2` describe a rectangle that would enclose the oval of which this arc is a part. Options to define the arc include the following.

| | |
|---|---|
| `-start angle` | The start location in degrees for this arc. The `angle` parameter is given in degrees. The 0-degree position is at 3:00 (the rightmost edge of the oval) and increases in the counterclockwise direction. The default is 0. |

| | |
|---|---|
| -extent *angle* | The number of degrees counterclockwise to extend the arc from the start position. The default is 90 degrees. |
| -style *styleType* | The style of arc to draw. This defines the area that will be filled by the -fill option. May be one of |

| | |
|---|---|
| pieslice | The ends of the arc are connected to the center of the oval by two line segments (default). |
| chord | The ends of the arc are connected to each other by a line segment. |
| arc | Draw only the arc itself. Ignore -fill options. |

| | |
|---|---|
| -fill *color* | The color to fill the arc, if -style is not arc. |

### 10.3.3 **The Rectangle Item**

***Syntax:*** *canvasName* create rectangle *x1 y1 x2 y2 ?options?*

Create a rectangle. The parameters x1 y1 x2 y2 define opposite corners of the rectangle. The rectangle supports the usual -fill, -outline, -width, and -stipple options.

### 10.3.4 **The Oval Item**

***Syntax:*** *canvasName* create oval *x1 y1 x2 y2 ?options?*

Create an oval. The parameters x1 y1 x2 y2 define opposite corners of the rectangle that would enclose this oval. The oval supports the usual -fill, -outline, -width, and -stipple options.

### 10.3.5 **The Polygon Item**

***Syntax:*** *canvasName* create polygon *x1 y1 x2 y2 ... xn yn ?options?*

Create a polygon. The x and y parameters define the vertexes of the polygon. A final line segment connecting xn, yn to x1, y1 will be added automatically. The polygon item supports the same -smooth and -splinesteps options as the line item, as well as the usual -fill, -outline, -width, and -stipple options.

### 10.3.6 **The Text Item**

**Syntax:**  *canvasName* `create text` *x y ?options?*

Create a `text` item. The `text` item has the following unique options:

`-anchor` *position*    Describes where the text will be positioned relative to the x and y locations.

The `position` argument may be one of

`center`
Center the text on the position (default).

`n s e w ne se sw nw`
One or more sides of the text to place on the position. If a single side is specified, that side will be centered on the x/y location. If two adjacent sides are specified, that corner will be placed on the x/y location. For example, if `position` is defined as `w`, the text will be drawn with the center of the left edge on the specified x/y location. If `position` is defined as `se`, the bottom rightmost corner of the text will be on the x/y location.

`-justify` *style*    If the text item is multi-line (has embedded `newline` characters), this option describes whether the lines should be `right` justified, `left` justified, or `center` justified. The default is `left`.

`-text` *text*    The text to display.

`-font` *fontDescriptor*    The font to use for this text.

`-fill` *color*    The color to use for this text item.

### 10.3.7 **The Bitmap Item**

**Syntax:**  *canvasName* `create bitmap` *x y ?options?*

Create a two-color bitmap image. Options for this item include

`-anchor` *position*    This option behaves as described for the `text` item.

`-bitmap` *name*    Defines the bitmap to display. May be one of

`@file.xbm`    Name of a file with bitmap data

`bitmapName`    Name of one of the predefined bitmaps

The Tcl 8.4 distribution includes the following bitmaps for the PC, Mac, and UNIX platforms.

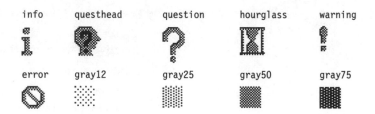

The Mac platform supports the following additional bitmaps.

## 10.3.8 The Image Item

**Syntax:** *canvasName* create image *x1 y1 ?options?*

Create a displayed image item. An image can be created from a GIF, PPM, PGM, or X-Bitmap image. The image command is discussed later in the chapter. The create image command was introduced several revisions after the create bitmap command. The create image is similar to the create bitmap command but can be used with more image formats and is more easily extended. The create image command uses the same -anchor option as the create bitmap. The image to be displayed is described with the -image options, as follows.

-image *imageName*    The name of the image to display. This is the
identifier handle returned by the image com-
mand.

### 10.3.9 An Example

The following example creates some simple graphic items to display a happy face.

**Example** 10.1

*Script Example*

```
# Create the canvas and display it.
canvas .c -height 140 -width 140 -background white
pack .c

# Create a nice big circle, colored gray

.c create oval 7 7 133 133 -outline black -fill gray80 -width 2

# And two little circles for eyes
.c create oval 39 49 53 63 -outline black -fill black
.c create oval 102 63 88 49 -outline black -fill black

# A Starfleet insignia nose
.c create polygon 70 67 74 81 69 77 67 81 -fill black

# A big Happy Smile!
.c create arc 21 21 119 119 -start 225 -extent 95 -style arc \
  -outline black -width 3
```

*Script Output*

## 10.4 More canvas Widget Subcommands

The create subcommand is only one of the subcommands supported by a canvas
widget. This section introduces some of them, with examples of how they can
be used.

### 10.4.1 **Modifying an Item**

You can modify a displayed item after creating it with the itemconfigure com-mand. This command behaves like the configure command for Tk widgets, except that it takes an extra argument to define the item.

*Syntax:* *canvasName* itemconfigure *tagOrId ?opt1? ?val1? ?opt2 val2?*

Return or set configuration values.

tagOrId Either the tag or the ID number of the item to configure.

opt1 The first option to set/query.

?val1? If present, the value to assign to the previous option.

## Example 10.2

### *Script Example*

```
# Create a canvas with a white background
set canv [canvas .c -height 50 -width 290 -background white]

# Create some text colored the default black.

set top [ $canv create text 145 20 \
  -text "This text can be seen before clicking the button"]

# Create some text colored white.
# It won't show against the background.

set bottom [ $canv create text 145 30 -fill white \
  -text "This text can be seen after clicking the button"]

# Create a button that will use itemconfigure to change the
# colors of the two lines of text.

set colorswap [button .b1 -text "Swap colors" \
  -command "$canv itemconfigure $top -fill white;\
      $canv itemconfigure $bottom -fill black;"]

# Pack them

pack $canv -side top
pack $colorswap -side bottom
```

### *Script Output*

Before click  After click

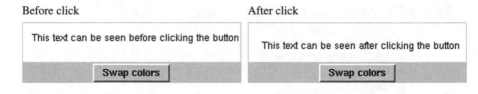

## 10.4.2 **Changing the Display Coordinates of an Item**

The previous happy face example simply displayed some graphic items but did not save the identifiers. The next example creates the happy face and saves the item for one eye to use with the canvas widget subcommand coords. The coords subcommand lets you change the coordinates of a drawable item after the item has been displayed. You can use this to move an item or change an item's shape.

*Syntax:* *canvasName* coords *tagOrId ?x1 y1? ... ?xn yn?*

Return or modify the coordinates of the item.

tagOrId     A tag or unique ID that identifies the item.

?x1
y1?...     Optional x and y parameters. If these arguments are absent, the current coordinates are returned. If these are present, they will be assigned as the new coordinates for this item.

**Example** 10.3

*Script Example*

```
################################################################
# proc wink {canv item }--
#    Close and re-open an 'eye' item.
# Arguments
#    canv  The canvas that includes this item.
#    item  An identifier for the 'eye' to wink
#
# Results
#    Converts Y coords for the specified item to center, then
#    restores them.
# The item is in its original state when this proc returns.

proc wink {canv item} {
  #
  # Get the coordinates for this item, and split them into
  #    left, bottom, right, and top variables.

  set bounding [$canv coords $item]
  set left [lindex $bounding 0]
  set bottom [lindex $bounding 1]
  set right [lindex $bounding 2]
  set top [lindex $bounding 3]
  set halfeye [expr int($top-$bottom)/2]

  # Loop to close the eye

  for {set i 1} {$i < $halfeye} {incr i } {
    $canv coords $item $left [expr $top - $i] $right \
```

```
        [expr $bottom + $i];
      update
      after 100
    }

    # Loop to re-open the eye

    for {set i $halfeye} {$i >= 0} {incr i -1} {
      $canv coords $item $left [expr $top - $i] \
        $right [expr $bottom + $i];
      update
      after 100
      }
}

# Create the canvas and display it.
canvas .c -height 140 -width 140 -background white
pack .c

# Create a nice big circle, colored gray
.c create oval 7 7 133 133 -outline black -fill gray80 -width 2

# And two little circles for eyes
.c create oval 39 49 53 63 -outline black -fill black
set righteye [.c create oval 102 63 88 49 -outline black \
  -fill black]

# A Starfleet insignia nose
.c create polygon 70 67 74 81 69 77 67 81 -fill black

# A big Happy Smile!
.c create arc 21 21 119 119 -start 225 -extent 95 -style arc \
  -outline black -width 3

# Now, wink at the folks

wink .c $righteye
```

### Script Output

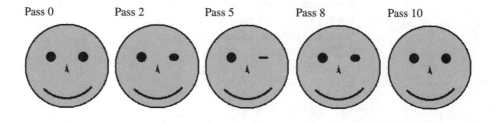

Pass 0      Pass 2      Pass 5      Pass 8      Pass 10

Note that the coords subcommand, like most of the canvas widget subcommands, will accept either an ID or a tag to identify the item. The righteye item could also have been created with the following line:

```
.c create oval 102 63 88 49 -outline black \
-fill black -tag righteye
```

The wink procedure is evaluated as follows:

```
wink .c righteye
```

Also notice the update command in the wink loops. If this were left out, the display would not update between changes. There would be a pause while the new images were calculated, but the display would never change.

### 10.4.3 **Moving an Item**

An item can be moved with the move subcommand, as well as with the coords subcommand. The move subcommand supports relative movement, whereas the coords command supports absolute positions.

> ***Syntax:*** *canvasName* move *tagOrId xoffset yoffset*
>
> Move an item a defined distance.
>
> *tagOrId*        A tag or unique ID that identifies the item.
>
> *xoffset yoffset*    The values to add to the item's current coordinates to define the new location. Positive values will move the item to the right and lower on the canvas.

For rectangle and oval items, the coordinates define the opposite corners and thus define the rectangle that would cover the item. In this case, it is easy to use the coords return to find the edges of the item.

If you have a multi-pointed polygon such as a star, finding the edges is a bit more difficult. The canvas widget subcommand bbox returns the coordinates of the top left and bottom right corners of a box that would enclose the item.

> ***Syntax:*** *canvasName* bbox *tagOrId*
>
> Return the coordinates of a box sized to enclose a single item or multiple items with the same tag.
>
> *tagOrId*    A tag or unique ID that identifies the item. If a tag is used and multiple items share that tag, the return is the bounding box that would cover all items with that tag.

The next example creates a star and bounces it around within a rectangle. Whenever the bounding box around the star hits an edge of the rectangle, the speed of the star is decreased and the direction is reversed.

## Example 10.4

*Script Example*

```
# Create the canvas and display it

canvas .c -height 150 -width 150
pack .c

# Create an outline box for the boundaries.

.c create rectangle 3 3 147 147 -width 3 -outline black \
  -fill white

# Create a star item

.c create polygon 1 15 3 10 0 5 5 5 8 0 10 5 16 5 12 10 \
  14 15 8 12 -fill black -outline black -tag star

# Set the initial velocity of the star

set xoff 2
set yoff 3

# Move the item

while {1} {
  set box [.c bbox star]
  set left [lindex $box 0]
  set top [lindex $box 1]
  set right [lindex $box 2]
  set bottom [lindex $box 3]

  # If the star has reached the left margin, heading left,
  # or the right margin, heading right, make it bounce.
  # Reduce the velocity to 90% in the bounce direction to
  # account for elasticity losses, and reverse the X
  # component of the velocity.
  #
  if {(($xoff < 0) && ($left <= 3)) ||
    (($xoff > 0) && ($right >= 147))} {
    set xoff [expr -.9 * $xoff]
  }

  # The same for the Y component of the velocity.

  if {(($yoff < 0) && ($top <= 3)) ||
    (($yoff > 0) && ($bottom >= 147))} {
    set yoff [expr -.9 * $yoff]
  }
```

```
.c move star $xoff $yoff
update
}
```

***Script Output***

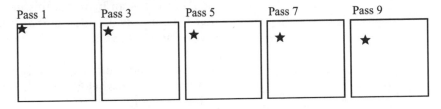

Tk stores the location of items in floating-point coordinates. Thus, the bouncing star does not completely stop until the *x* and *y* velocities fall below the precision of the floating-point library on your computer. The star will just move more and more slowly until you get bored and abort the program.

## 10.4.4 Finding, Raising, and Lowering Items

The canvas can be searched for items that meet certain criteria, such as their position in the display list, their location on the canvas, or their tags. The canvas widget subcommand that searches a canvas is the find subcommand. It will return a list of unique IDs for the items that match its search criteria. The list is always returned in the order in which the items appear in the display list, the first item displayed (the bottom if there are overlapping items) first, and so on.

The items in a canvas widget are stored in a display list. The items are rendered in the order in which they appear in the list. Thus, items that appear later in the list will cover items that appear earlier in the list. An item's position in the display list can be changed with the raise and lower subcommands.

***Syntax:*** *canvasName* raise *tagOrId ?abovetagOrId?*

Move the identified item to a later position in the display list, making it display above other items.

*tagOrId*   A tag or unique ID that identifies the item.

*?abovetagOrId?* The ID or tag of an item that this item should be above. By default, items are moved to the end position in the display list (top of the displayed items). With this option, an item can be moved to locations other than the top. In fact, you can raise an item to just above the lowest item, effectively lowering the item.

***Syntax:*** *canvasName* lower *tagOrId ?belowtagOrId?*

Move the identified item to an earlier position in the display list, making it display below other items.

*tagOrId*          A tag or unique ID that identifies the item.

*?belowtagOrId?*     The ID or tag of an item that this item should be directly below. By default, items are moved to the first position in the display list (bottom of the displayed items). With this option, an item can be moved to locations other than the bottom. You can lower an item to just below the top item, effectively raising the item.

***Syntax:*** *canvasName* find *searchSpec*

Find displayable items that match the search criteria and return that list.

searchSpec    The search criteria. May be one of

| | |
|---|---|
| all | Returns all items in a canvas in the order in which they appear in the display list. |
| withtag *Tag* | Returns a list of all items with this tag. |
| above *tagOrId* | Returns the single item just above the one defined by tagOrId. If a tag refers to multiple items, the last (topmost) item is used as the reference. |
| below *tagOrId* | Returns the single item just below the one defined by tagOrId. If a tag refers to multiple items, the first (lowest) item is used as the reference. |
| enclosed *x1 y1 x2 y2* | Returns the items totally enclosed by the rectangle defined by *x1, y1* and *x2, y2*. The *x* and *y* coordinates define opposing corners of a rectangle. |
| overlapping *x1 y1 x2 y2* | Returns the items that are partially enclosed by the rectangle defined by *x1, y1* and *x2, y2*. The *x* and *y* coordinates define opposing corners of a rectangle. |

closest *x y ?halo? ?start?*    Returns the item closest to the X/Y location described with the *x* and *y* parameters.

If more than one item overlies the X/Y location, the one that is later in the display list is returned. When using the closest search specifier, the halo parameter is a positive integer that is added to the actual bounding box of items to determine whether they cover the X/Y location.

The *start* parameter can be used to step through a list of items that overlie the X/Y position. If this is present, the item returned will be the highest item that is before the item defined by the *start* parameter. If the display list contained the item IDs in the order 1 2 3 4 9 8 7 6 5, and all items overlapped position 100,50, the command

```
$canvasName find -closest 100 50 0
```

would return item 1, the lowest object in the display table. The command

```
$canvasName find -closest 100 50 0 8
```

would return item 9, the item immediately below 8.

The next example shows some overlapping items and how their position in the display list changes the appearance of the display. This example redefines the default font for the text items. This is explained in the next section.

Note that the upvar command is used with the array argument. In Tcl, arrays are always passed by reference, not by value. Thus, if you need to pass an array to a procedure, you will call the procedure with the name of the array and use upvar to reference the array values.

## Example 10.5

### *Script Example*

```
###############################################################
# proc showDisplayList {canv array}--
#   Prints the Display List for a canvas.
#   Converts item ID's to item names via an array.
# Arguments
#   canv   Canvas to display from
#   array  The name of an array with textual names for the
#          display items
# Results
#   Prints output on the stdout.

proc showDisplayList {canv array} {
  upvar $array id
  set order [$canv find all]
```

```
      puts "display list (numeric): $order"
      puts -nonewline "display list (text): "
      foreach i $order {
        puts -nonewline "$id($i) "
      }
      puts ""
}

canvas .c -height 150 -width 170
pack .c

# create a light gray rectangle with dark text.

set tclSquare \
  [.c create rectangle 10 20 110 140 \
     -fill gray70 -outline gray70 ]
set tclText [.c create text 60 50 -text "Tcl\nIs\nTops" \
     -fill black -anchor n -font [list times 22 bold ] \
     -justify center ]

# create a dark gray rectangle with white text.

set tkSquare \
  [.c create rectangle 60 20 160 140 -fill gray30 \
     -outline gray30 ]
set tkText [.c create text 110 50 -text "Tk\nTops\nTcl" \
     -fill white -anchor n -font [list times 22 bold ] \
     -justify center ]

# Initialize the array with the names of the display items
#    linked to the unique number returned from the
#    canvas create.

foreach nm [list tclSquare tclText tkSquare tkText] {
  set id([subst $$nm]) "$nm"
}

# Update the display and canvas

update idle

# Show the display list
puts "\nAt beginning"
showDisplayList .c id

# Pause to admire the view

after 1000

# Raise the tclSquare and tclText items to the end \
#    (top) of the display list
.c raise $tclSquare
.c raise $tclText
```

```
# Update, display the new list, and pause again

update idle
puts "\nAfter raising tclSquare and tclText"
showDisplayList .c id
after 1000

# Raise the tkText to above the tclSquare (but below tclText)

.c lower $tkText $tclText

# Update and confirm.

update idle

puts "\nAfter 'lowering' tkText"
showDisplayList .c id
puts ""
puts "Find reports that $id([.c find above $tclSquare]) \
    is above tclSquare"
puts "Find reports that $id([.c find below $tclSquare]) \
    is below tclSquare"
puts "and items: [.c find enclosed 0 0 120 150] are \
    enclosed within 0,0 and 120,150"
```

***Script Output***

**At beginning**
**display list (numeric): 1 2 3 4**
**display list (text): tclSquare tclText tkSquare tkText**

**After raising tclSquare and tclText**
**display list (numeric): 3 4 1 2**
**display list (text): tkSquare tkText tclSquare tclText**

**After 'lowering' tkText**
**display list (numeric): 3 1 4 2**
**display list (text): tkSquare tclSquare tkText tclText**
**Find reports that tkText is above tclSquare**
**Find reports that tkSquare is below tclSquare**
**and items: 1 2 are enclosed within 0,0 and 120,150**

## 10.4.5 **Fonts and Text Items**

Fonts can be just as complex a problem as some 6,000 years of human endeavor with written language can make them. They can also be quite simple. The following discusses the platform-independent, simple method of dealing with fonts. Other methods are described in the on-line documentation under font. The pre-8.0 releases of Tk name fonts use the X Window system naming convention, as follows:

```
-foundry-family-weight-slant-setwidth-addstyle-pixel-point-
    resx-resy-spacing-width-charset-encoding.
```

If you need to work with a version of Tk earlier than 8.0, you are probably on a UNIX system and can determine a proper name of an available font with the X11 command xlsfonts or xfontsel. With the 8.0 release of Tcl and Tk, life became much simpler: a font is named with a list of attributes, such as family ?size? ?style? ?style? If the Tcl interpreter cannot find a font that will match the font you requested, it will find the closest match. It is guaranteed that a font will be found for any syntactically correct set of attributes.

family    The family name for a font. On all systems, times, helvetica, and courier are defined. A list of the defined fonts can be obtained with the font families command.

size    The size for this font. If this is a positive value, it is the size in points (1/72 of an inch). The scaling for the monitor is defined when Tk is initialized. If this value is a negative number, it will be converted to positive and will define the size of the font in pixels. Defining a font by point size is preferred and should cause applications to look the same on different systems.

style    The style for this font. May be one or more of normal (or roman), bold, italic, underline, or overstrike.

Information about fonts can be obtained with the font command. The following discusses only some of the more commonly used subcommands.

**Syntax:** font families ?-displayof *windowName?*

Returns a list of valid font families for this system.

-displayof *windowName*    If this option is present, it defines the window (frame, canvas, topwindow) to return this data for. By default, this is the primary graphics window ".".

The font measure command is useful when you are trying to arrange text on a display in an aesthetic manner.

**Syntax:** font measure *font* ?-displayof *windowName?* *text*

The font measure command returns the number of horizontal pixels the string text will require if rendered in the defined font.

| | |
|---|---|
| *font* | The name of the font, as described previously. |
| -displayof *windowName* | If this option is present, it defines the window (frame, canvas, topwindow) to return this data for. By default, this is the primary graphics window ".". |
| *text* | The text to measure. |

If Tk cannot obtain an exact match to the requested font on your system, it will find the best match. You can determine what font is actually being used with the font actual command.

**Syntax:** font actual *font* ?-displayof *windowName?*

Return the actual font that will be used when font is requested.

| | |
|---|---|
| *font* | The name of the requested font. |
| -displayof *windowName* | If this option is present, it defines the window (frame, canvas, topwindow) to return this data for. By default, this is the primary graphics window ".". |

With Tk 8.1, Tcl and Tk support the Unicode character fonts. These are encoded by preceding the four-digit Unicode value with \u. You can obtain information on the Unicode character sets at *http://Unicode.org.*

Unicode provides a standard method for handling letters other than the U.S. ASCII alphabet. The Unicode alphabet uses 16 bits to describe 65,536 letters. Each alphabet is assigned a range of numbers to represent its characters. With Unicode, you can represent Japanese Katakana, Korean Hangul, French, Spanish, Russian, and most other major alphabets.

The following example steps through the fonts available on a generic UNIX system and displays some sample text in ASCII and Unicode. Note that if the Unicode fonts are not supported in a given font, the Unicode numbers are displayed instead. This example was run using Tcl/Tk version 8.4a4.

## Example 10.6

***Script Example***

```
canvas .c -height 980 -width 860 -background white
grid .c -row 0 -column 0 -sticky news

set ypos 5
set ht [font metrics [list roman 16] -linespace]
set families [lsort [font families ]]

foreach family $families {
  .c create text 4 $ypos -font [list times 24 bold] \
    -text "$family" -anchor nw
```

```
.c create text 270 $ypos -font [list $family 24] \
  -text "test line -- UNICODE: \u30Ab \u042f \u3072" \
  -anchor nw
incr ypos [font metrics [list $family 24] -linespace]
.c create text 4 $ypos -font [list roman 16] \
  -text "[font actual [list $family 24]]" -anchor nw
incr ypos $ht
.c create line 4 $ypos 860 $ypos
incr ypos 10
}
```

## Script Output

## 10.4.6 **Using a Canvas Larger Than the View**

When you create a canvas, you can provide -width xsize and -height ysize arguments to define the size of the canvas to display on the screen. If you do not also use a -scrollregion argument, the canvas will be xsize by ysize in size, and the entire canvas will be visible. The -scrollregion command will let you declare that the actual canvas is larger than its visible portion. For example,

```
canvas .c -width 200 -height 150 -scrollregion {0 0 4500 2000}
```

creates a window 200 pixels wide and 150 pixels high into a canvas that is actually $4500 \times 2000$ pixels.

If you attach scrollbars to this canvas, you can scroll this $200 \times 150$ pixel window around the larger space. The -xscrollincrement and -yscrollincrement arguments will let you set how much of the canvas should scroll at a time. For instance, if you are displaying a lot of text in a canvas, you would want to set the -yscrollincrement to the height of a line. This will cause the canvas to display full lines of text, instead of displaying partial lines at the top and bottom of the canvas as you scroll through the text.

The next example shows a checkerboard pattern, with each square labeled to show its position in the grid. Because the -xscrollincrement is set to the size of a square, the full width of each square is displayed. Because the -yscrollincrement is half the size of a square, half the height of a square can be displayed.

Note that the -scrollregion can include negative coordinates as well as positive. You can draw any location in a canvas, but you will not be able to scroll to it unless you have set the -scrollregion to include the area you have drawn to. If you have a complex image to create, and you do not know what the size will be until it is drawn, you can draw the image to a canvas and then determine the bounding box for the image with the *canvasName* bbox command.

```
set coords[canvasName bbox all]
```

## Example 10.7

### *Script Example*

```
canvas .c -width 200 -height 150 \
  -scrollregion {-100 -200 4500 2000} \
  -yscrollcommand {.scrollY set} \
  -xscrollcommand {.scrollX set} \
  -xscrollincrement 50 -yscrollincrement 25
scrollbar .scrollY -orient vertical -command ".c yview"

scrollbar .scrollX -orient horizontal -command ".c xview"

grid .c -row 0 -column 0
grid .scrollY -row 0 -column 1 -sticky ns
grid .scrollX -row 1 -column 0 -sticky ew
```

```
for {set y -200} {$y < 2000} {incr y 50} {
  set bottom [expr $y + 50]
  for {set x -100} {$x < 4500} {incr x 50} {
    set right [expr $x+50]
    if {(($y + $x) % 100) == 50} {
      set textColor white
      set fillColor black
    } else {
      set textColor black
      set fillColor white
    }
    .c create rectangle $x $y $right $bottom \
      -fill $fillColor -outline gray30
    .c create text [expr $x+25] [expr $y+25] \
      -text "$x\n$y" -font \
      [list helvetica 18 bold] -fill $textColor
  }
}
```

*Script Output*

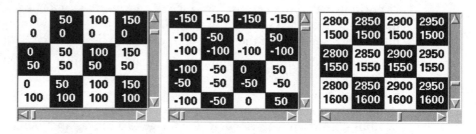

## 10.5 The bind and focus Commands

Section 10.1.3 mentioned that an event can be linked to a canvas item, and when that event occurs it can trigger an action. You can also bind actions to events on other widgets. This section discusses how this is done.

Most of the Tcl widgets have some event bindings defined by default. For example, when you click on a button widget, the default action for the ButtonPress event is to evaluate the script defined in the -command option.

### 10.5.1 The bind Command

The bind command links an event to a widget and a script. If the event occurs while the focus is on that widget, the script associated with that event will be evaluated.

*Syntax:*   bind *widgetName eventType script*

Define an action to be executed when an event associated with this widget occurs.

*widgetName*   The widget to have an action bound to it.

*eventType*   The event to trigger this action. Events can be defined in one of three formats:

alphanumeric
: A single printable (alphanumeric or punctuation) character defines a KeyPress event for that character.

*<<virtualEvent>>*
: A virtual event defined by your script with the event command.

*<modifier-type-detail>*
: This format precisely defines any event that can occur. The fields of an event descriptor are described in the following. Where two names are together, they are synonyms for each other. For example, either Button1 or B1 can be used to the left mouse button click.

*script*   The script to evaluate when this event occurs.

The most versatile technique for defining events is to use the <modifier-type-detail> convention. With this convention, an event is defined as zero or more modifiers, followed by an event-type descriptor, followed by a detail field.

*modifier*   There may be one or more occurrences of the *modifier* field, which describes conditions that must exist when an event defined by the type field occurs. For example, Alt and Shift may be pressed at the same time as a letter KeyPress . Not all computers support all available modifiers. For instance, few computers have more than three buttons on the mouse, and most general-purpose computers do not support a Mod key. The modifiers Double, Triple, and Quadruple define rapid sequences of two, three, or four mouse clicks. Valid values for modifier are as follows:

| | | | | |
|---|---|---|---|---|
| Button1 | Button2 | Button3 | Button4 | Button5 |
| B1 | B2 | B3 | B4 | B5 |
| Mod1 | Mod2 | Mod3 | Mod4 | Mod5 |
| M1 | M2 | M3 | M4 | M5 |
| Meta | Alt | Control | Shift | Lock |
| M | | | | |
| Double | Triple | Quadruple | | |

| | |
|---|---|
| *type* | This field describes the type of event. Only one type entry is allowed in an event descriptor. Valid values for type are as follows: |

| | | |
|---|---|---|
| Activate | Enter | Map |
| ButtonPress, Button | Expose | Motion |
| ButtonRelease | FocusIn | MouseWheel |
| Circulate | FocusOut | Property |
| Colormap | Gravity | Reparent |
| Configure | KeyPress, Key | Unmap |
| Deactivate | KeyRelease | Visibility |
| Destroy | Leave | |

| | |
|---|---|
| *detail* | The detail provides the final piece of data to identify an event precisely. The value the detail field can take depends on the content of the type field. |

| *type* | *detail* |
|---|---|
| ButtonPress | *detail* will be the number of a mouse button (1 through 5). |
| ButtonRelease | If the button number is specified, only events with that button will be bound to this action. If no *detail* is defined for a ButtonPress or ButtonRelease event, any mouse-button event will be bound to this action. |
| KeyPress | *detail* will specify a particular key, such as a or 3. |
| KeyRelease | Non-alphanumeric keys are defined by names such as Space or Caps_Lock. An X11 manual will list all of these. On a UNIX/Linux system you can run xkeycaps (*www.jwz.org/xkeycaps/*) to obtain a list of the available key types. If no *detail* is defined for a KeyPress or KeyRelease event, any keyboard event will be bound to this action. |

## Event Definition Examples

| **Event Definition** | **Description** |
|---|---|
| <B1-Motion> | This event is generated if the left mouse button is pressed and the mouse moves; that is, when you drag an item on a screen. |

| | |
|---|---|
| a | Generates an event when the A key is pressed. |
| Shift_L | This does not define an event. Shift_L is not an alphanumeric. |
| <Shift_L> | This event is generated when the left shift key is pressed. No event is generated when the key is released. |
| <KeyRelease-Shift_L> | Generates an event when the left shift key is released. |
| <Control-Alt-Delete> | Generates an event if all three are pressed simultaneously. Not a recommended event for PC-based hardware platforms. |

The bind command can pass information about the event that occurred to the script that is to be evaluated. This is done by including references to the events in the script argument to the bind command. The complete list of the information available about the event is defined in the bind on-line documentation. The information that can be passed to a script includes the following.

%x   The X component of the cursor's location in the current window when the event occurs.

%y   The Y component of the cursor's location in the current window when the event occurs.

%b   The button that was pressed or released if the event is a ButtonPress or ButtonRelease.

%k   The key that was pressed or released if the event is a KeyPress or KeyRelease.

%A   The ASCII value of the key pressed or released if the event is a KeyPress or KeyRelease.

%T   The type of event that occurred.

%W   The path name of the window in which the event occurred.

*bind .window <KeyPress> {keystroke %k}*

Will invoke the procedure keystroke with the value of the key when a KeyPress event occurs and .window has focus.

*bind .win <Motion> {moveitem %x %y}*

Will invoke the procedure moveitem with the x and y location of the cursor when a Motion event occurs and .win has focus.

## 10.5.2 **The canvas Widget bind Subcommand**

Events can be bound to a drawable item in a canvas, just as they are bound to widgets. The command to do this uses the same values for eventType and script as the bind command uses.

> *Syntax:* canvasName bind *tagOrId* *eventType* *script*
>
> Bind an action to an event and canvas object.
>
> *tagOrId*     The tag assigned when an object is created, or the object identifier returned when an object is created.
>
> *eventType*   The event to trigger on, as described previously.
>
> *script*     A Tcl script to evaluate when this event occurs.

The following example is a blueprint drawing with information attached to the items in the drawing, as was suggested in Section 10.1.1. When the cursor touches one of the lines, the room is highlighted, and information about the room is displayed in a label at the bottom of the display.

**Example** 10.8

***Script Example***

```
###################################################################

# proc drawRoom {cvs lineSegments name text }--
#   Draw a room and add bindings for <Enter> and <Leave>
# Arguments
#   cvs          The name of the canvas
#   lineSegments A list of start/end points for the line
#                segments that describe this room
#   name         The name of this room
#   text         The informational text to put in the label
#
# Results
#   Draws a room and assigns bindings

proc drawRoom {cvs lineSegments name text } {
  global highlight background normal

  # Draw the line segments.
  # Tag each one with the name of this room
  # Color them the 'normal' color (gray)

  foreach {stx sty ndx ndy} $lineSegments {
    $cvs create line $stx $sty $ndx $ndy \
      -tag $name -width 3 -fill $normal
  }

  # Place text down and to the right of the upper
  #   left corner of the room

  set txtPosx [expr [lindex $lineSegments 0] + 5]
  set txtPosy [expr [lindex $lineSegments 1] + 5]
```

```
$cvs create text $txtPosx $txtPosy -anchor nw -text $name

# Add a binding so that when the cursor enters a
#    line tagged with this name,
#    1) The info variable is assigned to the text
#    2) All line segments with this tag are raised
#    3) The color of these line segments becomes 'highlight'

$cvs bind $name <Enter> "[list set info $text]; \
    $cvs raise $name; \
    $cvs itemconfigure $name -fill $highlight;"

# return the color to normal and clear the info label
# when the cursor is not over this item

$cvs bind $name <Leave> ".c itemconfigure $name -fill $normal; \
    set info {}; "
}

# Define the background, highlight, and normal colors

set background white
set highlight black
set normal gray75

# Create a canvas and a label and display them.

canvas .c -background white
pack .c -side top

label .l -width 42 -textvar info -background white
pack .l -side top -anchor w

# Draw 4 rooms.

drawRoom .c {5 5 125 5 \
    125 5 125 25 125 75 125 105 \
    5 105 90 105 120 105 125 105 \
    5 5 5 20 5 50 5 105} "Den" "Paint off-white, hardwood floor"

drawRoom .c {125 5 205 5 \
    205 5 205 20 205 50 205 105 \
    125 105 205 105 \
    125 5 125 25 125 75 125 105} "Kitchen" "Tile floor"

drawRoom .c {5 105 90 105 120 105 145 105 \
    145 105 145 120 145 150 145 185 \
    5 185 145 185 \
    5 105 5 185} "BedRoom" "Hardwood floor"
```

```
drawRoom .c {145 105 205 105 \
    205 105 205 185 \
    145 185 205 185 \
    145 105 145 120 145 150 145 185} "bath" "Tile floor"
```

***Script Output***

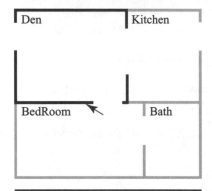

**Paint off-white, hardwood floor**

## 10.5.3 **Focus**

When a window manager is directing events to a particular item (window, widget, or canvas item), that window is said to have the focus. Some events are always passed to an item that requests them, whether the item is defined as having focus or not. The cursor entering an item always generates an event, and a destroy event will always be transmitted to any applicable item. The keyboard events, however, are delivered only to the widget that currently has the focus.

The window manager controls the top-level focus. The default behavior for Macintosh and MS Windows systems is to click a window to place the focus in a window. On UNIX/X Window systems, the window managers can be set to require a click or to place the focus automatically on the window where the cursor resides.

Within the Tcl application, the focus is in the top-level window, unless a widget explicitly demands the focus. Some widgets have default actions that acquire the focus. An entry widget, for instance, takes the focus when you click it or tab to that widget. If you want to allow KeyPress events to be received in a widget that does not normally gain focus, you must add bindings to demand the focus.

The next example shows a label widget .l with three events bound to it: Enter, Leave, and KeyPress. When the cursor enters the .l widget, it acquires the focus, and all KeyPress events will be delivered to the script defined in the bind .1 <KeyPress> command. When the cursor leaves label .1, no events are passed to this item.

The label .12 shares the same -textvariable as label .1. When lvar is modified in response to an event on .1, it is reflected in .12. However, .12 never grabs the focus, as .1 does. The bind .12 <KeyPress> {append lvar "L2";} command has no effect, since .12 never has focus.

**Example** 10.9

*Script Example*

```
label .l1 -width 40 -textvariable lvar -background gray80
label .l2 -width 40 -textvariable lvar

pack .l1
pack .l2

bind .l1 <KeyPress> {append lvar %A;}
bind .l1 <Enter> {puts "Enter Event - grabbing focus"; focus .l1}
bind .l1 <Leave> {puts "Leave Event - Returning focus"; focus .}
bind .l2 <KeyPress> {append lvar "L2";}
puts "These events are valid on label .l1: [bind .l1]"
```

*Script Output*

```
These events are valid on label .l1: <Leave> <Enter> <Key>

  # I moved the cursor into label .l1
Enter Event - grabbing focus
  # I typed "Label .l1 has focus"
  # I moved the cursor into label .l2
Leave Event - Returning focus
  # I typed "This has no effect"
```

# 10.6 Creating a Widget

Now that we know how to create drawable items in a canvas and bind actions to events in that canvas, we can create our own widgets. For example, suppose we want an Opera/Netscape–style button that does one thing when you click it and another if you hold down the mouse button for more than one second.

To create this we need to write a procedure that will create a canvas, draw something appropriate in that canvas, and bind scripts to the appropriate events. The following is a specification for a delayed-action button.

- Will be invoked as `delayButton name ?-option value?`
- Required options will be

  -bitmap *bitmapName*   The bitmap to display in this button.

  -command1 *script*   A script to evaluate when button is clicked.

  -command2 *script*   A script to evaluate when button is held down.

- Optional arguments will include

  | | |
  |---|---|
  | -height *number* | The height of the button. |
  | -width *number* | The width of the button. |
  | -foreground *color* | The foreground color for text and bitmap. |
  | -background *color* | The background color for the button and bitmap. |
  | -highlight *color* | The background color when the cursor enters the button. |
  | -text *Text to display below bitmap* | The optional text to display below the bitmap. |
  | -font *fontDescriptor* | The font for displayed text. |

- Clicking the widget with a left mouse button will invoke the *command1* script.
- Holding down the left mouse button will invoke the *command2* script.
- The button will default to 48 × 48 pixels.
- The button will default to a medium gray color.
- The highlight color will default to light gray.
- The button background will become the highlight color when a cursor enters the button.
- The button background will return to normal color when the cursor leaves the button.

This section shows a set of code that meets these specifications. The example shows the `delayButton` being used to display three simple buttons. There are a few things to notice in the next example. In the initialization, the configuration options are assigned default values before examining the argument list for modification. This lets the user override the defaults. Using the `info locals` to validate the options makes it easy to modify the code in the future. If a new configuration option becomes necessary (perhaps a -textColor instead of using the same color for the bitmap and text), you need only add a new default setting and change the code that uses the new value. The parsing code will not need to be modified.

In contrast, parsing for required options needs to have a list of required options to check against. When the required options are changed, this list must also be modified. After the button is created, event bindings can be assigned to it. These bindings cause the procedures in the delayButton namespace to be evaluated when the left mouse button is pressed or released. Note the way the after command is used to schedule the commands in scheduleCommand2, and to evaluate a command in invokeCommand1.

When button 1 is pressed, the scheduleCommand2 procedure is evaluated. This procedure schedules the *command2* script to be evaluated in one second and saves the identifier returned by the after command. It also appends a command that will delete the saved identifier when the command2 script is invoked.

When the button is released, the invokeCommand1 procedure will check to see if there is still an event identifier for this window in the afters array. If there is, the <ButtonRelease> event came before the after event was evaluated. In this case, the comamnd1 script will be evaluated, and the command2 event will be canceled. If there is no event identifier for this window in the afters array, it means the command2 script was already evaluated, and the procedure will return without evaluating the command1 script.

Also pay attention to the namespace commands. Because the after scripts are evaluated in global scope, full namespace identifiers are used for script names, and uplevel #0 is used to force scripts to evaluate in the global scope.

Putting the registerCommands, scheduleCommand2, cancelCommand2, and invoke-Command1 commands into a namespace protects these commands from possible collision with other commands and does not pollute the global space. Creating these procedures inside the namespace also allows them to create and share the associative arrays afters, command1Array, and command2Array without exposing these arrays to procedures executing outside this namespace.

The sample script for the delayButton does not include all the necessary procedures to use the menus or generate other data. It is only a skeleton to demonstrate the use of the delayButton.

## Example 10.10

### *Script Example*

```
##################################################################
# proc delayButton {delayButtonName args}--
#    Create a delayButton icon that will evaluate a command when
```

```
#    clicked and display an information label if the cursor
#    rests on it
#
# Arguments
#    delayButtonName  The name of this delayButton
#    args             A list of -flag value pairs
#
# Results
#    Creates a new delayButton and returns the name to the
#    calling script
#    Throws an error if unrecognized arguments or required args
#    are missing.

proc delayButton {delayButtonName args} {

    ## Initialization

    # define defaults
    set height 48
    set width 48
    set background gray80
    set highlight gray90
    set foreground black
    set text " "
    set command1 " "
    set command2 " "
    set bitmap " "
    set font {Helvetica 10}

    ## Parse for Unsupported Options

    # Step through the arguments.
    # Confirm that each -option is valid (has a default),
    # and set a variable for each option that is defined.
    #    The variable for -foo is "foo".

    foreach {option val} $args {
      set optName [string range $option 1 end]
      if {![info exists $optName]} {
          error "Bad argument $option - \
          must be one of [info locals]" \
          "Invalid option"
      }
      set $optName $val
    }

    ## Parse for Required Options

    # These arguments are required.

    set reqOptions [list -command1 -command2 -bitmap]
```

```
# Check that the required arguments are present
# Throw an error if any are missing.

foreach required $reqOptions {
  if {[lsearch -exact $args $required ] < 0} {
      error "delayButton requires a $required option" \
      "Missing required option"
  }
}

## Button Creation

# Create the canvas for this delayButton

canvas $delayButtonName -height $height -width $width \
  -background $background

# Place the bitmap in it.

$delayButtonName create bitmap [expr $width/2] \
  [expr $height/2] -bitmap $bitmap -foreground $foreground

# If there is text, it goes on the bottom.

if {![string match $text " "]} {
    $delayButtonName create text [expr $width/2] \
      [expr $height-1] \
      -text $text -fill $foreground \
      -font $font -anchor s
}

## Binding Definition

# Bind the button click to evaluate the $command
#    script in global scope

bind $delayButtonName <ButtonPress-1> \
  "::delayButton::scheduleCommand2 $delayButtonName"

bind $delayButtonName <ButtonRelease-1> \
  "::delayButton::invokeCommand1 $delayButtonName"

# Bind the background to change color when the
#    cursor enters

bind $delayButtonName <Enter> \
  "$delayButtonName configure -background $highlight"

# Bind the background to change color when the cursor
# leaves, and cancel any pending display of an info label.

bind $delayButtonName <Leave> \
```

```
        "$delayButtonName configure -background $background;\
        ::delayButton::cancelCommand2 $delayButtonName;"

    ## Command Registration

    # Register the commands
      ::delayButton::registerCommands $delayButtonName \
          $command1 $command2

    # And return the name

    return $delayButtonName
}

# The registerCommands, scheduleCommand2, cancelCommand2, and
# invokeCommand1 commands are defined within this namespace to
# 1) avoid polluting the global space.
# 2) make the "afters" array of identifiers returned by the
#     after command private to these procedures.
# 3) make the "afters" array persistent
# 4) protect the "command1Array" and "command2Array" variables
#     from the rest of the program
# 5) make the "command1Array" and "command2Array" variables
#     persistent

namespace eval delayButton {
    variable afters
    variable command1Array
    variable command2Array

#########################################################
# proc registerCommands {delayButtonName cmd1 cmd2}--
#    registers commands to be evaluated for this button
# Arguments
#    delayButtonName  The name of the delayButton
#    cmd1             Command to evaluate if clicked
#    cmd2             Command to evaluate if held
# Results
#    New entries are created in the command1Array
#    and command2Array variables.

proc registerCommands {delayButtonName cmd1 cmd2} {
    variable command1Array
    variable command2Array

    set command1Array($delayButtonName) $cmd1
    set command2Array($delayButtonName) $cmd2
}
```

```
############################################################
#   proc scheduleCommand2 {name }--
#   Cancel any existing "after" scripts for this button.
#
# Arguments
#   name  The name of this delayButton
#
# Results
#   Places an item in the "after" queue to be evaluated
#       1 second from now

proc scheduleCommand2 {delayButtonName } {
  variable afters
  variable command2Array

  cancelCommand2 $delayButtonName

  set afters($delayButtonName) \
    [after 1000 \
    $command2Array($delayButtonName) \; \
    [namespace current]::cancelCommand2 $delayButtonName]
}


############################################################
# proc cancelCommand2 {delayButtonName}--
#   Cancels the scheduled display of an Info label
# Arguments
#   delayButtonName The name of the delayButton
#
# Results
#   If this label was scheduled to be displayed,
#   it is disabled.

proc cancelCommand2 {delayButtonName} {
    variable afters
    if {[info exists afters($delayButtonName)]} {
        after cancel $afters($delayButtonName)
    }
    set afters($delayButtonName) ""
}


############################################################
#   proc invokeCommand1 {delayButtonName}--
#   Deletes the label associated with this button, and
#   resets the binding to the original actions.
# Arguments
#   delayButtonName  The name of the parent button
```

```
#
# Results
#    No more label, and bindings as they were before the
#    mouse paused
#    on this button

proc invokeCommand1 {delayButtonName} {
  variable afters
  variable command1Array

  # If there is nothing in the 'after' identifier
  # holder we've already done the 'command 2',
  # and this release is not part of a click.

  if {[llength $afters($delayButtonName)] == 0} {
      return
  }

  # Cancel the command 2 execution
  cancelCommand2 $delayButtonName

  # And do command 1
  uplevel #0 $command1Array($delayButtonName)
  }
}
```

The following script shows how the delayButton can be used.

```
##########################################################
# proc makeMenu {args}--
#    generate and post a demonstration menu
# Arguments
#    args  A list of entries for the menu
#
# Results
#    Creates a menu of command items with no commands associated
#    with them.

proc makeMenu {args} {
  catch {destroy .m}
  menu .m
  foreach item $args {
    .m add command -label $item
  }
  .m post [winfo pointerx .] [winfo pointery .]
}

# Create a button with text
delayButton .b1 -bitmap info -text "INFO" \
```

```
      -command1 {tk_messageBox -type ok -message "Information"} \
      -command2 {makeMenu "Tcl Info" "Tk Info" "BLT Info" "Expect Info"}
pack .b1 -side left

# Create a button without text

delayButton .b2 -bitmap hourglass \
   -command1 {tk_messageBox -type ok \
   -message [clock format [clock seconds]]} \
   -command2 {makeMenu "Time in London" \
      "Time in New York" "Time in Chicago"}
pack .b2 -side left

# Create a button with non-default colors

delayButton .b3 -bitmap warning \
         -command1 {reportLatestAlert} \
         -command2 {reportAllAlerts} \
         -background #000000 -foreground #FFFFFF \
         -highlight #888888
pack .b3 -side left
```

***Script Output***

Initial button state     Click on INFO     Hold button down on INFO

## 1O.7 A Help Balloon: Interacting with the Window Manager

It also would be useful to be able to attach pop-up help balloons to widgets. Tk does not include a pop-up help widget as one of the basic widgets, but one can be created with just a few lines of code. The help balloon in this example is derived from an example on the Tcl'ers Wiki site (*http://wiki.tcl.tk*). The behavior of the help balloon is as follows.

- Schedule a help message to appear after a cursor has entered a widget.
- Destroy a help message when the cursor leaves a widget.

Scheduling the window to appear, and destroying it when it is no longer required, can be done with the bind command, described previously. These bindings are established in the balloon procedure. When the cursor enters a widget, an after event is scheduled to display the help message, and the balloon is destroyed when the cursor leaves the requested window.

The %W argument to the bind command is replaced by the name of the window that generated the event. This lets the script connect the help balloon to the window that created it. Displaying a balloon requires the following steps.

**1.** Confirm that the cursor is still inside the window associated with this help balloon.

**2.** Destroy any previous balloon associated with this window.

**3.** Create a new window with the appropriate text.

**4.** Map this window to the screen in the appropriate place.

This is done in the balloon::show procedure. Confirming that the cursor is still inside the window associated with this help balloon and placing the help balloon in the correct location of the screen requires interacting with both the window manager and the Tk interpreter. The window manager controls how top-level windows are placed, whereas the Tk interpreter controls how widgets are placed within the application.

The Tk wm and winfo commands provide support for interacting with window features such as window size, location, decorations, and type. The wm command interacts with the window manager, whereas the winfo command interacts with windows owned by the wish interpreter.

On a Macintosh or Microsoft Windows platform, the window manager is merged into the operating system. On an X Window platform, the window manager is a separate program ranging from the simple wm and twm managers to the configurable modern window managers, such as Gnome/Enlightenment and CDE/KDE. There is a core of features supported by all window managers, and there are some subcommands supported only on certain platforms. Again, check the on-line documentation for your platform.

The wm command is used to interact with top-level windows, the root screen and system-oriented features such as the focus model. The syntax of the wm command is similar to other Tk commands, with the command name (wm) followed by a subcommand and a set of arguments specific to this subcommand.

> **_Syntax:_** wm *subcommand args*
>
> A few commonly used subcommands are examined in the following.
>
> The wm title command lets your script define the text in the top bar.

*Syntax:* `wm title` *windowName* `text`

Assigns *text* as the title displayed in the window manager decoration.

*windowName*    The window to set the title in.

*text*          The new title.

## Example 10.11

```
wm title . "Custom Title"
pack [label .l -text "Title Demonstration"]
```

The `wm geometry` command lets you control where windows are placed and how large they are. Note that all `wm` commands are "suggestions" to the window manager. If your program requests unsupported behavior, (like a 1280 × 1024 window on a 640 × 480 screen), the window manager may reject the request.

*Syntax:* `wm geometry` *windowName* *?geometryString?*

Queries or modifies the window's location or size.

*windowName*        The window to be queried or set.

*?geometryString?*  If this is defined, it instructs the window manager to change the size or location of the window. If not defined, the geometry of the window is returned.

The format of the returned geometry string will be

*width×height+xLocation+yLocation*

A geometry string defined by a user can include just the dimension information (i.e., 500 × 200) or the location information (i.e., + 50 + 200). The usual technique for defining location is with plus (+) markers, which denote pixels to the right and down from the top left corner. You can also describe the location with minus (−) markers, in which case the location is measured in pixels left or up from the bottom right corner.

## Example 10.12

```
# Retrieve the geometry
set g [wm geometry .]
```

```
# Parse it into width, height, x and y components
foreach {width height xloc yloc} [split $g {+x}] {}

# Move the window down and right
incr xloc 5
incr yloc 5

wm geometry . ${width}x${height}+${xloc}+${yloc}
```

The overrideredirect subcommand will turn off the decorative borders that let you resize and move windows. By default, top-level widgets are created with full decorations, as provided by the window manager.

**Syntax:** wm overrideredirect *windowName boolean*

Sets the override-redirect flag in the requested window. If true, the window is not given a decorative frame and cannot be moved by the user. By default, the override-redirect flag is false.

*windowName* The name of the window for which the override-redirect flag is to be set.

*boolean* A Boolean value to assign to the override-redirect flag.

The wm overrideredirect command should be given before the window manager transfers focus of a window. Unlike most Tcl/Tk commands, you may not be able to test this subcommand by typing commands in an interactive session. The difference between override-redirect true and false looks as follows.

## Example 10.13

*Script Example*

```
catch {destroy .t1 .t2}
toplevel .t1 -border 5 -relief raised
label .t1.1 -text "Reset Redirect True"
pack .t1.1
wm overrideredirect .t1 1

toplevel .t2 -border 5 -relief raised
label .t2.1 -text "Default Redirect"
pack .t2.1

wm geometry .t1 +300+300
wm geometry .t2 +300+400

raise .t1
raise .t2
```

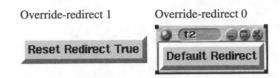

Override-redirect 1          Override-redirect 0

The `protocol` command allows a script to examine or modify how certain windowing system events are handled.

*Syntax:* `wm protocol` *window ?protocolName? ?script?*

> Return information about protocol handlers attached to a window, or assign a protocol handler to a window.

| | |
|---|---|
| `window` | The name of a top-level Tk window (the main window or one created with the `toplevel` command). |
| *?protocolName* | The name of an atom corresponding to a window manager protocol. The only protocol in common use is `WM_DELETE_WINDOW`, the notification that a window has received a delete signal. |
| | If this field is absent, report all protocols that have handlers associated with them. |
| *?script?* | A script to evaluate when the *protocolName* message is received. |
| | If this field is absent, return the script associated with the *protocolName* atom. |

The common use for the `wm protocol` command is to catch the `WM_DELETE_WINDOW` request, and give the user an option to save work before exiting (or abort the exit completely).

This is similar to using the `bind` command to catch the notification that a window has been destroyed: `bind . <Destroy> {cleanExit }`. The difference is that the `wm protocol WM_DELETE_WINDOW` command catches the request to delete a window, and can abort destroying the window, whereas the `bind . <Destroy>` command catches the notification that the window has already been destroyed.

## Example 10.14

### Script Example

```
# Confirm that a user wishes to exit the application.

proc confirmClose {} {
  set answer [tk_messageBox -type "yesno" \
      -message "Do you wish to exit" ]
  if {[string match $answer "yes"]} {
      # Might add call to a 'save' procedure here
```

```
        exit
  } else {
        return
  }
}

wm protocol . WM_DELETE_WINDOW confirmClose
puts "ALL Protocols with handlers: [wm protocol . ]"
puts "Handler for WM_DELETE_WINDOW: \
  [wm protocol . WM_DELETE_WINDOW]"
```

***Script Output***

**ALL Protocols with handlers: WM_DELETE_WINDOW**
**Handler for WM_DELETE_WINDOW: confirmClose**

---

The wm command gives the Tcl programmer access to information controlled by the window manager. The winfo command gives the Tcl programmer access to information controlled by the Tk application. This includes information such as what windows are children of another window, what type of widget a window is, the size and location of a widget, the location of the cursor, and so on.

The pointerxy subcommand will return the coordinates of the cursor.

***Syntax:*** winfo pointerxy *window*

Return the *x* and *y* location of the mouse cursor. These values are returned in screen coordinates, not application window coordinates.

*window*   The mouse cursor must be on the same screen as this window. If the cursor is not on this screen, each coordinate will be −1.

## Example 10.15

```
# Report the cursor location
label .l -textvar location
pack .l

while {1} {
  set location [winfo pointerxy .]
  update
  after 10
}
```

---

The containing subcommand will return the name of a window that encloses a pair of coordinates.

*Syntax:* `winfo containing` *rootX rootY*

Returns the name of the window that encloses the X and Y coordinates.

*rootX*   An X screen coordinate. (0 is the left edge of the screen.)

*rootY*   A Y screen coordinate. (0 is the top edge of the screen.)

## Example 10.16

```
# This label displays 'outside' when the cursor is outside
#   the label, and 'inside' when the cursor enters the window.

label .l -textvar where
pack .l

while {1} {
  set location [winfo pointerxy .]
  set in [eval winfo containing $location]
  if {[string match $in .l]} {
    set where inside
  } else {
    set where outside
  }
  update
  after 10
}
```

The winfo height, winfo width, winfo rootx, and winfo rooty return the same information as the wm geometry command. However, whereas the wm geometry command can only be used for top-level windows, the winfo commands can also be used for individual widgets.

*Syntax:* `winfo height` *winName*

*Syntax:* `winfo width` *winName*

Return height or width of a window.

*winName*   The name of the window.

## Example 10.17

```
puts "The main window is [winfo width .] x [winfo height .]"
```

*Syntax:* `winfo rootx` *winName*

*Syntax:* `winfo rooty` *winName*

Return $x$ or $y$ location of a window in screen coordinates.

*winName*    The name of the window.

**Example** 10.18

```
label .l
pack .l
puts "The label is at X: [winfo rootx .l] Y: [winfo rooty .l]"
```

The wm and winfo commands are used in the balloon::show procedure to confirm that a help balloon is still required and to map it to the correct location if it is. The first step, confirming that the cursor is still within the window, can be done with two winfo commands. The pointerxy subcommand will return the coordinates of the cursor, and the containing subcommand will return the name of a window that encloses a pair of coordinates.

A help balloon window should not have the decorations added by the window manager, as we do not want the user to be able to move this window, iconify it, and so on. The decorations are added by the window manager, not managed by Tk, so removing the decorations is done with the wm command. The subcommand that handles this is overrideredirect.

This example uses the message widget. A label displays only a single line of text, whereas a message widget displays multi-line text. The message is lighter weight than the text widget, discussed in the next chapter.

> **Syntax:** message *name ?options?*
>
> Create a message widget.
>
> *name*        A name for the message widget. Must be a proper window name.
>
> *?options?*    Options for the message include
>
> -text        The text to display in this widget.
>
> -textvar     The variable that will contain the text to display in this widget.
>
> -aspect      An integer to define the aspect ratio: (Xsize/Ysize) ∗ 100.
>
> -background  The background color for this widget.

The final step is to place the new window just under the widget that requested the help balloon. The window that requests the help will be a window managed by Tk, so we can use the winfo command to determine its height and X/Y locations. Placing a top-level window on the screen is a task for the window manager, so the wm geometry command gets used.

**Example** 10.19

*Script Example*
```
######################################################
# proc balloon {w help}--
#  Register help text with a widget
# Arguments
#  w     The name of a widget to have a help balloon
#        associated with it
#  help The text to associate with this window.
# Results
#  Creates bindings for cursor Enter and Leave to display
#  and destroy a help balloon.

proc balloon {w help} {
    bind $w <Any-Enter> "after 1000 [list balloon::show %W [list $help]]"
    bind $w <Any-Leave> "destroy % W.balloon"


}
namespace eval balloon {

######################################################
# proc show {w text }--
#   display a help balloon if the cursor is within window w
# Arguments
#  w      The name of the window for the help
#  text  The text to display in the window
# Results
#  Destroys any existing window, and creates a new
#      toplevel window containing a message widget with
#      the help text

proc show {w text} {

   # Get the name of the window containing the cursor.

   set currentWin [eval winfo containing [winfo pointerxy .]]

   # If the current window is not the one that requested the
   #  help, return.

   if {![string match $currentWin $w]} {
       return
   }

   # The new toplevel window will be a child of the
   #  window that requested help.
```

```
    set top $w.balloon

    # Destroy any previous help balloon

    catch {destroy $top}

    # Create a new toplevel window, and turn off decorations
    toplevel $top -borderwidth 1

    wm overrideredirect $top 1

    # If Macintosh, do a little magic.

    if {$::tcl_platform(platform) == "macintosh"} {

    # Daniel A. Steffen added an 'unsupported1' command
    # to make this work on macs as well, otherwise raising the
    # balloon window would immediately post a Leave event
    # leading to the destruction of the balloon... The
    # 'unsupported1' command makes the balloon window into a
    # floating window, which does not put the underlying
    # window into the background and thus avoids the problem.
    # (For this to work, appearance manager needs to be present.)
    #
    # In Tk 8.4, this command is renamed to:
    # ::tk::unsupported::MacWindowStyle

    unsupported1 style $top floating sideTitlebar
    }

    # Create and pack the message object with the help text

    pack [message $top.txt -aspect 200 -background lightyellow \
            -font fixed -text $text]

    # Get the location of the window requesting help,
    #  use that to calculate the location for the new window.

    set wmx [winfo rootx $w]
    set wmy [expr [winfo rooty $w]+[winfo height $w]]
    wm geometry $top \
      [winfo reqwidth $top.txt]x[winfo reqheight $top.txt]+$wmx+$wmy

    # Raise the window, to be certain it's not hidden below
    #  other windows.
    raise $top
      }
}
```

```
button  .b -text Exit -command exit
balloon .b "Push me if you're done with this"
pack    .b
```

***Script Output***

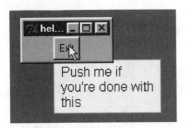

# 10.8 The image Object

Creating items such as lines and arcs on a canvas is one way of generating a picture, but for some applications a rasterized image is more useful. There are two ways of creating images in Tcl. The create bitmap canvas command will display a single color image on a canvas (as shown in Example 10.10). The create image canvas command will display an image object on the canvas.

The canvas bitmap item is easy to use but is not as versatile as the image object. You can use the image object to create simple bitmap images or full-color images. The full-color image objects can be shrunk, zoomed, subsampled, and moved from image object to image object. The image objects can be displayed in other widgets, including button, label, and text widgets.

The standard Tk distribution supports images defined in X-Bitmap, GIF, Portable Pixmap, and Portable GrayMap formats. Some extensions exist that provide support for other formats, such as JPEG and PNG. (See Chapter 14 for Jan Nijtmans's Img Extension, which adds more image support to Tk.) This section will explain how to create and use image objects.

## 10.8.1 The image Command

To create an image item on a canvas, you must first create an image object. The image command supports creating, deleting, and getting information about the image objects within the Tk interpreter. The image create command creates an image object from a file or internal data and returns a handle for accessing that object.

*Syntax:* `image create type ?name? ?options?`

Create an `image` object of the desired type, and return a handle for referencing this object.

| | |
|---|---|
| *type* | The type of `image` that will be created. Tk versions 8.0 and more recent support |

                    `photo`    A multicolor graphic.

                    `bitmap`   A two-color graphic.

*?name?*      The name for this `image`. If this is left out, the system will assign a name of the form `imageX`, where X is a unique numeric value.

*?options?*  These are options specific to the type of `image` being created. The appropriate options are discussed in regard to `bitmap` and `photo`.

An image can be deleted with the `image delete` command.

*Syntax:* `image delete name ?name?`

Delete the named image.

`name`   The handle returned by the `image create` command.

The `image` command can be used to get information about a single `image` or all images that exist in the interpreter.

*Syntax:* *image* `height` *name*

Return the height of the named image.

*Syntax:* *image* `width` *name*

Return the width of the named image.

*Syntax:* *image* `type` *name*

Return the type of the named `image`.

For each of these commands, the *name* parameter is the image name returned by the `image create` command. You can retrieve a list of existing image names with the `image names` command.

*Syntax:* `image names`

Return a list of the image object names.

As with the Tk widgets, when an image is created with the `image create` command, a command with the same name as the `image` is also created. This image object command can be used to manipulate the object via the *imageName* `cget` and *imageName* `configure` commands. These commands behave in the same way as other widget `cget` and `configure` subcommands. The configuration options that can be modified with the `configure` subcommand depend on the type of image created and are the same as the options available to that image create type command.

## 10.8.2 Bitmap Images

Bitmap images (which are different from a canvas bitmap item) are created with the command image create bitmap, as described previously. The options supported for this command include

-background *color*  The background color for this bitmap. If this is empty (the default), background pixels will be transparent.

-foreground *color*  The foreground color for this image. The default is black.

-data *data*  The data that defines this image. This must be in the same format as an X Window system bitmap file.

-file *filename*  A file containing the X-Bitmap data.

The X Window system bitmap file is quite simple. It was designed to be included in C programs and looks like a piece of C code. The format is as follows.

```
# define name_width width
# define name_height height
static unsigned char name_bits[] = {
 data1, data2, ...
};
```

The good news is that this is simple and easy to construct. The bitmap program on a UNIX system will let you construct an X-Bitmap file, or you can use the imagemagick or PBM utilities to convert an MS Windows or Mac bitmap file to an X-Bitmap file.

**Example** 10.20

*Script Example*

```
# Create and pack a canvas
pack [canvas .c -background white -height 60 -width 80]
# This is the hourglass bitmap from the predefined bitmaps in
# the Tk 8.0 distribution: tk8.0/bitmaps/hourglass.bmp

set hourglassdata {
# define hourglass_width 19
# define hourglass_height 21
static unsigned char hourglass_bits[] = {
 0xff, 0xff, 0x07, 0x55, 0x55, 0x05, 0xa2, 0x2a, 0x03, 0x66, 0x15, 0x01,
 0xa2, 0x2a, 0x03, 0x66, 0x15, 0x01, 0xc2, 0x0a, 0x03, 0x46, 0x05, 0x01,
 0x82, 0x0a, 0x03, 0x06, 0x05, 0x01, 0x02, 0x03, 0x03, 0x86, 0x05, 0x01,
 0xc2, 0x0a, 0x03, 0x66, 0x15, 0x01, 0xa2, 0x2a, 0x03, 0x66, 0x15, 0x01,
```

```
    0xa2, 0x2a, 0x03, 0x66, 0x15, 0x01, 0xa2, 0x2a, 0x03, 0xff, 0xff, 0x07,
    0xab, 0xaa, 0x02};
}

# Create a bitmap image from the hourglass data
set bm [image create bitmap -data $hourglassdata]

# And create a displayable canvas image item from that image.

.c create image 40 30 -image $bm

# And label the image.
.c create text 40 50 -text "bitmap image"
```

***Script Output***

Images displayed

bitmap image

---

## 10.8.3 Photo Images

The image data for a photo image may be PPM, PGM, or GIF. The data may be in binary form in a disk file or encoded as base64 data within the Tcl script. Base64 encoding is a technique for converting binary data to printable ASCII with the least expansion. This format is used by all e-mail systems that support the MIME (multipurpose Internet mail extensions) protocol (which most modern mail programs do). Strange as it sounds, the most portable way of converting a file from binary to base64 encoding is to mail it to yourself, save the mail, and extract the data you want from the saved mail file.

If you are running on a UNIX system, you may have the mmencode or mimencode program installed. These are part of the metamail MIME mail support. The companion CD-ROM includes scripts that will encode and decode base64 data within your script or in external files.

The tcllib (*http://tcllib.sf.net/*) collection of useful tools is included in the ActiveTcl distribution and includes the base64 package. This package includes encode and decode functions within the base64 namespace that will convert data to and from base64 format within a script.

```
package require base64
set b64Stream [base64::encode $binaryData]
```

The binary2b64.tcl program will convert a binary data file to base64 data. This program is in the *examples/random* directory on the companion CD-ROM. This script uses the b64tools.tcl package developed by Jan Wieck, which is also in that directory.

The image create photo command supports several options. These include

| | |
|---|---|
| -data *string* | The base64 encoded data that defines this image. |
| -file *filename* | A file that contains the image data in binary format. |
| -format *format* | The format for this image data. Tk will attempt to determine the type of image by default. The possible values for this option in version 8.4 are gif, pgm, and ppm. |

As with the image create bitmap command, this command creates a new command with the same name as the new image, which can be used to manipulate the image via the *imageName* cget and *imageName* configure commands.

The photo type images support other subcommands, including the following.

**Syntax:** *imageName* copy *sourceImage ?options?*

Copy the image data from *sourceImage* to the image *imageName*. Options include

| | |
|---|---|
| -from *x1 y1 x2 y2* | The area to copy from in the source image. The coordinates define opposing corners of a rectangle. |
| -to *x1 y1 x2 y2* | The area to copy to in the destination image. |
| -shrink | Shrink the image if necessary to fit the available space. |
| -zoom | Expand the image if necessary to fit the available space. |

**Syntax:** *imageName* get *x y*

Return the value of the pixel at coordinates x,y. The color is returned as three integers: the red, green, and blue intensities.

**Syntax:** *imageName* put *data ?-to x1 y1 ?x2 y2??*

Put new pixel data into an image object.

| | |
|---|---|
| *data* | The data is a string of color values, either as color names or in # rgb format. By default, these pixels will be placed from the upper left corner, across each line, and then across the next line. |
| -to *x1 y1 x2 y2* | Declares the location for the data to be placed. If only x1,y1 are defined, this is a starting point, and the edges of the image will be used as end points. If both x1,y1 and x2,y2 are defined, they define the opposing corners of a rectangle. |

The following example creates an image from base64 data, copies the date to another image, extracts some data (from the base of the T), and draws a box around the extracted data. In the extracted data, each pixel is grouped within curly braces and displayed as a red, blue, and green intensity value. The {0 0 0} pixels are black, and the {60 248 52} pixels are green.

**Example** 10.21

### *Script Example*

```
# Create a canvas

canvas .c -height 100 -width 300 -background white
pack .c

# Define an image - in base64 format
set img {
R01GODdhQAAwAKEAAP///wAAADz4NAD//ywAAAAAQAAwAAAC/oSPqcvtD6OctNqLs
16h+w+G4kiWAWOm6hqi7AuLbijU9k3adHxyYt0BBoQjokfAm4GQQeawZBw6X8riFH
q9sqo/rZQY9aq4NK3wPI1ufdilE/ORj9m5rNcoT5Hd/PIxb7IXZ9d1xOMh+Ne3CBh
IZ+UX1DR52KNgguOGBtToeFkJBWqZIJojmlgKipp6uDoyABsrGxCr+sgC25FLO6Db
W+kq8svr8bvbehtzXDyclOw7+9rsCw1DJos9TQ1yrK2XnB3Nrb3r/f35EY4dskxtf
k46rt5OLP/uGZ8+T8/fSz+Hjtk+duSM3RvBZV8/gsys3VI4TRyvYbXWBBQYjhXAJX
z61GmEh4BEto8bQ5JkFewkyAMqU6VsSWKDzJkOa9q8iTNnhQIAOw==
}

# Create an image from the img data

set i [image create photo -data $img]

# Now, create a displayable canvas image item from the image

.c create image 25 40 -image $i -anchor nw

# Create an image with no data,

set i2 [image create photo -height 50 -width 70]

# And copy data from the original image into it.
$i2 copy $i -from 1 1 50 40 -to 10 10 60 50

# Now display the image

.c create image 140 40 -image $i2 -anchor nw

# Display some of the values in the new image

puts "Values from 24 24 to 29 31"
for {set y 24} {$y < 31} {incr y} {
```

```
  for {set x 24} {$x < 29} {incr x} {
   puts -nonewline \
      "[format "% 12s" [list [$i2 get $x $y]]]"
   }
   puts ""
}

# Draw an outline around the area we sampled:

for {set x 24} {$x < 29} {incr x} {
  $i2 put {#FFF #FFF} -to $x 23
  $i2 put {#FFF #FFF} -to $x 30
}

for {set y 24} {$y < 31} {incr y} {
  $i2 put {#FFF} -to 22 $y
  $i2 put {#FFF} -to 23 $y
  $i2 put {#FFF} -to 29 $y
  $i2 put {#FFF} -to 30 $y
}

# And label the images.

.c create text 25 10 -text "Photo image 1" \
  -font {times 16} -anchor nw
.c create text 140 10 -text "Copied and \nmodified" \
  -font {times 16} -anchor nw
```

### Script Output

```
Values from 24 24 to 29 31
       {0 0 0} {60 248 52} {60 248 52}        {0 0 0}    {0 0 0}
       {0 0 0} {60 248 52} {60 248 52}        {0 0 0}    {0 0 0}
       {0 0 0} {60 248 52} {60 248 52}        {0 0 0}    {0 0 0}
       {0 0 0} {60 248 52} {60 248 52}        {0 0 0}    {0 0 0}
 {60 248 52} {60 248 52} {60 248 52} {60 248 52}    {0 0 0}
       {0 0 0}    {0 0 0}    {0 0 0}        {0 0 0}    {0 0 0}
       {0 0 0}    {0 0 0}    {0 0 0}        {0 0 0}    {0 0 0}
```

Images displayed

Photo image 1

Copied and
modified

Detail of copy/modified image

### 10.8.4 Revisiting the delayButton Widget

The bitmaps used in the delayButton example are all predefined in the Tk interpreter. If you have a bitmap of your own you would like to use, you would have to define it in a data file using the X Window system bitmap format. For example, if the bitmap image is in a file named *bitmap.xbm*, the delayButton could be created with the following command.

```
delayButton .f.bFile -bitmap @bitmap.xbm ...
```

Tk has no method for defining canvas bitmap item data in a script. Tk does allow you to define an image of type bitmap from data included in the script. The image command is the preferred way of dealing with images on canvases.

Unfortunately, you cannot access predefined bitmaps with the image command, though you can load data from the distribution (under the *TkDistribution/bitmaps* directory), as was just done in Example 10.20.

Following is a modified version of the toolbar procedure that uses an image instead of a bitmap and a script that creates its own bitmaps to display in the buttons. The code that executes within the delayButton namespace does not change.

The info and warning bitmap data are taken from the files *bitmaps/questhead.bmp* and *bitmaps/warning.bmp*. The data for the clockIcon is a base64 encoded GIF image. It may not be obvious in the book, but the clock has a red body, a blue border, and yellow hands. The points to note in this version of the script are as follows.

- The -bitmap options are replaced with -image options.
- The bitmap objects are replaced by image objects.
- The -foreground option is not supported in the canvasName create image command but is supported as a subcommand of the image object.

### Example 10.22

*Script Example*

```
#########################################################
# proc delayButton {delayButtonName args}--
```

```
#   Create a delayButton icon that will evaluate a command when
#   clicked and display an information label if the cursor
#   rests on it
#
# Arguments
#   delayButtonName  The name of this delayButton
#   args             A list of -flag value pairs
#
# Results
#   Creates a new delayButton and returns the name to the
#   calling script
#   Throws an error if unrecognized arguments or required args
#   are missing.

proc delayButton {delayButtonName args} {

    # define defaults
    set height 48
    set width 48
    set background gray80
    set highlight gray90
    set foreground black
    set text ""
    set command1 ""
    set command2 ""
    set image ""
    set font {Helvetica 10}

    # Step through the arguments.
    # Confirm that each -option is valid (has a default),
    # and set a variable for each option that is defined.
    #   The variable for -foo is "foo".

    foreach {option val} $args {
        set optName [string range $option 1 end]
        if {![info exists $optName]} {
            error "Bad argument $option - \
            must be one of [info locals]" \
            "Invalid option"
        }
        set $optName $val
    }

    # These arguments are required.

    set reqOptions [list -command1 -command2 -image]

    # Check that the required arguments are present
```

```
# Throw an error if any are missing.

foreach required $reqOptions {
    if {[lsearch -exact $args $required ] < 0} {
        error "delayButton requires a $required option" \
        "Missing required option"
    }
}

# Create the canvas for this delayButton

canvas $delayButtonName -height $height -width $width \
    -background $background

# Place the image in it.

$delayButtonName create image [expr $width/2] \
    [expr $height/2] -image $image

# If there is text, it goes on the bottom.

if {![string match $text ""]} {
    $delayButtonName create text [expr $width/2] \
        [expr $height-1] \
      -text $text -fill $foreground \
      -font $font -anchor s
}

# Bind the button click to evaluate the $command
#    script in global scope

bind $delayButtonName <ButtonPress-1> \
    "::delayButton::scheduleCommand2 $delayButtonName"

bind $delayButtonName <ButtonRelease-1> \
    "::delayButton::invokeCommand1 $delayButtonName"

# Bind the background to change color when the
#    cursor enters

bind $delayButtonName <Enter> \
    "$delayButtonName configure -background $highlight"

# Bind the background to change color when the cursor
#    leaves, and cancel any pending display of an info label.

bind $delayButtonName <Leave> \
    "$delayButtonName configure -background $background;\
    ::delayButton::cancelCommand2 $delayButtonName;"

# Register the commands
```

```
    ::delayButton::registerCommands $delayButtonName \
        $command1 $command2

    # And return the name

    return $delayButtonName
}
```

The following script shows how the delayButton can be used.

```
proc makeMenu {args} {
    catch {destroy .m}
    menu .m
    foreach item $args {
        .m add command -label $item
    }
    .m post [winfo pointerx .] [winfo pointery .]
}

# Create images for info, clock and warning
#  Use bitmap data for info and warning, and
#  a base64 GIF image for the clock

set info [image create bitmap -data {
# define info_width 8
# define info_height 21
static unsigned char info_bits[] = {
    0x3c, 0x2a, 0x16, 0x2a, 0x14, 0x00, 0x00, 0x3f, 0x15,
    0x2e, 0x14, 0x2c, 0x14, 0x2c, 0x14, 0x2c, 0x14, 0x2c,
    0xd7, 0xab, 0x55}

}]

set clock {
R0lGOD1hIAAgALMAANnZ2QD/////AAAAAD0ZmZmZmf8AAMwAAJmZAMz
MzP//////////////////yH5BAEAAAAALAAAAAAgACAAAAT/EA
AY5KTVXgDAvULAAYOcVBJQaxVi1BpARIYQQoFDT1rtCIEQEgIMZUAjJ
63WjEAICQGGAAY2ctNoZCCEhBDigkZMeISidgRACgxzQyEmPEGNQagKB
hIQQBjRyOiPEGJSaQCAhIYQBjZz0CDEGpSYQSEgIYUAjJz1CjEGpCQQ
SEkIYOMhJjxBjUGoCgYSEEAYOctIjxBiUmkAgISGEAY2c9AgxBqUmEE
hICGFAIyc9QoxBqQkEEhKEGNDISYUsRQghqIFBiBGEGNDIOY+QpQghx
IDDGBOEGGGMAY2c8giBEBxySmNMmCGEAY2c5ggBh5x0GGMCISQEGAYO
ch4hxphzjU4TIJEhhAGNlEeIMeacUwZIZAhhGGPMEWLAAY2ctAZCSAh
hUCjEGNDISasJhJAQwoBGGjHGnHNOGQgkJIQwoJGTVjsDISSEAAcOct
JqZyCEhBBggUZOWuOMhJAQAgwFGjlptSYRQggMctJqLSRShjDnnFKIM
ecOERCARE5ahRi1SgAAJHJSOsaolQAQAQA7
}

image create photo clockIcon -data $clock
```

```
unset clock

set warning [image create bitmap -data {
# define warning_width 6
# define warning_height 19
static unsigned char warning_bits[] = {
    0x0c, 0x16, 0x2b, 0x15, 0x2b, 0x15, 0x2b, 0x16, 0x0a,
    0x16, 0x0a, 0x16, 0x0a, 0x00, 0x00, 0x1e, 0x0a, 0x16,
    0x0a}
}]

delayButton .b1 -image $info -text "INFO" \
  -command1 {tk_messageBox -type ok -message "Information"} \
  -command2 {makeMenu "Tcl Info" "Tk Info" "Expect Info"}
pack .b1 -side left

delayButton .b2 -image clockIcon \
  -command1 {tk_messageBox -type ok \
      -message [clock format [clock seconds]]} \
  -command2 {makeMenu "Time in London" \
      "Time in New York" "Time in Chicago"}
pack .b2 -side left

delayButton .b3 -image $warning \
  -command1 {reportLatestAlert} \
  -command2 {reportAllAlerts} \
  -background #AAA -foreground #FFF -highlight #888
pack .b3 -side left
```

### Script Output

Start condition

After holding down button 1

As you can see, the results are the same with the -bitmap version and the -image version. The -image version of this widget needs more setup but is more versatile.

## 10.9 Bottom Line

- The canvas widget creates a drawing surface.

- The canvas widget returns a unique identifier whenever a drawable item is created.

- Drawable items may be associated with one or more tag strings.

- The coordinates of a drawable item can be accessed or modified with the *canvasName* coords command.

  ***Syntax:*** *canvasName* coords *tagOrId ?x1 y1?... ?xn yn?*

- A drawable item can be moved on a canvas with the *canvasName* move command.

  ***Syntax:*** *canvasName* move *tagOrId xoffset yoffset*

- The space occupied by a drawable item is returned by the *canvasName* bbox command.

  ***Syntax:*** *canvasName* bbox *tagOrId*

- A list of items that matches a search criterion is returned by the *canvasName* find command.

  ***Syntax:*** *canvasName* find *searchSpec*

- A drawable item's position in the display list can be modified with the *canvasName* raise command and *canvasName* lower command.

  ***Syntax:*** *canvasName* raise *tagOrId ? abovetagOrId?*

  ***Syntax:*** *canvasName* lower *tagOrId ? belowtagOrId?*

- A list of available fonts is returned with the font families command.

  ***Syntax:*** font families ?-displayof *windowName*

- The horizontal space necessary to display a string in a particular font is returned by the font measure command.

  ***Syntax:*** font measure *font* ?-displayof *windowName* ? *text*

- The closest match to a requested font is returned by the font actual command.

  ***Syntax:*** font actual *font* ?-displayof *windowName* ?

- Actions can be bound to events on a widget with the bind command.

  ***Syntax:*** bind *widgetName eventType script*

- Actions can be bound to events on a drawable item within a canvas widget, with the *canvasName* bind command.

  ***Syntax:*** *canvasName* bind *tagOrId eventType script*

- Two-color (bitmap) and multicolor (photo) images can be created with the image create command.

  ***Syntax:*** image create *type* *?name? ?options?*

- Images can be deleted with the image delete command.

  ***Syntax:*** image delete *name* *?name?*

- Information about an image is returned by the image height, image width, and image type commands.

  ***Syntax:*** image height *name*

  ***Syntax:*** image width *name*

  ***Syntax:*** image type *name*

- A list of images currently defined in a script is returned by the image names command.

  ***Syntax:*** image names

- Photo image pixel data can be copied from one image to another with the *imageName* copy command.

  ***Syntax:*** *imageName* copy *sourceImage* ? *options?*

- Photo image pixel data can be accessed or modified with the *imageName* get and *imageName* put commands.

  ***Syntax:*** *imageName* get *x y*

  ***Syntax:*** *imageName* put *data* ?-to *x1 y1 ?x2 y2??*

  - The canvas create bitmap command and the image create bitmap command are not the same but can be used to achieve equivalent results.

| canvas create bitmap | image create bitmap |
|---|---|
| Can access internal bitmaps | Can use data defined within a script |
| Can reference a data file via @filename | Can reference a data file via -file |
| Can modify foreground via cvsName create bitmap \ -foreground $newcolor | Can modify foreground via imageHandle configure \ -foreground $newcolor |

## 10.10 Problems

The following numbering convention is used in all Problem sections.

| Number Range | Description of Problems |
|---|---|
| 100–199 | These problems review the material covered in this chapter. They can be answered in a few words or a short (1–5-line) script. Each problem should take under a minute to answer. |
| 200–299 | These problems go beyond the details presented in this chapter. They may require some analysis of the material |

| Number Range | Description of Problems |
|---|---|
| | or command details not covered in the chapter. They may require reading a man page or making a web search. They can be answered with a few sentences or a 5–50-line script. Each problem should take under 10 minutes to answer. |
| 300–399 | These problems extend the material presented in this chapter. They may require referencing other sources. They can be answered in a few paragraphs or a few hundred lines of code. Each exercise may take a few hours to complete. |

**100.** Can an object drawn on a Tk canvas have more than one tag?

**101.** What command would draw a blue line from 20,30 to 50,90 on a canvas named .c?

**102.** How many colors can be included in a canvas bitmap object?

**103.** What command would cause all canvas graphic objects on a canvas named .c with the tag red to turn red when a cursor passes over them?

**104.** What command will cause keyboard events to be sent to a label named .l?

**105.** Can a canvas be linked with a scrollbar?

**106.** What command will create an image object?

**107.** What command will display an image object?

**108.** Can you access the data in a single pixel of a Tk image object?

**109.** If an application is running on a 1024 × 768 pixel display, what command would resize the application to fill the display?

**110.** What command will return the height of a window?

**200.** Write a script that creates a canvas and draws a 20 × 30 pixel blue rectangle with a 5-pixel-wide green border, a red oval with a 2-pixel-wide yellow border, and a 3-pixel-wide red line that connects them.

**201.** Create a bouncing ball animation by creating a canvas and an oval and changing the oval location every 10 milliseconds. Allow the bouncing ball to only bounce to 90% of the height of the starting location, to simulate a bouncing ball settling down.

**202.** Modify the Example 10.10 delayButton script to require text instead of a bitmap, and size the button to match the text, instead of using a fixed-size button.

**203.** Modify the Example 10.10 delayButton script to require a -helpText option, and automatically attach the help balloon described in Example 10.19 when the delayButton is created.

**204.** Lemon juice is a classic invisible ink. It dries invisibly until the paper is heated and the sugars in the lemon juice caramelize and turn brown. Write a Tcl script to simulate this by writing white text on a white background, and then slowly change the color using the `itemconfigure` command.

**205.** Modify the bouncing star Example (10.4) to include several non-moving circles. Highlight whichever circle is closest to the star as the star moves around.

**206.** Write a script that examines each pixel in an image object and counts the occurrences of pixels of different brightness values (referred to as "histogramming an image"). Display the results by printing the brightness value and count for any non-zero count.

**300.** Add bindings to the display in Problem 200 so that you can "grab" the rectangle or oval by placing the cursor on it and holding down the left mouse button, and "drag" it by moving the cursor while the button is depressed.

**301.** Modify the script in Problem 300 to update the line coordinates to always connect the two nearest edges of the rectangle and oval.

**302.** Create a simple "paint" package that will have radio buttons for select-drawing a rectangle or oval, and will allow a user to click on a location on the screen and drag a corner to define the size of the rectangle or oval.

**303.** The `winfo class` command will return the type of a window (`Button`, `Frame`, and so on). Use this command to write a recursive procedure that will place the names of all windows in an application into a tree data structure. Use the Tree example discussed in Chapter 8.

**304.** Write a Tk procedure that will display the elements in a tree data structure with each element on a single line, and indentation to denote how many levels deep a tree element is. You may need scrollbars to view an entire tree. The output should resemble the following:

```
.
.buttonFrame
  .buttonFrame.file
  .buttonFrame.edit
  .buttonFrame.view
.dataFrame
  .dataFrame.canvas
  .dataFrame.label
...
```

**305.** Modify the script created for Problem 206 to display the results as a bar chart. Scale the bars so that the longest is 90% of the canvas size, and use a scrollbar to display all bars.

# CHAPTER 11

# The text Widget and html_lib

The message, label, and entry widgets are useful for applications with short prompts and small amounts of data to enter; that is, for applications that resemble filling out a form. However, some applications need to allow the user to display, enter, or edit large amounts of text. The text widget supports this type of application. The text widget supports the following.

- Emacs-style editing
- Arrow-key–style editing
- Scrollbars
- Multiple fonts in a single document
- Tagging a single character or multiple-character strings (in a similar manner to the way tags are applied to canvas objects)
- Marking positions in the text
- Inserting other Tk widgets or images into the text display
- Binding events to a single character or a multiple-character string

Stephen Uhler used the text widget to construct the html_library for rendering HTML documents. This is not part of the Tcl/Tk distribution but can be found on the companion CD-ROM and is available via ftp at

   *http://noucorp.com/tcl/utilities/htmllib/htmllib-rel_0_3_4.zip*

This pure Tcl package will render HTML text and provides hooks for links and images. This chapter introduces the text widget and the html library.

## 11.1 Overview of the text Widget

An application may create multiple text windows, which can be displayed in either a top-level window, frame, canvas, or another text widget. The content of a text widget is addressed by line and character location. The text widget content is maintained as a set of lists. Each list consists of the text string to display, along with any tags, marks, image annotations, and window annotations associated with this text string.

The text widget displays text longer than the width of the widget in one of two ways. It can either truncate the line at the edge of the widget or wrap the text onto multiple lines. The widget can wrap the text at a word or character boundary.

When text wraps to multiple lines, the number of lines on the display will be different from the number of lines in the internal representation of the text. When referencing a location within the text widget, the line and character position refers to the internal representation of the text, not what is displayed.

When a scrollbar is connected to the text widget, the user can modify which lines are displayed on the screen. This does not affect the content of the text widget, and the line and character positions still reflect the internal representation of the text, not the displayed text. For example, if the user scrolls to the bottom of a document so that the top line is the fiftieth line of the document, the line number is still 50, not 1.

A text string can have a tag associated with it. Tags in a text widget are similar to tags in the canvas object. You can apply zero or more tags to an item of text and apply a given tag to one or more items of text. Tags are used to mark sections of text for special treatment (different fonts, binding actions, and so on). Tags are discussed in more detail later in this chapter.

A text widget can also have marks associated with it. Marks are similar to tags, except that where tags are associated with a text string, a mark is associated with a location in the text. You can have only a single instance of any mark, but you can have multiple marks referring to a single location. Marks are used to denote locations in the document for some action (inserting characters, navigating with a mouse, and so on). Marks are discussed in more detail later in this chapter.

### 11.1.1 Text Location in the text Widget

The text widget does not allow you to place text at any location the way a canvas widget does. A text widget "fills" from the top left, and you can address any position that has a character defined at that location. If a program requests a position outside the range of available lines and characters, the text widget will return the nearest location that has a character defined (usually the end). Tcl uses a list to define the index that describes a location in the text widget:

```
position ?modifier1 modifier2...modifierN?
```

The `position` field may be one of the following.

| | |
|---|---|
| `line.character` | The line and character that define a location in the internal representation of the text. Lines are numbered starting from 1 (to conform to the numbering style of other UNIX applications), and character positions are numbered starting from 0 (to conform to the numbering style of C strings). The `character` field may be numeric or the word end. The end keyword indicates the position of the `newline` character that terminates a line. |
| `@x.y` | The x and y parameters are in pixels. This index maps to the character with a bounding box that includes this pixel. |
| `markID` | The character just after the mark named `markID`. |
| `tagID.first` | The first occurrence of tag `tagID`. |
| `tagID.last` | The last occurrence of tag `tagID`. |
| `windowName` | The name of a window that was placed in this `text` widget with the `window create` widget command. |
| `imageName` | The name of an image that was placed in this `text` widget with the `image create` widget command. |
| `end` | The last character in the `text` widget. |

The modifier fields in an index may be one of

| | |
|---|---|
| `+num chars`<br>`-num chars`<br>`+num lines`<br>`-num lines` | The `location` moves forward or backward by the defined number of characters or lines. The plus symbol (+) moves the `location` forward (right or down), and the minus symbol (−) moves the `location` backward (left or up). |
| `linestart`<br>`lineend` | The index refers to the beginning or end of the line that includes the `location` index. NOTE: {1.0 `lineend`} is equivalent to {1.end}, and {1.0 `linestart`} is equivalent to {1.0}. |
| `wordstart`<br>`wordend` | The index refers to the beginning or end of the word that includes the `location` index. |

### Index Examples

The following are examples of valid and invalid index descriptions.

`0.0`

Not a valid index because line numbers start at 1. This will be mapped to the beginning of the text widget, index `1.0`.

{.b wordend}

> If a letter follows window .b, this refers to the location just before the first space after the .b window.
>
> If window .b is at the end of a word, this refers to the location just after the space that follows window .b.

1.0 lineend

> This is not a valid index; it is not a list.

[list mytag.first lineend -10c wordend]

> Sets the index to the end of the word that has a letter 10 character positions from the end of the line that includes the first reference to the tag mytag. Note that the index is evaluated left to right, as follows.
>
> **1.** Find the tag mytag.
>
> **2.** Move to the end of the line.
>
> **3.** Count back 10 characters.
>
> **4.** Go to the end of the word.

## 11.1.2 Tag Overview

The tag used in a text widget is similar to the tag used with the canvas object. A tag is a string of characters that can be used to identify a single character or text string. A tag can reference several text strings, and a text string can be referenced by multiple tags.

A tag's start and end locations define the text string associated with it. Note that the tag is associated with a location, not the character at a location. If the character at the location is deleted, the tag moves to the location of the nearest character that was included in a tagged area. If all the characters associated with a tag are deleted, the tag no longer exists.

Manipulating portions of text (setting fonts or colors, binding actions, and so on) is done by identifying the text portion with a tag and then manipulating the tagged text via the *textWidget* tag configure command. For instance, the command

```
$textWidget tag configure loud -font [times 24 bold]
```

will cause the text tagged with the tag loud to be drawn with large, bold letters. All text tagged loud will be displayed in a large, bold font.

The sel tag is always defined in a text widget. It cannot be destroyed. When characters in the text widget have been selected (by dragging the cursor over them with the mouse button depressed), the sel tag will define the start and end indices of the selected characters. The sel tag is configured to display the selected text in reverse video.

### 11.1.3 **Mark Overview**

A mark identifies a single location in the text, not a range of locations. Marks are associated with the spaces between the characters, instead of being associated with a character location. If the characters around a mark are deleted, the mark will be moved to stay next to the remaining characters. Marks are manipulated with the textName mark commands.

A mark can be declared to have gravity. The gravity of a mark controls how the mark will be moved when new characters are inserted at a mark. The gravity may be one of

left    The mark is treated as though it is attached to the character on the left, and any new characters are inserted to the right of the mark. Thus, the location of the mark on a line will not change.

right    The mark is treated as though it is attached to the character on the right, and new characters are inserted to the left of the mark. Thus, the location of the mark will be one greater character location every time a character is inserted.

The following two marks are always defined.

insert    The location of the insertion cursor.

current    The location closest to the mouse location. Note that this is not updated if the mouse is moved with button 1 depressed (as in a drag operation).

### 11.1.4 **Image Overview**

Images created with the image create command (covered in Chapter 10) can be inserted into a text widget. The annotation that defines an image uses a single character location regardless of the height or width of the image. The *textWidget* image create command can insert multiple copies of an image into a text widget. Each time an image is inserted, a unique identifier will be returned that can be used to refer to this instance of the image.

### 11.1.5 **Window Overview**

The *textWidget* window create command will insert a Tk widget such as a button, canvas, or even another text widget into a text widget. Only a single copy of any widget can be inserted. If the same widget is used as the argument of two textWidget window create commands, the first occurrence of the widget will be deleted, and it will be inserted at the location defined in the second command.

## 11.2 Creating a text Widget

Text widgets are created the same way as other widgets, with a command that returns the specified widget name. Like other widgets, the text widget supports defining the height and width on the command line. Note that the unit for the height and width is the size of a character in the default font, rather than pixels. You can determine the font being used by a text widget with the configure or cget widget command. (See Section 9.4.)

**Syntax:**  text *textName ?options ?*

Create a text widget.

*textName*    The name for this text widget.

?options?    Some of the options supported by the text widget are

-state *state*

Defines the initial state for this widget. May be one of

normal    The text widget will permit text to be edited.

disabled The text widget will not permit text to be edited. This option creates a display-only version of the widget.

-tabs *tabList*

Defines the tab stops for this text widget. Tabs are defined as a location (in any screen distance format, as described in Chapter 9) and an optional modifier to define how to justify the text within the column. The modifier may be one of

left    Left-justify the text.

right    Right-justify the text.

center    Center the text.

numeric    Line up a decimal point or the least significant digit at the tab location.

-wrap *style*

Defines how lines of text will wrap. May be one of

none    Lines will not wrap. Characters that do not fit within the defined width are not displayed.

word    Lines will wrap on the space between words. The final space on a line will be displayed as a newline, rather than leave a trailing space on the line before the wrap. Words are not wrapped on hyphens.

char     Lines will wrap at the last location in the text widget, regardless of the character. This is the default mode.

-spacing1 *distance*

Defines the extra blank space to leave above a line of text when it is displayed. If the line of text wraps to multiple lines when it is displayed, only the top line will have this space added.

-spacing2 *distance*

Defines the extra blank space to leave above lines that have been wrapped when they are displayed.

-spacing3 *distance*

Defines the extra blank space to leave below a line of text when it is displayed. If the line of text wraps to multiple lines when it is displayed, only the bottom line will have this space added.

## Example 11.1

### *Script Example*

```
# Create the text widget and pack it.

set txt [text .t -height 12 -width 72 -background white \
        -tabs {2.5i right 3i left 5.8i numeric}]
pack $txt

# Insert several lines at the end location. Each new line
# becomes the new last line in the widget.

$txt insert end "The next lines demonstrate tabbed text\n"
$txt insert end "\n"
$txt insert end "noTab \t Right Justified \t \
    Left Justified \t Numeric\n"
$txt insert end "\n"
$txt insert end "line1 \t column1 \t column2 \t 1.0\n"
$txt insert end "line2 \t column1 text \t column2\
  text \t 22.00\n"

$txt insert end "line3 \t text in column1 \t text\
  for column2 \t 333.00\n"

# Insert a few lines at specific line locations.
#   To demonstrate some location examples

$txt insert 1.0 "These lines are inserted last, but are\n"
$txt insert 2.0 "inserted at the\n"
```

```
$txt insert 2.end " beginning of the text widget\n"
$txt insert {3.5 linestart} "so that they appear first.\n"
$txt insert 4.0 "\n"
```

***Script Output***

```
These lines are inserted last, but are
inserted at the beginning of the text widget
so that they appear first.

The next lines demonstrate tabbed text

noTab    Right justified    Left justified    Numeric

line1             column1    column2               1.0
line2       column1 text    column2 text        22.00
line3    text in column1    text for column2   333.00
```

## 11.3 Text Widget Subcommands

This section describes several of the more useful subcommands supported by the text widget. See the on-line documentation for your version of Tk for more details and to see if other subcommands are implemented in the version you are using. The dump subcommand provides detailed information about the content of the text widget. Thus, it is very seldom used in actual programming. The dump subcommand is used in the following discussion of the text widget, as we examine how text strings, marks, and tags are handled by the text widget.

The dump subcommand returns a list of the text widget's content between two index points. Each entry in the list consists of sets of three fields: identifier, data, and index. The identifier may have one of several values that will define the data that follows. The data field will contain different values, depending on the value of the identifier. The index field will always be a value in line.char format. The values of identifier and the associated data may be one of the following.

text    The following data will be text to be displayed on the text widget. If there are multiple words in the text, the text will be grouped with curly braces.

tagon    Denotes the start of a tagged section of text. The data associated with this identifier will be a tag name. The index will be the location at which the tagged text starts.

| | |
|---|---|
| tagoff | Denotes the end of a tagged section of text. The data associated with this identifier will be a tag name. The index will be the location at which the tagged text ends. |
| mark | Denotes the location of a mark. The data associated with this identifier will be a mark name. The index will be the location to the right of the mark. |
| image | Denotes the location of an image to be displayed in the text widget. The index will be the index of the character to the right of the image. |
| window | Denotes the location of a window to be displayed in the text widget. The index will be the index of the character to the right of the window. |

## 11.3.1 Inserting and Deleting Text

The insert subcommand will insert one or more sets of text into the text widget. Each set of text can have zero or more tags associated with it.

**Syntax:** *textName* insert *index* *text* *?tags?* *?textN?* *?tagsN?* *?...?*

Insert text into text widget.

| | |
|---|---|
| *textName* | The name of the text widget. |
| *index* | The index at which to insert this text, formatted as described in Section 11.1.1. |
| *text* | A string of text to insert. If this text includes embedded newlines (\n), it will be inserted as multiple lines. |
| *tagList* | An optional list of tags to associate with the preceding text. |

The following example creates a text widget, inserts three lines of text, and displays a formatted dump of the text widget content. Notice the foreach command with three arguments in a list to step through the dump output. The ability to use a list of arguments to a foreach command was added in Tcl revision 7.4. The foreach with a list of iterator variables is a useful construct for stepping through data formatted as sets of items, instead of as a list of lists. (See Example 9.15 for an example of this form of the foreach command.)

## Example 11.2

### Script Example

```
text .t -height 5 -width 70 -background white
pack .t

.t insert end "This text is tagged 'TAG1'. " TAG1
.t insert end "This is on the same line, 'TAG2'\n" TAG2
.t insert end \
```

```
      "The newline after 'TAG2' puts this on a new line.\n"
.t insert 2.0 \
      "Line 2 becomes line 3 when this is inserted at 2.0\n" \
      INSERTED

set textDump [.t dump 1.0 end -all]

puts "[format "%-7s %-50s %6s\n" ID DATA INDEX]"

foreach {id data index} $textDump {
    puts "[format {%-7s %-50s %6s} \
        $id [string trim $data] $index]"
}
```

*Script Output*

| ID | DATA | INDEX |
|----|------|-------|
| tagon | TAG1 | 1.0 |
| text | This text is tagged 'TAG1'. | 1.0 |
| tagoff | TAG1 | 1.28 |
| tagon | TAG2 | 1.28 |
| text | This is on the same line, 'TAG2' | 1.28 |
| tagoff | TAG2 | 2.0 |
| tagon | INSERTED | 2.0 |
| text | Line 2 becomes line 3 when this is inserted at 2.0 | 2.0 |
| tagoff | INSERTED | 3.0 |
| text | The newline after 'TAG2' puts this on a new line. | 3.0 |
| mark | insert | 4.0 |
| mark | current | 4.0 |
| text | | 4.0 |

```
This text is tagged 'TAG1'. This is on the same line,  'TAG2'
Line 2 becomes line 3 when this is inserted at 2.0
The newline after 'TAG2' puts this on a new line.
```

In the previous example, all lines are shorter than the width of the text widget. Since none of the lines wrap, the text widget display resembles the internal representation. The first line of the example inserts a line with the text *This text is tagged 'TAG1'.* at the end of the text widget. Since there was no text in the widget, the end was also the beginning at that point. The dump shows that tag TAG1 starts at index 1.0 and ends at index 1.28. The text also starts at index 1.0.

Note that the second set of text is also inserted onto line 1. This is because the first set of inserted text did not have a newline character to mark it as terminating a line. The second set of text has a newline character at the end, which causes the next line to be inserted at index 2.0. However, the last insert command inserts text at location 2.0 and terminates that text with a newline, pushing the line that was at index 2.0 down to index 3.0.

The delete subcommand deletes the text between two locations.

*Syntax:*   textName delete *startIndex ?endIndex?*

Remove text from a text widget.

*startIndex*   The location at which to start removing characters.

*?endIndex?*   If *endIndex* is greater than *startIndex*, delete the characters after *startIndex* to (but not including) the character after *endIndex*. If *endIndex* is less than *startIndex*, no characters are deleted. If *endIndex* is not present, only the character after *startIndex* is deleted.

## 11.3.2 **Searching Text**

A script can search for text within a text widget using the *textWidget* search subcommand. This command will search forward or backward from an index point or search between two index points.

*Syntax:*   textName search *?options? pattern startIndex ?endIndex?*

*textName*   The name of the text widget.

search   Search the content of this text widget for text that matches a particular pattern.

*?options?*   Options for search include

| Search Direction | These are mutually exclusive options. |
| -forwards | The direction to search from the startIndex. |
| -backwards | |
| Search Style | These are mutually exclusive options. The default search style is to use glob rules. |
| -exact | Search for an exact match. |
| -regexp | Use regular expression rules to match the pattern to text. |
| -nocase | Ignore the case when comparing pattern to the text. |
| Other Options | These are not mutually exclusive options. |

| | |
|---|---|
| -count *varName* | The -count option must be followed by a variable name. If the search is successful, the number of characters matched will be placed in `varName`. |
| -- | Signifies that this is the last option. The next argument will be interpreted as a pattern, even if it starts with a "-", and would otherwise be interpreted as an option. As with the `switch` command, it is good style to use the "--"option whenever you use the `search` subcommand. This will ensure that your code will not generate an unexpected syntax error if it is used to search for a string starting with a "-". |
| *pattern* | A pattern to search for. May be a `glob` or `regexp` pattern or a text string. |
| *startIndex* | The location in the text widget to start searching from. |
| *?endIndex?* | An optional location in the text widget to stop searching at. |

## Example 11.3

### *Script Example*

```
# Create and pack a text widget
text .t -height 5 -width 68 -font {times 14}
pack .t

# Insert some text
.t insert end "The default style for the "
.t insert end "search" courier
.t insert end " command is to use"
.t insert end " glob " courier
.t insert end "rules.\n"
.t insert end "The"
.t insert end " -regexp " courier
.t insert end "flag will treat the pattern as a regular expression\n"
.t insert end "and, using the"
.t insert end " -exact " courier
.t insert end "flag will match an exact string."
.t tag configure courier -font {courier 14 }

# "Exact" doesn't exist in this text, search will return ""
```

```
set pos [.t search -exact -count matchchars -- "Exact" 1.0 end]
puts "Position of 'Exact' is '$pos' "

# "-exact flag" does exist. This will match 11 characters
# The two different fonts do not matter.

set pos \
   [.t search -exact -count matchchars -- "-exact flag" 1.0 end]
puts "Position of '-exact': $pos matched $matchchars chars"

# This regular expression search also searches for "-e"
# followed by any characters except a space .
# It will match to "-exact"

set pos [.t search -regexp -count matchchars -- {-e[^ ]+} 1.0 end]

puts "Position of '-e\[^ ]*': $pos matched $matchchars chars"

# This is an error - the lack of the "--" argument causes the
#   search argument "-e[^f]*" to be treated as a flag.

set pos [.t search -regexp -count matchchars {-e[^f]*} 1.0 end]
puts "This line is not evaluated."
```

***Script Output***

**Position of 'Exact' is "**
**Position of '-exact': 3.15 matched 11 chars**
**Position of '-e[^ ]*': 3.15 matched 6 chars**
**bad switch "-e[^f]*": must be --, -backward, -count, -elide,**
**  -exact, -forward, -nocase, or -regexp**

> The default style for the `search` command is to use `glob` rules.
> The `-regexp` flag will treat the pattern as a regular expression
> and, using the `-exact` flag will match an exact string.

### 11.3.3 **The** mark **Subcommands**

The *textName* mark subcommands are used to manipulate marks in the text
widget. Marks are used when you need to remember a particular location in the
text. For instance, you can use marks to define an area of text to highlight, for a
cut-and-paste operation, and so on. The *textName* mark set command defines a
mark.

*Syntax:* *textName* mark set *markName* *index*

Set a mark in the text widget textName.

*markName*    The name to assign to this mark.

*index*      The index of the character to the right of the mark.

## Example 11.4

```
# Put a mark at the beginning of the first three lines
for {set line 1} {$line <= 3} {incr line} {
    $textWidget mark set start_$line $line.0
}
```

The *textName* mark unset command will remove a mark.

*Syntax:* *textName* mark unset *markName* *?... markNameN?*

Remove a mark from the text widget textName.

*markName\**    The name or names of the mark to remove.

## Example 11.5

```
# Remove start_1, start_2, and start_3 marks
for {set line 1} {$line <= 3} {incr line} {
    $textWidget mark unset start_$line
}
```

You can obtain a list of all marks defined in a text widget with the *textName* mark names command.

*Syntax:* *textName* mark names

Return the names of all marks defined in the text widget textName.

## Example 11.6

```
# Remove all start_* marks
foreach mark [$textWidget mark names] {
  if {[string first start_ $mark] == 0} {
    $textWidget mark unset $mark
  }
}
```

You can search for marks before or after a given index position with the *textName* mark next and textName mark previous commands.

***Syntax:*** *textName* mark next *index*

***Syntax:*** *textName* mark previous *index*

Return the name of the first mark after (next) or before (previous) the *index* location.

*index*   The index from which to start the search.

## Example 11.7

***Script Example***

```
# Create a text widget for example
pack [set textWidget [text .t]]

# Insert 3 lines of text and put a mark at the
# beginning of each line
for {set line 1} {$line <= 3} {incr line} {
    $textWidget insert end "This is line $line\n"
    $textWidget mark set start_$line $line.0
}

# Step through the marks in a text widget
# Starting from the beginning

update idle;
set index 1.0
while {![string match $index ""]} {
    set index [$textWidget mark next $index]
    puts "Index is: $index"
}
```

***Script Output***

```
Index is: start_1
Index is: current
Index is: start_2
Index is: start_3
Index is: insert
Index is:
```

The next example shows how marks appear in a text widget.

## Example 11.8

***Script Example***

```
pack [text .t -height 5 -width 60]

.t insert end "A mark will be set in this line, \nas shown by dump"
```

```
.t mark set demoMark 1.2

puts "The first mark is: [.t mark next 1.0]"
puts "The last mark is: [.t mark previous end]"
set textDump [.t dump 1.0 end -all]
puts "[format "%-7s %-50s %6s\n" ID DATA INDEX]"
foreach {id data index} $textDump {
  puts "[format {%-7s %-50s %6s} $id [string trim $data] $index]"
}
```

***Script Output***

```
ID      DATA                                       INDEX

text    A                                            1.0
mark    demoMark                                     1.2
text    mark will be set in this line,              1.2
text    as shown by dump                             2.0
mark    insert                                      2.16
mark    current                                     2.16
text                                                2.16
```

```
A mark will be set in this line,
as shown by dump
```

## 11.3.4 Tags

Many of the interesting things that can be done with a text widget are done with tags. Tags define text that should be displayed in different fonts or colors, text with a highlighted background, text bound to an event, and so on.

### Creating and Destroying Tags

Tags can be attached to text when the text is inserted, as shown in Example 11.2, or they can be added later with the *textName* tag add command. The *textName* tag remove command will remove a tag from a specific set of characters, and the textName tag delete command will remove all occurrences of a tag.

**Syntax:** *textName* tag add *tagName startIndex1 ?end1? ?start2 ... endN?*

> *textName*    The text widget that will contain the tag.
>
> tag add    Add a tag at the defined index points.

startIndex ?end?   The tag will be attached to the character at startIndex and will contain all characters up to but not including the character at end. If the end is less than the startIndex, or if the start-Index does not refer to any character in the text widget, no characters are tagged.

## Example 11.9

```
# Tag the first letter of the page
$textWidget tag add "firstLetter" 1.0 1.1
```

---

**Syntax:** textName tag remove tagName start1 ?end1? ?start2 ... endN?

|  |  |
|---|---|
| textName | The text widget that contains the tag. |
| tag delete | Remove tag information for the named tags from characters in the ranges defined. |
| tagName | The names of tags to be removed. |
| start* ?end? | The range of characters from which to remove the tag information. |

## Example 11.10

```
# Remove the firstLetter tag on the first letter
$textWidget tag remove "firstLetter" 1.0 1.1
```

---

**Syntax:** textName tag delete tagName ?...tagnameN?

|  |  |
|---|---|
| textName | The text widget that contains the tag. |
| tag delete | Delete all information about the tags named in this command. |
| tagName* | The names of tags to be deleted. |

## Example 11.11

```
# Clear all tags in this widget
#  NOTE: "tag names" is described in the next section
eval $textWidget tag delete [$textWidget tag names]
```

---

### Finding Tags

Your script can get a list of tags that have been defined at a particular location, a range of locations, or an entire text widget. You can also retrieve a list of locations that are associated with a tag. Multiple tags can reference the same location in a text file. For instance, the first character of a paragraph may be in a different font, tagged to show that it is the start of a keyword, and tagged as the first character after a page break. You can obtain a list of the tags at a location with the tag names command.

> *Syntax:* textName tag names ?index?
>
> | textName | The text widget that contains the tags. |
> | tag names | Return a list of all tags defined at index. |
> | *index* | The index point to check for tags. If the index is not included, the list of all tags defined for this text widget is returned. |

## Example 11.12

```
# Display the tags at the start of line 2:
puts [$textWidget tag names 2.0]
```

When you are processing the content of a text widget, you may want to step through the widget looking at tags in the order in which they appear. The nextrange and prevrange commands will step through a text widget, returning the index points that fall within the requested range of characters.

Note that the prevrange and nextrange commands expect the start and end locations in the opposite order. For the prevrange command, startIndex is greater than endIndex, whereas for nextrange the endIndex is greater than startIndex.

> *Syntax:* textName tag nextrange *tagName startIndex ?endIndex?*
>
> *Syntax:* textName tag prevrange *tagName startIndex ?endIndex?*
>
> | *textName* | The text widget that contains the tags. |
> | tag nextrange | Return the first index defined after startIndex but before endIndex. |
> | tag prevrange | Return the first index defined before startIndex but after endIndex. |
> | *tagName* | The name of the tag to search for. |
> | *startIndex endIndex* | The index points that defined the boundaries for the search. |

## Example 11.13

### *Script Example*

```
# Create a text widget for example
pack [set textWidget [text .t]]
```

```
# Add tagged and untagged text text

for {set i 0} {$i < 3} {incr i} {
    $textWidget insert end "$i --" "myTag"
    $textWidget insert end "-$i\n"
}

# Initialize the "current" mark to the start of text

$textWidget mark set current 1.0

# Find the next range of the tag "myTag" after current

set tagRange [$textWidget tag nextrange "myTag" current]

# Loop until the nextrange returns an empty string

while {![string match $tagRange ""]} {
    # Do something interesting with the tag data here
    puts "Range for myTag: $tagRange"

    # Set the current mark to the end of the tagged area
    $textWidget mark set current [lindex $tagRange 1]

    # Find the next tagged range.
    set tagRange [$textWidget tag nextrange "myTag" current]
}
```

*Script Output*

**Range for myTag: 1.0 1.4**
**Range for myTag: 2.0 2.4**
**Range for myTag: 3.0 3.4**

---

The tag ranges command will return a list of all index ranges a tag references.

*Syntax:* *textName* tag ranges *tagName*

| | |
|---|---|
| *textName* | The text widget that contains the tags. |
| tag ranges | Return a list of index ranges that have been tagged with tagName. |
| *tagName* | The name of the tag to search for. |

## Example 11.14

*Script Example*

```
# Create a text widget for example
pack [set textWidget [text .t]]
```

```
# Add tagged and untagged text text
for {set i 0} {$i < 3} {incr i} {
    $textWidget insert end "$i --" "myTag"
    $textWidget insert end "-$i\n"
}

set tagRanges [$textWidget tag ranges "myTag"]
puts "The tagged ranges are: $tagRanges"
foreach {start end} $tagRanges {
    puts "'[$textWidget get $start $end]' is tagged"
}
```

### Script Output

**The tagged ranges are: 1.0 1.4 2.0 2.4 3.0 3.4**
**'0 --' is tagged**
**'1 --' is tagged**
**'2 --' is tagged**

---

The next example shows a more complex set of tags and text strings.

## Example 11.15

### Script Example

```
text .t -height 5 -width 70
pack .t
.t insert end \
  "Text can have multiple tags at any given index.\n" T1
.t insert end \
  "You can get a list of tags at an index with 'tag names'.\n" T2
.t insert end \
  "You can search the text with prevrange and nextrange.\n" T3
.t insert end "You can get the ranges where a tag is \
  defined with 'ranges'" T4

.t tag add firstchar 1.0
.t tag add firstline 1.0 {1.0 lineend}
.t tag add firstpage 1.0 end
.t tag add secondline 2.0
.t tag add firstchar 2.0
.t tag add firstchar 3.0
.t tag add firstchar 4.0

puts "These tags are defined:\n [.t tag names]\n"

puts "These tags are defined at index 1.0:"
puts " [.t tag names 1.0]\n"
```

```
puts "Tag firstchar is defined for these ranges:"
puts " [.t tag ranges firstchar]\n"

puts "Tag T2 is defined for the range:\n [.t tag ranges T2]\n"

puts "The first occurrence of firstchar after the"
puts " start of line 3 is:"
puts " [.t tag nextrange firstchar 3.0]\n"

puts "The first occurrence of firstchar before the"
puts " start of line 3 is:"
puts " [.t tag prevrange firstchar 3.0]\n"
```

*Script Output*

**These tags are defined:**
  **sel T1 T2 T3 T4 firstchar firstline firstpage secondline**

**These tags are defined at index 1.0:**
  **T1 firstchar firstline firstpage**

**Tag firstchar is defined for these ranges:**
  **1.0 1.1 2.0 2.1 3.0 3.1 4.0 4.1**

**Tag T2 is defined for the range:**
  **2.0 3.0**

**The first occurrence of firstchar after the**
  **start of line 3 is:**
  **3.0 3.1**

**The first occurrence of firstchar before the**
  **start of line 3 is:**
  **2.0 2.1**

```
Text can have multiple tags at any given index.
You can get a list of tags at an index with 'tag names'.
You can search the text with prevrange and nextrange.
You can get the ranges where a tag is defined with 'ranges'
```

## Using Tags

Tags are the interface into the text widget that allows you to bind actions to events on sections of text, set colors, set fonts, set margins, set line spacing, and so on. This section discusses a few of the things that can be done with tags and provides an example of how to use tags. The complete list of options you can set with a tag is in the on-line documentation. The tag bind command will bind an action to an event in a tagged area of text.

**Syntax:** *textName* tag bind *tagName ?eventType? ?script?*

    *textName*      The name of the text widget.

    tag bind      Bind an action to an event occurring on the tagged section of text, or return the script to be evaluated when an event occurs.

    *tagName*      The name of the tag that defines the range of characters that will accept an event.

    *?eventType?*      If the eventType field is set, this defines the event that will trigger this action. The event types are the same as those defined for canvas events in Section 10.5.

    *script*      The script to evaluate when this event occurs.

## Example 11.16

### Script Example

```
# Create a text widget for example
pack [set textWidget [text .t -height 10 -width 60]]

# insert some text
$textWidget insert end "This is text with a "
$textWidget insert end "secret" secretWord
$textWidget insert end " in it"

# Pop up a message box when someone clicks on the secret word

$textWidget tag bind secretWord <Button-1> \
        {tk_messageBox -type ok -message "You found the secret!"}
```

### Script Output

After clicking the word *secret*

The `tag configure` command will modify how tagged text is displayed. The `tag configure` command will allow you to set many of the options that control a display, including the following.

| | |
|---|---|
| `-foreground` *color* <br> `-background` *color* | The foreground and background colors for the text. |
| `-font` *fontID* | The font to use when displaying this text. |
| `-justify` *style* | How to justify text with this tag. May be `left`, `right`, or `center`. |
| `-offset` *pixels* | The vertical offset in pixels for this line from the base location for displaying text. A positive value raises the text above where it would otherwise be displayed, and a negative value lowers the text. This can be used to display subscripts and superscripts. |
| `-lmargin1` *pixels* <br> `-lmargin2` *pixels* <br> `-rmargin pixels` | The distance from the left and right edges to use as a margin. The `rmargin` value is a distance from the right edge of the text widget to treat as a right margin. |
| | The `lmargin1` is a distance from the left edge to treat as a margin for display lines that have not wrapped, and `lmargin2` is a distance to use as a margin for lines that have wrapped. |
| `-underline` *boolean* | Specifies whether or not to underline characters. |

The next example displays a few lines of text in several fonts and binds the creation of a label with more information to a button click on the word `tag`.

## Example 11.17

### *Script Example*

```
# Create and pack the text widget
text .t -height 5 -width 60
pack .t

# Insert some text with lots of tags.
.t insert end "T" {firstLetter} "he " {normal}
.t insert end "tag" {code action}
.t insert end " command allows you to create displays\n"
.t insert end "with multiple fonts" {normal} "1" {superscript}
.t insert end "\n\n"
.t insert end "1" {superscript}
.t insert end "Tcl/Tk for Real Programmers, " {italic} \
    "Clif Flynt, " {bold}
.t insert end "Academic Press, 1999"

# Set the fonts for the various types of tagged text
```

```
.t tag configure italic -font {times 14 italic}
.t tag configure normal -font {times 14 roman}
.t tag configure bold -font {times 14 bold}

# Set font and offset to make superscript text
.t tag configure superscript -font {times 10 roman} -offset 5

# Set font for typewriter style font
.t tag configure code -font {courier 14 roman underline}

# Define a font to make a fancy first letter for a word
.t tag configure firstLetter -font {times 16 italic bold}

# Bind an action to the text tagged as "action".
.t tag bind {action} <Button-1> {
  label .l -text "See Chapter 10" -relief raised;
  place .l -x 50 -y 10 ;
}
```

### Script Output

The _tag_ command allows you to create displays
with multiple fonts[1]

[1]_Tcl/Tk for Real Programmers_, **Clif Flynt**, Academic Press, 1999

The _ta_  See Chapter 10  ows you to create displays
with multiple fonts

[1]_Tcl/Tk for Real Programmers_, **Clif Flynt**, Academic Press, 1999

## 11.3.5 Inserting Images and Widgets into a text Widget

Following the pattern used by the canvas widget, you can insert an image created
with the image create command into a text widget with the *textName* image
create command, and other Tk widgets can be inserted into a text widget with
the *textName* window create command.

**Syntax:**  *textName* image create *index* ?*options*?

| | |
|---|---|
| *textName* | The name of the text widget this image will be placed in. |
| image create | Insert an image into a text widget. |
| *index* | The index at which to insert the image. |

| | |
|---|---|
| *?options?* | The options for the image create command include |

| | |
|---|---|
| -image *handle* | The image object handle returned when the Tk image object was created. (See Section 10.8.) |
| -name *imageName* | A name to use to refer to this image. A default name will be returned if this option is not present. |

## Example 11.18

### *Script Example*

```
# Create a bird graphic

set bird {
R0lGODlhIAAgAJEAANnZ2QAAAP///////yH5BAEAAAAALAAAAAAgACAAAAKWhI+p
y+0Po5y02qtIHIJvFD8IPhrFDwAAxCPwjeID3N3dEfiYFB/zCD4mxcdMgo9H8TGT
40NRfARAgo9pFP8IPqYaxccj+JhI8Y1gx93dHcUPgo+pSPGD4GMqUnyCj61J8Qk+
pibFJviYqhSb4GOqRlBC+Ji6EZQQPqZqBCWEj6kbQfAxdSOIPqYuBIXwMXW5/WGU
kz5SADs=
}

image create photo bird -data $bird

# Create and pack the text widget
text .t -height 2 -width 60 -background white -font {times 16 bold}
pack .t

.t image create 1.0 -image bird
.t insert 1.1 " Watch the birdie"
```

### *Script Output*

Watch the birdie

---

In the same fashion, another Tk widget (even another text widget) can be placed in a text widget with the window create object command.

***Syntax:*** *textName* window create *index ?options?*

| | |
|---|---|
| *textName* | The name of the text widget that this window will be inserted into. |
| window create | Insert a Tk widget into the text widget. |

| | |
|---|---|
| *index* | The index at which to insert the Tk widget. |
| *?options?* | The options for the window create command include |

| | |
|---|---|
| -window *widgetName* | The name given to this widget when it was created. |
| -create *script* | A script to evaluate to create the window if the -window option is not used. |

The text widget inserts the new image or widget at the requested index. It treats images and windows as if they were a single character. If the image or widget is inserted into an existing line, the height of the line will be increased to the size of the image. If you want to create a display with columnar format, you can use two text widgets and put the text for the left column in one text widget, and the text for the right column in the other, and then use window create to place the two text windows side by side.

### Example 11.19

#### Script Example

```
pack [text .t -width 60 -height 5 -background white]
label .l -text "label"
.t window create 1.0 -window .l
.t insert 1.1 " This is a label\n"
.t window create 2.0 -create {button .b1 -text "Button"}
.t insert 2.1 " This is a button\ndescribed on two lines"
```

#### Script Output

Notice in the previous example that *described on two lines* appears below the button, instead of having all text appear to the right. Images and windows appear on a line, just like text, and cannot span multiple lines. If you want to have an image that spans multiple lines, you must add a second text widget to hold the text, as shown in the next example.

The -borderwidth and -highlightthickness options are used with the second text widget to make it "invisible." By default, a text widget will have a border around it, which may not be the visual effect you wish.

**Example** 11.20

*Script Example*

```
set scroll {
R01GODdhNQC1AJEAAP///wAAAP///////ywAAAAANQC1AAAC/4SPqcvtD6OctNqL
s968+z8RsQk+pi43xccg+Ji6jBQfkeBj6rJRfEwj+Ji6S/GD4FNsgo+pqxSf4B/F
JviYukmxAQAOCEBEBMHH1M2gJABA8QEAjuBj6iLFBrgzICARQfAxdS8oCUBEBAGJ
MIugED6m7gU1AYgIICQRAAAUEz6m7gU1AYgAICRBsCOC4GPqX1ASiAgAQkKwI4Lg
Y+piUBKAiCD4FxGIiAghROIAXBB8iIhARIQQQiQOAFwAAaDYBB9TN4OSAABQfAyC
j6mrFBsA4O4IPqbuUmyCT7EJPqYuA8Um+Ji63EhxCD6mLjdSHIKPqcuNFJvgY+py
H8Um+P+YutxHsQk+pi73UWyCj6nLfRSf4GPqchvFJ/iYutxHsQk+pi73UWyCj6nL
fRSb4GPqch/FJ/iYutxG8Qk+pi63UXyCj6nLbRSf4GPqch/FJviYutxH8Qk+pi63
UXyCj6nLbRSf4GPqchvFJ/iYutxG8YPgY+pyA8UPgo+py20Un+Bj6nIbxSf4mLrc
RvEJPqYut1H8IPiYutxA8YPgY+pyA8UPgo+pyw0UPwg+pi43UHwj+Ji63EDxg+Bj
6nIDxQ+Cj6nLDRQ/CD6mLjdQ/CD4mLrcQPGN4GPqc1N8I/iYutwU3wg+pi43UPwg
+Ji63EDxjeBj6nJTfCP4mLrcFN//CD6mLjffFN4KPqctN8Y3gY+pyU/wj+Ji6zBT/
CD6mLjPFP4KPqctN8Y3gY+pyU/wj+Ji6zBT/CD6mLjPFP4KPqctM8Y/gY+oyU/wj
+Ji6zBQfCT6mLi/FR4KPqctL8ZHgY+oyU/wj+Ji6zBT/CD6mLjPFP4KPqctM8Y/g
Y+pyU3wj+Ji63BT/CD6mLjPFP4KPqctM8Y/gY+pyU3wj+Ji63BTfCD6mLjffFN4KP
qctN8Y3gY+pyA8U3go+pyO3xjeBj6nJTfCP4mLrcFN8IPqyuN8U3go+pywOUPwg+
pi43UPwg+Ji63EDxjeBj6nJTfCP4mLrcQPGD4GPqcgPFD4KP/6nLDRQ/CD6mLjdQ
/CD4mLrcQPGD4GPqchvFJ/iYutxG8YPgY+pyA8UPgo+pywOUPwg+pi63UXyCj6nL
bRSf4GPqchvFJ/iYutxG8Qk+pi73UXyCj6nLbRSf4GPqchvFJ/iYutxG8Qk+pi73
UWyCj6nLfRSb4GPqch/FJviYutxH8Qk+pi63UXyCj6nLfRSb4GPqch/FJviYutxH
sQk+pi73UWyCj6nLjRSH4GPqciPFJviYutxHsQk+pi73UWyCj6nLfRSb4GPqciPF
IfiYumwUh+BDRAQiIoQQQiS+EeyICIKPqbsUHwEAMAg+pm5SbAC4AAIQEUHwMXUx
KAnBj8GIuKAkBB9TF4MSwreIuKAkBB9T94KSAABEEJwwiAgK4WPqX1ACAIgIghNh
EUEhfEzdCOoAEBFBQCIMIighfEzdCOoAEBFASCIACgJwcfUvaAEABTfAACQ4GPq
X1ASAKD4BDsiguBj615QEgCACArhU2yCj6mLQUkIPgLFJviYukmxCf5SRfIKPqasU
m+BT/CD4mLpM8TGD4GPqslF8RIKPqctJ8ZHgY+pyA8Um+Ji63P4wykmrvTjrzbv/
YCiOZEcUADs=
}
```

```
 image create photo scroll -data $scroll

pack [text .t -width 60 -height 12 -background white]
.t image create 1.0 -image scroll
 text .t2 -width 35 -height 5 -background white \
     -font {times 16 bold} -borderwidth 0 \
     -highlightthickness 0

.t window create 1.1 -window .t2

.t2 insert 1.0 "When laying out pictures and text\n"
.t2 insert 2.0 "You may begin feeling quite vexed\n"
.t2 insert 3.0 "Put a window in line\n"
.t2 insert 4.0 "And the layout works fine\n"
.t2 insert 5.0 "And we'll render HTML next."
```

*Script Output*

When laying out pictures and text
You may begin feeling quite vexed
Put a window in line
And the layout works fine
And we'll render HTML next.

## 11.4 HTML Display Package

HTML is currently the most portable protocol for distributing formatted text, and the odds are good that HTML will continue to be important for many years. The text widget tags make it possible to use the text widget to display HTML text with little work.

Stephen Uhler wrote `html_library`, a library that will display HTML in a text widget. The `html_library` is a good example of what you can do with the text widget, so we will examine it. The HTML library is not a part of the standard Tk distribution. It is available on the companion CD-ROM and on the web at the following two addresses, among other locations.

- *http://wuarchive.wustl.edu/languages/tcl/html_library-0.3.tar.gz*
- *http://noucorp.com/*

The `htmllib` parsing engine is used in the `tcllib` (*http://tcllib.sf.net/*) `htmlparse` package.

### 11.4.1 Displaying HTML Text

Using the `html_library` package to display text is very simple, as follows.

| *Step* | *Example* |
| --- | --- |
| 1. Source the `html_library` code. | `source htmllib.tcl` |
| 2. Create a text widget to contain the displayed HTML text. | `text .t` |
| 3. Map the text widget to the display. | `pack .t` |
| 4. Initialize the HTML library by calling `HMinit_win`. | `HMinit_win .t` |
| 5. Display your HTML text by calling `HMparse_html`. | `HMparse_html $html "HMrender .t"` |

The following example shows a text window being used to display some HTML text and a dump of the first couple of lines. Note that the tags are used to define the indenting and fonts.

**Example** 11.21

*Script Example*

```
# Load the htmllib scripts
source "htmllib.tcl"

# Create and display a text widget:
pack [text .t -height 7 -width 50]

# Initialize the text widget
HMinit_win .t

# Define some HTML text
set txt {
<HTML><BODY>Test HTML
  <P><B>Bold Text</B>
  <P><I>Italics</I>
</BODY></HTML>
}

# and render it into the text widget
HMparse_html $txt "HMrender .t"

# Examine what's in the text widget
set textDump [.t dump 1.0 4.0 -all]
puts "[format "%-7s %-30s %6s\n" ID DATA INDEX]"
foreach {id data index} $textDump {
    puts "[format {%-7s %-30s %6s} $id [string trim $data] $index]"
}
```

*Script Output*

```
mark      current                        1.0
tagon                                    1.0
tagon     indent0                        1.0
tagon     font:arial:14:medium:r         1.0
text      Test HTML                      1.0
tagoff    indent0                        1.11
tagoff                                   1.11
tagon     space                          1.11
text                                     1.11
text                                     2.0
tagoff    space                          3.0
tagoff    font:arial:14:medium:r         3.0
tagon                                    3.0
```

| tagon  | indent0               | 3.0  |
|--------|------------------------|------|
| tagon  | font:arial:14:bold:r   | 3.0  |
| text   | Bold Text              | 3.0  |
| tagoff | font:arial:14:bold:r   | 3.9  |
| tagon  | font:arial:14:medium:r | 3.9  |
| text   |                        | 3.9  |
| tagoff | indent0                | 3.10 |
| tagoff |                        | 3.10 |
| tagon  | space                  | 3.10 |
| text   |                        | 3.10 |

Test HTML

**Bold Text**

*Italics*

You can see that the html library uses tags to define the fonts for the text widget to use to display the text.

## 11.4.2 Using html_library Callbacks: Loading Images and Hypertext Links

To display an image, the html_library needs an image widget handle. If the library tried to create the image, it would need code to handle all methods of obtaining image data, and the odds are good that the technique you need for your application would not be supported.

To get around this problem, the html_library calls a procedure that you supply (HMset_image ) to get an image handle. This technique makes the library versatile. Your script can use whatever method is necessary to acquire the image data: load it from the web, extract it from a database, code it into the script, and so on.

The requirements for handling hypertext links are similar. A browser will download a hypertext link from a remote site, a hypertext on-line help will load help files, and a hypertext GUI to a database engine might generate SQL queries. When a user clicks on a hypertext link, the html_library invokes the user-supplied procedure HMlink_callback to process the request.

Note that you must source html_library.tcl before you define your callback procedures. There are dummy versions of HMset_image and HMlink_callback in the html_library package that will override your functions if your script defines these procedures before it sources the html_library.tcl script.

One of the requirements of event-driven GUI programming is that procedures must return quickly. When the script is evaluating a procedure, it is not evaluating the event loop to see if the user has clicked a button (perhaps the Cancel button!). In particular, if the procedure acquiring image data is waiting for data to be read from a remote site, you cannot even use update to force the event loop to run. Therefore, the html_library package was designed to allow the script retrieving an image to return immediately and to use another procedure in the html_library to display the image when it is ready.

The following flowchart shows control flow when the html_library code encounters an <IMG> tag. Note that the creation of the image need not be connected to the flow that initiated the image creation (the HMset_image procedure). An outside event, such as a socket being closed, can invoke HMgot_image.

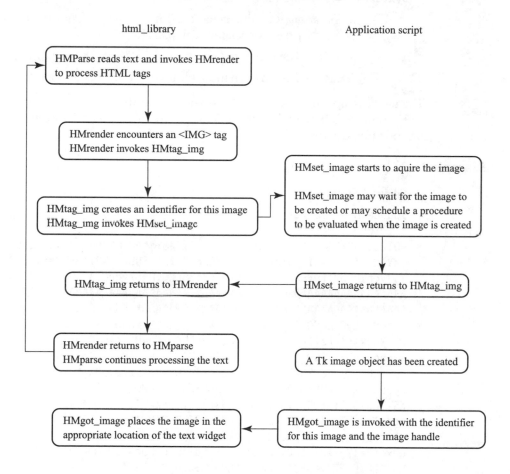

When HMset_image is called, it is passed a handle that identifies this image to the html_library. When the application script calls HMgot_image, it includes this handle and the image object handle of the new image object so that the html_library code knows which <IMG> tag is associated with this image object.

*Syntax:* HMset_image *win handle src*

Create an image widget from the appropriate data, and transfer that image widget back to the html_library by calling HMgot_image.

*win*    The name of the text widget that will ultimately receive the image.

*handle*    A handle provided by the html_library script that must be included with the image handle when HMgot_image is invoked.

*src*    The textual description of the image source. This is the content of the SRC="XXX" field.

*Syntax:* HMgot_image *handle image*

Maps an image widget handle into a text widget in the location defined by data associated with *handle*.

*handle*    The value that was passed to HMset_image as an argument.

*image*    The image handle returned by an image create command.

The next example displays the Tcl feather logo. In this example, the HMset_image call is done as a hard-coded image creation. In an actual application, this would be code to parse the src parameter, and so on.

## Example 11.22

### *Script Example*

```
source htmllib.tcl
set logo {
R0lGODdhKwBAAKUAAP////r6+vX19e3t7fPz8+jo6Obm5uDg4NXV1aurq56e
nnV1dcjIyOLi4ufn/5T09Ovr6+zs70Hh4Xt7e1JSUsXFxX9/f2FhYeTk5I+P
j3Jycn19fbW1tUVFRWtra5mZmY2Njd/f38LCwvHx8ZycnPf39wAAAAAAAAAA
AAAAAAAAAAAAAAAAAAAAAAAAAAAAAAAAAAAAAAAAAAAAAAAAAAAAAAAAAAAAA
AAAAAAAAAAAAAAAAAAAAAAAAAAAAAACwAAAAAKwBAAAAG/kCAcEgsEgOC
pGAgMDqLyCRhQCOYDtgDIsFNKL7fxKH5NAq84LR6zU4U1NNNqIZtk2+94tiCA
zvv/CgkAfICFeIIAfXYYLYAuMhmoIQopsDGAN1pBpBpB5N4AwyODg8NmpudbAsM
Awqpq6VpBkIIiwONjJ+PjayFBUIHiwygDA65uxBLhQO+wKwOoIOJexERCMV3
ygC/eQ5pCwkBEhMUFBWAZNrAxF/eAhLj4xbmy3cLzrkD7u8XgN9CBtuNMBh4
Ny5DGnsKuKVBBKAAQDADxL3TsCHNAGL1noUZ4hCPwgUH8o3bFwjis0xgJAlx
dSfTggISC2YoEODArTucVubRiIHg/rgJEyIMSKWQTU4ALPMk40BzXIcCAzxg
sgYml4s4/CT4OpXBBgM2ibHoJEcBPa1MQZxRoZIMNAFmsZn2GGIrSTtu3f8x+
iF1gl8h8ybv8wusCVg8QPBqjqGYL3kALCFkK8q0DJTj8hhPJQIVxBMtddfhgO
qqxmAYEIWjsX3IK1CGk1A7R2OCBi5IhqflQOed2ogNYLvn804G1qSGZ6wYGb
nUAAk07ReRZAYKp83IehrRn7WYCBqQWY4zhgD02k8SIEkilEHFcBguIlos1b
Tr+eAgn3WANoD12BgnqJFdiU335+HDDBf+0g8wdgSdGTwAQXxOZfAwrmwaBg
CnxQ3Uzj/v01RIOWPVYdBRMU8N4aBHy43RgfPFUbBR8I+EdbINo1wVP5hJDA
ibBxJNgBWjXgTomGtNXRHwZWMNAHuAEiFgD/FFKBkvZVxMsQFfoxUzyQWJUN
IACU8EUiuoSBx1FZ3gEAK2SG0Yd8YKAJhiB9eNHHmgoI8QieX7zFZ5xYgjEI
```

```
nOKkseYCeuZZaJ95VqabX4EEAMZbYo65kaBp1NHGEJAKgqkahKKxpp1kwcmQ
InxWeqcXiKIhpp14tjnnboamWukXt5bgaq64wkfrK5BcRhywdpAxLLFrNHEc
sgtCx6w8cLZxrB/K4NUFFgZAxcQeUSghQBxUDFDAuAZckYUWDQgoSOAS+pXh
7rtOBAEAOw==
}

set HTMLtxt {
<HTML>
<HEAD><TITLE>Example of Embedded image</TITLE></HEAD>
   <BODY>
   <B>Tcl</B>
   <IMG src="logo">
   <B>Powered</B>
   </BODY>
</HTML>
}
############################################################
# proc HMset_image {win handle src {speed {0}}}--
#  Acquire image data, create a Tcl image object,
#  and return the image handle.
#
# Arguments
#  win      The text window in which the html is rendered.
#  handle   A handle to return to the html library with
#           the image handle
#  src      The description of the image from:
#           <IMG src=XX>
#
# Results
#  This example creates a hard-coded image. and then invokes
#  HMgot_image with the handle for that image.

proc HMset_image {win handle src {speed {0}}} {
  global logo

  puts "HMset_image was invoked with WIN:\
    $win HANDLE: $handle SRC: $src"

  # In a real application this would parse the src, and load the
  # appropriate image data.

  set img [image create photo -data $logo]
  HMgot_image $handle $img
  return ""
}

text .t -height 6 -width 50
pack .t
```

```
HMinit_win .t
HMparse_html $HTMLtxt "HMrender .t"
```

*Script Output*

**HMset_image was invoked with WIN: .t HANDLE: .t.9 SRC: logo**

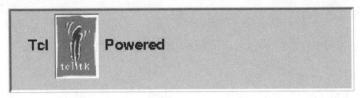

The html_library uses a technique similar to the image callback procedures to resolve hypertext links. When a user clicks on a hypertext link, the parsing engine invokes a procedure named HMlink_callback with the name of the text window and the content of the href=value field. The html_library provides a dummy HMlink_callback that does nothing. An application must provide its own HMlink_callback procedure to resolve hypertext links.

**Syntax:**  HMlink_callback *win href*

A procedure that is called from the html_library package when a user clicks on an <A href=value> field.

*win*     The text widget in which the new text can be rendered.

*href*    The hypertext reference.

The next example shows an HMlink_callback that will display the HTML text contained in a Tcl variable. In a browser application, the HMlink_callback procedure would download the requested URL, and in a help application it would load the requested help file.

## Example 11.23

*Script Example*

```
source htmllib.tcl

##############################################################
# proc HMlink_callback {win href}--
#  This procedure is invoked when a user selects a hypertext
#  link in the HTML display.
#
#  In an actual browser, the href field would contain the URL of
# the HTML page to retrieve. In this example, it contains the
# name of a Tcl variable.
```

```
#
# Arguments
#  win    The window in which the new page will be displayed
#  href   The hypertext reference.
# Results

proc HMlink_callback {win href} {
  global HTMLText2 HTMLText3
  puts "HMlink_callback was invoked with win: $win href: $href"

  # Clear the window
  HMreset_win $win
  # Display new text
  #  - href will be substituted to the name of a text string,
  #    and "set varName" returns the contents of a variable.
  #    "[set $href]" could also be written as "[subst $$href]"
  HMparse_html [set $href] "HMrender $win"
}

# Define three sets of simple HTML text to display
# This is the first text to display. It is an Unordered List of
#  hypertext links to the other two sets of HTML text.

set HTMLText1 {
<HTML>
<HEAD><TITLE> Initial Text </TITLE></HEAD>

<BODY>
  <UL>
   <LI>
     <A href=HTMLText2> Clicking this line will select text 2.</A>
   <LI>
     <A href=HTMLText3> Clicking this line will select text 3.</A>
  <UL>
</BODY> </HTML>
}

# This text will be displayed if the user selects the
#  top line in the list.
set HTMLText2 {
<HTML>
<HEAD><TITLE> Initial Text </TITLE></HEAD>
<BODY>
  <CENTER>This is text 2.</CENTER>
</BODY> </HTML>
}

# This text will be displayed if the user selects the
```

```
#  bottom line in the list.
set HTMLText3 {
<HTML>
<HEAD><TITLE> Initial Text </TITLE></HEAD>
<BODY>
  <CENTER>This is text 3.</CENTER>
</BODY> </HTML>
}

# Create the text window for this display
text .t -height 5 -width 60 -background white
pack .t

# Initialize the html_library package and display the text.
HMinit_win .t
HMparse_html $HTMLText1 "HMrender .t"
```

***Script Output***

**HMlink_callback was invoked with win: .t href: HTMLText2**

Before clicking a hypertext link

```
┌──────────────────────────────────────────────────┐
│  ○  Clicking this line will select text 2.         │
│  ○  Clicking this line will select text 3.         │
│                                                    │
└──────────────────────────────────────────────────┘
```

After clicking top hypertext link

```
┌──────────────────────────────────────────────────┐
│  This is text 2. │                                 │
│                                                    │
│                                                    │
└──────────────────────────────────────────────────┘
```

## 11.4.3 Interactive Help with the text Widget and htmllib

The next example shows how you can use the text widget bind command, an associative array, and the html library to create a text window in which a user can click on a word to get help. The tag bind command causes a mouse click event to invoke the ShowHelp procedure.

```
$textWin tag bind help <Button-1> \
   [list textWithHelp::ShowHelp $textWin %x %y]
```

When someone clicks on the text widget, the text widget invokes the textWith-Help::ShowHelp procedure with the name of the text widget and the X and Y cursor location. Within the ShowHelp procedure, the format converts the X and Y position to a text widget index.

```
# Convert the X and Y cursor location into a text index.
set index [format "@%d,%d" $x $y]
```

That index is used to identify the start and end locations of the word that was clicked and to get that word from the text widget with the following code:

```
# Get the word that surrounds that location from the text widget
set word [$txt get [list $index wordstart] [list $index wordend]]
```

By default, the text widget allows a user to edit the text with common emacs bindings or arrow keys. The last line,

```
$txtWin configure -state disabled
```

disables the editing, making the window read-only. This is appropriate for a display you do not want a user to modify.

In the following example, only the word text has help associated with it, and all words in the text widget are tagged with the string help. For other applications, you might add a tag configure command to the textWithHelp to make words with help highlighted and only tag the words that are in the index.

**Example** 11.24

*Script Example*

```
#############################################################
# proc textWithHelp {args}--
#     Creates a text widget with a binding for context
#        sensitive pop-up help
# Arguments
#     args  A list of arguments appropriate for the text widget
#
# Results
#     Creates a new text widget with a binding on the tag 'help'
#     Returns the name of the new widget

proc textWithHelp {args} {
    set textWin [eval text $args]
    $textWin tag bind help <Button-1> \
        [list textWithHelp::ShowHelp $textWin %x %y]
    return $textWin
}

namespace eval textWithHelp {
    variable helpDocs

#############################################################
# proc addHelp {key text}--
#     Add help text to the help database.
```

```
# Arguments
#    key     The keyword to identify this help message
#    text    An HTML text message.
# Results
#    Updates the helpDocs array.

  proc addHelp {key text} {
    variable helpDocs
    set helpDocs($key) $text
  }


##############################################################
# proc ShowHelp {txt x y}--
#    Finds the word with the cursor and checks that this word
#    is an index into the helpDocs array. If so, it
#    creates a popup window with a text widget, scrollbar, and
#    button. The text widget will display the HTML formatted
#    text indexed by the keyword.
#
# Arguments
#    txt The name of the parent window.
#    x   Cursor X location
#    y   Cursor Y location
# Results
#    Any old popup help window associated with this text widget
#        is destroyed
#    If the cursor is on a word with help, a new toplevel widget
#        is created with the help text.

  proc ShowHelp {txt x y} {
    variable helpDocs

    # Convert the X and Y cursor location into a text index.
    set index [format "@%d,%d" $x $y]

    # Get the word that surrounds that location from the text widget
    set word [$txt get [list $index wordstart] [list $index wordend]]

    # If the word exists, do stuff, else just return.

    if {[info exists helpDocs($word)]} {

        # Destroy any existing window.
        catch {destroy $txt.help}

        # Create a new toplevel, and title it appropriately
        set help [toplevel $txt.help]
```

```
            wm title $help "Help for $word"

            # Create a new text widget, scrollbar and exit button
            text $help.t -width 60 -height 10 \
                -yscrollcommand "$help.sb set"
            scrollbar $help.sb -orient vertical \
                -command "$help.t yview"
            button $help.b -text "Done" -command "destroy $help"

            # Map the widgets to the toplevel window
            grid $help.t -row 1 -column 1
            grid $help.sb -row 1 -column 2 -sticky ns
            grid $help.b -row 2 -column 1

            # Initialize the text widget for HTML and render the
            #   text
            HMinit_win $help.t
            HMparse_html $helpDocs($word) "HMrender $help.t"
        }
    }
}

# Example of use
source htmllib.tcl

# Add a help message to the help index.

textWithHelp::addHelp text \
    {<BODY>
        <CENTER><H4><CODE>text</CODE> widget</H4></CENTER>
        <P>
        <CODE><B>Syntax: </B>text <I>textName ?options?</I></CODE>
        <P>
        The text widget can be used to display and edit text.
    </BODY>}

# Create and map the text window
set txtWin [textWithHelp .txt -background white -height 5 \
    -width 60 -font {arial 16} ]

pack $txtWin

# Insert text into the text widget.
$txtWin insert end \
    "The text widget is part of the standard Tk toolkit." help

# Make the text window read only - disable editing.
$txtWin configure -state disabled
```

*Script Output*

After clicking on text

---

The previous example has hard-coded text to make an example that can be placed in the book. Your applications may use the http package to download pages from a remote site, load pages from a disk, generate pages from database records, or whatever technique your program specifications require. See the companion CD-ROM articles about the "Birthday Robot" and "Stock Robot" for more information about using the http package.

The ease with which HTML support is added to the text widget may make you think that it would be easy to write a full browser with Tk. Before you do too much work on that project, take a look at Steve Ball's plume browser at *http://tcltk.anu.edu.au/1.0a1/* and read Mike Doyle and Hattie Schroeder's book *Web Applications in Tcl/Tk*. Much of the work you will need to do to create a browser has already been done. Using a text widget to implement a browser display has the following problems.

■ *Performance:* Displaying HTML in a text widget requires a great deal of parsing HTML and calculating layout parameters. This can be compute intensive, and becomes slow when done in an interpreted language like Tcl.

■ *Layout limitations:* The text widget is optimized for pure text displays. As discussed in Section 11.3.5, you need to add extra windows to flow text around images, and so on.

D. Richard Hipp solved these problems with his TkHTML widget (*www.hwaci.com/sw/tkhtml/index.html*). This widget is the basis for several applications, including the full-featured BrowseX web browser (*http://browsex.com/*).

## 11.5 Bottom Line

■ The text widget will display formatted text.

- By default, the text widget allows the user to edit text.
- The text widget supports
    - Multiple fonts
    - Multiple colors for foreground and background
    - Varying margins
    - Varying line spacing
    - Binding actions to characters or strings
    - Including images and other Tk widgets in text
- Locations in the text widget are identified as line and character positions. Only locations where text exists can be accessed.
- Lines that are longer than the display can wrap. If this occurs, the line and character index points reflect the internal representation of the data, not the display.
- A text widget is created with the text command.

    ***Syntax:*** text *textName ?options?*

- Text is inserted into a text widget with the insert subcommand.

    ***Syntax:*** *textName* insert *index text ?tagList? ?moreText? ?moreTags?*

- An image is inserted into a text widget with the *textName* image create subcommand.

    ***Syntax:*** *textName* image create *index ?options?*

- A Tk widget can be inserted into a text widget with the *textName* window create subcommand.

    ***Syntax:*** *textName* window create *index ?options?*

- Text is deleted from a text widget with the delete subcommand.

    ***Syntax:*** *textName* delete *startIndex ?endIndex?*

- You can search for patterns in a text widget with the search subcommand.

    ***Syntax:*** *textName* search *?options? pattern startIndex ?endIndex?*

- A mark is placed with the mark set subcommand.

    ***Syntax:*** *textName* mark set *markName index*

- A mark is removed with the mark unset subcommand.

    ***Syntax:*** *textName* mark unset *markName ?...? ?markNameN?*

- You can get a list of marks with the mark names subcommand.

    ***Syntax:*** *textName* mark names

- You can iterate through the marks in a text widget with the mark next and mark previous subcommands.

> *Syntax:* `textName` mark next *index*

> *Syntax:* `textName` mark previous *index*

- You can add tags either in the `insert` subcommand or with the `tag add` subcommand.

  > *Syntax:* `textName` tag add *tagName startIndex1 ?end1? ?start2? ... ?endN?*

- You can remove a tag from a location with the `tag remove` subcommand.

  > *Syntax:* `textName` tag remove tagName *startIndex1 ?end1? ?start2? ... ?endN?*

- You can remove all references to a tag with the `tag delete` subcommand.

  > *Syntax:* `textName` tag delete *tagName ?tagname2? ... ?tagNameN?*

- You can get a list of tag names with the `tag names` subcommand.

  > *Syntax:* `textName` tag names *index*

- You can iterate through tag locations with the `tag nextrange` and `tag prevrange` subcommands.

  > *Syntax:* `textName` tag nextrange *tagName startIndex ?endIndex?*

  > *Syntax:* `textName` tag prevrange *tagName startIndex ?endIndex?*

- You can bind an event to an action that occurs on a character or string with the `tag bind` subcommand.

  > *Syntax:* `textName` tag bind *tagName ?eventType? ?script?*

- The `htmllib.tcl` library provides a set of procedures that will render HTML into a `text` widget. Images are inserted into the HTML document with the `HMset_image` and associated `HMgot_image` procedures.

  > *Syntax:* `HMset_image` *win handle src*

  > *Syntax:* `HMgot_image` *handle image*

- Hypertext links are inserted with a user-supplied `HMlink_callback` procedure.

  > *Syntax:* `HMlink_callback` *win href*

## 11.6 Problems

The following numbering convention is used in all Problem sections.

| *Number Range* | *Description of Problems* |
|---|---|
| 100–199 | These problems review the material covered in this chapter. They can be answered in a few words or a short (1–5-line) script. Each problem should take under a minute to answer. |

| 200–299 | These problems go beyond the details presented in this chapter. They may require some analysis of the material or command details not covered in the chapter. They may require reading a man page or making a web search. They can be answered with a few sentences or a 5–50-line script. Each problem should take under 10 minutes to answer. |
| --- | --- |
| 300–399 | These problems extend the material presented in this chapter. They may require referencing other sources. They can be answered in a few paragraphs or a few hundred lines of code. Each exercise may take a few hours to complete. |

**100.** What is the top line in a `text` widget?

**101.** What index string would match the start of a word that includes the index `2.22`?

**102.** What units are used to define the height and width of a `text` widget?

**103.** What command will return a list of all marks in a `text` widget?

**104.** Can a mark exist in multiple locations in a `text` widget?

**105.** Can a tag exist in multiple locations in a `text` widget?

**106.** What command would display characters tagged `bold` using the font `{times 16 bold}`?

**107.** What Tcl script library can be loaded to render HTML data?

**108.** What command would cause the procedure `highlightText` to be invoked when a user clicks on a word in the text widget `.t`?

**109.** What marks are always present in a `text` widget?

**110.** What tags are always present in a `text` widget?

**200.** Create a `text` widget and insert the text words *Hello,World* into the widget.

**201.** Create a `text` widget and vertical scrollbar. Add 100 lines of text into the `text` widget and confirm that the scrollbar will display them all.

**202.** Write a procedure `proc insertText {txtWin text}` that will accept the name of a `text` widget and a string of text. The procedure should tag the first character of each sentence as "red" and insert the text into the `text` widget. Use `tag configure` to make the first letter of each sentence appear red.

**203.** Write a procedure that will report all tags that overlap some section of text.

**204.** Write a script using the `text` widget (not canvas) that shows an image in the center of the `text` widget and text surrounding the image. There should be multiple lines displayed on each side of the image and multiple characters above and below the image.

**205.** Write a procedure proc highlightText {textName string} that will search a text widget for all occurrences of string and highlight those occurrences.

**300.** Write a set of scripts with a label and text widget. The label should display the word currently under the mouse cursor as the mouse is moved about a text widget.

**301.** Write a procedure that will accept the name of a text widget as an argument and modify the text in that widget to show what areas are tagged and what the tag is. This may require adding line feeds to the text to create blank lines to hold annotation.

**302.** Expand Example 11.24 by adding a procedure insertText helpTextName text that will check each word in the text string and underline all words for which help has been added.

**303.** Write an editor using a text widget, and a File menu that includes Load and Save options. The load and save commands can be implemented with a toplevel widget that contains an entry widget for the file name and a Done and Cancel button.

**304.** Write a multiple-choice test program that displays a set of questions, with a set of radiobutton widgets, for the user to select the answer.

# CHAPTER

## 12

# Tk Megawidgets

The widgets described in Chapter 9 are relatively small and simple objects created to serve a single purpose. They are designed to be combined into larger and more complex user interfaces in your application.

Many applications require more complex widgets. A program that allows a user to save or read data from a disk file will need a `file selection` widget that supports browsing. Many applications require a listbox or `text` widget that displays a scrollbar when the number of lines displayed exceeds the widget height.

Tk supports merging several widgets into a larger widget that can be reused in other applications. These compound widget interfaces are commonly called *megawidgets*.

The standard distribution of the Tk toolkit contains a few megawidgets, and many more megawidgets are supported in Tk extensions and packages, including `tix`(`<http://tix.sourceforge.net/>`), `iwidgets` (`<http://sourceforge.net/projects/incrtcl/>`), and `Bwidgets` (`<http://sourceforge.net/projects/tcllib/>`).

Megawidget packages can be created using only Tk or with C language extensions to `wish`. This chapter discusses the megawidgets included with the standard distribution and techniques for building megawidget libraries with Tk.

## 12.1 Standard Dialog Widgets

The standard distribution provides several megawidgets to simplify writing applications. These widgets extend the functionality of the Tk interpreter and save the script writer from having to reinvent some wheels.

The implementation of these widgets varies among the platforms Tcl supports. On the UNIX platform, they are all implemented as `.tcl` scripts in the

TK_LIBRARY directory. The Windows and Macintosh platforms include some of these widgets, in which case Tk uses the native implementation.

If you prefer to have your application use the Motif-style widgets instead of the native widgets (perhaps it is important to have the application appear the same across multiple platforms, rather than adhere to the platform look and feel), you can force the Motif look and feel by performing the following.

**1.** Set the global variable tk_strictMotif to 1.

**2.** Delete the compound widget commands you wish to have appear as Motif.

**3.** Source tk.tcl.

A code snippet to change the color selector will resemble the following.

```
set tk_strictMotif 1
rename tk_chooseColor ""
source [file join $tk_library tk.tcl]
```

### 12.1.1 tk_optionMenu

This menubutton widget displays the text of the selected item on the button. The widget creation command returns the name of the menu associated with the button name provided by the script.

> *Syntax:* tk_optionMenu *buttonName varName val1 ?val2...valN?*
>
> Create a menu from which to select an item.
>
> *buttonName*  A name for the button to be created. This name must not belong to an existing widget. Once the tk_optionMenu call has returned, this name can be used to display the widget.
>
> *varName*  The text variable to be associated with the menu. The selected value will be saved in this variable.
>
> *val\**  The values a user can select from on this menu. These values will become the elements in the menu, and the selected value will be displayed on the button face.

### Example 12.1

***Script Example***

```
tk_optionMenu .button varName Val1 Val2 Val3
pack .button
```

*Script Output*

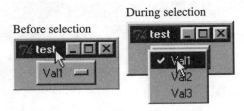

Before selection    During selection

## 12.1.2 `tk_chooseColor`

This color selector widget returns a properly formatted string that can be used for a color name. The string is the red-green-blue value displayed in the Selection field. This command creates a new window in the center of the screen and disables the other windows in the task that invoked it until interaction with this widget is complete.

> *Syntax:* `tk_chooseColor`

## Example 12.2

*Script Example*

```
tk_chooseColor
```

*Script Output*

UNIX

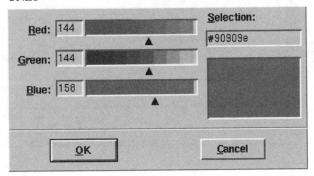

MS Windows

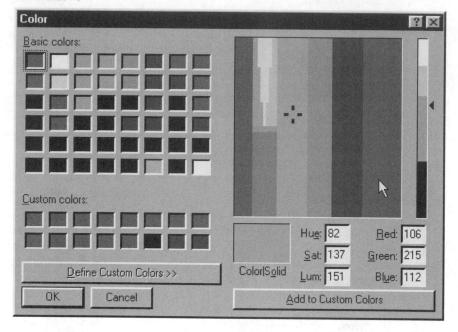

Macintosh

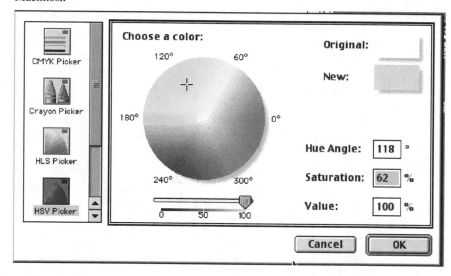

### 12.1.3 `tk_getOpenFile`

This `file browser` widget returns the name of a file that already exists. If the user
types in a nonexistent file name, an error message dialog box is displayed, and the

window focus is returned to the tk_getOpenFile window. This command creates a new window on the screen and disables the other widgets in the task that invoked it until interaction with this widget is complete.

*Syntax:* tk_getOpenFile *?option value?*

Create a file-browsing widget to find an existing file.

*?option value?*

The options supported by the tk_getOpenFile megawidget include

| | |
|---|---|
| -defaultextension *ext* | The *extension* string will be appended to a file name entered by users if they do not provide an extension. The default is an empty string. This option is ignored on the Macintosh. |
| -filetypes *patternList* | This list is used to create menu entries in the *Files of type:* menubutton. If file types are not supported by the platform evaluating the script, this option is ignored. |
| -initialdir *path* | The initial directory for the directory choice menubutton. Note that on the Macintosh the General Controls panel may be set to override application defaults, which will cause this option to be ignored. |
| -initialfile *fileName* | Specifies a default file name to appear in the selection window. |
| -parent *windowName* | Specifies the parent window for this widget. The widget will attempt to be placed over its parent but may be placed elsewhere by the window manager. |
| -title *titleString* | The title for this window. The window may be displayed without a title bar by some window managers. |

## Example 12.3

***Script Example***

```
set typeList {
  {{Include Files} {.h}}
  {{Object Files} {.o}}
  {{Source Files} {.c}}
  {{All Files} {.*}}
}
```

```
tk_getOpenFile -initialdir /usr/src/LOCAL/TCL/tk8.4a4/library \
  -filetypes $typeList
```

***Script Output***

UNIX

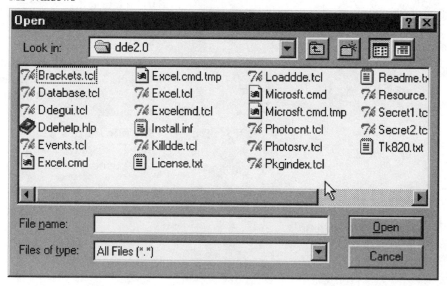

MS Windows

Macintosh

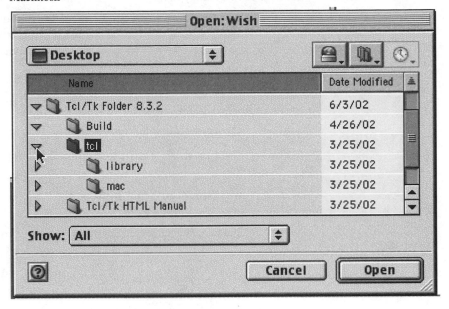

### 12.1.4 **tk_getSaveFile**

This file-browsing widget returns the name of a selected file. If the selected file already exists, users are prompted to confirm that they are willing to overwrite the file. This widget creates a new window that is identical to the window created by tk_getOpenFile.

*Syntax:*  tk_getSaveFile *?option value?*

Create a file-browsing widget to find an existing file or enter the name of a nonexistent file.

*?option value?*  The tk_getSaveFile megawidget supports the same options as the tk_getOpenFile widget.

### 12.1.5 **tk_messageBox**

The tk_messageBox command creates a dialog window in one of several predefined styles. This command returns the name of the button that was clicked. This command creates a new window that takes focus until interaction with this widget is complete.

*Syntax:* `tk_messageBox ?option value?`

Create a new window with a message and a set of buttons. When a button is clicked, the window is destroyed and the value of the button that was clicked is returned to the script that created this widget.

`option value`

Options for this widget include

| | |
|---|---|
| `-message` | The message to display in the box. |
| `-title` | The title to display in the window border. |
| `-type` | The type of message box to create. The type of box will determine what buttons are created. The options are |

| | |
|---|---|
| `abortretryignore` | Displays three buttons: `abort`, `retry`, and `ignore`. |
| `ok` | Displays one button: `ok`. |
| `okcancel` | Displays two buttons: `ok` and `cancel`. |
| `retrycancel` | Displays two buttons: `retry` and `cancel`. |
| `yesno` | Displays two buttons: yes and no. |
| `yesnocancel` | Displays three buttons: `yes`, `no`, and `cancel`. |

## Example 12.4

*Script Example*

```
tk_messageBox -message "Continue Examples?" -type yesno
```

*Script Output*

UNIX

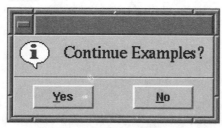

MS Windows

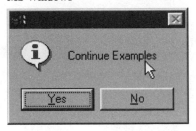

Macintosh

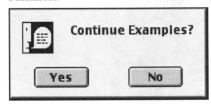

## 12.1.6 `tk_dialog`

The `tk_dialog` megawidget creates a message window with a line of text and one or more buttons labeled with text provided in the command line. When the user clicks a button, the button position is returned. The first button is number 0. If the user destroys the window, a –1 is returned. This command creates a new window in the center of the screen and disables the other windows in the task that invoked it until interaction with this widget is complete.

**Syntax:** `tk_dialog` *win title text bitmap default string1 ?... stringN?*

Create a dialog box and wait until the user clicks a button or destroys the box.

| | |
|---|---|
| *win* | The name for this dialog box widget. |
| *title* | A string to place in the border of the new window. Whether or not the window is displayed with a border depends on the window manager you are using. |
| *text* | The text to display in the message box. |
| *bitmap* | If this is not an empty string, it must be a bitmap object or bitmap file name (not an image object) to display. |
| *default* | A numeric value that describes the default button choice for this window. The buttons are numbered from 0. |
| *string\** | The strings to place in the buttons. |

**Example** 12.5

*Script Example*

```
tk_dialog .box "Example Dialog" \
  "Who's on first? " \
  questhead 0 "Yes" "No" "Don't Know"
```

*Script Output*

UNIX

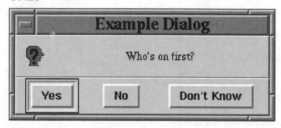

MS Windows

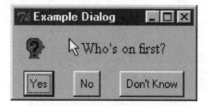

Macintosh

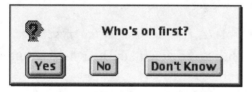

## 12.1.7 `tk_popup`

The `tk_popup` command creates a pop-up menu window at a given location on the display (not constrained within the `wish` window). The menu appears with a tear-off entry and takes focus. Note that this widget is not modal. The command after the `tk_popup` is evaluated immediately without waiting for the user to select an item from the menu. The following example shows the pop-up bound to a left button press to display a question based on the content of a `text` widget.

*Syntax:*  tk_popup *menu x y ?entry?*

| | |
|---|---|
| tk_popup | Create a pop-up menu somewhere on the display. This need not be within the Tcl/Tk application window. |
| *menu* | A previously defined menu object. |
| *x y* | The *x* and *y* coordinates for the menu in screen coordinates. |
| *?entry?* | A numeric value that defines a position in the menu. The defined position will be selected (active), and the menu will be placed with that entry at the x, y position requested. |

# Example 12.6

*Script Example*

```
proc question {} {
  global var;
  # Remove any existing .m menu.
  # Use catch in case there is no previous .m menu.
  catch {destroy .m}

  # Create a menu for this popup selector

  menu .m
  .m add radiobutton \
  -label "This dialog is from Abbott & Costello's \
    \"Who's on First?\" routine"\
    -variable var -value 1
  .m add radiobutton \
    -label "This dialog is from _War_and_Peace_" \
    -variable var -value 2
  .m add radiobutton -label \
    "This dialog is from Monty Python's Parrot sketch" \
    -variable var -value 3

  # Get the size and location of this window with the "winfo"
  #   command, which returns the geometry as
  #   WIDTHxHEIGHT+XPOS+YPOS
  # The scan command is similar to the C standard
  #   library "sscanf" function.

  scan [winfo geometry .] "%dx%d+%d+%d" \
    width height xpos ypos

  # Put the popup near the bottom right-hand
  #   edge of the parent window.

  tk_popup .m [expr $xpos + ($width/2) + 50 ] \
```

```
        [expr $ypos + $height - 40] 1
}

# Create a text window, display it, and insert some text
#    from a famous dialog.
text .t -height 12 -width 75
pack .t

set dialog {
  "C: Tell me the names of the ballplayers on this team.\n"
  "A: We have Who's on first, What's on second, "
  "I Don't Know is on third.\n"
  "C: That's what I want to find out.\n"
  "  I want you to tell me the names of the fellows"
  " on the team.\n"
  "A: I'm telling you. Who's on first, "
  "What's on second, I Don't\n"
  "  Know is on third --\n"
  "C: You know the fellows' names?\n"
  "A: Yes.\n"
  "C: Well, then who's playin' first.\n"
  "A: Yes.\n"
}

foreach line $dialog {
  .t insert end $line
}

# Bind the right button to a question about this dialog.
bind .t <Button-1> question
```

***Script Output***

UNIX

MS Windows

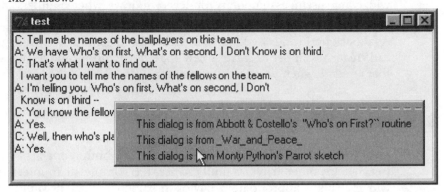

Macintosh

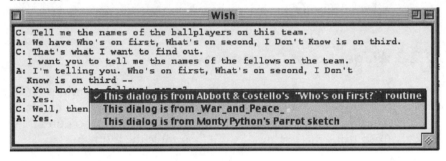

## 12.2 Megawidget Building Philosophy

The megawidgets included in the standard distribution are useful, but the odds
are good that you will end up needing to build your own widgets at some point.
You can design a megawidget library in a number of ways. Each technique has
features that may make it better or worse for your application. One of the primary
trade-offs is versatility and ease of use versus speed of construction. If you expect
to use the widget more than once, it is worthwhile to take the extra time to design
the widget library for versatility. Consider the points discussed in the sections that
follow when building your widget libraries.

### 12.2.1 Display in Application Window or Main Display?

The Tk distribution includes several megawidgets that open their own windows on
the primary display rather than being loaded into the application window. Some

widgets are useful as temporary top-level windows, whereas others are more useful if they can be packed into an application window.

A fallback position is to design a widget to be loaded in an existing window. You can create a wrapper to create a new `toplevel` window and `pack` the widget into that window when you need a pop-up.

## 12.2.2 Modal Versus Modeless Operation

Most of the megawidgets in the standard Tk distribution operate in a modal style, freezing any other activities until the user has completed an interaction with this widget. This is appropriate behavior in some circumstances but not in others. Consider the applications in which your megawidget will be used to determine whether modal or modeless operation is required, or if script writers should be able to define the behavior when they create the widget.

## 12.2.3 Widget Access Conventions

You can design a megawidget to follow its own conventions, or it can mimic the behavior of the standard Tk widgets. The widget creation command can return a handle that is used to identify this megawidget to procedures that manipulate it. Code using this technique would resemble the following.

```
set megaHandle [megaCreate -option value]
myMegaConfigureProc $megaHandle -newOption -newValue
```

The examples in this chapter demonstrate a better technique. They construct megawidgets that return the name of a procedure that accesses the megawidget. This technique mimics the behavior of the standard widgets and is implemented with the object-style technique introduced in Chapters 7 and 8. Code using this technique would resemble the following:

```
set mega [newMegaWidget -option value]
$mega configure -newOption -newValue
```

## 12.2.4 Widget Frames

Most megawidgets have a parent frame that holds their subwidgets. This frame can be created by the megawidget creation command or provided by the calling procedure. If the frame is created by the widget creation command, the calling script can provide the name (as names are given to Tk widgets), or the megawidget can generate a unique name.

If you provide the parent frame for the megawidget (instead of just providing a name), you can have the megawidget display itself in that frame automatically.

This is not generally a good technique. It restricts the usefulness of the widget to applications that have similar display requirements. This technique is useful for widgets such as toolbar buttons that are always displayed side by side in a frame.

## 12.2.5 Configuration

The next person who uses your megawidget library is guaranteed not to like the configuration options you chose. For instance, the dialog box that informs users that the nuclear reactor is about to explode and asks whether they would like to do something about it should probably be in a bright color with big letters, rather than the usual dull gray with small letters. Configuration options can be

- Set in a state variable and applied when the widget is created
- Set on the widget creation command line
- Set in a `configure` procedure associated with the widget
- Set with the `option add` command (discussed in Section 12.3.2) if the megawidget uses the `-class` option to define itself as a new class of widget

Supporting the second, third, and fourth options in the previous list is the most versatile design. This provides features that mimic the options supported by the normal Tk widgets.

## 12.2.6 Access to Subwidgets

A megawidget can be designed in an opaque manner, so that the component widgets cannot be accessed, or in a transparent manner, so that the component widgets can be accessed and modified. If the goal of this megawidget is to provide a uniform interface across all applications that use it, the widget should be designed to restrict programmers from modifying the options of the subwidgets. The message box and file browsers provided by the OS platform are examples of this style of widget.

If the goal for this megawidget is to provide a tool for a wide variety of applications, the megawidget should be designed to allow the application script writer access to the subwidgets. This allows the application writer to modify options such as background color and font. This can be handled by the techniques described in the following.

### *Naming Convention*

The megawidget creation command returns a base name for the megawidget. The subwidgets are accessed as `base.labelName`, `base.buttonOK`, and so on. This is the simplest technique to implement, although it may be difficult to use if you nest megawidgets within other megawidgets.

This technique's disadvantage is that it requires application-level code to know about the internals of the megawidget. This can make maintenance a headache.

### A Command to Return Subwidget Names

The megawidget package you design can include a subwidget command that will return the full name of a subwidget component of the megawidget. Code that uses this technique would resemble the following.

```
set button [$myMegaWidget subwidget buttonOK]
$button configure -text "A-OK"
```

### Pass Commands to the Subwidget

The widget procedure can accept a list of subwidgets and command strings to be evaluated by the subwidget. Code that uses this technique would resemble the following.

```
set myBigWidget [megawidget .bigwidget -option value]
$myBigWidget widgetcommand titleLabel configure -text "Big Widget"
```

### -subwidget Option

The widget procedures you create can accept (or require) a subwidget as an argument when they are invoked. Code that uses this technique would resemble the following.

```
$myMegawidget configure -subwidget buttonOK -text "A-OK"
```

## 12.2.7 Following Tk Conventions

The closer you follow the Tk conventions for names, options, and subcommands, the easier it is for script writers to use your megawidgets. If there are two equally good methods for creating the functionality you need, choose the one that mimics Tk.

# 12.3 Functionality That Makes Megawidgets Possible

Tcl/Tk provides three sets of functionality that make it easy to build megawidgets with pure Tcl. All of these pieces have other, perhaps more important, uses, but they work together synergistically when used to construct megawidgets. The three features are the rename command, the option command, and the -class option.

### 12.3.1 **The rename Command**

The rename command was discussed briefly in Chapter 7. The rename command is used to delete the procedure associated with a node when the node is destroyed.

We can also use the rename command to rename the command associated with a widget.

In the next example, a label named .1 is created with the command label .1 -text "original text". This creates both a widget named .1 and a command named .1. The rename command renames the procedure .1 to mylabel. The widget is still named .1, and that name must be used to pack the widget. However, the procedure is now named mylabel, and that is the name we must use to configure the widget.

```
label .1 -text "original text"
rename .1 mylabel
pack .1
mylabel configure -text "new text"
```

In Tk, procedure names and window names are resolved from separate tables. This allows the procedure to be renamed but still reference the original widget.

When creating megawidgets, we create a frame to hold the widget components, then rename that frame's procedure to something different, and define a new command with the original name of the frame as the widget command. The widget components are still children of the original frame and can be accessed using their original procedure name, the full window path.

Stripping it down below the bare essentials, the following shows what happens.

```
# Create a frame to hold the subwidgets.
frame .megawidget

# ... Build and display the subwidgets

# Rename the frame procedure to a new name.
rename .megawidget megaWidgetFrame

# Create a new procedure named for the original frame.
proc .megawidget {...} {...}
```

### 12.3.2 **The option Command**

The option command lets the Tcl programmer interact with the Tk option database. The option database is a collection of patterns and values. When the wish interpreter creates a new window, it examines the options database to see if this window has any configuration options that match a pattern in the database. The value from the database is applied to the widget if an option is matched. You can set a value in the option database with the option add command.

***Syntax:*** option add *pattern value ?priority?*

Add a definition to the options database.

*pattern*     The pattern describing the widget option to set.

*value*       A value to use when a widget that matches the pattern is created.

The form of a pattern is *application.widget.optionName*. The pattern tkcon. mybutton.background would match the background color of a button named .mybutton in an application named tkcon. The basic pattern supports a few variations to make it more versatile.

■ Any field can be replaced by a wildcard (*). Thus, *mybutton.background would match the background of any button named .mybutton.

■ Fields can be replaced by a generic name. The generic name will start with an uppercase letter. The generic name for a widget field is the name of the class of the object. For example, *Button.background will match the background of any button created in an application.

The Tcl interpreter will select options from the most specific pattern that matches a widget. Thus, using a widget name will override a generic widget option, as shown in the following example.

## Example 12.7

***Script Example***

```
# All labels have white background
option add *Label*background white

# All widgets named alert have black background
#  and white foreground
option add *alert*background black
option add *alert*foreground white

pack [label .l -text "normal colors"]
pack [label .alert -text "ALERT Inverted"]
```

***Script Output***

The option add command can be used in any application when you want to change the default value for a set of widgets. For example, if you want to make large buttons you might use the -font option for each button command, or you could set the *Button*Font option to a larger font. One advantage of using the option command is that it is faster than using *-option* in a widget creation command.

In an application with many widgets, this can noticeably affect how quickly windows are built.

### 12.3.3 The -class Option

The Tcl interpreter can assign a -class option to a new frame or toplevel widget. The default class for a frame is Frame, and the default class for a top-level window is Toplevel. (This information is returned by the winfo class *widgetName* command.)

If we include the -class option with the frame or toplevel command, our script can override this to become a new class. We can set options for all members of this new class with the option add command.

**Example** 12.8

*Script Example*

```
# A simple Label/Entry megawidget
proc LabelEntry {frameName labelText varName} {
  frame $frameName -class Labelentry
  pack [label $frameName.l -text $labelText] -side left
  pack [entry $frameName.e -textvar $varName] -side left
  return $frameName
}

# Labelentry widgets all use large font
option add *Labelentry*font {Times 24 bold}

pack [LabelEntry .le "Enter your Name" name]
```

*Script Output*

## 12.4 Building a Megawidget

The simple LabelEntry megawidget shown in the previous example makes it easier to develop a form-style application with many items to be filled out. Using this type of simple megawidget can make your applications easier to write and maintain. However, if you are developing a library of complex megawidgets for multiple projects, you will want them to be more flexible.

The first step in designing a library of megawidgets is deciding what sets of conventions you will follow. The actual conventions do not matter as much as consistently following the conventions. Consistency is one of the keys to creating a usable set of tools. This section describes building a modeless megawidget in a frame. This widget will behave like one of the basic Tk widgets. The conventions we will establish for this widget are as follows.

- The subwidget will create a new frame of class *Megawidget*.
- A configuration option can be defined for the entire megawidget, and it will be propagated to all appropriate subwidgets using the option command.
- A subwidget is identified by a unique identifier within the megawidget (e.g., .parentwindow.megawidget.subwidget will be identified as subwidget).
- A list of subwidget names will be returned by a names command, similar to array names.
- Subwidgets may also be accessed by full name. For example,

  .parentwindow.megawidget.subwidget

  may be identified as

  .parentwindow.megawidget.subwidget.

- A configuration option can be defined for a subwidget with a widgetconfigure command that duplicates the behavior of the configure command.
- A configuration option can be queried for a subwidget with a widgetcget command that duplicates the behavior of the cget command.
- A command can be passed to a subwidget with the widgetcommand command.
- Infrastructure data and procedures will be maintained in a namespace.

# 12.5 A Scrolling listbox Megawidget

This section shows how a megawidget can be built using the conventions described in Section 12.4. The first example creates a simple scrolling listbox megawidget. The next example enhances this widget into a more complex megawidget that can take selected items from one scrolled listbox and place them in another. The final example puts a wrapper around that megawidget to make a modal file selector.

## 12.5.1 scrolledListBox Description

The scrollable listbox megawidget we will construct will mimic the structure of the Tk widgets. The support procedures for this megawidget exist within a namespace. A single procedure (scrolledLB) exists in the global scope to create a scrolledLB megawidget.

The `scrolledLB` procedure will return the name of the new widget's parent frame and will create a procedure with that name in the global scope. This procedure will support several subcommands in the same manner as the Tk widgets.

The `scrolledLB` configuration options can be set by

- Using the `option add` command before constructing a `scrolledLB` widget
- Using new options defined for this megawidget
- Using the `widgetconfigure` widget subcommand after constructing a `scrolledLB` widget
- Retrieving the full path of a subwidget with the `subwidget` command and using that widget's `configure` subcommand

The `scrolledLB` procedure accepts any configuration values that are valid for a `frame` or that match specific options for this megawidget and uses those values to configure the `frame` or the `scrollbar` and `listbox` subwidgets. In addition, the `scrolledLB` command accepts an option to define whether the scrollbar should be on the left or right side of the listbox.

**_Syntax:_** `scrolledLB ?frameName? ?-option value?`

> Create a `scrolledLB` megawidget. Returns the name of the parent frame for this widget for use with the `pack`, `grid`, or `place` layout managers and creates a procedure with the same name to be used to interact with the megawidget.

> | | |
> |---|---|
> | *?frameName?* | An optional name for this widget. If this argument is not present, the widget will be created as a unique child of the root frame, ".". |
> | *?-option value?* | Sets of configuration values that can be applied to the scrollbar or listbox. |

The widget procedure created by the `scrolledLB` command will accept the subcommands `configure`, `widgetconfigure`, `widgetcget`, `widgetcommand`, `names`, `insert`, `delete`, `selection`, and `subwidget`.

The `scrolledLB` widget `widgetconfigure` and `widgetcget` subcommands are similar to the standard Tk `configure` and `cget` commands except that they accept a subwidget argument. The configuration options will be applied only to those subwidgets.

**_Syntax:_** `scrolledLBName widgetconfigure subwidget ?-option? ?value?`

> Return the value of an option, or set an option if a value is supplied.

> | | |
> |---|---|
> | *subwidget* | The name of a subwidget or subwidgets to be configured or queried. If the widget is being queried and multiple subwidget names are present, the return |

value will be a list of configurations in the order in which the subwidgets appear in the list.

*Note:* This field is different from standard widget usage.

*-option*     An option name. If multiple options are being set, there may be multiple *-option value* pairs. If the configuration is being queried, only one *-option* argument may be present.

*value*     The value to assign to a configuration option.

The insert and delete subcommands pass their arguments to the listbox subwidget with no further parsing. Thus, they duplicate the behavior of the listbox subcommands.

**Syntax:** `scrolledLBName insert index string`

Inserts an item into the listbox at the requested index position.

*index*     The location in the list before which this entry will be inserted. Any index value appropriate for a listbox widget may be used.

*string*     The text to insert into that location of the listbox.

**Syntax:** `scrolledLBName delete first ?last?`

Delete one or more items from the listbox.

*first*     The index of the first item to delete. The listbox items are numbered from 0.

*?last?*     The index of the last item in a range to delete. If this argument is not present, only the item identified by the *first* is deleted.

The selection subcommand returns the content of the selected entries of the listbox. Note that the listbox curselection subcommand returns a list of the indices of selected items, whereas this selection returns a list of the content.

**Syntax:** `scrolledLBName selection`

Returns the text of the selected item or items from the listbox.

The subwidget subcommand returns the full path name of a subwidget of the scrolledLB.

**Syntax:** `scrolledLBName subwidget name`

Returns the full name of a subwidget of this scrolledLB.

*name*     The name of the subwidget to return. May be one of

     *list*     The full name of the listbox widget.

| | |
|---|---|
| *scrollbar* | The full name of the scrollbar widget. |
| *title* | The full name of the label widget. |

## 12.5.2 Using the scrolledLB

The next example shows how to use the scrolled listbox. The widget creation command resembles that of a standard Tk widget.

**Example** 12.9

*Script Example*

```
# set the auto_path and declare that we require the
# scrolledLB package.
# The widget pkgIndex.tcl file is in the current directory

# Load the scrolledLB support
lappend auto_path .
package require scrolledLB

# The background of the listbox is white
# The other widgets are normal gray.

option add *Scrolledlb*Listbox*background white

# Create and pack the scrolled listbox
set lb [scrolledLB .sbox -listboxHeight 5 -listboxWidth 20 \
    -titleText "Pick your Banjo"]
pack $lb -side top

# Fill the listbox
foreach brand { {Bacon & Day} Epiphone Gibson \
    Ludwig Paramount Orpheum Vega Weymann} {
    $lb insert end $brand
    }

# Add a button to display the selection

set cmd [format {puts "Picking an [%s selection]"} $lb]

button .b -text "Output Selection" \
    -command $cmd
pack .b -side top
```

*Script Output*

**Picking an Orpheum**  ;# Printed when the button is clicked

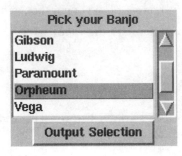

### 12.5.3 Implementing the Scrollable ListBox

The scrolledLB widget is implemented using the same code pattern that was described for the Tree object in Section 8.3. There is a set of support procedures for the scrolledLB in a private namespace and a procedure to create the widget in the global scope.

Creating a megawidget also creates a procedure in the global scope with the same name as the parent frame. The new procedure invokes support procedures in the widget namespace scope.

The scrolledLB megawidget is implemented with a state variable and three procedures. The state variable, scrolledLBState, exists within the scrolledLB namespace.

The scrolledLB procedure exists in the global scope. This provides the public API for creating a new instance of the widget. The MakescrolledLB and scrolledLBProc procedures exist in the scrolledLB namespace and perform the actual work of creating and manipulating the widget.

The scrolledLBState associative array holds the information that needs to be maintained between evaluations of the scripts in this package. This information includes a number used to create unique names for the scrolledLB widgets when no name is provided in the creation command line, and a lookup table to map simple subwidget names like list to the full widget path like .fileFrame.sbox.list.

The scrolledLB procedure exists in the global scope and invokes the MakescrolledLB procedure in the widget namespace. The MakescrolledLB procedure creates the new megawidget and returns the widget name to the scrolledLB procedure. The scrolledLB procedure uses that name to create a new procedure in the global scope that will interact with the new megawidget. The new procedure interacts with the widget by invoking the ScrolledLBProc procedure in the scrolledLB namespace.

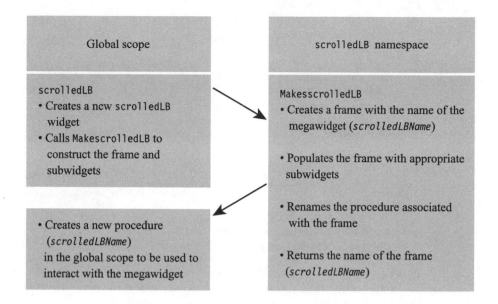

The Makescrolled LB procedure creates a frame to hold the subwidgets that constitute this megawidget. This frame will have the same name as the megawidget, making the subwidgets children of the parent megawidget.

The name conflict created by using the same name for both the megawidget and the frame that contains the megawidget components is resolved with the rename command, as described in Section 12.3.1.

For example, when a scrolledLB megawidget named .sbox is created, a frame named .sbox is created by MakescrolledLB. This creates both a window named .sbox and a procedure named .sbox. The procedure .sbox is renamed to .sbox.fr. The subwidgets are named .sbox.yscroll and .sbox.list. The subwidgets can be created either before or after renaming the procedure, since they are children of the window .sbox and are not affected by renaming the procedure .sbox. Being able to disconnect the frame .sbox from the procedure .sbox allows us to duplicate the Tk convention of declaring a name for the megawidget and then using that name as the widget procedure. If we didn't rename the frame widget procedure, there would be no way to interact with the frame after we create a new procedure with that name.

This naming convention makes the frame and subwidgets both appear as children to the megawidget. This is the way the megawidget and subwidgets are related to each other logically, although it is not the way the megawidget is implemented.

After the MakescrolledLB procedure creates and populates the frame, it renames the widget procedure associated with that frame. It returns the frame name to the scrolledLB procedure which is being evaluated in the global scope. The scrolledLB procedure creates the new procedure with the original name of the frame in the global scope.

The new procedure is a global scope kernel that simply invokes the scrolledLBProc procedure within the scrolledLB namespace. Script writers will use this procedure when they need to interact with the megawidget.

| *Global Scope* | scrolledLB *Namespace* |
|---|---|
| scrolledLBName | scrolledLBProc |
| Accepts the scrolledLB widget subcommands. | Performs the widget interactions requested by the widget subcommands. |
| Invokes scrolledLBProc to process the command with the name of the parent frame. | |

These procedures are all that is needed to create a scrolled listbox megawidget. The actual implementation is broken up into a few more procedures within the scrolledLB namespace just to make maintenance simpler.

## 12.5.4 The scrolledLB Code

The actual implementation of this code is broken up into a couple more procedures. Draw creates and maps the subwidgets into the parent frame, and DoWidgetCommand implements the widgetcommand subcommand.

**Example 12.10**

```
## Name: Scrolled LB. tcl
lappend auto_path .

package provide scrolledLB 1.0

####################################################################
# proc scrolledLB {args}
#    Create a scrolledLB megawidget
#    External entry point for creating a megawidget.
# Arguments
#    ?parentFrame?   A frame to use for the parent,
#                    If this is not provided, the megawidget
#                    is a child of the root frame (".").
# Results
#    Creates a procedure with the megawidget name for processing
#    widget commands
#    Returns the name of the megawidget
```

```
proc scrolledLB {args} {
  set newWidget [eval scrolledLB::MakescrolledLB $args]

  set newCmd [format {return [namespace eval %s %s %s $args ]}\
    scrolledLB scrolledLBProc $newWidget]

  proc $newWidget {args} $newCmd

  return $newWidget
}

namespace eval scrolledLB {
  variable scrolledLBState

  # Assign a couple defaults
  set scrolledLBState(unique) 0
  set scrolledLBState(debug) 0

  ##############################################################
  # proc MakescrolledLB {args}
  #    Create a scrolledLB megawidget
  # Arguments
  #    ?parentFrame?  A frame to use for the parent.
  #                   If this is not provided, the megawidget
  #                   is a child of the root frame (".").
  #    ?-scrollposition left/right?
  #                   The side of the listbox for the scrollbar
  # Results
  #    Returns the name of the parent frame for use as a
  #    megawidget

  proc MakescrolledLB {args} {
    variable scrolledLBState

    # Set the default name

    set holder .scrolledLB_$scrolledLBState(unique)
    incr scrolledLBState(unique)

    # If the first argument is a window path, use that as
    # the base name for this widget.
    if {[string first "." [lindex $args 0]] == 0} {
      set holder [lindex $args 0]
      set args [lreplace $args 0 0]
    }

    # Set Command line option defaults here,
    #   height and width are freebies
```

```
    set scrolledLBState($holder.height) 5
    set scrolledLBState($holder.width) 20

    set scrolledLBState($holder.scrollSide) 1
    set scrolledLBState($holder.listboxHeight) 10
    set scrolledLBState($holder.listboxWidth) 20
    set scrolledLBState($holder.listSide) 0
    set scrolledLBState($holder.titleText) title

    foreach {key val } $args {
      set keyName [string range $key 1 end]
      if {![info exists \
          scrolledLBState($holder.$keyName)]} {
        regsub -all "$holder." \
          [array names scrolledLBState $holder.*] \
          "" okList
        error "Bad option" \
          "Invalid option '$key'.\n\
          Must be one of $okList"
      }
      set scrolledLBState($holder.$keyName) $val
    }

    # Create master Frame

    frame $holder -height $scrolledLBState($holder.height) \
      -width $scrolledLBState($holder.width) \
      -class ScrolledLB

    # Apply invocation options to the master frame, as appropriate

    foreach {opt val} $args {
      catch {$holder configure $opt $val}
    }

    Draw $holder

    # We can't have two widgets with the same name.
    #   Rename the base frame procedure for this
    #   widget to $holder.fr so that we can use
    #   $holder as the widget procedure name
    #   for the megawidget.

    uplevel #0 rename $holder $holder.fr

    # When this window is destroyed,
    #   destroy the associated command.
```

```
    bind $holder <Destroy> "+ rename $holder {}"

    return $holder
}

##############################################################
# proc Draw {parent}--
#   creates the subwidgets and maps them into the parent
# Arguments
#   parent   The parent frame for these widgets
#
# Results
#   New windows are created and mapped.

proc Draw {parent} {
  variable scrolledLBState
  set tmp [scrollbar $parent.yscroll -orient vertical \
    -command "$parent.list yview" ]
  set scrolledLBState($parent.subWidgetName.yscroll) $tmp
  grid $tmp -row 1 -sticky ns \
    -column $scrolledLBState($parent.scrollSide)

  set tmp [listbox $parent.list \
    -yscrollcommand "$parent.yscroll set" \
    -height $scrolledLBState($parent.listboxHeight)\
    -width $scrolledLBState($parent.listboxWidth) ]
  set scrolledLBState($parent.subWidgetName.list) $tmp
  grid $tmp -row 1 -column $scrolledLBState($parent.listSide)

  set tmp [label $parent.title \
    -text $scrolledLBState($parent.titleText) ]
  set scrolledLBState($parent.subWidgetName.title) $tmp
  grid $tmp -row 0 -column 0 -columnspan 2
}

##############################################################
# proc DoWidgetCommand {widgetName widgets cmd}--
#   Perform operations on subwidgets
# Arguments
#   widgetName: The name of the holder frame
#   widgets:    A list of the public names for subwidgets
#   cmd:        A command to evaluate on each of these widgets
# Results
#   Does stuff about the subwidgets

proc DoWidgetCommand {widgetName widgets cmd} {
  variable scrolledLBState
```

```
      foreach widget $widgets {
        set index $widgetName.subWidgetName.$widget
        eval $scrolledLBState($index) $cmd
      }
    }

    proc selection {widgetName} {
      set lst [$widgetName.list curselection]
      set itemlst ""
      foreach l $lst {
        lappend itemlst [$widgetName.list get $l]
      }
      return $itemlst
    }


    #############################################################
    # proc scrolledLBProc {widgetName subCommand args}
    #    The master procedure for handling this megawidget's
    #    subcommands
    # Arguments
    #    widgetName:  The name of the scrolledLB
    #                 widget
    #    subCommand   The subCommand for this cmd
    #    args:        The rest of the command line
    #                 arguments
    # Default subCommands are:
    # configure - configure the parent frame
    # widgetconfigure - configure or query a subwidget.
    #            mega widgetconfigure itemID -key value
    #            mega widgetconfigure itemID -key
    # widgetcget - get the configuration of a widget
    #            mega widgetcget itemID -key
    # widgetcommand - perform a command on a widget
    #            mega widgetcommand itemID commandString
    # names - return the name or names that match
    #         a pattern
    #            mega names # Get names of all widgets
    #            mega names *a* # Get names of widgets
    #                          with an 'a' in them.
    # subwidget - return the full pathname of a
    #             requested subwidget
    # Results
    #    Evaluates a subcommand and returns a result if required.

    proc scrolledLBProc {widgetName subCommand args} {
      variable scrolledLBState
```

```
set cmdArgs $args

switch -- $subCommand {
configure {
       return [eval $widgetName.fr configure $cmdArgs]
}
widgetconfigure {
       set sbwid [lindex $cmdArgs 0]
       set cmd [lrange $cmdArgs 1 end]
       set index $widgetName.subWidgetName.$sbwid
       catch {eval \
         $scrolledLBState($index) configure $cmd} rtn
       return $rtn
}

delete -
insert {
       return [eval $widgetName.list $subCommand $cmdArgs]
}
selection {return [selection $widgetName]}

widgetcget {
       if {[llength $cmdArgs] != 2} {
         error "$widgetName cget subWidgetName -option"
       }
       set sbwid [lindex $cmdArgs 0]
       set index $widgetName.subWidgetName.$sbwid
       set cmd [lrange $cmdArgs 1 end]
       catch {eval \
         $scrolledLBState($index)\
         cget $cmd} rtn
       return $rtn
       }
  widgetcommand {
    return [eval DoWidgetCommand $widgetName $cmdArgs]
  }
  names {
       if {[string match $cmdArgs ""]} {
         set pattern $widgetName.subWidgetName.*
       } else {
         set pattern $widgetName.subWidgetName.$cmdArgs
       }
       foreach n [array names scrolledLBState $pattern] {
         foreach {d w s name} [split $n .] {}
         lappend names $name
       }
```

```
            return $names
    }
    subwidget {
            set name [lindex $cmdArgs 0]
            set index $widgetName.subWidgetName.$name
            if {[info exists scrolledLBState($index)]} {
              return $scrolledLBState($index)
            }
    }
    default {
            error "bad command" "Invalid Command: \
              $subCommand \n \
              must be configure, widgetconfigure, \
              widgetcget, names,\
              delete, insert, selection, \
              or subwidget"
    }
  }
 }
}
```

## 12.6 Namespaces and Tk Widgets

When the command associated with a Tk widget is evaluated, it is evaluated in the global namespace even if the widget is created inside a namespace. For example, the following code will not work.

```
namespace eval badCode {
  variable clicked 0
  button .b -text "Click me" -command "set clicked 1"
}
```

When the button is clicked, it will create and assign a 1 to the variable clicked in the global scope, not assign a 1 to the variable clicked in the namespace badCode. There are two namespace subcommands that provide the hooks for using Tk widgets and namespaces. The namespace current command will return the current namespace, and namespace code *script* will make a script that will be evaluated in the current namespace.

*Syntax:* namespace current

Returns the absolute name of the current namespace.

The previous example can be modified to use the `namespace current` command to set the correct variable. After performing substitutions, the script registered with the button is `set ::goodCode::clicked 1`.

**Example** 12.11

```
namespace eval goodCode {
  variable clicked 0
  button .b -text "Click me" \
    -command "set [namespace current]::clicked 1"
}
```

***Syntax:*** `namespace code` *script*

Returns a script that will be evaluated in the current namespace.

*script*   The script to be evaluated.

The first example can also be modified to work using the `namespace code` command. In the following example, the `namespace code {set clicked 1}` script is converted to `namespace inscope ::goodCode {set clicked 1}`, which is the script registered with the button. This is equivalent to `namespace eval ::goodCode {set clicked 1}`.

The `inscope` subcommand causes a script to be evaluated within an existing scope. It is usually used by the namespace procedures, not applications programmers.

```
namespace eval goodCode {
  variable clicked 0
  button .b -text "Click me" \
    -command "[namespace code {set clicked 1}]"
}
```

You will usually use `namespace current` when you need to provide a variable name to a Tk widget (for example, the `-textvariable` option) and `namespace code` with scripts associated with Tk widgets. If the script associated with a widget simply invokes a procedure within a namespace, you can use the `namespace current` command to add the namespace information to the procedure name. However, if you include Tcl commands such as `for`, `if`, `foreach`, and so on in your script, you must use `namespace code`.

Recommended procedure is to use `namespace code` for scripts associated with widgets. Since scripts associated with a widget tend to grow over time, it makes code maintenance easier.

## 12.6.1 Creating a Multiple-Language Megawidget

Many applications need to be distributed with support for multiple languages. Tcl has features that help make this easy. Tcl uses Unicode to store text strings, which makes it easy to represent non-Latin alphabets (see Section 10.4.5 for more discussion).

Tcl has supported a message catalog msgcat package to manage multiple languages since version 8.2. For simpler applications, you can use the associative array as a translation table.

The next example is a megawidget to create forms of label/entry widget pairs in which the label can be displayed in one of several languages. The label text is converted using an associative array as a lookup table. The Draw procedure uses both the namespace code command to invoke the worldForm::translate procedure when the translate button is clicked, and the namespace current command to link the variable worldFormState(language) to the tk_optionMenu widget.

```
proc Draw {parent} {
   variable worldFormState
   button $parent.translate \
         -text $worldFormState($parent.buttonText) \
         -command [namespace code [list translate $parent]]
   # ...
   tk_optionMenu $parent.options \
         [namespace current]::worldFormState(language) \
         French English German Spanish
   # ...
}
```

The following example shows the complete code for this megawidget and a short test example.

**Example** 12.12

### *Script Example 1*

```
## name: worldForm.tcl

package provide worldForm 1.0

#############################################################
# proc worldForm {args} -
#    Create a worldForm megawidget
#    External entry point for creating a megawidget.
# Arguments
#    ?parentFrame?  A frame to use for the parent,
#                   If this is not provided, the megawidget
#                   is a child of the root frame (".").
# Results
#    Creates a procedure with the megawidget name for processing
#    widget commands
```

```
#   Returns the name of the megawidget

proc worldForm {args} {
  set newWidget [eval worldForm::MakeworldForm $args]

  set newCmd [format {return [namespace eval %s %s %s $args ]} \
    worldForm WorldFormProc $newWidget]

  proc $newWidget {args} $newCmd

  return $newWidget
}

namespace eval worldForm {
  variable worldFormState
  # Assign a couple defaults
  set worldFormState(unique) 0

  ############################################################
  #     proc unique {}--
  #   Return a unique number
  # Arguments
  #   None
  #
  # Results
  #   Modifies stateVar(unique)
  #
  proc unique {} {
    variable worldFormState
    return [incr worldFormState(unique)]
  }

  ############################################################
  # proc MakeworldForm {args} -
  #   Create a worldForm megawidget
  # Arguments
  #   ?parentFrame?  A frame to use for the parent.
  #                  If this is not provided, the megawidget
  #                  is a child of the root frame (".").
  #   ? OTHER ARGS?
  # Results
  #   Returns the name of the parent frame for use as a
  #   megawidget

  proc MakeworldForm {args} {
    variable worldFormState

    # Set the default name
```

```
set holder .worldForm_$worldFormState(unique)
incr worldFormState(unique)
# If the first argument is a window path, use that as
# the base name for this widget.

if {[string first "." [lindex $args 0]] == 0} {
  set holder [lindex $args 0]
  set args [lreplace $args 0 0]
}

# Set Command line option defaults here,
#    height and width are freebies

set worldFormState($holder.height) 5
set worldFormState($holder.width) 20

set worldFormState($holder.buttonText) "translate"
set worldFormState($holder.row) 0
set worldFormState($holder.row) 0

set worldFormState($holder.row) 0
set worldFormState($holder.language) english

foreach {key val } $args {
  set keyName [string range $key 1 end]
  if {![info exists worldFormState($holder.$keyName)]} {
    regsub \
        -all "$holder." [array names worldFormState $holder.*] \
        "" okList
      error "Bad option" "Invalid option '$key'.\n Must be one \
        of $okList"
  }
  set worldFormState($holder.$keyName) $val
}

# Create master Frame
frame $holder -height $worldFormState($holder.height) \
  -width $worldFormState($holder.width) -class WorldForm

# Apply invocation options to the master frame, as \
  appropriate

foreach {opt val} $args {
  catch {$holder configure $opt $val}
}

Draw $holder

# We can't have two widgets with the same name.
#  Rename the base frame procedure for this
```

```
    #   widget to $holder.fr so that we can use
    #   $holder as the widget procedure name
    #   for the megawidget.

    uplevel #0 rename $holder $holder.fr

    # When this window is destroyed,
    #   destroy the associated command.
    bind $holder <Destroy> "+[namespace code [list rename \
      $holder {}]]"
    return $holder
}


############################################################
# proc Draw {parent}--
#   creates the subwidgets and maps them into the parent
# Arguments
#   parent   The parent frame for these widgets
#
# Results
#   New windows are created and mapped.

proc Draw {parent} {
  variable worldFormState
  set tmp [button $parent.translate \
    -text $worldFormState($parent.buttonText) \
    -command [namespace code [list translate $parent]] ]
  set worldFormState($parent.subWidgetName.translate) $tmp
  grid $parent.translate -row $worldFormState($parent.row) \
    -column 0

  set tmp [tk_optionMenu $parent.options \
    [namespace current]::worldFormState(language) \
    French English German Spanish ]
  set worldFormState($parent.subWidgetName.options) $tmp
  grid $parent.options -row $worldFormState($parent.row) \
    -column 1
}


############################################################
#   proc DoWidgetCommand {widgetName widgets cmd}--
#     Perform operations on subwidgets
# Arguments
#   widgetName:  The name of the holder frame
#   widgets:     A list of the public names for subwidgets
#   cmd:         A command to evaluate on each of these widgets
# Results
```

```
    #   Does stuff about the subwidgets

    proc DoWidgetCommand {widgetName widgets cmd} {
      variable worldFormState
      foreach widget $widgets {
        set index $widgetName.subWidgetName.$widget
        eval $worldFormState($index) $cmd
      }
    }


    ############################################################
    #     proc translate {parent}--
    #   Change the labels from one language to another
    # Arguments
    #   parent: The parent widget to examine for label widgets
    #
    # Results
    #   The labels are -configured with new text

    proc translate {parent} {
      variable worldFormState
      set language [string tolower $worldFormState(language)]
      foreach w [winfo children $parent] {
        if {[string match [winfo class $w] Label]} {
          set old [$w cget -text]
          $w configure -text $worldFormState($language.$old)
        }
      }
    }


    ############################################################
    #     proc updateXlateTable {lst}--
    #   Add index/value pairs to translation table
    # Arguments
    #   lst: List of language and word pairs
    #
    # Results
    #   The state array is updated

    proc updateXlateTable {lst} {
      variable worldFormState
      # sample: english Name french Nom spanish Nombre
      # array set State {
      #  english.Nom Name english.Nombre Name }
      # array set State {
      #  spanish.Nom Nombre spanish.Name Nombre}
      # For later xlate to english:
      #  "set word $State(english.$word)"
```

```
    foreach {lang word} $lst {
      set lookup ""
      foreach {l w} $lst {
        if {![string match $l $lang]} {
          lappend lookup $lang.$w $word
        }
      }
      array set worldFormState $lookup
    }
}

############################################################
#      proc insert {parent args}--
#    Insert a new Label/Entry pair
# Arguments
#    -width       Width of entry widget
#    \
     -alternates List of language alternates
                 {lang1 word1 lang2 \word2}
#    -text        Text for label
#    -textvar     Textvariable for entry widget
# Results
#    Adds new label/entry pair and increments the row pointer.

proc insert {parent args} {
  variable worldFormState
  set width 10
  incr worldFormState($parent.row)
  set alternates " "

  foreach {key val} $args {
    set varName [string range $key 1 end]
    set $varName $val
  }
   set w [entry $parent.e[unique] -textvariable $textvariable \
        -width $width]
  grid $w -row $worldFormState($parent.row) -column 1
  set w [label $parent.l[unique] -text $text]
  grid $w -row $worldFormState($parent.row) -column 0
  updateXlateTable $alternates
}

############################################################
# proc WorldFormProc {widgetName subCommand args}
#    The master procedure for handling this megawidget's
#    subcommands
# Arguments
```

```
#    widgetName:    The name of the worldForm
#                   widget
#    subCommand     The subCommand for this cmd
#    args:          The rest of the command line
#                   arguments
# Default subCommands are:
# configure - configure the parent frame
# widgetconfigure - configure or query a subwidget.
#         mega widgetconfigure itemID -key value
#         mega widgetconfigure itemID -key
# widgetcget - get the configuration of a widget
#         mega widgetcget itemID -key
# widgetcommand - perform a command on a widget
#         mega widgetcommand itemID commandString
# names - return the name or names that match
#       a pattern
#         mega names # Get names of all widgets
#         mega names *a* # Get names of widgets
#                         with an 'a' in them.
# subwidget - return the full pathname of a
#             requested subwidget
# Results
#    Evaluates a subcommand and returns a result if required.
proc WorldFormProc {widgetName subCommand args} {
  variable worldFormState
  set cmdArgs $args

  switch -- $subCommand {
    configure {
      return [eval $widgetName.fr configure $cmdArgs]
    }
    widgetconfigure {
      set sbwid [lindex $cmdArgs 0]
      set cmd [lrange $cmdArgs 1 end]
      set index $widgetName.subWidgetName.$sbwid
      catch {eval $worldFormState($index) configure $cmd} rtn
      return $rtn
    }
    insert {
      return [eval insert $widgetName $cmdArgs]
    }
    widgetcget {
      if {[llength $cmdArgs] != 2} {
        error "$widgetName cget subWidgetName -option"
      }
```

```
        set sbwid [lindex $cmdArgs 0]
        set index $widgetName.subWidgetName.$sbwid
        set cmd [lrange $cmdArgs 1 end]
        catch {eval $worldFormState($index) cget $cmd} rtn
        return $rtn
      }
      widgetcommand {
        return [eval DoWidgetCommand $widgetName $cmdArgs]
      }
      names {
        if {[string match $cmdArgs ""]} {
        set pattern $widgetName.subWidgetName.*
        } else {
        set pattern $widgetName.subWidgetName.$cmdArgs
      }
      foreach n [array names worldFormState $pattern] {
        foreach {d w s name} [split $n .] {}
        lappend names $name
      }
      return $names
      }
      subwidget {
        set name [lindex $cmdArgs 0]
        set index $widgetName.subWidgetName.$name
        if {[info exists worldFormState($index)]} {
          return $worldFormState($index)
        }
      }
      default {
        error "bad command" "Invalid Command: $subCommand \n \
            must be configure, widgetconfigure, widgetcget, names, \
            insert, or subwidget"
      }
    }
  }
 }
}
```

### Script Example 2

```
lappend auto_path .
package require worldForm
grid [worldForm .x]

.x insert -text Name -textvariable name \
  -alternates {english Name french Nom spanish Nombre german Name}

.x insert -text Address -textvariable address -width 20 \
```

```
-alternates {english Address french Adresse spanish Dirección
german Adresse}
```

***Script Output***

Initial                                    After click translate

After select Spanish                      After click translate

## 12.7 Incorporating a Megawidget into a Larger Megawidget

In this section, we will create a larger megawidget that contains two of the `scrolledLB` widgets, a `label`, a `button`, and an `entry` widget. This megawidget will allow a user to define a filter to extract a subset of the entries from the first listbox for display in the second listbox. When the widget is queried, it will return the selected items in the filtered listbox or the selected items in the unfiltered listbox if nothing was selected in the filtered box.

The justification for this widget is that sometimes there are too many items in a listbox to find those the user is interested in, but a simple filter could cut down the size to something manageable. This is similar to the effect that various file browsers get with the "filter" option, but this widget allows the user to see both the unfiltered list and the filtered list at the same time.

Like the `scrolledLB`, this megawidget is implemented as a procedure for creating the widget in the global scope with support procedures maintained in a namespace scope. As described in the previous section, there are some points to watch when using namespaces with Tk widgets. The button command string uses the `namespace code` command to cause the script to be evaluated in the current namespace.

If we knew that the `filteredLB` widget would always be defined at a top level, we could just define the command string as `::filteredLB::DoFilter`, but just as the `scrolledLB` megawidget is contained within the `filteredLB` widget, the filteredLB widget may be contained in a larger widget, as shown in the file browser megawidget example at the end of this section.

**Example** 12.13

*Script Example*

```
## Name: Filtered.tcl
lappend auto_path .
package provide filteredLB 1.0
package require scrolledLB

############################################################
# proc filteredLB {args}
#    Create a filteredLB megawidget
#    External entry point for creating a megawidget.
# Arguments
#    ?parentFrame?  A frame to use for the parent.
#                   If this is not provided, the megawidget
#                   is a child of the root frame (".").
# Results
#    Creates a procedure with the megawidget name for processing
#     widget commands
#    Returns the name of the megawidget

proc filteredLB {args} {
  set newWidget [eval filteredLB::MakefilteredLB $args]
  set newCmd [format {return [namespace eval %s %s %s $args ]}\
    filteredLB FilteredLBProc $newWidget]

  proc $newWidget {args} $newCmd

  return $newWidget
}

namespace eval filteredLB {
  variable filteredLBState

  # Assign a couple defaults
  set filteredLBState(unique) 0

  ############################################################
  # proc MakefilteredLB {args}
  #    Create a filteredLB megawidget
  # Arguments
  #    ?parentFrame?  A frame to use for the parent.
  #                   If this is not provided, the megawidget
  #                   is a child of the root frame (".").
  #    ?-scrollposition left/right?
```

```tcl
#                          The side of the listbox for the scrollbar
# Results
#    Returns the name of the parent frame for use as a
#    megawidget

proc MakefilteredLB {args} {
    variable filteredLBState

    # Set the default name

    set holder .filteredLB_$filteredLBState(unique)
    incr filteredLBState(unique)

    # If the first argument is a window path, use that as
    # the base name for this widget.

    if {[string first "." [lindex $args 0]] == 0} {
      set holder [lindex $args 0]
      set args [lreplace $args 0 0]
    }

    # Set Command line option defaults here,
    #    height and width are freebies

    set filteredLBState($holder.height) 5
    set filteredLBState($holder.width) 20

      set filteredLBState($holder.listbox1Height) 10
      set filteredLBState($holder.title1Text) title1
      set filteredLBState($holder.listbox1Width) 30
      set filteredLBState($holder.listbox2Height) 10
      set filteredLBState($holder.title2Text) title2
      set filteredLBState($holder.listbox2Width) 30
      set filteredLBState($holder.titleFont) {helvetica 20 bold}
      set filteredLBState($holder.titleText) title
      set filteredLBState($holder.patternVariable) filterVar
      set filteredLBState($holder.patternWidth) 10

    foreach {key val } $args {
        set keyName [string range $key 1 end]
        if {![info exists \
              filteredLBState($holder.$keyName)]} {
            regsub -all "$holder." \
               [array names filteredLBState $holder.*] \
          " " okList
      error "Bad option" \
        "Invalid option '$key'.\n\
        Must be one of $okList"
}
```

```
    set filteredLBState($holder.$keyName) $val
        }

    # Create master Frame

    frame $holder -height $filteredLBState($holder.height) \
        -width $filteredLBState($holder.width) \
        -class FilteredLB

    # Apply invocation options to the master frame, as appropriate

    foreach {opt val} $args {
      catch {$holder configure $opt $val}
    }

    Draw $holder

    # We can't have two widgets with the same name.
    #  Rename the base frame procedure for this
    #  widget to $holder.fr so that we can use
    #  $holder as the widget procedure name
    #  for the megawidget.

    uplevel #0 rename $holder $holder.fr

    # When this window is destroyed,
    #  destroy the associated command.

    bind $holder <Destroy> \
      "+ rename $holder {}"

    return $holder
}


##############################################################
# proc Draw {parent}--
#   creates the subwidgets and maps them into the parent
# Arguments
#   parent   The parent frame for these widgets
#
# Results
#   New windows are created and mapped.

proc Draw {parent} {
    variable filteredLBState

    image create photo arrow -data {
      R0lGOD1hEAAQAPABAAAAAP///yH5BAAAAAAALAAAAAAQABAAAAK
      RTJgwYcKECRMmTJgwYcKECRMmTJgwYcKECBMmTJgwYcKEABMmTJ
      gwYcKEABEmTJgwYcKEAAEmDAgQIECAAAEiDAgQIECAAAECDAgQI
```

```
        ECAAAEiTJgwYcKEAAEmTJgwYcKEABEmTJgwYcKEABMmTJgwYcKE
        CBMmTJgwYcKECRMmTJgwYcKECRMmTJgwYcKECRMmBQA7
        }

    set tmp [scrolledLB $parent.list1 \
      -listboxHeight $filteredLBState($parent.listbox1Height) \
      -titleText $filteredLBState($parent.title1Text) \
      -listboxWidth $filteredLBState($parent.listbox1Width)]
    set filteredLBState($parent.subWidgetName.list1) $tmp
    grid $tmp -row 2 -column 0 -rowspan 2

    set tmp [scrolledLB $parent.list2 \
      -listboxHeight $filteredLBState($parent.listbox2Height) \
      -titleText $filteredLBState($parent.title2Text) \
      -listboxWidth $filteredLBState($parent.listbox2Width)]
    set filteredLBState($parent.subWidgetName.list2) $tmp
    grid $tmp -row 2 -column 2 -rowspan 2

    set tmp [label $parent.title \
      -font $filteredLBState($parent.titleFont) \
      -text $filteredLBState($parent.titleText)]
    set filteredLBState($parent.subWidgetName.title) $tmp
    grid $tmp -row 0 -column 0 -columnspan 3

    set tmp [entry $parent.pattern \
      -textvar $filteredLBState($parent.patternVariable) \
      -width $filteredLBState($parent.patternWidth)]
    set filteredLBState($parent.subWidgetName.pattern) $tmp
    grid $tmp -row 1 -column 0 -columnspan 3

    set tmp [button $parent.go \
      -image arrow \
      -command "[namespace code [list DoFilter $parent]]"]
    set filteredLBState($parent.subWidgetName.go) $tmp
    grid $tmp -row 2 -column 1 -sticky n

}

############################################################
#    proc DoWidgetCommand {widgetName widgets cmd}--
#      Perform operations on subwidgets
# Arguments
#    widgetName: The name of the holder frame
#    widgets:    A list of the public names for subwidgets
#    cmd:        A command to evaluate on each of these widgets
# Results
#    Does stuff about the subwidgets
```

```
proc DoWidgetCommand {widgetName widgets cmd} {
  variable filteredLBState
  foreach widget $widgets {
    set index $widgetName.subWidgetName.$widget
    eval $filteredLBState($index) $cmd
  }
}

############################################################
# proc DoFilter {holder}--
#   Tests items in full listbox, and puts ones that match
#   a pattern into the second listbox.
#
# Arguments
#   holder  The name of the parent frame.
#
# Results
#   The second listbox (list2) may receive new entries.

proc DoFilter {holder} {
  variable filteredLBState
  set pattern [$filteredLBState($holder.subWidgetName.pattern) get]

  set fullListbox [[$holder subwidget list1] subwidget list]
  set filterListbox [[$holder subwidget list2] subwidget list]

  foreach item [$fullListbox get 0 end] {
    if {[string match $pattern $item]} {
        $filterListbox insert end $item
    }
  }
}

############################################################
# proc Selection {holder}--
#   Returns the selected items from the second listbox
#
# Arguments
#   holder  The name of the parent frame.
#
# Results
#   No changes to widget

proc Selection {holder} {
  set filterListbox [[$holder subwidget list2] subwidget list]

  set lst [$filterListbox curselection]
    set itemlst ""
```

```
      foreach l $lst {
        lappend itemlst [$filterListbox get $l]
      }
  if {[string match $itemlst ""]} {
  set fullListbox [[$holder subwidget list1] subwidget list]

  set lst [$fullListbox curselection]
    set itemlst ""
    foreach l $lst {
      lappend itemlst [$fullListbox get $l]
    }
  }
  return $itemlst
}


#############################################################
# proc FilteredLBProc {widgetName subCommand args}
#    The master procedure for handling this megawidget's
#    subcommands
# Arguments
#    widgetName:    The name of the filteredLB
#                   widget
#    subCommand     The subCommand for this cmd
#    args:          The rest of the command line
#                   arguments
# Default subCommands are:
# configure - configure the parent frame
# widgetconfigure - configure or query a subwidget.
#              mega widgetconfigure itemID -key value
#              mega widgetconfigure itemID -key
# widgetcget - get the configuration of a widget
#              mega widgetcget itemID -key
# widgetcommand - perform a command on a widget
#              mega widgetcommand itemID commandString
# names - return the name or names that match
#         a pattern
#              mega names # Get names of all widgets
#              mega names *a* # Get names of widgets
#                            with an 'a' in them.
# subwidget - return the full pathname of a
#             requested subwidget
# Results
#    Evaluates a subcommand and returns a result if required.

proc FilteredLBProc {widgetName subCommand args} {
  variable filteredLBState
```

```
set cmdArgs $args

switch -- $subCommand {
configure {
      return [eval $widgetName.fr configure $cmdArgs]
}
widgetconfigure {
      set sbwid [lindex $cmdArgs 0]
      set cmd [lrange $cmdArgs 1 end]
      set index $widgetName.subWidgetName.$sbwid
      catch {eval \
        $filteredLBState($index) configure $cmd} rtn
      return $rtn
}

delete -
insert {
      return [eval $widgetName.list1 $subCommand $cmdArgs]
}

selection {return [Selection $widgetName]}

widgetcget {
      if {[llength $cmdArgs] != 2} {
        error "$widgetName cget subWidgetName -option"
      }
      set sbwid [lindex $cmdArgs 0]
      set index $widgetName.subWidgetName.$sbwid
      set cmd [lrange $cmdArgs 1 end]
      catch {eval \
        $filteredLBState($index)\
        cget $cmd} rtn
      return $rtn
      }

widgetcommand {
  return [eval DoWidgetCommand $widgetName $cmdArgs]
}

names {
      if {[string match $cmdArgs ""]} {
        set pattern $widgetName.subWidgetName.*
      } else {
        set pattern $widgetName.subWidgetName.$cmdArgs
      }

  foreach n [array names filteredLBState $pattern] {
      foreach {d w s name} [split $n .] {}
```

```
                    lappend names $name
            }
        return $names
    }

    subwidget {
            set name [lindex $cmdArgs 0]
            set index $widgetName.subWidgetName.$name
            if {[info exists filteredLBState($index)]} {
              return $filteredLBState($index)
            }
    }

    default {
            error "bad command" "Invalid Command: \
              $subCommand \n \
              must be configure, widgetconfigure, \
              widgetcget, names,\
              delete, insert, selection, \
              or subwidget"
        }
      }
    }
  }
}
```

Using the `filteredLB` for the file browser is simple. You simply create the mega-widget, map it, and fill it with the appropriate values, as shown in the following example.

Note the `option add` commands. These set widgets associated with the `filteredLB` widget to a light gray and widgets associated with the `scrolledLB` widget to a darker gray. The `option` command will apply colors to the most specific option. The parts of the `filteredLB` widget that are implemented with the `scrolledLB` widget override the lighter gray to become darker, whereas the `title`, `entry`, and `button` widgets that are not part of a `scrolledLB` widget are assigned the light gray color.

### Example 12.14

***Script Example***

```
lappend auto_path .
package require filteredLB

option add *FilteredLB*Background #eee
option add *ScrolledLB*Background #ccc

set fb [filteredLB .dir -patternVariable tst \
```

```
   -title1Text "Original Data" -title2Text "Filtered Data" \
   -listbox1Height 5 -listbox2Height 5 \
   -titleText "Filtered directory contents" \
   -listbox1Width 15 -listbox2Width 15]

grid $fb

set path /bin
foreach f [glob $path/*] {
  .dir insert end $f
}
button .report -text "Report" \
  -command {tk_messageBox -type ok -message [.dir selection]}

grid .report
```

*Script Output*

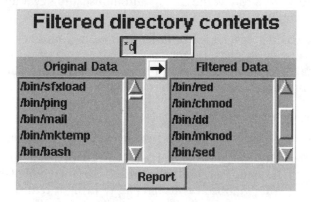

## 12.8 Making a Modal Megawidget: The grab and tkwait Commands

In this section we will take the filteredList megawidget we just developed and make a modal file selection widget. This widget is far from the last word in file selection widgets, but it makes a good example of how a modal widget can be constructed.

This widget is implemented as a single procedure that creates and displays the megawidget and returns the results of the user interaction when that interaction is complete. The condition for completion is that the user has either clicked the Quit button, clicked the OK button, or destroyed the widget using a window manager command.

This widget introduces the grab and tkwait commands that have not been used in previous examples. The grab command allows your application to examine and control how mouse and keyboard events are reported to the windows on your display. The tkwait command will cause a script to pause until an external event (such as a window being destroyed) occurs.

## 12.8.1 **The grab Command**

By default, whenever a cursor enters or leaves a widget, an Enter or Leave event is generated. When the cursor enters a widget, that widget is said to have focus, and all keystroke and button events will be reported to that widget. By using the grab command, you can declare that all keyboard and mouse events will go to a particular widget regardless of the location of the cursor. This requires a user to perform a set of interactions before your program releases the grab. Once the grab is released, the focus will follow the cursor, and mouse and keyboard events will be distributed normally.

The grab command has several subcommands that let you determine whether other grabs are already in place (in which case your program should save that state and restore it when it is done) and set a new state. You can learn what window is currently grabbing events with the grab current command.

*Syntax:* grab current ?*window*?

Returns a list of the windows that are currently grabbing events.

*window*    If *window* is defined and a child of *window* has grabbed events, that child will be returned. If no child of the window has grabbed events, an empty string is returned. If *window* is not defined, all windows in the application that have grabbed events will be reported.

A window can grab either all events for that application or all events for the entire system. The default mode is to grab only events for the current application. If you need to grab events for the entire system, this can be done with the -global flag when a grab is requested. If a grab is in effect, you can determine whether it is for a local (default) or global scope with the grab status command. The following example shows the focus being grabbed by a label, instead of the button. Since the label is grabbing focus, the button never responds to <Enter> or button events.

**Example** 12.15

*Script Example*

```
pack [button .b -text "Show" -command {puts [grab current]}]
pack [label .l -text "holding focus"]
grab .l
puts "Focus is held by: [grab current]"
```

*Script Output*

**Focus is held by: .1**

---

*Syntax:* `grab status` *window*

Returns the status of a grab on the defined window. The return will be one of

| | |
|---|---|
| `local` | The window is in local (default) mode. Only events destined for this application will be routed to this window. |
| `global` | The window is in global mode. All events in the system will be routed to this window. |
| *empty string* | There is no grab in effect for this window. |
| *window* | The window for which status will be returned. |

## Example 12.16

*Script Example*

```
pack [button .b -text "Show" -command {puts [grab current]}]
pack [label .1 -text "holding focus"]
grab .1
puts "Status for .1 is: [grab status .1]"
```

*Script Output*

**Status for .1 is: local**

---

You can declare that all events will go to a window with the `grab` or `grab set` command. These commands behave identically.

*Syntax:* `grab ?set?` *?-global? window*

Set a window to grab keyboard and mouse events.

| | |
|---|---|
| *-global* | Grab all events for the system. By default, only events generated while this application has the focus will be directed to this window. |
| *window* | The window to receive the events. |

## 12.8.2 The tkwait Command

Once all events in the system are directed to the modal widget, the widget has to know when the interaction is complete. We can force the Tcl interpreter to wait until the user has performed an interaction with the `tkwait` command. This command will wait until a particular event has occurred. The event may be a variable being modified (perhaps by a button press), a change in the visibility of a window, or a window being destroyed.

***Syntax:*** `tkwait EventType name`

Wait for an event to occur.

| | |
|---|---|
| `EventType` | A name describing the type of event that may occur. The content of *name* depends on which type of event has occurred. |

Valid events are

| | |
|---|---|
| `variable` *varName* | Causes `tkwait` to wait until the variable *varName* changes value. |
| `visibility` *windowName* | Causes `tkwait` to wait until the window *windowName* either becomes visible or is hidden. |
| `window` *windowName* | Causes `tkwait` to wait until the window named in *windowName* is destroyed. |

## Example 12.17

***Script Example***

```
# Create and display two widgets
pack [label .l -text "I'm the first .l"]
pack [button .b -text "Click to destroy label" -command "destroy .l"]

# The code pauses here until the window named .l is destroyed
# This will happen when the button is clicked.
tkwait window .l

# After the button is clicked, and .l is destroyed,
# a new .l is created and packed.
pack [label .l -text "I'm a new .l"]
```

***Script Output***

Before clicking button      After clicking button

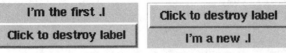

## 12.8.3 The Modal Widget Code

The next example shows how the `filtered listbox` megawidget can be used to create a modal file selection megawidget.

**Example** 12.18

*Script Example*

```
## Name: getFileList.tcl
lappend auto_path "."
package require filteredLB
package provide fileSel 1.0


#########################################################
# proc getFileList {directory}--
#  Returns a list of selected files from the requested
#  directory.
# Arguments
#  directory    The directory to return a list of files from
#
# Results
#  Creates a new window and grabs focus until user
#  interacts with it.
#  Returns a list of the selected files, or an empty list if:
#     no files are selected,
#     'QUIT' button is clicked,
#     window is destroyed.

proc getFileList {directory} {
  global popupStateVar

  # Find an unused, unique name for a toplevel window.
  # winfo children returns a list of child windows.

  set unique 0
  set childlist [winfo children .]
  while {[lsearch childlist .dirList_$unique]!= -1} {
    incr unique
  }

  # Create the new toplevel window that will hold this
  #  widget

  set win [toplevel .dirList_$unique -class Fileselector]

  # Create the widget as a child of the $win window
  # And configure the listboxes for multiple selections

  set fl [filteredLB $win.fl1 -titleText "Select Files" \
    -title1Text "Files in Directory" \
    -title2Text "Filtered list" ]

  [$fl subwidget list1] \
```

```
        widgetconfigure list -selectmode multiple
[$fl subwidget list2] \
        widgetconfigure list -selectmode multiple

# And fill the full list

foreach file [glob -nocomplain $directory/*] {
  $fl insert end [file tail $file]
}

# Pack the filteredList megawidget at the top of the
# new window

pack $fl -side top

# Create the buttons in a frame of their own, and pack them

set bframe [frame $win.buttons]
set quit [button $bframe.quit -text "QUIT" -command\
  {set popupStateVar(ret) ""}]

set ok [button $bframe.ok -text "OK" \
    -command \
    "set popupStateVar(ret) \[$fl selection\]"]

pack $quit -side left
pack $ok -side left
pack $bframe -side bottom

# bind the destroy event to setting the trigger variable,
# so we can exit properly if the window is destroyed by
# the window manager.

bind $win <Destroy> {set popupStateVar(ret) ""}

# The following code is adapted from dialog.tcl in the
# tk library. It sets the focus of the window manager
# on the new window, and waits for the value of
# popupStateVar(ret) to change.
#
# When the user clicks a button, or destroys the window,
# it will set the value of popupStateVar(ret),
# and processing will continue
# Set a grab and claim the focus.

set oldFocus [focus]
set oldGrab [grab current $win]
if {$oldGrab != ""} {
  set grabStatus [grab status $oldGrab]
}
```

```
        grab $win
        focus $win

        # Wait for the user to respond, then restore the focus
        # and return the index of the selected button. Restore
        # the focus before deleting the window, since otherwise
        # the window manager may take the focus away so we can't
        # redirect it. Finally, restore any grab that was in
        # effect.

        tkwait variable popupStateVar(ret)
        catch {focus $oldFocus}

        # It's possible that the window has already been
        # destroyed, hence this "catch". Delete the
        # <Destroy> handler so that popupStateVar(ret)
        # doesn't get reset by it.

        catch {
          bind $win <Destroy> {}
          destroy $win
        }

        if {$oldGrab != ""} {
          if {$grabStatus == "global"} {
            grab -global $oldGrab
          } {
            grab $oldGrab
          }
        }
        return $popupStateVar(ret)
}
```

### Example of Using *getFileList*

```
# The widgets pkgIndex.tcl file is in the current directory
# in this example.

lappend auto_path "."

# Include the widgets package to get the
#  fileSel megawidget.

package require fileSel

# Create a label and entry widget to get a base directory path

set dirFrame [frame .f1]
label $dirFrame.l1 -text "base directory: "
```

```
entry $dirFrame.e1 -textvariable directory

# Create buttons to invoke the getFileList widget.

set buttonFrame [frame .f2]
button $buttonFrame.b1 -text "Select Files" \
  -command {set filelist [getFileList $directory]}

# The selected files will be displayed in a label widget
# with the -textvariable defined as the filelist returned
# from the getFileList widget.

set selFrame [frame .sel]
set selectLabel [label $selFrame.label -text \
    "Selected files:"]
set selectVal [message $selFrame.selected \
    -textvariable filelist -width 100]

# and pack everything

pack $dirFrame.l1 -side left
pack $dirFrame.e1 -side right
pack $dirFrame -side top
pack $buttonFrame -side top
pack $buttonFrame.b1 -side left
pack $selFrame -side top
pack $selectVal -side right
pack $selectLabel -side left
```

***Script Output***

Initial window

base directory: /bin

Select Files

Selected files:

File selection window, after selections

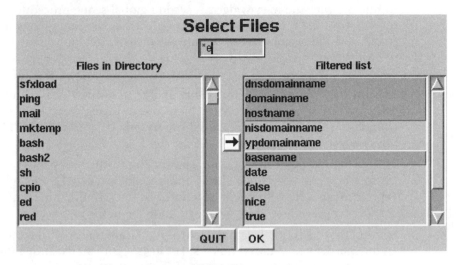

Initial window, after OK button clicked

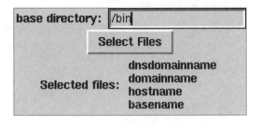

# 12.9 Automating Megawidget Construction

You may have noticed that the three megawidgets presented in this chapter are very similar. In fact, the bulk of the code in these widgets is identical. Building custom megawidgets can be automated in a few ways, by working from a skeleton and filling in the pieces, by further automating building from a skeleton with a configuration file and a Tcl script, or by assembling compound widgets on the fly with another set of procedures.

## 12.9.1 Building Megawidgets from a Skeleton

The architecture of these megawidgets is consistent. There is a procedure in the global scope to create a megawidget, which calls procedures in the appropriate namespace to populate the megawidget and return the name of the procedure to interact with the megawidget. A second global scope procedure is created to interact with the megawidget. This procedure has the same name as the parent frame, and will evaluate scripts within the megawidget namespace to implement the widget commands.

The unique part of each megawidget is the procedure to draw the subwidgets and the procedures that implement unique subwidget commands. The next example is a simple skeleton for these megawidgets. It is also found on the companion CD-ROM. Just replace the appropriate parts, and it will be a custom megawidget.

This skeleton uses a convention of starting lines with a semicolon (;) if they are instructions to the developer. These lines should be deleted or changed to normal Tcl comments. These lines will be ignored by the script that uses this skeleton to construct megawidgets from a configuration file in the next section.

Some of the procedure skeletons use args for the argument list and then have other arguments defined in the comments. The args argument list allows the procedure to accept any number of arguments, and the comments define what arguments are expected. If the argument defined in the comments is surrounded by question marks (?), it means the argument is optional.

All of these procedures use a convention of putting required arguments first and then optional arguments. The next example follows the normal Tk convention.

**Example 12.19**

```
lappend auto_path .

; Replace SkeletonPkg with name of package.
; Replace megaSkeletonDrawBody with body to draw widgets and
;    update state variable with widget paths.
; Replace megaSkeletonDefaults with default values for variables
;    that can be set on the command line.
; Replace SkeletonSubcommands with appropriate command/script
;    pairs for new widget commands.
; Replace SkeletonSubCmdNames with new commands.
; Replace SkeletonProcs with other support procs (for new
;    widget commands).
; Global replace SkeletonNameSpace with namespace identifier.
; Global replace SkeletonState with the name of a state array.
; Global replace SkeletonWidgetProc with widget procedure name.
; Replace megaSkeleton with widgetName.
; Replace Skeleton with name of widget.
; Make certain -class option is valid capitalization

package provide SkeletonPkg 1.0
```

```
#############################################################
# proc megaSkeleton {args}
#    Create a megaSkeleton megawidget
#    External entry point for creating a megawidget.
# Arguments
#    ?parentFrame?  A frame to use for the parent.
#                   If this is not provided, the megawidget
#                   is a child of the root frame (".").
# Results
#    Creates a procedure with the megawidget name for processing
#    widget commands
#    Returns the name of the megawidget
proc megaSkeleton {args} {
  set newWidget [eval SkeletonNameSpace::MakemegaSkeleton $args]

  set newCmd [format {return [namespace eval %s %s %s $args ]}\
    SkeletonNameSpace SkeletonWidgetProc $newWidget]

  proc $newWidget {args} $newCmd

  return $newWidget
}

namespace eval SkeletonNameSpace {
  variable SkeletonState

  # Assign a couple defaults
  set SkeletonState(unique) 0
  set SkeletonState(debug) 0

  #############################################################
  # proc MakemegaSkeleton {args}
  #    Create a megaSkeleton megawidget
  # Arguments
  #    ?parentFrame?  A frame to use for the parent.
  #                   If this is not provided, the megawidget
  #                   is a child of the root frame (".").
  #    ?-scrollposition left/right?
  #                   The side of the listbox for the scrollbar
  # Results
  #    Returns the name of the parent frame for use as a
  #    megawidget
  proc MakemegaSkeleton {args} {
    variable SkeletonState

    # Set the default name
```

```
        set holder .Skeleton_$SkeletonState(unique)
        incr SkeletonState(unique)

        # If the first argument is a window path, use that as
        # the base name for this widget.

        if {[string first "." [lindex $args 0]] == 0} {
            set holder [lindex $args 0]
            set args [lreplace $args 0 0]
        }

        # Set Command line option defaults here,
        #   height and width are freebies

        set SkeletonState($holder.height) 5
        set SkeletonState($holder.width) 20

        # Add more defaults following previous pattern.
megaSkeletonDefaults

        foreach {key val } $args {
          set keyName [string range $key 1 end]
          if {![info exists \
            SkeletonState($holder.$keyName)]} {
          regsub -all "$holder." \
            [array names SkeletonState $holder.*] \
            "" okList
          error "Bad option" \
            "Invalid option '$key'.\n\
            Must be one of $okList"
        }
          set SkeletonState($holder.$keyName) $val
        }

        # Create master Frame

        frame $holder -height $SkeletonState($holder.height) \
            -width $SkeletonState($holder.width) \
            -class megaSkeleton

        # Apply invocation options to the master frame, as appropriate

        foreach {opt val} $args {
          catch {$holder configure $opt $val}
        }

        Draw $holder

        # We can't have two widgets with the same name.
        #  Rename the base frame procedure for this
```

```
    #  widget to $holder.fr so that we can use
    #  $holder as the widget procedure name
    #  for the megawidget.

    uplevel #0 rename $holder $holder.fr

    # When this window is destroyed,
    #   destroy the associated command.

    bind $holder <Destroy> "+ rename $holder {}"
      return $holder
    }


    ############################################################
    # proc Draw {parent}--
    #   creates the subwidgets and maps them into the parent
    # Arguments
    #   parent   The parent frame for these widgets
    #
    # Results
    #   New windows are created and mapped.

    proc Draw {parent} {
        variable SkeletonState

#        variable filteredLBState
#        set tmp [button $parent.button1 \
#            -text $filteredLBState($parent.button1Text) ...
#        set filteredLBState($parent.subWidgetName.button1) $tmp
#        grid $tmp -row 2 -column 0 -rowspan 2

    megaSkeletonDrawBody
    }


    ############################################################
    # proc DoWidgetCommand {widgetName widgets cmd}--
    #   Perform operations on subwidgets
    # Arguments
    #   widgetName:  The name of the holder frame
    #   widgets:     A list of the public names for subwidgets
    #   cmd:         A command to evaluate on each of these widgets
    # Results
    #   Does stuff about the subwidgets

    proc DoWidgetCommand {widgetName widgets cmd} {
      variable SkeletonState
      foreach widget $widgets {
        set index $widgetName.subWidgetName.$widget
```

```
            eval $SkeletonState($index) $cmd
        }
    }
}

SkeletonProcs

###########################################################
# proc SkeletonWidgetProc {widgetName subCommand args}
#     The master procedure for handling this megawidget's
#     subcommands
# Arguments
#     widgetName:   The name of the megaSkeleton
#                     widget
#     subCommand    The subCommand for this cmd
#     args:         The rest of the command line
#                     arguments
# Default subCommands are:
# configure - configure the parent frame
# widgetconfigure - configure or query a subwidget.
#               mega widgetconfigure itemID -key value
#               mega widgetconfigure itemID -key
# widgetcget - get the configuration of a widget
#               mega widgetcget itemID -key
# widgetcommand - perform a command on a widget
#               mega widgetcommand itemID commandString
# names - return the name or names that match
#           a pattern
#               mega names # Get names of all widgets
#               mega names *a* # Get names of widgets
#                                   with an 'a' in them.
# subwidget - return the full pathname of a
#               requested subwidget
# Results
#     Evaluates a subcommand and returns a result if required.

proc SkeletonWidgetProc {widgetName subCommand args} {
    variable SkeletonState
    set cmdArgs $args

    switch -- $subCommand {
        configure {
            return [eval $widgetName.fr configure $cmdArgs]
        }
        widgetconfigure {
            set sbwid [lindex $cmdArgs 0]
            set cmd [lrange $cmdArgs 1 end]
            set index $widgetName.subWidgetName.$sbwid
```

```
        catch {eval \
          $SkeletonState($index) configure $cmd} rtn
        return $rtn
    }

SkeletonSubcommands

widgetcget {
    if {[llength $cmdArgs] != 2} {
        error "$widgetName cget subWidgetName -option"
    }
    set sbwid [lindex $cmdArgs 0]
    set index $widgetName.subWidgetName.$sbwid
    set cmd [lrange $cmdArgs 1 end]
    catch {eval \
      $SkeletonState($index)\
      cget $cmd} rtn
    return $rtn
}
widgetcommand {
    return [eval DoWidgetCommand $widgetName $cmdArgs]
}
names {
    if {[string match $cmdArgs ""]} {
        set pattern $widgetName.subWidgetName.*
    } else {
        set pattern $widgetName.subWidgetName.$cmdArgs
    }
    foreach n [array names SkeletonState $pattern] {
        foreach {d w s name} [split $n .] {}
        lappend names $name
    }
    return $names
}
subwidget {
    set name [lindex $cmdArgs 0]
    set index $widgetName.subWidgetName.$name
      if {[info exists SkeletonState($index)]} {
        return $SkeletonState($index)
      }
}
default {
    error "bad command" "Invalid Command: \
      $subCommand \n \
      must be configure, widgetconfigure, \
      widgetcget, names,\
```

```
                    SkeletonSubCmdNames \
                    or subwidget"
                }
            }
        }
    }
```

## 12.9.2 Building Megawidgets from a Configuration File

The next obvious step to automating the creation of megawidgets is to use a script to perform all substitutions, instead of your favorite editor. The next script will accept a few configuration lists and use them to construct a megawidget. The main procedure in this set of scripts is fillSkeleton. This script performs a set of regular expression substitutions to replace the Skeleton* strings with the appropriate scripts and names. The fillSkeleton procedure accepts four arguments.

- *WidgetName:* The name of the widget to create. This will be substituted for Skeleton where appropriate.

- *WidgetDef:* A list of lists in which each sublist is a list of keyword/value pairs that define a subwidget. The keywords supported by this are as follows.

| | |
|---|---|
| -name | The name of this subwidget. To be used when identifying this subcomponent for commands such as widgetconfigure. |
| -type | The type of widget (button, label, and so on). This is the Tk widget type, or may be another previously defined megawidget. |
| -gridoptions | The grid options to apply for this widget. These may include any grid options such as -row, -column, -rowspan, and so on. |
| -widgetoptions | Options to apply when creating this subwidget. These may include any valid option for this type of widget, such as -height, -width, -font, and so on. If it should be possible to define this value from the megawidget command line, it should be given a unique key, such as label1Text. In this case, rather than an absolute value, the value associated with this key/value pair must be a list in which the first element is the new option name (label1Text) and the second element is a default value for this option. For example, -height {%listboxHeight 10} sets the height of a subwidget to the value supplied with a -listboxHeight key, or the default value of 10. |

- *CmdSwitch:* A set of widget command names and scripts to evaluate to implement the command. This string will be inserted into the switch statement in SkeletonProc.

- *procs:* Any support procedures that should be included in the new widget namespace.

**Example** 12.20

```
#!tclsh

##############################################################
# proc fillSkeleton {widgetName widgetDef cmdSwitch procs} --
#   modify the megaSkeleton.tcl script to make a 'real'
#      compound megawidget
# Arguments
#   widgetName:  The name for the widget being defined
#   widgetDef: A list of keyword/value pairs
#     -name: name of subwidget
#     -type: Tk primitive - button, listbox, scrollbar, etc.
#     -widgetoptions: options to apply to the widget
#                      creation command
#     -gridoptions: Options to apply to the grid command
#
#     New widget-specific options can be declared as
#     arguments to a widgetoption or gridoption with a
#     {% newName defaultValue} list.
#     ie -widgetoptions {-width {%widgetWidth 50}}
#   cmdSwitch: A string to insert into the subcommand
#               switch statement. Should be a set of
#               match pattern/script pairs.
#   procs:     New procedure definitions to go into the
#               namespace. These will be invoked from the
#               subcommand procedure.
# Results
#   Creates a new .tcl file suitable for package require,
#   or source

proc fillSkeleton {widgetName widgetDef \
    {cmdSwitch {}} {procs {}} } {
  set if [open megaSkeleton.tcl r]
  set of [open $widgetName.tcl w]

  set capsName [string toupper \
    [string range $widgetName 0 0 ]][string range $widgetName 1 end]

  set drawBody [genDraw $widgetDef]

  set defaults [genDefaults $widgetDef]
```

```
    set subCmds [genSubcmds $cmdSwitch]

  while {[set len [gets $if line]] >= 0} {
    if {[string first ";" $line] == 0} {continue}
    regsub megaSkeletonDrawBody $line $drawBody line
    regsub megaSkeletonDefaults $line $defaults line
    regsub "SkeletonPkg" $line "$widgetName" line
    regsub SkeletonNameSpace $line $widgetName line
    regsub -all SkeletonState $line ${widgetName}State line
    regsub SkeletonWidgetProc $line ${capsName}Proc line
    regsub SkeletonSubcommands $line $cmdSwitch line
    regsub SkeletonSubCmdNames $line $subCmds line
    regsub SkeletonProcs $line $procs line
    regsub -- "-class megaSkeleton" $line "-class $capsName" line
    regsub megaSkeleton $line $widgetName line
    regsub Skeleton $line $widgetName line
    puts $of $line
  }
  return $of
}


##############################################################
# proc genDefaults {oList}--
#    Returns a list of defaults for inclusion in the
#    megawidget source file
# Arguments
#    oList       A list of widgetOptions
#
# Results
#    Returns a set of Tcl commands for insertion into the
#    megawidget creation procedure

proc genDefaults {oList} {
  set s "        "
  set optionList ""

  foreach def $oList {
    foreach {set values} $def {
      if {[string match $set "-widgetoptions"] ||
        [string match $set "-gridoptions"]} {
        foreach {key val} $values {
          if {[string first % $val] >= 0} {
            foreach {name dflt} $val {}
            set name [string trim $name "%"]
            append optionList \
```

```
            "$s set SkeletonState(\$holder.$name) \
            [list $dflt]\n"
        }
      }
    }
  }
}
  return $optionList
}

###########################################################
# proc genDraw {widgetDescList}--
#   Creates a draw procedure for the Megawidget creation
#   namespace
# Arguments
#   widgetDescList  A list of widget descriptors
#                      in a -key value format
#
# Results
#   Returns the body of a draw procedure

proc genDraw {widgetDescList} {
  array set settings {type "" name "" \
    widgetoptions "" gridoptions ""}

  set drawBody "variable SkeletonState\n"
  set s "        "
  foreach descr $widgetDescList {

    set opts " "
    foreach {key val} $descr {
      set index [string range $key 1 end]
      if {![info exists settings($index)]} {
        error "Bad Option" \
        "$index not supported - use one of \
        '[array names settings]'"
      }
      set settings($index) $val
    }

    foreach {key val} $settings(widgetoptions) {
      if {[string first % $val] >= 0} {
        foreach {name dflt} $val {}
        set name [string range $name 1 end]
        set val \$SkeletonState(\$parent.$name)
      }
```

```
        append opts " \\\n$s  $key $val"
      }

      while {[string first % $settings(gridoptions)] >= 0} {
        regexp {\{ *%([^ ]*) *([^ ^\}]+) *\}} \
          $settings(gridoptions) a b c
        regsub $a $settings(gridoptions) \
          "\$SkeletonState(\$parent.$b) " \
          settings(gridoptions)
      }

      append drawBody "$s set tmp \[$settings(type) \
        \$parent.$settings(name) $opts\]\n"
      append drawBody "$s set \
        SkeletonState(\$parent.subWidgetName.$settings(name)) \
        \$tmp\n"
      append drawBody "$s grid \$tmp $settings(gridoptions)\n\n"

    }
    return $drawBody
}

#############################################################
# proc genSubcmds {cmdSwitch}--
#    Convert a list of switch patterns and bodies into a
#    list of subcommands for the default branch error return.
# Arguments
#    cmdSwitch:  A set of pattern/script pairs
#
# Results
#    Returns a comma-delimited list of commands.

proc genSubcmds {cmdSwitch} {
    set cmds ""
    foreach {cmd body} $cmdSwitch {
      append cmds "$cmd, "
    }
    return $cmds
}
```

The next example shows how the fillSkeleton procedure can be used to create the scrolling listbox megawidget from Section 12.5.1.

**Example** 12.21

```
        # Define the widget name
        set widgetName scrolledList
```

```
# A descriptor set for a scrollbar, listbox, and label
set widgetDef {
  {
  -name yscroll
  -type scrollbar
  -widgetoptions {-orient vertical \
    -command {"$parent.list yview"} }
  -gridoptions {-row 1 -column {%scrollSide 1} -sticky ns}
  }
  {
  -name list
  -type listbox
  -widgetoptions {-yscrollcommand {"$parent.yscroll set"}
    -height {%listboxHeight 10} -width {%listboxWidth 20}}
  -gridoptions {-row 1 -column {%listSide 0}}
  }
  {
  -name title
  -type label
  -widgetoptions {-text {%titleText title}}
  -gridoptions {-row 0 -column 0 -columnspan 2}
  }
}

# Define the new pattern/script sets for the switch command
set switches {delete -
  insert {
          return [eval $widgetName.list $subCommand $cmdArgs]
  }
  selection {return [selection $widgetName]}
}

# Define a new procedure
set procDef {
  proc selection {widgetName} {
    set lst [$widgetName.list curselection]
    set itemlst ""
    foreach l $lst {
      lappend itemlst [$widgetName.list get $l]
    }
    return $itemlst
  }
}

# Generate a megawidget with the name from the command line

set of [fillSkeleton $widgetName $widgetDef $switches $procDef]
```

This script will generate a file named *scrolledList.tcl*, which can be used in a Tk script with the `source` command or can be indexed with `pkg_mkIndex`.

## 12.9.3 Another Technique for Building Megawidgets

The previous examples have been for megawidgets that exist in script files and can be loaded with `source` or `package require` commands. Jeffrey Hobbs, *jeff@hobbs.org*, created a different technique for automating megawidget creation with his `widget` package. His package will allow you to easily create a megawidget that uses a `subwidget` command or a naming convention to access the subwidgets. The subwidgets can be configured by accessing them as individual widgets, using either the name returned with the `subwidget` command or the subwidget naming convention to access the subwidgets. Configuration options related to the entire megawidget can be processed via the widget procedure, a procedure with the same name as that given to the megawidget.

You need only write the code to arrange the subwidgets to create a simple megawidget with this package. Optionally, you can add procedures to handle configuration options specific to your megawidget, special initialization, or widget destruction.

This package is found on the companion CD-ROM, with documentation and examples in the `widget.tcl` and `TOUR.tcl` programs. If you wish to use the package, you should read that documentation. This section will give you an overview and an example of how it works. To use this package to create a megawidget, you must

1. Invoke `widget create` to generate the widget creation procedure in the global scope and initialize the state variables.
2. Provide a `construct` procedure in the namespace for this class of megawidget. This namespace must be a child namespace of the `::Widget` namespace.
3. If the megawidget has options that are specific to the entire megawidget, rather than the subwidgets, provide a `configure` procedure within this megawidget's namespace.
4. If there are special initializations that need to be done before the widget is displayed, provide an `init` procedure within the megawidget namespace.
5. If you need to perform any special operations when the megawidget is destroyed, provide a `destruct` procedure in the megawidget namespace.

In addition, if this megawidget will be included in a package, you must write dummy megawidget creation commands so that `pkg_mkIndex` will index those procedures. The widget package generates the code for a megawidget at runtime. Thus, the actual megawidget creation commands do not exist when `pkg_mkIndex` is evaluated. If you create a dummy creation command, the dummy will be entered into the *pkgIndex.tcl* file, where it will be read by the `package require` command. When the script is evaluated, the dummy is replaced by the actual megawidget creation command.

The `widget create` command is the workhorse of this package. It takes several options that describe the megawidget being created.

**Syntax:** `widget create -options`

Generate a procedure to construct a megawidget. The procedure will be generated in the global namespace.

`-options`

The options for this command include

| | | |
|---|---|---|
| `-type ?type?` | The type of megawidget to create. The possible values for type are | |
| | `frame` | Return a frame that can be displayed with one of the layout managers (`pack`, `place`, or `grid`). |
| | `toplevel` | Return a top-level window that can be displayed outside the application window. |
| `-components list` | The components of this megawidget. Each component is defined in a list with the following fields: | |
| | `type` | The type of widget this will be: `button`, `label`, and so on. |
| | `name` | The name for this widget. |
| | `args` | A list of arguments that will be appended to the widget creation line when this widget is created. This is where arguments defining the relationship between a scrollbar and its target widget can be placed. |

The next example creates a megawidget that consists of a prompt and an entry widget. By default, the prompt will be on the left of the entry widget, but it can be configured to be on the right (to demonstrate using the `configure` command).

In most megawidgets created with this `widget` command, the layout of the individual widgets would be done in the `construct` procedure. Because this widget allows the user to define the layout of the prompt and entry widgets, that functionality is placed in a separate procedure that can be invoked from either the `construct` command or the `configure` command.

## Example 12.22

**Script Example**

```
# The widget package pkgIndex.tcl file is in the current directory.
```

```
lappend auto_path "."

# Uncomment these lines if this will be in a package.
# The dummy procedure will be indexed by pkg_mkIndex

# package provide PromptEntry 1.0
# PromptEntry args {}

# Generate the PromptEntry megawidget creation command

widget create PromptEntry -type frame \
  -components { {label prompt} {entry entry} } \
  -options { {-side Side side left} }

# The support functions for the PromptEntry megawidget

namespace eval ::Widget::PromptEntry {

##############################################################
# proc construct {w}--
# Called when a PromptEntry megawidget is created to handle
# widget-specific initializations.
# Arguments
# w    The window name for this megawidget.
#
# Results
# calls layout to specify the locations of the subwidgets.
#

  proc construct {w} {
    upvar [namespace current]::$w data

    # Initialize defaults
    set data(-side) left

    # Do initial layout
    layout $w
  }

##############################################################
# proc layout {w}--
# sets the location of the subwidgets
# Arguments
# w    The window name for this megawidget.
#
# Results
# packs the prompt and entry subwidgets in the locations
# defined by the -side option
```

```
proc layout {w} {
  upvar [namespace current]::$w data
  pack $data(prompt) -side $data(-side)
  pack $data(entry) -side $data(-side)
}

#############################################################
# proc configure {w args}--
# Process configuration commands that are specific to the
#   PromptEntry megawidget.
# Arguments
# w    The window name for this megawidget.
# args   A list of key/value pairs.
#
# Results
# Will either set the -side option to the requested value and
# rearrange the window, or throw an error.

proc configure {w args} {
  upvar [namespace current]::$w data
  foreach {key val} $args {
    switch -- $key {
      "-side" {
        set data(-side) $val
        layout $w
      }
      default {
        error "bad option - use -side"
      }
    } ;# switch
  } ;# foreach
} ;# End of configure procedure
} ;# End of namespace

# Example Script

# Create the widget and pack it.

set userInput [PromptEntry .pe]
pack $userInput

# Configure the base widget (the frame) to have a raised
# relief, with a 5-pixel border.

$userInput configure -relief raised -borderwidth 5

# Use the subwidget command to access the entry subwidget
# and change its width to 40 characters.
```

```
[.pe subwidget entry] configure -width 40

# Use the naming convention to set the background color
# to white, and define a textvariable for this widget.

$userInput.entry configure -background white \
  -textvariable peValue

# Use the subwidget command to set the text for the
# prompt

[$userInput subwidget prompt] configure -text "Enter Text: "

# The results label will echo the contents of the entry
# widget to demonstrate the PromptEntry widget behavior.

label .results -textvariable peValue -background gray80
pack .results
```

***Script Output***

| | |
|---|---|
| **Enter Text:** | Megawidgets facilitate prompt delivery. |
| | **Megawidgets facilitate prompt delivery.** |

# 12.10 Bottom Line

- This chapter has described the megawidgets included in the Tk distribution and shown how megawidgets can be constructed using Tk without any C language extensions. The megawidgets included in the Tk distribution are as follows:

  ***Syntax:*** tk_optionMenu *buttonName varName val1 ?val2...valN?*

  ***Syntax:*** tk_chooseColor

  ***Syntax:*** tk_getOpenFile *?option value?*

  ***Syntax:*** tk_getSaveFile *?option value?*

  ***Syntax:*** tk_messageBox *?option value?*

  ***Syntax:*** tk_dialog *win title text bitmap default \
          string1 ?... stringN?*

  ***Syntax:*** tk_popup *menu x y ?entry?*

- You can determine what windows (if any) have grabbed events with the grab current command.

  ***Syntax:*** grab current *?window?*

- You can determine whether a window that is grabbing events is grabbing them for the local task or all tasks with the grab status command.

  *Syntax:* grab status *window*

- A Tk window can be declared to be the recipient of all keyboard and mouse events with the grab command.

  *Syntax:* grab set *?-global? window*

- The rename command will change the name of a command.

  *Syntax:* rename *oldName ?newName?*

- You can define a default value for various options with the option add command.

  *Syntax:* option add *pattern value ?priority?*

- The namespace current command will return the full name of the current namespace.

  *Syntax:* namespace current

- The namespace code command will wrap a script so that it can be evaluated in the current space.

  *Syntax:* namespace code *script*

- A Tk script can be forced to wait for an event to occur with the tkwait command.

  *Syntax:* tkwait *EventType name*

- A megawidget can be made modal with the grab, focus, and tkwait commands.

- You can construct your own megawidgets by providing a wrapper procedure that arranges widgets within a frame.

- The name of a frame can be disassociated from the name of the procedure used to configure the frame.

- Megawidgets can be built using namespaces to conceal the internal structure of the megawidget.

- Megawidgets can be nested within other megawidgets to support more complex interactions.

## 12.11 Problems

The following numbering convention is used in all Problem sections.

| Number Range | Description of Problems |
|---|---|
| 100–199 | These problems review the material covered in this chapter. They can be answered in a few words or a short (1–5-line) script. Each problem should take under a minute to answer. |

| *Number Range* | *Description of Problems* |
|---|---|
| 200–299 | These problems go beyond the details presented in this chapter. They may require some analysis of the material or command details not covered in the chapter. They may require reading a man page or making a web search. They can be answered with a few sentences or a 5–50-line script. Each problem should take under 10 minutes to answer. |
| 300–399 | These problems extend the material presented in this chapter. They may require referencing other sources. They can be answered in a few paragraphs or a few hundred lines of code. Each exercise may take a few hours to complete. |

**100.** Which standard megawidget will allow a user to select an existing file from which to load data?

**101.** Which standard megawidget will allow a user to select a new file to which data can be written?

**102.** Which standard megawidget provides a generic dialog facility?

**103.** Can an application be written to use a Motif-style file selector on a Windows platform, instead of the native Windows-style file selector?

**104.** Which standard megawidget will give a user the option of selecting "Yes" or "No" as the answer to a question?

**105.** What two commands will follow this code fragment to

a. Configure the frame with a red background:

b. Grid the frame in row 1, column 2:

```
frame .f
rename .f myFrame
```

**106.** What command would set the font for all buttons to {times 24 bold}?

**107.** What command will force a Wish script to pause until the window .l is destroyed?

**108.** If the button .b is clicked after the following code fragment has executed, will the application exit? If not, why?

```
pack [entry .e -textvar tst]
pack [button .b -text "EXIT" -command "exit"]
update
grab set .e
```

**109.** What option to grab will cause all events to be trapped by an application?

**200.** Write a procedure that will accept a window name as an argument, and will create a `frame` with that name and `grid` a `text` widget and `scrollbar` into the `frame`. The procedure should return the name of the text widget.

**201.** Using the `fillSkeleton` procedure described in Section 12.9.2, construct a mega-widget with a label, and a canvas below it.

**202.** Modify the megawidget constructed in the previous exercise to accept the following options.

*-image imageName*
   An image to display in the canvas.

*-title text*
   Text to display in the `label` widget.

**203.** Write a procedure that will create a new top-level window and wait for a user to click one of two buttons. The return from the procedure will be the text of the button that was clicked.

**204.** Modal widgets are commonly created in a new top-level window. Can a modal widget be created within a frame? Why or why not?

**300.** Edit a copy of the megawidget skeleton described in Section 12.9.1 to create a megawidget with a prompt, an entry widget and a listbox. Allow a user to type a value into the `entry` widget or select a value from the listbox. When a listbox entry is selected, it should appear in the entry box. The widget should support the following widget procedures.

*insert value*
   Insert a value into the listbox.

*get*
   Get the content of the entry widget.

**301.** Create the megawidget described in Problem 300 using the `fillSkeleton` procedure, shown in Section 12.9.2.

**302.** Create the megawidget described in Problem 300 using the `widgets.tcl` package, described in Section 12.9.3.

**303.** The skeleton described in Section 12.9.1 will only create non-modal megawid-gets that are built within a frame. Modify the skeleton so that it can be used to build a modal megawidget in a top-level window. Name the new skeleton code `modalSkeleton.tcl`.

**304.** Modify the `fillSkeleton` procedure described in Section 12.9.2 to accept a `-modal` flag as the last parameter. If this is set, it should create a modal megawidget using the skeleton developed in the previous exercise.

CHAPTER

13

# Writing a Tcl Extension

One of the greatest strengths of the Tcl package is the ease with which it can be extended. By adding your own extensions to the interpreter you can

- Use compiled code to perform algorithms that are too computation intensive for an interpreted language.
- Add support for devices or data formats that are not currently supported by Tcl.
- Create a rapid prototyping interpreter for an existing C language library.
- Add Tk graphics to an existing application or set of libraries.
- Create a script-driven test suite for an application or library.

Extensions can be linked with the Tcl library to create a new `tclsh` or `wish` interpreter, or they can be loaded into a running `tclsh`. Note that support for loading binary objects into a running `tclsh` requires a version of the Tcl library that is more recent than 7.5 and an operating system that supports dynamic runtime libraries. Microsoft Windows, Macintosh OS, Linux, and many flavors of UNIX support this capability.

Whether you are building a new `tclsh` or a loadable binary package, and whether you are linking to an existing library or are writing your own functions, the steps to follow are the same. This chapter describes the components of an extension, steps through creating a simple Tcl extension, discusses how to move data between the Tcl interpreter and your C language functions, and discusses how to handle complex data such as structures.

In Tcl version 8.0 a major modification was introduced to the Tcl internals. Prior to this (Tcl 7.x and earlier), all data was stored internally as a string. When a script needed to perform a math operation, the data was converted from string to native format (integer, long, float, double, and so on), the operation was performed, and then the native format data was converted back to a string to be returned to the script. This procedure caused Tcl scripts to run rather slowly.

With Tcl revision 8.0 and later, the data is stored internally in a Tcl_Obj structure. The Tcl_Obj structure contains a string representation of the data and a native representation of the data. The two representations are kept in sync in a lazy manner; the native and string representations are calculated when needed and retained as long as they are valid.

This change improved the speed of the Tcl interpreter, while adding minimal complexity for extension writers. Most of the Tcl library functions that interface with data now come in two forms: one to deal with old-style string data and one to deal with new-style Tcl_Obj data.

If you are writing a new extension, you can use all of the new Tcl_Obj-oriented commands (which have the word Obj in their names). If you need to link with an earlier version of Tcl (for instance, if you need to use an extension that exists only for Tcl 7.5), you will need to use the older version of the commands.

This chapter covers both sets of commands. If you do not need to be able to link with an older version of Tcl, it is recommended that you use the Tcl_Obj objects for your data and the Tcl_Obj API to interface with the interpreter.

This chapter provides an overview of how to construct an extension, first from the functional viewpoint of what functionality is required in an extension and how the parts work together and then from the structural viewpoint of how the code modules should be assembled. This is followed by an example of a simple extension, and discussions of more advanced topics, such as using lists and arrays, and creating extensions with subcommands.

# 13.1 Functional View of a Tcl Extension

The interface between the Tcl library and an extension is implemented with several functions. On Windows systems these are documented under the Tcl Library Procedures entry in the Tcl Help menu. On UNIX systems, they are documented in files named *Tcl_*.3* in the *doc* directory. On the Macintosh these functions are documented under the *HTML DOCS* folder. The required commands are described in this chapter, but read the on-line documentation for more details.

The interface to the Tcl library includes several data types that are specific to Tcl. Those we will be dealing with are as follows.

| | |
|---|---|
| Tcl_Interp * | A pointer to a Tcl interpreter state structure. |
| Tcl_ObjCmdProc * | A pointer to a function that will accept Tcl objects as arguments. |
| Tcl_CmdProc * | A pointer to a function that will accept strings as arguments. |

ClientData A one-word value that is passed to functions but never used by the Tcl interpreter. This allows functions to use data that is specific to the application, not the interpreter. For instance, this argument could be used to pass a pointer to a database record, a window object, or a C++ this pointer.

### 13.1.1 Overview

An extension must implement the following sets of functionality.

- Initialize any persistent data structures.
- Register new commands with the Tcl interpreter.
- Accept data from the Tcl interpreter.
- Process the new commands.
- Return results to the calling scripts.
- Return status to the calling scripts.

### 13.1.2 Initialize Any Persistent Data Structures

Your extension must include an initialization function that will be called by the Tcl interpreter when the extension is loaded into the interpreter. The code that performs the initialization will depend on your application.

### 13.1.3 Register New Commands with the Interpreter

You register a new command with the Tcl interpreter by calling a function that will insert the name of the new command into the Tcl command hash table and associate that name with a pointer to a function to implement the command. There are two functions that can be invoked to register a new command with the Tcl interpreter. One will register the new command as a function that can use Tcl objects, and the other will register the new command as a function that requires string arguments. Extensions that are to be linked with versions of Tcl more recent than 8.0 should create Tcl object-based functions rather than string-based functions.

> *Syntax:* int Tcl_CreateObjCommand (*interp, cmdName, func, clientData, deleteFunc*)

> *Syntax:* int Tcl_CreateCommand (*interp, cmdName, func, clientData, deleteFunc*)

`Tcl_CreateObjCommand`
`Tcl_CreateCommand`

These functions register a new command with the Tcl interpreter. The following actions are performed within the Tcl interpreter.

- Register *cmdName* with the Tcl interpreter.

- Define `clientData` data for the command.

- Define the function to call when the command is evaluated.

- Define the command to call when the command is destroyed.

`Tcl_CreateCommand` is the pre-8.0 version of this command. It will still work with 8.0 and newer interpreters but will create an extension that does not run as fast as an extension that uses `Tcl_CreateObjCommand`.

`Tcl_Interp *interp`

This is a pointer to the Tcl interpreter. It is required by all commands that need to interact with the interpreter state. Your extensions will probably just pass this pointer to Tcl library functions that require a Tcl interpreter pointer. Your code should not attempt to manipulate any components of the interpreter structure directly.

`char *cmdName`

The name of the new command, as a NULL-terminated string.

`Tcl_ObjCmdProc *func`

The function to call when *cmdName* is encountered in a script.

`ClientData clientData`

A value that will be passed to *func* when the interpreter encounters *cmdName* and calls *func*. The `ClientData` type is a word, which on most machines is the size of a pointer. You can allocate memory and use this pointer to pass an arbitrarily large data structure to a function.

`Tcl_CmdDeleteProc *deleteFunc`

A pointer to a function to call when the command is deleted. If the command has some persistent data object associated with it, this function should free that memory. If you have no special processing, set this pointer to NULL, and the Tcl interpreter will not register a command deletion procedure.

These commands will return `TCL_OK` to indicate success or `TCL_ERROR` to indicate a failure. These are defined in the file `tcl.h`, which should be `#included` in your source.

```
Tcl_CreateObjCommand(interp, "demo", Demo_Cmd,
    (ClientData) NULL, NULL);
```

Modern Tcl extensions create the new commands in a namespace. To create new commands within a namespace, simply add the namespace identifier to the name of the command being added to the interpreter, as in the following example.

```
Tcl_CreateObjCommand(interp, "demoNamespace::demo", Demo_Cmd,
    (ClientData) NULL, NULL);
```

### 13.1.4 Accept Data from Tcl Interpreter

When a command is evaluated, the interpreter needs to pass data from the script to the function. The Tcl interpreter handles this with a technique similar to that used by the C language for receiving command line parameters. The function that implements the C command receives an integer argument count and an array of pointers to the Tcl script arguments. For example, if you register a command foo with the interpreter as

```
Tcl_CreateObjCommand(interp, "foo", fooCmd, NULL, NULL);
```

and later write a script command

```
foo one 1 two 2
```

fooCmd will be passed an argument count of 4 and an argument list that contains one, 1, two, and 2.

When the Tcl interpreter evaluates the Tcl command associated with a function in your extension, it will invoke that function with a defined set of arguments. If you are using Tcl 8.0 or newer and register your command using Tcl_CreateObjCommand, the Tcl command arguments will be passed to your function as an array of objects. If you are using an older version of Tcl or register your command using the Tcl_CreateCommand function, the arguments will be passed as an array of strings. The function prototype for the C function that implements the Tcl command will take one of these two forms:

**Syntax:** `int func clientData, interp, objc, objv)`

**Syntax:** `int func(clientData, interp, argc, argv)`

| | |
|---|---|
| *func* | The function to be called when *cmdName* is evaluated. |
| ClientData *clientData* | This value was defined when the command was registered with the interpreter. |
| Tcl_Interp *interp* | A pointer to the Tcl interpreter. It will be passed to Tcl library commands that need to interact with the interpreter state. |
| int *objc* | The count of objects being passed as arguments. |

| | |
|---|---|
| Tcl_Obj *objv[] | An array of Tcl objects that were the arguments to the Tcl command in the script. |
| int argc | In pre-8.0 versions of Tcl, this is the count of argument strings being passed to this function. |
| char *argv[] | In pre-8.0 versions of Tcl, this is an array of strings. Each array element is an argument passed to the Tcl command. Versions of Tcl prior to 8.0 used strings instead of objects for arguments. The objects are much more efficient and should be used unless you have compelling reasons for maintaining compatibility with older code. |

If you are using Tcl version 8.0 or newer and register the command with the Tcl_CreateObjCommand function, your function must accept an array of Tcl_Obj pointers. If you are using a version of Tcl older than 8.0, your function must accept arguments as an array of char pointers. In either case, the third argument will be an integer that describes the number of arguments in the array. Your function may return TCL_OK, TCL_ERROR, TCL_RETURN, TCL_BREAK, or TCL_CONTINUE. The most frequently used codes are TCL_OK and TCL_ERROR.

TCL_BREAK, TCL_RETURN, and TCL_CONTINUE are used for building program flow control commands such as looping or branching commands. Since Tcl already includes a complete set of looping and branching commands, if you think you need to implement a new flow control command, you may want to look at your application very closely to see if you have missed an existing command you could use.

### Converting Tcl Data to C Data

Once your function has been called, you will need to convert the data to the format your function (or the library calls it invokes) can use. In versions of Tcl earlier than 8.0, all data was stored as strings. Whenever data was needed in another format, it needed to be converted at that point, and the native format of the data was discarded when that use was finished.

With Tcl 8.0 and newer, the data is stored internally in a structure that maintains both a string and a native representation of the data. In this case, your function can use Tcl's support for extracting the values from the Tcl_Obj structure.

### Data Representation

In order to convert the data, you need to know a little about how the Tcl interpreter stores data internally. With versions of Tcl that pass the arguments as strings, you can convert the data from the Tcl script to native format (int, float, and so on) with the standard library calls sscanf, atof, atol, strtod, strtol, strtoul, and so on.

As of Tcl 8.0, the Tcl interpreter stores data in Tcl_Obj structures. The Tcl_Obj structure stores its data in two forms: a string representation and a native representation. The data in a Tcl_Obj object is accessed via a set of function calls that will be discussed later in this section.

It is not necessary to know the details of the Tcl_Obj structure implementation, because all interactions with a Tcl object will be done via Tcl library functions, but you will understand the function calls better if you understand the design of the Tcl_Obj structure. The two primary design features of the Tcl object are the data's dual-ported nature (the string and native representations) and the interpreter's use of references to objects rather than copies of objects.

A Tcl_Obj structure maintains a string representation of the data as well as the native representation. The conversion between these two representations of the data (the dual nature of the object) is handled in a lazy manner. The data is converted between formats only when necessary. When one representation of the data is modified, the other representation is deleted to indicate that it must be regenerated when needed again. For example, in the commands

    set x 12

> The Tcl interpreter creates an object and assigns the string representation to 12.

    puts "The value of X is: $x"

> The puts command does not require a conversion to native mode, so the string representation of $x is displayed and no conversion to integer is made.

    incr x 2

> The string representation of the data in the $x object is now converted to native (integer) representation, and the value 2 is added to it. The old string representation is cleared to show that the native representation is valid.

    set y [expr $x+2]

> When $x is accessed by the expr command, the object's native representation is used. After the addition is performed, a new object is created to hold the result. There is no need to convert the integer representation of x into a string, so it will be left blank. This new object is assigned to the variable y, with a native representation (integer) but no string representation defined.

    puts "The value of Y is: $y"

> When the puts is evaluated, the Tcl script needs a string representation of the object, the integer is then converted to a string, and the string representation is saved for future use.

If the value of $x were only displayed and never used for a calculation (as a report generator would treat the value), it would never be converted to integer format. Similarly, if the value of $y were never displayed (simply used in other calculations), the conversion to a string would never be made. Since most applications deal with data in native or string representation in batches, this lazy conversion increases the speed of the Tcl interpreter.

The reference counts associated with Tcl objects allow the Tcl interpreter to maintain pointers to objects, instead of making copies of any objects referenced in more than one location. This lets the interpreter maintain a smaller number of objects than would otherwise be necessary. When an object is created, it is assigned a reference count of 0.

When a Tcl object is referenced by other objects (for example, the object is associated with a variable), the reference counter is incremented. The reference counter will be incremented by one when a variable is declared as the -textvariable for a label or passed as an argument to a procedure. When an object that references another Tcl object is destroyed (with the unset command or by destroying an associated widget), the reference count for the associated object is decremented by one. If the reference count becomes 0 or less, the object is deleted and its memory is returned to the heap.

### Obtaining the Data

Since arguments are passed to your function in an array of pointers, the function can access data as argument[0], argument[1], and so on. For example, if you register your command using the Tcl_CreateCommand function, you could print out the arguments to a function with code such as the following.

```
int myFunc(ClientData data, Tcl_Interp *interp, int argc,
  char **argv) {
  int i;
  for (i=0; i<argc; i++) {
    printf("argument %d is %s\n", i, argv[i]);
  }
}
```

Recent versions of Tcl pass the data as an array of pointers to Tcl objects. In that case you need to use the Tcl conversion functions to extract either the string or native representation of the data.

***Syntax:*** int Tcl_GetIntFromObj (*interp, objPtr, intPtr*)

| | |
|---|---|
| Tcl_GetIntFromObj | Retrieve an integer from the object. |
| Tcl_Interp *interp | A pointer to the Tcl interpreter. |
| Tcl_Obj *objPtr | A pointer to the object that contains an integer. |
| int *intPtr | A pointer to the integer that will receive this data. |

*Syntax:* `int Tcl_GetDoubleFromObj (interp, objPtr, dblPtr)`

| | |
|---|---|
| `Tcl_GetDoubleFromObj` | Retrieve a double from the object. |
| `Tcl_Interp *interp` | A pointer to the Tcl interpreter. |
| `Tcl_Obj *objPtr` | A pointer to the object that contains a double. |
| `Double *dblPtr` | A pointer to the double that will receive this data. |

The `Tcl_GetIntFromObj` and `Tcl_GetDoubleFromObj` functions return a `TCL_OK` if they successfully extract a numeric value from the object, or return `TCL_ERROR` if they cannot generate a numeric value for this object. (For instance, if the object contains an alphabetic string, there is no integer or floating-point equivalent.)

Tcl data is always available as a string. When you need to get the string representation of an object's data, you use the `Tcl_GetStringFromObj` command.

*Syntax:* `char *Tcl_GetStringFromObj (objPtr, lengthPtr)`

| | |
|---|---|
| `Tcl_GetStringFromObj` | Retrieve a byte string from the object. |
| `Tcl_Obj *objPtr` | A pointer to the object that contains a string. |
| `int *lengthPtr` | A pointer to an `int` that will receive the number of characters in this data. If this value is `NULL`, the length will not be returned. |

Note that the `Tcl_GetStringFromObj` function does not follow the format of the previous `Get` functions. It returns the requested data as a `char` pointer rather than returning a status. Since the data is always available in a string format, this command can fail only if the object pointer is invalid, in which case the program has other problems and will probably crash.

The `Tcl_GetStringFromObj` command can place the number of valid bytes in the `char` pointer in an integer pointer (`lengthPtr`). The data in a string may be binary data (accessed via the Tcl `binary` command, for instance), in which case the length pointer is necessary to track the number of bytes in the string.

## 13.1.5 Returning Results

The function implementing a Tcl command can return results to a script in the following ways.

- Return a single value as the result.
- Return a list of values as the result.
- Modify the content of a script variable named as an argument.
- Modify the content of a known script variable.

If you desire to have your function return a value to the script as the result of evaluating the command (which is how most functions return their results), your code must call a function that sets the return to be a particular value. In old versions of Tcl, this can be done by passing a string. The modern Tcl interpreters require your code to create a new Tcl_Obj. The object created within the function will have a reference count of 0. If the return value from the function is assigned to a variable, the object's reference count will be incremented; otherwise, the object will be deleted when the command has finished being evaluated. You can create a new object with one of the following commands.

*Syntax:* Tcl_Obj *Tcl_NewIntObj (*intValue*)

*Syntax:* Tcl_Obj *Tcl_NewDoubleObj (*dblValue*)

*Syntax:* Tcl_Obj *Tcl_NewStringObj (*bytes, length*)

| | |
|---|---|
| Tcl_NewIntObj | Create a new Tcl object with an integer value. |
| Tcl_NewDoubleObj | Create a new Tcl object with a double value. |
| Tcl_NewStringObj | Create a new Tcl object from a byte string. |
| int *intValue* | The integer to assign to the new object. |
| double *dblValue* | The double to assign to the new object. |
| uchar *bytes* | An array of bytes to copy to the new object. |
| int *length* | The number of bytes to copy to the new object. If this is a negative value, all bytes up to the first NULL byte will be copied. |

In Tcl earlier than 8.0, since all variables were maintained as strings, a function could create an ASCII string to return with the sprintf command or could modify data in an existing string with the standard string library commands. After a return value has been created, it can be assigned with one of the following commands.

*Syntax:* void Tcl_SetObjResult (*interp, objPtr*)

*Syntax:* void Tcl_SetResult (*interp, string, freeProc*)

| | |
|---|---|
| Tcl_SetObjResult | Makes the Tcl interpreter point to *objPtr* as the result of this function. If this function has already had a result object defined, that object will be replaced by the object pointed to by objPtr. This function should be used with Tcl 8.0 and more recent versions. |
| Tcl_SetResult | Copies the string into the result string for this function, replacing any previous string that was there. This function is for use with pre-8.0 versions of Tcl. |

Tcl_Interp *interp    A pointer to the Tcl interpreter.

Tcl_Obj *objPtr    A pointer to the object that will become the result.

char *string    A string to copy to the object.

freeProc    The name of a procedure to call to free the memory associated with the string when this object is destroyed. Must be one of

TCL_STATIC

The string was defined in static memory and will remain constant.

TCL_DYNAMIC

The memory for the string was allocated with a call to Tcl_Alloc. It will be returned to the Tcl memory pool.

TCL_VOLATILE

The string was allocated from a nonpersistent area of memory (probably declared on the call stack) and may change when the function exits. In this case, the Tcl interpreter will allocate a safe space for the string and copy the memory content.

If the new command needs to return several pieces of information, you may prefer to pass the command the name of one or more Tcl variables to place the results in. This is similar to passing pointers to a C function. In this case, the code will modify the content of an existing Tcl variable.

The most generic function for modifying a Tcl variable is Tcl_SetVar. This function will accept the name of a variable and will either modify an existing variable or create a new variable by that name. The value to be assigned is passed to this function as a string, which can be easily obtained from a Tcl object, or generated as needed.

**Syntax:** char *Tcl_SetVar (*interp, varName, newValue, flags*)

Tcl_SetVar

Assign a value to a variable. Create a new Tcl variable if necessary.

Tcl_Interp *interp*

The pointer to the Tcl interpreter.

const char *varName*

A NULL-terminated string containing the name of the variable.

const char *newValue*

A NULL-terminated string containing the value to be assigned to this variable.

int *flags

One or more or'd-together flags to fine-tune the behavior of the assignment. By default (0), the value is assigned as a string to a variable in the current scope when the command is invoked. The flags may be one or more of

TCL_GLOBAL_ONLY
: When Tcl tries to resolve the name to a Tcl variable, it will look in the global scope, instead of the local scope.

TCL_NAMESPACE_ONLY
: Tcl looks for a variable defined only within the current namespace.

TCL_LEAVE_ERR_MSG
: If this is set and an error occurs, the error message is left in the interpreter's result string. The error message can be retrieved with the Tcl_GetObjResult or Tcl_GetStringResult function.

TCL_APPEND_VALUE
: Setting this bit causes the new value to be appended to the original data in the variable.

TCL_LIST_ELEMENT
: If this flag is set, the new value is converted to a valid Tcl list element before being assigned (or appended) to the variable.

If your code has access to a Tcl object, it can assign a native format value to the variable with one of the following commands.

**Syntax:** void Tcl_SetIntObj (objPtr, intValue)

**Syntax:** void Tcl_SetDoubleObj (objPtr, dblValue)

Tcl_SetIntObj
: Set the value of the integer representation of an object. If the object was not already an integer type, it will be converted to one if possible.

Tcl_SetDoubleObj
: Set the value of the integer representation of an object. If the object was not already a double type, it will be converted to one if possible.

Tcl_Obj *objPtr
: A pointer to the object that will contain the new value.

int intValue
: The integer to assign to this object.

double dblValue
: The double to assign to this object.

An object's string representation can be modified in several ways, either completely replacing one byte string with a new byte string, appending a single string, appending a string from another object, or appending a list of strings.

*Syntax:* `void Tcl_SetStringObj (`*objPtr, bytes, length*`)`

*Syntax:* `void Tcl_AppendToObj (`*objPtr, bytes, length*`)`

*Syntax:* `void Tcl_AppendObjToObj (`*objPtr, appendObjPtr*`)`

*Syntax:* `void Tcl_AppendStringsToObj (`*objPtr, string,* `..., NULL)`

| | |
|---|---|
| `Tcl_SetStringObj` | Redefine the string value of an object. |
| `Tcl_AppendToObj` | Append a string to the string representation of the data in an object. |
| `Tcl_AppendObjToObj` | Append the string representation of the value of one object to the string currently in an object. |
| `Tcl_AppendStringsToObj` | Append one or more strings to the string currently in an object. |
| `Tcl_Obj *`*objPtr* | A pointer to the object that contains the string. |
| `char *`*bytes* | An array of bytes to copy to the object. |
| `int `*length* | The number of bytes to copy to the new object. If this is a negative value, all the bytes up to the first NULL byte will be copied. |
| `Tcl_Obj *`*appendObjPtr* | A pointer to an object that contains a string to be appended. |
| `char *`*string* | A NULL-terminated string of characters. You may not use a binary string with the `Tcl_AppendStringsToObj` command. |

## 13.1.6 Returning Status to the Script

When a function returns execution control to the Tcl interpreter, it must return its status. The status should be either TCL_OK or TCL_ERROR. If the function returns TCL_OK, the object defined by `Tcl_SetObjResult` will be returned to the script, and the script will continue execution. If the function returns TCL_ERROR, an error will be generated, and unless your script is trapping errors with the `catch` command the execution will stop and error messages will be returned.

By default, the error messages returned will be the Tcl call stack leading to the Tcl command that caused the error. You may want to add other information to this, such as why a file write failed, what database seek did not return a value, or what socket can no longer be contacted. You can add more information to that message by invoking the function `Tcl_AddErrorInfo`, `Tcl_SetErrorCode`, `Tcl_AddObjErrorInfo`, or `Tcl_SetObjErrorCode`.

*Syntax:* void Tcl_AddErrorInfo (*interp, message*)

*Syntax:* void Tcl_SetErrorCode (*interp, element1, element2* ...NULL)

*Syntax:* void Tcl_AddObjErrorInfo (*interp, message, length*)

*Syntax:* void Tcl_SetObjErrorCode (*interp, objPtr*)

| | |
|---|---|
| Tcl_AddObjErrorInfo | Append additional text to the information object. This information object can be accessed within the Tcl script as the global variable errorInfo. |
| Tcl_AddErrorInfo | Append additional text to the information to be returned to the script. This function should be used with versions of Tcl before 8.0. |
| Tcl_SetObjErrorCode | Set the errorCode global variable to the value contained in the Tcl object. If the object contains a list, the list values are concatenated to form the return. By default errorCode will be NONE. |
| Tcl_SetErrorCode | Set the errorCode global variable to the value of the concatenated strings. |
| Tcl_Interp *interp | A pointer to the Tcl interpreter. |
| char *message | The message to append to the errorInfo global variable. This string will have a newline character appended to it. |
| Tcl_Obj *objPtr | A pointer to the object that will contain the error code. |
| char *element | A NULL-terminated ASCII string representation of a portion of the error code. |

If a system error occurs, your function can invoke Tcl_PosixError to set the errorCode variable from the C language global errno. The behavior of this command varies slightly for different platforms. You should check the on-line documentation for your platform and Tcl revision before using it.

## 13.1.7 Dealing with Persistent Data

There are circumstances in which an extension needs to maintain a copy of some persistent data separate from the script that is being evaluated, while allowing the script to describe the piece of data with which it needs to interact. For instance, a file pointer must be maintained until the file is closed, and a Tcl script may have several files open simultaneously, accessing one file and then another.

If your extension's data requirements are simple, it may be sufficient to allocate an array of items and assign them to scripts as necessary. For instance, if you write an extension that interfaces with a particular piece of hardware and there will never be more than one of these devices on a system, you may declare the control structure as a static global in your C code.

For more complex situations, the Tcl library includes functions that let you use a Tcl hash table to store key and value pairs. Your extension can allocate memory for a data structure, define a key to identify that structure, and then place a pointer to the structure in the hash table, to be accessed with the key. The key may be an alphanumeric string that can be returned to the Tcl script. When a Tcl script needs to access the data, it passes the key back to the extension code, which then retrieves the data from the hash table.

The Tcl hash table consists of a `Tcl_HashTable` structure that is allocated by your extension code and `Tcl_HashEntry` structures that are created as necessary to hold key/value pairs. You must initialize the hash table before using it with the functions that access hash table entries. Once the table is initialized, your code can add, access, or delete items from the hash table.

*Syntax:* `void Tcl_InitHashTable (tablePtr, keyType)`

> `Tcl_InitHashTable`
>
> > Initializes the hash table.
>
> `Tcl_HashTable *tablePtr`
>
> > A pointer to the `Tcl_HashTable` structure. The space for this structure must be allocated before calling `Tcl_InitHashTable`.
>
> `int keyType`
>
> > A Tcl hash table can use one of three different types of keys to access the data saved in the hash table. The acceptable values for *keyType* are

| | |
|---|---|
| `TCL_STRING_KEYS` | The hash table will use a NULL-terminated string as the key. This is the most commonly used type of hash key. The string representation of a `Tcl_Obj` object can be used as the key, which makes it simple to pass a value from a script to the Tcl hash table functions. |
| `TCL_ONE_WORD_KEYS` | The hash table will use a single-word value as the key. Note that if the word is a pointer, the value of the pointer is used as the key, not the data that the pointer references. |

*positiveInteger*      If a positive integer is used as the *keyType*, the key will be an array of the number of integers described. This allows complex binary data constructs to be used as keys. Note that the constructs used as keys must be the same size.

Once a hash table has been initialized, the `Tcl_CreateHashEntry`, `Tcl_FindHashEntry`, and `Tcl_DeleteHashEntry` commands can be used to create, query, or remove entries from the hash table.

**Syntax:** `Tcl_HashEntry *Tcl_CreateHashEntry (`*tablePtr*`, `*key*`, `*newPtr*`)`

**Syntax:** `Tcl_HashEntry *Tcl_FindHashEntry (`*tablePtr*`, `*key*`)`

**Syntax:** `void Tcl_DeleteHashEntry (`*entryPtr*`)`

| | |
|---|---|
| `Tcl_CreateHashEntry` | Allocates and initializes a new `Tcl_HashEntry` object for the requested key. If there was a previous entry with this key, `newPtr` is set to NULL. |
| `Tcl_FindHashEntry` | This function returns a pointer to the `Tcl_HashEntry` object that is associated with the key value. If that key does not exist in this hash table, this function returns NULL. |
| `Tcl_DeleteHashEntry` | This removes a hash table entry from the table. After this function has been called, `Tcl_FindHashEntry` will return a NULL if used with this key. This does not destroy data associated with the hash entry. Your functions that interact with the hash table must do that. |
| `Tcl_HashTable *`*tablePtr* | A pointer to a Tcl hash table. This table must be initialized by `Tcl_InitHashTable` before being used by these commands. |
| `char *`*key* | The *key* that defines this entry. This value must be one of the types described in the `Tcl_InitHashTable` call. |
| `int *`*newPtr* | This value will be 1 if a new entry was created and 0 if a *key* with this value already existed. |
| `Tcl_HashEntry *`*entryPtr* | A pointer to a hash table entry. |

A Tcl_HashEntry contains the key value that identifies it and a ClientData data object. The ClientData type is a word-sized object. On most modern machines, this is the same size as a pointer, which allows you to allocate an arbitrary data space and place the pointer to that space in a Tcl_HashEntry. You can manipulate a Tcl_HashEntry object with the Tcl_SetHashValue and Tcl_GetHashValue commands.

*Syntax:* ClientData TclGetHashValue (*entryPtr*)

*Syntax:* void TclSetHashValue (*entryPtr, value*)

| | |
|---|---|
| TclGetHashValue | Retrieve the data from a Tcl_HashEntry. |
| TclSetHashValue | Set the value of the data in a Tcl_HashEntry. |
| Tcl_HashEntry *entryPtr* | A pointer to a hash table entry. |
| ClientData *value* | The value to be placed in the clientData field of the Tcl_HashEntry. |

The following code will create a hash table, add an entry, and retrieve the data.

## Example 13.1

*Code Example*

```
void hashSnippet () {

    // The hash table pointer
    Tcl_HashTable *hashTable;

    // firstEntry will point to a hash entry we create
    Tcl_HashEntry *firstEntry;

    // secondEntry will point to a hash entry extracted from
    // the table
    Tcl_HashEntry *secondEntry;

    int isNew;
    char *insertData, *retrievedData;
    char *key;

    key = "myKey";
    insertData = "This is data in the hash table";

    // Allocate the space and initialize the hash table

    hashTable = (Tcl_HashTable *)
      malloc(sizeof(Tcl_HashTable));
    Tcl_InitHashTable(hashTable, TCL_STRING_KEYS);
```

```
// Get a hash Entry for the key, and confirm it is a
// new key

firstEntry = Tcl_CreateHashEntry(hashTable, key, &isNew);

if (isNew == 0) {
  printf("Bad key - this key already exists!");
  return;
}

// Define the value for this entry.

Tcl_SetHashValue(firstEntry, insertData);

/*--------------------------------------------------------
 * At this point, the data has been placed in the hash
 * table. In an actual application, these sections of
 * code would be in separate functions.
 *-------------------------------------------------- */

// Retrieve the hash entry with the key.

secondEntry = Tcl_FindHashEntry(hashTable, key);
  if (secondEntry == (Tcl_HashEntry *) NULL) {
  printf("Failed to find %s\n", key);
  return;
}

// Extract the data from the hash entry

retrievedData = (char *)Tcl_GetHashValue(secondEntry);

// Display the data, just to prove a point

printf("Retrieved this string from hashTable: \n%s\n",
  retrievedData);
}
```

***Code Output***

```
Retrieved this string from hashTable:
This is data in the hash table
```

## 13.2 Building an Extension

The bulk of your extension may be a library of code that has already been developed and tested, a library you need to test and validate, or a set of code you will write for this specific extension. In each of these cases, you will use the functions described previously to connect the application code to the interpreter. The next step is the mechanics of constructing the extension.

## 13.2.1 Structural Overview of an Extension

An extension consists of one or more source code files, one or more include files, and a Makefile or VC++, Borland, or CodeWarrior project files. The source code files must contain a function with initialization code, and that function must conform to the naming conventions described in Section 13.2.2.

The source code files will include at least one function that adds new commands to the interpreter and at least one function to implement the new commands. A common structure is to create two files: one with the initialization function that adds the new commands to the interpreter and a second file with the functions that implement the new commands.

All code that uses functions from the Tcl library will need to include tcl.h. The tcl.h file has all the function prototypes, #define, data definitions, and so on required to interact with the Tcl library functions.

## 13.2.2 Naming Conventions

There are a few naming conventions involved with writing a Tcl extension. Some of these are required in order to interact with the Tcl interpreter, and some are recommended in order to conform to the appearance of other Tcl extensions. If you write your extension to conform to the recommended standards, it will be easier for your extension to be used and maintained by others.

These conventions are described in the *Tcl/Tk Engineering Manual* and the *Tcl Extension Architecture* (TEA) guide, found on the companion CD-ROM included with this book. They can also be acquired from *www.tcl.tk/doc/*. Most of the conventions mentioned in these documents are discussed in this chapter, but you should check the source documents for more details. It may save you from having to rewrite your code later.

In the following tables, you should replace the string *ExtName* with the name of your extension. Note the capitalization, which is part of the naming convention.

### Function Names

The extension initialization function is expected to have a specific name in order for it to be automatically found by the Tcl extension loading commands.

| Function Name | Description |
|---|---|
| *ExtName*_Init | This function is required. It initializes an extension by creating any persistent data objects and registering |

|  |  |
|---|---|
|  | new commands with the Tcl interpreter. This entry point is used to initialize the extension when a DLL (Dynamic Link Library) or shared library is loaded. The capitalization is important. For example, for an extension named ext the Init function would be Ext_Init. |
| *ExtName*_AppInit | This function is called to initialize a stand-alone tclsh interpreter with the extension compiled into it. This is not needed when you compile a loadable extension. |
| *extNameCommand*_Cmd | These entry points are optional, but this is the naming convention used for the C code that will be invoked when the command *command* is evaluated by a Tcl script. For example, if the extension named ext implements the Tcl command foo, you would put the code implementing the foo command in the function extFoo_Cmd. |

## File Names

There are certain conventions followed in Tcl to make it easier for other maintainers to work with your code. Your extension will still work if you do not follow these guidelines, but consistency is a good thing.

| *File Names* | *Description* |
|---|---|
| *extName*Int.h | This file is required. It will contain the #include statements, #define statements, data structure definitions, and function prototypes that are used by the code in this extension. This is for the package's internal use. This file will be included by all extension code files. |
| *extName*.h | This file is optional. If your extension includes a library with a C interface, the external API definitions should be in this file. |
| *extName*.c | This file is recommended. It will contain the C language functions that implement the extension. If your extension is small, it may also include the *ExtName*_Init function. |
| *extName*_Init.c | This file is optional. If your extension is medium sized, you may use a file named like this for the *ExtName*_Init function and put the functions that implement the extension into the *extName*.c file, or further subdivide the extension as shown in the following. |
| *extName*Cmd.c | This file is optional. If the code to interface between Tcl and the C code is large, you may want to separate the code that creates the new commands in the Tcl interpreter from the *extName*.c file and place that code in a separate file. |

| | |
|---|---|
| *extName*CmdAL.c<br>*extName*CmdMZ.c | These files are optional. If you have a truly large extension, it can make the code easier to follow if you split the functions that implement the commands into smaller files. One convention used for this is to put the commands that start with the letter A through some other letter in one file, and those that start with a character after the breakpoint letter in another file. |
| *extName*Command.c | These files are optional. If your extension has commands that accept a number of subcommands, or if the command is implemented with several functions, it can make the code easier to follow if you split the functions that implement a command into a separate file. Thus, the functions that implement command foo would be in extFoo.c, whereas those that implement command bar would be in extBar.c. |
| *extName*.dll<br>*extName*.lib<br>*extName*.so | A file in one of these formats will be created for your extension when you have completed compiling your extension. |
| *extName*.shlb<br>*extName*.sl<br>*extName*CFM68K.shl | The Tcl interpreter will use the extName part of the extension to find the default *ExtName*_Init function. |

If you cannot follow this naming convention for the extension loadable library file, you can force the Tcl interpreter to find the initialization function by declaring the extension name in the load command as follows:

```
load wrongname.dll myextension
```

Not following the naming convention for the extension library will make it impossible to use pkg_mkIndex to construct a tclIndex file, but you can build the index line with a text editor if necessary.

### Directory Tree

The *Tcl Extension Architecture* (TEA) document defines a directory tree for Tcl extensions. Again, you do not need to follow these guidelines to make a working extension, but it will be easier to maintain and port your package if you follow them. The templates and skeletons included with the TEA materials on the companion CD-ROM (also available at *www.tcl.tk*) can make writing an extension easier. Your extension directory should be parallel to the Tcl and Tk directories. This allows simple relative addressing to be used by the makefiles to find the appropriate files.

```
%>ls sources
myExtension   tcl8.4.4   tk8.4.4
```

The following files should be placed at the top level of your directory.

README A short discussion of what the package does and what the user may expect to find in this directory.

license The distribution license for this package. Tcl is distributed with the Berkeley license, which is very open. You may elect to use the same licensing for your extension, the more restrictive GNU Copyleft, or your corporation's license agreement.

changes A list of changes that have happened in the package. This should tell a user what to expect when they upgrade to a new version.

There will be several subdirectories under the main directory. These may include the following.

generic This directory will contain C source code files that are not platform dependent. The *extName*Int.h file and *extName*_Init.c files, and the files that implement the extension functionality, should be here.

unix Any UNIX-specific files should be in this directory. If there are platform-specific functions (perhaps using system libraries), a copy of the functions for the UNIX systems should be here. A UNIX-compatible Makefile or configure file should be included in this directory.

win Any MS Windows–specific files should be in this directory. An nmake-compatible Makefile or the VC++ or Borland project files should be included.

mac Any Macintosh-specific files should be in this directory. A Mac-specific Makefile or CodeWarrior project files should also be included here.

compat If your extension requires certain library features that may not exist, or are broken on some platforms, put source code files that implement the library calls in this directory.

doc The documentation files should be put here. The standard for documenting Tcl packages is to use the UNIX nroff macros used with the main Tcl documentation. These can be converted to machine-native formats as necessary.

tests It is good policy to have a set of regression tests to confirm that the package works as expected.

library If your package has Tcl scripts associated with it, they should go here.

## 13.3 An Example

This section constructs a simple extension that will demonstrate the mechanisms discussed in this chapter. On the companion CD-ROM you will find this demo code, the sampleextension from SourceForge, and a dummyTclExtension kit with a Tcl script that will create a skeleton extension similar to the demo extension. This example follows the coding standards in the *Tcl/Tk Engineering Manual*, which is included on the companion CD-ROM. Where the manual does not define a standard, it is noted that this convention is mine, not the Tcl standard. Otherwise, the naming conventions and so on are those defined by the Tcl community.

This demo extension does not perform any calculations. It just shows how an extension can be constructed and how to acquire and return data using the hash functions. The demo package implements one Tcl command and five subcommands. The subcommands are debug, create, get, destroy, and set.

***Syntax:*** demo debug *level*

| | |
|---|---|
| demo debug | Sets a static global variable in the C code that turns on or off internal debug output. |
| *level* | The level to assign to this variable. A value of zero will disable the debugging output, and a non-zero value will enable that output. |

***Syntax:*** demo create *key raw_message*

| | |
|---|---|
| demo create | Create a hash table entry. |
| *key* | The key for this hash table entry. |
| *raw_message* | The string to assign to this hash. |

***Syntax:*** demo get *key*

| | |
|---|---|
| demo get | Retrieves the value of an entry from the hash table and returns the string saved with that key. |
| *key* | The key for the entry to return. |

***Syntax:*** demo destroy *key*

| | |
|---|---|
| demo destroy | Deletes an entry in the hash table. |
| *key* | The key that identifies which entry to delete. |

***Syntax:*** demo set *arrayName index Value*

| | |
|---|---|
| demo set | An example of how to set the values in an associative array. It sets the requested index to the requested value and sets the index alpha of the array to the value NewValue. The index alpha and value NewValue are hard-coded in the procedure Demo_SetCmd. This subcommand executes the C code equivalent of |

```
set arrayName(index) Value
```

For example, the command

```
demo set myArray myIndex "my Value"
```

is equivalent to

```
set myArray(myIndex) "my Value"
```

Both commands will return the string "my Value".

*arrayName*    The name of a Tcl array. It need not exist before calling this subcommand.

*index*    An index into the array. This index will have Value assigned to it.

*Value*    The value to assign to *arrayName*(*index*).

The demo extension is arranged in the style of a large package with many commands, to show how the functionality can be split across files and functions. It consists of the following files.

demoInt.h    This include file has the definitions for the structures used by this extension and the function prototypes of the functions defined in demoInit.c, demoCmd.c, and demoDemo.c.

demoInit.c    This file contains the Demo_Init function.

DemoCmd.c    This file contains the Demo_Cmd function, which is invoked when a demo Tcl command is evaluated in a script.

This file also includes the descriptions of the subcommands associated with the demo command.

demoDemo.c    This file contains the functions that implement the demo subcommands.

### 13.3.1 demoInt.h

The demoInt.h include file will be included by all the source files in the demo extension. It includes the version number information for this extension, the include files that will be used by other functions, some magic for Microsoft VC++, definition of data structures used by the demo extension, and the function prototypes.

### Example 13.2

demoInt.h

```
/*
 * demoInt.h --
 *
 *    Declarations used by the demotcl extension
 *
 */
#ifndef _DEMOINT
#define _DEMOINT

/*
1
```

```
 * Declare the #includes that will be used by this extension
 */
#include <tcl.h>
#include <string.h>

/*
2
 * Define the version number.
 * Note: VERSION is defined as a string, not integer.
 */
#define DEMO_VERSION "1.0"

/*
3
 * VC++ has an alternate entry point called
 * DllMain, so we need to rename our entry point.
 */
#if defined(__WIN32__)
# define WIN32_LEAN_AND_MEAN
# include <windows.h>
# undef WIN32_LEAN_AND_MEAN
# if defined(_MSC_VER)
#   define EXPORT(a,b) __declspec(dllexport) a b
#   define DllEntryPoint DllMain
# else
#   if defined(__BORLANDC__)
#     define EXPORT(a,b) a _export b
#   else
#     define EXPORT(a,b) a b
#   endif
# endif
#else
# define EXPORT(a,b) a b
#endif

/*
4
 * The CmdReturn structure is used by the subroutines to
 * pass back a success/failure code and a Tcl_Obj result.
 *
 * This is not an official Tcl standard return type. I
 * find this works well with commands that accept subcommands.
 */
  typedef struct cmd_return {
    int status;
    Tcl_Obj *object;
} CmdReturn;
```

```
/*
5
 * Function Prototypes for the commands that actually do the
 * processing.
 * Two macros are used in these prototypes:
 *
 * EXTERN EXPORT is for functions that must interact with the
 *   Microsoft or Borland C++ DLL loader.
 * ANSI_ARGS is defined in tcl.h
 *   ANSI_ARGS returns an empty string for non-ANSI C
 *   compilers, and returns its arguments for ANSI C
 *   compilers.
 */

EXTERN EXPORT(int,Demo_Init) _ANSI_ARGS_ ((Tcl_Interp *));
EXTERN EXPORT(int,Demo_Cmd) _ANSI_ARGS_
    ((ClientData, Tcl_Interp *, int, Tcl_Obj **));
CmdReturn *demo_GetCmd _ANSI_ARGS_ ((ClientData,
    Tcl_Interp *, int, Tcl_Obj **));
CmdReturn *demo_SetCmd _ANSI_ARGS_ ((ClientData,
    Tcl_Interp *, int, Tcl_Obj **));
CmdReturn *demo_CreateCmd _ANSI_ARGS_ ((ClientData,
    Tcl_Interp *, int, Tcl_Obj **));
CmdReturn *demo_DestroyCmd _ANSI_ARGS_ ((ClientData,
    Tcl_Interp *, int, Tcl_Obj **));
void demo_InitHashTable _ANSI_ARGS_ (());

#define debugprt if (demoDebugPrint>0) printf

/* End _DEMOINT */

#endif
```

Note the following regarding the previous example:

1. The demoInt.h file has the #include definitions that will be used by the source code files in the demo package. If the extension requires several include files, this convention makes it easier to maintain the list of include files. (See Example 13.2, Section 1.)

2. The DEMO_VERSION string will be used in the Demo_Init function to define the script global variable demo_version. All packages should include a *packageName*_version variable definition. Defining this variable allows scripts to check the version of the package they have loaded. (See Example 13.2, Section 2.)

3. There are some conventions that Microsoft VC++ demands for code that will be dynamically loaded. If your extension will need to compile only on UNIX or Macintosh, you may delete this section and simplify the function prototypes. (See Example 13.2, Section 3.)

4. The CmdReturn structure is not a part of the Tcl standard. I use it to allow functions that implement subcommands to return both a status and a Tcl_Obj to the function that implements the primary command. The status field will be assigned the value TCL_OK or TCL_ERROR. The object field will be a pointer to a Tcl Object or NULL if the function has no return. If you find another convention more suited to your needs, feel free to use that instead. (See Example 13.2, Section 4.)

5. These are the function prototypes. All of the functions in the source code files should be declared here. (See Example 13.2, Section 5.)

### 13.3.2 demoInit.c

The demoInit.c file is one of the required files in an extension. At a minimum this file must define the Demo_Init function, as shown in the following example.

**Example** 13.3

demoInit.c

```
#include "demoInt.h"
/* CVS Revision Tag */
#define DEMOINIT_REVISION "$Revision: 1.5 $"
/*
 *------------------------------------------------------------
 *
 * Demo_Init
 *
 *   Called from demo_AppInit() if this is a stand-alone
 *   shell, or when the package is loaded if compiled
 *   into a binary package.
 *
 * Results:
 *   A standard Tcl result.
 *
 * Side effects:
 *   Creates a hash table.
 *   Adds new commands
 *   Creates new Tcl global variables for demo_version and
 *     demoInit_revision.
 *
 *------------------------------------------------------------
 */
int Demo_Init (Tcl_Interp *interp) {
/* interp   Current interpreter. */
```

```
    /*
    1
     * If this application will need to save any
     * data in a hash table initialize the hash table.
     */
    Demo_InitHashTable ();

    /*
    2
     * Call Tcl_CreateCommand for commands defined by this
     * extension
     */

    Tcl_CreateObjCommand(interp, "demo", Demo_Cmd,
        (ClientData) NULL, NULL);

    /*
    3
     * Define the package for pkg_mkIndex to index
     */

    Tcl_PkgProvide(interp, "demo", DEMO_VERSION);

    /*
    4
     * Define the version for this package
     */
    Tcl_SetVar((Tcl_Interp *) interp, "demo_version",
        DEMO_VERSION, TCL_GLOBAL_ONLY);

    /*
    5
     * Not a requirement. I like to make the source code
     * revision available as a Tcl variable.
     * It's easier to track bugs when you can track all the
     * revisions of all the files in a release.
     */

    Tcl_SetVar((Tcl_Interp *) interp, "demoInit_revision",
        DEMOINIT_REVISION, TCL_GLOBAL_ONLY);

    /*
    6
     */
      return TCL_OK;
    }
```

Note the following regarding the previous example:

**1.** Tcl allows any package to create its own hash table database to store and retrieve arbitrary data. If a package needs to share persistent information with scripts, you will probably need to save that data in a hash table and return a key to the script to identify which data is being referenced. The hash table is discussed in more detail with the functions that actually interact with the table. (See Example 13.3, Section 1.)

**2.** The `Tcl_CreateObjCommand` function creates a Tcl command demo and declares that the function `Demo_Cmd` is to be called when this command is evaluated. (See Example 13.3, Section 2.)

**3.** The `Tcl_PkgProvide` command declares that this package is named demo, and the revision defined by `DEMO_VERSION`. `DEMO_VERSION` is `#defined` in `demoInt.h`. (See Example, 13.3, Section 3.)

**4.** This `Tcl_SetVar` command defines a global Tcl variable demo_version as the version number of this package. This definition allows a script to check the version number of the demo package that was loaded. (See Example 13.3, Section 4.)

**5.** This is not part of the Tcl standard. My preference is to include the source control revision string in each module to make it easy to determine just what versions of all the code were linked into a package. This is particularly important when in a crunch phase of a project and making several releases a day to testers who are trying to convey what behavior was seen on what version of the code. (See Example 13.3, Section 5.)

**6.** Finally, return `TCL_OK`. None of these function calls should fail. (See Example 13.3, Section 6.)

### 13.3.3 `demoCmd.c`

The `demoCmd.c` file is where most of your extension code will exist. For small extensions, this file will contain all of the code that implements your package functionality. The `Demo_Cmd` function introduces a couple of new Tcl library functions.

The `Tcl_GetIndexFromObj` function searches a list of words for a target word. This function will return the index of the word that either exactly matches the target word or is a unique abbreviation of the target word. This function is used in this example to extract a subcommand from a list of valid subcommands.

> ***Syntax:*** int Tcl_GetIndexFromObj (*interp, objPtr, tblPtr, msg, flags, indexPtr*)
>
> > `Tcl_GetIndexFromObj` sets the variable pointed to by *indexPtr* to the offset into *tablePtr* of the entry that matches the string representation of the data in *objPtr*. An item in *tablePtr* is defined as a match if it is either an exact match to a string in the table or a unique abbreviation

for a string in the table. This function returns TCL_OK if it finds a match or TCL_ERROR if no match is found. If Tcl_GetIndexFromObj fails, it will set an error message in the interpreter's result object.

| | |
|---|---|
| Tcl_Interp *interp | A pointer to the Tcl interpreter. |
| Tcl_Obj *objPtr | A Tcl_Obj that contains the string to be searched for in the table. |
| const char *tablePtr | A pointer to a NULL-terminated list of strings to be searched for a match. |
| const char *msg | A string that will be included in an error message to explain what was being looked up if Tcl_GetIndexFromObj fails. The error message will resemble the following. |

bad *msg* "*string*": must be *tableStrings*

| | |
|---|---|
| *msg* | The string defined in the msg argument. |
| *string* | The string representation of the data in objPtr. |
| *tableStrings* | The strings defined in *tablePtr*. |

| | |
|---|---|
| int *flags* | The *flags* argument allows the calling code to define what matches are acceptable. If this flag is TCL_EXACT, only exact matches will be returned, rather than allowing abbreviations. |
| int *indexPtr | A pointer to the integer that will receive the index of the matching field. |

The demoCmd.c file contains the C functions that are called when demo commands are evaluated in the Tcl script. In a larger package with several commands, this file would contain several entry points.

## Example 13.4

```
#include "demoInt.h"

/*
1
 * Define the subcommands
 *
 * These strings define the subcommands that the demo command
 * supports.
 *
 * To add a new subcommand, add the new subcommand string,
 * #define, and entry in cmdDefinition.
 *
 * Note: Order is important.
```

```
 *
 * These are the subcommands that will be recognized
 *
 */

static char *subcommands[] = {
   "create", "set", "get", "debug", "destroy", NULL};
/*
2
 * These #defines define the positions of the subcommands.
 * You can use enum if you are certain your compiler will
 * provide the same numbers as this.
 */

#define M_create 0
#define M_set 1
#define M_get 2
#define M_debug 3
#define M_destroy 4

/*
3
 * The cmdDefinition structure describes the minimum and
 * maximum number of expected arguments for the subcommand
 * (including cmd and subcommand names), and a usage message
 * to return if the argument count is outside the expected
 * range.
 */

typedef struct cmd_Def {
char *usage;
int minArgCnt;
int maxArgCnt;
} cmdDefinition;

static cmdDefinition definitions[5] = {
  {"create key raw_message", 4 , 4},
  {"set arrayName index Value", 5, 5},
  {"get key ", 3, 3},
  {"debug level", 3, 3},
  {"destroy key", 3,3}
};

/*
4
 * If demoDebugPrint != 0, then debugprt will print debugging
 * info. This value is set with the subcommand debug.
 */
```

```
int demoDebugPrint = 0;

/*
5
 * ----------------------------------------------------------------
 *
 * Demo_Cmd --
 *
 *    Demo_Cmd is invoked to process the "demo" Tcl command.
 *    It will parse a subcommand, and perform the requested
 *    action.
 *
 * Results:
 *    A standard Tcl result.
 *
 * Side effects:
 *
 * ----------------------------------------------------------------
 */

int Demo_Cmd (ClientData demo,
              Tcl_Interp *interp,
              int objc,
              Tcl_Obj *objv[]) {
/* ClientData demo;         /* Not used. */
/* Tcl_Interp *interp;      /* Current interpreter. */
/* int objc;                /* Number of arguments. */
/* Tcl_Obj *CONST objv[];   /* Argument objects. */
int cmdnum;
int result;
Tcl_Obj *returnValue;
CmdReturn *returnStruct;
ClientData info;

/*
 * Initialize the return value
 */

returnValue = NULL;
returnStruct = NULL;

/*
6
 * Check that we have at least a subcommand,
 * else return an Error and the usage message
 */

if (objc < 2) {
  Tcl_WrongNumArgs(interp, 1, objv,
```

```
       "subcommand ?options?");
    return TCL_ERROR;
}

/*
7
 * Find this demo subcommand in the list of subcommands.
 * Tcl_GetIndexFromObj returns the offset of the recognized
 * string, which is used to index into the command
 * definitions table.
 */

result = Tcl_GetIndexFromObj(interp, objv[1], subcommands,
            "subcommand", TCL_EXACT, &cmdnum);

/*
8
 * If the result is not TCL_OK, then the error message is
 * already in the Tcl Interpreter, this code can
 * immediately return.
 */

if (result != TCL_OK) {
return TCL_ERROR;
}

/*
9
 * Check that the argument count matches what's expected
 * for this Subcommand.
 */

if ((objc < definitions[cmdnum].minArgCnt) ||
  (objc > definitions[cmdnum].maxArgCnt) ) {
  Tcl_WrongNumArgs(interp, 1, objv,
        definitions[cmdnum].usage);
  return TCL_ERROR;
}

result = TCL_OK;

/*
10
 * The subcommand is recognized, and has a valid number of
 * arguments Process the command.
 */

switch (cmdnum) {
  case M_debug: {
```

```
        char *tmp;
        tmp = Tcl_GetStringFromObj(objv[2], NULL);
        if (TCL_OK !=
          Tcl_GetInt(interp, tmp, &demoDebugPrint)) {
          return (TCL_ERROR);
        }
        break;
    }
    case M_destroy: {
      returnStruct =
        Demo_DestroyCmd((ClientData) &info,
          interp, objc, objv);
        break;
    }
    case M_create: {
      returnStruct =
        Demo_CreateCmd((ClientData) &info,
          interp, objc, objv);
        break;
    }
    case M_get: {
      returnStruct =
        Demo_GetCmd((ClientData) &info,
          interp, objc, objv);
        break;
    }
    case M_set: {
      returnStruct =
        Demo_SetCmd((ClientData) &info,
          interp, objc, objv);
        break;
    }
    default: {
      char error[80];
      sprintf(error,
        "Bad sub-command %s. Has no switch entry",
        Tcl_GetStringFromObj(objv[1], NULL));
      returnValue = Tcl_NewStringObj(error, -1);
      result = TCL_ERROR;
    }
}

/*
11
 * Extract an object to return from returnStruc.
 * returnStruct will be NULL if the processing is done
```

```
 * in this function and no other function is called.
 */
if (returnStruct != NULL) {
  returnValue = returnStruct->object;
  result = returnStruct->status;
  free (returnStruct);
}

/*
12
 * Set the return value and return the status
 */
if (returnValue != NULL) {
  Tcl_SetObjResult(interp, returnValue);
}
return result;
}
```

---

Note the following regarding the previous script example:

1. This array of strings will be passed to the Tcl_GetIndexFromObj function that will identify a valid subcommand from this list. (See Example 13.4, Section 1.)

2. These #defines create a set of textual identifiers for the positions of the sub-commands in the list. They will be used in a switch command in the main code to select which function to call to implement the subcommands. (See Example 13.4, Section 2.)

3. The cmdDefinition structure is one that I prefer. It is not part of the official Tcl coding standards. It is strongly recommended that functions check their arguments and return a usage message if the arguments do not at least match the expected count. This can be done in each function that implements a sub-command, or in the function that implements the main command. I prefer to use this table to define the maximum and minimum number of arguments expected and the error message to return if the number of arguments received is not within that range. (See Example 13.4, Section 3.)

4. There is a #define macro used to define debugprt in demoInt.h. This will reference the demoDebugPrint global variable. This is not part of the official Tcl coding standards. I find it convenient to use printf for some levels of debugging. (See Example 13.4, Section 4.)

5. This is the standard header for a C function in a Tcl extension, as recommended in the *Tcl/Tk Engineering Manual*. (See Example 13.4, Section 5.)

6. If there are not at least two arguments, this command was not called with the required subcommand argument. (See Example 13.4, Section 6.)

7. The `Tcl_GetIndexFromObj` call will set the cmdnum variable to the index of the subcommand in the list, if there is a match. (See Example 13.4, Section 7.)

8. If the `Tcl_GetIndexFromObj` call returned TCL_ERROR, it will have set an error return as a side effect. If the return value is not TCL_OK, this function can perform any required cleanup and return a TCL_ERROR status. The interface with Tcl interpreter is already taken care of. (See Example 13.4, Section 8.)

9. This section of code is not part of the official Tcl coding standard. The tests can be done here or in the individual functions that will be called from the `switch` statement. The call to `Tcl_WrongNumArgs` sets the return value for this function to a standard error message and leaves the interface with the interpreter ready for this function return. (See Example 13.4, Section 9.)

10. When the execution has reached this point, all syntactical checks have been completed. The subcommand processing can be done in this function, as is done for the `demo debug` command, or another function can be called, as is done for the other subcommands.

    The functions that implement the commands are named using the naming convention Demo_*subcommand* Cmd.

    Note that this `switch` statement does not require a default case statement. This code will be evaluated only if the `Tcl_GetIndexFromObj` function returned a valid index. This code should not be called with an unexpected value in normal operation.

    However, most code will require maintenance at some point in its life cycle. If a new command were added, the tables updated, and the `switch` statement not changed, a silent error could be introduced to the extension. Including the default case protects against that failure mode. (See Example 13.4, Section 10.)

11. The `CmdReturn` structure is not part of the official Tcl coding style. I find it useful to return both status and an object from a function, and this works. You may prefer to transfer the status and object with C variables passed as pointers in the function argument list. (See Example 13.4, Section 11.)

12. The `returnValue` is tracked separately from the `returnStruct` so that subcommands processed within this function as well as external functions can set the integer result code and `returnStruct` object to return values to the calling script. (See Example 13.4, Section 12.)

## 13.3.4 `demoDemo.c`

The demoDemo.c file has the functions that implement the subcommands of the demo command. The naming convention is that the first demo indicates this is part of the demo package, and the second demo indicates that this file implements the demo command. If there were a foo command in this demo package, it would be implemented in the file demoFoo.c.

Most of these functions will be called from demoCmd.c. The exception is the `Demo_InitHashTable` function, which is called from `Demo_Init`. This function is included in this file to allow the hash table pointer (demo_hashtbl) to be a static global and keep all references to it within this file.

### Demo_InitHashTable

This function simply initializes the Tcl hash table and defines the keys to be NULL-terminated strings.

**Example** 13.5

```
#include "demoInt.h"
static Tcl_HashTable *demo_hashtblPtr;

extern int demoDebugPrint;

/* -----------------------------------------------------------
 * void Demo_InitHashTable ()--
 *    Initialize a hash table.
 *    If your application does not need a hash table, this may be
 *    deleted.
 *
 * Arguments
 *    NONE
 *
 * Results
 *    Initializes the hash table to accept STRING keys
 *
 * Side Effects:
 *    None
 ------------------------------------------------------------ */

void Demo_InitHashTable () {
  demo_hashtblPtr = (Tcl_HashTable *)
    malloc(sizeof(Tcl_HashTable));
  Tcl_InitHashTable(demo_hashtblPtr, TCL_STRING_KEYS);
}
```

### Demo_CreateCmd

This function implements the create subcommand. Demo_CreateCmd is the first function we have discussed that checks arguments for more than syntactic correctness and needs to return status messages other than syntax messages provided by the Tcl interpreter.

This function uses both the `Tcl_AddObjErrorInfo` and the `Tcl_AddErrorInfo` function to demonstrate how each can be used. The error messages are appended to the return value for `Demo_CreateCmd` in the order in which the error functions are called.

The `Tcl_SetErrorCode` function concatenates the string arguments into the Tcl script global variable `errorCode`. It adds spaces as required to maintain the arguments as separate words in the `errorCode` variable.

## Example 13.6

```
/* ------------------------------------------------------
 * CmdReturn *Demo_CreateCmd ()--
 *    Demonstrates creating a hash entry.
 *    Creates a hash entry for Key, with value String
 * Arguments
 *   objv[0]: "demo"
 *   objv[1]: "create"
 *   objv[2]: hash Key
 *   objv[3]: String
 *
 * Results
 *    Creates a new hash entry. Sets error if entry already
 *    exists.
 *
 * Side Effects:
 *    None
 ------------------------------------------------------- */

CmdReturn *Demo_CreateCmd (ClientData info,
                           Tcl_Interp *interp,
                           int objc,
                           Tcl_Obj *objv[]) {
Tcl_HashEntry *hashEntryPtr;
CmdReturn *returnStructPtr;
char *returnCharPtr;
char *tmpString;
Tcl_Obj *returnObjPtr;
char *hashEntryContentsPtr;
char *hashKeyPtr;
int isNew;
int length;

/*
1
 * Print that the function was called for debugging
```

```
         */
        debugprt("Demo_CreateCmd called with %d args\n", objc);

        /*
2
         * Allocate the space and initialize the return structure.
         */

        returnStructPtr = (CmdReturn *) malloc(sizeof (CmdReturn));
        returnStructPtr->status = TCL_OK;
        returnCharPtr = NULL;
        returnObjPtr = NULL;

        /*
3
         * Extract the string representation of the object
         * argument, and use that as a key into the hash table.
         *
         * If this entry already exists, complain.
         */

        hashKeyPtr = Tcl_GetStringFromObj(objv[2], NULL);
        hashEntryPtr = Tcl_CreateHashEntry(demo_hashtblPtr,
            hashKeyPtr, &isNew);

        if (!isNew) {
            char errString[80];

            sprintf(errString,
                "Hashed object named \"%s\" already exists.\n",
                hashKeyPtr);

            /*
4
             * Both of these strings will be added to the Tcl script
             * global variable errorInfo
             */

            Tcl_AddErrorInfo(interp, "error in Demo_CreateCmd");

            Tcl_AddObjErrorInfo(interp, errString,
                strlen(errString));

            /*
5
             * This SetErrorCode command will set the Tcl script
             * variable errorCode to "APPLICATION" "Name in use"
             */
```

```
        Tcl_SetErrorCode(interp, "APPLICATION", \
            "Name in use", (char *) NULL);

        /*
         * This defines the return string for this subcommand
         */

        Tcl_AppendResult(interp, "Hashed object named \"",
            hashKeyPtr, "\" already exists.", (char *)  NULL);

        returnStructPtr->status = TCL_ERROR;
            goto done;
    }

    /*
6
     * If we are here, then the key is unused.
     * Get the string representation from the object,
     * and make a copy that can be placed into the hash table.
     */

    tmpString = Tcl_GetStringFromObj(objv[3], &length);
    hashEntryContentsPtr = (char *) malloc(length+1);
    strcpy(hashEntryContentsPtr, tmpString);
    debugprt("setting: %s\n", hashEntryContentsPtr);
    Tcl_SetHashValue(hashEntryPtr, hashEntryContentsPtr);

    /*
7
     * Set the return values, clean up and return
     */

done:
    if ((returnObjPtr == NULL) && (returnCharPtr != NULL)) {
      returnObjPtr = Tcl_NewStringObj(returnCharPtr, -1);
    }
    returnStructPtr->object = returnObjPtr;
    if (returnCharPtr != NULL) {free(returnCharPtr);}
    return returnStructPtr;
    }
```

Note the following in regard to the previous example:

**1.** This is not a part of the Tcl standard. I find that in many circumstances he needs to generate execution traces to track down the types of bugs that show up once every three weeks of continuous operation. Real-time debuggers are not always appropriate for this type of problem, whereas log files may help pinpoint the problem. I like to be able to enable an output message whenever a function is entered. (See Example 13.6, Section 1.)

**2.** The `returnStructPtr` is initialized in each of the functions that process the subcommands. It will be freed in the `Demo_Cmd` function after this function returns. (See Example 13.6, Section 2.)

**3.** If the `hashKeyPtr` already exists, `isNew` will be set to zero, and a pointer to the previous `hashEntryPtr` will be returned. If your code sets the value of this entry with a `Tcl_SetHashValue` call, the old data will be lost. (See Example 13.6, Section 3.)

**4.** Note that the `sprintf` call in this example is error prone. If the key is more than 37 characters, it will overflow the 80 characters allocated for `errString`. A robust application would count the characters, allocate space for the string, invoke `Tcl_AddError` to copy the error message to the error return, and then free the string. (See Example 13.6, Section 4.)

**5.** Each time `Tcl_AddError` or `Tcl_AddObjError` is called, it will append the argument, followed by a `newline` character to the end of the global script variable `errorInfo`.

The `Tcl_SetErrorCode` function treats each string as a separate list element. The first field should be a label that will define the format of the following data. (See Example 13.6, Section 5.)

**6.** Note that the string data in the third argument to the `create` subcommand is copied to another area of memory before being inserted into the hash table. The argument object is a temporary object that will be destroyed, along with its data, when the demo `create` command is fully evaluated.

The `Tcl_HashEntry` structure accepts a pointer as the data to store. It retains the pointer, rather than copying the data to a new place. Thus, if the string pointer returned from the `Tcl_GetStringFromObj(objv[3],...` call were used as the data in the `Tcl_SetHashValue` call, the string would be destroyed when the command completed, and the data in those memory locations could become corrupted. (See Example 13.6, Section 6.)

**7.** All of the functions that implement the demo subcommands use a flow model of testing values, setting failure values if necessary, and using a `goto` to exit the function. This can also be done using a structured programming flow, but becomes complex and difficult to follow when there are multiple tests. (See Example 13.6, Section 7.)

### Demo_GetCmd

The `Demo_GetCmd` will return the string that was inserted into the hash table with a demo `create` command. This function follows the same flow as the `Demo_CreateCmd` function.

**Example** 13.7

```
/* -----------------------------------------------------------
 * CmdReturn *Demo_GetCmd ()--
 *    Demonstrates retrieving a value from a hash table.
 *    Returns the value of the requested item in the hash table
 *
 * Arguments
 *  objv[0]: "demo"
 *  objv[1]: "get"
 *  objv[2]: hash Key
 *
 * Results
 *  No changes to hash table. Returns saved value, or sets error.
 *
 * Side Effects:
 *  None
 * -----------------------------------------------------------*/

CmdReturn *Demo_GetCmd (ClientData info,
                        Tcl_Interp *interp,
                        int objc,
                        Tcl_Obj *objv[]) {
Tcl_HashEntry *hashEntryPtr;
CmdReturn *returnStructPtr;
char *returnCharPtr;
Tcl_Obj *returnObjPtr;
char *hashKeyPtr;
debugprt("Demo_GetCmd called with %d args\n", objc);

/*
 * Allocate the space and initialize the return structure.
 */

returnStructPtr = (CmdReturn *) malloc(sizeof (CmdReturn));

returnStructPtr->status = TCL_OK;
returnStructPtr->object = NULL;
returnCharPtr = NULL;
returnObjPtr = NULL;

/*
 * Get the key from the argument
 * and attempt to extract that entry from the hashtable.
 * If the returned entry pointer is NULL, this key is not in
 * the table.
 */
```

```
hashKeyPtr = Tcl_GetStringFromObj(objv[2], NULL);
hashEntryPtr =
    Tcl_FindHashEntry(demo_hashtblPtr, hashKeyPtr);
if (hashEntryPtr == (Tcl_HashEntry *) NULL) {
  char errString[80];
  Tcl_Obj *objv[2];
  Tcl_Obj *errCodePtr;

 /*
1
  * Define an error code as a list. Set errorCode.
  */

  objv[0] = Tcl_NewStringObj("APPLICATION", -1);
  objv[1] = Tcl_NewStringObj("No such name", -1);

  errCodePtr = Tcl_NewListObj(2, objv);

 /*
  * This string will be placed in the global variable
  * errorInfo
  */

sprintf(errString,
  "Hash object \"%s\" does not exist.", hashKeyPtr);
Tcl_AddErrorInfo(interp, errString);

/*
 * This string will be returned as the result of the
 * command.

 */

  Tcl_AppendResult(interp,
      "can not find hashed object named \"",
      hashKeyPtr, "\"", (char *) NULL);
  returnStructPtr->status = TCL_ERROR;
  goto done;
}

/*
2
 * If we got here, then the search was successful and we can
 * extract the data value from the hash entry and return it.
 */

returnCharPtr = (char *)Tcl_GetHashValue(hashEntryPtr);
debugprt("returnString: %s\n", returnCharPtr);
```

```
    done:
      if ((returnObjPtr == NULL) && (returnCharPtr != NULL)) {
       returnObjPtr = Tcl_NewStringObj(returnCharPtr, -1);
      }

      returnStructPtr->object = returnObjPtr;
      if (returnCharPtr != NULL) {free(returnCharPtr);}
      return returnStructPtr;
    }
```

Note the following in regard to the previous example:

**1.** Demo_GetCmd uses the Tcl_SetObjErrorCode function to set the global script variable errorCode. This function assigns the errCodePtr to the error code. It does not make a copy of the object. (See Example 13.7, Section 1.)

**2.** The character pointer returnCharPtr will be set to point to the string that was stored in the hash table. This is not a copy of the data. The data is copied when returnObjPtr is created with the Tcl_NewStringObj(returnCharPtr, -1) function. (See Example 13.7, Section 2.)

### Demo_DestroyCmd

The Demo_DestroyCmd function will remove an item from the hash table and release the memory associated with it. This example uses yet another technique for setting the error returns. The default behavior is to set the global script variable errorInfo with the same string as the function return and to set the errorCode value to NONE. This function simply allows that to happen.

**Example** 13.8

```
/* ----------------------------------------------------------
 * CmdReturn *Demo_DestroyCmd ()--
 *   Demonstrate destroying an entry in the hash table.
 * Arguments
 *   objv[0]: "demo"
 *   objv[1]: "destroy"
 *   objv[2]: hash Key
 *
 * Results
 *   Deletes the hash table entry and frees the memory
 *   associated with the hash object being stored.
 *
 * Side Effects:
 *   None
 * ---------------------------------------------------------- */
```

```
CmdReturn *Demo_DestroyCmd (ClientData info,
                            Tcl_Interp *interp,
                            int objc,
                            Tcl_Obj *objv[]) {
  Tcl_HashEntry *hashEntryPtr;
  CmdReturn *returnStructPtr;
  char *returnCharPtr;
  Tcl_Obj *returnObjPtr;
  char *hashEntryContentsPtr;
  char *hashKeyPtr;
  debugprt("Demo_DestroyCmd called with %d args\n", objc);

  /*
   * Allocate the space and initialize the return structure.
   */

  returnStructPtr = (CmdReturn *) malloc(sizeof (CmdReturn));

  returnStructPtr->status = TCL_OK;
  returnStructPtr->object = NULL;
  returnCharPtr = NULL;
  returnObjPtr = NULL;

  /*
   * Extract the string representation from the argument, and
   * use it as a key into the hash table.
   */

  hashKeyPtr = Tcl_GetStringFromObj(objv[2], NULL);
  hashEntryPtr = Tcl_FindHashEntry(demo_hashtblPtr,
        hashKeyPtr);

  /*
1
   * If the hashEntryPtr returns NULL, then this key is not in
   * the table. Return an error.
   */

  if (hashEntryPtr == (Tcl_HashEntry *) NULL) {
  /*
   * Tcl_AppendResult sets the return for this command.
   * The script global variable errorInfo will also be
   * set to this string.
   * The script global variable errorCode will be set to
   * "NONE"
   */

  Tcl_AppendResult(interp,
      "cannot find hashed object named \"",
```

```
        hashKeyPtr, "\"", (char *) NULL);
    returnStructPtr->status = TCL_ERROR;
    goto done;
}

/*
 2
  * Retrieve the pointer to the data saved in the hash table
  * and free it. Then delete the hash table entry.
  */

    hashEntryContentsPtr =
      (char *)Tcl_GetHashValue(hashEntryPtr);
    free(hashEntryContentsPtr);

    Tcl_DeleteHashEntry(hashEntryPtr);

done:
    if ((returnObjPtr == NULL) && (returnCharPtr != NULL)) {
      returnObjPtr = Tcl_NewStringObj(returnCharPtr, -1);
    }

    returnStructPtr->object = returnObjPtr;

    if (returnCharPtr != NULL) {free(returnCharPtr);}

    return returnStructPtr;
}
```

Note the following in regard to the previous example:

**1.** This function allows the interpreter to set the `errorInfo` and `errorCode` values. The string `cannot find hashed object...` will be returned as the result of the command and will also be placed in the `errorInfo` variable. (See Example 13.8, Section 1.)

**2.** The data saved in the hash table is the pointer to the string that was created in the `Demo_CreateCmd` function. Once the `Tcl_HashEntry` pointer is destroyed, that pointer will be an orphan unless there is other code that references it. In this example, there is no other code using the pointer, so the memory must be released. (See Example 13.8, Section 2.)

### Demo_SetCmd

The `Demo_SetCmd` demonstrates creating or modifying an array variable in the calling script. By default, the variable will be set in the scope of the command that calls the demo set command. If demo set is called from within a procedure, the variable will exist only while that procedure is being evaluated. The Tcl interpreter will take care of releasing the variable when the procedure completes.

Demo_SetCmd uses the Tcl_ObjSetVar2 function to set the value of the array variable. The Tcl_ObjSetVar2 and Tcl_ObjGetVar2 functions allow C code to get or set the value of a Tcl script variable. Tcl_ObjSetVar2 and Tcl_ObjGetVar2 are the functions called by the Tcl interpreter to access variables in a script. Any behavior the Tcl interpreter supports for scripts is also supported for C code that is using these functions. You can modify the behavior of these commands with the *flags* argument. By default, the behavior is as follows.

- When accessing an existing variable, the Tcl_ObjGetVar2 command first tries to find a variable in the local procedure scope. If that fails, it looks for a variable defined with the variable command in the current namespace. Finally, it looks in the global scope.

- The Tcl_ObjSetVar2 function will overwrite the existing value of a variable by default. The default is not to append the new data to an existing variable.

- When referencing an array, the array name and index are referenced in separate objects. By default, you cannot reference an array item with an object that has a string representation of name(index).

*Syntax:* char *Tcl_SetVar2 (*interp, name1, name2, newstring, flags*)

*Syntax:* char *Tcl_GetVar2 (*interp, name2, name1, flags*)

| | |
|---|---|
| Tcl_SetVar2 | Creates or modifies a script variable. The value of the referenced variable will be set to *newstring*. This function returns a char * pointer to the new value. This function is for use with versions of Tcl older than 8.0. |
| Tcl_GetVar2 | Returns the string value for the variable or array reference identified by the string values in *name1* and *name2*. This function is for use with versions of Tcl older than 8.0. |
| Tcl_Interp *interp | A pointer to the Tcl interpreter. |
| char *name1 | A string that references either a simple Tcl string variable or the name of an associative array. |
| char *name2 | If this is not NULL, it is the index of an array variable. If this is not NULL, *name1* must contain the name of an array variable. |
| char *newstring | A string that contains the new value to be assigned to the variable described by *name1* and *name2*. |

int *flags*

The *flags* parameter can be used to tune the behavior of these commands. The value of flags is a bitmap composed of the logical OR of the following fields:

TCL_GLOBAL_ONLY

Setting this flag causes the variable name to be referenced only in the global scope, not a namespace or local procedure scope. If both this and the TCL_NAMESPACE_ONLY flags are set, this flag is ignored.

TCL_NAMESPACE_ONLY

Setting this flag causes the variable to be referenced only in the current namespace scope, not in the current local procedure scope. This flag overrides TCL_GLOBAL_ONLY.

TCL_LEAVE_ERR_MSG

This flag causes an error message to be placed in the interpreter's result object if the command fails. If this is not set, no error message will be left.

TCL_APPEND_VALUE

If this flag is set, the new value will be appended to the existing value, instead of overwriting it.

TCL_LIST_ELEMENT

If this flag is set, the new data will be converted into a valid list element before being appended to the existing data.

TCL_PARSE_PART1

If this flag is set and the *id1Ptr* object contains a string defining an array element (*arrayName(index)*), this will be used to reference the array index, rather than using the value in *id2Ptr* as the index.

***Syntax:*** Tcl_Obj *Tcl_ObjSetVar2 (*interp, id1Ptr, id2Ptr, newValPtr, flags*)

***Syntax:*** Tcl_Obj *Tcl_ObjGetVar2 (*interp, id1Ptr, id2Ptr, flags*)

| | |
|---|---|
| Tcl_ObjSetVar2 | Creates or modifies a Tcl variable. The value of the referenced variable will be set to the value of the *newValPtr* object. The Tcl_Obj pointer will be a pointer to the new object. This may not be a pointer to *newValPtr* if events triggered by accessing the *newValPtr* modify the content of *newValPtr*. This can occur if you are using the trace command to observe a variable. See the discussion on using trace in Section 16.1 and read about the trace command in your on-line help to see how this can happen. |
| Tcl_ObjGetVar2 | Returns a Tcl object containing a value for the variable identified by the string values in *id1Ptr* and *id2Ptr*. |
| Tcl_Interp *interp | A pointer to the Tcl interpreter. |
| Tcl_Obj *id1Ptr | An object that contains the name of a Tcl variable. This may be either a simple variable or an array name. |
| Tcl_Obj *id2Ptr | If this is not NULL, it contains the index of an array variable. If this is not NULL, *id1Ptr* must contain the name of an array variable. |
| Tcl_Obj *newValPtr | A pointer to an object with the new value to be assigned to the variable described by *id1Ptr* and *id2Ptr*. |
| int *flags* | The *flags* parameter can be used to tune the behavior of these commands. The value of flags is a bitmap composed of the logical OR of the fields described for Tcl_SetVar2 and Tcl_GetVar2. |

## Example 13.9

```
/* ----------------------------------------------------
 * CmdReturn *Demo_SetCmd ()--
 *   Demonstrates setting an array to a value
 * Arguments
 *   objv[0]: "demo"
 *   objv[1]: "set"
 *   objv[2]: arrayName
 *   objv[3]: Index
 *   objv[4]: Value
 *
 * Results
 *   Sets arrayName(Index) to the Value
```

```
         *  Also sets arrayName(alpha) to the string "NewValue".
         *  Returns the string "NewValue"
         *
         * Side Effects:
         *  None
         ---------------------------------------------------------- */

        CmdReturn *Demo_SetCmd (ClientData info,
                                Tcl_Interp *interp,
                                int objc,
                                Tcl_Obj *objv[]) {
          Tcl_Obj *returnObjPtr;
          Tcl_Obj *indexObjPtr;
          Tcl_Obj *arrayObjPtr;
          Tcl_Obj *valueObjPtr;
          CmdReturn *returnStructPtr;
          debugprt("Demo_SetCmd called with %d args\n", objc);

          /*
           * Allocate the space and initialize the return structure.
           */
          returnStructPtr = (CmdReturn *) malloc(sizeof (CmdReturn));
          returnStructPtr->status = TCL_OK;
          returnObjPtr = NULL;

          /*
    1
           * Use Tcl_ObjSetVar2 to set the array element "Index" to
           * "Value"
           */
          arrayObjPtr = objv[2];
          Tcl_ObjSetVar2(interp, arrayObjPtr, objv[3], objv[4], 0);

          /*
    2
           * Create two new objects to set a value for index "alpha"
           * in the array.
           */
          indexObjPtr = Tcl_NewStringObj("alpha", -1);
          valueObjPtr = Tcl_NewStringObj("NewValue", -1);

          returnObjPtr = Tcl_ObjSetVar2(interp, arrayObjPtr,
              indexObjPtr, valueObjPtr, 0);

          returnStructPtr->status = TCL_OK;
          returnStructPtr->object = returnObjPtr;

          /*
```

```
3
    * Delete the temporary objects by reducing their RefCount
    *   The object manager will free them, and associated
    * memory when the reference count becomes 0.
    */

Tcl_DecrRefCount(indexObjPtr);

/*
4
    * Don't delete valueObjPtr - it's the returnObjPtr
    * object. The task will core dump if you clear it,
    *  and then use it.
    *  Tcl_DecrRefCount(valueObjPtr);
    */

return(returnStructPtr);
}
```

Note the following in regard to the previous example:

1. This code implements the equivalent of set *arrayName(Index) Value*. (See Example 13.9, Section 1.)

2. This section of code implements the equivalent of set *arrayName*(alpha) "NewValue". The value assigned to returnObjPtr is a pointer to valueObjPtr, because there is no extra processing attached to the valueObjPtr variable. (See Example 13.9, Section 2.)

3. Note that you should use the Tcl_DecrRefCount function to free Tcl objects. Do not use the free function. (See Example 13.9, Section 3.)

4. The valueObjPtr is also created in this function. A pointer to this object will be returned by the Tcl_ObjSetVar2 call, but the reference count for this object is not incremented.

    Since this object is being returned as the returnObjPtr, the reference count should not be decremented. If a pointer to this object is passed to Tcl_DecrRefCount, the object will be destroyed, and returnObjPtr will point to a nonexistent object. When the Tcl interpreter tries to process the nonexistent object, it will not do anything pleasant. (See Example 13.9, Section 4.)

## 13.4 Complex Data

If you need to handle complex data (such as a structure) in your extension, there are some options.

- You can define the structure in your Tcl script as a list of values and pass that list to extension code to parse into a structure.

- You can use an associative array in the Tcl script, where each index into the associative array is a field in the structure.

- You can create a function that will accept the values for a structure in list or array format, parse them into a structure, place that structure in a hash table, and return a key to the Tcl script for future use.

The following example shows how a Tcl associative array can be used to pass a structure into a C code extension. The code expects to be called with the name of an array that has the appropriate indices set. The indices of the array must have the same names as the fields of the structure.

## Example 13.10

*Script Example*

```
...
  Tcl_Obj    *indexPtr;
  Tcl_Obj    *structElementPtr;

  struct demo {
    int     firstInt;
    char  *secondString;
    double thirdFloat;
  } demoStruct;

  /*
   * The names of the fields to be used as array indices
   */

  char *fields[] = {"firstInt", "secondString",
            "thirdFloat", NULL };

  /*
   * Create an object that can be used with
   * Tcl_ObjGetVar2 to find the object identified with
   * the array and index names
   */

  indexPtr = Tcl_NewStringObj(fields[0], -1);

  /*
   * Loop through the elements in the structure /
   * indices of the array.
   */

  for (i=0; i<3; i++) {

    /*
```

```
 * Set the index object to reference the field
 * being processed.
 */

Tcl_SetStringObj (indexPtr, fields[i], -1);

/*
 * Get the object identified as arrayName(index)
 * If that value is NULL, there is no
 * arrayName(index): complain.
 */

structElementPtr =
    Tcl_ObjGetVar2(interp, objv[2], indexPtr, 0);
if (structElementPtr == NULL) {
  Tcl_AppendResult(interp,
    "Array Index \"", fields[i],
    "\" is not defined ", (char *) NULL);
  returnStructPtr->status = TCL_ERROR;
  goto done;
}

/*
 * This is a strange way to determine which structure
 * element is being processed.
 *
 * The advantage is that it works in a loop.
 *
 * If an illegal value is in the object, the error
 * return will be set automatically by the interpreter.
 */

switch (i) {
case 0: {
     int t;
     if (TCL_OK !=
       Tcl_GetIntFromObj(interp,
          structElementPtr, &t)) {
           returnStructPtr->status = TCL_ERROR;
           goto done;
       } else {
         demoStruct.firstInt = t;
       }
    break;
    }
case 1: {
     char *t;
     if (NULL == (t =
```

```
              Tcl_GetStringFromObj(structElementPtr,
                  NULL))) {
                  returnStructPtr->status = TCL_ERROR;
                  goto done;
          } else {
              demoStruct.secondString=
                      (char *)malloc(strlen(t)+1);
              strcpy(demoStruct.secondString, t);
          }
      break;
      }
   case 2: {
          double t;
          if (TCL_OK !=
              Tcl_GetDoubleFromObj(interp,
                      structElementPtr, &t)) {
                  returnStructPtr->status = TCL_ERROR;
                  goto done;
          } else {
              demoStruct.thirdFloat = t;
          }
      break;
      }
  }
 }

/*
 * print contents of structure for example code
 */

printf("demoStruct assigned values: \n %d\n %s\n %f\n",
  demoStruct.firstInt, demoStruct.secondString,
  demoStruct.thirdFloat);
...
```

---

The following example demonstrates populating a structure using the `arraystr` subcommand.

**Example** 13.11

### *Script Example*

```
set struct(firstInt) "12"
set struct(secondString) "Testing"
set struct(thirdFloat) "34.56"
demo arraystr struct
```

*Script Output*

```
demoStruct assigned values:
  12
  Testing
  34.560000
```

The next example demonstrates a pair of functions that use a list to define the elements of a structure and save the structure in a hash table. These functions implement two new subcommands in the demo extension: demo liststr *key list* and demo getstr *key*.

These functions introduce the Tcl list object. A Tcl list object is an object that contains a set of pointers to other objects. There are several commands in the Tcl library API to manipulate the list object. This example introduces only a few that are necessary for this application.

**Syntax:** int Tcl_ListObjLength (*interp, listPtr, lengthPtr*)

Places the length of the list (the number of list elements, not the string length) in the *lengthPtr* argument. This function returns either TCL_OK or TCL_ERROR.

Tcl_Interp *\*interp*  A pointer to the Tcl interpreter.

Tcl_Obj *\*listPtr*  A pointer to the list object.

int *\*lengthPtr*  A pointer to the integer that will receive the length of this list.

**Syntax:** int Tcl_ListObjIndex (*interp, listPtr, index, elementPtr*)

Places a pointer to the object identified by the *index* argument in the *elementPtr* variable. The function returns either TCL_OK or TCL_ERROR.

Tcl_Interp *\*interp*  A pointer to the Tcl interpreter.

Tcl_Obj *\*listPtr*  A pointer to the list object.

int *index*  The index of the list element to return.

Tcl_Obj *\*\*elementPtr* The address of a pointer to a Tcl_Obj that will be set to point to the Tcl_Obj that is referenced by *index*.

**Syntax:** Tcl_Obj* Tcl_NewListObj (*count, objv*)

Returns a pointer to a new Tcl_Obj that is a list object pointing to each of the objects in the *objv* array of objects.

int *count*  The number of objects defined in the *objv* array of objects.

Tcl_Obj *\*objv[ ]* An array of pointers to Tcl objects that will be included in this list.

**Example** 13.12

*Code Example*

```
/* ---------------------------------------------------------
 * CmdReturn *Demo_ListstrCmd (ClientData info--
 *   Accepts a key and a list of data items that will be used to
 *   fill a predefined structure.
 *   The newly filled structure pointer is saved in a hash
 *   table, referenced by 'key_Value'.
 *
 * Arguments:
 *   objv[0] "demo"
 *   objv[1] "liststr"
 *   objv[2] key_Value
 *   objv[3] structure_List
 *
 * Results:
 *   Places a structure pointer in the hash table.
 *
 * Side Effects:
 *   None
 * --------------------------------------------------------- */

CmdReturn *Demo_ListstrCmd (ClientData info,
                            Tcl_Interp *interp,
                            int objc,
                            Tcl_Obj *objv[]) {
Tcl_HashEntry *hashEntryPtr;
CmdReturn *returnStructPtr;
char *returnCharPtr;
Tcl_Obj *returnObjPtr;
Tcl_Obj *listElementPtr;
int listlen;
int isNew;
int length;
char *tmpString;
int i;
char *hashEntryContentsPtr;
char *hashKeyPtr;
struct demo {
  int    firstInt;
  char   *secondString;
  double thirdFloat;
} *demoStruct;
debugprt("Demo_ListstrCmd called with %d args\n", objc);

/*
 * Allocate the space and initialize the return structure.
```

```
    */

    returnStructPtr = (CmdReturn *) malloc(sizeof (CmdReturn));

    returnStructPtr->status = TCL_OK;
    returnStructPtr->object = NULL;
    returnCharPtr = NULL;
    returnObjPtr = NULL;

    /*
     * Allocate space for the structure
     */

    demoStruct = (struct demo *) malloc(sizeof (struct demo));

    /*
     * Get the length of the list, then step through it.
     */

    Tcl_ListObjLength(interp, objv[3], &listlen);

    for(i=0; i< listlen; i++) {
    /*
     * Extract a list element from the list pointer
     */
    Tcl_ListObjIndex(interp, objv[3], i, &listElementPtr);

    debugprt("Position: %d : Value: %s\n",
      i, Tcl_GetStringFromObj(listElementPtr, NULL));

      /*
       * A strange way to determine which structure element
       * is being processed, but it works in the loop.
       * If an illegal value is in the object, the error
       * return will be set automatically by the interpreter.
       */

    switch (i) {
    case 0: {
        int t;
        if (TCL_OK !=
          Tcl_GetIntFromObj(interp,
            listElementPtr, &t)) {
           returnStructPtr->status = TCL_ERROR;
           goto done;
        } else {
          demoStruct->firstInt = t;
        }
      break;
      }
```

```
    case 1: {
        char *t;
        if (NULL == (t =
          Tcl_GetStringFromObj(listElementPtr,
              NULL))) {
           returnStructPtr->status = TCL_ERROR;
           goto done;
        } else {
          demoStruct->secondString=
            (char *)malloc(strlen(t)+1);
          strcpy(demoStruct->secondString, t);
        }
    break;
    }

    case 2: {
        double t;
        if (TCL_OK !=
          Tcl_GetDoubleFromObj(interp,
            listElementPtr, &t)) {
           returnStructPtr->status = TCL_ERROR;
           goto done;
        } else {
          demoStruct->thirdFloat = t;
        }
    break;
    }

  }
}

/*
 * Extract the string representation of the object
 * argument, and use that as a key into the hash table.
 *
 * If this entry already exists, complain.
 */

hashKeyPtr = Tcl_GetStringFromObj(objv[2], NULL);
hashEntryPtr = Tcl_CreateHashEntry(demo_hashtblPtr,
    hashKeyPtr, &isNew);

if (!isNew) {
  char errString[80];
  sprintf(errString,
```

```
      "Hashed object named \"%s\" already exists.\n",
      hashKeyPtr);

   /*
    * Both of these strings will be added to the Tcl
    * script global variable errorInfo
    */

   Tcl_AddObjErrorInfo(interp, errString,
       strlen(errString));
   Tcl_AddErrorInfo(interp, "error in Demo_CreateCmd");

   /*
    * This SetErrorCode command will set the Tcl script
    * variable errorCode to "APPLICATION {Name exists}"
    */

   Tcl_SetErrorCode(interp, "APPLICATION", "Name exists",
       (char *) NULL);

   /*
    * This defines the return string for this subcommand
    */

   Tcl_AppendResult(interp, "Hashed object named \"",
       hashKeyPtr, "\" already exists.", (char *) NULL);

   returnStructPtr->status = TCL_ERROR;
   goto done;
}

/*
 * If we are here, then the key is unused.
 * Get the string representation from the object,
 * and make a copy that can be placed into the hash table.
 */

tmpString = Tcl_GetStringFromObj(objv[3], &length);
hashEntryContentsPtr = (char *) malloc(length+1);
strcpy(hashEntryContentsPtr, tmpString);
debugprt("setting: %s\n", hashEntryContentsPtr);
Tcl_SetHashValue(hashEntryPtr, demoStruct);

done:
   if ((returnObjPtr == NULL) && (returnCharPtr != NULL)) {
       returnObjPtr = Tcl_NewStringObj(returnCharPtr, -1);
   }

   returnStructPtr->object = returnObjPtr;
   if (returnCharPtr != NULL) {free(returnCharPtr);}
```

```
        return returnStructPtr;
}

/* --------------------------------------------------------
 * CmdReturn *Demo_GetstrCmd ()--
 *  Demonstrates retrieving a structure pointer from a hash
 *  table, and returning the content as a list.
 *
 * Arguments
 *  objv[0]: "demo"
 *  objv[1]: "getstr"
 *  objv[2]: hash_Key
 *
 * Results
 *  No changes to hash table. Returns saved value, or sets error.
 *
 * Side Effects:
 *  None
 * -------------------------------------------------------- */

CmdReturn *Demo_GetstrCmd (ClientData info,
                           Tcl_Interp *interp,
                           int objc,
                           Tcl_Obj *objv[]) {
Tcl_HashEntry *hashEntryPtr;
CmdReturn *returnStructPtr;
char *returnCharPtr;
Tcl_Obj *returnObjPtr;
Tcl_Obj *listPtrPtr[3];
char *hashKeyPtr;
struct demo {
  int    firstInt;
  char   *secondString;
  double thirdFloat;
} *demoStruct;
debugprt("Demo_GetCmd called with %d args\n", objc);

/*
 * Allocate the space and initialize the return structure.
 */

  returnStructPtr = (CmdReturn *) malloc(sizeof (CmdReturn));

  returnStructPtr->status = TCL_OK;
  returnStructPtr->object = NULL;
  returnCharPtr = NULL;
  returnObjPtr = NULL;
```

```
      /*
       * Get the key from the argument
       * And attempt to extract that entry from the hashtable.
       * If the returned entry pointer is NULL, this key is not
       * in the table.
       */

    hashKeyPtr = Tcl_GetStringFromObj(objv[2], NULL);
    hashEntryPtr = Tcl_FindHashEntry(demo_hashtblPtr,
        hashKeyPtr);

    if (hashEntryPtr == (Tcl_HashEntry *) NULL) {
      char errString[80];
      Tcl_Obj *errCodePtr;

      /*
       * This string will be returned as the result of the
       * command.
       */

      Tcl_AppendResult(interp,
          "can not find hashed object named \"",
          hashKeyPtr, "\"", (char *) NULL);
      returnStructPtr->status = TCL_ERROR;
      goto done;
    }
    /*
     * If we got here, then the search was successful and we
     * can extract the data value from the hash entry and
     * return it.
     */

  demoStruct = (struct demo *)Tcl_GetHashValue(hashEntryPtr);

    /*
     * Create three objects with the values from the structure,
     * and then merge them into a list object.
     *
     * Return the list object.
     */

  listPtrPtr[0] = Tcl_NewIntObj(demoStruct->firstInt);
  listPtrPtr[1] =
    Tcl_NewStringObj(demoStruct->secondString, -1);
  listPtrPtr[2] =
    Tcl_NewDoubleObj((double) demoStruct->thirdFloat);

  returnObjPtr = Tcl_NewListObj(3, listPtrPtr);
```

```
    debugprt("returnString: %s\n", returnCharPtr);

done:
    if ((returnObjPtr == NULL) && (returnCharPtr != NULL)) {
      returnObjPtr = Tcl_NewStringObj(returnCharPtr, -1);
    }
    returnStructPtr->object = returnObjPtr;
    if (returnCharPtr != NULL) {free(returnCharPtr);}
    return returnStructPtr;
}
```

The following script example demonstrates using the `liststr` and `getstr` subcommands.

**Example** 13.13

*Script Example*

```
demo liststr key1 [list 12 "this is a test" 34.56]
demo getstr key1
```

*Script Output*

```
12 {this is a test} 34.56
```

## 13.5 Bottom Line

- A Tcl extension can be built for several purposes, including the following:
   a. Adding graphics to an existing library
   b. Adding new features to a Tcl interpreter
   c. Creating a rapid prototyping interpreter from a library
   d. Creating a script-driven test package for a library
- A Tcl extension must include the following:
   a. An *ExtName_*Init function
   b. Calls to `Tcl_CreateCommand` to create new Tcl commands
   c. Code to implement each new Tcl command
- A Tcl extension should also include the following:
   a. An include file named *extName*Int.h
   b. A `makefile` `codewarrior` or IDE project files

   c. Separate directories for generic code, platform-specific files, documentation, and tests

A Tcl extension may include other files as necessary to make it a maintainable, modular set of code.

- New Tcl commands are defined with the `Tcl_CreateObjCommand` or `Tcl_CreateCommand` command.

  ***Syntax:*** `int Tcl_CreateObjCommand (`*`interp, cmdName, func, clientData, deleteFunc`*`)`

  ***Syntax:*** `int Tcl_CreateCommand (`*`interp, cmdName, func, clientData, deleteFunc`*`)`

- The C function associated with the new Tcl command created by `Tcl_Create...Command` should have a function prototype that resembles the following.

  `int funcName (`*`clientData, interp, objc, objv`*`)`

- You can get a native or a string representation from a Tcl object with the `Tcl_GetIntFromObj`, `Tcl_GetDoubleFromObj`, or `Tcl_GetStringFromObj` command.

  ***Syntax:*** `int Tcl_GetIntFromObj (`*`interp, objPtr, intPtr`*`)`

  ***Syntax:*** `int Tcl_GetDoubleFromObj (`*`interp, objPtr, doublePtr`*`)`

  ***Syntax:*** `char *Tcl_GetStringFromObj (`*`objPtr, lengthPtr`*`)`

- You can create a new object with one of the following functions.

  ***Syntax:*** `Tcl_Obj *Tcl_NewIntObj (`*`intValue`*`)`

  ***Syntax:*** `Tcl_Obj *Tcl_NewDoubleObj (`*`doubleValue`*`)`

  ***Syntax:*** `Tcl_Obj *Tcl_NewStringObj (`*`bytes, length`*`)`

- You can modify the content of an object with one of the following functions.

  ***Syntax:*** `void Tcl_SetIntObj (`*`objPtr, intValue`*`)`

  ***Syntax:*** `void Tcl_SetDoubleObj (`*`objPtr, doubleValue`*`)`

  ***Syntax:*** `void Tcl_SetStringObj (`*`objPtr, bytes, length`*`)`

  ***Syntax:*** `void Tcl_AppendToObj (`*`objPtr, bytes, length`*`)`

  ***Syntax:*** `void Tcl_AppendObjToObj (`*`objPtr, appendObjPtr`*`)`

  ***Syntax:*** `void Tcl_AppendStringsToObj (`*`objPtr, string, ..., NULL`*`)`

- The results of a function are returned to the calling script with the functions `Tcl_SetObjResult` and `Tcl_SetResult`.

  ***Syntax:*** `void Tcl_SetObjResult (`*`interp, objPtr`*`)`

  ***Syntax:*** `void Tcl_SetResult (`*`interp, string, freeProc`*`)`

- The status of a function is returned to the calling script with the functions `Tcl_AddObjErrorInfo`, `Tcl_AddErrorInfo`, `Tcl_SetObjErrorCode`, and `Tcl_SetErrorCode`, which set the `errorCode` and `errorInfo` global Tcl variables.

*Syntax:* void Tcl_AddObjErrorInfo (*interp, message, length*)

*Syntax:* void Tcl_AddErrorInfo (*interp, message*)

*Syntax:* void Tcl_SetObjErrorCode (*interp, objPtr*)

*Syntax:* void Tcl_SetErrorCode (*interp, element1, element2...NULL*)

■ Tcl provides an interface to fast hash table database functions to allow tasks to save and retrieve arbitrary data based on keys. A hash table must be initialized with the Tcl_InitHashTable function.

*Syntax:* void Tcl_InitHashTable (*tablePtr, keyType*)

■ Hash table entries may be manipulated with the following functions.

*Syntax:* Tcl_HashEntry *Tcl_CreateHashEntry (*tablePtr, key, newPtr*)

*Syntax:* Tcl_HashEntry *Tcl_FindHashEntry (*tablePtr, key*)

*Syntax:* void Tcl_DeleteHashEntry (*entryPtr*)

■ Data may be retrieved or deposited in a Tcl_HashEntry with the following functions.

*Syntax:* ClientData TclGetHashValue (*entryPtr*)

*Syntax:* void TclSetHashValue (*entryPtr, value*)

■ A match to a string can be found in an array of strings with the Tcl_GetIndexFromObj function.

*Syntax:* int Tcl_GetIndexFromObj (*interp, objPtr, tblPtr, msg, flags, indexPtr*)

■ The content of Tcl variables can be accessed with the following functions.

*Syntax:* Tcl_Obj *Tcl_ObjGetVar2 (*interp, id1Ptr, id2Ptr, flags*)

*Syntax:* char *Tcl_GetVar2 (*interp, name2, name1, flags*)

■ The content of Tcl script variables can be set with the following functions.

*Syntax:* Tcl_Obj *Tcl_ObjSetVar2 (*interp, id1Ptr, id2Ptr, newValPtr, flags*)

*Syntax:* char *Tcl_SetVar2 (*interp, name1, name2, newstring, flags*)

■ A Tcl list is implemented with a Tcl object that contains an array of pointers to the elements of the list. You can create a Tcl list within a C function with the Tcl_NewListObj function.

*Syntax:* Tcl_Obj* Tcl_NewListObj (*count, objv*)

■ You can get the length of a list with the Tcl_ListObjLength function.

*Syntax:* int Tcl_ListObjLength (*interp, listPtr, lengthPtr*)

■ You can retrieve the list element from a particular index in a list with the Tcl_ListObjIndex function.

*Syntax:* int Tcl_ListObjIndex (*interp, listPtr, index, elementPtr*)

# 13.6 Problems

The following numbering convention is used in all Problem sections.

| Number Range | Description of Problems |
|---|---|
| 100–199 | These problems review the material covered in this chapter. They can be answered in a few words or a short (1–5-line) script. Each problem should take under a minute to answer. |
| 200–299 | These problems go beyond the details presented in this chapter. They may require some analysis of the material or command details not covered in the chapter. They may require reading a man page or making a web search. They can be answered with a few sentences or a 5–50-line script. Each problem should take under 10 minutes to answer. |
| 300–399 | These problems extend the material presented in this chapter. They may require referencing other sources. They can be answered in a few paragraphs or a few hundred lines of code. Each exercise may take a few hours to complete. |

**100.** If you have a stand-alone application with no source code or library documentation, is this a likely candidate for a Tcl extension? Why or why not?

**101.** What Tcl library call adds a new command to a Tcl interpreter?

**102.** What Tcl command will return the integer value of the data in a Tcl object? What will be returned if the object does not contain integer data?

**103.** What data format is always valid for Tcl data?

**104.** Can the `Tcl_SetVar` function be used to assign a value to a variable that does not exist?

**105.** Can you assign a string of binary (not ASCII) data to a Tcl object?

**106.** What value should a successful command return?

**107.** What command will add a string to the `errorInfo` global variable?

**108.** Given an extension named `checksum`, what should the initialization function be named?

**109.** What would be the path and name of the include file for internal use by the extension `foo`? (Following the TEA path and name conventions.)

**110.** Which library command will append a string onto the data in a Tcl object?

**111.** Which library command will create a new Tcl object with an integer value?

**112.** Which library command will append a new list element to a Tcl list variable?

**200.** If you have an application built from an internally developed function library, describe how you could use a Tcl extension to perform automated integration and unit testing for the package.

**201.** Find the sample extension code on the companion CD-ROM and compile that on your preferred platform.

**202.** Write a Tcl extension that will calculate and return a simple checksum (the sum of all bytes) of the content of a Tcl variable.

**203.** Write a Tcl extension that will return a string formatted with the `sprintf` command. This new command will resemble the Tcl `format` command.

**300.** Write a Tcl extension that will save data in a structure, as shown in Example 13.10. Add a subcommand to retrieve the values from the structure and populate a given array.

**301.** Port the extension written for Problem 202 to at least one other platform: MS Windows, UNIX, or Macintosh.

**302.** Write a set of test scripts for the extension written in Problem 203 to exercise the `sprintf` function and prove that it behaves as documented.

**303.** Port the extension and tests written in Problems 203 and 302 to another platform. Confirm that `sprintf` behaves the same on both platforms.

# CHAPTER 14

# Extensions and Packages

The previous chapters described building Tcl packages and C language extensions to Tcl. Using these techniques, you can create almost any application you desire.

In many cases your applications will require features that have already been developed. You can save time by using existing extensions and packages for these features. Using existing extensions not only saves you development time but reduces your maintenance and testing time.

This chapter provides an overview of a few extensions and packages. It is not possible to cover all of the extensions and packages written for Tcl. The Tcl FAQ (frequently asked questions) lists over 700 extensions, and more are being written. Before you write your own extension, check to see if one already exists.

The primary archive for Tcl extensions and packages is *www.sourceforge.net*. Most extensions are also announced in comp.lang.tcl or comp.lang.tcl.announce. You can use the Google News Search engine (*www.google.com/advanced_group_search*) to limit your search to those newsgroups. Finally, many of the extensions are described in the Tcl/Tk FAQ (*www.purl.org/NET/Tcl-FAQ*) and discussed on the Tcl'ers Wiki (*http://wiki.tcl.tk/itcl*).

Although extensions can save you a great deal of development time, there are some points to consider when using extensions and packages.

- Extensions tend to lag behind the Tcl core.

  Most of these packages are developed by Tcl advocates who work in their spare time to maintain the packages. It can take weeks or months before they have time to update their package after a major change to the Tcl internals.

  Commercial extensions can also lag behind the core. Frequently, a commercial user of Tcl will decide to freeze their application at a particular level, rather than try to support multiple levels of code at their user sites.

In particular, the change from Tcl 7.6 to Tcl 8.0 introduced some API changes requiring enough rewriting that some less popular extensions have not yet been ported beyond revision 7.6.

Most popular and commercial packages, however, have been updated to take advantage of the 8.0 improvements.

■ Not all extensions are available on all platforms.

Many packages were developed before Tcl was available on Macintosh and Windows platforms, and they may have some UNIX-specific code in them. Similarly, there are Windows-specific and Mac-specific extensions that interface with other platform-specific applications.

■ All extensions may not be available at your customer site.

Installing extensions takes time, and keeping multiple versions of libraries and extensions consistent can create problems for system administrators. Thus, the more extensions your application requires, the more difficult it may be for users to install your application.

If you are writing an application for in-house use (and your system administrators will install the extensions you need), this is not a problem. However, if you write an application you would like to see used throughout your company or distributed across the Internet, the more extensions it requires, the less likely someone is to be willing to try it.

If you need an extension, by all means use it. However, if you can limit your application to using only core Tcl or a single extension, you should do so.

The ActiveTcl (or *Batteries Included*) Tcl distribution from ActiveState provides many of the popular extensions and is becoming the de facto standard Tcl distribution. If your application requires these extensions, odds are good that it will run on your client systems.

Wrapping an application with the Tcl interpreter and required extensions to make a single executable module is another distribution option. Some of these options are discussed in the next chapter. Packages written in Tcl are more easily distributed than extensions written in C.

Whereas many sites may not have an extension, any site that is interested in running your Tcl application can run Tcl packages. You can include the Tcl packages your script needs with the distribution and install them with your application. For example, the HTML library discussed in Chapter 11 has been included in several other packages, including TclTutor.

This chapter introduces the following packages.

[incr Tcl]   The previous chapters have shown how object-oriented techniques can be used with pure Tcl. The [incr Tcl] extension provides a complete object-oriented extension for the Tcl developer. It supports classes; private, public, and protected scopes; constructors; destructors; inheritance; and aggregation.

| expect | expect automates procedures that have a character-based interaction. It allows a Tcl script to spawn a child task and interact with that task as though the task were interacting with a human. |
| --- | --- |
| TclX | This is a collection of new Tcl commands that support system access and reduce the amount of code you need to write. Many of the TclX features have been integrated into the more recent versions of Tcl. |
| SybTcl | The SybTcl extension provides an interface to a Sybase database server. |
| OraTcl | The OraTcl extension provides an interface to an Oracle database server. |
| mysqltcl | The mysqltcl extension provides an interface to a MySql database server. |
| VSdb | This is a pure Tcl database package that is very portable. It is easy to set up and use, and is well suited to tasks that do not require a relational database server. |
| BWidgets | The Bwidgets package provides several compound widgets and versions of standard Tk widgets with extended features. This is a pure Tcl package that can be used on multiple platforms. |
| BLT | A set of Tcl and Tk extensions that include support for treating numeric lists as high-speed vectors and creating graphs and bar charts. |
| Img extension | This extension adds support for more image file formats to the Tcl image object. |

# 14.1 [incr Tcl]

| Language | C |
| --- | --- |
| Primary Site | *http://incrtcl.sourceforge.net/* |
| Contact | *mmclennan@cadence.com,* Michael McLennan |
| Tcl Revision Supported | Tcl: 7.3-8.4 and newer; Tk: 3.6-8.4 and newer |
| Supported Platforms | UNIX, MS Windows, Mac 68K, Mac PowerPC |
| Mailing List | *incrtcl-users-request@lists.sourceforge.net* with a subject of: subscribe |
| Other Book References | *Tcl/Tk Tools*<br>*[incr Tcl/Tk] from the Ground Up* |

[Incr Tcl] is to Tcl what C++ is to C, right down to the pun for the name. It extends the base Tcl language with support for the following:

■ Namespaces

■ Class definition with

   ■ Public, private, and protected class methods

   ■ Public, private, and protected data

   ■ Inheritance

   ■ Aggregation

   ■ Constructors

   ■ Destructors

   ■ Variables attached to a class rather than a class instance

   ■ Procedures attached to a class rather than a class instance

The namespace commands were first introduced into Tcl by [incr Tcl]. The [incr Tcl] namespace command has the same basic format as the namespace command in Tcl. One difference is that [incr Tcl] allows you to define items in a namespace to be completely private. A pure Tcl script can always access items in a Tcl namespace using the complete name of the item.

Previous chapters showed how you can use subsets of object-oriented programming techniques with Tcl. With [incr Tcl] you can perform pure object-oriented programming. The following example is adapted from the [incr Tcl] introduction (itcl-intro/itcl/tree/tree2.itcl). It implements a tree object, similar to that developed in Chapters 6, 7 and 8.

There are man pages and MS Windows help files included with the [incr Tcl] distribution. A couple of commands used in this example include class and method. The class command defines a class. In the example that follows, this defines a Tree class with the private data members key, value, parent, and children.

> **Syntax:** class *className* { *script* }
>
> Define an [incr Tcl] class.
>
> *className* A name for this class.
>
> {*script*}   A Tcl script that contains the commands that define this class. These commands may include procedure (method) definitions, variable declarations, and inheritance and access definitions.

The class methods are defined with the method command and can be defined either in-line (as the methods add, clear, and parent are defined) or similarly to function prototypes (as the get method is defined). When a method is defined as a function prototype, the code that implements the method can be placed later in the script or in a separate file.

***Syntax:*** method *name* { *args* } { *body* }

Define a method for this class.

*name*  The name of this method.

*args*  An argument list, similar to the argument list used with the proc command.

*body*  The body of this method. Similar to the body of a proc.

## Example 14.1

***Script Example***

```
package require Itcl
namespace import itcl::*

class Tree {
  private variable key ""
  private variable value ""
  private variable parent ""
  private variable children ""

  # Assign a key and value in the constructor

  constructor {n v} {
    set key $n
    set value $v
  }

  # The destructor calls 'clear' to recursively
  # destroy child nodes

  destructor {
    clear
  }

  # Destroy any children of this node
  # Note that this is recursive.

  method clear {} {
    if {$children != ""} {
      eval delete object $children
    }
    set children {}
  }

  # Add a new child object to the current object.

  method add {obj} {
    $obj parent $this
```

```
      lappend children $obj
   }

   # Assign the parent for this node

   method parent {pobj} {
      set parent $pobj
   }

   # A forward declaration to return information associated
   #    with this node.

   public method get {{option -value}}

}

#########################################################
# body Tree::get {{option -value}}--
#    Return information associated with this node
# Arguments
#    option : A flag to determine whether to return the
#             key, value, or parent associated with this node.
#
# Results

body Tree::get {{option -value}} {
   switch -- $option {
      -key { return $key }
      -value { return $value }
      -parent { return $parent }
      -children {return $children}
   }

   error "bad option \"$option\""
}
```

The following example shows how this tree object could be used.

## Example 14.2

### *Script Example*

```
# Create a Tree

Tree topNode key0 Value0

# Add two children

topNode add [Tree childNode1 key1 Value1]
```

```
topNode add [Tree childNode2 key2 Value2]

# Display some values from the tree.

puts "topNode's children are: [topNode get -children]"
puts "Value associated with childNode1 is \
  [childNode1 get -value]"
puts "Parent of childNode2 is: [childNode2 get -parent]"
```

*Script Output*

**topNode's children are: childNode1 childNode2**
**Value associated with childNode1 is Value1**
**Parent of childNode2 is: ::topNode**

# 14.2 expect

| | |
|---|---|
| Language | C |
| Primary Site | *http://expect.nist.gov/* |
| Contact | *libes@nist.gov*, Don Libes |
| Tcl Revision Supported | Tcl: 7.3-8.4 and newer; Tk: 3.6-8.4 and newer |
| Supported Platforms | UNIX<br>Windows NT |
| Unofficially<br>Supported Platforms | *http://bmrc.berkeley.edu/people/chaffee/expectnt.html* |
| Other Book References | *Exploring Expect, Tcl/Tk Tools* |

Expect adds commands to Tcl that make it easy to write scripts to interact with programs that use a character-based interface. This includes programs such as telnet and FTP that use a prompt/command type interface or even keyboard-driven spreadsheet packages such as sc.

Expect can be used for tasks ranging from changing passwords on remote systems to converting an interactive hardware diagnostics package into an automated test system. When you load both the expect and Tk extensions simultaneously, you have a tool that is ideal for transforming legacy applications that use dialogs or screen menus into modern GUI-style applications. There are three indispensable commands in expect.

*Syntax:* spawn *options commandName commandArgs*

Starts a new process and connects the process's stdin and stdout to the expect interpreter.

| | | |
|---|---|---|
| *options* | The spawn command supports several options, including | |
| | -noecho | The spawn will echo the command line and arguments unless this option is set. |
| | *-open fileID* | The -open option lets you process the input from a file handle (returned by open) instead of executing a new program. This allows you to use an expect script to evaluate program output from a file as well as directly controlling a program. |
| *commandName* | The name of the executable program to start. | |
| *commandArgs* | The command line arguments for the executable program being spawned. | |

## Example 14.3

```
# Open an ftp connection to the Red Hat update site

spawn ftp updates.redhat.com
```

---

**Syntax:** expect *?-option? pattern1 action1 ?-option? pattern2 action2 ...*

Scan the input for one of several patterns. When a pattern is recognized, evaluate the associated action.

| | | |
|---|---|---|
| *-option* | Options that will control the matching are | |
| | -exact | Match the pattern exactly. |
| | -re | Use regular expression rules to match this pattern. |
| | -glob | Use glob rules to match this pattern. |
| *pattern* | A pattern to match in the output from the spawned program. | |
| *action* | A script to be evaluated when a pattern is matched. | |

## Example 14.4

```
# Expect the "Name" prompt.
# Generate an error if the prompt does not appear
#   within 10 seconds.
# Generate an error if the connection is dropped.
expect {
  {Name (updates.redhat.com:clif):} {
    exp_send "anonymous\n"
  }
}
```

```
expect {
  {ssword} {
    exp_send "user@example.com\n"
  }
  timeout {
    # Read all available input
    expect *

    # Generate an error
    error "Timed out" \
      "Expected: 'password prompt. Saw: $expect_out(buffer)"
  }
  eof {
    # Read all available input
    expect *

    # Generate an error
    error "Connection Closed" \
      "Expected: '$prompt'. Saw: $expect_out(buffer)"
  }
}
```

*Syntax:* `exp_send` *string*

Sends *string* to the slave process.

*string*    The string to be transmitted to the slave process. Note that a `newline` character is not appended to this text.

## **Example** 14.5

```
# Download the readme file
exp_send "get README\n"
```

When expect finds a string that matches a pattern, it stores information about the match in the associative array expect_out. This array contains several indices, including the following.

`expect_out(buffer)`    All characters up to and including the characters that matched a pattern.

`expect_out(0,string)`    The characters that matched an exact, `glob`, or regular expression pattern.

`expect_out(#,string)`    The indices `(1,string)-(9,string)` will contain the characters that match regular expressions within parentheses. The characters that match the first expression within parentheses are assigned to expect_out(1,string), the characters that match the next parenthetical expression are assigned to expect_out(2,string), and so on.

Red Hat maintains an ftp server for upgrades to the Red Hat Linux distribution. You can visit the site every few days to see if there are any new upgrades you need for your system, or you could use expect to automate this process. The following example shows how to automate this task.

This script will log into the ftp server and check the files in the *SRPMS* directory against the files already downloaded, and download any new files. In the following example, note the timeout and eof patterns in the expect commands. If a pattern is not recognized within a defined length of time, the timeout action will be evaluated. If the connection to the spawned process is closed, the eof action will be evaluated. This is similar to the behavior of the default pattern in the switch command. As with the default option, you do not need to check for the timeout and eof conditions, but you will eventually regret it if you do not.

## Example 14.6

*Script Example*

```
#!/usr/local/bin/expect

# Open a connection to Red Hat
spawn ftp updates.redhat.com

# Set the timeout for 10 seconds.
set timeout 10000

##############################################################
# proc dialog {prompt send}--
#    Generalize a prompt/response dialog
# Arguments
#    prompt: The prompt to expect
#    send:   The string to send when the prompt is received
# Results
#    No valid return
#    Generates an error on TIMEOUT or EOF condition.

proc dialog {prompt send } {
  expect {
    $prompt {
      sleep 1;
      exp_send "$send\n"

    }
    timeout {
      expect *
```

```
            error "Timed out" \
               "Expected: '$prompt'. Saw: $expect_out(buffer)"
         }
         eof {
            expect *
            error "Connection Closed" \
               "Expected: '$prompt'. Saw: $expect_out(buffer)"
         }
      }
   }
}

# Expect "Name", send "anonymous"
dialog "Name" anonymous

# Expect the password prompt, and send a mail address
dialog "ssword" "user@example.com"

# Change to the Red Hat 7.3 Source RPMS directory
dialog "ftp>" "cd 7.3/en/os/SRPMS"

# Get a list of the available files
dialog "ftp>" "ls -latr"

set files ""

# Loop until a break condition is reached
# Read lines looking for words (file names)
#    that end in .rpm

while {1} {
   expect {
      -re {([^ ]*rpm)} {
         # Recognized an rpm file. Check to see if we
         # already have it.

         if {![file exists $expect_out(1,string)]} {
            # No, we don't have this one, append it
            # to a list to download.
            lappend files $expect_out(1,string)
         }
      }
      ftp> {
         # At the end of the file list, this is a new prompt
         break;
      }
      timeout {
         error "Connection Timed out!"
      }
      eof {
```

```
        error "Connection Closed!"
      }
    }
}

# We collected the ftp> prompt to find the end of the
#   'ls' data.
# Send a newline to generate a new prompt.

exp_send "\n"

# For each file in our list of files to collect,
#   Get the file.

foreach file $files {
  dialog "ftp>" "get $file"

}
```

*Script Output*

```
spawn ftp updates.redhat.com
Connected to updates.redhat.com.
220 Red Hat FTP server ready. All transfers are logged.
530 Please login with USER and PASS.
530 Please login with USER and PASS.
KERBEROS_V4 rejected as an authentication type
Name (updates.redhat.com:clif): anonymous
331 Please specify the password.
Password:
230-  THE SOFTWARE AVAILABLE FROM THIS SITE IS PROVIDED AND LICENSED
230-  "AS IS" WITHOUT WARRANTY OF ANY KIND, EITHER EXPRESSED OR
230-  IMPLIED, INCLUDING, BUT NOT LIMITED TO, THE IMPLIED WARRANTIES
230-  OF MERCHANTABILITY AND FITNESS FOR A PARTICULAR PURPOSE.
230 Login successful. Have fun.
Remote system type is UNIX.
Using binary mode to transfer files.
ftp> cd 7.3/en/os/SRPMS
250 Directory successfully changed.
ftp> ls -latr
227 Entering Passive Mode (66,77,185,39,48,234)
150 Here comes the directory listing.
-rw-rw-r--  1 2220  235   894372  Jun 27 16:34 openssh-3.1p1-6.src.rpm
-rw-rw-r--  1 2220  235  1324660  Jun 28 19:12 squid-2.4.STABLE6-6.7.3.src.rpm
drwxrwsr-x  2 0     235     4096  Jul 08 10:17 .
226 Directory send OK.
ftp>
```

```
ftp> get openssh-3.1p1-6.src.rpm
local: openssh-3.1p1-6.src.rpm remote: openssh-3.1p1-6.src.rpm
227 Entering Passive Mode (66,77,185,39,50,89)
150 Opening BINARY mode data connection for openssh-3.1p1-6.src.rpm
          (894372 bytes).
226 File send OK.
894372 bytes received in 29 seconds (30 Kbytes/s)
ftp>
```

## 14.3 TclX

| | |
|---|---|
| Language | C |
| Primary Sites | *http://tclx.sourceforge.net/* |
| | *http://wiki.tcl.tk/tclx/* |
| | *www.maths.mq.edu.au/~ steffen/tcltk/tclx/* |
| | (TclX for Macintosh) |
| Contact | *markd@grizzly.com*, Mark Diekhans |
| Tcl Revision Supported | Tcl: 7.3-8.4 and newer; Tk: 3.6-8.4 and newer |
| Supported Platforms | UNIX, MS Windows, Mac OS |
| Other Book References | *Tcl/Tk Tools* |

The TclX extension is designed to make large programming tasks easier and to give the Tcl programmer more access to operating system functions such as chmod, chown, and kill. TclX contains a large number of new commands. Many of the best features of Tcl (sockets, time and date, random numbers, associative arrays, and more) were introduced in TclX. There are still many features provided by TclX that are not in the Tcl core. TclX features include the following:

- Extended file system interaction commands
- Extended looping constructs
- Extended string manipulation commands
- Extended list manipulation commands
- Keyed lists
- Debugging commands
- Performance profiling commands
- System library interface commands
- Network information commands
- Help

Using TclX can help you in the following ways.

- TclX gives you access to operating system functions that are not supported by the Tcl core. Using core Tcl, you would need to write stand-alone C programs (or your own extensions) to gain access to these.

- TclX scripts are smaller than pure Tcl scripts, because TclX has built-in constructs you would otherwise need to write as procedures.

- TclX commands run faster than the equivalent function written as a Tcl procedure, because the TclX command is written in C and compiled instead of interpreted.

The following example uses the recursive file system looping command for_recursive_glob to step through the files in a directory, and the three text search commands scancontext, scanmatch, and scanfile.

The addDirToTree procedure uses the foreach, glob, and file type commands to build a recursive directory search procedure. The for_recursive_glob command provides these features in a single loop.

*Syntax:* for_recursive_glob *var dirlist globlist code*

> Recursively loops through the directories in a list looking for files that match one of a list of glob patterns. When a file matching the pattern is found, the script defined in *code* is evaluated with the variable *var* set to the name of the file that matched the pattern.

> *var*      The name of a variable that will receive the name of each matching file.

> *dirlist*      A list of directories to search for files that match the *globlist* patterns.

> *globlist*      A list of glob patterns that will be used to match file names.

> *code*      A script to evaluate whenever a file name matches one of the patterns in *globlist*.

Many applications require searching a large number of files for particular strings. A pure Tcl script can perform this operation by reading the file and using string first, string match, or regexp. This type of solution uses many interpreter steps and can be slow. The TclX scancontext, scanmatch, and scanfile commands work together to optimize file search applications.

*Syntax:* scancontext create

> Create a new scan context for use with the scanfile command. Returns a *contextHandle*.

The *contextHandle* returned by the scancontext create command can be used with the scanmatch command to link in a pattern to an action to perform.

*Syntax:* scanmatch *contextHandle ?regexp? code*

Associate a regular expression and script with a *contextHandle*.

*contextHandle*  A handle returned by `scancontext create`.

*regexp*  A regular expression to scan for. If this is blank, the script is assigned as the default script to evaluate when no other expression is matched.

*code*  A script to evaluate when the *regexp* is matched.

When a regular expression defined with `scanmatch` is recognized, information about the match is stored in the associative array variable `matchInfo`, which is visible to the `code` script. The `matchInfo` variable has several indices with information about the match.

The `scanfile` command will examine a file's content and invoke the appropriate scripts when patterns are matched.

**Syntax:** `scanfile` *contexthandle fileId*

Scan a file for lines that match one of the regular expressions defined in a context handle. If a line matches a regular expression, the associated script is evaluated.

*contextHandle*  The handle returned by the `scancontext create` command.

*fileId*  A file channel opened with read access.

## Example 14.7

### *Script Example*

```
#!/usr/local/bin/tcl
proc scanTreeForString {topDir pattern matchString \
    filesWith filesWithout} {
  upvar $filesWith with
  upvar $filesWithout without

  set with ""

  # Create a scan context for the files that will be scanned.

  set sc [scancontext create]

  # Add an action to take when the pattern is recognized
  # in a file. If the pattern is recognized, append the
  # file name to the list of files containing the pattern
  # and break out of the scanning loop. Without the "break",
  # scanfile would process each occurrence of the text that
  # matches the regular expression.

  scanmatch $sc "$matchString" {
    lappend with [file tail $filename]
```

```
      break;
   }

   # Process all the files below $topDir that match the
   # pattern

   for_recursive_glob filename $topDir $pattern {
     set fl [open $filename RDONLY]
     scanfile $sc $fl
     close $fl
     # If there were no lines matching the $matchString,
     # there will be no $filename in the list "with".
     # In that case, add $filename to the list of files
     # without the $matchString.
     if {[lsearch $with [file tail $filename]] < 0} {
       lappend without [file tail $filename]
     }
   }

   # Clean up and leave

   scancontext delete $sc
}
scanTreeForString /usr/src/TCL/tcl8.4a4 *.c Tcl_Obj hasObj noObj

puts "These files have 'Tcl_Obj' in them: $hasObj"
puts "These files do not: $noObj"
```

*Script Output*

```
These files have 'Tcl_Obj' in them: tclLoadAout.c
tclLoadDl.c tclLoadDld.c tclLoadDyld.c tclLoadNext.c
tclLoadOSF.c tclLoadShl.c tclUnixChan.c tclUnixFCmd.c
tclUnixFile.c tclUnixInit.c tclUnixPipe.c tclBasic.c
tclBinary.c tclClock.c tclCmdAH.c tclCmdIL.c tclCmdMZ.c
tclCompCmds.c tclCompile.c tclEncoding.c tclEnv.c tclEvent.c
tclExecute.c tclFCmd.c tclFileName.c tclHistory.c tclIO.c
tclIOCmd.c tclIOGT.c tclIOUtil.c tclIndexObj.c tclInterp.c
tclLink.c tclListObj.c tclLiteral.c tclLoad.c tclLoadNone.c
tclMain.c tclNamesp.c tclObj.c tclParse.c tclPipe.c tclPkg.c
tclProc.c tclRegexp.c tclResult.c tclScan.c tclStringObj.c
tclStubInit.c tclTest.c tclTestObj.c tclTestProcBodyObj.c
tclThreadTest.c tclTimer.c tclUtil.c tclVar.c tclWinChan.c
tclWinDde.c tclWinFCmd.c tclWinFile.c tclWinInit.c
tclWinLoad.c tclWinPipe.c tclWinReg.c tclWinTest.c
tclMacBOAMain.c tclMacChan.c tclMacFCmd.c tclMacFile.c
tclMacInit.c tclMacLibrary.c tclMacLoad.c tclMacResource.c
tclMacUnix.c pkga.c pkgb.c pkgc.c pkgd.c
```

These files do not: `tclAppInit.c` `tclLoadAix.c` `tclMtherr.c`
`tclUnixEvent.c` `tclUnixNotify.c` `tclUnixSock.c` `tclUnixTest.c`
`tclUnixThrd.c` `tclUnixTime.c` `tclXtNotify.c` `tclXtTest.c`
`regc_color.c` `regc_cvec.c` `regc_lex.c` `regc_locale.c` `regc_nfa.c`
`regcomp.c` `rege_dfa.c` `regerror.c` `regexec.c` `regfree.c`
`regfronts.c` `tclAlloc.c` `tclAsync.c` `tclCkalloc.c` `tclCompExpr.c`
`tclDate.c` `tclGet.c` `tclHash.c` `tclIOSock.c` `tclNotify.c`
`tclPanic.c` `tclParseExpr.c` `tclPosixStr.c` `tclPreserve.c`
`tclResolve.c` `tclStubLib.c` `tclThread.c` `tclThreadJoin.c`
`tclUniData.c` `tclUtf.c` `fixstrtod.c` `gettod.c` `memcmp.c`
`opendir.c` `strftime.c` `strncasecmp.c` `strstr.c` `strtod.c`
`strtol.c` `strtoll.c` `strtoul.c` `strtoull.c` `tmpnam.c` `waitpid.c`
`cat.c` `stub16.c` `tclAppInit.c` `tclWin32Dll.c` `tclWinConsole.c`
`tclWinError.c` `tclWinMtherr.c` `tclWinNotify.c` `tclWinSerial.c`
`tclWinSock.c` `tclWinThrd.c` `tclWinTime.c` `tclMacAlloc.c`
`tclMacAppInit.c` `tclMacBOAAppInit.c` `tclMacDNR.c` `tclMacEnv.c`
`tclMacExit.c` `tclMacInterrupt.c` `tclMacNotify.c` `tclMacOSA.c`
`tclMacPanic.c` `tclMacSock.c` `tclMacTest.c` `tclMacThrd.c`
`tclMacTime.c` `tclMacUtil.c` `man2tcl.c` `pkge.c` `pkgf.c`

---

# 14.4 Sybtcl and Oratcl

| | |
|---|---|
| Language | C |
| Primary Site | Oratcl *http://sourceforge.net/projects/oratcl/* |
| | Sybtcl *http://sourceforge.net/projects/sybtcl/* |
| Original Author | Tom Pointdexter |
| Contact | OraTcl: *tmh@purdue.edu*, Todd Helfter |
| | SybTcl: *dhagberg@millibits.com*, D. J. Hagberg |
| Tcl Revision Supported | Tcl: 7.3-8.4 and newer; Tk: 3.6-8.4 and newer |
| Supported Platforms | UNIX, MS Windows |
| Other Book References | *Tcl/Tk Tools* |

Sybtcl and Oratcl are Tcl interfaces to the Sybase and Oracle database libraries. These packages allow you to use Tcl to write programs that interact with a database server. In general, these two packages follow the same style of interaction with the Tcl interpreter and the database libraries. This consistency makes it easy to convert an application from one brand of database server to another.

The Oratcl extension was reworked extensively between revisions 3 and 4. Oratcl 4.0 has asynchronous processing as well as being thread safe and slave interp safe. The following describes both the older version of Oratcl and the 4.0 and newer interface.

The packages maintain the flavor of the C library for their respective servers. Hence, there are some optimized database access techniques that are available in one extension that are not available in the other. Both of the packages support the following primitive functions.

| Function | Sybase | Oracle |
|---|---|---|
| Connect to server | sybconnect *id password* | oraconnect *id/password@server* |
| Send SQL to server | sybsql *$handle $sqlString* | orasql *$cursor \$sqlString* |
| Fetch rows | sybnext *$handle* | orafetch *$cursor* |
| Close connection | sybclose *$handle* | oralogoff *$logon_connection* |

Both packages support returning status and other information from the database server to the Tcl script.

| Information Variables | Sybase | Oracle | Oracle 4.0 |
|---|---|---|---|
| Status number | $sybmsg(dberr) | $oramsg(rc) | [oramsg $cursor rc] |
| Status message | $sybmsg(errortxt) | $oramsg(errortxt) | [oramsg $cursor error] |

The following example scripts show how simple Sybtcl and Oratcl scripts can connect to a book database with rows for titles and authors.

**Example** 14.8

**Database Content**

| Title | Author |
|---|---|
| *The Three Musketeers* | Alexandre Dumas |
| *Great Expectations* | Charles Dickens |
| *Tcl/Tk: A Developer's Guide* | Clif Flynt |

```
# Sybtcl Script
set handle [sybconnect $id $password]
sybsql $handle "select * from titles"
set row [sybnext $handle]
while {$sybnext(nextrow) == "REG_ROW"} {
  puts "column 1 = [lindex $row 0]"
  puts "column 2 = [lindex $row 1]"
  set row [sybnext $handle]
}
```

```
# Oratcl 3.X Script
set lda [oralogon $id/$pass@server]
set cursor [oraopen $lda]
orasql $cursor "select * from titles"
while {[set row [orafetch $cursor]] != " "} {
  puts "column 1 = [lindex $row 0]"
  puts "column 2 = [lindex $row 1]"
}
oraclose $cursor
oralogoff $lda

# Oratcl 4.0 Script
set lda [oralogon $id/$pass@$server]
set cursor [oraopen $lda]
oraparse $cursor {select * from titles}
oraexec $cursor
while {[orafetch $cursor -datavariable row] == 0} {
    puts "column 1 = [lindex $row 0]"
    puts "column 2 = [lindex $row 1]"
}
oraclose $cursor
oralogoff $lda
```

***Script Output***

```
column 1 = The Three Musketeers
column 2 = Alexandre Dumas
column 1 = Great Expectations
column 2 = Charles Dickens
column 1 = Tcl/Tk: A Developer's Guide
column 2 = Clif Flynt
```

# 14.5 mysqltcl

| | |
|---|---|
| Language | C |
| Primary Site | *www.xdobry.de/mysqltcl/* |
| Contact | *mail@xdobry.de*, Artur Trzewik |
| Tcl Revision Supported | Tcl: 8.0-8.4 and newer; Tk: 8.0-8.4 and newer |
| Supported Platforms | *UNIX, MS Windows* |

The mysqltcl package allows Tcl scripts to interact with the MySql database
server, popular on many small UNIX and Windows systems. The mysqltcl

package uses a different paradigm from other database packages. Rather than creating a new Tcl command for each database connection, this package returns a handle for each open connection, similar to the behavior of the Tcl channel commands.

Another difference between mysqltcl and the Oratcl, Sybtcl, and some other DB extensions is that mysqltcl will generate a Tcl error when an exception is thrown by the database engine. The other extensions generate Tcl errors when errors occur in the Tcl interpreter, but the script must examine the status returns to confirm that there were no database engine exceptions. This package includes many commands for getting status and information and stepping through the data. The essential commands for mysqltcl are as follows.

**Syntax:** mysqlconnect *?options?*

Connect to a mysql database server. By default, on the current machine, as the current user.

*options*    Options to control which server, database, and so on to use. There are several options, including

-host *hostname*    The host to attach to. By default, the local host is used.

-db *dbName*    The database to connect to. There is no default. If this option is not used, the database must be connected to using the mysqluse command.

-user *userName*    The name of the user to connect as.

-password *password*    The password to use for this user.

**Syntax:** mysqlsel *handle command ?option?*

Execute an SQL command that may return rows of data.

*handle*    The handle returned by the mysqlconnect command.

*command*    An SQL command.

*option*    An option to control how the data is returned. By default, this command returns the number of rows that match the command, and the script should step through the rows using mysqlnext. If the command is not a SELECT command, the returned value will always be −1. The options for this command are

-list    Return each row as a list, with each field being a list element within the row.

-flatlist    Returns the data as a list of fields. There will be NumRows * NumFields elements in the list.

*Syntax:* `mysqlexec` *handle command*

Execute an SQL command that does not select rows. The `mysqlsel` command can be used with commands that do not select any data. Returns the number of rows affected (for DELETE or UPDATE commands), or returns 0 for commands that do not affect rows of data (TABLE CREATE, and so on).

*handle*    The handle returned by the `mysqlconnect` command.

*command*    An SQL command.

The following example shows how to connect to a MySql server, create a couple of tables, insert data, select lines, and generate a simple report.

## Example 14.9

*Script Example*

```
load /usr/local/lib/libmysqltcl.so

# Connect to database
set handle [mysqlconnect -db clif1]

# Create two new tables

set createCmds {
  {CREATE TABLE books (
    first CHAR(20), last CHAR(20), title CHAR(50),
    publisher INTEGER, ID INTEGER);}
  {CREATE TABLE publishers (
    name CHAR(50), id INTEGER);}
}

foreach createCmd $createCmds {
  set result [mysqlexec $handle $createCmd]
  puts "Create Table result: $result"
}

# Define data for tables

set bookData {
  {'Brent', 'Welch', \
    'Practical Programming in Tcl/Tk', 2, 1}
  {'Dave', 'Zeltserman', \
    'Building Network Management Tools with Tcl/Tk', 2, 2}
  {'Mike', 'Doyle', \
    'Interactive Web Applications with Tcl/Tk', 1, 3}
  {'Clif', 'Flynt', \
```

```
      'Tcl/Tk: A Developer\'s Guide', 1, 4}
}

set publisherData {
  {'Morgan Kaufmann', 1}
  {'Prentice Hall', 2}
}

# Insert data into the tables.

foreach book $bookData {
  set result [mysqlexec $handle "INSERT INTO books VALUES ($book)"]
  puts "Insert result: $result"
}

foreach pub $publisherData {
  mysqlexec $handle "INSERT INTO publishers VALUES ($pub)"
}

# And now extract data and generate a simple report.

set fail [catch \
    {mysqlsel $handle "SELECT * FROM books" -list } bookList]

if {$fail} {
    error "SQL error number $mysqlstatus(code) message: $bookList" ""
}

foreach book $bookList {
    foreach {first last title pubId id} $book {}
    foreach {pubName pubID} [mysqlsel $handle \
      "Select * from publishers where ID=$pubId" -flatlist] {}
    puts [format "%-12s %-30s \n    %-30s" \
      $last $title $pubName]
    }
```

*Script Output*

```
Create Table result: 0
Create Table result: 0
Insert result: 1
Insert result: 1
Insert result: 1
Insert result: 1
Welch        Practical Programming in Tcl/Tk
             Prentice Hall
Zeltserman   Building Network Management Tools with Tcl/Tk
             Prentice Hall
Doyle        Interactive Web Applications with Tcl/Tk
```

Flynt

**Academic Press Professional**
**Tcl/Tk, A Developer's Guide**
**Morgan Kaufmann**

## 14.6 VSdb Package

| | |
|---|---|
| Language | Tcl |
| Primary Site | *http://sourceforge.net/projects/tclvs/* |
| Original Author | Steve Wahle |
| Contact | *creat@lowcountry.com*, Scott Beasley |
| Tcl Revision Supported | Tcl: 8.x; Tk: 8.x |
| Supported Platforms | UNIX, Windows |

The VSdb package is a small, pure Tcl database package that can easily be merged into an application that needs to be portable. It has support for multiple databases and tables, and can perform simple text searches. It is useful for projects that need a more complex database tool than a simple text file, but you do not want to require that MySQL, Access, or Oracle be available.

The model is a set of rows and named columns. You can select rows by index number (starting from 1) or perform a text search to retrieve a set of index numbers. When you retrieve a row, all fields will be retrieved. Data is read from, and written to, the databases by placing the values in appropriately named associative array indices. The VSdb package is documented with README files and short examples. A few of the commands are described in the following.

*Syntax:* dbCreate *path handleName tableName fieldList*

Create a new empty database table.

*path* The directory path to the database files. May be "." for current directory.

*handleName* The name for the associative array that will be associated with this table. This array name can be treated as a handle that will be passed to all other VSdb procedures. This variable should be in the global scope or a namespace in order to be persistent.

*tableName* The name for this database table. This name will be used to access data in this table.

*fieldList* A list of the fields to define for this table. The order is unimportant, since the data will be saved and retrieved in an associative array.

### Example 14.10

```
# Create a DB named contacts with fields for name and phone
dbCreate /home/bases dbArray contacts {Name Phone}
```

---

**Syntax:** dbOpen *path handleName*

Open an existing database.

*path*      The directory path to the database files. May be "." for current directory.

*handleName*  The name for the associative array that will be associated with this table. This array name can be treated as a handle that will be passed to all other VSdb procedures. This variable should be in the global scope or a namespace in order to be persistent.

### Example 14.11

```
# Open the previously created database
dbOpen /home/bases dbArray
```

---

**Syntax:** dbNewRow *handleName tableName*

Create a new row to receive data.

*handleName*  The name for the associative array that will be associated with this table. This array name can be treated as a handle that will be passed to all other VSdb procedures. This variable should be in the global scope or a namespace in order to be persistent.

*tableName*  The name for this database table. This name will be used to access data in this table.

### Example 14.12

```
# New row:
dbNewRow dbArray contacts
```

---

**Syntax:** dbPutRow *handleName tableName*

Write a row to the database. Similar to a commit in other database systems.

*handleName*  The name for the associative array that will be associated with this table. This array name can be treated as a handle that will be passed to all other VSdb procedures. This variable should be in the global scope or a namespace in order to be persistent.

*tableName* The name for this database table. This name will be used to access data in this table.

## Example 14.13

```
# Create a New row:
dbNewRow dbArray contacts

# Set the field values
set dbArray(contacts,Name) "Clif Flynt"
set dbArray(contacts,Phone) "123-456-789"

# Commit the data
dbPutRow dbArray contacts
```

---

***Syntax:*** dbGetRow *handleName tableName rowIndex*

Retrieve a row from the database.

*handleName* The name for the associative array that will be associated with this table. This array name can be treated as a handle that will be passed to all other VSdb procedures. This variable should be in the global scope or a namespace in order to be persistent.

*tableName* The name for this database table. This name will be used to access data in this table.

*rowIndex* The index number for this row.

## Example 14.14

```
dbGetRow dbArray contacts 1

puts "$dbArray(contacts,Name) - $dbArray(contacts,Phone)"
```

---

***Syntax:*** dbuSearchString *handleName tableName fieldName string args*

Returns a list of row indices that match the search constraints.

*handleName* The name for the associative array that will be associated with this table. This array name can be treated as a handle that will be passed to all other VSdb procedures. This variable should be in the global scope or a namespace in order to be persistent.

| | |
|---|---|
| *tableName* | The name for this database table. This name will be used to access data in this table. |
| *fieldName* | The name of the field to search for the string, as defined with the `dbCreate` command. |
| *string* | A string to search for in the named field. This may be an exact string or a `glob` pattern. |
| *args* | Two flags to define whether the match is to be exact or use `glob` rules, and if the match should be case free or use case. The values are |

| | |
|---|---|
| CASE | Use case in comparison. |
| NOCASE | Use a case-free comparison. |
| EXACT | Accept only an exact match. |
| LIKE | Use `glob` rules for matching. |

### VSdb Example

**Example** 14.15

***Script Example***

```
lappend auto_path /usr/local/lib

package require TclVSdb
namespace import TclVSdb::*

# Connect to the dB.

if {![file exists "synopsis.idx"]} {
  dbCreate . dbhnd synopsis {Title Descr Text}
} else {
  dbOpen . dbhnd
}

# Add new data to the database.

proc addRow {title descr text} {
  global dbhnd

  # Create a new row

  dbNewRow dbhnd synopsis

  # Set the data variables in this connection's array

  foreach index {Title Descr Text} \
        var {title descr text} {
    set dbhnd(synopsis,$index) [set $var]
  }
```

```
     # Put this data into the new row.

        dbPutRow dbhnd synopsis

}

# Retrieve a row by index number and convert the data to a list

proc getRow {num} {
  global dbhnd

  dbGetRow dbhnd synopsis $num
  foreach index {Title Descr Text} {
    lappend values $dbhnd(synopsis,$index)
  }
  return $values
}

# Add two rows of data
addRow {Chapter 1: Why Tcl/Tk} \
  {Introduces the Tcl/Tk to the new reader} \
  {Your first question is likely to be \
  "What features does Tcl/Tk offer me that other \
  languages don't?" This chapter will give you an \
  overview of the Tcl/Tk features...}

addRow {Chapter 2: Mechanics of Using the Tcl and Tk Interpreters} \
  {Describes how to use the Tcl and Wish interpreters} \
  {The first step in learning a new computer language is \
  learning to run the interpreter/compiler...}

# Search for a row and display some info from it.

set i [dbuSearchString dbhnd synopsis Title \
    "* Mechanics *" LIKE CASE]

set lst [getRow $i]

puts "The mechanics of using the Tcl interpreter \
    are described in"
puts "[lindex $lst 0]"
puts "This chapter [lindex $lst 1]"
```

***Script Output***

**The mechanics of using the Tcl interpreter are described in**
**Chapter 2: Mechanics of Using the Tcl and Tk Interpreters**
**This chapter Describes how to use the Tcl and Wish interpreters**

## 14.7 BWidgets

| | |
|---|---|
| Language | Tcl |
| Primary Site | *http://sourceforge.net/projects/tcllib/* |
| Tcl Revision Supported | Tcl: 8.0-8.4 and newer; Tk: 8.0-8.4 and newer |
| Supported Platforms | UNIX, MS Windows, Macintosh |

Chapter 12 described how to create complex megawidgets from the simple Tk widgets. The BWidgets package provides many of the commonly used megawidgets (such as tab notebooks and a tree display widget) and versions of standard Tk widgets with expanded features, including buttons and labels with pop-up help, resizeable frames, and more. The BWidgets package includes extensive documentation as HTML files. The following examples demonstrate using a few of the widgets and commands.

A tabbed notebook has become a standard widget for GUI programs. It provides a good way to present different sets of related information to a user. The BWidgets package includes a NoteBook widget that can be configured to appear as you wish for your application.

***Syntax:*** NoteBook *widgetName ?option value?...*

Create a tabbed notebook widget.

*widgetName*   The name for this widget, following normal Tk window naming rules.

*option value*   A set of options and values to fine-tune the widget. The options include

-font *fontDesc*   The font to use for the notebook tabs.

-height *height*   The height of the tab notebook.

-width *width*   The width of the tab notebook.

-arcradius *number*   Describes how round the corners of the tabs should be.

A NoteBook widget supports many subcommands to manipulate it, including the following.

***Syntax:*** *notebookName* insert *index id ?option value?*

Insert a new tab page into the notebook. This command returns a frame to hold the content for the new page.

*notebookName*   The name of a previously created tab NoteBook widget.

*index*   The location of the new tab. May be an integer or end.

*id*   An identifier for this page.

option value    A set of options and values to fine-tune the widget. The
                options include

-text *text*          The text to display in the tab.

-createcmd *script*   A script to evaluate the first time
                      the tab is raised.

-raisecmd *script*    A script to evaluate each time the
                      tab is raised.

**Syntax:** *notebookName* raise *id*

Raise a notebook page to the top.

*notebookName*  The name of a previously created tab NoteBook widget.

*id*            An identifier for this page.

## Example 14.16

### Script Example

```
set nb [NoteBook .nb -height 100 -width 250]
grid $nb
set p1 [$nb insert end page1 -text "Page 1"]
set p2 [$nb insert end page2 -text "Page 2"]

label $p1.1 -text "Page 1 label" -relief raised
pack $p1.1

$nb raise page1
```

### Script Output

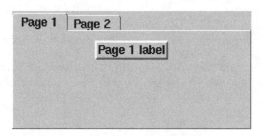

In any form-type application, you end up with many sets of labels and associated
entry widgets. The LabelEntry widget provides a simple way of creating label and
entry pairs with automatic help displays.

**Syntax:** LabelEntry *widgetName* *option value*

Create a label and entry pair.

*option value*    A set of options and values to fine-tune the widget. The options supported by the Tk `label` and `entry` widgets are supported, as well as the following.

| | |
|---|---|
| `-label` *text* | The text to display in the label portion of this widget. |
| `-helptext` *text* | Text to display when the cursor rests on the label for a period of time. |
| `-font` *fontDesc* | Defines the font for the entry portion of this widget. This may be different from the font used by the `label` widget. |
| `-labelfont` *fontDesc* | Defines the font for the label portion of this widget. This may be different from the font used by the `entry` widget. |

### Example 14.17

*Script Example*

```
LabelEntry .le -font {arial 16} \
    -labelfont {Times 18} \
    -label "Name: " \
    -helptext "What is your name?"
grid .le
```

*Script Output*

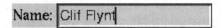

Another common need is a window with a scrollbar. The Bwidget `ScrolledWindow` widget provides a window in which the scrollbar appears when the data exceeds the display area, and vanishes if there is no need for a scrollbar.

*Syntax:*   `ScrolledWindow` *widgetName ?option value?*

Create a window that will hold a scrollable widget (`canvas`, `text`, or `listbox` widget) and display scrollbars when needed.

*widgetName*    The name for this widget, following normal Tk window naming rules.

*option value*   A set of options and values to fine-tune the widget. The options include

         `-auto` *type*   Specifies when to draw scrollbars. The *type* field may be

| | |
|---|---|
| none | Always draw scrollbars. |
| horizontal | Horizontal scrollbar is drawn as needed. |
| vertical | Vertical scrollbar is drawn as needed. |
| both | Both scrollbars are drawn as needed. This is the default. |

The setwidget subcommand will assign a widget to be the scrolled widget in a ScrolledWindow megawidget.

**Syntax:** *widgetName* setwidget *subWindowName*

Assign *subWindowName* as the scrolled window in the *widgetName* ScrolledWindow widget.

*widgetName*  The name for the ScrolledWindow widget, following normal Tk window naming rules.

*subWindowName*  The name for the window to be scrolled. This window must be a child of *widgetName*.

## Example 14.18

### Script Example

```
# Create the ScrolledWindow and grid it
set sw [ScrolledWindow .sw]
grid .sw -sticky news

# Create a child to be held in the window
canvas $sw.cvs -height 60 -width 80 -background white

# Map the child into the ScrolledWindow
$sw setwidget $sw.cvs

# Put some graphics into the canvas
$sw.cvs create rectangle 3 3 40 40 -fill black
$sw.cvs create oval 40 40 80 80 -fill gray50

# Define the scrollregion to cover everything drawn.
$sw.cvs configure -scrollregion [$sw.cvs bbox all]
```

### Script Output

Using the BLT widgets, a GUI for the previous VSdb example could resemble that shown in the following example.

**Example** 14.19

*Script Example*

```
lappend auto_path /usr/local/ActiveTcl/lib
package require BWidget 1.6

###########################################################
# proc updateScan {rowNum}--
#    Updates the scan window
# Arguments
#    rowNum: The number of this row of data to display.
#
# Results
#    Modifies global variables, clears the $textScan text
#    widget and updates the widget with new text.

proc updateScan {rowNum} {
  global values textScan

  # Get a list of the contents in this row of data
  set l [getRow $rowNum]

  # Assign the first two fields to the appropriate
  # array index.
  set values(Title) [lindex $l 0]
  set values(Desc) [lindex $l 1]

  # Clear the text widget and display this paragraph
  $textScan delete 0.0 end
  $textScan insert end [lindex $l 2]
}

# source the vsdb Demo to load the addRow and getRow
#    procedures, and open/populate a sample database.

source vsdbDemo.tcl

# Create a tabbed notebook widget

grid [set nb [NoteBook .nb -height 200 -width 250]]

# Create a page to enter new data into the database.

set page1 [$nb insert end entry -text "Entry"]

# Create and grid a set of LabelEntry widgets for Title
#    and a short description

set row 0
```

```
set w [LabelEntry $page1.l1 -label "Title: " \
  -helptext "Title of this Chapter" \
   -textvariable values(Title)]
grid $w -row [incr row] -column 0 -sticky ew

set w [LabelEntry $page1.l2 -label "Description: " \
  -helptext "Brief Description" \
  -textvariable values(Descr)]
grid $w -row [incr row] -column 0 -sticky ew

# Now, a label over a text widget, and then a text
#   widget to enter the first paragraph.

set w [label $page1.l3 -text "First Paragraph:"]
grid $w -row [incr row] -column 0 -sticky ew

set textEntry [text $page1.txt -height 5 -width 50]
grid $textEntry -row [incr row] -column 0 -sticky ew

# And a button to commit the data

set w [Button $page1.b1 -text Insert \
  -command {addRow $values(Title) $values(Descr) \
    [$textEntry get 0.0 end]}]

grid $w -row [incr row] -column 0 -sticky ew

# Next, a notebook page to scan through the chapters

set page2 [$nb insert end scan -text "Scan"]

set pn [PanedWindow $page2.pn -side right]
set title [$pn add]
set descr [$pn add]
set text [$pn add]
set control [$pn add]

grid $pn

grid [label $title.lbl -textvariable values(Title) \
  -width 50 -relief ridge -border 2]

grid [message $descr.lbl -textvariable values(Desc) \
  -width 300 -relief ridge -border 2]

set sw [ScrolledWindow $text.txt]

set textScan [text $sw.txt -width 50 -height 8 \
  -relief ridge -border 2]
grid $sw
$sw setwidget $textScan

set w [scale $control.sc -from 1 -to 16 -variable rowNum \
  -command {updateScan} -orient horizontal]
```

```
grid $w -row 0 -column 0

$nb compute_size

getRow 1
$nb raise entry
```

***Script Output***

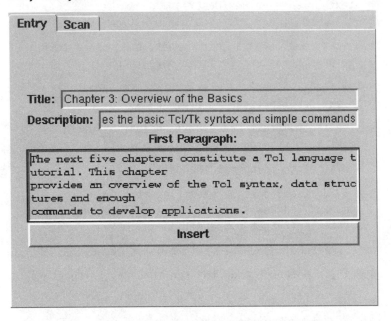

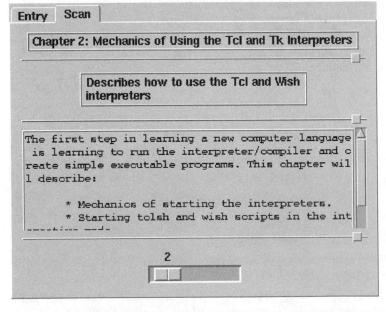

# 14.8 BLT

| | |
|---|---|
| Language | C |
| Primary Site | *http://sourceforge.net/projects/blt/* |
| Contact | *gah@siliconmetrics.com*, George A. Howlett |
| Tcl Revision Supported | Tcl: 7.5-8.4 and newer; Tk: 4.1-8.4 and newer |
| Supported Platforms | UNIX, MS Windows |
| Other Book References | *Tcl/Tk Tools* |

BLT adds several useful new graphical features to Tk, including the following:

- Commands to draw graphs and bar charts
- Commands to manipulate vectors of numeric data
- Commands to manage widget layout in a tabular fashion
- Commands to better integrate with the X server
- Commands to manipulate bitmaps
- Drag-and-drop support

The BLT extension introduced a tabular layout manager named `table` to Tk. The `table` commands were modified and merged into the core Tk interpreter as the `grid` layout manager in version 4.1.

The BLT graphing commands let you easily construct and customize graphs and bar charts. The vector support is integrated with graph and bar chart support to improve the graphing performance. If you have spent any time converting data from a report into a format for other graphing programs, you will enjoy having a full interpreter available to process your input. This makes data presentation tasks much simpler.

BLT widgets follow the same conventions as the primitive Tk widgets. When a new graph or bar-chart widget is created, a new command is created to interact with that widget.

***Syntax:*** `barchart` *widgetName ?options?*

***Syntax:*** `graph` *widgetName ?options?*

| | |
|---|---|
| `barchart` | Create a bar-chart widget. |
| `graph` | Create a graph widget. |
| *widgetName* | A name for this widget. This name should follow the standard Tk naming convention. |
| *options* | The widget appearance can be configured with the usual `-height` and `-width` options, as well as widget-specific options such as |
| | `-title` *text*   A title for the graph. |

-plotbackground *color*    The color of the graph background.

-invertxy                 Invert the X and Y axes.

The data to be displayed on a graph is grouped in graph elements. A graph element describes the data to be plotted on an axis, the appearance of the plot, and information for the graph legend. A graph element's data may be defined as a single point of data, a list, or as a BLT vector. If the data are defined using a vector, the graph will automatically update when vector content is modified.

***Syntax:*** *widgetName* create element *elementName ?options?*

| | |
|---|---|
| *widgetName* | The name of a BLT widget (graph or barchart). |
| create element | Create a graph element that will contain data to be graphed. |
| *elementName* | An identifying string for this element. This is a descriptive name. It need not follow Tk naming conventions. |
| *options* | The options for the element creation command include |

-xdata *?value?*
> Defines the data to plot along the X axis. The argument for this option may be a single value, a Tcl list of numbers, or the name of a previously defined BLT vector.

-ydata *?value?*
> Defines the data to plot along the Y axis. The argument for this option may be a single value, a Tcl list of numbers, or the name of a previously defined BLT vector.

-background *color*
> The background color for the plotted data points.

-foreground *color*
> The foreground color for the plotted data points.

-label *text*
> The label to use to describe this data in the graph legend.

The next example generates a bar chart of the page hits reported by the Apache hypertext transfer protocol (HTTP) server. It creates BLT vectors as new pages appear in the data. As you can see, most of the code deals with extracting the information to be graphed from the report. Having the data extraction and graphing tool in a single package makes generating plots like this easier than reformatting the data with one program and visualizing it with another.

## Example 14.20

*Script Example*

```
#!/usr/local/bin/wish

lappend auto_path /usr/lib

# The BLT commands are maintained in the ::blt
# namespace.
package require BLT
namespace import blt::*

# create a barchart, titled "Downloads"
#  display bars for a given day side by side
# Display the graph widget.

barchart .html -title Downloads -width 600 -height 300 \
   -barmode aligned
pack .html

# Place the legend on the top.

.html legend configure -position top

# Define a list of colors used to select contrasting colors
# for the bars

set colors [list black red green yellow orange blue purple]

# Make the vectors 32 days long because vectors count from 0
# while days of the months count from 1.

set days 32
# Vector x will be the x axis variable.

vector x($days)

# Read in lines of data from stdin.
# Each line is a logfile entry.

while {![eof stdin]} {
   # Data is read in from stdin.
   # Read lines, and skip any short ones immediately.

   set len [gets stdin line]
   if {$len > 4} {

   # A log entry resembles this:
   # tarantula.av.pa-x.dec.com - - [01/Jan/1998:04:18:19 \
```

```
# -0500] www.msen.com "GET /~clif/TclTutor.html HTTP/1.0"
# 304 - "-" "Web21 CustomCrawl bert@web21.com"

# Parse out the IP address date, page and status with
# a regular expression

regexp {([^ ]+).*\[([^:]*).*"(GET|HEAD) ([^ ]*).*" ([0-9]*) }\
  $line all ip date action page stat

if {$stat != 200} {continue}

    # The date format is: [31/Jan/1998:15:07:47 -0500]
    # The regexp reduces this to 31/Jan/1998
    # Extract the day by converting to a list, and using
    #    lindex to grab the first element

    set day [string trimleft [lindex [split $date /] 0] 0]

    set x($day) $day

    set name [file tail $page]
    regsub -all -- {[\."-:\?~]} $name "_" id

    # If we've already seen this page, increment the days
    # page count. This is done with "expr" instead of
    # "incr" because the vectors store their data as
    # floating-point numbers, and incr will only deal with
    # integers.

    if {[info exists $id]} {
      set ${id}($day) [expr $${id}($day) +1]
    } else {
      # This is a new page.
      # Create a new vector for this page, and assign
      #  the hit count to 1

      vector ${id}($days)
      set ${id}($day) 1

      # Select the next color from the list, and
      #  rotate the list

      set c [lindex $colors 0]
      set colors "[lrange $colors 1 end] $c"

      # Create a new element in this barchart.
      # The x position will be the x vector.
      # The height of the bars (ydata) is the newly
      #    created vector.
      # The color is set to the new contrasting color
      # The label for the legend is the page name.
```

```
        .html element create $id -xdata x -ydata $id \
          -background $c -foreground $c -label $name
      }
    }
  }

# The bars are centered around their X value,
# The min X must be one lower than the actual
# Minimum X value to show these.

set min [lindex [array names x] 0]

foreach v [array names x] {
  if {$v < $min} {set min $v}
}

incr min -1

# Configure the min X and Y values for the charts

.html axis configure x -min $min
.html axis configure y -logscale 0 -min 0
```

***Script Output***

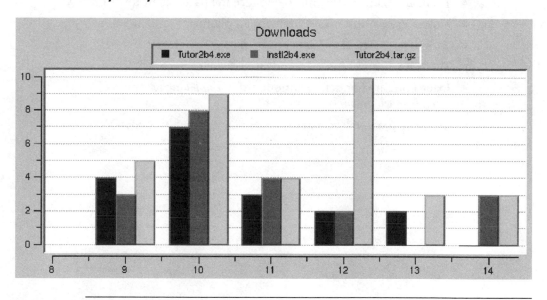

# 14.9 Graphics Extensions: img

| | |
|---|---|
| Language | C |
| Primary Site | *http://sourceforge.net/projects/tkimg/* |

| | |
|---|---|
| Contact | *Jan.Nijtmans@wxs.nl*, Jan Nijtmans |
| Tcl Revision Supported | Tcl: 7.6p2-8.4 and newer; Tk: 4.2p2-8.4 and newer |
| Supported Platforms | UNIX, MS Windows |

The Img extension adds support for BMP, XBM, XPM, GIF (with transparency), PNG, JPEG, TIFF, and PostScript images to the Tk image object (described in Chapter 10). You must have the *libtiff*, *libpng*, and *libjpg* libraries available on your system to read TIFF, PNG, or JPEG image files. These libraries are all public domain and easily acquired from the SourceForge tkimg site or from these sites:

- TIFF library code: *ftp://ftp.sgi.com/graphics/tiff/*
- PNG library code: *ftp://ftp.uu.net/graphics/png*
- JPEG library code: *ftp://ftp.uu.net/graphics/jpeg*

## 14.10 Bottom Line

- There are many extensions to enhance the base Tcl/Tk functionality.
- Not all extensions are available for all platforms and all Tcl revisions.
- Tcl extensions tend to lag behind the core Tcl releases.
- The primary archive for Tcl code is *www.sourceforge.net*.
- Extensions are frequently announced in *comp.lang.tcl* or *comp.lang.tcl.announce*.
- Many frequently used extensions are mentioned in the FAQ.

# CHAPTER

## 15

# Programming Tools

One of the tricks to getting your job done efficiently is having the right tools for the job. There are plenty of tools available for developing Tcl applications.

This chapter provides a quick description of several program development tools that are in use in the Tcl community. It is not a complete listing of tools. If the tool you need is not mentioned here, try checking the Tcl Resource Center at *www.tcl.tk/resource/*, the announcements in `comp.lang.tcl`, the FAQs at *www.purl.org/NET/Tcl-FAQ*, or the Tcl'ers Wiki (*http://mini.net/tcl/*).

Development tools for Tcl are rapidly changing and improving. This chapter discusses the versions of the tools that were available in August 2002. New versions of many of these packages will be available before the book and companion CD-ROM are published.

The Open Source community is generating new ideas and packages, and commercial developers such as ICEM, ActiveState, Neatware, and others have released full-featured toolkits that are constantly being improved. These options provide the Tcl developer with tools that can be configured to your needs and high-quality, commercially supported tools.

The ICEM (*www.icemcfd.com*) Tcl Compiler supports multiple back ends, allowing it to generate machine-independent Tcl object code, Java code, or C code. This product was originally a commercial product and has been re-released as freeware on selected platforms.

The TclPro development suite is a full development package, including a GUI-based debugger, a static code checker, a wrapper tool for creating self-extracting Tcl applications, and a byte-code compiler that will produce machine-independent Tcl object code. Originally developed by Scriptics Corporation as a commercial product, this package has been released to open source and is maintained on SourceForge (*http://sourceforge.net/projects/tclpro/*).

Neatware (*www.neatware.com/*) and ActiveState (*www.activestate.com*) have each taken portions of the TclPro suite and enhanced them for new commercial products. Neatware has developed a Tcl-oriented IDE that includes a context-sensitive editor, debugger, code checker, byte-code compiler, and more. Active-State has enhanced the TclPro suite of tools and renamed it Tcl Dev Kit. The Tcl Dev kit extends the TclPro suite by

- providing support for

| | | | |
|---|---|---|---|
| Tcl 8.3 and 8.4 | TkTable 2.8 | BWidgets 1.4.1 | Tk 8.3 and 8.4 |
| Tcllib 1.3 | TclXML 2.0 | TclX c8.3 | TclDOM 2.0 |
| TclSOAP 1.6.5 | [incr Tcl] 3.2 | [iner Tk] 3.2 | Img 1.2.4 |
| IWidgets 4.0.0 | Snack 2.1.6 | TkHTML 2.0 | TkCon 2.3 |
| Tcom 3.7 (Windows only) | Expect 5.38 (UNIX only) | | |

- adding GUI front ends to the TclPro compiler and wrapper
- providing code coverage and hot spot profiling support in the debugger
- providing binaries for Linux, HP-UX, Solaris, and MS Windows

The Tcl Dev kit is designed to work with the Komodo Integrated Development Environment. Komodo includes a context-sensitive editor that supports Tcl, Perl, Python, Ruby, C, C++, HTML, and many other languages; real-time syntax checking; a debugger; and support for large projects. This chapter briefly covers the following.

### Code Formatters

| | |
|---|---|
| frink | Reformats code into a standard style for easy comprehension. |

### Code Checkers

| | |
|---|---|
| tclCheck | Checks for balanced brackets, braces, and parentheses. |
| ice_lint | Checks for syntax errors, unset or nonexistent variables, incorrect procedure calls, and more. |
| procheck | Part of the TclPro suite. Checks for syntax errors, unset or nonexistent variables, incorrect procedure calls, and more. |

### Debuggers

| | |
|---|---|
| Don Libes's Debugger | This is a text-oriented package with support for setting breakpoints, examining data, and so on. |
| tuba | A GUI-based package with multiple windows for both Tcl and Tk. |
| prodebug | Part of the TclPro suite. A GUI-based debugger with multiple windows that can debug remote or embedded applications, as well as those on the local host. |

### *GUI Generators*

| | |
|---|---|
| SpecTcl | SpecTcl creates a GUI skeleton for a Tk program. |
| Visual GIPSY | Visual GIPSY generates a GUI skeleton and templates for creating reusable objects. |

### *Tcl Compilers*

| | |
|---|---|
| ICEM Tcl Compiler | The ICEM Tcl compiler translates Tcl code into C code to improve performance. |
| procomp | Part of the TclPro suite. TclPro Compiler converts Tcl scripts into Tcl byte-code files. |

### *Packaging Tools*

| | |
|---|---|
| prowrap | Part of the TclPro suite. This wrapper works with [incr Tcl] as well as other extensions. |
| freewrap | Wraps a tclsh or wish interpreter with your application for distribution. |
| Starkit | Starkit wraps the entire Tcl/Tk distribution into a single file with hooks to evaluate scripted documents. This provides a middle ground between a fully wrapped and fully scripted package. |

### *Tcl Extension Generators*

| | |
|---|---|
| SWIG | SWIG creates Tcl extensions from libraries of C functions by reading the function and data definitions from an include file. |
| CriTcl | CriTcl generates a loadable Tcl extension from C code embedded into a Tcl script. |

### *Integrated Development Environments*

| | |
|---|---|
| ASED | ASED is a pure Tcl IDE that runs on many platforms. |
| Komodo | The Komodo IDE supports Tcl and other languages on UNIX and Windows platforms. |
| MyrmecoX | The MyrmecoX IDE is optimized for the Windows platform and supports several packages. |

## 15.1 Code Formatter

Despite our best efforts, after several hours of refining our understanding of the problem (i.e., hacking code), we usually end up with badly formatted code. Incorrectly formatted code makes the logic difficult to follow and hides logical or syntax errors caused by misplaced braces. Reformatting the code can frequently help you find those errors.

## 15.1.1 `frink`

The `frink` program will reformat a Tcl script to make it more comprehensible and can also check syntax.

| | |
|---|---|
| Language | C |
| Primary Site | *ftp://catless.ncl.ac.uk/pub/frink.tar.gz* |
| Contact | *Lindsay.Marshall@newcastle.ac.uk* |
| Tcl Revision Supported | `Tcl:` 7.3-8.4 and newer; `Tk:` 3.6-8.4 and newer |
| Supported Platforms | UNIX, MS Windows, Mac |

`Frink` will convert your script to a format that closely resembles the recommended style for Tcl scripts described in the *Tcl Style Guide*. As added benefits, `frink` will check the script for syntactic errors while it is reformatting the scripts, and the reformatted script will run faster. `Frink` supports several command line options to define how the code will be formatted.

| | |
|---|---|
| `-a` | Add spaces after { } and "" when processing `-command` (default = OFF). |
| `-A` | Turn OFF special processing of `expr` commands. |
| `-b` | Add braces (see manual page for details) (default = OFF). |
| `-B` | Turn OFF processing code passed to the bind command. |
| `-c <n>` | Set further indent for continuations to `n` (default = 2). |
| `-d` | Remove braces in certain (safe) circumstances (default = OFF). |
| `-e` | Produce "else" (default = OFF). |
| `-E` | Extract constant strings (not implemented yet). |
| `-f` | Rewrite some strings to use `msgcat`. |
| `-F<n>` | Selectively control which heuristics are used. Currently, the parameter is a single hex-coded number, with each bit representing a test. The values you need to know are |

        00001 append parameter testing

        00002 `lappend` parameter testing

        00004 `set` parameter testing

        00008 `regexp` parameter testing

        00010 `return` checks

        00020 check for : or ::: in names

        00040 `expr` checks

        00080 `foreach var` checking

        00100 check missing parameters

        00200 check `-switches` on commands (not tk options)

|          | 00400 check for abbreviations of options |
|----------|-----------|
|          | 00800 check for unused variables |
|          | 01000 check for bad name choice |
|          | 02000 check for array usage |
| -g       | Indent switch cases (default = OFF). |
| -h       | Print information about options. |
| -H       | Turn on heuristic tests and warnings (default = OFF). |
| -i \<n\> | Set indent for each level to n (default = 4). |
| -I       | Treat elseif and else the same way (default = OFF). |
| -j       | Remove nonessential blank lines (default = OFF). |
| -J       | Just do checks, no output (default = OFF). |
| -k       | Remove nonessential braces (default = OFF). |
| -K \<f\> | Specify file of extra code specs. |
| -l       | Try for one-liners. |
| -m       | Minimize the code by removing redundant spacing (default = OFF). |
| -M       | Warn about switch statements with no -- (default = OFF). |
| -n       | Do not generate tab characters (default = OFF). |
| -N       | Do not put a newline out before elseif (default = OFF). |
| -o       | Obfuscate: (default = OFF). |
| -O \<t\> | Don't format lines starting with token "t". |
| -p \<v\> | If v is a number, produce that many blank lines after each proc definition; otherwise, produce whatever format the code indicates. No codes are defined yet..... (default = do nothing). |
| -P       | Turn off processing of "time" command (default = OFF). |
| -q       | Add spaces around the conditions in if and while statements (default = OFF). |
| -r       | Remove comments (default = OFF). |
| -s \<c\> | Format according to style name "c" (no style names defined yet). |
| -S       | Stop preserving end-of-line comments (default = OFF). |
| -t \<n\> | Set tabs every n characters. |
| -T       | Produce "then" (default = OFF). |
| -u       | Safe to remove brackets from around elseif conditions (default = OFF). |
| -U       | Hardline checking enabled. Will be strict about presence of --. Complains about switches with no default. Complains about 1 used without brackets in while/for condition (default = OFF). |

| | |
|---|---|
| -v | Put { } around variable names where appropriate. |
| -V | The current version number. |
| -w \<n> | Set line length (default = 80). |
| -W | Halt on warning. |
| -x | Produce "xf-style" continuations. |
| -X | Recognize tclX features. |
| -y | Don't process -command (default = OFF). |
| -Y | Try to process dynamic code (default = OFF). |
| -z | Put a single space before the\character on continuations. |
| -Z | Control heuristics that are tested. (-H turns on all tests). |

Frink is distributed as source code with a configure file for Posix-style systems. You can compile and link this program under Microsoft Visual C++ with the following procedure.

1. Get a copy of Gnu getopt.c and getopt.h. (I found a good copy in the Gnu C library and as part of the Gnu m4 distribution.)
2. Copy getopt.c and getopt.h to the frink source code directory.
3. Within Visual C++ create a Win32 Console Application ( File > New > Projects).
4. Add the files ( Project > Add To Project > Files).
5. Build all.

The following example shows frink being used to reformat a poorly formatted piece of code.

**Example** 15.1

```
$> cat badfmt.tcl
proc checksum \
  {
    txt
  } \
  {
    set sum 0;    foreach l [split $txt ""] \
    {
        binary scan $l c val
        set sum [expr {($sum >> 1)+($sum^$val)}]
    };    return $sum
}

set data "123456789012345678901234567890123456789 01234567890"
puts [time {checksum $data} 100]
$> frink badfmt.tcl > goodfmt.tcl
```

```
*** badfmt.tcl Warning : variable "val" might be used
    before being set (line 9)
$> cat goodfmt.tcl
proc checksum {txt} {
    set sum 0
    foreach l [split $txt ""] {
        binary scan $l c val
        set sum [expr {($sum≫1) + ($sum^$val)}]
    }
    return $sum
}

set data "12345678901234567890123456789012345678901234567890"
puts [time {checksum $ data} 100]
```

The frink program can also perform syntax checking. You can enable various tests with the -F flag and add more command syntax definitions with the -K flag. The format for a syntax definition is as follows.

**Syntax:** cmdName { *arg1 ...argN* }

    cmdName    The name of the command.

    *arg\**    An argument definition. May be one of

        var    Argument is the name of a variable.

        any    Argument may be any value.

        args    Any number of arguments. This value can only be the last element in the argument list.

The following example shows frink being used to examine a buggy code fragment.

**Example** 15.2

```
$> cat badcode.tcl
# The next line is missing a closing quote
proc foo {a b} {puts "a $b}

# The next line has too few arguments
foo b

$> cat syntaxdef
foo {any any}

$> frink -K /tmp/syntaxdef badcode.tcl

# The next line is missing a closing quote
*** /tmp/error2.tcl Warning : Missing " in proc foo (line 2)
proc foo {a b} {
    puts "a $b"
}
```

```
# The next line has too few arguments
*** /tmp/error2.tcl Warning : Call of foo with
    too few parameters (line 5)
foo b
```

## 15.2 Code Checkers

One drawback of interpreted languages, as opposed to compiled languages, is that a program can run for months without evaluating a line of code that has a syntax error. This situation is most likely to occur in exception-handling code, since that is the code least often exercised. A syntax error in this code can cause your program to do something catastrophic while attempting to recover from a minor problem.

There are several code checkers that will examine your script for syntax errors, and more are being developed. Although none of these is perfect (Tcl has too many ways to confuse such programs), these will catch many bugs before you run your code.

### 15.2.1 `tclCheck`

| | |
|---|---|
| Language | C |
| Primary Site | *http://catless.ncl.ac.uk/Programs/tclCheck/* |
| Contact | *Lindsay.Marshall@newcastle.ac.uk* |
| Tcl Revision Supported | `Tcl: 7.3-8.4` and newer; `Tk: 3.6-8.4` and newer |
| Supported Platforms | UNIX |

This program checks for matching parentheses, braces, and brackets and a few other common programming errors. Most Tcl syntax errors are caused by these easy-to-catch errors (or syntax problems that are identified by `frink`). `TclCheck` and `frink` can save you hours of time you would otherwise spend staring at your code and counting braces.

`TclCheck` supports several command line flags to fine-tune its behavior. These include the following.

-c      By default `tclCheck` attempts to recognize comments so as to permit unmatching brackets in them. This flag turns this behavior off.

-e      This flag enables checking for lines that have a \ followed by spaces or tabs at their end. By default, this test is not carried out.

-g      By default, `tclCheck` pops its stack of brackets to a find a match with } > ] > ). This flag turns this off.

-i      This flag stops the printing of error messages beginning "Inside a string".

-j     Generates a compressed skeleton printout where indentation is ignored when matching brackets (see -1).

-1     Generates a compressed skeleton printout where nested matching lines are paired up and removed. Matching includes any indentation.

-m     Removes from the skeleton printout bracket pairs that match up directly on lines.

-q     Do not generate any output unless exceptions are detected.

-s     Generate a printout of the bracket skeleton of the entire program.

-t     Tiger mode. This will flag any single " that occurs in places where tcl would not detect the start of a string. By default this is turned off, but it can be very useful for tracking down some problems that are difficult to find.

TclCheck is distributed as C source code with a Makefile. Like frink, it will compile under Windows if you get a copy of Gnu getopt.c to link with it.

**Example** 15.3

*Script Example*

```
# The next line is missing a closing quote
proc foo {a b} {puts "a $b}

# The next line has too few arguments
foo b
```

*Script Output*

```
File ../buggy.tcl:
Inside a string: unmatched } on line 3 char 27
" missing, opened on line 3 char 22
} missing, opened on line 3 char 16
```

---

## 15.2.2 ICEM ice_lint

| | |
|---|---|
| Language | executable |
| Primary Site | *http://icemcfd.com/tcl/ice.html* |
| Contact | *tcl@icemcfd.com* |
| Tcl Revision Supported | Tcl: 7.3-8.4 and newer; Tk: 3.6-8.4 and newer |
| Supported Platforms | DEC OSF1 V4.0, HP-UX 9.01, 10.0, IBM AIX 3.2, 4.0, 4.1, Linux (ELF), SGI IRIX 5.X+, Solaris 5.3+, MS Windows |

The ice_lint program is part of the ICEM Tcl compiler package. It can be licensed without charge. The ice_lint program uses the same sophisticated parser as the

The ICEM Tcl compiler and does an excellent job of detecting many different types of errors, including the following:

- Parsing errors
- Unset or nonexistent variables
- Incorrect usage of built-in and user-defined procedures
- Possibly illegal arithmetic statements
- A control command with an empty body
- A nonparsable statement

## Example 15.4

*Script Example*

```
# The next line is missing a closing quote
proc foo {a b} {puts "a $b}

# The next line has too few arguments
foo b
```

*Script Output*

```
ice_lint.2.0.2 bug.tcl
In proc "foo":
--- ERROR ---: missing "
file "bug.tcl" line 2.
At or near: "puts "a $b"
In proc "__temp_tclc_temp_proc_name0":
--- ERROR ---: Illegal # args to proc "foo" = 1.
Usage : "foo arg arg "
file "bug.tcl" line 5.
At or near: "foo b"
Finished with compilation!
```

## 15.2.3 procheck

| | |
|---|---|
| Language | Tcl and C |
| Primary Site | *http://sourceforge.net/projects/tclpro/* |
| Tcl Revision Supported | Tcl: 7.3–8.4 and newer; Tk: 3.6–8.4 and newer |
| Supported Platforms | UNIX, MS Windows, Mac, Mac OS X |

The TclPro procheck program checks for many types of errors, including incorrect argument counts, obsolete paradigms, mismatched braces, quotes, and more. This program is available from SourceForge. Enhanced versions of this program are distributed by ActiveState and Neatware.

**Example** 15.5

*Script Example*

```
# The next line is missing a closing quote
proc foo {a b} {puts "a $b}

# The next line has too few arguments
foo b
```

*Script Output*

```
scanning: /tmp/error2.tcl
checking: /tmp/error2.tcl
/tmp/error2.tcl:2 (parse) parse error: missing "
puts "a $b
     ^
/tmp/error2.tcl:5 (procNumArgs) wrong # args for
    user-defined proc: "foo"
foo b
```

# 15.3 Debuggers

Again, despite our best efforts, we spend a lot of time debugging code. These debuggers range from lightweight, compiled extensions such as Don Libes's debug package to full-featured GUI-based debuggers.

There are many debuggers not covered here, some of which are tailored to work with specific Tcl extensions. If the debuggers described here do not meet your requirements, use the search engine at *http://www.tcl.tk*.

## 15.3.1 debug

| | |
|---|---|
| Language | C |
| Primary Site | *http://expect.nist.gov/* |
| Contact | *libes@nist.gov* |
| Tcl Revision Supported | Tcl: 7.3-8.4 and newer; Tk: 3.6-8.4 and newer |
| Supported Platforms | UNIX |
| Other Book References | *Exploring Expect* |

This text-oriented debugger is distributed by Don Libes as part of the expect extension. Your script can load the expect extension to gain access to this feature without using the rest of the expect commands. The code for the debugger is in the files Dbg.c, Dbg.h, and Dbg_cf.h. With a little tweaking you can merge this debugger into other extensions.

This extension adds a debug command to the Tcl language. The command debug 1 allows you to interact with the debugger; the command debug 0 turns the debugger off. This debugger supports stepping into or over procedures and viewing the stack. This debugger supports setting breakpoints that stop on a given line and breakpoints with a command to evaluate when the breakpoint is hit. The complete Tcl interpreter is available for use while in debugger mode, so you can use normal Tcl commands to view or modify variables, load new procedures, and so on. The on-line help lists the available commands in this debugger.

```
dbg1.1> h

s [#]              step into procedure
n [#]              step over procedure
N [#]              step over procedures, commands, and arguments
c                  continue
r                  continue until return to caller
u [#]              move scope up level
d [#]              move scope down level
                   go to absolute frame if # is prefaced by "#"
w                  show stack ("where")
w -w [#]           show/set width
w -c [0|1]         show/set compress
b                  show breakpoints
b [-r regexp-pattern]   [if expr] [then command]
b [-g glob-pattern]     [if expr] [then command]
b [[file:]#]            [if expr] [then command]
                   if pattern given, break if command resembles pattern
                   if # given, break on line #
                   if expr given, break if expr true
                   if command given, execute command at breakpoint
b -#               delete breakpoint
b -                delete all breakpoints
```

While in debugging mode, the normal prompt resembles Dbg2.3>, where the digit 2 represents the current stack level and the 3 represents the number of interactive commands that have been executed. In the sample debugging session shown next, the optional patterns and if/then statements are used with the break command to display the content of the variable lst when the breakpoint is encountered.

## Example 15.6

### *Script Example*

```
% cat test.tcl
proc addList {lst} {
   set total 0;
   foreach num $lst {
```

```
      set total [expr $total + $num]
    }
    return $total
}
proc mean {lst} {
    set sum [addList $lst]
    set count [llength $lst]
    set mean [expr $sum / $count]
    return $mean
}
set lst [list 2 4 6 8]
puts "Mean $lst : [mean $lst]"
```

***Debugging Session***

```
$> expect
expect1.1> debug 1
0
expect1.2> source /tmp/test.tcl
1: history add {source /tmp/test.tcl
}
dbg1.1> b -g "*set count*" if {[llength $lst] < 10} {
 puts "LIST: $lst"}
0
dbg1.2> c
LIST: 2 4 6 8
3: set count [llength $lst]
dbg3.3> w
 0: expect
*1: mean {2 4 6 8}
 3: set {count} {4}
dbg3.4> n 2
3: set mean [expr $sum / $count]
dbg3.5> w
0: expect
*1: mean {2 4 6 8}
 3: set {mean} {5}
dbg3.6> c
Mean 2 4 6 8 : 5
```

## 15.3.2 Graphic Debuggers

There are several GUI-oriented debuggers available for Tcl, ranging from free packages to the commercial debuggers included with the ActiveState Tcl Dev Kit and Komodo IDE or the Neatware MyrmecoX IDE.

### Tuba

| | |
|---|---|
| Language | Tcl/C++ |
| Download From | *www.go.dlr.de/fresh/unix/src/misc/* |
| Tcl Revision Supported | Tcl: 8.0-8.4 and newer; Tk: 8.0-8.4 and newer |
| Supported Platforms | UNIX, MS Windows |

This package uses multiple windows to display the code being debugged, allow the user to display and modify variable content, step into or through procedures, and set breakpoints by line, procedure, or when a variable is set. The GUI is very friendly and includes balloon pop-ups to describe the tool buttons.

Tuba includes an extended update command and some parsing code to enable it to control the code being debugged. These functions are written in both C++ and Tcl. The Tcl code and the C++ libraries have the same functionality, but the compiled code runs much faster. If you cannot compile the C++ libraries, the Tcl libraries are acceptably fast.

The first image to follow shows the main window and file selection window. The second image shows the source code window with a variable monitor window displayed on top of it.

Main window and file selection box

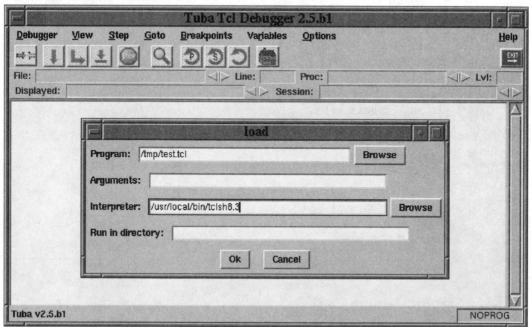

Testing with breakpoint and variable monitor window

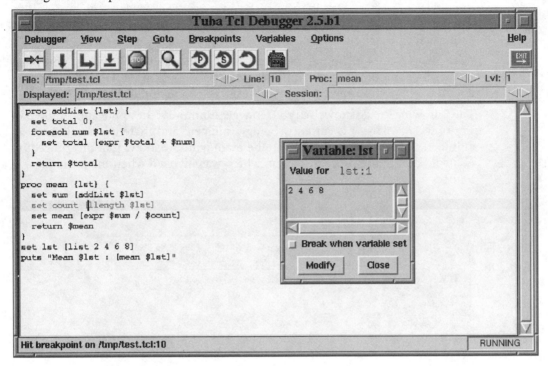

### TclPro prodebug

| | |
|---|---|
| Language | C and Tcl |
| Primary Site | *http://sourceforge.net/projects/tclpro/* |
| Tcl Revision Supported | Tcl: 7.6-8.4 and newer; Tk: 4.2-8.4 and newer |
| Supported Platforms | UNIX, MS Windows, Mac, Mac OS X |

The prodebug program is part of the TclPro development suite. This debugger can be used to debug local, embedded, and remote applications written in either straight Tcl or [incr Tcl]. When a program is loaded into prodebug, it is checked for correctness. If prodebug finds a syntax error, it will display a window with a description of the error and mark the offending line in the main window.

The main window of the TclPro Debugger displays the content of the local variables, the stack, the code being evaluated, and the visible breakpoints. You can open other windows to display all breakpoints, display variables being watched, select procedures to display in the main window, or enter commands that can be evaluated at different procedure scopes in the stack.

The prodebug program supports stepping into, over, or out of Tcl procedures; setting breakpoints on lines of Tcl code; setting variable breakpoints that stop execution when a variable is set; viewing variable data; and viewing the Tcl stack.

When the evaluation is halted at a breakpoint, you can step up and down through the Tcl call stack to examine the program state. The prodebug debugger also displays the "hidden" stack levels such as the uplevel that occurs when the script associated with a button is evaluated.

In order to use the debugger with remote or embedded applications, you must add a small amount of initialization code to your application. Once this is done, a remote application can be debugged just like a local application.

The following image shows TclPro Debugger examining the application shown in Example 15.6. Line 4 is currently being evaluated, and there is a breakpoint set at line 9. The Stack Frame display in the main window shows that this procedure is invoked from the procedure mean, which was invoked when the program was loaded.

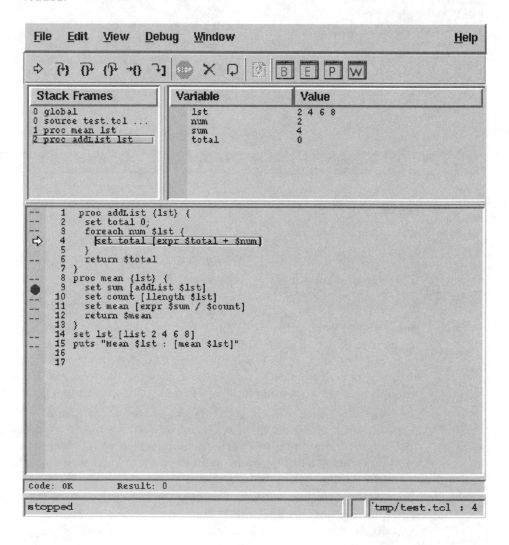

```
proc addList {lst} {
  set total 0;
  foreach num $lst {
    set total [expr $total + $num]
  }
  return $total
}
proc mean {lst} {
  set sum [addList $lst]
  set count [llength $lst]
  set mean [expr $sum / $count]
  return $mean
}
set lst [list 2 4 6 8]
puts "Mean $lst : [mean $lst]"
```

# 15.4 GUI Generators

If you are developing a GUI-intensive application, you can spend a lot of time rearranging the widgets trying to get the appearance you want. Alternatively, you can use one of the GUI generator programs to create a GUI skeleton that you can populate with your application code. There are many other GUI builders available. You should check *www.tcl.tk,* SourceForge, or *comp.lang.tcl* for other generators that may suit your needs better.

## 15.4.1 SpecTcl

| | |
|---|---|
| Language | Tcl |
| Primary Site | *http://sourceforge.net/projects/spectcl/* |
| Tcl Revision Supported | Tcl: 7.6-8.1; Tk: 4.2-8.1 |
| Supported Platforms | UNIX, MS Windows, Mac |

SpecTcl can generate the skeleton of a GUI program. It lets you position any of the standard Tcl widgets within a grid, define the properties for the widgets, test the appearance of the GUI, and save the GUI description and the Tcl (or Java) code.

Chapters 9 through 12 discussed several of the widget properties that can be defined when a widget is created or with the configure subcommand. Double clicking on a widget within SpecTcl will open a window that displays all of a widget's properties and allows you to modify them.

The following image shows SpecTcl creating a GUI front end for the Tcl script used for demonstrating the debuggers. The tool buttons along the left side select the Tcl widget to be inserted into the GUI. The tool buttons along the top allow you to set options that are likely to be consistent among your widgets, such as foreground color, background color, and font. The window displaying the button properties was placed over the main window for this image.

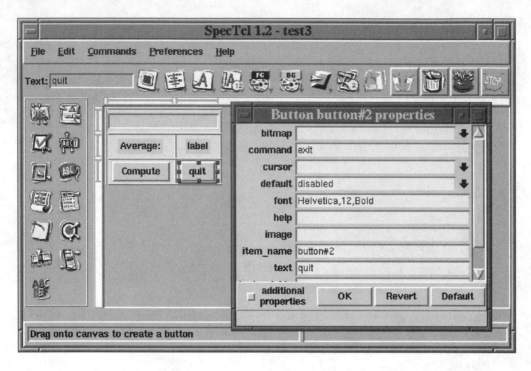

This session resulted in the following code. Adding the procedure definitions for main and addList completes the application.

**Example** 15.7

```
#! /bin/sh
# the next line restarts using wish \
exec wish "$0" "$@"

# interface generated by SpecTcl version 1.2 from /tmp/IDE/SpecTcl/bin/test3.ui
#   root    is the parent window for this user interface

proc test3_ui {root args} {
# this treats "." as a special case

if {$root == "."} {
    set base ""
} else {
    set base $root
}

entry $base.entry#1 \
      -textvariable lst

label $base.label#1 \
      -text Average:
```

```
label $base.label#2 \
      -text label \
      -textvariable mean

button $base.button#1 \
      -command {set mean [mean $lst]} \
      -text Compute

button $base.button#2 \
      -text quit

# Add contents to menus

# Geometry management

grid $base.entry#1 -in $root -row 1 -column 1 \
      -columnspan 2
grid $base.label#1 -in $root  -row 2 -column 1
grid $base.label#2 -in $root  -row 2 -column 2
grid $base.button#1 -in $root -row 3 -column 1
grid $base.button#2 -in $root -row 3 -column 2

    # Resize behavior management

    grid rowconfigure $root 1 -weight 0 -minsize 30 -pad 0
    grid rowconfigure $root 2 -weight 0 -minsize 30 -pad 0
    grid rowconfigure $root 3 -weight 0 -minsize 30 -pad 0
    grid columnconfigure $root 1 -weight 0 -minsize 30 -pad 0
    grid columnconfigure $root 2 -weight 0 -minsize 30 -pad 0
# additional interface code
# end additional interface code

}

# Allow interface to be run "stand-alone" for testing

catch {
  if [info exists embed_args] {
    # we are running in the plugin
    test3_ui .
  } else {
    # we are running in stand-alone mode
    if {$argv0 == [info script]} {
       wm title . "Testing test3_ui"
       test3_ui .
    }
  }
}
```

## 15.4.2 **Visual GIPSY**

| | |
|---|---|
| Language | Tcl |
| Primary Site | *www.prs.de* |
| Contact | *vg-support@prs.de* |
| Tcl Revision Supported | Tcl: 8.0-8.4+; Tk: 8.0-8.4+ |
| Supported Platforms | UNIX, Windows, Macintosh |
| Patzschke + Rasp Software | (*www.prs.de*) provide the Visual GIPSY program as a free offering. |

Visual GIPSY is a full-featured GUI development system that supports many options, including the following:

- Megawidget packages (including BWidgets and Tix)
- Pack, place, or grid geometry managers
- Defining a GUI within main, frame, or top-level windows
- Defining a GUI within canvas or text widgets
- Defining reusable GUI components

The following image shows Visual GIPSY creating a GUI front end for the Tcl script used for demonstrating the debuggers. The buttons all have tool tip pop-ups to explain what the button does. The buttons under Tookit 8.3.4, Menu Items, and Graphic Objects will create new widgets or graphic objects. If you select BWidget or other package support, those buttons will be placed in a new section with the appropriate label.

The Object Inspector window provides access to all options that can be set for a widget. You can select individual object settings or propagate a set of values (for example, background color) to all widgets with the Apply Attribute global button.

The window to the right shows a tree representation of the windows defined in this GUI. In this example, there is only one layer of windows. More complex GUIs may have multiple levels of frame, canvas, text, and menu widgets. The top-level window displays how the GUI will appear and allows the designer to drag and drop widgets to rearrange the appearance.

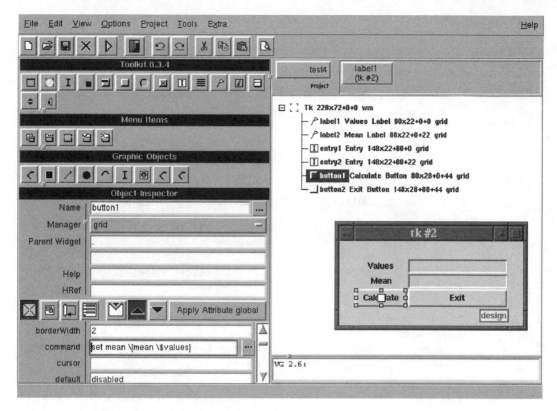

The following example is the code generated by this session.

**Example** 15.8

```
 # !/bin/sh
# start with WISH8.3\
      exec wish8.3 "$0" $ {1+"$@"}
###############################################################
# Edited with VisualGIPSY 2.6.3 on Wed Aug 21 12:58:35 EDT 2002
###############################################################

#### VG-START####

#### VG-CODE:simple####

#-------------------------------------------------------------
# Definition of Graphical User Interface
# Designed with VisualGIPSY
# Tk widget hierarchy section
#-------------------------------------------------------------
proc gui {} {
```

```
                  label .label1;

                  grid .label1 -column 0 -row 2 -sticky nesw;
                  label .label2;

                  grid .label2 -column 0 -row 3 -sticky nesw;
                  entry .entry1 -textvariable "values";

                  grid .entry1 -column 1 -row 2 -sticky nesw;
                  entry .entry2 -textvariable "mean";

                  grid .entry2 -column 1 -row 3 -sticky nesw;
                  button .button1 -command "set mean \[mean\$values\]";

                  grid .button1 -column 0 -row 4 -sticky nesw;
                  button .button2 -command "exit";

                  grid .button2 -column 1 -row 4 -sticky nesw;
          }

  #-----------------------------------------------------------
  # non widget area, used to create
  # images      : composed or referenced bitmap objects
  # fonts       : composed font objects
  # bindgroups : not supported yet!
  #-----------------------------------------------------------

  #-----------------------------------------------------------
  # Store tk database entries ...
  #-----------------------------------------------------------
  option add *label1.text {Values};
  option add *label2.text {Mean};
  option add *button1.text {Calculate};
  option add *button2.text {Exit};

  #-----------------------------------------------------------
  # Create the Graphical User Interface as designed with VisualGIPSY
  #-----------------------------------------------------------
  gui;

  ####VG-STOP####
```

## 15.5 Tcl Compilers

One problem with using Tcl in the commercial world is that when you distribute your application as a set of scripts your end users (and competitors) can read and modify the code. These compilers convert readable Tcl scripts to Tcl byte-code files that will conceal your source. The compiled versions of applications also load and run slightly faster than pure Tcl scripts.

## 15.5.1 **ICEM Tcl Compiler**

| | |
|---|---|
| Language | `executable` |
| Primary Site | *http://icemcfd.com/tcl/ice.html* |
| Contact | *tcl@icemcfd.com* |
| Tcl Revision Supported | `Tcl: 7.4-8.0; Tk: 4.0-8.0` |
| Supported Platforms DEC | OSF1 V4.0, HP-UX 9.01, 10.0, IBM AIX 3.2, 4.0, 4.1, Linux (ELF), SGI IRIX 5.X and above, Sparc Solaris 5.3 and up, MS Windows |

Interpreted code is fast to develop but runs slowly, whereas compiled code runs quickly but is slow to develop. The ICEM Tcl compiler helps you get the best of both worlds.

The compiler comes in two varieties. The version 1.3 compiler compiles Tcl 7.X scripts into C. This can speed up your 7.X script by factors between 5 and 15, depending on the script. The C output is compiled and linked with Tcl libraries to create an executable. The compiled C code produced by the 1.3 compiler is about 50% faster than the byte-interpreted Tcl 8.0 code.

The version 2.0 compiler will generate Tcl object code, Java code, or C object code and will perform compiler optimizations, including constant folding, subexpression elimination, and loop unrolling. The `tcl_compiler` application will generate a new module with a suffix of `.ptcl`, which can be evaluated by the `tclsh` or `wish` supplied with the ICEM compiler.

**Example** 15.9

```
$> cat speed.tcl
proc checksum {txt } {
   set sum 0
   foreach 1 [split $txt ""] {
      binary scan $1 c val
      set sum [expr {($sum >> 1) + ($sum ^ $val)}]
   }
   return $sum
}

set data "12345678901234567890123456789012345678901234567890"
puts "checksum takes [time {checksum $data} 100]"

$> tcl_compiler speed.tcl
$> ls -l speed*
```

```
-rw-r--r--    1 clif     users     1807 Aug 17 23:28 speed.ptcl
-rw-r--r--    1 clif     users      285 Aug 17 23:28 speed.tcl

: Standard 8.4 Tclsh interpreter
$> tclsh speed.tcl
```
**checksum takes 248 microseconds per iteration**

```
: ICEM 8.0 Tclsh interpreter
$> tclsh speed.ptcl
```
**checksum takes 172 microseconds per iteration**

### 15.5.2 TclPro procomp

| | |
|---|---|
| Language | executable |
| Primary Site | *http://sourceforge.net/projects/tcl* |
| Tcl Revision Supported | Tcl: 7.3–8.4 and newer; Tk: 3.6–8.4 and newer |
| Supported Platforms | UNIX, MS Windows, Mac, Mac OS X |

The TclPro procomp compiler will turn a Tcl script into a set of Tcl byte codes that can load and run on any platform. The byte-code files can be read with an extension that is part of the TclPro package. This extension may be distributed by developers but is not part of the standard Tcl 8.x releases. The TclPro procomp uses .tbc for the suffix to distinguish between pure Tcl scripts and compiled scripts.

The primary purpose for a byte-code-compiled script is to conceal the actual Tcl code. The byte-code files may run faster than pure script programs, since there is no need for the just-in-time compilation. The following example uses the same speed.tcl as the previous example.

**Example 15.10**

```
$> procomp speed.tcl

TclPro Compiler -- Version 1.4.1
Copyright (C) Ajuba Solutions 1998-2002. All rights reserved.
This product is registered to: clif
$> ls -latr speed*
-rw-r--r--    1 clif     users      278 Aug 18 11:01 speed.tcl
-rw-r--r--    1 clif     users      839 Aug 18 11:05 speed.tbc
$> tclsh speed.tbc
```
**checksum takes 243 microseconds per iteration**

# 15.6 Packaging Tools

One of the other problems with distributing scripted applications has been associated with distribution and installation. Most corporations do not want to distribute their product in an easily read script format, and interpreting the scripts requires that the end user has all the required interpreters and extensions on their system.

Wrapping an application with the Tcl interpreter solves both of these problems. The script is converted to a compiled or g-zipped format, making it difficult to read, and the correct revision of the interpreter is distributed with the application. The size of a wrapped Tcl application is very similar to a compiled application linked with the appropriate libraries.

## 15.6.1 TclPro prowrap

| | |
|---|---|
| Language | executable |
| Primary Site | *http://sourceforge.net/projects/tclpro/* |
| Tcl Revision Supported | Tcl: 7.3-8.4 and newer; Tk: 3.6-8.4 and newer |
| Supported Platforms | UNIX, MS Windows, Mac, Mac OS X |

The TclPro prowrap combines a set of Tcl script files, Tcl byte-code files, images, and so on into a single executable file that combines the functionality of an archive and an application. You can even include your own tclsh (or wish) interpreter and libraries in this executable file.

You can declare one script file within the bundle of files combined by TclPro Wrapper to be evaluated by the Tcl interpreter. This file may be evaluated by the interpreter included in the bundle or by an interpreter already resident on the user's system. The other files in the bundle can be accessed as though they were in the directory with the script being evaluated and can be accessed with the open and source command, as image files, and so on.

This is a clean way of packaging a set of scripts and their associated files. It solves the installation problems that have plagued Tcl developers over the years.

## 15.6.2 freewrap

| | |
|---|---|
| Language | executable |
| Primary Site | *http://sourceforge.net/projects/freewrap/* |
| Contact | *freewrapmgr@users.sourceforge.net* |

| | |
|---|---|
| Tcl Revision Supported | Tcl: 8.0-8.4 and newer; Tk: 8.0-8.4 and newer |
| Supported Platforms | UNIX, MS Windows, Mac, Mac OS X |

The `freewrap` wrapper uses the zip file feature of including an executable preamble. The `freewrap` application adds support for treating a zip file as a file system to the Tcl interpreter and then adds that interpreter to a zip file, creating a compressed executable program.

One nice feature of this technique is that if you have a copy of `freewrap` that was compiled on a target platform, you can use that copy to create an executable for that platform from any other platform. For instance, you can create Windows and Solaris executables on a Linux platform.

### 15.6.3 Starkit and Starpack

| | |
|---|---|
| Language | C, Tcl |
| Primary Site | *www.equi4.com/starkit/* |
| Contact | *jcw@equi4.com, steve@digital-smarties.com* |
| Tcl Revision Supported | Tcl: 8.1-8.4 and newer; Tk: 8.1-8.4 and newer |
| Supported Platforms | UNIX, MS Windows, Mac, Mac OS X |

The standard Tcl installation includes two executable programs (`tclsh` and `wish`), a few configuration files, and several Tcl script files. The normal Tcl distribution installs all of these files in a painless fashion. However, if you are intending to distribute a simple application, you may not wish to make your end user install Tcl first.

The `TclKit` package merges all of the Tcl and Tk executable programs and support files into a single module using a virtual file system that mirrors a directory tree within a compressed zip file. The package provides tools to wrap all files involved in an application into a single file called a Starkit (STand-Alone Runtime Kit). This allows you to deploy an application with just two files (the `TclKit` interpreter and your kit), instead of many files.

`Starpacks` extend this idea and allow you to wrap both the TclKit executable and your Starkit into a single executable file. The program that generates Starkits and Starpack is `sdx`, which is available from *www.equi4.com/starkit*. Like many Tcl commands, the `sdx` program supports several subcommands.

**Syntax:** sdx qwrap *file.tcl ?name ?*

> Wraps the *file.tcl* script into a `Starkit` named `file.kit`, suitable for evaluating with a `tclkit` interpreter.
>
> *file.tcl*   A file with a Tcl script in it.
>
> *name*   An optional name to use instead of *file* for the name of the resulting Starkit.

**Example** 15.11

```
$> cat test.tcl
package require Tk
grid [button .b -text "QUIT" -command exit]

$> sdx qwrap test.tcl
3 updates applied
$> ls -latr test*
-rw-r--r--      1 clif     users           64 Aug 17 16:44 test.tcl
-rwxr-xr-x      1 clif     users          746 Aug 17 16:44 test.kit
$> ./test.kit    ;# Displays a button
```

*Syntax:* sdx unwrap *file.kit*

Unwraps a Starkit into a directory named file.vfs.

*file.kit*    The name of a previously wrapped TclKit.

**Example** 15.12

```
$> sdx unwrap test.kit
$> ls -ltr test*
-rw-r--r--      1 clif     users           64 Aug 17 16:44 test.tcl
-rwxr-xr-x      1 clif     users          746 Aug 17 16:44 test.kit

test.vfs:
total 16
-rw-r--r--      1 clif     users          109 Aug 17 16:44 main.tcl
drwxr-xr-x      2 clif     users         4096 Aug 17 16:56 lib
```

A stand-alone Starpack can be built from the files in a .vfs directory tree with the sdx wrap command. The easiest way to construct this tree is to use sdx qwrap to wrap a file into a Starkit, then unwrap the Starkit using the sdx unwrap command, and finally wrap a full stand-alone Starpack with the sdx wrap command.

*Syntax:* sdx wrap *dirName* -runtime *TclKitName*

Wrap the files in *dirName*.vfs into a Starpack stand-alone, executable program.

*dirName*    The prefix of a directory named *dirName*.vfs. All files in the *dirName*.vfs/lib directory will be placed in the virtual file system built into the Starpack.

*tclkitName*    The name of a TclKit executable. This file can be for a platform other than the platform creating the wrap. Thus, you can create MS Windows or Linux executable programs on a Solaris platform, and so on.

**Example** 15.13

```
$> sdx wrap test -runtime tclkit.linux
 2 updates applied
$> ls -ltr test*

-rw-r--r--    1 clif     users          64 Aug 17 16:44 test.tcl
-rwxr-xr-x    1 clif     users         746 Aug 17 16:44 test.kit
-rwxr-xr-x    1 clif     users     2874580 Aug 17 17:03 test

test.vfs:
total 8
-rw-r--r--    1 clif     users         109 Aug 17 16:44 main.tcl
drwxr-xr-x    2 clif     users        4096 Aug 17 16:56 lib

$>  ./test  ;# Displays button widget
```

If an application requires several .tcl files (and perhaps a pkgIndex.tcl), they can all be placed in the *dirName*.vfs/lib directory. Note that the TclKit provided in the -runtime option should not be the same TclKit used to evaluate sdx. This should be a copy of the stand-alone tclkit.

## 15.7 Tcl Extension Generators

Chapter 13 described how to build a Tcl extension. Although the Tcl interface is very easy to work with, building an extension around a large library can mean writing a lot of code. The SWIG and CriTcl packages allow you to construct Tcl extensions without needing to learn the details of the Tcl interface. The SWIG package is designed to create a Tcl extension from a library of existing code, whereas the CriTcl package is ideal for smaller, special-purpose extensions that provide one or two new commands.

### 15.7.1 SWIG

| | |
|---|---|
| Language | C++ |
| Primary Site | *www.swig.org* |
| Contact | *beazley@cs.uchicago.edu* |
| Tcl Revision Supported | Tcl: 8.0 and newer; Tk: 8.0 and newer |
| Supported Platforms | UNIX (gcc), MS Windows, Mac (PowerPC) |

The SWIG (Simplified Wrapper and Interface Generator) program reads a slightly modified include file and generates the Tcl interface code to link to the library API that the include file defined. SWIG will create Tcl commands that can access pointers and structures, as well as the standard Tcl data types. With a command line option, SWIG can put the new commands into a private namespace. SWIG can generate interfaces for almost any data construct. The package is very rich and complete.

The following example demonstrates how easily an extension can be created with SWIG. This example shows a subset of what SWIG can do. If you have an image analysis library, it would probably have a function to translate points from one location to another. The function and data definitions in the include file might resemble the following.

```
typedef struct point_s {
  float x;
  float y;
} point;

int translatePoint(float xOffset, float yOffset,
  point *original, point *translated);
```

To convert the structure and function definition into a SWIG definition file, you would add the following items to an include (.h) file:

- A module definition name

  %module *three_d*

- An optional command to generate the AppInit function

  %include tclsh.i

- In-line code for the include files that will be required to compile the wrapper

  %{
  # include "imageOps.h"
  %}

- Dummy constructor/destructor functions for structures for which SWIG should create interfaces

When this is done, the definition file would resemble the following:

```
%module imageOps

%include tclsh.i
%{
#include "imageOps.h"
%}
typedef struct point_s {
  float x;
  float y;
  point();
  ~point();
} point;
```

```
int translatePoint(float xOffset, float yOffset,
    point *original, point *translated);
```

This input is all SWIG needs to generate code to create the structures and invoke the translatePoint function. The last steps in creating a new extension are compiling the wrapper and linking with the Tcl libraries.

```
$> swig imageOps.i
$> cc imageOps_wrap.c -limageOps -ltcl -ldl -lm
```

When this is done, you are ready to write scripts to use the new commands. The new extension has the following new commands.

*Syntax:* new_point

Create a new point structure, and return the handle for this structure.

*Syntax:* point_x_set *pointHandle value*

*Syntax:* point_y_set *pointHandle value*

Sets the value of the *member* field of the point structure.

*pointHandle*   The handle returned by the new_point command.

*value*          The value to assign to this member of the structure.

*Syntax:* point_x_get *pointHandle*

*Syntax:* point_y_get *pointHandle*

Returns the value of the *member* member of the point structure.

*pointHandle*   The handle returned by the new_point command.

*Syntax:* delete_point *pointHandle*

Destroys the point structure referenced by the handle.

*pointHandle*   The handle returned by the new_point command.

*Syntax:* translatePoint *xOffset yOffset originalPoint translatedPoint*

Translates a point by xOffset and yOffset distances and puts the new values into the provided structure.

*xOffset*          The distance to translate in the X direction.

*yOffset*          The distance to translate in the Y direction.

*originalPoint*    The handle returned by new_point with the location of the point to translate.

*translatedPoint* The handle returned by new_point. The results of the translation will be placed in this structure.

A script to use these new commands would resemble the following.

**Example** 15.14

*Script Example*

```
 # Define the original point
point original
original configure -x 100.0 -y 200.0

# Create a point for the results
point translated

# Perform the translation
translatePoint 50 -50 original translated

# Display the results
puts "translated position is: \
   [translated cget -x] [translated cget -y]"
```

*Script Output*

**translated position is: 150.0 150.0**

## 15.7.2 CriTcl

| | |
|---|---|
| Language | Tcl |
| Primary Site | *www.equi4.com/critlib/* |
| Contact | *jcw@equi4.com, steve@digital-smarties.com* |
| Tcl Revision Supported | Tcl: 8.0–8.4 and newer; Tk: 8.0–8.4 and newer |
| Supported Platforms | UNIX (gcc), MS Windows (Mingw) |

One of the advantages of Tcl is that you can do your development in an easy-to-use interpreter, profile your code, and then recode the computer-intensive sections in C. CriTcl (Compiled Runtime In Tcl) makes this very easy.

CriTcl adds a new command `critcl::cproc` to allow a script to define in-line C code. When the script needs to use the C function defined by the cproc command, it is either generated and compiled on the fly or loaded from a shared library generated when the application was run previously.

**Syntax:** `critcl::cproc` *name arguments return body*

Define an in-line C procedure.

| | |
|---|---|
| *name* | The name of the new Tcl command to create from the C code. |
| *arguments* | A C function argument definition. |
| *return* | The return type of the C function. |
| *body* | The body of a C function. |

**Example** 15.15

```
critcl::cproc add {int x int y} int {
    return x + y;
}
```

The next example shows the same procedure for generating a simple 8-bit check-sum written in both C and Tcl. Note in the next example that the char pointer is defined as a char*. CriTcl expects single-word data types.

**Example** 15.16

### *Script Example*

```
package require critcl

proc checksum {txt } {
    set sum 0
    foreach l [split $txt ""] {
    binary scan $1 c val
    set sum [expr ($sum >> 1) + ($sum ^ $val)]
  }
  return $sum
}

critcl::cproc checksum_c {char* txt} int {
  int sum = 0;
  char *l;

  l = txt;

  while (*l != 0) {
    sum = (sum >> 1) + (sum ^ *l);
    l++;
  }
  return sum;
}

set data "12345678901234567890123456789012345678901234567890"
puts "Tcl Checksum: [checksum $data]"
puts "C Checksum: [checksum_c $data]"

puts "Pure Tcl takes [time {checksum $data} 1000]"
puts "C code takes [time {checksum_c $data} 1000]"
```

### *Script Output*

```
Tcl Checksum: 53
C Checksum: 53
```

```
Pure Tcl takes 1484 microseconds per iteration
C code takes 2 microseconds per iteration
```

CriTcl is deployed as a single cross-platform Starpack, which is interpreted using TclKit. CriTcl is also able to generate packaged extensions (with cross-platform support) suitable for inclusion in Starkits or other wrapping mechanisms. There is more information about these packages on the companion CD-ROM.

## 15.8 Integrated Development Environments

The Tcl language is easy to work with, and the interpreted nature of the language makes the edit/test sequence quick. This leads many folks to stick with traditional development tools such as the emacs Tcl mode or other simple text editors.

There are several freeware IDEs (such as ASED) that support TCL, as well as at least two commercial IDEs. Again, if you do not find anything listed here that suits your needs, check for new developments at *www.tcl.tk or comp.lang.tcl.announce*. These packages have some unique and some similar features. The following table provides an overview of the functionality.

| *Feature* | *ASED* | *Komodo* | *MyrmecoX* |
|---|---|---|---|
| Highlighted commands | First | Y | Y |
| Command syntax hint | N | Y | Y |
| Command completion | N | Pull-down | Pull-down |
| Automatic quote/brace/bracket | Y | Y | N |
| Show matching quote/brace/bracket | Y | Y | N |
| Auto indent | Y | Y | N |
| Highlight runtime errors | N | Y | N |
| Syntax checker | N | Y | Y |
| Code browse | Y | N | N |
| Expand/shrink code segments | N | Y | N |
| Integrated console | Y | N | Y |
| Integrated debugger | N | Y | Y |

### 15.8.1 ASED

| | |
|---|---|
| Language | Tcl |
| Primary Site | *www.mms-forum.de/ased/asedhome.htm* |
| Contact | *andreas.sievers@t-on-line.de* |

| Tcl Revision Supported | Tcl: 8.1-8.4 and newer; Tk: 8.1-8.4 and newer |
| Supported Platforms | UNIX, MS Windows |

ASED is a pure Tcl package, making it portable to many platforms and relatively easy for a user to modify. The Options menu allows a user to select which editing options they prefer. The code browser window (on the left side of the following image) allows you to easily find a procedure in the application you are editing.

The active Tcl console (bottom window) allows the programmer to interact with the application during test runs. You can use this feature, for instance, to enter code such as set argv foo to simulate running the application from a command line with an argument. The following image shows the results of running a test on the code in the right-hand window. The highlight on proc: addList indicates that the edit cursor is within the addList procedure.

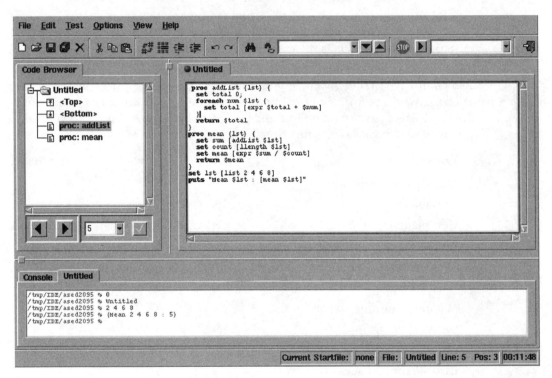

## 15.8.2 **Komodo**

| Language | compiled |
| Primary Site | *www.activestate.com/Products/Komodo/* |
| Contact | *Komodo-feedback@ActiveState.com* |
| Tcl Revision Supported | Tcl: 8.0-8.4 and newer; Tk: 8.0-8.4 and newer |
| Supported Platforms | Linux, MS Windows |

The Komodo IDE supports many languages, including Perl, Python, Tcl, PHP, XSLT, JavaScript, Ruby, Java, and others. It includes an integrated debugger, GUI layout tool, and a tool for testing and tuning regular expressions.

The context-sensitive editor will underline sections of code with syntax errors while you are typing them, to provide immediate feedback about problems. If you pause, the GUI will open a pop-up syntax reminder or provide a pull-down menu to select subcommands. The built-in debugger supports breakpoints, stack display, variable monitoring, and other features.

The following image shows Komodo being used to debug an application. The mean procedure is rolled up to save space in the edit window. The execution is currently halted at the breakpoint on line 9, with the bottom debug window displaying the current state of the program.

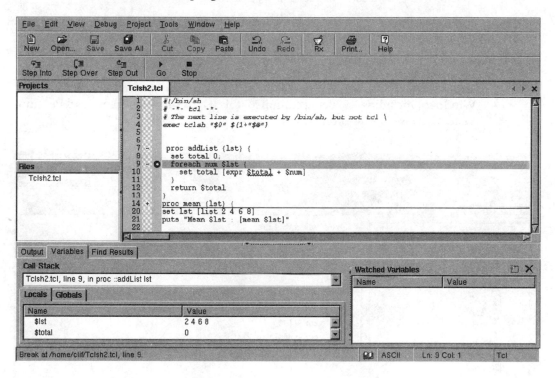

### 15.8.3 **MyrmecoX**

| | |
|---|---|
| Language | Compiled |
| Primary Site | *www.neatware.com* |
| Contact | *changl@neatware.com* |
| Tcl Revision Supported | Tcl: 8.0–8.4 and newer; Tk: 8.0–8.4 and newer |
| Supported Platforms | MS Windows |

The MyrmecoX IDE extends the TclPro tool set (including the byte-code compiler) to work within the framework of an IDE. The IDE supports context-sensitive editing with knowledge of the following packages.

| | |
|---|---|
| Kernel/Util | Tcl/Tk8.3.4, TclX/TkX 8.3, Tcllib0.8 |
| GUI | BLT 2.4, BWidget 1.2.1, IWidget 3.0, Img 1.2, Tktable 2.6, tkWizard1.0m, xWizard 2.0 |
| Object | [incr Tcl] 3.2, [incr Tk] 3.2 |
| Web | TclSoap 1.6.1, TclXML 2.0, TclDom 2.0 |
| Database | TclODBC 2.1, Oratcl 3.3 |
| COM | TCOM (Windows only) |
| Automation | Expect 5.2.1 (Windows only) |
| Java | TclBlend |
| Security | TLS 1.4 |

The package is developed for MS Windows and supported on all flavors of Windows, including XP. Being compiled, this IDE is suitable for low-end Pentium systems, as well as 64-bit Itaniums.

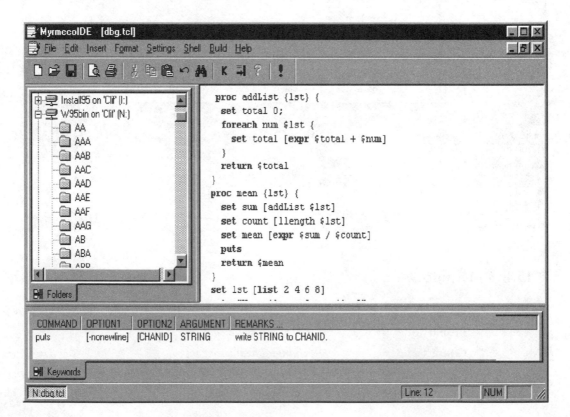

# 15.9 Bottom Line

- There are many tools available to help you develop Tcl/Tk applications. Information about tools and extensions can be found at *www.tcl.tk*, the announcements in the newsgroup `comp.lang.tcl`, the FAQs at *www.purl.org/ NET/Tcl-FAQ*, and the Tcl'ers Wiki at *http://mini.net/tcl/*.

- You can reformat your Tcl code with `frink`.

- You can check your code for syntax errors with `tclCheck`, `frink`, `ice_lint`, and `procheck`.

- You can debug Tcl scripts with `debug`, `tuba`, and `TclPro Debugger`.

- You can shorten your GUI development time with the GUI generators `SpecTcl`, Komodo, and `Visual GIPSY`.

- You can convert scripts to executable binary code with the ICEM compiler, the TclPro compiler, Freewrap, or TclKit.

- You can develop extensions quickly with the SWIG extension generator.

- You can improve an application's speed by embedding C code using CriTcl.

- Tcl can be developed using the ASED, Komodo, or MyrmecoX IDE tools.

# CHAPTER

# 16

# Tips and Techniques

Every language has its strengths and weaknesses, and every programmer develops ways to take advantage of the strengths and work around the weaknesses. This chapter covers some of the ways you can use Tcl more effectively to accomplish your tasks. This chapter discusses debugging, some common mistakes, some techniques to make your code more maintainable, and a bunch of odds and ends that have not been covered in previous chapters.

## 16.1 Debugging Techniques

The debuggers discussed in Chapter 15 are very useful tools but are not the only way to debug code. Tcl has some features that make it easy to debug code. The interpreted nature of Tcl makes it easy to do much of your debugging without a debugger. Since there is no separate compilation stage in Tcl, you can easily add a few debugging lines and rerun a test. The following discusses techniques for debugging code without a debugger.

### 16.1.1 Examine the Call Stack with the `info level` Command

Sometimes a bug appears in a procedure that is invoked with bad arguments. In order to fix the bug, you need to know which code invoked the procedure. You can learn this with the `info level` command.

> *Syntax:* `info level ?levelValue?`
>
> If invoked with no *levelValue* argument, `info level` returns the stack level currently being evaluated. If invoked with a *levelValue*

argument, `info level` returns the name and arguments of the procedure at that stack level.

*levelValue*    If *levelValue* is a positive value, it represents the level in the procedure stack to return. If it is a negative value, it represents a stack location relative to the current position in the stack.

Example 16.1 displays up to two levels of the procedure call stack, and Example 16.4 includes code to display a complete call stack.

## 16.1.2 Examine Variables When Accessed with trace Command

Sometimes you know that variable foo has an invalid value by the time it is used in procedure bar. You know the value of foo was valid when it was set in procedure baz, and something changed the value but you do not know what. The trace command will let you evaluate a script whenever the variable foo is accessed. This makes it easy to track which procedures are using (and changing) variables.

**Syntax:** `trace variable` *name operations command*

Puts a `trace` on a variable that will cause a procedure to be evaluated whenever the variable is accessed.

*name*    The name of the variable to be traced.

*operations*    Whenever a selected operation on the variable occurs, the *command* will be evaluated. `Operation` may be one of

r    Evaluate the command whenever the variable is read.

w    Evaluate the command whenever the variable is written.

u    Evaluate the command whenever the variable is unset.

*command*    A command to evaluate when the variable is accessed. The command will be invoked with the following three arguments.

name    The name of the variable.

index    If the variable is an associative array, this will be the index of the associative array. If the variable is a scalar variable, this will be an empty string.

operation    A single letter to denote the operation that triggered this evaluation.

The following example shows how the trace command can be used with a procedure (traceProc) to display part of the call stack and the new value when a variable is modified. If you find yourself using traces frequently, you may want to examine the OAT extension and TclProp package from the University of Minnesota (*www.cs.umn.edu/research/GIMME/tclprop.html*). The OAT extension enhances the trace command, allowing all Tcl and Tk objects (such as widgets) to be traced. The TclProp package (among other features) lets you watch for variables being changed with a single line command instead of needing to declare a script.

## Example 16.1

### Script Example 1

```
# The procedure to invoke from trace

proc traceProc {varName index operation} {
  upvar $varName var
  set lvl [info level]
  incr lvl -1;
  puts "Variable $varName is being modified in:
    '[info level $lvl]'"
  if {$lvl > 1} {
    incr lvl -1;
    puts " Which was invoked from: '[info level $lvl]'"
  }
  puts "The current value of $varName is: $var\n"
}
```

### Script Example 2

```
# A procedure to modify the traced Variable

proc modifyVariable {newVal} {
  global tracedVariable
  set tracedVariable $newVal
}

# A procedure to call the variable changing procedure,
#  to demonstrate getting information further up the
#  call stack.

proc otherProc {newVal} {
  modifyVariable $newVal
}

# A variable to watch.

global tracedVariable

# Create a trace on the tracedVariable variable
```

```
trace variable tracedVariable w traceProc

# Now, modify the variable, twice within procedures,
# and once from the global scope.

# This will modify the variable two levels deep
# in the call stack.

otherProc One

# This will modify the variable one level down the call stack.

modifyVariable Two

# Notice that the change from global scope reports itself as
# coming from the 'traceProc' command

set tracedVariable Three
```

***Script Output***

**Variable tracedVariable is being modified in:**
**    'modifyVariable One'**
**  Which was invoked from: 'otherProc One'**
**The current value of tracedVariable is: One**

**Variable tracedVariable is being modified in:**
**    'modifyVariable Two'**
**The current value of tracedVariable is: Two**

**Variable tracedVariable is being modified in:**
**    'traceProc tracedVariable {} w'**
**The current value of tracedVariable is: Three**

---

## 16.1.3 **Run Script in Interactive Mode**

You can invoke a script from a tclsh or wish interpreter with the source command. When a script is invoked with the source command, the interpreter returns you to the interactive prompt instead of exiting on an error. The tkcon program described in Chapter 2 is an excellent tool to use for interactive mode debugging. The ability to recover previous commands and edit them slightly makes it easy to run multiple tests and observe how a procedure behaves.

If your script requires command line arguments, you can set the argv and argc variables before you source the script, as shown in the following example. The example shows a simple debugging session that tries to open a nonexistent file, and then evaluates the procedure that would be called if a valid file name were provided.

**Example** 16.2

*Script Example*
```
proc processLineProcedure {line} {
  puts "Processing '$line'"
}

puts "There are $argc arguments to this script"
puts "The arguments are: $argv"

set fileName [lindex $argv 0]
set infile [open $fileName "r"]
while {![eof $infile]} {
  set len [gets $infile line]
  if {$len > 0} {
    processLineProcedure $line
  }
}
```

*Debugging Session*
```
$> tclsh
% set argv [list badFileName -option value]
 badFileName -option value
% set argc 3
3
% source e_16_2.tcl
There are 3 arguments to this script
The arguments are: badFileName -option value
couldn't open "badFileName": no such file or directory
% set errorInfo
couldn't open "badFileName": no such file or directory
  while executing
"open $fileName "r""
  invoked from within
"set infile [open $fileName "r"]"
  (file "e_16_2.tcl" line 9)
  invoked from within
"source e_16_2.tcl"
```

## 16.1.4 Use puts to Print the Value of Variables or Lines to Be Evaluated

This technique may not be elegant, but it works in all environments. You may need to print the data to a file instead of the screen if you are trying to debug an application that runs for a long time, does something strange, recovers, and continues running. Some of the variants on using puts to track program flow and variables include a conditional puts in a procedure, a bitmapped conditional, and printing every line.

### A Conditional puts in a Procedure

This technique is useful while you are in the latter stages of debugging a system. With this technique you can leave your debugging code in place, while confirming the behavior without the extra output.

**Example** 16.3

```
proc debugPuts {args} {
  global DEBUG
  if { [info exists DEBUG] && $DEBUG } {
    puts "$args"
  }
}
```

### A Bitmapped Conditional

A bitmap can be used to control how much information is printed while the script is running. This is another technique that is useful when you do not always want to see a lot of output, but for tracking down some bugs you need all the help you can get.

The next example shows a procedure that will print different amounts of information, depending on the value of stateArray(debugLevel). If bit 8 is set, a call stack is displayed. Note that a positive (absolute) level is used for the info level command rather than a negative (relative) level. This is a workaround for the fact that Tcl generates an error when you try to access level 0 via a relative level offset but will accept 0 as an absolute level.

For example, a procedure that is called from the global level is at level 1 (as returned by [info level]). If the info level command is invoked within that procedure as info level −1, Tcl will generate an error. However, if the info level command is invoked as info level 0, Tcl will return the procedure name and argument that invoked the procedure.

**Example** 16.4

### Script Example 1

```
proc debugPuts {args} {
  global stateArray

  # If low-order bit set, print the message(s)
```

```
      if {$stateArray(debugLevel) & 1} {
        puts "DEBUG Message: $args"
      }

      # If bit two is set, print the proc name and args that
      #   invoked debugPuts

      if {$stateArray(debugLevel) & 2} {
        set level [info level]
        incr level -1

        puts "DEBUG Invoked from:: [info level $level]"
      }

      # If bit four is set, print the contents of stateArray

      if {$stateArray(debugLevel) & 4} {
        foreach index [array names stateArray] {
          puts "DEBUG: stateArray($index): $stateArray($index)"
        }
      }

      # If bit 8 is set, print the call stack

      if {$stateArray(debugLevel) & 8} {
        set level [info level]
        for {set l 1} {$l < $level} {incr l} {
          puts "DEBUG CallStack $l: [info level $l]"
        }
      }
    }
```

***Script Example 2***

```
proc topProc {arg1 arg2} {
  lowerProc three four five
}

proc lowerProc {args} {
  debugPuts "Message from a proc called from a proc"
}

set stateArray(debugLevel) 15
topProc one two
```

***Script Output***

```
DEBUG Message: {Message from a proc called from a proc}
DEBUG Invoked from:: lowerProc three four five
DEBUG: stateArray(debugLevel): 15
```

```
DEBUG CallStack 1: topProc one two
DEBUG CallStack 2: lowerProc three four five
```

---

### *Printing Every Line*

To debug some nasty problems, you may want to display each line before it is evaluated. Sometimes, seeing the line with the substitutions done makes the script's behavior obvious. You can modify your script to display each line before executing it by duplicating each line of code and adding a string resembling

```
puts "WILL EVAL:
```

to the beginning of the duplicated line, and a close quote to the end of the line. This modification is easily done with an editor that supports macros (such as Emacs). Alternatively, you can modify your script with another Tcl script. The caveat with this technique is to be careful that you do not accidentally perform an action within your puts. Consider the following example.

### Example 16.5

```
# This will evaluate the modifyDatabase procedure.
#  It will print the status return, not the procedure call.
puts "WILL EVAL set status [modifyDatabase $newData]"

# This prints the command and the value of newData
puts "WILL EVAL: set status \[modifyDatabase $newData\]"
set status [modifyDatabase $newData]
```

---

## 16.1.5 Extract Portions of Script for Unit Testing

Since Tcl does not have a separate compilation stage, unit testing can be more easily performed in Tcl than in languages such as C, which might need to have more of the program infrastructure in place in order to link a test program.

## 16.1.6 Attach a tkcon Session to Application

The tkcon application can attach itself to another running a wish interpreter, providing a console interface to a running application. With this console you can examine global variables, check the status of after events, interact with windows, and so on. This is an excellent way of examining the state of an application running outside a debugger that displays an unexpected error. The following illustration shows how to attach a TkCon console to another wish application.

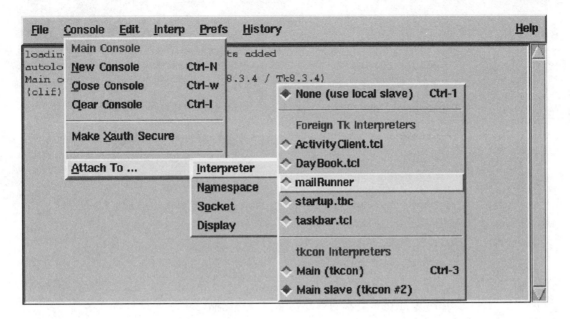

### 16.1.7 **Create a New Window (Using the `toplevel` Command) to Interact with Your Application**

If you cannot use the `tkcon` program, you can add code to a script that will allow you to evaluate commands within the running application and display results.

The `makeInteractionWindow` procedure in the following example creates a new top-level window that accepts Tcl commands, evaluates them, and displays the results. The images show this procedure being used to examine a `radiobutton` application.

**Example** 16.6

*Script Example*

```
# interactive Window

# Create a window to use to interact with the running script

proc makeInteractionWindow {} {
  # Can't have two toplevels open at once.
  if {[winfo exists .topInteraction]} {return}

  # Create a toplevel window to hold these widgets
  set topWindow [toplevel .topInteraction]

  # Create an entry widget for commands to execute,
  #   and a label for the entry widget
```

```
    set cmdLabel [label $topWindow.cmdLabel -text "Command"]

    set cmd [entry $topWindow.cmd -textvariable cmdString \
      -width 60]

    grid $cmdLabel -row 0 -column 0
    grid $cmd -row 0 -column 1 -columnspan 3

    # Create a scrolling text window for the command output,

    set outputLabel [label $topWindow.outputLabel \
      -text "Command Result"]

    set output [text $topWindow.output -height 5 -width 60 \
      -relief raised]

    set sb [scrollbar $topWindow.sb -command "$output yview"]
    $output configure -yscrollcommand "$sb set"

    grid $outputLabel -row 1 -column 0
    grid $output -row 1 -column 1 -columnspan 3
    grid $sb -row 1 -column 4 -sticky ns

    # Create buttons to clear the command,
    #   execute the command and
    #   close the toplevel window.

    set clear [button $topWindow.clear -text "Clear Command" \
        -command { set cmdString "" }]

    # The command for the $go button is placed in quotes to
    #   allow "$output" to be replaced by the actual output
    #   window name. "$output see end" scrolls the window to
    #   the bottom after each command (to display the command
    #   output).

    set go [button $topWindow.go -text "Do Command" \
      -command "$output insert end \"\[uplevel #0 \
        \[list eval \$cmdString\]\n\]\"; \
          $output see end; \
        "]

    set close [button $topWindow.close -text "Close" \
      -command "destroy $topWindow"]

    grid $clear -row 2 -column 1
    grid $go -row 2 -column 2
    grid $close -row 2 -column 3

    # bind the Return key in the command entry widget to
```

```
  #  behave the same as clicking the $go button.
  #  NOTE: <Enter> is the "cursor enters widget"
  #  event, NOT the Enter key

  bind $cmd "<Return>" "$go invoke"
}

############################################################
# Application starts here

if {[lsearch $argv -debug] != -1} {
    makeInteractionWindow
}

# Update the text displayed in a label

proc updateLabel {myLabel item} {
  global price;
  $myLabel configure -text \
  "The cost for a potion of $item is $price gold pieces"
}

# Create and display a label

set l [label .l -text "Select a Potion"]
grid $l -column 0 -row 0 -columnspan 3

# A list of potions and prices

set itemList [list "Cure Light Wounds" 16 "Boldness" 20 \
  "See Invisible" 60]
set position 0

foreach {item cost} $itemList {
  radiobutton .b_$position -text $item -variable price \
  -value $cost -command [list updateLabel $l $item]
  grid .b_$position -column $position -row 1
    incr position
}
```

**Script Output**

Application

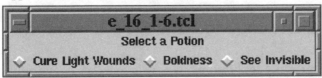

Debugging window

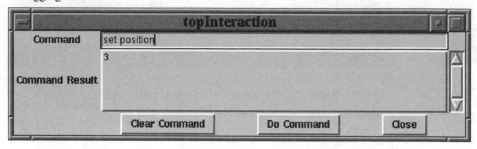

### 16.1.8 **Use a Second** wish **Interpreter for Remote Debugging**

The send command allows you to send a command from one wish interpreter to another. The command will be evaluated in the target interpreter, and the results will be returned to the source interpreter. This feature lets you use one wish interpreter in interactive mode to debug a script running in another interpreter. You can display variables, evaluate procedures, load new procedures, and so on.

*Syntax:* send *interp cmd*

Send a command to another wish interpreter, and return the results of that command.

*interp* The name of the destination interpreter. You can get a list of the wish interpreters currently running on a system with the winfo interps command.

*cmd* A command to be evaluated in the destination interpreter. Remember to enclose the cmd string in curly braces if you want substitutions to be performed in the destination interpreter, not the source interpreter.

All of the preceding techniques can be done in a remote interpreter using the send command. You can print out data, invoke procedures, check the state of the after queue, or even source new versions of procedures. Note that using the send command on a UNIX system requires that you use xauth security (or build wish with a reduced security). Under Windows, versions of Tk prior to 8.1 do not support the send command.

## 16.2 **Tcl As a Glue Language: The exec Command**

Although almost any application can be written in Tcl, not all applications should be written in Tcl. Some applications should be written using Tcl with an extension, and some should be written using Tcl as a glue language to join other stand-alone programs.

Scripting languages are extremely useful for applications that require gluing several pieces of functionality into a new application. They are less well suited to creating base functionality such as the following:

- Arithmetic-based algorithms (generating checksums or compressing files)
- Large data applications (subsampling images)
- Controlling hardware (device drivers)

Tcl/Tk's strength is how easy it makes merging several libraries and stand-alone programs into a complex application. This merging can be done by creating new Tcl extensions or by using Tcl to glue several stand-alone programs into a new application. If the functionality you need involves several functions and is available in an existing library, it is probably best to make a Tcl extension wrapper to access the library. See Chapter 13 on writing extensions and Chapter 15 on the SWIG and CriTcl packages to automate creating extensions from libraries.

The extensions you create can either be linked into a new interpreter or merged at runtime with the load command. Note that you can use the load command only if your operating system supports dynamically loaded libraries (.so under Linux and Solaris, .dll under Windows). If stand-alone applications exist that perform a subset of what you need, you can use these existing applications with a Tcl script to control and extend them to perform the tasks you need done.

Many applications are easily written using Tcl and extensions for some functionality and invoking stand-alone programs for other functionality. For example, I use a Tk script to control the PPP connections on a UNIX system. It uses the BLT extension to create an activity bar chart, invokes several stand-alone programs to initiate PPP connections and monitor the activity, and has some Tcl code that tracks the number of connection hours.

The caveat with calling stand-alone programs from your script is that it can limit the portability of the script. For instance, a script that uses ps to monitor active processes and display the top CPU users will require different ps arguments for BSD and System V-based UNIXes and will not run at all on a Macintosh or Windows platform.

The command that lets you merge existing stand-alone programs into a new application is the exec command. The exec command will invoke new programs in a subprocess and return the program output to the Tcl interpreter as the result of the command. If the subtask exits with a non-zero status (an error status), the exec command will generate an error. You can invoke a single program with the exec command, or a series of commands where the output of one program becomes the input to the next program with the UNIX pipe symbol (|). The argument to the exec command is either an exec option, a command to execute as a subprocess, an argument for the commands, or a pipeline descriptor.

*Syntax:* exec *?-options? arg1 ?arg2...argn?*

Execute arguments in a subprocess.

-options   The exec command supports two options:

> -keepnewline   Normally, a trailing newline character is deleted from the program output returned by the exec command. If this argument is set, the trailing newline is retained.
>
> --   Denotes the last option. All subsequent arguments will be treated as subprocess program names or arguments.

*arg\**   These arguments can be either a program name, a program argument, or a pipeline descriptor. There are many pipeline descriptors. Some of the commonly used ones are

> |   Separates distinct programs in the command line. The standard output of the program on the left side of the pipe symbol (|) will be used as the standard input for the program on the right of the pipe symbol.
>
> < *fileName*   The first program in the list will use the content of fileName as the standard input.
>
> > *fileName*   The standard output from the last program in the list will be written to *fileName*.

The following examples create compressed archives of files in a directory under UNIX or Windows using the exec command.

## 16.2.1 Creating a G-zipped tar Archive Under UNIX

This script will create a gzipped tar archive on systems that include the tar and gzip programs.

**Example** 16.7

```
# This script is called with the name of a directory to
#  archive as the first argument in the command line,
#  and the name of the archive as the second argument.

set directory [lindex $argv 0]
set archive [lindex $argv 1]

# Get a list of the files to include in the archive.
```

```
set fllst [glob $directory/*]

# Create the tar archive, and gzip it.

eval exec tar -cvf $archive $fllst
exec gzip $archive
```

## 16.2.2 Creating a Zip Archive Under Windows

This script will create a zip archive on systems that include the zip program.

**Example** 16.8

```
# This script is called with the name of a directory to
#  archive as the first argument in the command line,
#  and the name of the archive as the second argument.

set directory [lindex $argv 0]
set zipfile [lindex $argv 1]

# The file "distfiles" will contain a list of files for
#  this archive.

set outfl [open distfiles "w"]

# Get a list of the files to include in the archive.

set fllst [glob $directory/*]

# And write that list into the content file, one
# file name per line

foreach fl $fllst {
  puts $outfl "$fl"
}

close $outfl
# Execute the winzip program to make an archive.
eval "exec C:/winzip/winzip32.exe -a $zipfile @distfiles"
```

## 16.3 Common Mistakes

There are several common mistakes programmers make as they learn Tcl. Cameron Laird has collected many of these from the questions and answers posted in comp.lang.tcl, at *http://Starbase.NeoSoft.COM/~claird/comp.lang.tcl/fmm.html*). This section is a sampling of common errors not discussed in the previous chapters.

## 16.3.1 Problems Using the exec Command

The previous description of the exec command looks straightforward, but there are some common mistakes people make trying to use the exec command.

### The tclsh Shell Is Not the UNIX Shell

Many problems appear when people try to use shell expansions or shell escapes with the exec command. For example, the wrong way to write the exec tar... command in the previous example would be

```
exec tar -cvf $archive $directory/*
```

In this case, the tclsh shell would substitute the name of the directory (for example, foo) for $directory and would pass that string (foo/* ) to the tar program. The tar program would fail to identify any file named "*" in that directory.

When you type a command with a "*" at the shell prompt (or in an sh script), the shell automatically expands the * to the list of files. Under Tcl, this expansion is done by the glob command.

In the same way, if you try to group an argument to exec with single quotes, it will fail. The single quote has meaning to the UNIX shell interpreter (disable substitutions) but is just another character to the Tcl interpreter.

### The tclsh Shell Is Not COMMAND.COM

This is the Windows equivalent of the previous mistake. Remember that the DIR, COPY, and DEL commands are part of COMMAND.COM, not stand-alone programs. You cannot get a directory within a Tcl script with a command such as the following.

```
# Won't work
set filelist [exec dir C:*.*]
```

There is no DIR.EXE or DIR.COM for the Tcl shell to execute. The best solution is to use the Tcl glob, file copy, file delete, and file rename commands. If you really need the DIR output you can exec the COMMAND.COM program with the /C option. This option tells the COMMAND.COM program to evaluate the string after the /C as though it had been typed in at a command prompt.

```
# This will get a list of files
set filelist [glob C:/*.*]
```

```
# This will get the output of the dir command
set filelist [exec COMMAND.COM /C dir C:*.*]
```

Note that `filelist` will contain all the output from the DIR, not just a list of the files.

### A Tcl List Is Passed as a Single Argument to a Procedure

Notice the `eval` in the `eval exec tar -cvf $archive $fllst` line in the previous UNIX example (Example 16.7). If you simply used

```
# won't work.
exec tar -cvf $archive $fllst
```

the content of `fllst` would be passed as a single argument to the `exec` command, which would pass them as a single argument to the `tar` program. Since there is no file named `file1 file2 file3..`, this results in an error.

The `eval` command concatenates all of the arguments into one string and then evaluates that string. This changes the list from a single argument to as many arguments as there are file names in the list.

```
# will work.
eval exec tar -cvf $archive $fllst
```

### Changing the Directory Is Done Within a *tclsh* (or *sh*) Shell; It Is Not a Stand-Alone Program

The command `exec cd $newDirectory` is probably not what you want.

The change `directory` command is a part of a shell. It changes the current directory within the shell. It is not an external program. Use the built-in `Tcl` command `cd` if you want to change the working directory for your script.

## 16.3.2 Calculating the Time: Numbers in Tcl

Numbers in Tcl can be represented in octal, decimal, or hexadecimal. The base of a number is determined by the first (or first two) digits. If the first digit is not a 0, the number is interpreted as a decimal number. If the first digit is a 0 and the second character is x, the number is interpreted as a hexadecimal number. If the first digit is a 0 and the second digit is between 1 and 7, the number is interpreted as an octal number. If the first digit is a 0 and the second digit is 8 or 9, this is an error.

In versions of Tcl without the `clock` command, it was common to split a time or date string and try to perform calculations on the parts of the time. This would work most of the time. Note that at 08:00 the command

```
set minutes [expr [lindex [split $time ":"] 0]*60]
```

will generate an error, since 08 is not a valid octal number. If you need to convert a time/date to seconds in versions of Tcl more recent than 7.5, you should use the `clock format` and `clock scan` commands.

If you need to process time and date in an older version of Tcl, or if you are reading data that may have leading zeros (the number of cents in a commercial transaction, for instance), use the `string trimleft` command to remove the leading zeros. In the following example, note the test for an empty string. If the initial value is all zeros (000, for instance), the `string trimleft` command will remove all the zeros, leaving an empty string. An empty string will generate an error if you try to use it in a calculation.

```
set value [getNumberWithLeadingZeros]
set value [string trimleft $value "0"]
if {$value == ""} {set value 0}
```

### 16.3.3 `set`, `lappend`, `append`, and `incr` Are the Only Tcl Commands That Modify an Argument

The commands `lreplace`, `string`, and `expr` all return a new value without modifying any original argument.

```
# This WON'T remove the first list entry
lreplace $list 0 0 ""

# This WILL remove the first list entry
set list [lreplace $list 0 0 ""]

# This WON'T shorten the string
string range $myString 5 end

# This WILL shorten the string
set myString [string range $myString 5 end]

# This WON'T change the value of counter
expr $counter + 1

# These commands WILL change the value of counter
set counter [expr $counter + 1]
incr counter
```

### 16.3.4 The `incr` Command Works Only with Integers

Some commands (for example, commands that return locations and widths of objects on a canvas) return float values that `incr` will not handle. You can convert a floating-point number to an integer with the `expr round` and `expr int` commands, or you can use the `expr` command to increment a variable. Remember that you must reassign the new value to the variable when using the expr command.

```
set variable [expr $variable + 1.0]
```

### 16.3.5 The upvar Command Takes a Name, Not a Value

When you invoke a procedure that uses the upvar command, you must pass the variable name, not *$varName*.

```
proc useUpvar {variableName} {
  upvar $variableName localVariable
  set localVariable 0
}

# This will set the value of x to 0
useUpvar x

# This will not change the value of x
useUpvar $x
```

### 16.3.6 Changes to Widgets Do Not Appear Until the Event Loop Is Processed

If your wish script is making many modifications to the display within a procedure, you may need to add the update command to the looping. This will not only update the screen and show the progress but also scan for user input (such as someone clicking an abort button). This is discussed in detail in Chapter 9.

### 16.3.7 Be Aware of Possible % Sign Reduction

The bind and format commands both use the % as a marker for special characters. If you combine the two commands, the % will be substituted twice. For example, a bind command that should set a value when an entry field is entered might resemble the following:

```
bind .entry <Enter> {set defaultVal [format %%f6.2 $value]}
```

Note that there are two percent signs. When the cursor enters .entry, the script registered with the bind command will be evaluated. The first phase of this evaluation is to scan the script for % patterns and substitute the appropriate values. The %% pair will be replaced with a single %. When the script is evaluated, the format command resembles the following, which is a valid command.

```
format %f6.2 $value
```

If only a single % had been used, it would have been discarded during the first evaluation, and the argument for the format command would have been simply f6.2.

# 16.4 Coding Tips and Techniques

There are many ways to write a program. Some techniques work better with a particular language than others. The following describe techniques that work well with Tcl.

## 16.4.1 Use the Interpreter to Parse Input

Tcl is one of the very few languages that provides the script writer with access to a parse engine. This can save you time (and help you write more robust code) in several ways.

### Use Procedures Instead of *switch* Statements to Parse Input

If you are accustomed to C programming, you are used to constructs such as the following:

```
while {[gets stdin cmdLine]} {
  set cmd [lindex $cmdLine 0]
  switch $cmd {
    "cmd1" {cmd1Procedure $cmdLine}
    "cmd2" {cmd2Procedure $cmdLine}
    ...
  }
}
```

Whenever you add a new command using a switch statement, you need to add a new pattern to the switch command. In Tcl, you can write a loop to parse input such as the following:

```
while {[gets stdin cmdLine]} {
  set cmd [lindex $cmdLine 0]
  set cmdName [format "%sProcedure" $cmd]
  # Confirm that the command exists before trying to eval it.

  if {[info command $cmdName] != ""} {
    eval $cmdName $cmdLine
  }
}
```

When the requirements change and you need to add a new command, you simply add a new procedure without changing the command parsing code.

### Use the `info complete` Command to Match Quotes, Braces, and Brackets

The `info complete` command will return a 1 if a command is complete, and a 0 if there are opening quotes, braces, or brackets without the appropriate closing quotes, braces, or brackets. The `info complete` command is designed to determine whether a Tcl command has unmatched quotes, braces, or brackets, but it can be used to test any line of text that may include nested braces, and so on.

### Use `eval` to Set Command Line Arguments

Again, if you are familiar with C, you are familiar with parsing command line arguments using code that resembles the following:

```
foreach arg $argv {
  switch $arg -- {
    "-alpha" {set alphaMode 1}
    "-debug" {set debugMode 1}
    ...
  }
}
```

When you need to add a new command line option, you need to add new code to the `switch` statement. In Tcl, you can write code that resembles the following:

```
foreach arg $argv {
  set varName [format "%sMode" $arg]
  eval set $varName 1
}
```

With this technique, adding new options does not require changing the parse code. Alternatively, if you have more complex command line requirements, you can use a first-letter convention to define how an argument should be processed. The following are examples.

*-SvarName Value*    Set the variable *varName* to *Value*.

*-Aindex Value*    Set the state array *index* to *Value*.

The code to parse this style of command line would resemble the following:

```
foreach {arg value} $argv {
  set type [string range $arg 1 1]
  set name [string range $arg 2 end]
  switch $type {
    "A" {
      set stateArray($name) $value
    }
    "S" {
      set $name $value
    }
```

```
        default {
            error "Unrecognized option: $arg"
        }
    }
}
```

With this style of command line parsing, you can set any variable from the command line without changing any code. Note that this technique will not generate an error if you misspell the index or variable name in the command line. The error will be silent, and evaluating the script may produce unexpected results because the command line initialized a variable that was never used.

One method of protecting against this failure mode is to set default values for all the parameters that may be set from a command line and allow only existing variables and array indices to be modified. Code for this would resemble the following:

```
proc setDefaults {} {
    global stateArray
    set stateArray(firstIndex) 1
    set stateArray(secondIndex) 2
    # ...
}

foreach {arg value} $argv {
    set type [string range $arg 1 1]
    set name [string range $arg 2 end]
    switch $type {
        "A" {
            if {[info exists stateArray($name)]} {
                set stateArray($name) $value
            } else {
                puts "$name is an invalid index"
                puts "Use one of [array names stateArray]"
            }
        }
        "S" {
            if {[info exists $name]} {
                set $name $value
            } else {
                puts "$name is an invalid variable name"
            }
        }
        default {
            error "Unrecognized option: $arg"
        }
    }
}
```

### Use a Single Array for Global Variables

Rather than use simple variables for global variables, group all shared variables that a set of procedures will need in a single-array variable. This technique reduces the possibility of variable name collisions when you merge sets of code and makes it easy to add new variables when necessary without requiring changes to the global commands in all procedures that will use the new value.

```
# Don't use this technique
proc initializeParameters {
  global height width linecolor
  set height 100
  set width 200
  set linecolor blue
}

# Use this technique
proc initializeParameters {
  global globalParams
  set globalParams(height) 100
  set globalParams(width) 200
  set globalParams(linecolor) blue
}
```

Using a single associative array lets you save the program's state with a single command, as in the following:

```
puts $saveFile "array set myStateArray \
  [list [array get myStateArray ]]"
```

This also lets you reload the settings with a simple source command. Saving the state in a data-driven loop allows you to add new indices to the state variable without needing to modify the save and restore state functions.

### Declare Globals in a Single Location

If you use more than a few global variables, it can become difficult to keep all procedures that use them in sync as new variables are added. The names of the global variables can be kept in a single global list, and that list can be evaluated to set the global variables.

```
set globalList {errorInfo errorCode argv argc stateArray1 \
  stateArray2}

proc someProcedure {args} {
  global globalList ; eval global $globalList
}
```

### *Generate a GUI from Data, Not from Code*

Some parts of a GUI need to be generated from code, but others can be generated on the fly from lists. For example, a menu can be generated with a set of commands such as the following:

```
set cmdButton [menubutton .cmdButton -text "Select cmds" \
  -menu .cmdButton.mnu]
set cmdMenu [menu $cmdButton.mnu]

$cmdMenu add command -label {Selection One} -command ProcOne
$cmdMenu add command -label {Selection Two} -command ProcTwo
```

Or a menu could be generated with a loop and a list, such as the following:

```
set cmdMenuList [list \
  {Selection One} {procOne} {Selection Two} {procTwo}]

set cmdButton [menubutton .cmdButton -text "Select cmds" \
   -menu .cmdButton.mnu]
set cmdMenu [menu $cmdButton.mnu]

foreach {label cmd} $cmdMenuList {
  $cmdMenu add command -label $label -command $cmd
}
```

If there are more than three items in the menu, the list-driven code is smaller. The list-driven code is also simpler to maintain, because the list of labels and commands is more tightly localized. If the list can be generated at runtime from other data, it can reduce the amount of code that needs to be modified when the program needs to be changed.

## 16.4.2 Handling Platform-Specific Code

Tcl has excellent multiple-platform support. In many circumstances you can use built-in Tcl commands that are identical across all platforms. However, sometimes there are spots where you need to write platform-specific code. For instance, in TclTutor, you can click on a word to get on-line help. Under UNIX, this is done using exec to run TkMan as a subprocess. Under Windows, the exec command invokes winhlp32.exe.

The tcl_platform(platform) array variable (discussed in Chapter 5) contains the name of the platform where your code is being evaluated. Once you have determined the platform, there are several options for evaluating platform-specific code.

■ Place platform-specific scripts in a variable, and evaluate the content of the variable in the mainline code. This works well when the platform-specific script is short.

```
switch $tcl_platform(platform) {
  "unix" {
```

```
        set helpString "TkMan $topic"
        }
        "win" {
        set helpString "winhlp32 -k$topic $helpFile"
        }
    }
    ...
    if {[userRequestsHelp]} {eval exec $helpString}
```

■ Place platform-specific code within tcl_platform(platform) test. If the platform-specific code is more complex, you may prefer to put a script within the test, as follows.

```
    if {[userRequestsHelp]} {
      switch $tcl_platform(platform) {
        "unix" {
              exec TkMan $topic
        }
        "win" {
              exec winhlp32 -k$topic $helpFile
        }
      }
    }
    ...
```

■ If there are large amounts of platform-specific code, those scripts can be placed in separate files and loaded at runtime, as follows.

```
    # A platform-specific procedure named HelpProc is defined in
    # each of these script files.
    switch $tcl_platform(platform) {
      "unix" {
        source "unix_Procedures.tcl"
      }
      "win" {
        source "win_Procedures.tcl"
      }
      "mac" {
        source "mac_Procedures.tcl"
      }
    }
    if {[userRequestsHelp]} {HelpProc}
```

## 16.5 Bottom Line

This chapter has discussed several tricks, techniques, and tips for writing efficient and maintainable Tcl scripts. These include the following.

■ You can use other wish interpreters or new windows to debug a wish application.

- Some applications should be written as separate programs, invoked with `exec`, rather than as extensions or Tcl scripts.

- The Tcl interpreter is not the UNIX command shell or `COMMAND.COM`.

- Be aware of possible leading zeros in numbers.

- Most Tcl commands do not modify the content of their arguments. `append`, `lappend`, `set`, and `incr` are exceptions.

- Use the Tcl interpreter to parse data whenever possible, rather than writing new code to parse data.

- Use a single global array for shared data instead of many variables. If you must use many variables, group them into a global list and evaluate that list to declare the globals in procedures.

# About the CD-ROM

The CD-ROM supplied with *Tcl/Tk: A Developer's Guide* is more than just an extension of the book. The CD-ROM includes all code described in the book, Tcl/Tk source code, binary distributions, additional tutorials (in several languages),extra documentation and articles about using Tcl/Tk, development tools, Tcl extensions, and a full extra bonus book.

For the beginner, the tutorials will get you programming in just a few hours. For the experienced user, the development tools will help you to program better and faster. The articles and chapters of case studies discussing how Tcl/Tk is used in the real world will help advanced users see how to apply Tcl/Tk to their needs. The material on the CD-ROM makes *Tcl/Tk: A Developer's Guide* a one-stop shopping spree for anyone interested in using Tcl/Tk.

Recent Tcl/Tk distributions from ActiveState are on the CD-ROM, ready for installation on a Mac, Windows, or UNIX machine. If you need Tcl/Tk on a platform that is not normally supported, the complete sources are also included.

The tutorials on the CD-ROM will help you learn the basics of Tcl/Tk quickly. There are PDF and HTML-based tutorials from the Net, some discussions of Tcl tricks from *comp.lang.tcl* and *Tcler'sWiki*, and a copy of TclTutor, a computer-aided instruction package. If you find that one tutorial does not explain something the way you would like, look at the others. With several different authors presenting the same material from different angles, you will be certain to find one that explains what you need to know. The bonus book chapters and magazine articles discuss how Tcl and Tk have been used in the real world, how to build extensions with C++ libraries, and how to use Tcl/Tk to build web and e-mail applications, news robots, and more.

## A.1 How Do I Find Those Extra Goodies?

On most platforms, inserting the CD-ROM into your CD-ROM drive will automatically start an application to view the content of the CD-ROM. On some UNIX systems, the browsing application may not start. In that case, mount the CD-ROM and invoke */mnt/cdrom/autorun.sh* to start the application.

If the application does not start, you can browse the files on the CD-ROM with an HTML browser such as Netscape, Opera, Mozilla, or Internet Explorer. The initial file is *index.htm* on the root folder of the CD-ROM.

To install the packages, you will need to know the directory layout. See Appendix B for instructions on installing the Tcl/Tk distributions. See Appendices C and D for instructions on installing the extensions and packages. Finally, see Appendix E for information about accessing the *Real World* Tcl chapters and tutorials.

The CD-ROM also includes binaries for tclkit for many platforms, and a selection of Tcl applications developed with tclkit, which can be run from the CD-ROM. More information about TclKits and Starkits is available at *www.equi4.com/tclkit*. The CD-ROM contains the following directories.

| | |
|---|---|
| appendic | Copies of the installation appendices |
| bin | TclKits used by the browsing application |
| distr | Tcl/Tk distributions, including ActiveTcl for Windows, Linux, Solaris, and HP-UX, and binaries for Macintosh, FreeBSD, and Windows |
| docco | Additional documentation, including the engineering and style guides from U.C. Berkeley, Sun, Scriptics and Ajuba, Paul Raines's *Tcl/Tk Reference Guide*, the *Real World* Tcl chapters, magazine articles, and some how-to guides |
| examples | The examples from *Tcl/Tk: A Developer's Guide* |
| packages | Tcl/Tk extensions and packages described in Chapters 14 and 15 |
| skeltns | Bare-bones skeletons for writing C extensions, client-server code, megawidgets, and so on |
| src | The sources for Tcl and Tk |
| tclkits | Executable binaries of TclKit for various platforms, demonstration kits, and documentation on TclKit, Starkit, and Starpacks |
| tclpkg | A collection of pure Tcl packages described in the book |
| tools | A collection of development tools described in Chapter 15 |
| tutorial | A collection of HTML-based Tcl tutorials |

# APPENDIX B

# Installing Tcl/Tk Distributions

The companion CD-ROM contains binary distributions for revisions 8.3 and 8.4 Macintosh, Linux, FreeBSD, Solaris, HP-UX, and Windows platforms. Source code distributions are provided for revisions 7.6, 8.3, and 8.4. To facilitate matters, the Tcl and Tk distributions are compiled under FreeBSD UNIX and made a g-zipped tar file (.tgz) that can be extracted into the */usr/local* directory.

The companion CD-ROM includes executable Starkits (see Chapter 15) and a custom browser application that will run on many platforms. This browser provides simple HTML viewing and knows how to run the various installation files found on the companion CD-ROM.

The 8.4.1 release on the companion CD-ROM is the most recent stable release of Tcl/Tk. Unless you have a compelling reason to use 7.6 (you are working with an old extension that has 7.x series dependencies), you should install the 8.4.1 release. The examples in the following material assume 8.4. If you want to install 7.6 or 8.1, just change the numbers.

## B.1 Installing Tcl/Tk on a Macintosh

The Tcl/Tk distribution for the Macintosh is created as a self-extracting BinHex archive. Installing Tcl/Tk from this file is a two-step process. The first step is to convert the packed file into an installation file using the Aladdin Systems StuffIt Expander package. The StuffIt Expander program is distributed with Netscape, or it can be obtained from *www.aladdinsys.com*.

The second step is to run the installation program to perform the Tcl/Tk installation. To unpack the distribution using the StuffIt Expander, perform the following steps.

1. Place the companion CD-ROM in the CD-ROM drive and confirm that it creates a CD-ROM icon on your screen when it loads.

2. Double click the CD-ROM icon, and then double click the *distr* folder and the *mac.bin* folder.

3. Double click the file you wish to install. This example installs the 8.3.5 runtime package *(MacTclTk_8.3.5_FullInstall.bin)*.

4. Double clicking this icon will bring up a new window for selecting a destination folder to unpack the *binhex* file to. You may select a new folder (as shown in the following illustration), or put the installation file into an existing folder (perhaps *installers*).

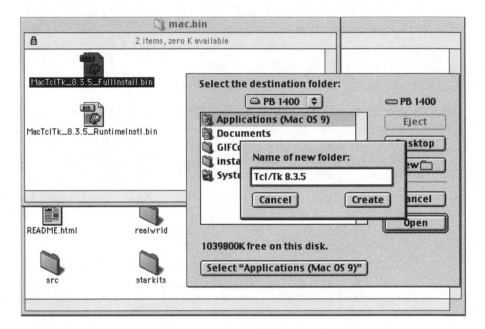

5. Click the bottom button (Select "*folder*"), and you should see the window shown in the following illustration.

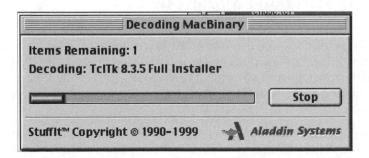

**6.** When the *binhex* file has been unpacked, the target directory should resemble that shown in the following illustration.

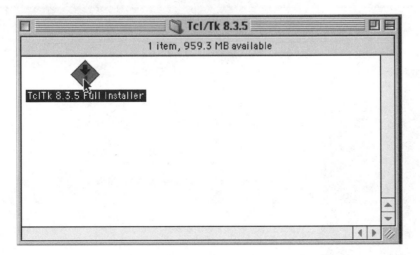

**7.** Double click the Tcl/Tk Installer icon. This starts the Tcl/Tk installation.

**8.** There may be a couple of windows describing the installer being used for this distribution, followed by a window with the Tcl license agreement, shown in the following illustration. Double click the Accept button to continue.

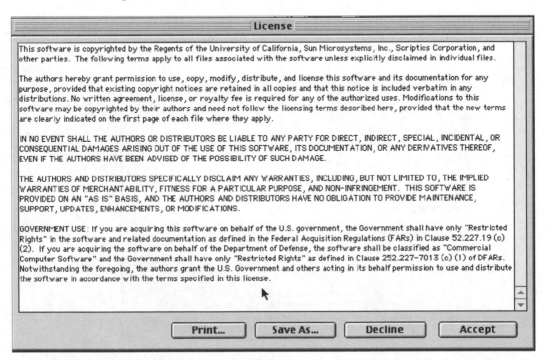

**9.** The next window may be the *Readme* file. This varies with different revisions. Click the Continue button.

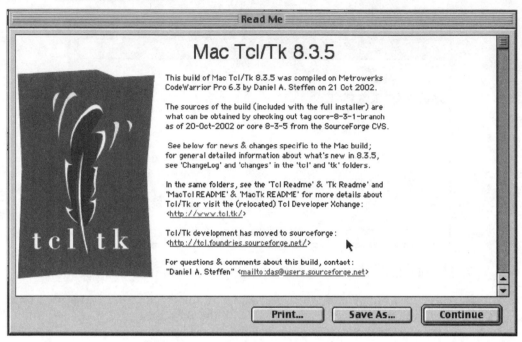

**10.** If you are installing the full package, the next window will give you a chance to select which items you wish to install. The minimal installation is the Runtime and Script libraries, as shown in the following illustration.

If you will be developing a C language extension, you will need the Developers, Tests, and Sources packages. If you do not want the default installation directory, you can click the Select Folder or Switch Disk buttons. After you have selected the workspace for Tcl/Tk (or kept the default), click the Install button.

**11.** While the installation is running, you will see a progress bar such as that shown in the following illustration.

Finally, you will see a completion window, as shown in the following illustration.

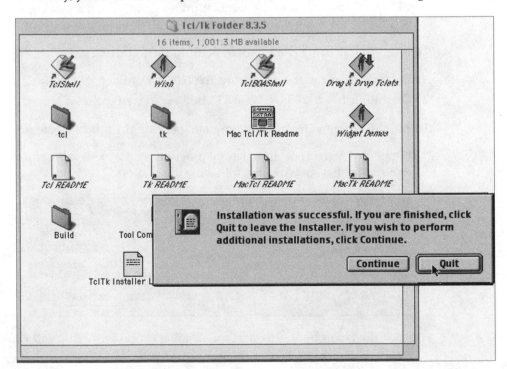

**12.** When you double click the Wish icon, it will open two windows: an image window and a command window. You can use these windows to create wish programs, as described in Chapter 2.

## B.2 Installing Tcl/Tk on MS Windows

The companion CD-ROM contains the ActiveTcl release from ActiveState (*www.activestate.com*). This is a *Batteries Included* release with many extensions, the tcllib packages, and more. When you place the *Tcl/Tk: A Developer's Guide* CD-ROM in the CD-ROM drive, a browsing application will start automatically. You can use this application to step to the appropriate installation file, you can use File Explorer to browse to the appropriate directory, or you can use your normal browser to view the *index.htm* file on the CD-ROM.

The browsing application on the CD-ROM and the File Explorer can run the installation program directly from the CD-ROM. If you use another browser, you may need to copy the file to your hard drive and invoke it from there. To install Tcl/Tk using a browsing application, perform the following steps.

**1.** Scroll down to the Binary Distributions link, and click that link.

**2.** The next page is titled *Tcl Binary Distributions*. Scroll to and click the 8.4.1 link, and then select Windows.

**3.** Click the Windows link. If you are using the browsing application on the CD-ROM, this will start the installation program. If you are using a browser, you may need to copy the file to your hard drive and execute it from there.

To install Tcl/Tk using File Explorer, perform the following steps.

**1.** Enter or browse to the *distr\Active.Tcl\Tcl8_4.1\* folder.

**2.** Double click *ActiveTcl8.4.1.0-win32-ix86.exe* to start the installation.

To run the Windows installation program, perform the following steps.

**1.** When the ActiveState installation program starts, you will see a window resembling that shown in the following illustration.

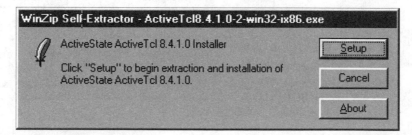

Click the Setup button to start the installation process. This will extract the installation files to a temporary location on your hard drive.

**2.** Once the files have been extracted, a window displaying the packages to be installed will be displayed. Click the Next button to proceed.

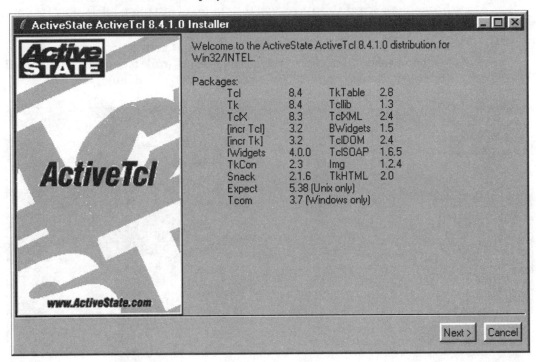

**3.** The next screen is the license agreement. Click the *I accept the terms in the License Agreement* option to continue, and then click the Next button.

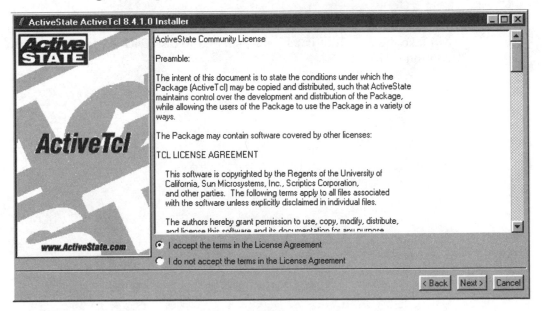

4. The next two screens allow you to select the folders for the Tcl/Tk interpreters to be installed in. You can take the defaults, or enter a folder you prefer. The first of these screens also gives you the option of installing Tcl/Tk only for your use or for all users on this system.

If the system you are installing Tcl/Tk onto is used by several users, you may want to install for all users. If this is a personal workstation, select the *Install for current user only* option. Click the Next button to continue.

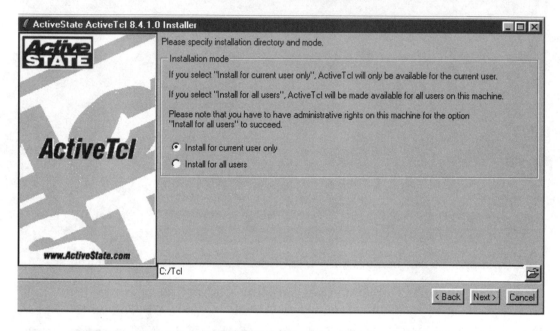

5. The next screen allows you to select the folder for the demo scripts. Again, you can take the default or enter your preferred folder. Click the Next button to continue.

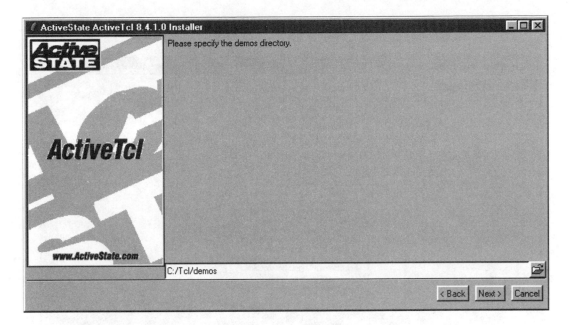

6. The next screen confirms your choices, and gives you a final chance to go back and change them. Click the Next button to continue.

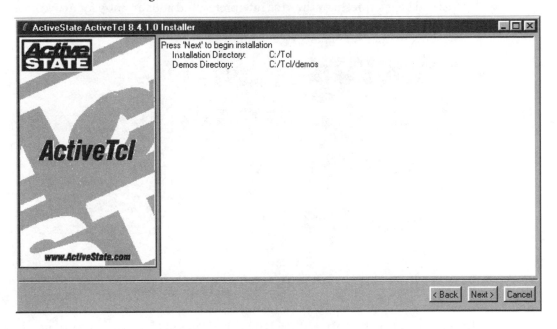

**7.** The installation program will display the files as it installs them, as shown in the following illustration.

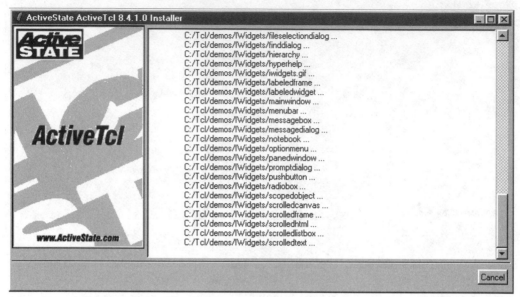

**8.** The last step of the Tcl installation adds an association so that files ending in .*tcl* will be interpreted by the wish interpreter, and adds an entry for ActiveState to the Start/Programs menu. You can click the wish or tkcon entries under this window to open an interactive session.

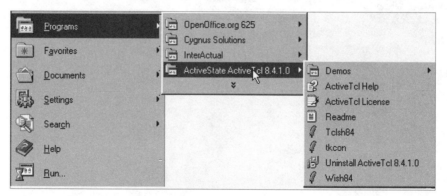

## B.3 Installing Tcl/Tk on UNIX/Linux Systems

The traditional method of installing Tcl/Tk on a UNIX or Linux system is to compile the code. The companion CD-ROM contains copies of the Tcl/Tk sources that can be unpacked and compiled. Pre-compiled versions of the Tcl/Tk interpreters are also provided for many common platforms.

Invoking the autorun.sh script will attempt to run the custom browser for your platform. If your platform is not supported, you can view the *index.htm* file with your preferred browser, or change to the appropriate directories to install the interpreters.

The companion CD-ROM contains the ActiveTcl release from ActiveState (*www.activestate.com*) for the platforms they support. This is a *Batteries Included* release with many extensions, the packages, and more. The ActiveTcl distribution uses a script that allows Tcl to be installed wherever the user has permissions.

Binary versions of the Tcl/Tk interpreters for several other platforms are provided pre-compiled and ready to be installed into */usr/local/bin*. These distributions are provided as simple tar files and cannot be relocated.

### B.3.1 Installing ActiveTcl

To install ActiveTcl, perform the following steps.

**1.** If you use the browser on the companion CD-ROM (run autorun.sh), you can select the green Binary Distributions, and then click on the release you wish to install. Finally, click your platform (for instance, Solaris/Sparc). This will un-tar the installation file to your */tmp* directory, and start the installation script. Alternately, you can use your normal browser to select these links, and copy the appropriate ActiveTcl *tar.gz* file to a temporary location to install from. The installation files are located in *distr/Active.Tcl/Tcl8_4.1*. Once you have unpacked the installation script, run install.sh to start the ActiveTcl installer.

**2.** The first window displays the packages that are provided in this ActiveTcl installation. Click the Next button to continue.

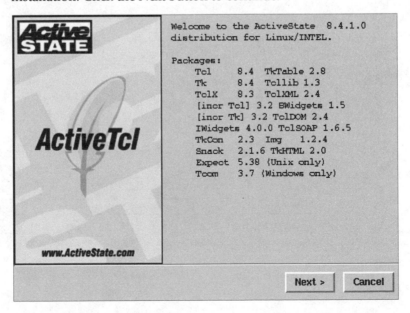

**3.** The next window will display the ActiveTcl license. Accept the terms, and click Next to continue.

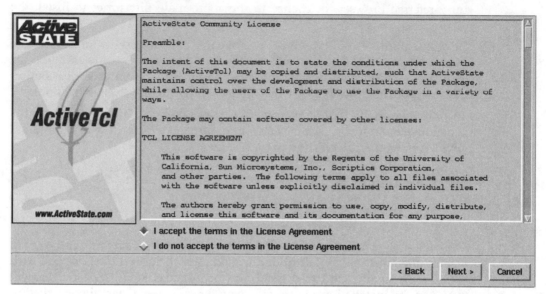

**4.** The next window lets you select the installation directory. You may accept the default, type in your preferred path, or click the Open Folder icon to open a browser. Note that you must have write permission to install into system directories. Click Next to continue.

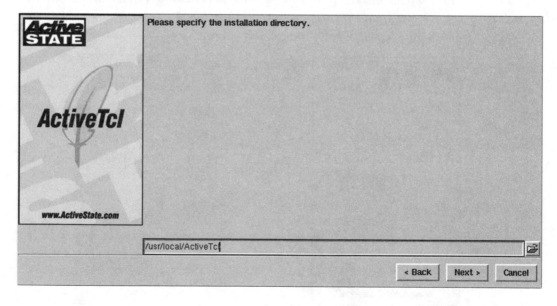

**5.** You can install the demo scripts into the same directory tree as the Tcl interpreter and libraries, or you can define another path to use. Click Next to continue.

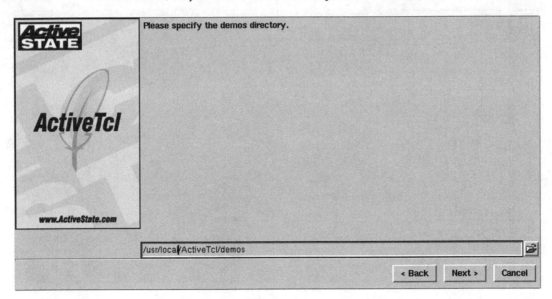

**6.** The next window lets you select a runtime installation directory. Accept the default by clicking Next to continue.

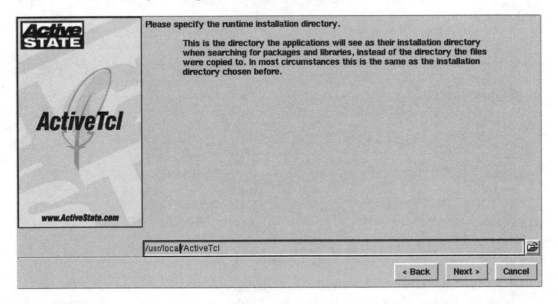

**7.** The next window summarizes your choices and gives you an opportunity to back up and modify the installation. Click Next to continue.

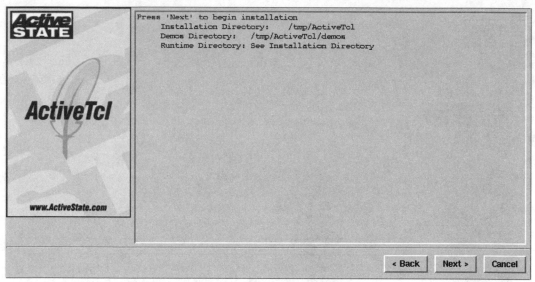

**8.** The installation script lists the files as they are being installed. Click Next to continue.

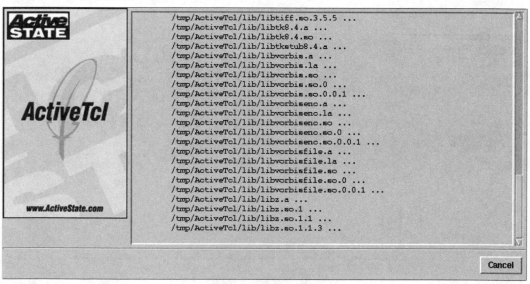

**9.** The final window reminds you of changes you will need to make (as follows) to your environment variables to find the new Tcl interpreters and documentation. Click Finish.

```
For a csh or compatible perform
    setenv PATH "/tmp/ActiveTcl/bin:$PATH"
```

```
For a sh or similar perform
    PATH="/tmp/ActiveTcl/bin:$PATH"
    export PATH
```

```
Some shells (bash for example) allow
    export PATH="/tmp/ActiveTcl/bin:$PATH"
```

```
Similar changes are required for MANPATH
```

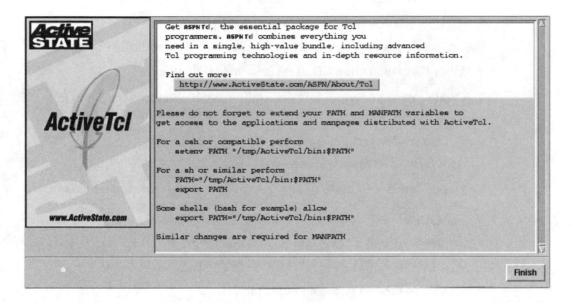

## B.3.2  Installing Other Compiled Tcl/Tk Distributions

Compiled copies of the Tcl/Tk interpreters are provided for a few other platforms, including FreeBSD. These are compiled to be installed into *usr/local* and are archived as tar files with absolute paths.

You can unpack these (using the browsing application on the companion CD-ROM) by running the autorun.sh script, clicking the green Binary Distributions entry, selecting the revision you wish to install, and then clicking the appropriate red label for the distribution. These archives are described as installing into *usr/local*. If you use the application, the packages will be unpacked into *usr/local*, and the results will be displayed in a pop-up window. The archives are located in the *distr/XX.bin* directories, where *XX* is the name of the platform. You can install one of these (for example, the FreeBSD distribution) with the following commands.

```
cd /
tar -xvof /cdrom/distr/freebsd.bin/Tcl8_4_1-freebsd-ix86.tar
```

### B.3.3 **Compiling Tcl/Tk**

If there are no binaries for your platform, you can compile the Tcl interpreters for your system. The source files are found on the companion CD-ROM in the *src/tcltk* directory. To compile the Tcl/Tk distributions, you will need the following:

- a C compiler (gcc is good, and even the portable C compiler will work)
- gunzip (to uncompress the distribution)
- tar (to unpack the distribution)

You must compile the Tcl distribution before you can compile the Tk distribution.

1. Mount the companion CD-ROM (mounted on */cdrom*).

2. Create a parent directory for the distributions, if necessary. I prefer to keep all Tcl distributions under */usr/src/TCL* instead of just */usr/src*.

3. Change to the parent directory for this distribution.

   ```
   $> cd /usr/src/TCL
   ```

4. Unpack the distributions. (Note that true tar uses -xvof, whereas pax-based tar does not use the -o flag, and some modern tar programs do not require the dash.)

   ```
   $> gzcat /cdrom/src/tcltk/tcl8.4.1-src.tar.gz | tar -xvf -
   ```

   ```
   $> gzcat /cdrom/src/tcltk/tk8.4.1-src.tar.gz | tar -xvf -
   ```

5. Change to the *distribution/unix* directory.

   ```
   $> cd tcl8.4/unix
   ```

6. Run configure, which will examine your system and create a Makefile.

   ```
   $> ./configure
   ```

   You can get a list of options to set when configure is run with the -help flag.

*Generates Output*

```
$> configure -help
```

*Output*

```
Usage: configure [options] [host]
Options: [defaults in brackets after descriptions]
Configuration:
  --cache-file=FILE   cache test results in FILE
  --help              print this message
  --no-create         do not create output files
  --quiet, --silent   do not print 'checking...' messages
  --version           print the version of autoconf that created configure
```

Directory and file names:
```
  --prefix=PREFIX           install architecture-independent files in PREFIX
                            [/usr/local]
  --exec-prefix=EPREFIX     install architecture-dependent files in EPREFIX
                            [same as prefix]
  --bindir=DIR              user executables in DIR [EPREFIX/bin]
  --sbindir=DIR             system admin executables in DIR [EPREFIX/sbin]
  --libexecdir=DIR          program executables in DIR [EPREFIX/libexec]
  --datadir=DIR             read-only architecture-independent data in DIR
                            [PREFIX/share]
  --sysconfdir=DIR          read-only single-machine data in DIR [PREFIX/etc]
  --sharedstatedir=DIR      modifiable architecture-independent data in DIR
                            [PREFIX/com]
  --localstatedir=DIR       modifiable single-machine data in DIR [PREFIX/var]
  --libdir=DIR              object code libraries in DIR [EPREFIX/lib]
  --includedir=DIR          C header files in DIR [PREFIX/include]
  --oldincludedir=DIR       C header files for non-gcc in DIR [/usr/include]
  --infodir=DIR             info documentation in DIR [PREFIX/info]
  --mandir=DIR              man documentation in DIR [PREFIX/man]
  --srcdir=DIR              find the sources in DIR [configure dir or ..]
  --program-prefix=PREFIX   prepend PREFIX to installed program names
  --program-suffix=SUFFIX   append SUFFIX to installed program names
  --program-transform-name=PROGRAM
                            run sed PROGRAM on installed program names

Host type:
  --build=BUILD             configure for building on BUILD [BUILD=HOST]
  --host=HOST               configure for HOST [guessed]
  --target=TARGET           configure for TARGET [TARGET=HOST]
Features and packages:
  --disable-FEATURE         do not include FEATURE (same as --enable-FEATURE
                            =no)
  --enable-FEATURE[=ARG]    include FEATURE [ARG=yes]
  --with-PACKAGE[=ARG]      use PACKAGE [ARG=yes]
  --without-PACKAGE         do not use PACKAGE (same as --with-PACKAGE=no)
  --x-includes=DIR          X include files are in DIR
  --x-libraries=DIR         X library files are in DIR
--enable and --with options recognized:
  --enable-man-symlinks     use symlinks for the manpages
--enable-man-compression=PROG
                            compress the manpages with PROG
  --enable-threads          build with threads
  --enable-langinfo         use nl_langinfo if possible to determine
                            encoding at startup, otherwise use old heuristic
  --enable-shared           build and link with shared libraries
                            [--enable-shared]
```

```
--enable-64bit          enable 64bit support (where applicable)
--enable-64bit-vis      enable 64bit Sparc VIS support
--disable-load          disallow dynamic loading and load command
--enable-symbols        build with debugging symbols [--disable-symbols]
--enable-framework      package shared libraries in frameworks
                        [--disable-framework]
```

The configuration options you are likely to want to set include the following.

`--disable-load`  If the computer's operating system does not support runtime-linked shared libraries, you cannot use the `load` command, and you may as well disable it. BSDI BSD/OS 2.x and 3.x do not support runtime-linked shared libraries. Linux, Solaris, SunOS 4.1.3, and HP-UX do support runtime-linked shared libraries.

`--enable-shared`  If your computer's operating system supports linked, shared libraries, you can create a `libtcl` that can be linked into your other applications.

`--prefix=PREFIX`  By default, Tcl installs itself in */usr/local/bin* and */usr/local/lib*. If you need to install Tcl elsewhere and you want the Tcl interpreter to find its initialization files in default locations, you can either define the prefix with this option or edit the `Makefile` after the `configure` is complete.

**7.** Modify the `Makefile`, if required. For most installations, the `Makefile` that is created by `configure` can be used as is.

**8.** Make the distribution.

```
$> make
```

**9.** Test that the compile worked.

```
$> make test
```

On some systems, the floating-point tests will fail. This is usually not a real bug, but reflects slight differences in floating-point emulation on different machines.

**10.** Install the Tcl interpreter, libraries, and man pages.

```
$> make install
```

To compile and install the Tk distribution, change to the *unix* directory under the Tk distribution, and repeat steps 6 through 10.

## B.3.4 **Large Systems Installation**

If you need to install Tcl/Tk on many machines, you will not want to compile Tcl/Tk on each machine and perform the install. The best solution is probably to NFS-mount a common bin and library directory tree. If that is not possible, you can distribute the software across your network using packages such as rdist and surd.

If neither of these options is appropriate for your site, the Tcl Makefile can be used to install the Tcl package in a directory other than the one it was compiled for. For example, this lets you compile Tcl for *usr/local* and install it under *tmp/usr/local*. You can then make an installation tar file from *tmp* to use when installing binaries on other systems. The steps for doing this are as follows.

**1.** Unpack and configure, as described previously.

**2.** Edit the Makefile.

**3.** Add a path for the temporary directory to the INSTALL_ROOT parameter. For example:

```
INSTALL_ROOT = /tmp
```

**4.** Make the distribution.

**5.** Create the empty directory tree for the installation.

```
mkdir /tmp/usr

mkdir /tmp/usr/local
```

**6.** Make install.

**7.** Change to the parent of the temporary directory.

```
cd /tmp/usr/local
```

**8.** Create a tar archive.

```
tar -cvf tcl.install.tar
```

**9.** Copy the tar archive to the destination system and un-tar it.

```
bar> rlogin foo

foo> cd /usr/local
foo> ftp bar
ftp> ...
ftp> get tcl.install.tar
ftp> quit
foo> tar -xvf tcl.install.tar
```

# APPENDIX C

# Installing Tcl/Tk Extensions

The companion CD-ROM contains several extensions to Tcl. Most of these are distributed as source code to be compiled with the Tcl library to create a new Tcl interpreter or loadable library. Many of the extensions are supported on MS Windows and are distributed as loadable libraries, and some are also supported for the Macintosh and are distributed as .bin, hqx, or .sit archives.

When building extensions, the best directory structure is to have the extension directory in the same directory as your Tcl and Tk distributions. Build the Tcl and Tk extensions before you compile the extension (see Appendix B for a description of how to compile Tcl and Tk). The directory tree should resemble the following.

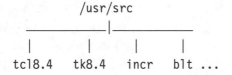

```
                    /usr/src
        _____|_____
       |       |        |       |
     tcl8.4  tk8.4     incr    blt ...
```

## C.1 Installing the BLT Extension

The BLT extension included on the companion CD-ROM is revision 2.4z, which can be used with Tk revisions 4.1, 4.2, 8.0, and more recent. This version is supported only for UNIX, Linux, and so on. To use BLT, you will first need to install Tcl/Tk on your system. See Appendix B for instructions on installing Tcl/Tk. To install BLT, perform the following steps (modified from the INSTALL file).

**1.** Uncompress and un-tar the distribution file. The browsing application can be used to extract the files to your target directory, or you can change to the directory you wish to unpack the distribution to and extract the files with unzip, as follows.

```
unzip/cdrom/packages/blt/BLT2.4z.zip
```

This will create a directory *blt2.4z*, with the subdirectories shown in the following.

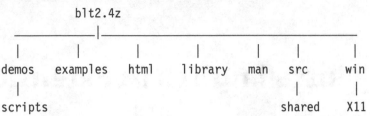

**2.** Change directories to the *blt2.4z* directory, as follows.

```
cd blt2.4z
```

**3.** Run ./configure. Invoke the auto-configuration script (./configure). The configure script supports command line options to define the locations of the Tcl and Tk header files and libraries. For example, you can define the Tcl file locations with the --with-tcl=*dir* switch, as follows.

```
./configure --with-tcl=/util/lang/tcl
```

| | |
|---|---|
| --with-tcl=dir | Top-level directory in which the Tcl and/or Tk header files and libraries are installed. Will search both $dir/include and $dir/lib. |
| --with-tk=dir | Top-level directory in which the Tk header files and libraries are installed. |
| --with-cc=program | Lets you specify the C compiler, such as acc or gcc. |
| --prefix=path | By default, the bltwish demo program, the BLT header files, libraries, scripts, and manual pages are installed in */usr/local/blt*. This lets you pick another location. |

The configure script creates a header file src/bltConfig.h. It will also generate new Makefiles from their respective templates (Makefile.in).

**4.** Compile the libraries and build the demonstration program bltwish.

```
make
```

**5.** Test by running the demos.

Go into the demos directory, as follows,

```
cd demos
```

and run the test scripts, as follows,

```
./graph
```

If your system does not support #! in shell scripts, run the test script as follows:

```
../bltwish ./graph
```

**6.** Install BLT, as follows:

```
make install
```

The directories shown in the following will be created when BLT is installed. By default, the top directory is *usr/local/blt*.

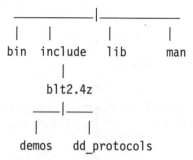

**7.** You can change the top directory by supplying the --prefix=dir switch to ./configure .

**8.** (Optional) Compile BLT into your own custom wish. If your version of wish supports dynamic loading of packages, you can simply add the following to the start of your script:

```
package require BLT
```

If your operating system does not support dynamic loading, you must compile a special *swiss-army* style wish with the extensions you need linked in. You can add BLT to a custom wish by modifying the tkAppInit.c file. To include BLT, add the following lines to your program's Tcl_AppInit routine in tkAppInit.c, as follows:

```
if (Blt_Init(interp) != TCL_OK) {
    return TCL_ERROR;
}
```

Then link with libBLT.a. And that is all there is to it. This revision of BLT places the new commands in the blt:: namespace. Earlier versions of BLT created the new commands (graph, vector, and so on) in the global scope.

## C.2 Installing the expect Extension

The expect extension is supplied as source code to be compiled for UNIX systems and as a zip archive for Windows NT. The NT port is several years old and may require tweaking for newer versions of Tcl/Tk and Windows. The NT port is provided as both a binary and sources.

### C.2.1 **Building the expect Extension Under UNIX or Mac OS X**

The steps for building expect under UNIX or Linux are as follows.

1. Build and install Tcl/Tk as described in Appendix B.
2. Mount the companion CD-ROM, and unpack the expect distribution. The browsing application can be used to extract the files to your target directory, or you can change to the directory you wish to unpack the distribution to and extract the files using unzip, as follows:

   ```
   unzip/cdrom/packages/expect/expect_5_38.zip
   ```
3. Change to the expect-5.38 directory, as follows:

   ```
   cd /usr/src/expect-5.38
   ```
4. Run the configure script to create a new Makefile. To generate a shared library, you must include the --enable-shared flag, as follows:

   ```
   ./configure --enable-shared
   ```
5. Make the package, as follows:

   ```
   make
   ```
6. Test the package, as follows:

   ```
   make test
   ```
7. Install the package, as follows:

   ```
   make install
   ```

### C.2.2 **Installing the expect Extension Under Windows NT**

The binary support for expect under Windows NT is provided in a self-extracting zip archive and install shield installation package.

1. Mount the *Tcl/Tk: A Developer's Guide* CD-ROM.
2. Using File Explorer, select packages/expect/expect-5.21r1b1-setup.exe, or using the provided browsing application select *Expect 5.21 for Windows NT: Binary*. This will start the installation program.
3. When the procedure is complete, it will have installed a new copy of wish8.0 and a Tcl 8.0 shell with expect.

## C.3 **Installing the img Extension**

The companion CD-ROM contains the complete sources for the img wish extensions (tkimg1.3rc2.zip) and the binaries for MS Windows platforms in a self-extracting zip file (img124.exe). The img zip archive (tkimg1.3rc2.zip) distribution includes distributions for the jpeg, tiff, and png image libraries, and code and patches to link these libraries into a new wish interpreter with support for jpeg, tiff, and png image types.

### C.3.1 Installing the img Extension Under MS Windows

The image libraries and the img library files are included in the file img124.exe. This executable will install the 1.2.4 release of the img package. The image format libraries will be installed into a new directory named Img1.2, under your existing Tcl\lib directory. You may need to rebuild the pkgIndex.tcl file that is distributed in this .EXE.

The new image formats can be accessed once you load the revision of the img library for the version of wish you are running. The Img extension can be loaded with a Tcl command resembling the following:

```
load C:/Tcl/lib/img1.2/img12.dll
```

### C.3.2 Building the img Extension Under UNIX

To build the img extensions under UNIX, perform the following steps.

**1.** Mount the companion CD-ROM and extract the source code. The browsing application can be used to extract the files to your target directory, or you can change to the directory you wish to unpack the distribution to and extract the files with zip, as follows:

```
unzip /cdrom/packages/img/tkimg1.3rc2.zip
```

Unpack the img code in the same directory level as your Tcl and Tk distributions. The same directory level is not required, but it makes life simpler. When this done, your build directory should resemble the following.

```
            /usr/src
    ————————|————————
    |       |       |       |
  tcl8.4  tk8.4   img     ...
```

**2.** Configure and build Tcl following the instructions in Appendix B.

**3.** Configure and build Tk following the instructions in Appendix B.

**4.** Make the libimg library.

Change to the tkimg directory. Execute the configure script and run make.

Note that you may need write access to /usr/local/lib and /usr/local/include for a build using the default configuration values.

This creates a loadable library that can be inserted into your wish interpreter with the load command or by creating a package index file (as described in Chapter 8) and including a package require Img command in your script.

If your system does not support runtime linking, you'll need to create a non-shared library. To do this set, the --disable-shared flag when you run the configure script.

```
./configure --disable-shared
```

## C.4 Installing the [incr Tcl] Extension

The [incr Tcl] extension is supported for UNIX, Macintosh, and MS Windows platforms. The ActiveTcl distributions included on the companion CD-ROM include the [incr Tcl] libraries.

If you cannot use the ActiveTcl distributions, the companion CD-ROM includes source code for [incr Tcl] and binary distributions for Macintosh and Windows. This version of [incr Tcl] supports Tcl/Tk revision 8.0 and newer.

### C.4.1 Installing [incr Tcl] on a Macintosh

The [incr Tcl] distribution for the Macintosh is created as a self-extracting BinHex archive. The [incr Tcl] extension can be installed from this file using the Aladdin Systems StuffIt Expander package. The StuffIt Expander program is distributed with Netscape and can be obtained from *www.aladdinsys.com*. To unpack the distribution using the StuffIt Expander, perform the following steps.

1. Place the *Tcl/Tk: A Developer's Guide* CD-ROM in the CD-ROM drive and confirm that it creates an icon on your screen when it loads.

2. Open the CD-ROM and select the packages:incr_tcl:Mac_Itcl3.1_8.3.2p1. sit.bin, packages:incr_tcl:incr_tcl/MacItcl2.2p2PPC.sea.hqx, or packages:incr_tcl:incr_tcl/MacItcl2.2p268k.sea.hqx archive. If you get an error opening these, you must use the StuffIt Expander to unpack them, as follows.

   a. Start the StuffIt Expander program.
   b. Click on the File menu in the upper left-hand corner of the screen.
   c. Click on the Expand menu option from that menu. Clicking on the Expand option will bring up a file-browsing window for selecting the installation file.
   d. Select the file to be extracted.

3. Select the destination directory for the [incr Tcl] package. This should be the library directory under the Tcl folder.

**4.** When the `StuffIt Expander` is finished with a 2.2 installation, you will have a new icon for [`incr Tcl`] and new interpreters to use.

After installing the 3.1 [`incr Tcl`] package, there will be a new set of folders, including the files `-> Extensions:-> Tool Command Language Folder:Itcl3.1.shlb` and `-> Extensions:-> Tool Command Language Folder :Itk3.1.shlb`. The SHLB libraries can be loaded into a Tcl shell with the load command (`load tcl:library:-> Extensions:-> Tool Command Language Folder:Itk3.1.shlb`) or moved to another directory for use. You can create a package index file, as described in Chapter 8.

## C.4.2 Installing the [`incr Tcl`] Extension Under MS Windows

If you have installed the ActiveTcl distribution, you will already have [`incr Tcl`] installed on your system. If you have another Tcl distribution and need the [`incr Tcl`] package, you can use a zip distribution of the 3.2 release (the most recent, for Tcl/Tk 8.2 and more recent) or a self-installing `.EXE` distribution of the 2.2 release for Tcl 7.6.

### Installing the 3.2 Release for Tcl Version 8.2 and Newer

The zip file for the 3.2 release is `packages/incr_tcl/itcl32.zip`. This file should be unzipped to a subdirectory named `incr` in the *lib* folder for your Tcl installation. Depending on the Tcl release, this may be the folder that includes `init.tcl` or the parent of that folder. You can find `init.tcl` using the Windows `Search` facility or by starting a `tclsh` or `wish` shell and using the `info library` command.

Once you have identified the destination, you can use Winzip or File Explorer to install the `itcl32.zip` file. Alternatively, you can use the browser application that comes with the companion CD-ROM to browse to the *Incr Tcl 3.2.1 Compiled for Windows* entry and select it.

### Installing the 2.2 Release for Tcl Version 7.6

This [`incr Tcl`] installation kit is created with `InstallShield`. You can install [`incr Tcl`] by executing the `itcl22.exe` file. You can execute this file using File Explorer to select `packages/incr_tcl/itcl22.exe` or by using the browser application to select *Incr Tcl 2.2 Compiled for Windows* under the *Extensions and Packages* link.

When you execute the `itcl2.2.exe` program, you will see the familiar blue screen. If you choose the defaults, this program will install [`incr Tcl`] in `C:\Program Files\Itcl2.2`. The new interpreters will be named `itclsh.exe` and `itkwish.exe`. These files will be placed in the `bin` subdirectory of the installation directory you specified during installation (by default, this will be `C:\Program Files\Itcl2.2\bin`).

### C.4.3 **Installing [incr Tcl] Under UNIX**

The source distribution of [incr Tcl] is a zip file (packages/incr_tcl/itcl3_2_1.zip). The following procedure will create the [incr Tcl] extension.

1. Create a directory path that includes the Tcl/Tk sources for your machine. The directory tree should resemble the following.

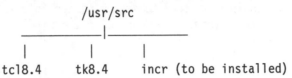

```
              /usr/src
   _____|_____
   |           |           |
 tcl8.4      tk8.4      incr (to be installed)
```

2. Change to the parent directory for tcl8.4 and tk8.4.
3. Mount the *Tcl/Tk: A Developer's Guide* CD-ROM.
4. Unpack the [incr Tcl] source files with unzip, as follows:

   unzip -c /cdrom/packages/incr_tcl/itcl3_2_1.zip

   This will create a new directory itcl3.2.1.
5. Change to the itcl3.2.1 directory.
6. Run the configure script to create the Makefile.
7. Run make to make the libraries. On BSD/OS systems you may need to manually add -ldl to the Makefile after configure.
8. Run make install to install the libraries. You may need to be root to do this.

### C.4.4 **Installing iwidgets**

The iwidgets package is a collection of megawidgets written in [incr Tcl]. The package is distributed as a zip file (packages/incr_tcl/iwidgets-4.0.1.zip), which can be extracted with Stuffit Expander, winzip, unzip, or the browsing application on the companion CD-ROM.

This file should be unzipped to a subdirectory in the *lib* folder for your Tcl installation. The *lib* directory should be the parent of the folder that includes init.tcl. You can find init.tcl using the Windows Search facility or the UNIX find command, or by starting a tclsh or wish shell and using the info library command. To install using the browsing application on the companion CD-ROM, browse to *Extensions and Packages* and select *Incr Widgets: MegaWidget package written in [incr tk]: As zip*.

## C.5 **Installing the MySqlTcl Extension**

The MySqlTcl extension is provided as source and as an RPM for Linux distributions. The steps for building MySqlTcl under UNIX or Linux are as follows.

1. Build and install Tcl/Tk as described in Appendix B.

2. Mount the *Tcl/Tk: A Developer's Guide* CD-ROM.

3. Unpack the MySqlTcl distribution, as follows:

   ```
   unzip /cdrom/packages/mysqltcl/mysqltcl-2.0rc15.zip
   ```

4. At this point the directory tree should resemble the following.

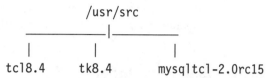

5. Change to the mysqltcl-2.0rc15 directory.

6. Run the configure script to create a new Makefile.

7. Make the package.

8. Use make install to install the package. Note that you may need superuser privileges for this.

To install the RPM, use the RPM manager for your version of Linux, and point it at /cdrom/packages/mysqltcl/mysqltcl-2.0rc15-0.i386.rpm.

# C.6 Installing the oratcl Extension

Two revisions of the oratcl extension are provided on the *Tcl/Tk: A Developer's Guide* CD-ROM. The 2.5 release supports Tcl revisions 7.6 and 8.0 and Tk revisions 4.2 and 8.0 on UNIX, Macintosh, and Windows platforms. To use this extension you must also have access to an Oracle server (version 6, 7.0, 7.1, 7.2, or 7.3). The 4.0 release is provided for Windows and UNIX, and will work with Tcl 8.2 and more recent, and Oracle 8.x and 9.x.

## C.6.1 Installing the 2.5 oratcl Extension Under MS Windows

The oratcl DLL files are stored in the zip file packages\oratcl2.5\oratcl25.zip. To use oratcl you must also have the Oracle DLLs installed. This installation requires that you unzip the files into a temporary directory, and then run the oratcl installation script install.tcl to copy the appropriate files to your Tcl directories. To install the oratcl DLLs, perform the following steps.

1. Place the *Tcl/Tk: A Developer's Guide* CD-ROM in the CD-ROM drive.

2. Extract the zip file (extensn\oratcl\oratcl25.zip) with Winzip, File Explorer, or the browsing application provided on the CD-ROM. You can extract these files to any folder. This example assumes the code is extracted to C:\oratmp.

3. Change to the `C:\oratmp\win` directory, as follows:

   `cd C:\oratmp\win`

4. Run the `install.tcl` script, which will determine which version of Tcl you are running and will copy the appropriate version of the `oratcl` DLL to a new directory named `oratcl25` under your Tcl installation `lib` directory.

You may need to add the new directory to the `auto_path` variable in your scripts in order to load `oratcl` with a `package require Oratcl` command.

### C.6.2 Installing the 2.5 `oratcl` Extension Under UNIX

The `oratcl` source code is provided in a zip archive. To build this package you will need to have the Oracle C libraries installed on your system. The steps for building `oratcl` under UNIX or Linux are as follows.

1. Build and install Tcl/Tk as described in Appendix B.

2. Mount the *Tcl/Tk: A Developer's Guide* CD-ROM.

3. Unpack the `oratcl` distribution, as follows:

   `unzip /cdrom/packages/oratcl2.5/oratcl25src.zip`

4. At this point the directory tree should resemble the following.

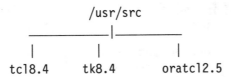

```
              /usr/src
      ————————|————————
      |         |          |
    tcl8.4    tk8.4     oratcl2.5
```

5. Change to the `oratcl-2.5` directory.

6. Run the `configure` script to create a new `Makefile`.

7. Make the package.

8. Use `make install` to install the package. Note that you may need superuser privileges for this.

### C.6.3 Installing the 4.0 `oratcl` Extension Under MS Windows

The `oratcl` DLL files are stored in the zip file `packages\oratcl4.0\oratcl40-win.zip`. To use `oratcl` you must also have the Oracle DLLs installed.

This file should be unzipped to a subdirectory in the *lib* folder for your Tcl installation. The *lib* directory should be the parent of the folder that includes `init.tcl`. You can find `init.tcl` using the Windows Search facility or the UNIX `find` command, or by starting a `tclsh` or `wish` shell and using the `info library` command. To install the `oratcl` DLLs, perform the following steps.

1. Place the *Tcl/Tk: A Developer's Guide* CD-ROM in the CD-ROM drive.

2. Extract the zip file (`extensn\oratcl\oratcl25.zip`) with Winzip, File Explorer, or the browsing application provided on the CD-ROM. You can extract these files to any folder. This example assumes the code is extracted to `C:\oratmp`.

3. Change to the `C:\oratmp\win` directory, as follows:

   `cd C:\oratmp\win`

4. Run the `install.tcl` script, which will determine which version of Tcl you are running and will copy the appropriate version of the `oratcl` DLL to a new directory named `oratcl25` under your Tcl installation `library` directory.

You may need to add the new directory to the `auto_path` variable in your scripts in order to load `oratcl` with a `package require Oratcl` command.

### C.6.4 Installing the 4.0 oratcl Extension Under UNIX

The `oratcl` source code is provided in a zip archive. To build this package you will need to have the Oracle C libraries installed on your system. The steps for building `oratcl` under UNIX or Linux are as follows.

1. Build and install Tcl/Tk as described in Appendix B.

2. Mount the *Tcl/Tk: A Developer's Guide* CD-ROM.

3. Unpack the `oratcl` distribution, as follows:

   `unzip /cdrom/packages/oratcl4.0/oratcl40src.zip`

   At this point the directory tree should resemble the following.

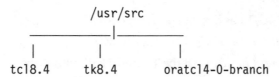

```
                  /usr/src
        _____|_____
       |           |           |
     tcl8.4      tk8.4        oratcl4-0-branch
```

4. Change to the `oratcl-4-0-branch` directory.

5. Run the `configure` script to create a new `Makefile`.

6. Make the package.

## C.7 Installing the sybtcl Extension

The `sybtcl` extension is provided compiled for MS Windows systems or as source for UNIX systems. To use `sybtcl` you must also have the Sybase runtime libraries (`libsybdb.dll`) installed.

### C.7.1 **Installing the sybtcl Extension Under MS Windows**

The sybtcl DLL files are stored in the zip file packages\sybtcl\sybtcl-3.0rc2.zip. To use sybtcl you must also have the Sybase DLLs (libsybdb.dll) installed.

This installation requires that you unzip the files into a temporary directory, and then run the sybtcl installation script install.tcl to copy the appropriate files to your Tcl directories. To install the sybtcl DLLs, perform the following steps.

1. Place the *Tcl/Tk: A Developer's Guide* CD-ROM in the CD-ROM drive.
2. Extract the zip file (extensn\oratcl\oratcl25.zip) with Winzip, File Explorer, or the browsing application provided on the CD-ROM. You can extract these files to any folder. This example assumes the code is extracted to C:\sybtmp.
3. Change to the C:\sybtmp\win directory, as follows:

   cd C:\sybtmp\win

4. Run the install.tcl script, which will determine which version of Tcl you are running and will copy the appropriate version of the oratcl DLL to a new directory named sybtcl30 under your Tcl installation lib directory.

### C.7.2 **Installing the sybtcl Extension Under UNIX**

The sybtcl source code is provided in a zip archive. To build this package you will need to have the Sybase C libraries (libsybdb.a) installed on your system. The steps for building sybtcl under UNIX or Linux are as follows.

1. Build and install Tcl/Tk as described in Appendix B.
2. Mount the *Tcl/Tk: A Developer's Guide* CD-ROM.
3. Change to the parent directory of the Tcl and Tk distributions.
4. Unpack the sybtcl distribution, as follows.

   unzip /cdrom/packages/sybtcl/sybtcl-3.0rc2.zip

5. At this point the directory tree should resemble the following.

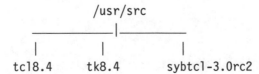

6. Change to the sybtcl-3.0rc2 directory.
7. Run the configure script to create a new Makefile.
8. Make the package.

## C.8 Installing the VSdb Package

The vsdb package is a pure Tcl database package suitable for portable, lightweight applications. It is distributed as a zip file that can be unpacked into a temporary location with winzip, unzip, Stuffit Expander, or the browsing application on the CD-ROM.

After unpacking the files to a temporary directory, evaluate the insvsdb.tcl file to install the TclVSdb package into the proper folder on your system. This may require an administrative privilege level. After the installation, you can remove the temporary folder. Including package require TclVSdb in a script should load the package.

# C.9 Installing the Tc1X Extension

The TclX extension is supported on UNIX, Macintosh, and Windows systems. This extension is bundled into the ActiveTcl distributions for Windows and several UNIX systems. (See Appendix B for information on installing the ActiveTcl distributions.) A compiled version for the Macintosh and source are provided on the companion CD-ROM.

## C.9.1 Installing the Tc1X Extension on a Macintosh

The TclX distribution for the Macintosh is created as a self-extracting Bin-Hex archive. The TclX extension can be installed from this file using the Aladdin Systems StuffIt Expander package. The StuffIt Expander program is distributed with Netscape and can be obtained from *www.aladdinsys.com*. To unpack the distribution using the StuffIt Expander, perform the following steps.

**1.** Place the *Tcl/Tk: A Developer's Guide* CD-ROM in the CD-ROM drive and confirm that it creates an icon on your screen when it loads.

**2.** Open the CD-ROM and select the packages:tclx:Mac_TclX8.3_8.3.2p1.sit. bin archive. If you get an error opening this, you must use the StuffIt Expander directly to unpack it, as follows.

   a. Start the StuffIt Expander program.

   b. Click on the File menu in the upper left-hand corner of your screen.

   c. Click on the Expand menu option from that menu. Clicking on the Expand option will bring up a file-browsing window to select the installation file.

   d. Select the file to be extracted.

3. Select the destination directory for the TclX package. This should be the library directory under the Tcl folder.

4. When StuffIt Expander is finished there will be a new set of folders, including the file Mac TclX8.3 for 8.3.2p1 -> Extensions:-> Tool Command Language Folder:TclX.shlb). The *.shlb* library can be loaded into a Tcl shell with the load command load tcl:library:-> Extensions:-> Tool Command Language Folder:TclX.shlb, or moved to another directory for use. You can create a package index file, as described in Chapter 8.

## C.9.2 Installing the TclX Extension Under UNIX

To configure and compile the TclX extension, you need to have the appropriate version of Tcl and Tk already compiled. The following procedure will generate the TclX extension on your system.

1. Mount the *Tcl/Tk: A Developer's Guide* CD-ROM.

2. Extract the Tcl and Tk distributions. The browsing application can be used to extract the files to your target directory, or you can change to the directory you wish to unpack the distribution to and extract the files with zip, as follows.

   unzip /cdrom/packages/tclx/tclx835-src.zip

   Unpack the TclX code in the same directory level as your Tcl and Tk distributions. The same directory level is not required, but it makes life simpler. When this is done, your build directory should resemble the following.

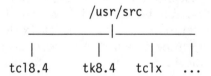

```
                  /usr/src
      _____|_____
     |        |        |       |
   tcl8.4   tk8.4    tclx    ...
```

3. Build the Tcl and Tk interpreters as described in Appendix B.

4. Change to the tclx8.3.5/unix subdirectory.

5. Generate the Makefile by running the configure script, as follows:

   $> configure

6. Make the interpreters, as follows:

   $> make

7. Test the new Tcl interpreter, as follows:

   $> make test

8. Install the new Tcl interpreters, as follows:

   $> make install

## C.10 Installing the BWidget Package

The BWidget package is a collection of pure Tcl megawidgets. These provide a professional look and feel without platform dependencies. The package is distributed as a zip file that can be unpacked into your Tcl library location with `winzip, unzip, Stuffit Expander`, or the browsing application on the companion CD-ROM.

The library directory should be the parent of the folder that includes `init.tcl`. You can find `init.tcl` using the Windows Search facility or the UNIX `find` command, or by starting a `tclsh` or `wish` shell and using the `info library` command.

# APPENDIX D

# Installing Tcl/Tk Applications

## D.1 Starkit

Starkits (STand-Alone Runtime kits) for Tcl allow you to package a collection of scripts and libraries for easy distribution. The Starkits include a small database engine and support for mounting and reading zip files as virtual file systems. Starkits are made using the `sdx.kit` program and the Tclkit appropriate to your platform. Tclkits for many platforms are provided on the *Tcl/Tk: A Developer's Guide* CD-ROM under the `tclkits` folder.

### D.1.1 Installing the Tclkit

To install Tclkit, perform the following steps.

**1.** Mount the *Tcl/Tk: A Developer's Guide* CD-ROM.

**2.** Copy the appropriate Tclkit for your platform from `D:/tclkits` (or `/cdrom/tclkits` for UNIX users) to a directory in your search path.

**3.** Copy the `sdx.kit` file from the `tclkits` directory to a directory in your PATH, rename this to `sdx`, and (on UNIX systems) use `chmod` to add execute permission.

### D.1.2 More Information

For more information on using Starkits, see the discussion in Chapter 15 or the Starkit articles under the *Documentation* heading (`docco/starkit`).

## D.2 TkCon

The TkConsole program can be run on the Macintosh or under MS Windows or UNIX. This package is distributed in a zip archive. To install it, perform the following steps.

1. Place the *Tcl/Tk: A Developer's Guide* CD-ROM in the CD-ROM drive.
2. Extract the zip file (tools\tkcon\tkcon.zip) with Winzip, File Explorer, or the browsing application provided on the CD-ROM. On UNIX systems, extract to a bin directory. This may be your $HOME bin or a system bin (if you have superuser permissions). For Windows and Macintosh, you may extract *TkCon.tcl* to any directory. On Windows boxes, you may want to make a shortcut to the tkcon.tcl application, and on Macintosh platforms you should use the Drag-N-Drop Tclets application to make the console easily executed.

## D.3 frink

The frink program will check Tcl/Tk programs for correctness and reformat them for readability. The companion CD-ROM includes binaries for Linux, Windows, Solaris, and HP-UX (PaRisc).

### D.3.1 Installing a Precompiled frink Package

To install a precompiled frink package, perform the following steps.

1. Place and/or mount the *Tcl/Tk: A Developer's Guide* CD-ROM in your CD-ROM drive.
2. Extract the appropriate zip file for your platform (tools\frink\frink-*platform*.zip) with Winzip, unzip, or the browsing application provided on the CD-ROM. You should extract these files to a folder in your search path.

### D.3.2 Compiling frink Under MS Windows

To compile this package with VC++ 5.0, perform the following steps.

1. Place the *Tcl/Tk: A Developer's Guide* CD-ROM in your CD-ROM drive.
2. Extract the zip file (tools\frink\frink-2_1_5.zip) with Winzip or the browsing application provided on the CD-ROM. You can extract these files to any folder. This example assumes the code is extracted to C:\frink.

**3.** Start up VC++.

**4.** Create a new project (File > New > Project Workspace).

**5.** Select `Console Application` from the listbox, and check win32 under Platform.

**6.** Type in the path to the directory you created (but not the directory itself) in the Location entry box (i.e., if you created a new directory `C:\frink`, type `C:` in the Location entry box).

**7.** Type the name of the directory you created in the Name entry box.

**8.** Click on the Create button. The new project will now be created. Wait until the progress bars have been erased from your screen.

**9.** Open the Insert Files into the Project window (Insert > Files into Project). With the Ctrl key depressed, click on each of the *.c* and *.h* files with the left mouse button, and then click on the Add button.

**10.** Click on the Build menubutton and select Build All.

### D.3.3 Compiling `frink` Under UNIX

To compile `frink` on a UNIX/Linux system, perform the following.

**1.** Mount the *Tcl/Tk: A Developer's Guide* CD-ROM.

**2.** Change the directory to the top of your source tree, as follows:

```
cd /home/example/src
```

**3.** Unpack the `frink` source distribution, as follows:

```
unzip /cdrom/tools/frink/frink-2_1_5.zip
```

**4.** Change to the `frink-2.1.5` directory, as follows:

```
cd frink-2.1.5
```

**5.** Run the `configure` script, as follows:

```
./configure
```

**6.** Make the `frink` executable by clicking on the `Make` button.

**7.** Install with the `Install` button.

## D.4 `tclCheck`

TclCheck is distributed as a gzipped tar archive (`tclCheck-1-1-13.zip`) with a configure script for UNIX systems. A compiled version of `tclCheck` is in the `tools\tclCheck\tclCheck_win.zip` file.

### D.4.1 **Installing a Precompiled tclCheck Package**

To install a precompiled tclCheck package, perform the following steps.

1. Place and/or mount the *Tcl/Tk: A Developer's Guide* CD-ROM in your CD-ROM drive.

2. Extract the appropriate zip file for your platform (tools\tclCheck\tclCheck-*platform*.zip) with Winzip, unzip, or the browsing application provided on the CD-ROM. You should extract these files to a folder in your search path.

### D.4.2 **Compiling tclCheck Under MS Windows**

To compile this package with VC++ 5.0, perform the following steps.

1. Place the *Tcl/Tk: A Developer's Guide* CD-ROM in your CD-ROM drive.

2. Extract the zip file (tools\tclCheck\tclCheck-1-1-13.zip) with Winzip or the browsing application provided on the CD-ROM. You can extract these files to any folder. This example assumes the code is extracted to C:\tclCheck.

3. Start up VC++.

4. Create a new project (File > New > Project Workspace).

5. Select Console Application from the listbox, and check win32 under Platform.

6. Type in the path to the directory you created (but not the directory itself) in the Location entry box (i.e., if you created a new directory C:\tclCheck, type C: in the Location entry box).

7. Type the name of the directory you created in the Name entry box.

8. Click on the Create button. The new project will now be created. Wait until the progress bars have been erased from your screen.

9. Open the Insert Files into the Project window (Insert > Files into Project). With the Ctrl key depressed, click on each of the .c and .h files with the left mouse button, and then click on the Add button.

10. Click on the Build menubutton and select Build All.

### D.4.3 **Compiling tclCheck Under UNIX**

To compile tclCheck on a UNIX/Linux system, perform the following steps.

1. Mount the *Tcl/Tk: A Developer's Guide* CD-ROM.

2. Change the directory to the top of your source tree, as follows:

```
cd /home/example/src
```

3. Unpack the `tclCheck` source distribution, as follows:

   `unzip /cdrom/tools/tclCheck/tclCheck-1-1-13.zip`

4. Change to the `tclCheck-1.1.13` directory, as follows:

   `cd tclCheck-1-1-13`

5. Compile the `tclCheck.c` program, as follows:

   `gcc -o tclCheck tclCheck.c`

## D.5 ICEM Lint

The ICEM Lint program (`icelint`) is available precompiled for IBM Risc, DEC Alpha, SGI, and Solaris systems. To install this package on a UNIX system, unzip the appropriate zip archive with unzip or the browser application on the companion CD-ROM, and then copy the binary files to your path.

## D.6 TclPro Suite

The TclPro suite is a collection of development tools including a debugger, wrapper, lint, and compiler. It is provided on the companion CD-ROM as precompiled installations for HP-UX (PaRisc), SGI Irix, Solaris, Linux, FreeBSD, and MS Windows.

### D.6.1 Installing the TclPro Suite on UNIX Platforms

To install the `TclPro` suite on a UNIX platform, perform the following steps.

1. Mount the *Tcl/Tk: A Developer's Guide* CD-ROM.
2. Extract the zip file (`tools\tclpro\tclpro*.PLATFORM.zip`) with unzip or the browsing application provided on the CD-ROM.
3. Examine the README file for more platform-specific instructions, or evaluate the `setup.sh` script.
4. The `setup.sh` script will install the TclPro suite on your system. If you are prompted for a license, use `1094-320C-1G38-2U24-P8YY`. This license has been granted to the public domain for using TclPro.
5. Add the installation directory to your PATH.

### D.6.2 Installing the TclPro Suite on MS Windows

To install the `TclPro` suite on MS Windows, perform the following steps.

1. Place the *Tcl/Tk: A Developer's Guide* CD-ROM in the CD-ROM drive.

2. Select the self-executing zip file `tools\tclpro\tclpro141.exe` by browsing with the File Explorer, the Run command, or the browser utility on the CD-ROM.

3. The installation program will install the TclPro suite on your system. If you are prompted for a license, use `1094-320C-1G38-2U24-P8YY`. This license has been granted to the public domain for using TclPro.

## D.7 Tuba

The Tuba debugger is a Tcl language package supported on UNIX/Linux and MS Windows platforms. This revision does not work under Macintosh. This distribution of Tuba is packaged as a zip file with the generic Tcl-based parser.

### D.7.1 Installing the tuba Debugger

To install the `tuba` debugger, perform the following steps.

1. Place the *Tcl/Tk: A Developer's Guide* CD-ROM in the CD-ROM drive, and/or mount the *Tcl/Tk: A Developer's Guide* CD-ROM.

2. Extract the zip file (`tools\tuba\tuba-2.5.b1.zip`) with Winzip, File Explorer, or the browsing application provided on the CD-ROM.

3. On UNIX systems, add the directory to your PATH. On Windows systems you may want to make a shortcut to the `tuba` application.

## D.8 tcl-debug

The `tcl-debug` distribution is found on the companion CD-ROM in the file `tools/dbg/tcldb_17.zip`.

### D.8.1 Compiling tcl-debug Under UNIX

The `tcl-debug` package is distributed as a zip archive with a `configure` file. To compile `tcl-debug` on a UNIX/Linux system, perform the following steps.

1. Mount the *Tcl/Tk: A Developer's Guide* CD-ROM.

2. Change the directory to the top of your source tree, as follows:

```
cd /home/example/src
```

**3.** Unpack the `tcl-debug` source distribution, as follows, or by using the browsing application on the CD-ROM:

`unzip /cdrom/tools/dbg/tcldb_17.zip`

**4.** Change to the `tcl-debug` directory, as follows.

`cd tcl-debug-1.7`

**5.** Create the `Makefile` by running the `configure` script, as follows.

`configure`

**6.** Make the `tcl-debug` executable, as follows.

`make`

# D.9 SpecTcl

The SpecTcl distribution is done as a zip archive for UNIX systems, as a self-extracting zip file for MS Windows systems, and as a self-extracting BinHex archive (to be unpacked with the `StuffIt Expander` for the Macintosh).

## D.9.1 Installing SpecTcl Under MS Windows

The SpecTcl installation program (`D:\tools\spectcl\spectcl.exe`) is generated with `InstallShield`. When you invoke the program, you will see the familiar blue screen. To install `SpecTcl` from the `D:\tools\spectcl\spectcl.exe` file, perform the following steps.

**1.** Place the *Tcl/Tk: A Developer's Guide* CD-ROM in your CD-ROM drive. The rest of these instructions assume that this is drive D.

**2.** You can use File Explorer, the Run option, or the browsing application to start the `D:\tools\spectcl\spectcl.exe` installer, as follows.

    a. Using Run, select Start and then Run from the Windows task button. Enter or browse to `D:\tools\spectcl\SpecTcl1.1.exe` and run that program.

    b. Using File Explorer, browse to the `D:\tools\spectcl` directory and double click on `SpecTcl1.1.exe`.

    c. Using the browsing application, browse to the Tools selection, and click on *Spectcl for Windows*.

        i. The initial screen will inform you that this application will install `SpecTcl` onto your computer. Click on the OK button.

        ii. The next screen contains the license agreement. Click on the Accept button.

        iii. The next screen contains a browser to allow you to select the destination for the SpecTcl installation. Select the location for this installation and click on the OK button.

        iv. After you click on the OK button, you will see the familiar progress bar as SpecTcl is installed.

        v. When SpecTcl has been installed in the selected directory, a window will be displayed that asks if you would like to have a shortcut for SpecTcl created. Click on the Yes button.

The final window will tell you how you can invoke SpecTcl.

## D.9.2 **Installing SpecTcl Under UNIX**

To install `SpecTcl` under UNIX, perform the following steps.

**1.** Mount the *Tcl/Tk: A Developer's Guide* CD-ROM.

**2.** Change the directory to the directory in which you wish to install `SpecTcl`.

**3.** Unpack the `SpecTcl` distribution, as follows:

```
unzip /cdrom/tools/spectcl/spectcl1_2a3.zip
```

**4.** Change to the `SpecTcl/bin` directory.

**5.** Edit `specTcl` and `specJava`.

    a. Set the `DIR` variable to point to the current directory.

    b. Optionally set the `WISH` variable to point to the version of `wish` you want to use.

    c. Add the `$DIR/SpecTcl1.1/bin` path to your `$PATH` environment variable, or copy the `specTcl` and `specJava` variables to a directory in your search path.

## D.9.3 **Installing SpecTcl on a PPC-based Macintosh**

The `SpecTcl` distribution for the Macintosh is a self-extracting BinHex archive. This file includes a stub for the Power PC version of the Macintosh. The first step is to convert the packed file into an installation file using the Aladdin Systems `StuffIt Expander` package. The `StuffIt Expander` program is distributed with Netscape and can be obtained from *www.aladdinsys.com*.

The second step is to run the installation program to install `SpecTcl`. To unpack the distribution using the `StuffIt Expander`, perform the following steps.

**1.** Place the *Tcl/Tk: A Developer's Guide* CD-ROM in the CD-ROM drive and confirm that it creates an icon on your screen when it loads.

**2.** Start the `StuffIt Expander` program by double clicking on the Expander icon.

**3.** Click on the File menu in the upper left-hand corner of your screen.

**4.** Click on the Expand menu option from that menu.

**5.** Clicking on the Expand option will bring up a file-browsing window to select the installation file. The following steps describe selecting the file:

a. Select the desktop.

b. Double click on the name of the CD-ROM.

c. Double click on *tools*.

d. Double click on *spectcl*.

e. Double click on the entry *SpecTcl1.1.sea.hqx*.

f. Click on the Desktop button. The content of the desktop will now appear in the window, and the Unstuff button will no longer be grayed out.

g. Click on the Unstuff button, or press the Return key.

h. StuffIt Expander will now convert the distribution file to an executable program on your desktop area.

6. When StuffIt Expander has completed the expansion of the distribution file, there will be a new icon on your desktop named SpecTcl 1.1 Installer.

7. Click on the SpecTcl 1.1 Installer icon. This starts the SpecTcl installation.

8. The first window you will see will have the Tcl/Tk license agreement. Click on the Continue button.

9. The next screen informs you that this installation program will install the SpecTcl GUI Builder. Click on the Install button.

10. The next window will allow you to select where you would like to place the Tcl/Tk package.

11. After you have selected the workspace for SpecTcl (perhaps the main desktop), click on the Install button.

After your system has rebooted, there will be an icon named SpecTcl Folder in the workspace you selected for the installation. You can now drag the SpecTcl 1.1 Installation icon to the trash bin. You will not need it again.

# D.10 Visual GIPSY

Visual GIPSY, by Patzschke Rasp Software AG, is a cross-platform GUI builder for Tcl/Tk applications. It is provided on the companion CD-ROM as a zip archive for UNIX, Windows, and Macintosh systems, and as a self-installing archive for Windows.

## D.10.1 Installing Visual Gipsy Under MS Windows

The Visual Gipsy installation program (D:\tools\gipsy\vg263.exe) is generated with InstallShield. When you invoke the program, you will see the familiar blue screen. To install Visual Gipsy from the D:\tools\gipsy\vg263.exe file, perform the following steps.

1. Place the *Tcl/Tk: A Developer's Guide* CD-ROM in your CD-ROM drive. The rest of these instructions assume that this is drive D.

2. You can use File Explorer, the Run option, or the browsing application to start the D:\tools\gipsy\vg263.exe installer, as follows.

   a. Using Run, select Start and then Run from the Windows task button. Enter or browse to D:\tools\gipsy\gipsy.exe and run that program.

   b. Using File Explorer, browse to the D:\tools\gipsy directory and double click on gipsy.exe.

   c. Using the browsing application, browse to the Tools selection, and click on *Visual GIPSY for Windows*.

   ■ The initial screen will inform you that this application will install Visual GIPSY onto your computer. Click on the OK button.

   ■ The next screens allow you to select the installation directory, Program groups, and so on.

   Follow the instructions on the screens to install Visual GIPSY.

### D.10.2 Installing Visual GIPSY Under UNIX, Linux, Mac OS, and So On

To install Visual GIPSY, perform the following steps.

1. Place and/or mount the *Tcl/Tk: A Developer's Guide* CD-ROM in your CD-ROM drive.

2. Extract the tools/gipsy/vg269.zip file with unzip, Winzip, Stuffit Expander, or the browsing application provided on the CD-ROM.

3. Extracting this file will create a vg269 directory that contains the libraries, examples, and executables. Add this directory to your path to be able to run vg.tcl.

## D.11 Freewrap

The Freewrap package will combine a Tcl interpreter and Tcl scripts into a single executable. The companion CD-ROM includes executable packages for Windows and Linux (x86) and the source code as zip archives.

### D.11.1 Installing Freewrap Under MS Windows

The Freewrap distribution is packaged as a zip file that can be unpacked with Winzip or the browsing application on the CD-ROM.

1. Place the *Tcl/Tk: A Developer's Guide* CD-ROM in your CD-ROM drive. The rest of these instructions assume that this is drive D.
2. Unpack the archive, as follows.
   a. To unpack with Winzip, extract the file
   `D:\tools\freewrap\freewrap53b_win.zip`
   b. To unpack with the browsing tool, browse to the Tools selection and click on *Freewrap for Windows*.

This will unpack `freewrap.exe` and a documentation folder into the selected directory.

## D.11.2 Installing Freewrap Under Linux

To install `Freewrap` under Linux, perform the following steps.

1. Mount the *Tcl/Tk: A Developer's Guide* CD-ROM.
2. Change the directory to the directory in which you wish to install Freewrap.
3. Unpack the Freewrap source distribution, as follows.
   `unzip /cdrom/tools/freewrap/freewrap53b_linux-x86.zip`
   Alternatively, you can use the browsing tool on the CD-ROM by executing `autorun.sh` and selecting Tools and Freewrap for Linux.

This will unpack Freewrap and a documentation folder into the selected directory.

## D.11.3 Installing and Compiling Freewrap Under UNIX

To install Freewrap under UNIX, perform the following steps.

1. Mount the *Tcl/Tk: A Developer's Guide* CD-ROM.
2. Change the directory to the directory in which you wish to install Freewrap.
3. Unpack the Freewrap source distribution, as follows:
   `unzip /cdrom/tools/freewrap/freewrap53b_src.zip`
   Alternatively, you can use the browsing tool on the CD-ROM by executing `autorun.sh` and selecting *Tools* and *Freewrap Source*.
4. Change to the `freewrap` directory. Check the `README` file for more options. To make a default installation, continue these instructions.
5. Create the `Makefile` by running `configure`, as follows:
   `./configure`
6. Make the `freewrap` executable with `make`, as follows:
   `make`
7. Install the new executable with `make install`.

## D.12 CriTcl

The CriTcl package allows you to embed C language functions into a Tcl script. These functions are compiled on the fly into libraries that are then loaded to provide performance improvements. This version of Critlib is only supported for the gcc compiler, either on a UNIX system or a Windows platform with the cygwin tools installed. This critlib package is provided as a zip file that can be extracted with unzip or the browsing application on the companion CD-ROM.

### D.12.1 Installing CriTcl

To install CriTcl, perform the following steps.

**1.** Mount the *Tcl/Tk: A Developer's Guide* CD-ROM.

**2.** Change the directory to the directory in which you wish to install CriTcl. The best location for these files is in the Tcl library folder. This path is returned by the info library command when you start your Tcl or Wish interpreter.

**3.** Unpack the critlib source distribution, as follows:

```
unzip /cdrom/tools/critcl/critlib.zip
```

Alternatively, you can use the browsing tool on the CD-ROM by executing autorun.sh and selecting *Tools* and *CriTcl package*.

This will unpack CriTcl and a documentation folder into the selected directory.

## D.13 SWIG

The SWIG distribution is done as a zip archive for UNIX and Windows systems and as a self-extracting BinHex archive for the Macintosh.

### D.13.1 Installing SWIG Under MS Windows

The SWIG distribution is packaged as a zip file that can be unpacked with Winzip or the browsing application on the CD-ROM.

**1.** Place the *Tcl/Tk: A Developer's Guide* CD-ROM in your CD-ROM drive. The rest of these instructions assume that this is drive D.

**2.** Unpack the archive, as follows.

   a. To unpack with Winzip, extract the file D:\tools\swig\swigwin-1.3.17.zip.

   b. To unpack with the browsing tool, browse to the Tools selection, and click on *SWIG for Windows*.

See the documentation file for more details on using SWIG with Windows, and read the chapter in the "Real World" section of the companion CD-ROM for more details on SWIG.

## D.13.2 Installing SWIG Under UNIX

To install SWIG under UNIX, perform the following steps.

1. Mount the *Tcl/Tk: A Developer's Guide* CD-ROM.
2. Change the directory to the directory in which you wish to install SWIG.
3. Unpack the swig source distribution, as follows:

   `unzip /cdrom/tools/swig/swig1_3_17.zip`

   Alternatively, you can use the browsing tool on the CD-ROM by executing `autorun.sh` and selecting *Tools* and *SWIG for Unix* (*as zip*).
4. Change to the SWIG1.1.3.17 directory. Check the README file for more options. To make a default installation, continue these instructions.
5. Create the Makefile by running `configure`, as follows:

   `./configure`
6. Make the swig executable with make, as follows:

   `make`
7. Install the new executable with `make install`.

## D.13.3 Installing SWIG on a Macintosh

The SWIG distribution for the Macintosh is a self-extracting BinHex archive. Note that this distribution is for a Power PC–based Macintosh. This executable will not work on a $680 \times 0$–based Macintosh.

The first step is to convert the packed file into an installation file using the Aladdin Systems StuffIt Expander package. The StuffIt Expander program is distributed with Netscape and can be obtained from *www.aladdinsys.com*.

The second step is to run the installation program to install SWIG. To unpack the distribution using the StuffIt Expander, perform the following steps.

1. Place the *Tcl/Tk: A Developer's Guide* CD-ROM in the CD-ROM drive and confirm that it creates an icon on your screen when it loads.
2. Start the StuffIt Expander program by double clicking on the Expander icon. Click on the File menu in the upper left-hand corner of the screen. Click on the Expand menu option from that menu. Clicking on the Expand option will bring up a file-browsing window for selecting the installation file.
3. Perform the following steps to select the file to be extracted.

a. Select the desktop.

b. Double click on the name of the CD-ROM.

c. Double click on *tools*.

d. Double click on *swig*.

e. Double click on the entry *SWIG-1.3.11.sit.hqx*.

f. Click on the Desktop button. The content of the desktop will now appear in the window, and the Unstuff button will no longer be grayed out.

g. Click on the Unstuff button, or press the Return key.

StuffIt Expander will now convert the distribution file to an executable program on your desktop area.

4. When StuffIt Expander has completed the expansion of the distribution file, there will be a new icon on your desktop. Verify that this is the case.

5. Click on the New icon. This starts the SWIG installation.

6. The first window you will see has the information about the package used to create the archive. Click on the Continue button.

7. The next window contains a file browser widget that will allow you to select where you wish to have SWIG installed. After you have selected the workspace for SWIG (perhaps the main desktop), click on the Save button.

SWIG will be unpacked into the directory you selected.

# D.14 megaWidget

Jeff Hobbs's megaWidget package is included in the tools/hobbs directory. This package is discussed in Chapter 12. This package is being distributed as a zip archive.

## D.14.1 Unpacking the megaWidget Distribution

This package is distributed as a zip archive. To install it, perform the following steps.

1. Place the *Tcl/Tk: A Developer's Guide* CD-ROM in the CD-ROM drive.

2. Extract the zip file (tools\tkcon\tkcon.zip) with Winzip, File Explorer, or the browsing application provided on the CD-ROM. The best location for these files is in the Tcl library folder. This path is returned by the info library command when you start your Tcl or Wish interpreter.

Run the *TOUR.tcl* example with a command resembling the following:

```
C:\progra~1\tcl\bin\wish80 tour.tcl
```

# D.15 ASED

Andreas Siever's ASED package provides a pure Tcl, cross-platform IDE for developing Tcl applications.

## D.15.1 Unpacking the ASED Distribution

This package is distributed as a zip archive. To install it, perform the following steps.

1. Place the *Tcl/Tk: A Developer's Guide* CD-ROM in the CD-ROM drive. On Linux systems, mount the CD-ROM.

2. Extract the zip file (`tools\ased\ased2097.zip`) with Winzip, Stuff-It Expander, File Explorer, or the browsing application provided on the CD-ROM. This will create a folder named `ased2097` with the various files ASED needs to run, including the main file `ased.tcl`. On Linux systems, add this directory to your PATH. On Windows systems, you can create a shortcut to this file.

# D.16 ActiveState Komodo IDE

The ActiveState Komodo demo version is provided as a gzipped `tar` file for Linux and as a Microsoft Installation file for Windows platforms. You must contact ActiveState to receive an activation key to run these demos. You can retrieve a key from *www.ActiveState.com/Komodo/Download*.

## D.16.1 Installing Komodo Under Windows

To install Komodo under Windows, perform the following steps.

1. Place the *Tcl/Tk: A Developer's Guide* CD-ROM in the CD-ROM drive.

2. Using File Explorer, the Run menu, or the browsing application, execute `D:\tools\komodo\Komodo-Personal-2.0.1-49959.msi`.

3. Follow the instructions.

## D.16.2 Installing Komodo Under Linux

To install Komodo under Linux, perform the following steps.

1. Mount the *Tcl/Tk: A Developer's Guide* CD-ROM.

2. Change the directory to a temporary directory with at least 100 M of free space.

**3.** Unpack the Komodo source distribution, as follows:

```
tar -xvzof /cdrom/tools/komodo/Komodo-Personal-2.0.1-49987.tar.gz
```

**4.** Evaluate the Installation script (`install.sh`) and follow the instructions.

```
$> sh install.sh
Install script for ActiveState's Komodo.
Enter the directory for the Komodo installation,
or press Enter to accept the default [~/Komodo-2.0]./opt/Komodo

Installing Komodo to '/opt/Komodo'.

Komodo installation requires about 100 megabytes. Please
make sure enough free space is available before continuing.
Would you like to proceed? [Y/n] y

Installing Komodo (this may take a couple of minutes)...
Relocating siloed Perl...
Creating XPCOM registry...
registerSelf for remoteControl
*** Registering -venkman handler.
*** Registering CommandLine JS components

Finished installing Komodo.

Please report any problems to komodo-feedback@ActiveState.com
or log a bug at http://bugs.ActiveState.com/Komodo
And please include the install log, "koinstall.log", with your bug report.

Ensure you put '/opt/Komodo' on your PATH.
Enjoy!
```

## D.17 Neatware MyrmecoX IDE

The Neatware MyrmecoX demo version is provided as a Microsoft Installation file that can be executed directly from the companion CD-ROM. This demo package will run for one month after you install it and does not require an activation key. To install MyrmecoX, perform the following steps.

**1.** Place the *Tcl/Tk: A Developer's Guide* CD-ROM in the CD-ROM drive.

**2.** Using File Explorer, the Run menu, or the browsing application, execute `D:\tools\neatware\MP32DEMO.msi`.

**3.** Follow the instructions. You may receive an error resembling the following. It is safe to ignore this error and continue the installation.

```
  Could not write value DefaultFeature to key
UNKNOWN\Features\6C24324FC2F98084EBE902EBC0D2DE3E
  Verify that you have sufficient access to that key, or contact
  your support personnel.
```

# APPENDIX E

# Bonus Book and Tutorials

*Tcl/Tk: A Developer's Guide* includes a bonus book. Several chapters that were originally written for a book about using Tcl/Tk in the real world have been added to the companion CD-ROM. The CD-ROM also includes several tutorials, four reference guides, and several articles and how-to documents.

## E.1 Accessing the *Real World Tcl* Chapters

To access these chapters, perform the following steps.

1. Load the CD-ROM into your CD-ROM drive.
2. Invoke the browsing application or your preferred browser.
3. View the file `index.htm`.
4. Select *More documentation and articles*.
5. Select *Real World Tcl*.
6. Select the article you want to read.

## E.2 Accessing the Tutorials

The companion CD-ROM contains textual and HTML-based tutorials and the TclTutor package.

### E.2.1 **Accessing the Textual and HTML-based Tutorials**

The textual and HTML-based tutorials are referenced from the opening HTML page on the companion CD-ROM. To access these tutorials, simply load the CD-ROM into your CD-ROM drive and point your browser at the file `index.htm` on that device and follow the references.

## E.3 TclTutor

TclTutor is a computer-aided instruction package for learning Tcl. It provides a brief description and an interactive example for all Tcl commands. Experience has shown that people completely unfamiliar with Tcl can complete the tutorial and be performing productive programming in just a few hours.

The TclTutor source is distributed as a zip file and is also distributed as a Starkit that can be run directly from the companion CD-ROM. For Windows, TclTutor is available as a single executable file. If you want to install the TclTutor source onto your hard drive, you must have `wish` installed on your system before starting the installation.

### E.3.1 **Installing TclTutor Under MS Windows**

To install TclTutor under MS Windows, perform the following steps.

**1.** Place the *Tcl/Tk: A Developer's Guide* CD-ROM in your CD-ROM drive.

**2.** Using File Explorer, browse to `CDROM\tutorial\tcltutor`.

**3.** Drag the `TclTutor.exe` icon to your desktop.

**4.** The tutor can be run by double clicking on this icon.

### E.3.2 **Installing TclTutor Under UNIX**

TclTutor is distributed as source in a zip file or as a Starkit that can be copied to your hard disk or run directly from the companion CD-ROM.

To run it from the CD-ROM, perform the following steps.

**1.** Mount the *Tcl/Tk: A Developer's Guide* CD-ROM.

**2.** Invoke the `tcltutor.sh` script. This script will try each of the TclKits provided on the CD-ROM to see which will work for your platform. If your platform is supported, TclTutor will start.

To install `tcltutor.kit` on your hard drive, perform the following steps.

**1.** Identify the proper TclKit for your platform by name. The TclKits are in `/cdrom/tclkits`, with names that include the platform and architecture they are compiled for.

**2.** Copy the appropriate Tclkit to a directory in your PATH and rename it `tclkit`.

**3.** Copy `/cdrom/tutorial/tcltutor/tutor2b6.kit` to a directory in your path and rename it `tcltutor`.

**4.** Set the +x mode for these files.

At this point, you should be able to invoke the tutorial as `tcltutor` from a shell window.

To install TclTutor on a UNIX/Linux system, perform the following steps. If there is no TclKit for your platform available, you can install the TclTutor source. Note that you must have a `wish` interpreter more recent than release 8.0 installed on your system to use TclTutor.

**1.** Mount the *Tcl/Tk: A Developer's Guide* CD-ROM.

**2.** Change the directory to the top of your source tree, as follows:

```
cd /usr/src/LOCAL
```

**3.** Unpack the `TclTutor` distribution, as follows:

```
unzip /cdrom/tutorial/tcltutor/tutor2b6.zip
```

**4.** Add this directory to your PATH environment variable.

### E.3.3 Installing TclTutor on a Macintosh

TclTutor is packaged in a zip archive (`tcltutor::tutor266.zip`) for the Macintosh. You can drag and drop this file to the `StuffIt Expander` icon to unpack the files. This version of TclTutor can be run by starting a `wish` session, using the Tcl `cd` command to change to the directory where TclTutor is installed, and then source TclTutor, as follows:

```
% cd ..

% ls
  Tcl/Tk Folder
  TclTutor
% cd TclTutor

% source TclTutor.tcl
```

## E.4 Accessing the Extra Documentation

The `docco/tcl_eng` directory contains additional documentation about Tcl/Tk engineering as PDF documents. These files include the following.

| | |
|---|---|
| `eng_man.pdf` | These documents describe the conventions used for cre- |
| `tea.pdf` | ating Tcl extensions. |
| `tea_tcl2k.pdf` | |

| | |
|---|---|
| `style.pdf` | The Tcl script style manual. |
| `tkref40.zip` | Paul Raines's Tcl/Tk pocket reference guide for Tcl revision 7.4 and Tk revision 4.0. |
| `tkref80.tgz` | Paul Raines's Tcl/Tk pocket reference guide for Tcl and Tk revision 8.0. |

## E.5 Accessing the Extra Articles

Clif Flynt, Cameron Laird, Will Duquette, Steve Landers, Mark Roseman, and others have written articles and how-tos for various facets of Tcl. The articles are found in subdirectories under /docco, or you can follow the links from the main index.htm document.

# Index of Commands

Page references point to examples in which these commands are used.

# Index

Bold page references point to definitions.

# Additional Acknowledgments

- The tutorial from *www.etsimo.uniovi.es/tcl/tutorial/* copyright © 1995–1998 Eliseo Vergara, Antonio Bello, César Menéndez, and Francisco Ortega, the University of Oviedo, Spain (*mailto:Antonio@zeus.estimo.uniovi.es*). Included with permission.

- "A Non-Programmer's Introduction to Tcl/Tk" copyright © 1998–2001 Chris Palmer (*www.Ardenstone.com*). Used with permission.

- Splash screen and ray-trace graphics courtesy of Robert Wenzlaff (*www.soylent-green.com*).